FOOD FUNDAMENTALS

Also by Margaret McWilliams
Nutrition for the Growing Years
Illustrated Guide to Food Preparation
Kotschevar, L. and M. McWilliams Understanding Food
Stare, F. and M. McWilliams Living Nutrition
McWilliams, M. and L. Davis Food for You

Food Fundamentals

SECOND EDITION

Margaret McWilliams
California State University, Los Angeles
Los Angeles, California

John Wiley & Sons, Inc., New York • London • Sydney • Toronto

To Kathy

Library of Congress Cataloging in Publication Data:

McWilliams, Margaret.
Food Fundamentals.

Bibliography: p.
1. Food.   I. Title.

TX354.M28 1974   641   73–22144
ISBN 0–471–58736–2

Printed in the United States of America

10 9 8 7 6 5

Preface

This book provides a broad background of knowledge to aid students in developing their ability to prepare and evaluate nourishing and satisfying foods. Today's consumers are faced with choices in food preparation that require an appraisal of individual priorities, economic resources, knowledge, time, abilities, and needs. Persons with a thorough understanding of the many factors underlying these choices will be able to tailor their approach to food preparation to meet individual situations.

Food, like many other facets of our lives, has been undergoing many changes in the variety, form, preparation, and even in its meanings to people. Economic problems and politics have influenced the role of food; rising costs have caused formerly casual consumers to take a sharp look at the foods they select and to make modifications in their diets. A combination of the forces of higher living costs and the women's liberation movement has moved many women from the home into the dual role of worker and homemaker, a change that limits time for homemaking and increases purchasing power. For their families, meal preparation may focus on convenience foods, tender cuts of meat requiring brief preparation, and frequent meals eaten away from home. For other people, these same social and economic pressures are being met by placing an increased value on food produced in the home.

Food preparation in the home now is a matter of choice for large numbers of people. Not too long ago, cooking was a necessity to feed one's family. Today's families have the choice of merely opening cans and packages to provide a wide range of foods or the option of creating their own food adventures by utilizing foods from all over the world. The creativity found in food preparation is a joy to increasing numbers of men and women, while others may prefer to rely on food processors for day-to-day meals. Either route can satisfactorily provide the body's need for nutrients.

This new edition has been revised extensively to provide a broader base of information on food buying. Consumers need to know about seasonal variations, nutrition labeling, alternatives for high priced foods, cooking characteristics of different varieties of produce, and other aspects of food marketing that confront the supermarket shopper.

In addition to the increased emphasis on consumer issues, the sections on fish and poultry have been expanded, a modification reflecting the nutritional emphasis that is being given to increasing their utilization in the diet. Another feature of this edition is the chapter on food preservation, a change dictated by modifications in consumer interests and practices as economic conditions have changed. The discussion of crystallization has been broadened to include frozen foods as well as sugar cookery. The special section on the scientific basis of food preparation has been expanded to include the chapter on colloids.

This revision has been done with the goals of developing an appreciation of good food and a knowledge of how food of high quality is prepared. I hope that the discussions and illustrations in this edition of *Food Fundamentals* will stimulate interest and guide students in their progress toward these goals. The accompanying laboratory manual, *Illustrated Guide to Food Preparation* (Plycon Press), is coordinated with this revision of *Food Fundamentals* and is a complementary component of this complete system for guiding students in the laboratory and individual study.

August 1973   Margaret McWilliams
Fullerton, California

Preface to the First Edition

The current trend toward more extensive use of mixes, of processed and of prepared foods underlines the need for increased emphasis on the interrelationships between basic physical and chemical principles and food preparation. This book focuses attention on this interdisciplinary approach and provides a broad basis for the study of food.

This book is designed for a college level beginning food preparation course of four semester units or six quarter units. Since the unit allotment for such a course is variable from one university to another, it may be necessary to delete some of the material included in this text. The chapter on Meal Management can appropriately be omitted in colleges where this topic is studied as a separate course. In some instances where time is restricted, it may be necessary to consider pectin, gelatin, or perhaps other chapters only summarily. In such a situation, it may be suitable to study these chapters in more detail in a subsequent course.

The sequence of topics for a particular class is certainly best judged by its teacher. Therefore, each chapter has been written as a unit to permit maximum flexibility of arrangement. For instance, sugar cookery could conveniently be studied after starch cookery; Chapter 16 might well be studied concurrently with both Chapters 8 and 9.

Students who have had a year of college chemistry will find that the chapters on the Science of Food (Chapters 16, 17, and 18) add a depth of understanding to the material considered in Chapters 1 through 15 and serve as a useful reference in more advanced courses. However, the first fifteen chapters provide a readily understandable basis for a beginning college level course in food preparation for the student who has not taken a fundamental course in chemistry.

I wish to generally acknowledge the corporations who have contributed illustrations used in the text. Some of the chapters in this book were influenced by courses I took under Miss Helen Charley and Dr. Andrea Mackey at Oregon State University. For professional advice and encouragement in the preparation of the manuscript, I would like to specifically thank Mrs. Bertha Gregory, Mrs. Mary Kramer, Dr. Naoma Norton, and Mrs. Betty Garrett of California State College at Los Angeles; and my family of Los Angeles, Calif.

Margaret E. McWilliams

Los Angeles, California
October 1965

Contents

1. Food Preparation Today   1
2. Important Factors in Food Preparation   7

Part I Food Preparation   21

3. Beverages   23
4. Vegetables   51
5. Fruits   96
6. Salads and Salad Dressings   124
7. Cereals and Starch Cookery   145
8. Milk and Cheese   175
9. Meats, Fish, and Poultry   203
10. Eggs   266
11. Leavening Agents   295
12. Baked Products   309
13. Crystallization: Sugar Cookery and Frozen Desserts   355

Part II Food Management   377

14. Food Preservation   379
15. Food Sanitation Problems   400
16. Meal Management   417

Contents

Part III Food Science   449

  17. Colloids   451
  18. Carbohydrates   459
  19. Fats   472
  20. Proteins   490

Appendix A Nutritive Values of the Edible Part of Foods   A1

Appendix B Consumer Buying Guides   A39

Appendix C Suggested Sources of Educational Materials about
        Materials about Food   A45

Appendix D Pigment Structures   A47

Appendix E   A49

Glossary   G1

Photo Acknowledgments   P1

Index   I1

FOOD FUNDAMENTALS

FIGURE 1.1   Arab bread or Khaubz Araby and shish kebabs are within easy reach of today's armchair traveler and gourmet as the horizons of home food preparation expand.

CHAPTER 1
Food Preparation Today

Food preparation, in the contemporary context of an increasingly impersonal and pressured society, is undergoing philosophical as well as technological change. The current concern about ecological problems has caused many people to reflect on the simpler life that existed early in this century and to place increasing value on foods prepared in the home. To a growing number of consumers, convenience foods and highly processed foods are "chemical fare" to be viewed with skepticism and distrust. For them, food preparation beginning with the basic ingredients is almost a religion. Home-baked bread is emerging once again as the symbol of wholesome food in tune with the environment. The rising cost of convenience foods is yet another factor that motivates consumers to do their own food preparation.

The "do-it-yourself" philosophy in the kitchen also is gaining renewed vigor from the many people who are discovering the pleasure of creativity in the kitchen. Both men and women are finding that food preparation provides a sense of accomplishment and identity consistent with their life-styles. Foreign and exotic recipes are the forte of the sophisticated chef and gourmet. For others, satisfaction is gained by adding individualized touches to convenience foods purchased in the grocery store.

Although more leisure time is a part of the changing living patterns, there still are many who find their time too limited for some of the recipes favored by food hobbyists. Many women have the dual responsibility of homemaker and wage earner. Their goal in the kitchen may need to be confined to the preparation of nourishing and well-prepared, but not elaborate meals. For these women, time management, wise shopping, and efficient food preparation principles and techniques are essential.

Men are expanding their role in food preparation in many families. The

1

trend in family life is toward greater sharing of routine responsibilities, with grocery shopping and food preparation becoming tasks undertaken by many men. Outside the home, large numbers of men (and women) are employed as chefs in restaurants, as dietitians, and as food technologists in the food production industry.

Since food is important to all people for psychological as well as physiological reasons, consumers need extensive, yet basic information on food purchasing, sanitation, preparation, and service. Knowledge of nutritional needs is fundamental to good menu planning, but the achievement of good nutrition is dependent on numerous factors; and one of the most important factors is quality food preparation.

Preparation techniques are geared toward enhancing the sensory appeal of foods. Food that is well prepared will appeal to the diner's senses of smell and sight and will set the stage for the enjoyment of a meal. When the food is being eaten, the senses of taste and touch are also involved. In fact, a few crisp products even promote an awareness of the sound of food.

Acceptance of food is based on the impression the product makes on these senses. A full and pleasing aroma is generally preferred to a strong, acrid odor. Bright, natural colors in fruits and vegetables are accepted by many people in preference to faded or distorted colors. The shapes and arrangement of food on the plate contribute significantly to the visual appeal. Flavor evaluation is a combination of the taste and aroma of individual foods. This aspect requires consideration of the overall flavor of food mixtures as well as the contribution of individual ingredients. Texture may seem to be a rather subtle quality that is hardly noticed by some people, and yet the toughness or mushiness of a vegetable may have a definite influence on its acceptance. Foods that retain their crispness, water chestnuts for example, are sometimes used in recipes to provide textural interest.

Optimum quality in food preparation, that is, food with maximum appeal to the senses, can be achieved when the physical and chemical factors involved in the cooking processes are understood. To illustrate, the colors and flavors in vegetables can be modified by controlling the medium in which they are prepared and the length of time that they are heated. An understanding of the chemical nature of proteins and the changes effected in them by heat facilitates egg, meat, and milk cookery. Knowledge of the factors involved in modifying boiling temperatures is an aid in preparing candies.

Such illustrations show clearly the close link between the various areas of the physical sciences and the science of food preparation. By tracing the application of the physical sciences to food preparation back through history to the eighteenth century, one discovers a creative and imaginative gentleman, Count Rumford. The double boiler, a piece of equipment valued even today for heating foods without scorching, was one of his famous inventions. In addition to this and other pieces of kitchen equipment, he is famous for his pioneer work in developing some of the basic principles involved in feeding large groups of people. His contributions mark the period when food preparation first began to develop as a science.

An understanding of the science of food preparation is a distinct asset in home preparation, in institutional settings, and in the food industry. In all of these situations, the professional is required to analyze food problems and solve them. Recipes must be evaluated, and errors in procedure or ingredients must be recognized and corrected. Good products are not due to mere chance, but are the result of deliberate, intelligent planning and analytical evaluation.

The world of food is changing rapidly. Social forces have done much to shape the changes. The consumer movement has awakened the average consumer to a high level of concern about the additives in his food, the freshness of products, the complexities of unit pricing, and the numerous roles of government in protecting and aiding him in the marketplace. The far-reaching results of this new awareness cannot be assessed at the present time, but the effects are being felt throughout the nation. New legislation, increasing public relations efforts by the food industry, and consumer education programs are only a few manifestations of this movement.

The high level of employment among women, particularly the increasing rate among those who have young children, is influencing food practices. A higher fraction of meals is being eaten in restaurants. The higher income and reduced amount of time available for meal preparation encourage use of convenience foods. In some families, greater use is made of the exotic and more expensive produce and canned foods. Menus are becoming more cosmopolitan.

Many of the changes in the foods consumed are the result of technological advances in the food industry. Food scientists have been successful in perfecting techniques to cook starch products, dehydrate them, and then reconstitute them quickly just prior to serving them. The result has been the numerous instant cereal products, instant mashed potatoes, and instant rice—all of them time-savers for people with little time to spend in the kitchen. Through research, manufacturers have overcome many of the difficult and complex problems associated with the production and storage of mixes. As these problems have been solved, acceptance has become more widespread. Public interest and the wide use of convenience foods have triggered further research directed toward increasing the variety of mixes and improving their quality still more. These products are a boon to individuals with limitations either in culinary ability or time.

As a consequence of the rapid strides in commercial food science, the study of food preparation today has expanded to include the grocery store and food processing plants as extensions of the laboratory. Much can be

FIGURE 1.2   Much of the food eaten in the home today is produced in modern factories that bear little resemblance to the family kitchen.

learned by careful and thorough study of the numerous food products available to the consumer. He is faced with many decisions that traditionally had been solved by preparing the food from its basic components. Just to serve potatoes at a meal the consumer makes the choice of baked potatoes, stuffed baked, hash browns, mashed, scalloped, au gratin, boiled, in salad (hot or cold), french fried, and many other variations. As if this were not enough of a dilemma, he must make other decisions at the market. If he chooses to prepare the fresh product, immediately the question becomes: What variety is best for the recipe being prepared? For those electing to use a convenience-food approach to potatoes for dinner, choices must be made between dehydrated and frozen products. Prices and brands are also involved as a part of the decision. Yet another dimension of the consumer's shopping experience is the frequent addition of new products. These new food items add to the complexity of selection by requiring continual reassessment of food purchasing decisions.

New food products have been a creative force in the diets of many people. In the vegetable category, considerable creativity in the food industry has expanded the choices among frozen vegetable products significantly. These tempting and easily prepared items provide a positive, albeit expensive step toward promoting greater use of vegetables. Even if these products are not purchased, the displays and packages provide suggestions for preparing similar recipes in one's own kitchen. Packaged casseroles add a creative and cosmopolitan potential for the consumer. Bags of sauce mixes encourage the use of different herbs and spices to increase interest in a meal. Frozen doughs, ready-to-eat baked products, and refrigerated oven-ready quick bread variations afford additional opportunities for adding a home-baked flavor without beginning the preparation from the basic ingredients. Frozen dinners offer a quick and easy solution for those who are limited in time and/or ability in the kitchen.

FIGURE 1.3   Many a homemaker meets the challenge of time pressures while satisfying the family's desire for good food by modifying commercial products with her own personal touches.

The alternatives and choices in food preparation are many. The actual solution for the individual will be based on the practical factors that include the amount of money available for food, the skill in food preparation, the time that can be devoted to food preparation, food preferences of the individual and his family, and the amount of satisfaction provided by creative experiences in the kitchen. The common denominator among all consumers is that food is essential for survival. Beyond that point, innumerable avenues are available for preparing and serving food. By studying food preparation and becoming thoroughly familiar with the foods and food products that can be utilized, individuals can adapt and develop patterns of preparation that are satisfying nutritionally, aesthetically, gustatorily, and economically.

Never before in history has food preparation offered such a potential for enjoyment in the kitchen. The equipment available today is both functional and beautiful. Ranges are designed for eye appeal and easy cleaning as well as convenience and performance. Ovens that clean themselves are a functional development appreciated by many people. Timed outlets and ovens add significantly to scheduling freedom for busy people who need to be doing other things at the time a meal should be started. Blenders, portable oven-broiler units, and other small electric appliances afford the opportunity for variety in preparation and convenience. Teflon coating on pans and waffle irons provides an assist in preparation and maintenance tasks. Microwave ovens, particularly the smaller countertop version, have begun to gain acceptance and meet a real need for families with time limitations for food preparation. And one of the brightest pleasures in the modern kitchen comes from the colorful equipment—utensils that promote the beauty of food for the cook as well as the diner. Beautiful, yet functional kitchenwares subtly promote pleasure and confidence in preparing food.

With the abundant support provided by the retail food, food production, and equipment industries, anyone can prepare nourishing and attractive meals. However, food selection, planning, sanitation, and preparation are greatly aided by studying these many facets of food and nutrition. The remainder of this book is devoted to helping students learn not only the "how to's," but also the "why's." An understanding of principles is essential if consumers are to be able to adapt in a meaningful way to the many changes that will occur in the years ahead.

BIBLIOGRAPHY

Brown, S. C. *Count Rumford.* Doubleday. Garden City, N. Y. 1962.
Kramer, M., and M. Spader. *Contemporary Meal Management.* Wiley, New York, N. Y. 1972.

CHAPTER 2
Important Factors in Food Preparation

TEMPERATURE SCALES

Today in the United States, three different temperature scales are in common use: Kelvin, Celsius (Centigrade), and Fahrenheit. Although the Kelvin scale is convenient for physicists because of its construction with zero at absolute zero, this scale has not been adopted widely by other groups. Food researchers and many other scientists use the Celsius (also referred to as Centigrade) scale. This scale, with its zero point defined as the freezing temperature of water and with the boiling point of water at sea level being designated as 100, is a logical system well suited to their needs in the laboratory. The Fahrenheit scale is presently used by most of the other people in the United States. However, there is some dissatisfaction with this scale because of the values of the freezing point of water (32°F) and the boiling point (212°F).

At this time, recipes for home use are usually based on the Fahrenheit scale. Candy and deep-fat frying thermometers are marked in this scale; oven regulators are keyed to the Fahrenheit scale. Despite such evidence of acceptance of this somewhat cumbersome scale, a change to the Celsius scale is in progress. Even at the present time, anyone working in food research and consumer products needs to be able to interpret temperatures by using both the Fahrenheit and Celsius scales. The following equations and examples illustrate the calculations required.

To convert a temperature reported in the Fahrenheit scale to the Celsius scale, the following equation is used:

$$X°C = \frac{5}{9}\left[(Y°F) - 32 \right]$$

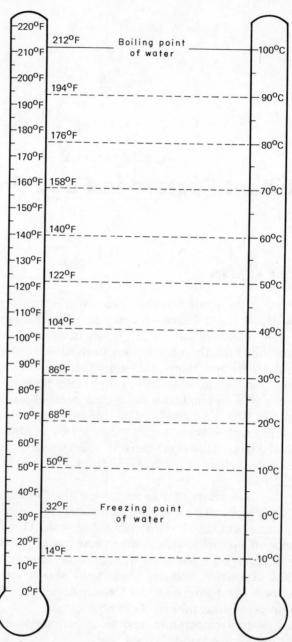

FIGURE 2.1 The Fahrenheit temperature scale, generally used in food preparation in the United States, is now being challenged by the Celsius scale, whose supporters favor the convenience of 0°C as the freezing point of water and 100°C as the boiling point at sea level.

For example, to convert 140°F to the Celsius scale:

$$X°C = \frac{5}{9}\left[(140°F) - 32\right]$$
$$= \frac{5}{9}(108)$$
$$= 60°C$$

Conversion from the Celsius scale to the Fahrenheit scale is done by using this equation:

$$Y°F = \frac{9\,(X°C)}{5} + 32$$

Thus, 60°C is converted to the Fahrenheit scale as follows:

$$Y°F = \frac{9\,(60°C)}{5} + 32$$
$$= 108 + 32$$
$$= 140°F$$

Table 2.1 provides a useful comparison of numerical values in these two temperature scales.

TEMPERATURES USED IN FOOD PREPARATION

The temperatures used in food preparation range from temperatures somewhat below the freezing point of water to those used in deep-fat frying

Table 2.1. Comparison of Numerical Values of Temperatures in the Fahrenheit and Celsius Scales

°F	°C	°F	°C
−10	−23.3	160	71.1
0	−17.8	170	76.7
10	−12.2	180	82.2
20	− 6.7	190	87.8
30	− 1.1	200	93.3
40	4.4	210	98.9
50	10.0	220	104.4
60	15.6	230	110.0
70	21.1	240	115.6
80	26.7	250	121.1
90	32.2	300	148.9
100	37.8	325	162.8
110	43.3	350	176.7
120	48.9	375	190.5
130	54.4	400	204.4
140	60.0	425	218.3
150	65.6	450	232.2

(190°C or 375°F) and baking (as high as 220°C or 425°F). Through skillful use and understanding of the temperatures involved, excellent food products can be prepared. The person who has a knowledge of factors that influence crystallization and freezing points is able to apply the appropriate theories to prepare frozen desserts and other frozen products with desirable textural characteristics. When temperature control in the intermediate temperature range between freezing and boiling is utilized, foods can be stored to minimize the growth of microorganisms, successful yeast products can be prepared, and tender protein foods can be the end product. Higher temperatures are utilized in sugar cookery, baking, and frying.

Freezing Temperatures

The freezing point of water is the temperature at which a transition is made from a liquid to a solid. The heat released during this transformation is called the *heat of solidification*. Eighty calories per gram are released during this process. Freezing of pure water occurs at 0°C (32°F). The addition of a material that forms a true solution lowers the temperature at which this phenomenon occurs. As is true with the boiling point, an electrolyte (a material such as salt which ionizes or dissociates) will cause a greater change than a substance that dissolves but does not ionize. Sugar and salt are common materials capable of lowering the freezing point of a solution below that of pure water. Therefore a frozen dessert with a high sugar content will melt more quickly and be more difficult to serve than a less sweet mixture. To minimize the complications of serving frozen desserts in warm weather, the sugar content of the recipe should be limited to just the amount absolutely required for a satisfactory flavor. As the quantity of sugar increases, the freezing temperature is lowered, and the dessert may be too soft to hold its shape satisfactorily when served.

A practical application of the decrease in the freezing temperature of water with the addition of a solute is made in preparing ice cream in an ice cream freezer. The ice cream mixture is placed in a container that is surrounded by a mixture of salt and ice. This brine solution is much colder than the ice alone would be. Consequently, the ice cream will freeze more rapidly than it will when no salt is added to the ice.

Intermediate Temperatures

Successful holding of meats, milk, eggs, fish, poultry, and food mixtures containing these items is based on avoiding the temperature range between 40°F and 120°F (4°–49°C). Microorganisms grow rapidly in these types of food within this range. However, refrigerator storage does not favor growth of microorganisms and the storage life before microorganism levels become dangerous is lengthened. High temperatures, that is temperatures above 49°C (120°F), are also outside the favorable temperature range for reproduction of microorganisms. Consequently, these types of foods may be held safely for an extended serving period in a warming oven or other heating unit that maintains the food above this upper limit. Of course, there are many fresh fruits and vegetables and dried products that do not favor the growth of microorganisms; these items are safely stored at room temperature without serious concern for microbiological contamination under ordinary home conditions (see Chapter 15).

Temperature is obviously an important consideration when food is to be prepared by heating. A few foods require careful control of heat. For a stirred custard, for example, sustained low heat is essential to the preparation of a smooth, yet well thickened product. This control can be achieved by heating the mixture in a double boiler, with the mixture suspended over simmering water. Some recipes recommend that milk be scalded or that almonds be blanched. Again, such procedures require the ability to recognize the approximate temperature of the liquid and careful control of the heating mixture. Intermediate temperatures include scalding, lukewarm, and simmering.

The coolest of the intermediate temperatures is lukewarm, the term used to designate a temperature of 40°C (104°F). Since this is just above body temperature, lukewarm water feels just slightly warm to the touch. As water is heated beyond lukewarm, scalding temperatures are reached. At scalding (65°C or 149°F), large bubbles collect on the sides and bottom of the pan. With still more heating, water will reach simmering, defined as the range between 82 and 99°C (180 to 211°F). Simmering water has large bubbles that form and rise almost to the suface of the water, but rarely break the surface.

Boiling Temperatures

Boiling is the physical phenomenon in which a liquid changes to the vapor state, as occurs when water boils. The temperature at which this occurs is the point at which the vapor pressure (the pressure of the liquid upward) just exceeds atmospheric pressure (downward pressure). Vapor pressure is the force that the molecules of the liquid exert in their attempt to leave the liquid. Up to the boiling point, an increase in the heat input raises the temperature of the liquid and increases the vapor pressure. When the vapor pressure is sufficiently high, the liquid will boil. At sea level water boils at 100°C (212°F).

Increasing the rate of boiling will not raise the temperature of the water. It simply means that the increased amount of heat going into the water causes a more rapid rate of evaporation. The heat required to change boiling water to water vapor is called the heat of vaporization; 540 kilocalories are required to convert one gram of boiling water to water vapor.

Atmospheric pressure varies with altitude and causes the boiling temperature of water to vary. Atmospheric pressure is decreased with an increase in elevation. Since the pressure exerted downward on the liquid is less, the vapor pressure will not need to be as great for boiling to occur. The boiling point of water decreases 1°F for every 500 feet rise in elevation (1°C for every 960 feet). In practice, this means that vegetables and other foods cooked in boiling water in the mountains will need to be boiled a longer time than at sea level because they are actually being heated in water that is not as hot. A remarkable illustration of this change in temperature is noted in accounts of mountaineering expeditions on Mount Everest, where the extemely high elevations and the very low atmospheric pressure cause such a decrease in the boiling temperature of water that it is possible to put one's hand in hot tea and not even be burned.

Atmospheric pressure may be altered in food preparation through the use of special equipment. In a pressure cooker or pressure saucepan, downward pressure is artificially increased and, as a result, the boiling point of water is elevated. This is true because the increased downward pressure necessitates an increased vapor pressure if boiling is to occur. The increased vapor pressure is achieved as the liquid reaches temperatures above the normal boiling point. The elevated temperatures that can be reached in a pressure saucepan cause foods to become tender more quickly than they would in an unpressurized pan.

In industry a partial vacuum may be used to advantage in processing certain products. An important illustration is the production of frozen orange juice concentrate, a product requiring the removal of a large quantity of water without imparting a cooked flavor. By reducing atmospheric pressure through development of a partial vacuum, water can be evaporated at a temperature sufficiently low to avoid a cooked flavor.

Vapor pressure of water may be altered by adding certain substances to the water. Particles that dissolve in water will reduce the vapor pressure, and thus elevate the boiling temperature of the mixture. Substances with particles smaller than one millimicron in diameter will form such true solutions. Particles larger than one millimicron do not elevate the boiling point since they are too large to go into true solution.

Sugar can be dissolved in water to cause a decrease in vapor pressure and an elevation of the boiling point. The greater the amount of sugar that is in solution, the higher the boiling point will be. Salt has a greater influence than sugar on the boiling point of water because it ionizes into sodium and chloride ions. The many small sodium and chloride ions together are noticeably more effective in raising the boiling point than the relatively fewer, but

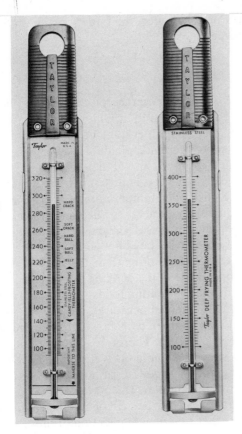

FIGURE 2.2 Candy thermometers are scaled to more than 300°F and deep-frying thermometers to 400°F so that the high temperatures reached in sugar cookery and frying may be measured accurately.

larger, molecules of sugar. The small amount of salt used in boiling vegetables, however, has a very limited effect on the boiling point. With larger quantities of salt or sugar, as suggested in the experiments at the end of this chapter, the solution will have a higher boiling point than water. The boiling temperatures of sugar mixtures will be considered at greater length in Chapter 13.

Active boiling can be reached and maintained readily when the pan is placed directly on the heating unit. However, liquids will not boil in the top of a double boiler because it is not possible to transmit enough heat energy through the water in the lower portion to raise the vapor pressure of the liquid in the top unit of the double boiler to the boiling point. No matter how much steam is circulating in the bottom portion, the liquid in the top will not boil. To boil food in the top of a double boiler, the upper portion must be placed directly over the heat source.

Frying Temperatures

As we have just noted, the usual temperature of the cooking liquid when water is the medium is approximately 100°C. Only when sugar solutions become very concentrated will the temperature of the solution rise significantly above this point unless pressure is applied. However, when the cooking medium is oil or hot fat, the vapor pressure of these materials is very low. As a result, they may be heated to very high temperatures without boiling. Frying generally requires a controlled temperature of approximately 190°C (375°F) for optimum food quality, but the fat can become much hotter and still boiling does not occur. From a practical viewpoint, foods that are fried will cook much more quickly than will those boiled in water because the fat will be approximately 65C° (150F°) hotter than the boiling water.

In addition to the obvious importance of the cooking temperatures that can be reached by using different media for heating foods, two other aspects of significance should be mentioned. The temperatures of pans in which foods have been fried are much hotter than are pans in which only the boiling temperature of water has been reached. Therefore, kitchen counters other than those made of stainless steel or ceramic tile will be damaged when pans used for frying or for heating concentrated sugar solutions are transferred directly from the hot range to the counter. In contrast, pans containing foods cooked in water generally can be placed on kitchen counters without defacing the surface. The other practical application of these different temperatures is concerned with safety. Of course, boiling water is sufficiently hot to cause serious burns, but the higher temperatures of boiling candies and frying fats and oils present a still more serious hazard.

WATER IN FOOD PREPARATION

Water, one of the most important materials used in food preparation, can transfer heat, act as a solvent, and/or serve as a dispersing medium. Water is used to heat and cook foods because it can transfer heat from the pan to the foods which it surrounds. Palatability of foods is greatly influenced by the ability of water to act as a solvent. For example, most people find foods rather unpalatable without salt, but salt must be dissolved if its flavor is to be imparted to foods. Water also serves as the solvent to dissolve baking powder and activate the reaction that releases carbon dioxide to leaven quick breads and cakes. Finally, water is used to distribute other food substances such as cereal granules, starch in a pudding, and flour in batters and doughs.

SOFT WATER

Soft water contains few, if any, insoluble salts and is therefore ideal for food preparation. The water available in many areas, however, is naturally high in insoluble salts and is less desirable. This hard water may be improved by a variety of water-softening techniques. In lieu of a means of softening, distilled water may be a suitable choice at times.

Falling rain is said to be soft because there are no insoluble salts in it, but rainwater dissolves some minerals as it passes through the soil. The types of salts dissolved in the water as it filters through the soil determine whether the water will become temporarily or permanently hard.

TEMPORARY HARDNESS

Bicarbonate $(-HCO_3)$ salts of calcium and magnesium cause temporary hardness. These salts, calcium bicarbonate $(Ca(HCO_3)_2)$ and magnesium bicarbonate $(Mg(HCO_3)_2)$, are removed by boiling the water. During boiling these salts are changed to insoluble calcium and magnesium salts which precipitate to form the lime $(CaCO_3)$ deposits found in tea kettles. The reaction is as follows:

$$Ca(HCO_3)_2 + Mg(HCO_3)_2 \rightarrow CaCO_3 \downarrow + MgCO_3 \downarrow + 2H_2O + 2CO_2$$

PERMANENT HARDNESS

Water is permanently hard when sulfate (SO_4) or chloride (Cl) salts of calcium (Ca), iron (Fe), and magnesium (Mg) are present. These substances may be dissolved in water as it filters through the ground. To soften this water, sodium (Na) salts are introduced. Sodium, being highly reactive, replaces the calcium or magnesium ion in the salt. The resultant calcium and magnesium carbonates $(-CO_3)$ precipitate and the soluble sodium sulfate or sodium chloride remains in the water.

$$CaSO_4 + MgSO_4 + 2Na_2CO_3 \rightarrow CaCO_3 \downarrow + MgCO_3 \downarrow + 2Na_2SO_4$$

This is the type of reaction that occurs in commercial or home water softeners.

Water should be softened if results in food preparation are to be optimum. The alkaline reaction of hard water causes a yellowish color in vegetables containing flavone pigments. Pectic substances in vegetables and fruits react with the salts in hard water and thus prolong the cooking time. Cloudy tea and coffee are the result of using hard water to brew the beverage.

MEASURING PROCEDURES

Careful measuring is essential if foods of superior quality are to be produced. Traditionally, ingredients in the home have been measured by the use of volumetric equipment, including glass cups, graduated measuring cups, and measuring spoons. Various ingredients have been measured according to the standardized procedures outlined below. Experimental food research has long been based on weights because of the greater precision and reproducibility of results that is effected by weighing.

The traditional home techniques are about to be modified as a result of the United States Metric Study, which led to the recommendation in 1971 that the United States, through a nationally coordinated and systematic program, convert to the International Metric System during the next 10 years. This conversion will touch innumerable facets of American life, and certainly will lead to changes in measuring techniques in food preparation.

Conventional Techniques

Dry Ingredients. The presently accepted technique for measuring dry ingredients requires the use of either graduated, measuring cup sets (Mary Ann cups) or measuring spoons and a straight-edged spatula. Dry ingredients are not measured in a glass measuring cup because there is no precise way to level the surface of the ingredients without packing. With the exception of brown sugar, dry ingredients are lightly spooned into the measuring device until the measure is more than full. The measurement is completed by scraping the straight edge of a metal spatula across the top to remove the excess.

Many dry ingredients have a tendency to pack together. The degree of packing is variable, so that the most reliable results are achieved by stirring the contents of the package to eliminate packing before measuring the ingredient. This is particularly important when measuring cornstarch, which usually packs heavily during shipping and storage.

Flour is another dry ingredient that has a tendency to pack. The recommended practice has been to sift flour once prior to lightly spooning it into the measure. This is the procedure that is the basis for the quantities indicated in recipes. Arlin et al. (1964) found that the cup weights of flour sifted and spooned into the measures ranged in weight from 92 to 120 grams, flour measured without being sifted ranged from 121 to 144 grams per cup, and flour dipped into a measuring cup without sifting ranged from 130 to 150 grams. Clearly, the method of measuring used will significantly influence the amount of flour actually incorporated in a specific product. Even when using flour labeled as "presifted," Mathews and Batcher (1963) demonstrated that the practice of sifting flour prior to measuring was more accurate than was the method of simply measuring unsifted flour. The frequently observed practice of using one cup minus two tablespoons of unsifted flour in place of one cup of sifted flour is definitely lacking in precision.

The different types of sugars used in food preparation require somewhat different measuring techniques. Granulated sugar should be stirred to lighten it and break up any lumps before being spooned into the measuring device. In contrast, powdered sugar is measured more precisely by sifting it once before measuring. The amount of brown sugar specified in a recipe ordinarily is based on the premise that the brown sugar will be packed just firmly enough into the measuring cup so that the sugar will hold the shape of the cup when removed.

Liquids. Liquids are most easily measured in a standard glass measuring cup that rests on a level surface. This type of measurement is sufficiently accurate for home use. All readings should be made by bending over until the eye is at the same level as the cup. The measurement is completed when the bottom of the meniscus (curved surface of the liquid) is level with the desired mark on the glass.

Fats and Oils. Oils or melted shortening are treated as any other liquid and are measured in a glass measuring cup.

Solid fats may be measured in two ways. In the preferred method, firm fats are measured in graduated cups or in measuring spoons by pressing the fat firmly into the appropriate measure until all air spaces are eliminated. The surface is then leveled with the straight edge of a spatula. This technique is somewhat laborious, but is sufficiently accurate for home use.

Solid fats for products that are unaffected by a few extra drops of water are sometimes measured by the water displacement method. In this method, which is faster but distinctly less accurate, a glass measuring cup is filled with water to the appropriate level and then fat is pressed into the cup until the water level rises to the one-cup mark. For example, to measure two-thirds cup of fat it would be necessary to first fill the measuring cup with one-third cup of water. Fat would then be placed in the cup until the water level rose to the one-cup mark. Care must be exercised to push the fat below water level if this method is to achieve any degree of accuracy. Some water will cling to the fat when it is transferred from the water in the measuring cup to the food mixture, but this small amount of moisture will not be detrimental to some products. Pastry, however, will be toughened if extra water is added with the fat. Therefore the first method, that is, measuring in the appropriate graduated equipment, is mandatory for measuring shortening for pastry.

USING THE INTERNATIONAL METRIC SYSTEM

The use of the metric system in home food preparation will require that recipes be converted to metric measures and that a balance (and probably a modified metric cup, too) be substituted for the measuring cups now in use. Although this transition will require extensive educational efforts to convert consumer orientation from the present units of measure to the metric system and may also involve shifting from the present practice of volume measures to the use of weights, the accuracy provided by metric weights is a compelling reward in food preparation.

In practice, ingredients generally could be weighed or else be measured volumetrically, following final implementation of the metric system. Miller and Trimbo (1972) recommend the practice of weighing all solids, with the possible exception of small quantities of seasonings. These workers also suggest that the weighing of liquids might be preferable to the use of a graduated cylinder. The customary graduated cylinder is designed with priority being given to accuracy rather than to security. In anticipation of the breakage and spillage that doubtless would occur in the home kitchen if conventional graduated cylinders were used for measuring liquids, the

Table 2.2. Prefixes Utilized in the Metric System

Multiples and Submultiples	Symbols	Prefixes
$1,000,000,000,000 = 10^{12}$	T	Tera
$1,000,000,000 = 10^{9}$	G	Giga
$1,000,000 = 10^{6}$	M	Mega
$1,000 = 10^{3}$	k	Kilo
$100 = 10^{2}$	h	Hecto
$10 = 10^{1}$	da	Deka
$0.1 = 10^{-1}$	d	Deci
$0.01 = 10^{-2}$	c	Centi
$0.001 = 10^{-3}$	m	Milli
$0.000,001 = 10^{-6}$	μ	Micro
$0.000,000,001 = 10^{-9}$	n	Nano
$0.000,000,000,001 = 10^{-12}$	p	Pico

Table 2.3. Common Equivalents and Conversions

Equivalents

(Weights)
↓

    1 kilogram = 2.21 pounds
    453.59 grams = 1 pound
    28.35 grams = 1 ounce
    1 gram = 0.035 ounce
              (Measures)
                 ↓
    1 liter = 1.06 quarts
    1 gallon = 3.785 liters
    1 quart = 946.4 milliliters
    1 cup = 236.6 milliliters
    1 fluid ounce = 29.6 milliliters
    1 tablespoon = 14.8 milliliters

Conversions

    Quarts × 0.946 = liters
    Gallons × 0.0037 = cubic meters
    Ounces (avdp) × 28.35 = grams
    Pounds (avdp) × 0.454 = kilograms

    Liters × 1.056 = quarts
    Cubic meters × 264.172 = gallons
    Grams × 0.035 = ounces (avdp)
    Kilograms × 2.204 = pounds (avdp)

---

suggestion has been made by Miller and Trimbo (1972) that a plastic cylinder with a height:diameter ratio of 2:1 could be used with minimum hazard and sufficient accuracy for domestic purposes.

The prefixes utilized in the metric system are shown in Table 2.2. Some of the equivalencies important to food preparation are presented in Table 2.3.

BIBLIOGRAPHY

Arlin, M. L., M. M. Nielsen, and F. T. Hall. The effect of different methods of flour measurements on the quality of plain two-egg cakes. *J. Home Econ. 56:*339. 1964.

DeSimone, D. V. *A Metric America: A Decision Whose Time Has Come.* National Bureau of Standards Special Publication No. 345. 1971.

Mathews, R. H., and O. M. Batcher. Sifted versus unsifted flour. *J. Home Econ. 55:*123. 1963.

Mathews, R. H. and E. H. Bechtel. Viscosity of white sauces made with wheat flours from different U.S. regions. *J. Home Econ. 58:*392. 1966.

McWilliams, M. *Illustrated Guide to Food Preparation.* Plycon Press, Fullerton, Calif. 1972.

Meyer, L. H. *Introductory Chemistry.* Macmillan, New Yk, NY. 1959.

Miller, B. S., and H. B. Trimbo. Use of metric measurements in food preparation. *J. Home Econ. 64,* No. 2:20. 1972.

Purchase, M. E. Metric measures: their use in the United States and in the Home Economics Research Journal. *H. E. Research J.* 1:133. 1972.

Warning, M. Start now to think metric. *J. Home Econ.* 64, No. 9:18. 1972.

SUGGESTIONS FOR STUDY

1. Convert the following temperatures to degrees Fahrenheit: −10°C, 5°C, 18°C, 63°C, 115°C.

2. Convert the following temperatures to degrees Celsius: −15°F, 8°F, 39°F, 68°F, 225°F.

3. Measure two cups of water into a one quart saucepan and note the temperature of the water when it boils. By tablespoons add the amounts of sugar suggested below. Note the temperature at a full boil after each addition. Using separate saucepans, repeat the experiment with salt, gelatin, and corn meal in the indicated amounts.

Sugar	Salt	Gelatin (hydrated)	Corn Meal
1 Tbsp	1 Tbsp	1 Tbsp	1 Tbsp
2 Tbsp	2 Tbsp	2 Tbsp	2 Tbsp
3 Tbsp	3 Tbsp	3 Tbsp	3 Tbsp
4 Tbsp	4 Tbsp		
5 Tbsp	5 Tbsp		
6 Tbsp	6 Tbsp		

4. Heat two cups of water in the top part of a double boiler (over boiling water) until the temperature reaches a maximum. Note the temperature.

5. Gradually heat water in a pan and observe the appearance of the water at lukewarm, scalding, and simmering.

6. Heat one cup of oil in a small saucepan to 375°F. Use a deep-fat frying thermometer to follow the temperature rise. Describe the difference in the behavior of the oil and the water observed in activities 4 and 5.

PART I

Food Preparation

CHAPTER 3

Beverages

COFFEE

A cup of coffee is the symbol of hospitality in the United States and other countries of the world, for when friends gather, coffee frequently appears, its tempting aroma and flavor serving as catalysts stimulating conversation. In the front offices of business executives and at break time on industrial production lines, coffee often is served. Coffee is synonymous with friendship and relaxation, yet its stimulating qualities are utilized by students who are existing on long hours of study and few hours of sleep.

Coffee is served in many different ways throughout the world: Greeks and Turks brew a very strong, sweet coffee syrup that is boiled; Syrians add cracked cardamom seed and rose water or orange-blossom water to boiled coffee; Italians prefer a well-roasted coffee followed by fine grinding to produce a very strong beverage; the French favor café au lait, a combination using half coffee and half hot milk; Spaniards use boiled milk instead of water to make coffee; in Vienna a favorite beverage is strong coffee served with whipped cream; South Americans frequently prepare a quantity of very strong coffee to be mixed when needed with hot boiled milk; in the southern United States chicory is usually blended to produce a viscous coffee.

Production of Coffee

The coffee available in vacuum-sealed cans at the market has been transported thousands of miles and has undergone many processing steps

FIGURE 3.1　Coffee cherries require about six months on the tree to mature to their deep purple to red harvest color.

before reaching the consumer. It represents the finest coffee that agriculturists and food scientists have been able to develop.

Much of the coffee available in the United States markets is imported from Brazil, for the climate and soil of its mountainous regions have combined to make Brazil the most famous coffee-producing nation of the world. Brazilian coffees are classified according to the area in which they are grown: Santos, Rio, Victoria, and Bahia. In South America coffee production is not unique to Brazil, however. Fine coffees from other South American countries have also found favor on the world market and are often blended with Brazilian coffees. Other notable coffees are exported from such widely scattered points as Kenya in Africa, the East and West Indies, Hawaii, Arabia, and Turkey.

All areas in which coffee is grown commercially have a moist, warm climate that is particularly suited to the horticultural needs of the coffee tree. Ideally the temperature should range from 65 to 75°F; there should be some sun each day as well as frequent showers.

The production of the raw material for coffee is similar to that of other fruits—first the tree forms blossoms which in turn give way to a slowly developing fruit. When this fruit (cherry) is about six months old, it will become a deeper purple to red color. At this stage the cherries are harvested and then processed by either the wet or dry method to remove the desired beans from the pulp of the cherries. The dried green coffee beans are then shipped to various importers in other countries.

Coffee in the market is a blend of several varieties of coffee which may have originated in quite diverse regions of the world. The blending for a desired flavor is a highly developed skill based on the knowledge derived from years of experience. The varieties presently favored are *Coffea*

FIGURE 3.2   After harvesting, the coffee cherries are separated from other material by sluicing.

arabicas, Coffea liberica, and *Coffea canephora*, although some other types may be developed, with the aid of science, into valued commercial coffees (Table 3.1). Only after careful blending are the beans ready for roasting.

Roasting, the most exacting production step, is done in the country where the coffee will be consumed. The extent of roasting varies according to the country: Brazilians and Turks prefer a darkly roasted bean as do the French and Italians, whereas Americans prefer lighter roasting for their coffees. Within each country variations are available, of course, to suit individual tastes. For instance, a lighter roast is frequently found on the West Coast of the United States as contrasted with a darker roast in the South and a medium color in the East.

During roasting, several important chemical and physical changes take place. An obvious change is the browning of the bean as the sugars caramelize and the starch begins to dextrinize. These chemically simpler substances contribute a definite brown color and distinctive odor and flavor that are characteristic of the roasted beans. An appreciable (16 percent) loss of moisture and a limited loss of other volatile compounds occur during roasting. These combined changes create the desired flavor, a quality that is at its peak immediately following roasting.

Grinding of the beans, the next step after roasting, increases the surface area immensely and thus facilitates brewing of the beverage. Unfortunately, increasing the surface area by grinding the beans accelerates the losses of aromatic flavoring compounds. Flavor retention is maximized by quickly packaging the ground coffee in hermetically sealed cans. For optimum flavor, the roasted beans may be purchased at the market and then ground at home as needed.

Table 3.1. Coffee Varieties of Commercial Importance

Variety	Amount of Cherries To Equal 1 lb Coffee Beans[a]	Flavor	Acceptance
Coffea arabicas	5 lb	Pleasing	Widespread, but tree susceptible to rust
Coffea liberica (Liberica)	10 lb	Bitter	Limited
Coffea canephora (also called *Coffea robusta* or Robusta)	4 lb	Neutral to sweet	Good; tree is hardy

[a]F. L. Wellman, *Coffee.* Interscience Publishers. New York. 1961.

Constituents of Coffee

The flavor of coffee is influenced significantly by the oil content. Natural oils carry and hold the volatile flavoring compounds well, but they can have the negative effect of contributing a stale, somewhat rancid taste to the beverage. Stale character is partially the result of oxidation of the oils, a change that begins when the beans are ground. Since the amount of exposed surface area influences the rate of oxidation and the development of rancidity in the oils, changes occur more readily in fine grind than in the coarser regular grind. This problem is minimized by vacuum packing of the coffee immediately after grinding. Another approach to prolonging the quality of the beverage is to grind the beans in the market or at home. The value of grinding the coffee at the market is partially offset by the usual practice of packaging the product in paper containers which are easily penetrated by air, thus readily permitting oxidation of the oils.

Caffeine, the stimulating substance in coffee, is found in abundance in the green coffee bean, but roasting volatilizes some of it. During the brewing period, some of the remaining caffeine is extracted into the beverage, resulting in a stimulating beverage. The actual amount of caffeine in the beverage is influenced by the strength of the brew, but is not significantly altered by the use of a dripolator, percolator, or vacuum pot during its preparation. A comparison between the caffeine content of various beverages, including coffee, is shown in Table 3.2.

The flavor of coffee is the result of many different compounds. Caffeine appears to contribute some bitterness to the beverage. A particularly important contributor to the flavor bouquet is caffeol, which actually is a group of compounds that develop rather prominently during roasting. Polyphenols, also called tannins, form another group of compounds that contribute to the

Table 3.2. Caffeine Content of Selected Beverages[a,b]

Beverage	Caffeine (mg)
Coffee	90–125
Tea	30–70
Cocoa, breakfast	1.1–3.2
Chocolate	7.8
Cola drink	
Brand 1	36.3
Brand 2	38.9

[a]From the Pan-American Coffee Bureau. New York, N. Y.
[b]Figures are for a five-ounce cup of beverage.

flavor profile of the beverage. Very limited extraction of polyphenols during the brewing period may yield just enough of these astringent compounds to help in rounding out the flavor. However, boiling temperatures readily release the polyphenols from the grounds, resulting in a distinctly bitter and less mellow flavor. By brewing the beverage at temperatures just below boiling, the astringent character due to extracted polyphenols is minimized.

Flavor preferences vary from individual to individual and from one cultural group to another. As a result, there are many different methods presently being used for brewing coffee. Methods generally preferred by people in the United States are directed toward minimizing the extraction of polyphenols and optimizing the caffeol content of the finished beverage.

FIGURE 3.3 The root of chicory is included in some coffee blends and is particularly popular in the South.

However, the Italian way of preparing coffee, that is of making espresso, is specifically designed to enhance the bitterness of the product. The high extraction of polyphenols in espresso is accomplished by forcing steam through finely ground coffee that has been deeply roasted.

Buying Coffee

The choices confronting the consumer in the market are becoming increasingly varied, and the choices in types of coffee are no exception. Not only are there choices between brands, but there are also selections to be made between ground coffees and soluble coffees. The first decision is whether to buy the soluble coffees, which highlight convenience of preparation, or ground coffees, which require more time in preparation but which also boast a better and fuller flavor. The fact that so many consumers have opted for the soluble coffees has provided stimulus for extensive research to produce instant and freeze-dried coffees with better flavor retention.

Soluble coffees. Soluble coffees would appear to be a product of the fast-moving culture of this century. Surprisingly, the earliest versions of soluble coffees can be traced back to 1771 in England, and records indicate that a soluble coffee was field tested during the Civil War in the United States. Despite this long record of experience in developing these coffees, the ultimate goal of researchers in this field, the achievement of a soluble product that is comparable in color, flavor, and appearance to the beverage brewed fresh from the ground beans, still has not been reached.

Soluble coffees are marketed as *instant coffee* or *freeze-dried coffee.* Until 1965, the soluble coffees on the market were spray dried, and those labeled *instant coffee* still are produced in this manner from coffee that is prepared by extracting the original brew from ground coffee by the use of boiling water. Freeze-drying techniques for the production of soluble coffee have been devised and utilized extensively by the coffee industry in the United States. In summary form, the freeze-drying process is accomplished in four steps: (1) freezing, (2) heat transfer of the heat of sublimation, (3) moving the water vapor through the dried portions from the subliming ice crystals, and (4) taking away the water vapor that emerges above the surface. This is a time-consuming process despite the fact that modifications in the procedure have reduced drying time from 20 hours to as little as 4 hours.

One of the problems of interest in the production of soluble coffees has been the achievement of a particle size that is roughly that of ground coffee. The large particle has the practical advantage of being sufficiently heavy to sink through the water to the bottom of a cup, thus facilitating its solution to yield a nonlumpy beverage. The process that makes these larger particles from the original fine powder is called agglomeration. Other refinements utilized in preparing freeze-dried coffees include aromatization and recovery of aromatic volatiles. Attempts to recover the volatile flavoring substances that are lost during processing of the coffee brew are reasonably successful now. These substances then can be added to freeze-dried coffee to yield a product with a flavor approaching that of fresh coffee.

Technologists also have developed a decaffeinated soluble coffee for persons seeking a beverage with only a very limited amount of caffeine. Caffeine can be removed from the green beans or from the liquid extracts prior to the drying of soluble coffees. The chief problem in preparing a satisfactory decaffeinated soluble coffee is loss of the volatile flavoring substances and an accompanying loss of aroma and flavor. However, all but 1 to 2 percent of the caffeine is removed.

Ground coffees. The consumer selecting ground coffees has the choice of a variety of brands and, within these brands, a choice of grinds or particle size. The various producers select a blend of such types of coffee as "Brazils," "Milds" (all other varieties except the Robustas), and "Robustas." Robustas are generally more harsh in flavor and are of limited use in blends for the ground coffee market.

Ground coffees generally are available as fine grind (the smallest particle size), drip grind, and regular grind (large particle size). Some companies also market a coarser grind specifically designed for use in electric percolators. The different grinds provide a varying amount of surface area for extraction of the water-soluble components. Fine grind has the greatest amount of surface area in a given measure and is considered to be best suited to brewing coffee in a vacuum pot where the grounds are freely circulating in the water during the brief extraction period. Drip grind is the grind of choice when using a dripolator type of coffee maker. In this method, water just below boiling temperature filters through a bed of the drip-grind coffee. Regular grind and the coarser electric percolator grind have a proportionately smaller amount of surface area as a result of their larger particle size. This grind does have sufficient area available for extraction as the water passes repeatedly through the basket of grounds.

Preparation of the Beverage

Preparation of a cup of coffee of high quality is a simple task when four fundamental requirements are met: (1) fresh coffee of the appropriate grind for the pot being used, (2) soft water with a pleasing flavor, (3) a clean pot, and (4) controlled heat. If any of these essentials is missing, the beverage will be less pleasing. Fortunately, all of these requirements can be controlled.

The keys to having fresh coffee for preparing the beverage are to buy the quantity that will be used within a couple of weeks and to store the opened can of coffee properly. Coffee begins to deteriorate in quality once the can is opened. The tantalizing aroma that issues from the can unfortunately is lost forever and is unavailable for enhancing the flavor of the finished beverage. These volatile, yet important flavor constituents can be retained effectively if the can is stored tightly covered and opened just long enough to measure out the coffee. In addition to the flavor change due to loss of volatiles during storage, there is the gradual oxidation of the oils, a change that leads to a rancid flavor quality. Development of rancidity is minimal within the first few days after the can has been opened, but does develop during long storage. For consumers who use coffee only on occasion, refrigerator storage in a tightly covered container will retard rancidity.

Flavor of the water used in the beverage is important to the final flavor bouquet of the beverage despite the fact that considerable flavor is extracted from the coffee grounds during the brewing period. The flavor overtones from the water still will carry through and influence the quality. In some areas, the solution to satisfactory coffee flavor may be provided by the use of bottled water. However, municipal water supplies usually are satisfactory for the preparation of coffee with good flavor.

The hardness of water is of interest when evaluating coffee on the basis of appearance. Hard water precipitates the polyphenols released from the coffee during the extraction period, and the beverage will become rather murky. The most sparkling appearance is obtained by using distilled water, but distilled water does have the disadvantage of being less flavorful than water containing small amounts of soluble mineral salts.

To suggest the need for a clean pot almost seems superfluous, and yet this is the problem that is limiting the quality of the beverage in many instances. Coffee leaves an oily film on the walls of the coffee maker, and these oils become rancid if they are not removed by washing in hot, soapy water. Obviously, any rancid oils remaining in a pot will contribute to the total flavor of the beverage prepared in it. When coffee pots have metal seams in them, the oil film that collects in the seams is particularly difficult to remove. The simplest guide to the cleanliness of the pot is the odor that can be noted when the cover is removed. If an unpleasant, somewhat rancid odor can be detected, the pot is not clean, and the beverage prepared in it will have a poor flavor which reflects the nature of the pot.

Temperatures between 85 and 95°C (185-203°F) are optimum for preparing coffee. This temperature range extracts the caffeol and caffeine while keeping the polyphenol concentration to a minimum. The pleasing flavor from the caffeol and the stimulating effect of the caffeine blend to make a beverage enjoyed by many.

The use of filter paper during the brewing period is an aid in preventing the coffee particles from falling into the beverage. By filtering out any particles, the sediment that is noted in the beverage will be greatly reduced, and the coffee will have a more translucent quality. Also, the flavor of the beverage will not be impaired by the continuing extraction of polyphenols from grounds that collect in the finished product.

Cookbooks suggest using two tablespoons of coffee grounds to make one cup of the beverage (three-fourths cup of water). Some people, however, prefer the weaker brew that results from using one tablespoon of the ground beans. Experience shows that less than two tablespoons of grounds per cup will be needed to make coffee in large quantities; the exact amount varies with the individual coffeemaker and the quantity being prepared. Table 3.3 provides a convenient guide for the preparation of coffee in large quantities. Results for small or large amounts will be improved if the pot is filled to at least three-fourths of its capacity.

In the United States four basic types of coffee are prepared: vacuum, dripolator, percolator, and steeped ("boiled") coffee. With the exception of steeped coffee, which is prepared in a conventional kettle, these coffees are prepared in devices designed specifically for brewing the beverage.

Vacuum coffee is made in a two-part container. By heating water in the lower portion of the pot, sufficient pressure is created in the bottom container to force the water into the upper portion where fine-grind coffee has been placed. The water and grounds are in contact usually for a period of approximately three minutes or less. This contact period may be altered to suit individual preferences for a weaker or stronger beverage. After the brewing is completed and the heat is reduced on the lower container, the pressure drops and the brewed coffee is pulled back down to the bottom container. The upper portion and grounds may then be removed easily. Sometimes a tight seal may fail to be established between the upper and lower containers, thus prohibiting the vacuum required to draw the beverage back down into the lower pot following the brewing period. This condition is corrected by twisting the containers until a tight seal is obtained and then

Table 3.3. Proportions Suitable for Making Coffee in Large Quantities

Number of People	Number of Servings,[a] 5½ oz Each	Coffee Needed, Pounds	Water Needed, Gallons
25	40	1	2
50	80	2	4
75	120	3	6
100	160	4	8
125	200	5	10
150	240	6	12

[a]Based on the average number of servings consumed by a given number of people. (Permission from the Pan-American Coffee Bureau, 120 Wall St., New York 5, N. Y. 1960.)

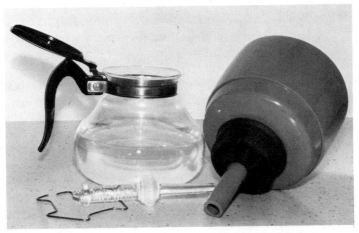

FIGURE 3.4a   The parts of a typical vacuum coffeemaker. Water is measured into the lower container, and the coffee grounds are placed in the upper chamber. Note the wire trivet used when Pyrex is to be placed on an electric surface unit.

FIGURE 3.4b   The assembled vacuum coffeemaker. Automatic electric vacuum coffeemakers also are available for home use.

reheating briefly before cooling the lower pot. The advantage of vacuum coffee is its convenient preparation; its disadvantage is that the coffee will be slightly bitter because the water and grounds are in contact for a few minutes at a high temperature.

A dripolator is composed of three parts: the lower portion to collect the finished product, the center basket for the coffee grounds, and the upper portion to hold the heated water. The basic design for this type of coffee-maker is credited to Count Rumford in the late eighteenth century. To make dripolator coffee, drip-grind coffee is placed in the center container and freshly boiling water is measured into the top portion. The water then drips through the grounds to the bottom of the pot. Coffee made in a dripolator usually has better flavor than coffee made by any other method because the hot water and coffee grounds are in contact just once and then only briefly. In addition, the water is in the optimum temperature range when it is in contact with the grounds. The chief disadvantage of making coffee in a dripolator is the inconvenience of heating the water in a separate container. Also, it may be necessary to reheat the beverage since some cooling will occur during the brewing period.

Percolator coffee is made by measuring regular-grind coffee into a basket suspended on a stem near the top of the pot and cold water into the percolator itself. When hot, a small amount of water constantly circulates up through the stem and trickles down through the grounds. The usual per-colation time is 6 to 8 minutes. This type of coffee is likely to be somewhat bitter because very hot water goes through the grounds several times. In addition, the amount of air introduced during the percolation period may cause some loss of flavor.

The method that is sometimes used for making large quantities of coffee is called "boiling." Actually a more accurate name is "steeped coffee" since the beverage should not be boiled at any time during its preparation. Steeped coffee is made by heating water and then adding regular-grind coffee either loose or tied in a cloth bag. If the grounds are loose they may be settled after the steeping period by adding some egg shells, some slightly beaten egg whites, or some cold water to the beverage. If the grounds are in a bag they should be removed when the coffee is brewed to the proper strength. Removal of the grounds is a great aid in making acceptable steeped coffee. This method of making coffee is sometimes convenient, if not impera-tive, since no special equipment is required. Unfortunately, good coffee does not always result when the steeping method is used because the precautions mentioned above are not always observed. Such coffee then tends to be very strong and bitter.

FIGURE 3.5a   The parts of a dripolator. The coffee grounds are placed in the basket (shown in front) which then is attached to the upper container before being placed on the pot. Boiling water is measured into the upper container after the pot is assembled.

FIGURE 3.5b   The assembled dripolator.

FIGURE 3.6*a* The parts of a percolator. Water is measured into the pot and the grounds into the basket.

FIGURE 3.6*b* The assembled percolator. Automatic electric percolators also are marketed for home use.

A Good Cup of Coffee

The many different coffee traditions in various parts of the world lead to diverse standards for evaluating a good cup of coffee. Americans generally prefer a clear beverage with a delightful aroma and a full flavor. The coffee should not be bitter, and there should not be any sediment in the bottom of the cup. For optimum enjoyment, hot coffee should be served steaming hot. Freshly made coffee has the optimum flavor; coffee that is held at serving temperature for long periods of time gradually loses some of the more volatile, yet highly desirable flavor constituents.

If the brewed beverage is not as described above, preparation can be improved by: more careful measuring of the grounds and the water; maintaining a sparklingly clean pot; using freshly ground or newly opened coffee; and using filter paper. Coffee, despite the fact that it is consumed by a large segment of the population, still needs to be prepared with careful attention to detail if it is to be of top quality when served.

Espresso

One of the results of the increasing numbers of people from the United States traveling to Europe has been the broadening of food tastes to include many foreign foods. A beverage that has been growing in popularity is espresso, the strong coffee variation from Italy. The preparation of espresso requires a special machine (viewed by many with a blend of awe and terror)

FIGURE 3.7 An espresso machine brews strong coffee through a combination of steam and hot water.

which brews the beverage a cup at a time. The flavor quality is derived from brewing the finely ground beans with a mixture of steam and hot water. Traditionally, this very strong and somewhat bitter beverage is served black.

Iced Coffee

Iced coffee, although not as popular as iced tea, is a popular summertime beverage in the United States. Preparation is accomplished by simply preparing a somewhat stronger brew and then pouring the hot beverage over a generous supply of ice to chill and dilute the beverage. Suggestions for the actual strength of the hot coffee range from using one and one-half to two times as much ground coffee as is normally used to prepare the hot beverage, that is, three to four tablespoons of coffee grounds per cup. By using more of the grounds to offset the dilution that will take place as the ice melts in the hot beverage, a pleasing iced beverage with a distinctive flavor will result without extracting the bitter quality that comes from a longer brewing period.

Alternative methods for making iced coffee also are available. Coffee of regular strength can be poured over cubes of frozen coffee. Instant coffee or freeze-dried coffees may be added to hot water and then poured over ice cubes for quick preparation. Of course, between one and one-half to two times the amount of soluble coffee ordinarily used will need to be added to compensate for the dilution due to the melting ice. Iced coffee should have a distinct, coffee-like flavor without bitterness, and the beverage should be sparklingly translucent.

TEA

Tea has been widely used in the Orient since 350 A.D. Apparently the Chinese were the first to use tea and then it was adopted by the Japanese. From Japan, tea was gradually introduced to the Arabs, Venetians, English, and Portuguese. The first reports of the use of tea in the United States date back to the mid-seventeenth century. Probably the most notable mention of tea in America was in connection with the Boston Tea Party in colonial times.

Tea has become a national institution in Japan and in nations influenced strongly by the British. The tea ceremony as performed by a Japanese woman is a precise and beautiful ritual. The unhurried performance of the tea ceremony, a delightful contrast to the informality of modern America, embodies Japanese graciousness and love of tradition.

The British are known for their afternoon tea, a custom that is observed daily in British countries and on British ships. Traditionally, tea and cakes or biscuits of some type are served in the late afternoon. Such nourishment is almost a necessity if one is to conform to the British schedule of a late

FIGURE 3.8   Tea bushes are continually pruned so that workers can pluck 70 to 80 pounds of the most desirable, young tea leaves each day.

evening meal. The brewing of tea is done with more conviction and enthusiasm in England than in many countries. As served in England, tea is a strong, somewhat bitter-flavored beverage to which milk and/or lemon juice are added.

Like coffee, tea thrives in a tropical climate and at altitudes up to 6000 feet. Most of the tea used by the non-Communist nations comes from Japan, India, Ceylon, and the East Indies, where the climate is appropriate for the cultivation of tea. However, some tea is produced in the United States in South Carolina. On an experimental basis, tea also has been produced in the San Joaquin and Sacramento valleys of California. Although tea requires as much as 68 inches of water per year for good production levels, irrigation is a practical solution for meeting this need. Perhaps domestic production will grow in importance; production costs in the United States presently are less than half the price that is paid for imported tea.

A great deal of human labor is required to produce a pound of tea. Three years of careful cultivation and pruning are required before the plant is ready to be plucked for the first time. To maintain a convenient height of three to five feet, this evergreen shrub is continually pruned during its 25 to 50 years of productive life. Picking the tea leaves, the portion of the plant that is of commercial importance, is a slow task requiring manual labor. One worker can pluck only enough in a day to produce slightly more than nine pounds of marketable tea leaves.

Classification of Tea

Tea is classified into one of three groups depending on the method of processing the leaves. Black tea has gained the widest acceptance in the United States, but the other two types, oolong and green teas, also are available here. A brief discussion of processing techniques will reveal the reasons for the different characteristics of the three types.

Further subclassification is made within each type according to size of the leaf, variety of tea leaf, area in which it was grown, and added flavoring substances.

Black Tea. Tea leaves, thinly spread on racks, are slowly withered as the first step in the production of black tea. The withered leaves are then rolled to break open the cells and release the juices and enzymes. The different rolling techniques used in the various countries are partially responsible for the different flavor characteristics inherent in the various teas.

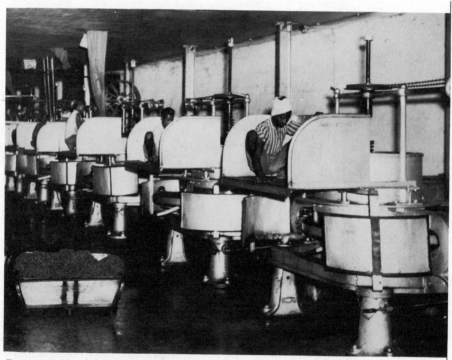

FIGURE 3.9a After the leaves have been withered, the tea leaves are rolled to break up the cells and liberate the juices to aid in developing the flavor qualities of black tea.

FIGURE 3.9*b* Fermenting, the next step, takes place in cool, humid rooms. The chemical changes during fermentation result in the change in leaf color and flavor from the characteristics of green teas to those of black teas.

As soon as rolling is completed, the leaves are sifted and spread thinly on trays where the juices and enzymes, released by rolling, begin the fermentation process. The oxidation of the various polyphenols that takes place during fermentation results in a color change in the leaf as well as in the infusion made from the leaf. A long fermentation period at temperatures between 70 and 80°F oxidizes the various polyphenols to produce a mild, deep-colored beverage. Two of the important polyphenols are catechin and gallocatechin.

Drying or firing, the final step in the processing of tea, is accomplished by passing the fermented leaves through a chamber in which hot air is circulating. At the entrance to the chamber the temperature is 200°F, but it drops to about 120°F near the exit. Besides halting the fermentation process, firing causes some caramelization to occur, resulting in the characteristic black color of black tea leaves.

Quality in black tea is directly related to the polyphenol content and enzyme activity of the leaves selected for processing. The buds and the next two leaves are considered to be most desirable portions of the tea plant since they are high in polyphenols and in the copper-containing oxidase prominent in the oxidation of catechins and gallocatechins. Cognizance is taken of the higher quality of these leaves in the grading system that has been established. Broken Orange Pekoe, the top grade, contains primarily the buds. In order of decreasing quality, other grades are Broken Pekoe, Orange

FIGURE 3.9c   Firing halts the fermentation process and dries the leaves.

Pekoe, Pekoe, Souchong; Broken Orange Pekoe Fannings, and Fannings and Dustings. Orange Pekoe and Pekoe grades, when blended, are well accepted in the United States.

India and Ceylon are famous for their black teas. Darjeeling, named for its district of production, is recognized as the finest tea from India.

Green Tea. Green tea leaves are steamed initially rather than withered in order to inactivate the enzymes that would cause fermentation. The other processing steps, namely rolling and firing, are the same as in the production of black tea. The aroma, flavor, and color of green tea are significantly different from black tea because fermentation has been prevented. Japan is noted for its production of green tea.

Oolong Tea. Oolong teas are intermediate between green and black tea. The initial processing of oolong tea, a brief fermentation, is done on the tea farms prior to collection for a subsequent firing in the town.

Oolong tea has color, flavor, and aroma characteristics reminiscent of both black and green teas because of its partial fermentation. Formosa is particularly noted for the production of fine oolong tea.

Preparation of the Beverage

Tea is served in a variety of ways depending on the country in which it is prepared. In Japan and China tea is intended primarily to be a thirst quencher.

In England and various member nations of the British Commonwealth a much stronger and more stimulating brew is considered to be the standard. By using a longer steeping time and a hotter brewing temperature, the British achieve a more stimulating and more bitter beverage than tea as prepared in America.

A good cup of tea, which contains a maximum of caffeine and a minimum of polyphenols, may be produced by using soft water that has been freshly boiled. Freshly boiled water is important, since it still contains enough oxygen to give the tea a fresh, pleasant flavor. Very hard water will react with the polyphenols, causing them to precipitate and form an extremely disagreeable film that floats on the surface of the tea and coats the cup.

To make tea according to American tastes, the freshly boiled water is poured into a china or glass teapot containing the appropriate amount of tea leaves and is then steeped with the leaves for three to five minutes with no additional heating. One teaspoonful of tea leaves makes one cup of tea. Research has shown that temperatures between 180°F and 212°F are optimum for steeping the tea leaves because at these temperatures the leaves open and provide more surface area for extraction. Preheating the teapot with boiling water is an aid in keeping the tea within this temperature range during the steeping period.

Chemists have demonstrated that a three-minute extraction period will result in maximum caffeine and minimum polyphenols in the beverage. Tea, steeped for three minutes will thus be stimulating, but not astringent. Many people, however, prefer the somewhat stronger flavor achieved by a longer steeping period.

At the end of the steeping period the leaves should be removed to avoid the bitterness that accompanies the continuing extraction of caffeine and polyphenols. Teabags made of parchment provide an easy means of removal as do metal teaballs that hold bulk tea leaves together. Any container for tea leaves should be somewhat larger than the measure of leaves to allow space for swelling of the leaves and circulation of water during the steeping process.

A Good Cup of Tea

A well-prepared cup of tea will be sparklingly clear and will have no suggestion of a surface film. The color will be typical for the type of tea: amber for black tea, an intermediate light brownish-green for oolong, and a pale greenish-yellow for green tea. The flavor of black tea should be brisk and full with no trace of bitterness; the aroma should be distinctive and tempting. The mild aroma and slightly bitter flavor of oolong tea are intermediate between black and green tea. Green tea has little aroma; the flavor, rather than being full and mild, is slightly bitter.

FIGURE 3.10 Tea can serve as the base for a variety of beverages, including hot spiced tea.

The quality of the tea beverage is dependent on the quality of tea leaves used in the preparation. However, tea, whether merchandised as tea bags or loose bulk tea, has a much longer shelf life than coffee. The lack of oils in tea eliminates the concern for avoiding the onset of rancidity during shelf storage. This difference and the limited volatility of its flavoring components make it possible to store tea leaves for several weeks to a period of several months in a closed container without serious changes in the flavor of the beverage brewed from these leaves. Because of this fact, several varieties of tea (including green, black, oolong, and variations such as jasmine and mint) can conveniently be stored for subsequent home use.

Iced Tea

Iced tea may be made by two basic methods. Tea may be prepared as it is for hot tea and then thoroughly chilled, or a concentrated hot tea may be prepared and poured over ice while it is still hot. The latter method is certainly much faster. To make the concentrate, use twice as much tea as for hot tea and brew the beverage for three to five minutes. This results in a very dark beverage that will dilute to normal strength as the ice melts. By this method a nonastringent but flavorful glass of iced tea may be prepared quickly.

Cloudiness is frequently a problem in iced tea, particularly if hard water is used. Clear iced tea can be made even with hard water by letting tea leaves float in water at room temperature for a twelve-hour period. This method is almost too lengthy to be practical, but it does present a solution to the problem of cloudy iced tea when suitable water is not available.

Instant Tea

Instant tea, a counterpart of instant coffee, is available in the markets today. Its widest acceptance has been in making iced tea because of its solubility in cold water. The flavor of instant tea is not as full and pleasing as the beverages made from the tea leaves.

FIGURE 3.11   Iced tea is prepared by using twice as large a measure of tea to make a strong infusion which is diluted by pouring over ice.

COCOA AND CHOCOLATE

Processing of Cocoa and Chocolate

Hot chocolate and cocoa are two beverages that are enjoyed by many, particularly in the winter. The source of the chocolate and cocoa used in their preparation is the bean contained in the pod which forms on the *Theobroma cacao* tree. The preferred sources of the cacao beans are Java, Ceylon, and Samoa, where the mature cacao pods are harvested, and the beans removed preparatory to roasting. Roasting is the stage of the production process that develops the characteristic chocolate aroma of the nibs (the fleshy part of the beans). In addition to the flavor change that occurs during roasting, the heat also drives off some of the moisture and other volatile substances and causes changes in the chemical structures of the polyphenols, producing less astringent compounds. The roasted nibs are then blended with others and stone ground to produce a chocolate liquor that may be marketed as bitter chocolate or altered by the addition of cocoa butter (fat) and sugar to give other familiar chocolate products. Table 3.4 lists the ratio of the various substances in four familiar chocolate products.

The nibs themselves contain cocoa butter, starch, theobromine, caffeine, and pigments of the anthocyanin group identified as cocoa red and cocoa purple. The two fatty acids occurring in the largest percentages in the nibs are oleic acid (38.1 percent) and stearic acid (35.4 percent); palmitic acid and linoleic acid are also present at levels of 24.4 percent and 2.1 percent, respectively.

Cocoa is made by pressing ground nibs to remove much of the cocoa butter. Some of this cocoa butter is added to chocolate to raise the quantity of fat. Milk chocolate results when milk solids and sugar are added.

Cocoa and chocolate are classified as natural or Dutch processed, depending on whether an alkali has been added to the nibs during roasting. The addition of alkali produces a pH of 6.0-8.8 in Dutch processed chocolate

Table 3.4. Composition of Four Types of Chocolate[a]

Type of Chocolate	White Milk Solids, %	Sugar, %	Fat, %
Bitter	0	0	50–56
Bittersweet	0	5–20	40–50
Sweet	0	40–55	32–42
Milk	12	35–55	28–39

[a]F. Fiene and S. Blumenthal. *Handbook of Food Manufacture.* Chemical Publishing Co. New York. 1942.

as compared with the pH range of 5.2-6.0 in natural processed chocolate. Because of the reduced acidity of alkaline treated products, less soda is needed for neutralization reactions than would be needed if natural cocoa or chocolate were used. In addition, alkaline processed chocolate has a reduced tendency to settle out of liquid products.

The appearance of chocolate is altered under adverse storage conditions. When chocolate is exposed to reasonably warm, summerlike temperatures, the fat softens, causing a color change that is referred to as fat bloom. Sugar bloom on chocolate changes the chocolate to a white or light gray and is caused by moisture collecting on the surface.

Chocolate products of higher quality are produced by two important steps in the production of chocolate: conching and tempering. The melted chocolate is kept in motion for 36 to 72 hours in machines called conches which hold the temperature between 43°C (110°F) and 99°C (210°F). Conching is followed by tempering in big kettles. The temperature of the liquid chocolate is gradually reduced to 29-30°C (84-86°F), causing very small fat crystals to form (see Chapter 19). The combination of these two processes produces a very velvety chocolate that is much less likely to develop bloom.

Preparation of the Beverage

The preparation of either cocoa or hot chocolate takes advantage of the fact that these products contain starch which, when heated to boiling, will gelatinize and help to reduce the amount of sediment that settles from either of these beverages. When chocolate is to be used, the solid chocolate must first be melted carefully to avoid scorching. This step is eliminated if fluid chocolate is utilized in the preparation. The cocoa or chocolate, sugar, salt, and water are then mixed together and heated to boiling. When the starch is gelatinized, milk is added gradually and heated to serving temperature. This procedure eliminates raw starch flavor, minimizes sedimentation of the chocolate or cocoa solids, and produces a minimum amount of scum formation from precipitated milk proteins. In addition to keeping the heating period and temperature for the milk carefully controlled, scum formation is further discouraged by beating the beverage with a rotary beater just prior to serving.

Cocoa now is prepared easily in the home by using any of the several instant cocoa mixes available on the market. These blend easily with water or milk (either hot or cold) and require only heating to be ready to serve as the hot beverage. Scum formation is not a problem when these mixes are used.

Occasionally, cocoa may need to be substituted for chocolate in a recipe. A satisfactory substitution can be made by substituting three and one-half tablespoons of cocoa and one-half tablespoon of margarine or butter for one ounce of chocolate. An ounce of chocolate is the same as a square of chocolate, and it requires both halves of the divided square to equal this amount. Ordinarily, unsweetened chocolate is marketed with each ounce being wrapped individually.

Evaluation of the Beverage

A good cup of hot chocolate or cocoa should be pleasing in flavor, free of sediment, and devoid of scum. The flavor is a combination resulting from proper measuring of the cocoa or unsweetened chocolate, selection of the desired chocolate product (natural or alkaline processed), and careful heating to avoid any scorching of the chocolate or milk. A minimum of sediment is obtained by being careful to gelatinize the small amount of starch in the chocolate-water mixture. Scum formation is promoted by an extended heating period and too high a temperature. By simply heating the beverage to the desired serving temperature, beating briefly with a rotary beater, and then serving immediately, scum formation will be held at an absolute minimum. The garnishing of the beverage with a marshmallow or a dollop of whipped cream also combats this problem. A more extensive discussion of scum formation in milk products is found in Chapter 8.

SUMMARY

Coffee is a popular beverage served in many areas of the world. The beverage is prepared by brewing roasted, ground coffee beans in a coffee maker to which water has been added. Fine-grind coffee is used in a vacuum coffee maker to prepare the beverage. Other common preparation methods include using drip-grind coffee in a dripolator and regular-grind coffee in a percolator. The ideal beverage will have a maximum amount of caffeol extracted to enhance the flavor, a suitable amount of caffeine to provide the stimulant, and a minimum amount of polyphenols extracted to avoid bitterness. In addition to the conventional ground coffees, soluble coffees are available in the forms of instant coffees and freeze-dried coffees.

Tea, in contrast to coffee, can be stored for relatively long periods of time because the leaves do not contain the oils that cause coffee to acquire an off flavor rather quickly. Tea leaves can be dried and marketed as green tea, fermented briefly, and then dried for marketing as oolong tea, or fermented more extensively before being dried and packaged as black tea. These tea leaves may be left intact or broken into the broken grades that are sold in tea bags. As can be noted by the consumer, broken grades contribute significant coloring material to the beverage. In addition to the variations that are provided by the differences in processing, flavoring substances such as dried flower petals and leaves can be added to contribute still other flavor modifications. Only one teaspoon of tea leaves is required to prepare a cup of the beverage, in contrast to the two tablespoons of ground coffee that are recommended. Both beverages are prepared by extracting flavor and color constituents from the roasted beans or leaves.

Hot chocolate and cocoa are similar beverages prepared by adding milk to a gelatinized blend of chocolate (or cocoa), sugar, and water. The problem of excessive sediment in the finished beverage is minimized by boiling the chocolate and water mixture. Scum formation is held to a minimum by keeping the beverage below boiling and avoiding prolonged heating. Instant cocoa mixes are popular because of their ease of preparation.

BIBLIOGRAPHY

Allen, A. B. Caffeine identification, differentiation of synthetic and natural caffeine. *J. Agr. Food Chem. 9*, No. 4:294. 1961.

Bate-Smith, E. C. Flavonoid compounds in food. *Adv. Food Res. 5*:261. 1954.

Brown, S. C. *Count Rumford*. Doubleday. Garden City, N. Y. 1962.

Crocker, E. C. and M. P. Vucassovich. Non-alcoholic beverages. *Food Tech. 4*:14. 1949.

Eden, T. *Tea*. Longmans, Greens. New York, N. Y. 1958.

Harler, C. R. *The Culture and Marketing of Tea*. Oxford University Press. New York, N. Y. 1956.

McWilliams, M. *Illustrated Guide to Food Preparation*. Plycon Press, Fullerton, Calif. 1970.

Pan-American Coffee Bureau. *Coffee, Please!* Pan-American Coffee Bureau. 120 Wall St., New York, N. Y. 1960.

Pintauro, Nicholas. *Soluble Coffee Manufacturing Processes*. Noyes Development Corp., Park Ridge, N. J. 1969.

Pintauro, Nicholas. *Soluble Tea Production Processes*. Noyes Development Corp., Park Ridge, N. J. 1970.

Rhoades, J. W. Coffee volatiles, analysis of volatile constituents of coffee. *J. Agr. Food Chem. 8*, No. 2:136. 1960.

Sivetz, M. and H. E. Foote. *Coffee Processing Technology*. Vol. 1 and Vol. 2. Avi Publishing Co., Westport, Conn. 1963.

Uribe, C. A. *Brown Gold*. Random House, New York, N. Y. 1954.

Wellman, F. L. *Coffee*. Interscience Publishers, New York, N. Y. 1961.

Wolfrom, M. L. *et al*. Coffee constituents, carbohydrates of the coffee bean. *J. Agr. Food Chem. 8*, No. 1:58. 1960.

SUGGESTIONS FOR STUDY

1. Prepare three cups of coffee in a dripolator using *(a)* tap water and *(b)* distilled water. Is there an observable difference between the two beverages? What is the reason for the difference?

2. Prepare coffee using *(a)* a percolator, *(b)* a dripolator, *(c)* a vacuum pot, and *(d)* the steeping method. What are the advantages and disadvantages of each method?

3. Prepare *(a)* decaffeinated, *(b)* instant, *(c)* freeze-dried coffee. Compare these beverages with the ones prepared above for flavor, aroma, appearance, and cost.

4. Using fine, drip, and regular grinds, prepare coffee in different kinds of coffeemakers. What grind is best suited to the *(a)* vacuum pot, *(b)* percolator, and *(c)* dripolator?

5. Compare the color, flavor, and aroma of black, oolong, and green teas. Explain the reasons for these differences.

6. Prepare two cups of tea using *(a)* distilled water and *(b)* tap water. Note and explain any observed differences.

7. Prepare two cups of each of the following: *(a)* cocoa made with alkaline processed cocoa, *(b)* cocoa made with natural cocoa, *(c)* hot chocolate made with unsweetened chocolate and *(d)* instant cocoa mix. Compare the color, flavor, sedimentation and cost of the various beverages.

CHAPTER 4

Vegetables

Vegetables are defined as plants, usually herbaceous, that contain an edible portion which suitably is served with the main course of a meal. Although the line between fruits and vegetables is sometimes vague, the stipulation that the plant should be herbaceous helps to clarify the issue; beans, corn, and practically all of the vegetables die down when the growing season is over, a characteristic of herbs. Typically, vegetables are served with the main course or in a salad rather than at the close of a meal. This practice is perpetuated because of the preference for or the tradition of ending a meal with a sweet taste, a characteristic generally lacking among the vegetables. The above definition is useful in classifying some of the plant foods that might otherwise be confusing. For example, tomatoes are conveniently designated as vegetables because they grow on a vine that withers at the end of the growing season, and they generally are served with the main course rather than as a dessert. A contrast is presented by rhubarb, which does grow vigorously and then wither; but this plant food is classified as a fruit because its common use is in desserts such as pies and sauces.

A second definition of a vegetable is suggestive of the challenge presented by vegetable cookery. Although the usage of the word "vegetable" to designate a person leading a "dull or merely physical existence" is not intended to reflect gastronomic qualities, the very fact that this is an accepted use of the word speaks clearly of common attitudes toward vegetables as food. Too often vegetables are prepared with loud overtones of duty and virtue, but with little intention of providing delight. Well prepared vegetables can be the highlight of a meal: their bright colors give a welcome lift to a meal that might otherwise appear to be drab; their varied textures add interest to a meal; their many shapes afford a means of creating a more attractive plate; and their diverse flavors may be used effectively to complement other foods in the meal. In addition, vegetables are important sources of minerals, vitamins, and bulk in the diet.

SURVEY OF VEGETABLES

Classification of vegetables frequently is done on the basis of the portion of the plant that is consumed. In plants such as onions and shallots, the bulb is eaten. The root of beets and carrots is the portion utilized as food. Other portions of the plant that are eaten include leaves and stems (lettuce and parsley), fruits (green peppers and sweet corn), seeds (legumes), and tubers (potatoes). Illustrations of this means of classifying vegetables are listed in Table 4.1.

Fresh vegetables in increasing variety are available to the consumer and present an opportunity for considerable variations in menu planning. The following overview of several of the vegetables that may be available will provide a guide to their use.

Anise or sweet fennel could be described as licorice-flavored celery. The bulb can be eaten raw, or it may be cut up and cooked by boiling, steaming, or braising. Refrigerator storage in the hydrator drawer is recommended.

Artichokes are of two types. The Globe artichoke is the edible flowerhead of a thistlelike plant. The edible portion consists of the base of the

FIGURE 4.1 Examples of vegetables classified according to the part of the plant commonly eaten: *(a)* bulb—onion; *(b)* root—radish; *(c)* leaves and stems—Brussels sprouts; *(d)* seeds-peas; *(e)* fruits-corn.

FIGURE 4.2 Globe artichokes are a vegetable with a delicious pulp at the base of each leaf and in the heart. The sharp tip of each leaf hints of its thistle origins.

leaves and the heart that is found under the choke (the fuzzy portion). This vegetable can be stored in the refrigerator for a few days prior to being boiled or stuffed. The cooked vegetable may be served chilled or hot. Jerusalem artichokes bear a misleading name, since they are a native tuber of North America. Use ranges from raw slices in salads and garnishes to boiling or broiling for service as an alternative to potatoes in the meal.

Asparagus is related botanically to the onion, although the flavor and appearance are distinctly different. There are two basic types of asparagus — white and green. The green asparagus, which is the type commonly marketed, is very perishable and needs to be kept refrigerated with its cut end contin-

Table 4.1. Classification of Vegetables

Portion of Plant	Examples
Bulb	Onions, garlic
Root	Beets, carrots, radishes, parsnips, turnips, sweet potatoes
Tubers[a]	White potatoes, Jerusalem artichokes
Leaves and stems	Cabbage, Brussels sprouts, celery, Chinese cabbage, endive, parsley, lettuce, other salad greens
Fruits	Tomatoes, eggplant, peppers, okra, sweet corn, squash, cucumbers
Seeds	Legumes[b] (lima beans, kidney beans, red beans, pinto beans, peas, navy beans)

[a]Enlarged fleshy stems that grow under the ground.
[b]Seeds from the *Leguminosae* family are commonly called legumes.

ually damp until it is cooked. Preferred preparation methods are boiling and stir frying. Although boiled asparagus frequently is served hot, its use in chilled salads also is popular.

Beans of many different types are available in the market. Fresh beans that may be purchased include green, string beans, yellow or wax beans, lima beans, and fava beans (somewhat similar to the lima bean). Popular dry beans range from kidney, pinto, black, garbanzo, red, pink, navy, and white to lima beans. Fresh beans require refrigerator storage for optimum retention of quality, but dry beans may be stored several months simply by covering them tightly and holding them at temperatures somewhat below room temperature.

Beets, when marketed young, are used as cooked greens and even as salad greens. More commonly, the root is boiled, then peeled and sliced to be served either with butter or as Harvard beets. Beet pickles are popular, too.

Broccoli is a colorful vegetable whose "flowers" and stalks provide an interesting addition to the eye appeal of a meal. When the stalks are topped by heads of blue-green buds, the vegetable is tender when boiled. Yellowing of the heads indicates that the vegetable is too mature, and the stem will begin to be woody. Refrigerator storage for a brief time will be satisfactory.

Brussels sprouts frequently are dubbed "little cabbages," and certainly both flavor and appearance support this title. This food forms along the stem of the plant. Prime quality is typified by a fresh, bright green color and a compact head. Refrigerator storage until the sprouts are cooked is recommended.

Cabbage ranges in color from the familiar green cabbage to the deep purple tones of red cabbage. Red cabbage and green cabbage heads are firm and solid, with the leaves heavily ribbed, yet smooth in texture. A distinct contrast is found in Savoy cabbage, a cabbage head with a very loose structure and leaves with a crinkled appearance. Chinese cabbage has an elongated head and a very prominent central rib in the leaves. Yet another

FIGURE 4.3 Green, red, and Savoy cabbages are popular vegetables in salads or cooked in a variety of recipes.

variation is represented by kohlrabi, which is characterized by its turnip-shaped edible stem. Cabbages are palatable in their cooked forms, but they are also very popular as raw salad ingredients. All types of cabbage should be stored in the hydrator drawer of the refrigerator to help maintain crisp freshness.

Carrots have a mild, sweet flavor and bright color. Their use in food preparation ranges from raw carrot curls and sticks as snack and salad ingredients, to boiled carrots served plain or with a variety of sauces, and even to desserts as a principal ingredient in carrot cake. The lacy leaves of carrots support their inclusion as a member of the parsley family. Other relatives in this family are celery and parsnips.

Cauliflower is named for its appearance of being a cabbage flower, and truly is a descendant of cabbage. Typically, its white, tight head occasionally interspersed with a few small leaves has been popular in this country for nearly half a century. However, there has been continuing experimentation with breeding, which has led to a light green variety that is a cross between cauliflower and broccoli. Such successes presumably will lead to additional variations in fresh produce available to the consumer.

Celery is widely available for use as the raw vegetable, as an ingredient in stews and pot roasts, or stir fried. The common variety available is Pascal celery, preferred because of its minimal stringiness. A relative of celery is celeriac or celery root. In contrast to celery, celery root is prized for its bulblike root, and is served as a substitute for potatoes after it has been boiled. Another use is as marinated, raw julienne strips. Another interesting relation of celery that may become available fresh in the markets is a Chinese product called celtuce, a cross between lettuce and celery.

Corn, white or yellow, is one of the particularly popular vegetables that is available fresh and in abundance during the summer months. Winter supplies are limited and, therefore, more costly. Many varieties have been developed, but all varieties are best when cooked very soon after being picked. The flavor of the corn cooked immediately after picking will be sweeter because the sugar will not have had an opportunity to be converted to starch.

Eggplant, originally found in India and China, is an eye-catching vegetable with a deep purple, glossy skin. Other varieties may be red or cream colored. Typically, the purple-skinned eggplants will range between four and six inches in diameter. Sautéing or baking should be done soon after purchase, because this vegetable is best when stored only briefly in the warmer part of the refrigerator.

Greens may be defined simply as green, leafy vegetables served either raw or cooked. Included in this group are endive, kale, lettuce, mustard and beet tops, dandelions, and spinach. Endive is a green with a somewhat bitter flavor quality. Curly endive has rather scratchy leaves with an almost finger-like appearance. Its narrow projections are in contrast to the broad leaves of escarole, another variety of endive. French endive develops in an upright stalk rather than in the bushy form of curly endive and escarole. Actually, French endive is a form of chicory related to the chicory that is dried and used occasionally as a coffee extender. The many different forms of lettuce may be grouped into five categories: leaf or bunching, crisphead, romaine,

FIGURE 4.4 The prickly character of curly endive distinguishes it from escarole, a type of endive with broader, less jagged leaves.

butterhead, and stem. The most commonly used lettuce is the crisphead, more frequently marketed as iceberg. Leaf lettuce and red leaf lettuce are favorites of gardeners, but also are often available in the produce section of supermarkets. Butterhead lettuces are rather loosely headed and their leaves are more pliable and less crisp than crisphead. The leaves have a somewhat oily feel. Familiar varieties of this delicate lettuce are Boston and Bibb, which sometimes is called "limestone." Romaine has an elongated shape to its head and a leaf that is deceptive in appearance. Although the leaf looks coarse and somewhat tough, top quality romaine has a tender leaf with a pleasing crispness. The stem lettuce is represented by celtuce.

Mushrooms are fungi that are highly prized as a complement to steaks, in sauces and gravies. Commercial production of this delicacy requires careful control of humidity, temperature, and ventilation, but the financial rewards have proved to be sufficient to compensate producers for the care required to grow mushrooms. Storage in the refrigerator should be limited to no more than five days to insure optimum quality.

Okra is a vegetable considered to be synonymous with Creole cookery. The pods are commonly used in soups and gumbos.

Onions are used in many different varieties in food preparation. The dry onions available to the shopper may be flat, as is true of the popular white onion, or globe-shaped. The larger ones commonly are chopped or minced to add flavoring to a wide variety of dishes. Very large dry onions are well suited to making onion rings. Red onions, because of their attractive appearance and pleasing flavor, are a useful ingredient in raw vegetable salads. Small dry onions just over an inch in diameter are popular as "boiling" onions to be served creamed, buttered, or as a component of kabobs. Green onions are onions that are harvested green before the bulb develops fully. Scallions are shoots harvested before the white onion bulb develops. Chives are very tiny onions whose tops are snipped fine and added to sour cream and other foods to provide an onionlike flavor and a green garnish. Leeks are appropriately described as very large green onions with flat leaves and a rather thick stalk. Green onions are best stored in the refrigerator's hydrator drawer for only short periods of time. In fact, chives are ideal when they are snipped directly from the plant just prior to being served. Dry onions should be stored in a spot cooler than room temperature and with relatively low humidity to delay root growth and decay.

Peppers add a bright touch of red or green to the menu. Their flavor contribution may be sweet and delicate or surprisingly hot, depending on the type of pepper used. Red and green sweet peppers, commonly referred to as bell peppers, are useful raw in salads, parboiled and stuffed, or diced and added to a wide variety of hot dishes. The paprika pepper is a mild red pepper that is ground and canned for marketing as paprika. The hot pepper varieties are chili, pimiento, and cayenne peppers.

Potatoes are extremely versatile in their preparation and have a well established place in the diet. Many different varieties of potatoes are available throughout the country, and their cooking characteristics are quite

FIGURE 4.5 Butterhead lettuces include the larger Boston (left) and Bibb or "limestone" (right).

variable. The selection of a variety for a specific use is discussed in the section on selection of vegetables.

Sweet potatoes are native to the Western Hemisphere and were noted as long ago as Columbus' voyages to this continent. The dry-meated sweet potatoes generally have a tan or light-colored skin. The deeper colored, moist-meated sweet potatoes are often called yams, although actually yams are a different class. Generally, the medium-sized sweet potatoes that are bulky in the center and tapered toward the ends are of excellent quality as long as the ends are firm and free of spoilage.

Peas are difficult to market fresh because of the rapid change from sugar to starch unless they are cooled very rapidly and kept cold until cooked. Preferably they are stored as short a time as possible and are kept in the pod, being shelled just before boiling them. A variety of increasing interest in this country is the Snow pea, a pea noted for its very tender pod. Snow peas and the somewhat smaller China pea are cooked whole, the crisp pod being served along with the peas themselves.

Rutabagas have been widely utilized for many years because of their excellent keeping qualities. Usually they are dipped in wax to extend their storage life, and the wax is removed when the rutabaga is peeled before being boiled.

Squash generally is divided into summer squash and winter squash,

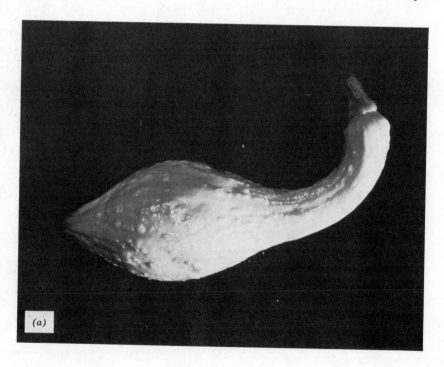

(a)

FIGURE 4.6   Summer squash: *(a)* yellow crookneck; *(b)* zucchini; *(c)* scallop.

terms that have little relation to their availability in the market. The summer squash varieties have a soft rind and rather limited storage life in the refrigerator. In contrast, winter squash generally can be typified by a hard shell and a storage life of three months or longer. Favored varieties of summer squash are yellow crookneck, yellow straightneck, zucchini, scallops or pattypan, and cocozelle. Varieties of winter squash commonly available are Hubbard, acorn (table queen), buttercup, butternut, and banana.

Tomatoes are actually the fruit of the tomato plant, but their common usage in the main part of the meal causes them to be classified as a vegetable today. The versatility of the tomato as a raw vegetable served simply sliced or as a component of vegetable salads or cooked in many sauces and casseroles has resulted in a very large market for this food. Yet its fragile qualities have caused some difficulties in marketing the fresh vegetable. Several varieties have been developed for particular requirements. The cherry tomato is a very popular variety for use in salads.

COMPOSITION

Although the percentage composition will vary, certain substances are common to all vegetables. Water content is high in most vegetables, but it is particularly high in greens and tomatoes. Water constitutes over 90 per cent of the edible portion of these vegetables. Greens rely on water in the cells for their crispness. Partial dehydration of the cells of lettuce and other greens is accompanied by a change from a crisp to a limp leaf. Since the cell walls of greens are structurally weak, rigidity is achieved only when the cells are filled with water.

Cellulose, the structural carbohydrate in the cell walls of all plants, occurs in slightly different forms in various parts of the plant. A stalk of asparagus serves as a good illustration. The tip is tender but the cellulose changes to a rather woody material that is considerably tougher at the lower end of the stalk.

The cell walls are cemented with a group of compounds called pectic substances (see Chapter 18). In immature vegetables most of the pectic substances present will be in the form of protopectin. Protopectin is converted to pectin in the mature vegetable and then to pectic acid in overripe vegetables. As the transition from protopectin to pectic acid progresses, the vegetable softens, at least in part as a result of the increased solubility of the pectic substances.

Some vegetables such as corn and potatoes contain a high percentage of carbohydrate in the form of starch. In immature vegetables this carbohydrate is primarily in the form of sugar, and the sugar gradually changes to the related carbohydrate, starch, as the vegetable matures.

The caloric value of vegetables comes largely from their carbohydrate content; analysis of a number of vegetables reveals that there is almost no fat in them and, with the exception of the legumes, there is also little protein in vegetables. Legumes, however, are an important source of vegetable proteins. The composition of several common vegetables is compiled in Table 4.2.

NUTRITIONAL SIGNIFICANCE OF VEGETABLES

The nutritional contribution of different vegetables is sufficiently varied that it is wise to serve a variety of vegetables to ensure that all the necessary nutrients from the vegetable category are included in the diet. Most vegetables are an important source of minerals, vitamins, and cellulose, and certain vegetables such as potatoes contribute appreciable quantities of starch. Legumes are a good source of protein, but it should be noted that

Table 4.2. Approximate Composition of Some Vegetables Commonly Used in the United States[a]

Vegetable, 1 Cup	Water, %	Protein, Grams	Fat, Grams	Total Carbohydrate, Grams
Asparagus, cooked	92	4	Trace	6
Green beans, cooked	92	2	Trace	6
Beets, cooked	88	2	Trace	16
Broccoli, cooked	90	5	Trace	8
Brussels sprouts, cooked	85	6	1	12
Cabbage, raw	92	1	Trace	5
Carrots, cooked	92	1	1	9
Cauliflower, cooked	92	3	Trace	6
Sweet corn, cooked	76	2	1	16
Lettuce, raw	95	5	1	13
Lima beans, cooked mature	64	16	1	48
Onions, cooked	90	2	Trace	18
Peas, cooked	82	8	1	19
Potatoes, baked	75	3	Trace	21
Spinach, cooked	91	6	1	6
Split peas, cooked mature	70	20	1	52
Sweet potatoes, baked	64	2	1	36
Tomatoes, raw	94	2	Trace	6

[a]Compiled from *Food, the Yearbook of Agriculture, 1959*, pp. 249-253. U. S. Government Printing Office. Superintendent of Documents. Washington, D. C. 1959.

FIGURE 4.7 Swiss chard is one of the dark green, leafy vegetables contributing carotene (provitamin A), ascorbic acid, calcium, and iron.

vegetable proteins are classified as incomplete proteins. Incomplete proteins are well utilized by the body, but should be supplemented with proteins from animal sources (eggs, milk, cheese, meats, poultry, or fish).

Calcium and iron are two minerals found in significant amounts in vegetables. Beans, peas, broccoli, and greens contain important amounts of these essential minerals. Spinach contains an appreciable quantity of calcium, but the oxalic acid in spinach combines with the calcium to form an insoluble salt, calcium oxalate, which cannot be absorbed by the body. Vegetables also help to meet the body's need for sodium, chlorine, cobalt, copper, magnesium, manganese, phosphorus, and potassium.

Carotenes (precursors of vitamin A) and ascorbic acid are abundant in many vegetables; vitamin D is notably low. Orange-colored vegetables and dark-green leafy vegetables are excellent sources of carotenes. Leafy vegetables are also good sources of ascorbic acid.

Vegetables are useful in the diet for their cellulose content. Very little, if any, cellulose is digested in the body, but cellulose provides the roughage necessary to promote motility of food through the intestines.

Not only do different vegetables contribute a variety of nutrients, but the same kind of vegetable will vary in the amount of the nutrients. The nutritive value of a particular kind of vegetable is influenced by the variety of vegetable, the growing conditions, and the treatment from the field to the table.

Knowledge of the nutrients available in different varieties of a vegetable is being utilized in programs designed to alleviate malnutrition where it exists in the free world. Through programs administered by agencies of the United Nations, farmers are being encouraged to plant particularly nutritious varieties of crops indigenous to a country because these foods will be accepted by the people. By growing more nutritious varieties of an accepted food it is possible to improve nutrition without markedly altering dietary patterns.

The term "growing conditions" encompasses the natural mineral content of the soil, fertilizing programs, and climate. Fertility of the soil has a strong influence on the total crop yield per acre. The level of iodine in the soil determines the amount of iodine in vegetables grown there. In addition, a boron deficiency in the soil reduces the carotene and riboflavin levels of tomatoes.

Studies have shown that ascorbic-acid levels are influenced by rainfall and sunlight during development of the vegetable. Long exposure to sunlight is conducive to a high ascorbic-acid level in a vegetable and is more beneficial than simply having the plant in indirect light. The influence of temperature on ascorbic-acid content is controversial: some studies have demonstrated a reduced ascorbic-acid level with an increase in temperature, whereas others have shown a higher ascorbic-acid content. Carotene levels are influenced by rainfall, amount of sunlight, and the season of the year. These factors, however, have not been analyzed sufficiently to permit definitive separation of their effects.

Considerable confusion among consumers has developed as a result of the promotion of "organically grown" vegetables. Supposedly, organically grown produce has been grown with the use of natural fertilizers and without chemical fertilizers or insecticides. First, there presently (1973) is no legal definition of "organically grown," although such legislation has been proposed and discussed heatedly. Consequently, any produce can legally be identified in this manner if one wishes to do so. Furthermore, no evidence has yet shown that produce grown only with natural fertilizers is more nourishing than that grown with chemical fertilizers, although yields clearly are greater with appropriate chemical fertilizer programs. The result is that a greater volume of produce, and thus more nutrients can be produced from an acre of land through the controlled use of fertilizers and pesticides.

The loss of nutrients in relation to marketing and preparation of vegetables will be considered later in this chapter.

FIGURE 4.8 Plump and firm vegetables free of blemishes provide optimum quality and nutrition. Through good harvesting and marketing practices zucchini, tomatoes, onions, corn, and many other fresh vegetables are now available to consumers.

MARKETING

Good farming practices are certainly important, but farmers alone are not responsible for the nutritive content of vegetables. There are two important links between the farmer and the consumer, and at both of these times careful storage of the food is vital if vitamin losses are to be minimized. One of these times is during the shipment of vegetables from the farm to the market.

When fresh vegetables are crated, the temperature in the crate slowly begins to rise and the quality of the food starts to diminish. It has been shown that the temperature in a crate of spinach will rise to 85-100°F, at which time a soft rot develops. The respiration rate in leafy vegetables is higher than for other vegetables; hence, the temperature rise in the crate is rather rapid. However, the temperature rise in the crate also presents a problem to a lesser degree in other vegetables such as broccoli, asparagus, peas, and corn. The temperature change may be controlled by packing the vegetables loosely in the crates and by putting some crushed ice inside the field crates.

The vegetables ordinarily are loaded into refrigerated trucks or refrigerated railroad cars. Such trucks or cars work in opposite roles at different seasons of the year for in summer they chill the vegetables and in winter they may be equipped with heaters to prevent freezing.

Refrigerator cars should be packed so that there are channels between and above the rows of food to permit good air circulation and to maintain a relatively uniform temperature throughout the car. Properly iced, high-quality vegetables from the West Coast will arrive at Eastern markets in excellent condition. A comparison made between vegetables carefully shipped from the West Coast to an Eastern market and vegetables grown locally near the same market which were not chilled revealed that the quality of the Western vegetables was high even after the long trip, whereas the uniced local vegetables showed distinct loss of quality.

Proper storage in the market is the second important step in making high-quality vegetables available to the consumer. Adequate cold-storage space is essential for holding vegetables until they are placed in display areas. A good fresh-produce section is an attraction that is not overlooked by competent grocers.

SELECTION

Selection of vegetables is an important part of meal preparation for it is impossible to serve tasty, appetizing vegetables if they are not of high quality before being prepared. Quality guides are available to the consumer to aid in the selection not only of fresh vegetables but also of canned and frozen products. Actually, the first step in selection is the decision between purchasing the vegetable fresh, frozen, or canned. Individual preference may influence this decision, but price and availability of the fresh vegetable often play significant roles, too. When a vegetable is in season so that the quality is high and the price is low, the homemaker may purchase the fresh vegetable. Others may elect to buy canned and frozen vegetables year-round because of the convenience in preparation this provides.

Fresh Vegetables

The United States, under the Consumer and Marketing Service of the United States Department of Agriculture, has established grade standards for most fresh vegetables. In most instances, there are at least two grades provided, with U.S. No. 1 or U.S. Fancy being the highest grade. However, there are variations in grade terminology from one vegetable to another. For example, the highest grade for potatoes is U.S. Extra No. 1. This terminology may be found on produce packages in the market on occasion, but the main use of grades is found in the marketing chain between the grower, shipper, wholesaler, and retailer. The use of federal grades is not required by federal law, but a few states have legislation requiring their use.

The quality of fresh vegetables is influenced by the season of the year and the handling from the time of harvest until the produce is purchased by the consumer. When the vegetable is harvested during the normal peak of production for its type, quality generally will be optimal. Table 4.3 provides a guide to the usual availability of fresh vegetables. This serves as a key to the vegetables that are likely to be of high quality in the fresh produce section of the market at any particular time of year. In addition to this guide, consumers also will need to examine vegetables carefully with attention to the purchasing guides suggested in Table 4.4 In addition to the specifics mentioned for the vegetables in Table 4.4, vegetables should be examined for their freshness, as indicated by color and crispness, and their freedom from rot and other blemishes.

Sometimes different grades or different sizes of the same vegetable will be available to the shopper, thus offering an opportunity to select on the basis of both quality and price. An example might be asparagus of different sizes. Jumbo asparagus, the size designation for stalks not less than 13/16 of an inch in diameter, is higher in price than smaller asparagus, but may be sufficiently important for special occasions to warrant the greater cost. On the other hand, the less expensive sizes may be of equally fine quality and well suited to the type of recipe for which they are being selected. Carrots are another type of vegetable in which size must be considered. Small carrots may be cooked and served whole with a pot roast, but only large carrots are satisfactory when curls are to be made from the carrots.

Table 4.3. A Guide to Average Monthly Availability of Fresh Vegetables[a]

Vegetable	Jan. (%)	Feb. (%)	Mar. (%)	Apr. (%)	May (%)	June (%)	July (%)	Aug. (%)	Sept. (%)	Oct. (%)	Nov. (%)	Dec. (%)	Total (million lbs)
Artichoke	6	8	13	21	15	5	3	3	4	6	9	6	59
Asparagus		2	20	34	27	16	1			*	*		109
Beans (all)	6	5	6	8	10	13	12	11	9	9	7	6	396
Beets	4	4	5	5	7	13	15	13	12	11	7	4	99
Broccoli	10	10	12	11	9	5	4	4	6	10	11	9	59
Brussels sprouts	14	11	7	3	2	1	*	2	10	17	19	15	20
Cabbage	9	8	10	9	9	9	8	7	8	8	8	8	1860
Carrots	10	9	10	9	8	8	8	7	8	8	8	8	1365
Cauliflower	8	7	8	7	5	5	4	5	11	19	14	8	198
Celery	8	8	9	9	8	8	8	7	7	8	10	10	1326
Corn	2	2	3	6	16	17	17	18	11	10	7	1	196
Cucumbers	5	4	5	8	12	13	13	10	8	8	8	6	613
Eggplant	8	6	7	7	7	8	8	12	12	9	8	8	79
Endive Belgian	9	16	15	14	11	1			4	9	9	12	3
Endive escarole	8	7	9	8	7	9	9	9	9	10	8	7	158
Garlic	5	8	8	9	6	7	11	11	13	9	8	6	59
Greens	10	9	11	10	8	7	6	6	7	8	8	9	289
Lettuce	8	7	9	9	9	9	9	9	8	8	8	8	4214
Mushrooms	10	9	10	10	8	7	6	5	6	8	10	11	48
Okra	*	*	1	4	10	18	23	21	13	7	3	1	38
Onions, dry	8	7	8	9	9	10	9	9	9	8	8	7	2300
Onions, green	6	6	8	9	10	11	11	10	8	7	7	7	188
Parsnips	13	11	11	9	7	5	3	3	7	13	11	9	32
Peas, green	7	9	11	14	12	14	12	9	5	3	2	3	20
Peppers	7	6	7	7	9	10	10	10	10	9	8	7	533
Potatoes	9	7	9	9	9	9	8	8	8	8	8	8	13870
Radishes	6	6	8	9	11	12	11	9	8	7	7	7	294
Spinach	10	9	10	10	10	9	6	5	7	9	9	8	105
Squash	7	6	6	7	8	9	9	9	10	11	11	8	327
Sweet potatoes	9	8	9	7	5	2	3	6	10	12	17	13	989
Tomatoes	6	6	8	8	11	12	11	10	8	8	6	6	2434
Turnips-rutabagas	12	11	10	6	5	4	4	5	9	12	13	11	224

[a]Adapted from *Guide to Average Monthly Availability of Fresh Fruits and Vegetables*. United Fresh Fruit and Vegetable Association, 777 14th St., N.W. Washington, D.C. 20005. 7th rev. ed. 1969.
*Indicates supply is less than 0.5 percent of annual total.

Table 4.4. Guide to Selection of Fresh Vegetables

Vegetable	Criteria
Artichoke	Plump, firm, heavy in comparison with size, green scales with absence of brown discoloration
Asparagus	Good green color extending down much of stalk, closed and compact tips, crisp and tender stalk
Beans (green and wax)	Bright color for the variety, pods that are firm and crisp rather than flabby
Beets	Fresh-looking tops if still attached, surface that is smooth and deep red, firm and round with slim tap root
Broccoli	Dark green to purplish color with no trace of yellow in bud clusters, smooth stalks of moderate size with no traces of spoilage
Brussels sprouts	Fresh green color void of yellow leaves, tight outer leaves free of injury, tight heads
Cabbage	Firm head, fresh color in outer leaves, crisp leaves
Carrots	Crisp rather than flabby, good orange color free from sunburned green at top
Cauliflower	Uniform creamy white color with no trace of dark discoloration, solid and compact head, fresh leaves if attached
Celery	Crisp stalks with a solid feel, glossy surface on stalk, crisp leaves, no discoloration on inside surface of large outer stalks
Corn	Ear well covered with plump young kernels, fresh husks that are green and unwilted, silks free of decay
Cucumbers	Firm, moderate size, green color all over
Eggplant	Smooth and firm with deep purple skin free of blemishes
Greens	Crisp appearance with good green color typical of the type of green, free from rust and other blemishes, no wilted or decaying areas

Table 4.4. Guide to Selection of Fresh Vegetables (continued)

Vegetable	Criteria
Lettuce	Crisp quality to leaves, with butter lettuces being somewhat less crisp, but still succulent, free of decay, good color for the variety
Mushrooms	Caps closed around the stem, surface of cap light-colored and gills (if showing under cap) should be light rather than dark, smooth and firm cap with no suggestion of drying out
Okra	Pods tender enough to bend under some pressure, less than 4½ inches long, fresh green color, no blemishes
Onions, dry	Firm and dry with small necks, no decay
Onions, green	Crisp, bright green tops, free from decay
Parsnips	Smooth and firm, small to medium size, free from blemishes
Peas	Crisp pods with fresh green color, pods full but not bulging
Peppers	Firm, deep color, no trace of flabbiness or decay
Potatoes	Firm, free from sunburned green areas, no decay, skin intact and free from blemishes
Radishes	Medium size, firm and plump, fresh red color
Squash	Well developed with no soft areas, firm, summer squash has glossy and tender skin, winter squash has tough and hard skin
Sweet potatoes	Firm, good color, no signs of decay at ends
Tomatoes	Smooth, good color for stage of ripeness, firm if not fully ripe, slightly soft if ripe, free from blemishes
Turnips and rutabagas	Firm and smooth, free of blemishes

Selection of the proper variety is necessary for optimum preparation of some vegetables. Tomatoes provide a useful illustration. Meaty varieties such as beefsteak tomatoes are particularly well suited for salads and broiling, whereas a less expensive, juicy variety will suffice for stewing and casseroles. Cherry tomatoes are well suited to the preparation of kabobs and salads, but are not practical when tomato slices are required.

Some Chinese recipes require a special pea, the Chinese pea, which has such a tender pod that the entire pea and its pod are served. For these recipes, the ordinary garden varieties of peas are entirely unsuitable because of the tough nature of the pod.

Potatoes provide a particularly outstanding illustration of the importance of selecting the variety of a vegetable that is best suited to the preparation for which it is intended. Some potatoes are relatively high in sugar content and low in starch; these are designated as waxy potatoes. Nonwaxy potatoes are just the reverse, that is, they are high in starch and low in sugar in comparison with the waxy potatoes. Another designation for nonwaxy potatoes is mealy potatoes. A comparison of a boiled waxy potato with a boiled nonwaxy potato will quickly illustrate the significance of the difference in composition. Starch granules in the potatoes swell as they take up water during cooking; more swelling occurs in the nonwaxy potato than in the waxy potato because of the greater starch content in the nonwaxy potato. The result is that the cell walls begin to rupture in the nonwaxy potato and pieces of the potato slough off into the cooking water, while the waxy potato remains intact.

Since the waxy potato holds its shape well if it is not overcooked, this type of potato is well suited to the preparation of recipes requiring distinct pieces of potato. Potato salad, boiled potatoes, scalloped potatoes, and parsley potatoes are typical of the preparations for which waxy potatoes are best suited. Nonwaxy potatoes, when used in these types of recipes, result in products with indistinct outlines and reduced eye appeal.

Nonwaxy potatoes, because of their high starch content and resultant cooking characteristics, are well suited to baking and mashing. The white, light, and fluffy mashed potatoes resulting from the use of nonwaxy potatoes contrast clearly with the darker, more compact, and rather gummy mashed potatoes prepared using waxy potatoes.

This compositional difference is also of interest when selecting potatoes for frying. The best french fried potatoes are produced with nonwaxy potatoes; their lower sugar content means a slower rate of browning, thus insuring sufficient time for cooking the potato slice throughout before the surface becomes the desired golden brown. When waxy potatoes are used for deep-fat frying, the high sugar content causes excessive browning and a burned flavor because the sugar caramelizes too much on the surface before the interior of the potato is cooked sufficiently. An additional bonus for selecting nonwaxy potatoes is that the most common variety, the Russet Burbank, is long and flat, a shape particularly well suited to easy cutting for french fries.

The varieties of potatoes that commonly are available in markets vary from one part of the country to another. The Russet Burbank is a nonwaxy potato variety that is found in many areas; Red Pontiac is a familiar example of a waxy potato variety. Some potatoes possess some characteristics of the waxy potato and some of the cooking quality of nonwaxy potatoes. These potatoes are considered to be all-purpose potatoes, yielding satisfactory, but not outstanding finished products. They are useful when only one kind of potato is being purchased, but the plans for preparation range from mashed and baked to boiled and scalloped. Table 4.5 is a guide to the types of preparation best suited to several varieties of potatoes available in markets around the country.

An accurate way of predicting the cooking quality of potatoes is based on their specific gravity. Even within a variety, the specific gravity of potatoes will vary, and this variation is reflected by a difference in cooking quality. Potatoes with a low specific gravity were found (Mackey and Joiner, 1960) to have a waxy texture and quality, while potatoes with a higher

Table 4.5. Varieties of Potatoes and the Types of Preparation to which They Are Best Suited[a]

Variety	Suitable Types of Preparation
Cherokee	Boiling, baking
Chippewa	Boiling
Cobbler	Boiling, medium acceptability baked
Green Mountain	Boiling, baking
Hunter	Boiling, baking
Katahdin	Boiling, french frying
Kennebec	Boiling, baking, french frying
Keswick	Boiling, baking
Norgold Russet	Boiling, french frying
Norland	Boiling
Pungo	Boiling, baking
Red LaSoda	Boiling
Red Pontiac	Boiling
Russet Burbank	Baking, french frying
Sebago	Boiling, baking
White Rose	Boiling

[a]Adapted from *Buying Guide for Fresh Fruits, Vegetables, and Nuts.* Blue Goose, Inc., Fullerton, Calif. 1971. Page 84.

FIGURE 4.9 The potato at the bottom of the container has a high solids content and is good for baking; the one at the top has a low solids content, suiting it well to boiling and use in salads.

specific gravity (high solids content) possessed the cooking qualities of nonwaxy potatoes. Potatoes can be separated readily on the basis of specific gravity simply by placing them in a solution containing 11 cups of water and one cup of salt. The potatoes that float have a low specific gravity (less than 1.08) and will behave as waxy potatoes; those that sink have a high specific gravity with a high solids content and are categorized as nonwaxy. Although this simple method of providing useful information to the consumer is not yet being utilized in markets, there is some possibility that it may be adopted.

Since 1971, revised standards for grading potatoes have been in effect. The new top grade is designated as U.S. Extra No. 1, a rating that requires a minimum size of $2\frac{1}{4}$ inches in diameter (or five ounces in weight), with a variation limit of $1\frac{1}{4}$ inches, and a minimum of internal defects or sprouts. U. S. No. 1 is now the second grade, but still is somewhat stronger in its quality definition than was the U. S. Fancy, formerly the top grade. The grading of potatoes is an optional service except where it is required by state law. Potatoes may also be designated by size. Under federal standards, small potatoes range from a minimum of $1\frac{3}{4}$ inches in diameter to a maximum of $2\frac{1}{2}$ inches; medium vary between $2\frac{1}{4}$ and $3\frac{1}{4}$ inches; and large range from 3 to $4\frac{1}{4}$ inches. If size of U. S. No. 1 potatoes is not designated, the potatoes must be a minimum of $1\frac{7}{8}$ inches in diameter. No maximum diameter is stated.

Frozen and Canned Vegetables

Three grades have been established on a national basis to designate quality of frozen and canned vegetables. U. S. Grade A or Fancy vegetables are of top quality and are selected on the basis of color, tenderness, and freedom from blemishes. The next grade, U. S. Grade B or Extra Standard, is characterized as being usually slightly more mature and less carefully selected for color and tenderness than Grade A. U. S. Grade C or Standard is the lowest grade and is indicative of less uniformity of color and flavor. However, this grade is less expensive and of sufficiently high quality for use in soups and some casseroles. Grading by U. S. grade standards is optional, but products bearing the official U. S. grade names are packed under constant inspection by representatives of the United States Department of Agriculture. Products designated simply as Fancy or Grade A are required to meet the standards of U. S. Grade A, but federal inspection is not necessarily conducted during processing of these foods. Brand names rather than grade names are frequently used as indicators of quality.

Product labels must indicate the usual name for the product and also the net contents in ounces (if less than four pounds). The style must also be indicated, but this can be done by picture or word; an illustration would be to designate frozen green beans as cut green beans or to show a picture of the cut product. Additional recipe information on the label is optional.

Regulations regarding nutrition labeling of foods, including vegetable products have been emerging, spurred by the consumer interest growing out of the 1969 White House Conference on Food, Nutrition, and Health. Nutrition labeling, under the jurisdiction of the Food and Drug Administration, is being implemented to serve two purposes:

1. To improve the nutritional information on food labels.
2. To make information on food labels more meaningful to the public.

Nutrition labeling regulations make this a voluntary procedure for most foods; mandatory labeling of nutrients is required when (1) a nutrient is added (even when it is added to replace one lost during processing), or

(2) a nutritional claim is made for the food either in advertising or on its label. The final required implementation date for this type of labeling is December 31, 1974.

Regulations for nutrition labeling require the following information presented in this standard format:

"Nutrition Information per Serving"
1. Serving size.
2. Servings per container.
3. Caloric content or calories.
4. Protein content or protein.
5. Carbohydrate content or carbohydrate.
6. Fat content or fat.
7. Percentage of United States Recommended Daily Allowances (U. S. RDA).

Ordinarily, the levels of vitamin A, vitamin C, thiamin, riboflavin, niacin, calcium, and iron must be included. Twelve other vitamins and minerals also *may* be listed. An example of this type of labeling is shown in Figure 4.10.

Table 4.6 provides a comparison of yield obtained from canned and frozen vegetables and is a useful guide for purchasing these items.

FIGURE 4.10 An example of the format for nutrition labeling.

NUTRITION INFORMATION
(PER SERVING)
SERVING SIZE = 8 OZ.
SERVINGS PER CONTAINER = 1

CALORIES............... 560	FAT (PERCENT OF
PROTEIN................. 23 GM	CALORIES 53%)....... 33 GM
CARBOHYDRATE ..... 43 GM	POLYUNSAT-
	URATED .... 2 GM
	SATURATED........ 9 GM
	CHOLESTEROL*
	(20 MG/100 GM) ...... 40 MG
	SODIUM (365 MG/
	100 GM)................. 830 MG

PERCENTAGE OF U.S. RECOMMENDED DAILY
ALLOWANCES (U.S. RDA)

PROTEIN 35	RIBOFLAVIN.................... 15
VITAMIN A 35	NIACIN........................... 15
VITAMIN C	CALCIUM 2
(ASCORBIC ACID)....... 10	IRON.............................. 25
THIAMIN (VITAMIN	
B₁) 15	

*Information on fat and cholesterol content is provided for individuals who, on the advice of a physician, are modifying their total dietary intake of fat and cholesterol.

Table 4.6. Approximate Amount of Cooked Vegetables Obtained from Canned and Frozen Vegetable Containers[a]

Vegetable	Yield From Cans (Drained)		Yield From Frozen Packages	
	Can Size	Cups	Package Size	Cups
Asparagus, cut	14 oz (no. 300)	1 1/3	10 oz	1 1/4
Beans, green or wax, cut	15½ oz (no. 300)	1 3/4	9 oz	1 2/3
Beans, lima	16 oz (no. 303)	1 3/4	10 oz	1 2/3
Beets, sliced, diced or whole	16 oz (no. 303)	1 3/4	—	—
Broccoli, cut	—	—	10 oz	1 1/2
Carrots, diced or sliced	16 oz (no. 303)	1 3/4	10 oz	1 2/3
Cauliflower	—	—	10 oz	1 1/2
Corn, whole	16 oz (no. 303)	1 2/3	10 oz	1 1/2
Peas	16 oz (no. 303)	1 3/4	10 oz	1 2/3
Spinach	15 oz (no. 300)	1 1/3	10 oz	1 1/4
Tomatoes (undrained)	16 oz (no. 303)	1 7/8	—	—

[a]Adapted from E. R. Thompson, *How to Buy Canned and Frozen Vegetables.* Consumer and Marketing Service Home and Garden Bulletin No. 167. Washington, D. C. 1969.

New products on the market present new decisions for the consumer. Many frozen vegetable combinations, complete with a wide selection of sauces, have added significantly to consumer interest in vegetables. The high relative cost of some of these gourmet foods may tend to limit their use by some budget-minded shoppers. However, they suggest many ways of glamorizing vegetables during home preparation. To cite another example, one may now buy potatoes fresh, frozen, or dehydrated. Decision among these types will need to be based on a cost comparison between the fresh and the prepared products, a consideration of the time available for meal preparation, and an evaluation of the commercially prepared product versus the home-prepared food.

The development of new vegetable products has been the goal of considerable research. Frozen vegetables are consistent with consumer demand for easy-to-store and quick-to-prepare foods. The bulkiness of potatoes was an important motivation for developing convenience forms of this vegetable to ease storage and transportation problems. The process has been refined to the point where 48 cubic feet of fresh potatoes may now be packaged in 12.5 cubic feet. The nonwaxy potatoes are preferable for dehydrated potato products.

Dehydrated potato flakelets are manufactured in the following steps: steam cooking the potatoes until soft; ricing them; drum-drying the riced mixture in a thin sheet; fragmenting of the thin sheet; sifting of the flakes; and packaging. These processes are used to make the mashed potato flakes that are now available. Other dehydrated potato products include scalloped potatoes, potatoes au gratin, and hash browns.

Precooked french fries and stuffed baked potatoes are frozen and require only reheating before they are ready to be served. Frozen grated potato patties and hash brown potatoes are ready to be fried. In fact, potato-containing convenience items have been so successful that the total consumption of potatoes has stopped declining and is now undergoing a healthy rise in the United States.

STORAGE

Most homemakers in the United States do not shop daily and therefore must store fresh vegetables prior to their preparation. Since a good vegetable cannot be prepared from one of poor original quality, it is important to preserve the quality of a vegetable during the storage period. Any spoiled portions should be removed before storage. Excess foliage such as carrot tops or leaves surrounding a head of cauliflower use valuable refrigerator space and may well be discarded before storing the vegetable.

The vegetables should be stored in the refrigerator to retard respiration and the deteriorative changes accompanying this process. The advantage gained from the cool temperature is partially offset by the extremely dry atmosphere unless vegetables are stored in the hydrator drawers or in plastic bags.

Successful storage of succulents (vegetables that rely on water for firmness and crispness) depends particularly on control of evaporation from the plant cells. Since cool air can hold less water than warm air, less water will be evaporated from foods stored in a cool environment. Covering foods also retards evaporation.

Optimum storage of salad greens requires a cool temperature and a small, tightly closed container. Some water will evaporate from the lettuce until a balance is reached between the moisture in the leaves and the air of the container. This balance will be reached with less total water lost from the lettuce if there is only a small amount of cold air surrounding the vegetable.

The chief exceptions to the rule of storing fresh vegetables in the refrigerator hydrator drawers are found in storing dry onions, dry legumes, winter squash, and potatoes. These are staple items and may be stored for reasonably long periods of time. Oxidative changes due to the respiration of potatoes may markedly alter the proportions of starch and sugar if prolonged storage occurs at improper temperatures. Temperatures around 45°F are favorable for the accumulation of a high sugar level at the expense of starch. Temperatures in the range from 50 to 70°F promote a higher level of starch. Optimum storage temperature for potatoes is about 60°F since this temperature does not greatly change the character of either waxy or mealy potatoes.

VEGETABLES IN THE MEAL

Acceptability of a vegetable is often determined by the meal planner's skill in selecting a vegetable that complements the rest of the meal. Consideration must be given to the shape, color, texture, and flavor of the vegetable in relation to the rest of the meal. A vegetable should be selected to present a contrast in shape to the other foods on the plate. Stuffed tomatoes and baked potatoes are monotonous compared to sliced tomatoes with a baked potato or potato chips with a stuffed tomato.

A colorful vegetable adds a festive touch to an otherwise drab plate. Buttered carrots garnished with parsley enhance a dinner of sliced turkey, dressing, and mashed potatoes. Crisp celery sticks would provide a pleasing contrast in texture for this dinner.

Mild-flavored vegetables are particularly pleasing when the other foods in a meal have strong flavors. The mild flavor of refried beans is appreciated as a contrast to the spiciness of highly seasoned enchiladas.

Some vegetables provide more interest if a special seasoning, sauce, or garnish is served with it. Sjöström and Crocker, in testing the effect of monosodium glutamate as a seasoning for vegetables, found that the compound intensified sweet and salt flavors. Only a small amount is needed for a bland vegetable; more may be used for vegetables with strong flavors. Flavor may be heightened by adding other ingredients such as mint leaves to peas, sherry to baked beans, or an egg yolk garnish on spinach.

Since vegetables are so important in fulfilling the dietary needs of the body, it is necessary to ensure their consumption through careful planning, selection, and preparation.

PRINCIPLES UTILIZED IN VEGETABLE COOKERY

Nutritional Aspects

Two considerations are of paramount importance when planning vegetable preparation. Careful attention should be given to the maintenance of good flavor and color. Second, preparation should conserve nutritive content as much as possible without having a detrimental influence on appearance or flavor.

Fresh vegetables will be most nutritious if they are consumed soon after harvesting. Oxidative changes occur during storage which result in some loss of vitamin A and ascorbic acid. Since cut surfaces increase the loss of water-soluble vitamins (the B vitamins and ascorbic acid), nutrients are conserved when vegetables are cooked whole and unpared (see Table 4.7).

Heating vegetables in water causes some loss of ascorbic acid and thiamin, but heating in a slightly alkaline medium hastens this loss. Vitamin A is quite stable and riboflavin and niacin are reasonably stable during cooking. Long cooking should be avoided from the standpoint of nutritive value as well as palatability. The long time required to bake vegetables causes some vitamin losses.

A pressure saucepan, because of the reduced cooking time, is helpful in minimizing some vitamin losses of vegetables that ordinarily require a long time to become tender. McIntosh and Jones, however, have demonstrated that ascorbic-acid retention in most vegetables is lower in the pressure cooker than in a saucepan.

Texture Changes

As a vegetable is heated, certain changes occur in the structure: protopectin undergoes a change to a more soluble substance, pectin; some softening of the cellulose takes place; starch takes up moisture and swells; and the protein coagulates. The first two changes, that is, the conversion of protopectin and the softening of cellulose, are responsible for the softening evident in cooked vegetables. This change in texture, caused by heating, increases the palatability of some vegetables.

Altering the pH of the water used to boil a vegetable will have a definite

Table 4.7. Properties of Vitamins Important in Food Preparation

Vitamin	Solubility in Water	Sensitivity to:			
			Heat in Presence of:		
		Oxidation	Acid	Alkali	Light
Vitamin A	No	Sensitive	Stable	Stable	Sensitive
Thiamin	Yes	Stable	Sensitive	Sensitive	Stable
Riboflavin	Yes	Stable	Stable	Sensitive	Sensitive
Niacin	Yes	Stable	Stable	Stable	Stable
Ascorbic acid	Yes	Sensitive	Sensitive	Sensitive	Sensitive
Vitamin D	No	Stable	Stable	Stable	Stable

influence on the softening that occurs. In an alkaline medium the structure begins to lose its integrity and the vegetable becomes mushy and unattractive in outline. An acid medium retards softening of the structure and greatly increases the time required for a vegetable to become tender. Indeed, softening may not occur if sufficient acid is added to a vegetable.

During cooking, some of the natural organic acids in vegetables are released into the boiling water so that the vegetable is actually being heated in a very mild acid. Such acids are not strong enough to prevent softening, but they can influence the color of the vegetable.

Color Considerations

Vegetables contain various chemical compounds that are responsible for the wide range of colors found in raw and cooked vegetables. The basic classifications of pigments are the chlorophylls, carotenoids, and flavonoids. Chemically, each of the specific compounds within a pigment class is related to the others. For example, all of the pigments categorized as flavonoids are chemically related to a phenolic compound known as flavone, chlorophylls are based on a porphyrin structure, and carotenoids are related to carotene. Examples of the chemical structures of selected compounds are included in the Appendix. Table 4.8 lists several common pigments and illustrations of vegetables in which they are found. Although one pigment generally predominates in a vegetable, several pigments may occur together to achieve the blending of color that is observed in the fresh vegetable. These compounds can undergo certain chemical changes during heating that may enhance or harm the color of the finished product. Therefore, an appropriate preparation procedure should be selected to preserve or heighten the pigments.

Vegetables lose some of their organic acids into the water when they are boiled, causing a weakly acid medium to develop. By using a cover on the pan, these volatile acids will be trapped in the pan and the vegetables will then be cooked in a mild acid solution. If the color of the vegetable is undesirable in acid, it is preferable to use a more neutral medium. In actual practice this is achieved when the volatile acids are allowed to escape by boiling the vegetable without using a lid. A survey of the color reactions of the common vegetable pigments will indicate which vegetables will be more attractive if boiled without being covered.

Chlorophyll, the pigment found in all green vegetables, is slightly water soluble. In an acid medium, chlorophyll is converted to pheophytin (Table 4.8), producing an olive green color in the vegetable. However, in an alkaline medium, the chlorophyll is a bright green (Table 4.9). This intense green color in alkali prompted some people to use soda in the cooking water a few years ago. Unfortunately, the alkaline medium favored the destruction of

Table 4.8. Common Vegetable Pigments

Pigment	Color	Vegetable
Chlorophylls		
Chlorophyll a	Intense blue green	Lettuce, spinach,
Chlorophyll b	Yellow green	peas, green beans, broccoli
Pheophytin a	Pale green-gray	Green vegetables
Pheophytin b	Olive green	cooked more than 7 minutes
Carotenoids		
Carotenes		
α-carotene	Yellow orange	Winter squash, carrots
β-carotene	Red orange	Carrots, sweet potatoes
Lycopene	Red	Tomatoes, rutabagas
Xanthophylls		
Cryptoxanthin	Yellow	Sweet corn
Lutein	Orange	Spinach
Flavonoids		
Anthocyanins	Red, purple, blue	Red cabbage
Anthoxanthins	White	Cauliflower, white onions, turnips

both ascorbic acid and thiamin. In addition, soda caused some destruction of cellulose, resulting in a rather mushy texture and limp appearance.

Owing to the undesirable color change when chlorophyll is in an acid medium, the use of a lid on fresh green vegetables has been debated. Some workers prefer to boil green vegetables uncovered to permit the escape of volatile organic acids and thus minimize the acidity of the vegetable. Others advocate the use of a cover to minimize the time required to bring the vegetable to a boil; prolonged boiling allows some decomposition of chlorophyll and results in a color change similar to the olive green produced in the presence of acid.

The keen observer will note an intensification of the color when a green vegetable is placed in boiling water; a partial explanation is that air is lost in the layer of cells just under the outer covering of the vegetable, and also that chlorophyll reacts with slightly alkaline water.

Color changes in frozen green vegetables occur much less readily during heating than is true of chlorophylls in fresh vegetables. Consequently, frozen green vegetables will retain their desired green color when cooked with a cover (unless the cooking period is prolonged). In canned green vegetables, chlorophylls are changed to pheophytins by the long cooking period and high temperature required for preventing botulism. This pigment change cannot be reversed to restore the green of chlorophyll.

The carotenoids encompass a variety of colors from yellow to red. Xanthophyll and lycopene are carotenoid pigments found in tomatoes. Different amounts of these pigments will be formed, depending on the light conditions under which they are ripened. Tomatoes protected from intense light will develop a high lycopene content (reddish color), whereas a more yellow color will dominate under conditions with more intense light. When tomatoes are ripened at temperatures consistently higher than 40°C (104°F), carotenoids are not developed, and the chlorophyll of the green tomato does not decompose.

The orange-colored vegetables, such as sweet potatoes, carrots, and rutabagas, contain carotenes. This pigment group not only provides the attractive color of these vegetables, but several of its members are nutritionally important as precursors of vitamin A. β-carotene is a particularly valuable form. Carotenoids are relatively unchanged in color in the presence of dilute acid or alkali. Therefore, these vegetables may be cooked with a cover without modifying the color.

The anthoxanthins form a segment of a large group of pigments called the flavonoids. These particular compounds are virtually colorless in acid, but turn to a distinct yellow color in an alkaline medium. In vegetables containing anthoxanthins, the color is more acceptable if the vegetable is cooked in the acidic medium created by covering the pan.

Anthocyanins, another group of pigments classified as flavonoids, are responsible for the dark red color found in some vegetables. Anyone who

Table 4.9. Color Reactions of Vegetable Pigments

Pigment	Example	Color in Acid	Color in Alkali	Color Reaction to Metals
Chlorophyll	Broccoli	Olive green	Bright green	Copper, iron: bright green
Carotenoids	Carrots	Orange	Orange	
Flavonoids:				
Anthoxanthins	Cauliflower	Colorless, white	Yellow	Aluminum: yellow Iron: brown
Anthocyanins	Red cabbage	Red	Blue to green	Iron: blue Tin: purple

has boiled red cabbage will attest to the highly soluble nature of this group of pigments. Red cabbage effectively demonstrates the color range possible in anthocyanins with the use of acid or alkali. The color changes of rubro-brassyl chloride, the particular pigment in red cabbage, parallel the reaction of litmus paper, that is, red in acid and blue (or blue green) in alkali. Because of the unpleasant colors developed in alkali, red cabbage should be cooked in a mild acid, such as is formed by adding tart apples to the boiling cabbage.

The summary statement may be made that, with the exception of chlorophyll, the pigments are attractive in an acid medium. In practice, this means that all chlorophyll-containing vegetables may be boiled uncovered in order to decrease the acidity of the medium. Vegetables in which any of the other pigments predominate will be a pleasing color in the weak acid medium created when the volatile organic acids are retained by covering the boiling vegetable with a lid. The color changes of the pigments are summarized in Table 4.9.

Flavor Considerations

Pigment reactions clearly influence the decision regarding the use of a cover when cooking vegetables. However, flavor also must be considered before making the final decision about covering fresh vegetables. Strong-flavored vegetables such as cabbage and onions will have a milder flavor if the volatile aromatic compounds are allowed to escape. Conversely, mild-flavored vegetables will retain their volatile flavor compounds better if a cover is used.

Onions will develop a milder flavor with a longer boiling period. Carson and Wong have demonstrated that propionaldehyde, hydrogen sulfide, and sulfur dioxide are important flavoring substances in onions. These compounds are volatile so they will be lost to an increasing degree with longer cooking time if onions are cooked without a cover.

Members of the cabbage family develop a stronger flavor as cooking time elapses. Raw cabbage contains sinigrin, a glycoside found in the cabbage family. In the presence of water and heat, sinigrin is converted to allyl isothiocyanate which in turn is converted to hydrogen sulfide, a strong and unpleasant-smelling compound. The longer the cooking time, the greater will be the development of this strong flavor and odor. For this reason, as well as for optimum nutritive value, these vegetables should be cooked a minimum length of time. Starting the vegetable in boiling water will facilitate this.

From the preceding discussion it is apparent that the pigments and flavors of vegetables are of importance in the decision to boil a vegetable covered or uncovered. If either color or flavor considerations dictate omission of a lid, the vegetable should be boiled uncovered to achieve maximum palatability. If neither flavor nor color is adversely affected by a cover, it is preferable to use a lid. These suggestions are based on the theory that good nutrition results from the consumption, not merely the presentation, of an adequate diet.

The amount of water to be used in vegetable cookery is a controversial subject since the strength of flavors and the vitamin content will be influenced by the quantity of water used in vegetable cookery. A minimum amount of water is certainly preferred for mild-flavored vegetables to reduce the loss of soluble flavoring compounds into the water. These vegetables may be suitably prepared by adding just enough water to bubble over the vegetable. Spinach is an exception: the freshly washed vegetable is placed in a covered pan without adding water and heated until the leaves wilt down, at which time the cover is removed.

Strong-flavored vegetables of the cabbage and onion families will be milder in flavor if enough water is used to cover the vegetable with about one-half inch of water. A summary of the amount of water, the use of a cover, and the approximate boiling time for selected fresh vegetables is given in Table 4.10.

For several years "waterless cookery" has been widely touted. The idea of the conservation of the water soluble vitamins by cooking with a very limited amount of water is nutritionally sound. This method, however, requires the use of a tightly fitting lid. For the reasons already discussed, this method may not always produce the most palatable vegetable.

PREPARATION PROCEDURES

Careful washing is the first step in the actual preparation of all fresh vegetables. For many vegetables, washing is done by scrubbing each vegetable under cold, running water. A vegetable brush or plastic scouring pad is a useful device, particularly when scrubbing potatoes and other vegetables to which dirt adheres tenaciously. Greens require special attention, since the convolutions of the leaves trap dirt and sand quite tightly. Spinach and other leafy vegetables are washed most effectively by filling the sink with cold water, splashing the leaves up and down vigorously in the water, draining the water from the sink, rinsing the sand and dirt from the bottom of the sink, and then repeating the entire process until no more sediment collects in the bottom of the sink. Unless the leaves are unusually dirty, two or three rinsings should be sufficient.

The next step is a thorough inspection and removal of all blemishes. Also trimming, paring, and cutting need to be done judiciously for various vegetables. These steps vary significantly from one vegetable to another. Corn on the cob requires careful removal of all of the silks, removal of the stem, and cleavage of the end of the cob if the ear has not filled well. In

Table 4.10. Applications of the Theories on Promoting Optimum Color and Flavor of Selected, Boiled Fresh Vegetables

Vegetable	Use of Cover	Reason to Cover or to Uncover	Total Amount of Water	Size of Piece	Boiling Time, minutes[a]
Artichoke (Globe)	Covered[b]	Steam needed in pan	3/4 in.	Whole	35–45
Asparagus	Uncovered	Green color	Small[c]	Tips, stalks	5–10 10–20
Beans, string	Uncovered	Green color	Small	Whole	20–30
Beets	Covered	Mild flavor	Small	Whole	30–90
Broccoli	Uncovered	Green color, strong flavor	—[d]	Split stalk	10–20
Brussels sprouts	Uncovered	Green color, strong flavor	Large[e]	Whole	10–20
Cabbage, green	Uncovered	Green color, strong flavor	Large	Wedge	7–15
Cabbage, red	Uncovered	Strong flavor	Large	Wedge	10–15
Carrots	Covered	Mild flavor	1/2 in.	Small, whole	15–30
Cauliflower	Uncovered	Strong flavor	Large	Whole, flower	15–25 8–15
Corn	Covered	Mild flavor	1/2 in.	Kernels	5–7
Corn, on the cob	Covered	Mild flavor	To cover	Whole	5–10
Onions	Uncovered	Strong flavor	Large	Whole	15–40
Parsnips	Uncovered	Strong flavor	Large	Whole	20–40
Peas	Uncovered	Green color	Small	Whole	10–20
Potatoes	Covered	Mild flavor	Small	Whole	25–40
Spinach	Covered to wilt, then uncovered	Green color	Clings to leaves	Leaves	5–10
Sweet potatoes	Covered	Mild flavor	Small	Whole	25–40
Tomatoes	Covered	Mild flavor	None	Whole	7–15

[a]Variation in cooking time depends on size and maturity of vegetables as well as personal preference.
[b]Chlorophyll turns olive green with or without a cover because of the long cooking time needed for artichokes, so cover is used to trap steam in the pan to aid in retaining the flavor.
[c]Just enough water is used to bubble to the top of the vegetable when the water is boiling gently.
[d]Water to within 1/4 in. of flowers when broccoli is standing upright in water.
[e]Enough water is used to provide an extra 1/2 in. of water over the vegetable.

addition, long ears usually need to be broken in half. Green beans are trimmed at both ends and then either left whole or cut into the desired shape.

Cauliflower is prepared by cutting off the stem as close to the head as is possible and then either cutting into flowerets or leaving the head whole, as desired. Brussels sprouts are trimmed to the base of the individual heads and any undesired leaves are removed. Broccoli and asparagus are prepared by cutting off the woody lower portions of the stalks. Large stalks of broccoli are split lengthwise, either in halves or quarters, up to the branching area. Cabbage is either shredded or cut into wedges, depending on the preparation technique planned. If cabbage is cut into wedges for boiling, care should be taken to include a portion of the core in each wedge so that the wedge will hold together. Wedges with a very heavy core, may be improved by trimming the core to a strip just thick enough to retain the wedge during boiling.

Beets should be left whole, including the root, and the stem should be trimmed to about one inch. Care must be taken to avoid cutting or damaging the skin of beets because the pigments then escape readily into the water and the cooked beets will be very dull in color. Spinach and other greens are prepared by breaking off the roots and any woody stems. Carrots and potatoes, if they are to be peeled, are pared most effectively by using a vegetable peeler with a floating blade. Less loss occurs with this device than results from the use of a paring knife. The ends of carrots and any blemishes are then removed, using a paring knife.

Potatoes often discolor after they are pared, a problem that is caused by enzymatic action leading to the formation of the pigment melanin from the amino acid tyrosine. This color change, which progresses through a brownish pink ultimately to a gray color, is minimized by paring the potatoes just prior to heating or by placing them in water immediately after paring. Since the water soak is detrimental to retention of the water soluble vitamins, this practice should be avoided as much as possible.

When one is deciding how to cut vegetables, the type of preparation contemplated, the maturity of the vegetable, and the shapes of other foods being served on the same plate should all be considered. Vegetables to be deep-fat fried must be cut into portions of narrow diameter so that they will be softened and heated in the center before they become too dark on the surface. Boiled vegetables may be cut into a variety of shapes, but cutting into small pieces greatly increases the surface area, thus increasing the loss of water soluble and/or easily oxidized vitamins. On the other hand, vegetables to be panned or stir-fried must be cut into thin pieces so that they will cook quickly without burning. The very rapid heating time and the absolute minimum of water used help to offset the vitamin loss that might be expected from the relatively large proportion of cut surfaces. Very large, mature vegetables may need to be cut to reduce their cooking time and make them easier to manage in the pan.

The last factor, that of shape, is of particular interest in preparing elongated or large vegetables. For instance, asparagus and carrots are complimentary in appearance when asparagus is served as spears and carrots are sliced crosswise. French cut green beans are more interesting in appearance when they are served along with a baked acorn squash half than when they are served with cole slaw.

Vegetables may be cooked by a variety of methods, including boiling, steaming, broiling, baking, stir-frying (panning), and frying. In any method the ultimate objective is to prepare an appetizing, nutritious food. Cooking of vegetables will soften the cellulose, alter the flavor, improve digestibility, and gelatinize the starch. Table 4.11 suggests suitable methods for cooking some of the common vegetables.

Table 4.11. Suggested Methods for Preparing Various Vegetables

Vegetable	Raw	Boiled or Steamed	Broiled	Baked	Fried	Stir-fried
Artichoke, Globe		X				
Asparagus		X				X
Beans, string		X				X
Beans, dried lima		Simmered		X		
Beans, fresh lima		X				
Beets		X		X		X
Broccoli		X			X	X
Brussels sprouts		X				X
Cabbage, green	X	X				X
Cabbage, red	X	X				
Carrots	X	X		X		
Cauliflower	X	X			X	X
Celery	X	X				X
Corn		X		X		
Eggplant				X	X	
Mushrooms	X		X		X	X
Okra		X			X	
Onions	X	X	X	X	X	
Parsnips		X		X	X	
Peas		X				
Potatoes		X		X	X	
Spinach	X	X				X
Squash, acorn				X		
Squash, summer		X				
Sweet potatoes		X		X		
Tomatoes	X	X	X	X	X	
Zucchini		X		X	X	

Boiling

Boiling is probably the method most often used for cooking vegetables since most vegetables may be suitably prepared in this manner. The decisions involved in boiling vegetables are the use of a lid and the amount of water to use. These problems were considered in the previous section.

Water should be brought to a boil before adding the vegetable so that the vegetable is in water for a minimum length of time. It should be remembered that a vegetable will not cook any faster when the water is boiling vigorously than when the water is boiling gently. The minimal agitation caused by a gentle boil will cause little disruption of the outline of a vegetable boiled the appropriate length of time and will reduce the likelihood of burning the vegetable by evaporating all the water from the pan.

Care should be taken to avoid overcooking vegetables to prevent an adverse effect on texture, flavor, color, and nutritive value. Vegetables should be boiled until they are just tender enough to be cut easily with a fork, but are not at all mushy. Best results will be obtained if the vegetables are uniform in size so that all will be done at the same time.

Broccoli presents a special problem since the stem requires a longer cooking time than the flowers. This may be overcome by splitting the stems and placing the vegetable upright in the pan with the flowers extending above the water. When the stems are almost tender, the broccoli is pushed over sideways so that the flowers are also in the water. This brief period in the water will be sufficient to cook the tender flower portion.

Steaming

Steaming requires a two-part device: a pan in which to boil the water and a basket to hold the food above the water. Some companies manufacture a unit that fits tightly above a saucepan. This unit has many perforations in the bottom to permit the steam from the saucepan to circulate in the upper area. A variation of the steamer is an adjustable perforated basket. A lid is required to trap the steam in the upper unit containing the vegetables. Because of this physical limitation (lid must be used), green or strong-flavored vegetables are not optimum when a steamer is used. Other vegetables may suitably be prepared in a steamer. Mild-flavored, sweet vegetables are particularly adaptable to steaming. Since the vegetable is not placed in water, the loss of water-soluble nutrients is reduced. Steaming time, however, is appreciably longer than boiling time for a vegetable.

Simmering

Dried legumes such as navy beans, lima beans, and pinto beans are heated in simmering water to permit coagulation with minimum toughening of the protein, and to hasten rehydration and softening of the cellulose. A long cooking period is required to replace the water in dried legumes, but this may be shortened somewhat by soaking for a period of three hours to overnight before simmering. The addition of molasses or the use of hard water will lengthen cooking time because the calcium from the molasses or water will react with the pectic substances in the beans, causing slower softening of the legumes.

Broiling

Tomatoes typify a vegetable that may be broiled for they not only soften quickly, but also may be sliced thinly so that the heat can penetrate completely before the exterior becomes too dark. Some vegetables such as onions may be broiled if they have been parboiled (boiled until partially cooked). Broiling is a quick method of preparing vegetables because the heat is very intense.

Baking

Some vegetables such as winter squash and potatoes are suitable for baking because their skins will protect them from drying while baking; other

FIGURE 4.11   Stuffed green peppers are prepared by parboiling the pepper, stuffing with any of a variety of stuffings, and then baking until tender.

vegetables that may appropriately be cooked in a covered container may be peeled and sliced, then baked in a covered casserole. In the latter situation the cover holds in the moisture of the vegetable and prevents the dry air of the oven from reaching the vegetables.

Baked vegetables require a longer heating period than boiled vegetables. Baking is usually done at rather high oven temperatures of 175-220°C (350-425°F). Acceptable baked vegetables may be prepared, however, at meat-roasting temperatures of 150-165°C (300-325°F) if it is convenient to bake them with the meat. Extra time should be added to the regular baking time to compensate for the lower oven temperature.

Frying

A variety of vegetables may be fried plain or dipped in batter and fried. French fried potatoes, eggplant, and batter-dipped onion rings are familiar examples of fried vegetables.

Deep-fat and shallow-fat frying are two methods of frying vegetables. Shallow-fat frying generally is done in a frying pan on top of the range, with the temperature being controlled at a point low enough to keep the fat from smoking. Deep-fat frying is done by completely immersing the vegetable in hot (usually maintained at 190°C or 375°F) fat. The temperature for deep-fat frying should be controlled carefully either by use of a thermostat or by manual regulation with the aid of a thermometer. Fat that is too cool will soak into the food and cause unnecessary absorption of grease, whereas very hot fat browns vegetables excessively before the interior is cooked sufficiently.

Stir-Frying or Panning

The method of vegetable preparation known as stir-frying or panning is one borrowed from Oriental cookery. Stir-frying can be done satisfactorily either in a wok or a frying pan. This method requires thinly sliced vegetables or greens so that the heat will penetrate quickly throughout the vegetable to achieve the softened, yet slightly crisp texture that is characteristic of well prepared stir-fried vegetables. Stir-frying is done by melting a small amount of butter or margarine or heating a little vegetable oil in the pan. The vegetables are added and stirred to promote uniform heating of all of the vegetables. Some very thinly sliced vegetables and greens may be stir-fried uncovered, with frequent stirring until done. Larger pieces may be stir-fried more satisfactorily by covering the pan at all times except when the vegetable is being stirred. If necessary, a very small amount of water may be added to prevent burning. However, the water naturally present in most vegetables being stir-fried is sufficient to avoid scorching if the heat is properly controlled.

FIGURE 4.12 Brussels sprouts are but one of many vegetables amenable to stir-frying.

Variations Using Special Equipment

If pressure saucepans or electronic ranges are available, additional variations for vegetable preparation then are possible. A pressure saucepan may be viewed as a variation on the technique of steaming vegetables. The significant feature is that the temperature is much higher than is possible in a nonpressurized container. As a result, the cooking time is dramatically reduced. At the usual pressure of 15 pounds in a pressure saucepan, the cooking medium is at a temperature of approximately 250°F, compared with the temperature of boiling water (212°F at sea level). The pressure saucepan may be used to advantage in any region, but it is of particular value when vegetables are to be boiled at high elevations where the temperature of boiling water is reduced significantly. The long boiling times can be decreased greatly through the use of a pressure saucepan.

Microwave cooking of vegetables has been studied for more than two decades. Although the design of the electronic ranges has undergone some change, this appliance consistently has proved to be a satisfactory device for preparing vegetables. One of the most significant features is its speed in comparison with other methods. This saving in time is directly correlated with the quantity of food being heated in the cavity at one time. When Bowman et al. (1971) compared microwave, pressure saucepan, and conventional vegetable cookery techniques at high altitude, no consistent preference was found for any one of the three methods tested. All three were found to produce satisfactory results.

SUMMARY

Vegetables are valuable in a meal because of nutritive value, color, shape, and texture. Fresh vegetables of many kinds are now available throughout the year as a result of continuing improvements in agricultural production, harvesting, and marketing operations. Through careful selection of fresh, frozen, and canned vegetables, proper storage, and skillful preparation, consumers can elevate vegetables to a position of importance in a meal. Attentive and imaginative preparation may change the consumption of vegetables from that of duty status to the level of gourmet appreciation. Variety in meals may be obtained by preparing vegetables in many different ways, including boiling, steaming, simmering, baking, broiling, frying, and stir-frying. Various seasonings, sauces, and garnishes also are effective in heightening the interest of vegetables in a meal.

BIBLIOGRAPHY

Bate-Smith, E. C. Flavonoid compounds in food. *Adv. Food Res.* 5:261–295, 1954.

Bowman, F. et al. Microwave vs. conventional cooking of vegetables at high altitude. *J.A.D.A.* 58:427. 1971.

Brown, H. D. Problems of the potato chip industry—processing and technology. *Adv. Food Res. 10*:181–226, 1960.

Carson, J. F., and F. F. Wong. Onion flavor and odor, volatile flavor components of onions. *J. Agr. Food Chem. 9, 2*:140–143. 1961.

Clifcorn, L. E. Factors influencing the vitamin content of canned foods. *Adv. Food Res. 1*:39–105. 1948.

Chapman, V. J. et al. Electronic cooking of fresh and frozen broccoli. *J. Home Econ. 52*:161. 1960

Consumer and Food Economics Research Division. *Conserving the Nutritive Values in Foods.* Home and Garden Bulletin No. 90. U. S. Department of Agriculture, Washington, D. C. Rev. 1971.

Consumer and Food Economics Research Division. *Vegetables in Family Meals* Home and Garden Bulletin No. 105. U. S. Department of Agriculture, Washington, D. C. Rev. 1971.

Consumer and Marketing Service. *How to Buy Dry Beans, Peas, and Lentils.* Home and Garden Bulletin No. 177. U. S. Department of Agriculture, Washington, D. C. 1970.

Eskew, R. K., and F. H. Drazza. Potato flakelets—a new dense product from flakes. *Food Tech. 16, 4*:99-101. 1962.

Farrer, K. T. H. Thermal destruction of vitamin B₁ in foods. *Adv. Food Res.* 6: 285-293. 1955.

Food and Drug Administration. *Facts from FDA.* DHEW Publication No. (FDA) 73–2036. 5600 Fishers Lane, Rockville, Md. 20852. April 1973.

Gordon, J., and I. Noble. Effect of cooking method on vegetables. *J.A.D.A.* 35: 578. 1959.

Gordon, J., and I. Noble. "Waterless" vs. boiling water cooking of vegetables. *J.A.D.A.* 44:378. 1964.

Howard, F. D., J. H. MacGillivray, and M. Yamaguchi. *Nutrient Composition of Fresh California-grown Vegetables.* Calif. Ag. Expt. Sta. Bull. 788. Davis, Calif. 1962.

Ide, L. E. *How to Buy Potatoes.* Home and Garden Bulletin No. 198. USDA, Washington, D. C. 1972.

Lee, F. E., Vegetables and mushrooms. Chapter 27 in *Chemistry and technology of food and food products,* ed. by M. B. Jacobs, Vol. 3, 2nd ed. Interscience Publishers, New York, N. Y. 1951.

Mackey, A. Recent research with potatoes. *Proc. Sixth Annual Washington State Potato Conference.* 1967.

Mackey, A., and S. Joiner. *Science in Cooking—Potatoes.* Circular of Information 600, Agricultural Experiment Station, Oregon State University, Corvallis. 1960.

Moyer, W. C. *The Buying Guide.* Blue Goose. Fullerton, Calif. 4th ed. 1971.

Olson, R. L., and W. O. Harrington. Potato granules, development and technology of manufacture. *Adv. Food Res.* 6:231–253. 1955.

Robinson, T. *Organic Constituents in Higher Plants.* Burgess Publishing Co., Minneapolis. 1963.

Smith, M. E. *How to Buy Fresh Vegetables.* Home and Garden Bulletin No. 143. U. S. Department of Agriculture, Washington, D. C. 1967.

Somers, G. F., and K. C. Beeson. Influence of climate and fertilizer practices upon vitamin and mineral content of vegetables. *Adv. Food Res.* 1:291–324. 1948.

Sweeney, J. P., and M. E. Martin. Stability of chlorophyll in vegetables as affected by pH. *Food Tech.* 15:263. 1961.

Thompson, E. R. *How to Buy Canned and Frozen Vegetables.* Home and Garden Bulletin No. 167. U. S. Department of Agriculture, Washington, D. C. 1969.

United Fresh Fruit and Vegetable Assoc. *Fruit and Vegetable Facts and Pointers.* 777 14th St., N. W. Washington 5, D. C.

SUGGESTIONS FOR STUDY

1.   Compare the cost and palatability of fresh, frozen, and canned: corn, green beans, peas, and carrots. Also compare frozen vegetables with sauces or other gourmet touches.

2.   Prepare a small sample of each of the suggested fresh vegetables (chlorophyll, broccoli; carotinoid, carrots; anthocyanin, red cabbage; anthoxanthin, white onion) by each of the four methods indicated below:

Pan 1. Add one tablespoon lemon juice. Use just enough water to boil over the vegetable.

Pan 2. Add one tablespoon baking soda. Use just enough water to boil over the vegetable.

Pan 3. Use just enough water to boil over the vegetable.

Pan 4. Fill pan with water to one and a half inches below the top of the pan. Compare: (a) the boiling time required in each treatment to appropriately soften the vegetable; (b) the color of each pigment in treatments 1 and 2; (c) the texture of each vegetable in treatments 1 and 2; (d) the flavor of the mild- and strong-flavored vegetables in treatments 3 and 4.

3. For each of the following vegetables decide whether a lid should be placed on the pan and how much water should be used: corn, peas, broccoli, white onions, red cabbage, spinach, Brussels sprouts, cauliflower, beets, carrots. Give reasons for your answers.

4. Which type of potato would you select for use in preparing the following: (a) mashed potatoes, (b) boiled potatoes, (c) scalloped potatoes, (d) potato salad, (e) french fried, (f) baked potatoes, (g) fried potatoes. Explain the reason for your answers.

CHAPTER 5

Fruits

During the past few years, progress in transportation and technology have combined to make a wide variety of fruits and fruit products available in most markets throughout the year. Fresh fruits grown in widely scattered parts of the world now reach consumers at prices within the average family's budget. No longer is winter fare restricted to oranges and apples. The opportunities for livening meals with fruits are many.

A fruit is the edible, more or less succulent product of a tree or plant, consisting of the ripened seeds and adjacent tissues. This group of foods presents a wide gamut of flavors, colors, and textures. The resultant versatility of fruits is appreciated in meal planning, for many intriguing recipes have been created which prominently utilize fruits in all portions of the menu from soup through dessert.

CLASSIFICATION

Fruits may be divided into groups or families according to such differences as shape, cell structure, type of seed, or natural habitat. One system of categorizing fruits includes the following groups: berries, citrus fruits, drupes, grapes, melons, pomes, and tropical and subtropical fruits.

Berries

Berries typically have a fragile cell structure that is easily damaged by rough handling or freezing. This large classification includes blackberries, loganberries, boysenberries, red and black raspberries, youngberries, blueberries, cranberries, gooseberries, huckleberries, and strawberries. As a general group, berries are excellent for use in desserts, either as the fresh fruit or in various baked products such as pies.

Raspberries, blueberries, and strawberries have gained wide acceptance in the frozen-food market. Blueberries are even being marketed in blueberry muffin mixes. With the increase in popularity of pancakes as a restaurant specialty, several berry syrups have gained favor with the American public. Most of these berries make excellent jams and jellies.

Cranberries enjoy wide popularity in the fall when they are available as the fresh fruit. Year around, various canned cranberry products such as cranberry sauce, jelly, and juice have a wide sale.

Citrus Fruits

Citrus fruits are almost synonymous with breakfast in many American homes. The common citrus fruits are grapefruit, oranges, lemons, and limes; less well-known members in this family are kumquats, citron, and tangerines. These fruits, all members of the genus *Citrus*, are characterized by their tough peel.

The two common types of oranges are Valencias and Navels. Valencia oranges, preferred for juice, can be distinguished from Navel oranges by looking at the bottom of the orange. The Navel orange is characterized by an umbilical formation at this point as contrasted with the smooth area on Valencias. This growth in the Navel orange is actually the beginning of an orange inside an orange. Navels are seedless and may be used to advantage for slicing.

The bright color and pleasing flavor of oranges have combined to make them a favorite fruit whether they are served as juice or in slices. Commercially, the production of orange juice to be sold fresh, canned, or frozen is a large-scale operation.

Oranges have a high pectin content in the albedo (white portion), which is valued by manufacturers of commercial pectin (see Chapter 14) and producers of orange marmalade.

Another type of citrus fruit is the tangerine. This fruit has the shape of a slightly flattened orange and is appreciated for the ease with which it may be peeled and sectioned. One type of tangerine, commonly marketed as canned mandarin oranges, has found wide acceptance as a salad and dessert ingredient.

The enjoyment of grapefruit is not limited to the United States for, in addition to the groves in Florida, California, Texas, and Arizona, it is grown in South Africa, Israel, and the West Indies. The tartness of either the white or pink grapefruit is particularly pleasing for breakfast.

Lemons, also noted for their tartness, have a unique ability to brighten

FIGURE 5.1 Citrus fruits grow in abundance on trees of medium height in areas having a very mild climate.

food flavors. Lemon meringue pies are high on the list of favorite desserts; a slice of lemon is a pleasing garnish on fish; lemonade is a delightful thirst quencher; and these are only three of the more common uses for lemons. Most of the lemons used in this country are grown in California.

Kumquats are a small citrus fruit that may be consumed raw, preserved, or candied. Because of their petite size, they may be appropriately served as a garnish for an entree or as a focal point of a salad.

Citron is a citrus fruit resembling a large avocado. The thick-skinned fruit is picked while it is still green and the peel is candied. Candied citron peel is diced for use in fruit cakes and cookies.

Drupes

Drupes are fruits containing a single seed surrounded by an edible fleshy portion. Apricots, cherries, peaches, and plums as well as prunes are classified as drupes. These five fruits are popular as fresh fruits in season, as frozen and canned foods, or as jams and jellies. The familiar Maraschino cherries are made by bleaching sweet cherries with sulfur dioxide prior to the addition of food coloring. Apricots, peaches, and prunes are frequently dried.

Grapes

Many varieties of grapes are marketed for dessert and salad preparation. Concord, Thompson seedless, Flame Tokay, Emperor, Muscat, Malaga, and Catawba are varieties familar to many shoppers. These are classified as either American or European grapes. Characteristically, European grapes are oval in shape as compared with the round American grapes. The names of these two groups are misleading since many European grapes are grown in the United States.

The many commercial uses for Concord grapes are well known today. Grape jelly, jam, conserves, and preserves are widely sold. Canned grape juice and frozen grape juice are popular beverages which are an appropriate alternate for citrus juices when ascorbic acid is added.

An important industry stemming from the production of European grapes is the wine industry. The different varieties provide the raw materials for making many wines in the United States as well as in Europe. American wine production dates back to the mission days of early California when the Spanish friars introduced grapes to that region. This heritage has passed continuously through history, and is exemplified today in wines produced by a California monastery.

Thompson seedless grapes are canned in fruit cocktail and as spiced grapes. Raisins are made by sun drying the Thompson seedless and Muscat grapes; and dried small grapes are marketed as dried currants.

Melons

A type of fruit that to date has remained a somewhat seasonal food is the melon. Since melons come from many areas of the United States, they ripen at various times, depending on the growing season in a particular area. The ripe melons are shipped to distant markets. California, because of its extended distance from north to south, illustrates the range of seasons well. The Imperial Valley in southern California harvests melons from the middle of May until early July, at which time northern California takes over the market only to relinquish it again to the Imperial Valley for a fall crop.

The melon group is divided into watermelons and muskmelons which include cantaloupe, honeydew, Persian, Casaba, honey ball, and Crenshaw. As can be seen, the name cantaloupe is not synonymous with muskmelon, but is a particular type of muskmelon.

A close relative of the cantaloupe is the thick-fleshed Persian melon. The flesh of the Casaba is soft and creamy in color. The Casaba and Persian melons were crossed to produce the rich flavor and salmon color of the Crenshaw melon. In contrast to the cantaloupe and Persian melons, which develop optimum flavor when ripened on the vine, Casabas and Crenshaws are of excellent quality when ripened off the vine.

The delicate green interior and very sweet flavor of honeydews are a contrast to the other melons. The exterior of a honey ball melon resembles a honeydew and the interior is similar to a mild-flavored cantaloupe.

Melons are particularly palatable when served as the fresh fruit, for their pleasing flavors and colors blend well with mixtures of melons or with other fruits. In addition, watermelon rind can also be pickled and served throughout the year.

Pomes

All members of the botanical family *Malaceae,* including the quince, pear, and apple, are classified as pomes. Pomes are characterized by a central core (containing five encapsulated seeds) surrounded by an edible fleshy layer. Apples are a particularly useful fruit due to their great versatility and excellent keeping qualities. Because of their retention of quality during cold storage, apples were virtually considered as staples before modern transportation and production made other fruits readily available in the winter. Commercially, apples are dried, made into juice and vinegar, preserved as jelly and apple butter, canned as applesauce and pie filling, or frozen in pies. Many recipes in the home utilize apples in a large variety of ways.

Fresh or canned pears are well suited for use in fruit salads, as a tinted garnish for a meat platter, or in pear pie. Quince is most commonly marketed as preserves or jelly.

Tropical and Subtropical Fruits

Several tropical and subtropical fruits such as the avocado, banana, date, fig, pineapple, and pomegranate are commonly available today. The consumption of avocados has increased as more recipes have been developed for their use. The Fuerte is an abundant variety suitable for making chip dips, sandwich fillings, salads, and ices. The mild flavor and high fat content (25 percent) of avocados make them excellent carriers of seasonings.

Bananas have been a favorite fruit for years in the United States even though they have to be imported from Central and South America. The variety most commonly available in the United States is the Gros Michel. Occasionally, markets will also have a smaller, sweet banana with a red skin. Common uses for bananas include breads, cakes, pies, fritters, salads, and desserts.

FIGURE 5.2 Pineapples grow in neat, close-packed rows in Hawaii. This fruit flourishes in a tropical climate.

For centuries dates have been grown in Iran, Iraq, and North Africa. Now a variety, the Deglet Noor, is raised in significant quantities in California. During their development, dates pass through three distinct stages: khalal, the color change from green to yellow or red; rutab, the period of softening; and tamar, the time when the fruit is cured. Dates are used in baked products, in milk drinks, in salads, and as a confection.

Figs are grown in the southern section of the United States as well as in the Mediterranean area where they originated. Several varieties of figs are produced, but probably the most familiar canned fig is the Kadota. Fresh and canned figs are used in salads and desserts; and dried figs are utilized by commercial bakers in the production of fig bar cookies.

Although pineapple was originally found in Central America, it is now produced on a large scale in Hawaii and Cuba, with Puerto Rico and Florida also making their contributions to the American scene. Pineapple packing is a very important industry in Hawaii where pineapple juice is preserved in both the canned and frozen form for wide distribution. In addition, pineapple is canned in spears, rings, chunks, and the crushed or grated form.

Papayas are a tropical fruit being shipped in increasing quantities from Hawaii to the conterminous United States. The delicate flavor makes this fruit a welcome addition in fruit salads, or it may be served alone with a dash of lime juice for a flavor accent. Surprisingly, even the seeds of the papaya are useful, for they can be ground and used in salad dressing. The papaya is also important as the source of papain, an enzyme widely used in tenderizing less tender cuts of meat.

Pomegranates are valued for their seeds, which contain a reasonably large amount of juice. Juice may be extracted from the seeds for use in fruit juices and grenadine. The dark red seeds make an attractive addition to various fruit combinations.

COMPOSITION OF FRUITS

Fruits in general contain a high percentage of water: muskmelons and watermelons are approximately 92 percent water; most other fruits have a water content ranging between 80 and 90 percent; and in dried fruits, water constitutes about 25 percent of the edible weight of the fruit. Fruits are notably low in protein and also in fat, with the exception of the avocado which contains up to 25 percent fat. Table 5.1 lists average values for the composition of some fruits commonly used in the United States.

Although the total amount of carbohydrate remains constant, the form varies with the maturity of the fruit. Starch content is relatively high in immature fruit, but is very low in mature fruits, since a majority of this carbohydrate is converted to sugar as the fruit ripens. Cellulose and pectic substances, which are classified as carbohydrates, are important structural components of fruits (see Chapter 14).

Various sugars are found in fruits at levels ranging from 61 percent for dates to less than 1 percent for avocados. The sugar content of all varieties of dates is considerably higher than in most other fruits. Some dates, however, contain sucrose as the principal sugar, whereas others, when ripe, have an abundance of invert sugar which has been formed due to the enzyme action of invertase on sucrose (see Chapter 13).

Other important constituents in fruits are enzymes and organic acids. The enzymes are important because they effect chemical changes in the maturing fruit. Organic-acid levels are high in fruits; this acidity causes canned and frozen fruits to be less susceptible to spoilage than vegetables.

PIGMENTS IN FRUITS

The pigments of fruits are classified in the same manner as the vegetable pigments discussed in the preceding chapter. Oranges offer an interesting combination of the various pigments. The rind (flavedo) of most

Table 5.1. Average Values Obtained in the Analysis of Selected Fruits Available in the United States[a]

Fruit[b]	Water %	Calo-ries	Carbo-hydrate, grams	Vitamin A Value, I. U.	Ascorbic Acid, mg
Apples, 1 medium	85	70	18	50	3
Apricots, 3	85	55	14	2890	10
Avocado, ½ of 10-oz	74	185	6	310	15
Banana, 1 medium	76	85	23	170	10
Cantaloupe, ½ of 5-in.	94	40	9	6590	63
Grapefruit, ½ medium	89	50	14	10	50
Navel orange, 1 large	86	70	17	270	83
Peach, 1 medium	89	35	10	1320	7
Pear, 3 × 2½ in.	83	100	25	30	7
Pineapple, 1 c, diced	85	75	19	180	33
Strawberries, 1 c	90	55	12	90	89
Watermelon, 4 × 8 slice	92	120	29	2530	26

[a]Selected from the table "Nutrients in Common Foods in Terms of Household Measures," *Food, the Yearbook of Agriculture, 1959,* U. S. Department of Agriculture, Washington, D. C.
[b]All values are for the raw fruits.

oranges reveals some chlorophyll in addition to the characteristic carotenoid pigments. A particular kind of orange, the blood orange, also contains anthocyanins. The white area (albedo) just under the flavedo of all varieties of oranges contains anthoxanthin pigments.

Although the number of vegetables containing anthocyanins is distinctly limited, there are several fruits that provide illustrations of this group of flavonoid pigments. The anthocyanin-containing fruits range in color from the deep blue of Concord grapes to the bright red of fresh strawberries (Table 5.2). This color range is due to the presence of chemically related compounds, which have sufficient structural differences to produce the

subtle variations noted between fruits. These compounds, like the anthocyanin present in red cabbage, will undergo color changes if the pH of the
fruit is changed. When fruit juices containing anthocyanins are quite acidic,
as is the case when lemon juice is used in a significant amount, the juices
will have their red color enhanced. In contrast, a distinctly bluish quality
becomes apparent when the mixture is brought to a more alkaline pH.

Table 5.2. Anthocyanin Pigments in Fruits

Anthocyanin compound	Color	Example in fruit
Delphinidin	Blue	Concord grape
Cyanidins	Purple to deep red	Bing cherries, sour cherries, blueberries, black raspberries, boysenberries
Pelargonidin	Red	Strawberries, red raspberries

Yet another possible factor in determining the actual color of a fruit mixture
containing flavonoid pigments is the change that may be caused by contact
with metals. When flavonoids come in contact with aluminum, iron, or tin,
the pigment will form a complex with the metal, and undesirable color shifts
to blues and greens occur.

In the intact fruit, the pigments add considerable beauty and appeal.
However, an undesirable brown color begins to develop in some fruits, such
as peaches and apples, after they are cut. This browning is the result of
oxidation of certain flavonoid compounds, phenolic substances such as
catechin and leucoanthocyanins. The reaction is catalyzed by phenol oxidase
enzymes naturally present in the fruits. Prevention of browning may be
achieved by covering the fruit with an acidic juice or a sugar syrup, thus
blocking air from the surface and suppressing enzyme activity.

NUTRITIVE VALUE OF FRUITS

Some fruits are nutritionally useful as an excellent source of ascorbic
acid, and the yellow fruits such as apricots, peaches, and cantaloupe contain
carotene, the precursor of vitamin A. The actual contributions of these
vitamins depend on several factors such as maturity, storage conditions,
climate, and amount of sunshine, as well as the manner in which the foods
are prepared in the home.

Citrus fruits are an excellent year-around source of ascorbic acid although experiments have shown that fruits grown late in the season contain less ascorbic acid than the fruits that mature earlier. It is also of interest that fruits from the center of the tree are lower in ascorbic acid than fruits grown at the ends of the branches.

Apples are a variable source of ascorbic acid, with the highly colored apples at the end of the season being appreciably higher in ascorbic acid than green apples. There is also a variation among varieties of the same fruit as illustrated by comparing test levels in three varieties: Jonathan, 7.0-8.2 milligrams of ascorbic acid per 100 grams of fruit; Delicious, 8.0-9.6 milligrams per 100 grams of apples; and Winesap, 9.6-13.9 milligrams for the same quantity of fruit.

The ascorbic acid content of the various berries is a helpful supplement to the daily requirement since the average level of ascorbic acid in berries, with the exception of strawberries, is only slightly less than half of the value for citrus fruits. Strawberries, an outstanding source of ascorbic acid, actually contain more ascorbic acid than oranges.

The iron and calcium content of the diet may be increased by judicious selection of fruits. Dried fruits are good sources of iron, as are fresh fruits if they are eaten in large quantities. Oranges and figs contain appreciably more calcium than do the other fruits.

An additional contribution of fruits is their high cellulose content which provides needed roughage or bulk in the diet. Of course, their sugar content is a useful source of energy.

SOME COMMERCIAL ASPECTS OF FRUIT PRODUCTION

Fruits are consumed fresh in large quantities, frequently at a great distance from the production area. For maximum desirability, raw fruits should be of excellent quality. The maintenance of this quality during shipping can be achieved by the use of refrigerated cars and trucks.

Control of humidity is vital to achieve a favorable balance between the moisture level that would cause mold formation and the arid condition that would dehydrate and shrivel fruits. High humidity in the atmosphere during storage promotes retention of water in the cells whereas low humidity increases water loss. In fruits such as strawberries, which depend on cellular water for plumpness, humidity control is essential during storage.

Another means of slowing deterioration is the controlled addition of carbon dioxide to the atmosphere surrounding the fruit, for carbon dioxide gas inhibits yeast and mold growth. A low oxygen, high carbon dioxide environment also decreases spoilage by retarding the ripening process, but too much carbon dioxide will cause alcohol to form in apples and pears. Sulfur dioxide, another gas, is used as a fumigant to retard mold growth in grapes during shipping.

FIGURE 5.3   Mature fruit and blossoms frequently occur at the same time on citrus trees.

Growers are concerned with environmental circumstances affecting their crop. Irrigation is used to ensure adequate moisture for many crops. Temperature is more difficult to control, but smudge pots are used with some degres of success in citrus groves to combat a mild freeze. Occasional freezes occurring in citrus-growing areas, however, cause considerable damage to the crop. It is interesting to note that, although the frozen fruit may continue to increase in size because of a thickening of the rind, the juice volume is greatly reduced since freezing ruptures interior membranes and permits evaporation of the juice.

Considerable research has been conducted on the chemical reactions that occur during the ripening of various fruits. It has been shown that some fruits such as the avocado and banana have a greatly increased rate of respiration accompanied by a change in color as the fruit matures. This respiration change occurs even after the fruit has been picked, hence the practice of picking these fruits while still green does not impair the ripening process and has the advantage of facilitating shipping procedures. Some other fruits such as citrus fruits, pineapple, and some melons are definitely harmed by early picking because the chemical changes needed to produce the typical ripened flavor will not occur once the fruit is picked. The rise in sugar content in some melons (cantaloupes and Persian melons) which normally occurs in the vine-ripened fruit will not take place when these fruits are picked green, and the low sugar level is detrimental to flavor.

Color of food definitely influences its acceptance, and the color of fruit is no exception. The fruit industry has long recognized this and has constantly sought ways to improve the color of marketed fruits. For many years ethylene gas has been used as an effective means of hastening the ripening and accompanying color development of fruits. This is still the common means of ripening tomatoes, bananas, and several other fruits. The presence of ethylene decomposes the chlorophyll which obscures the carotenoid pigments in some oranges. The orange color revealed after the chlorophyll is eliminated makes the oranges more marketable even though the flavor is unchanged.

To enhance the eye appeal of citrus fruit, the practice of waxing was developed in 1922. A thin film of carnauba wax (from palm fronds), paraffin, or other approved coatings now may be applied not only to citrus fruits, but also to apples, cantaloupes, and peaches, as well as several vegetables. Actually, so little wax is used that only one gallon of the wax will suffice for five tons of apples; an orange is treated with about six drops of the wax. This small quantity of wax, when buffed with brushes, adds significantly to the eye appeal of the fruit. Perhaps more importantly, wax serves as a protective coating to prevent decay at the stem end of melons, to reduce skin damage during shipping, and retard moisture loss and shriveling of fruit. The use of wax makes it possible to store apples for long periods of time and to ship oranges all around the world.

SELECTION

Fresh Fruits

When buying fresh fruits, the consumer should select fruit that is fresh, free from bruises and blemishes, of an appropriate size for its intended use, and of a preferred degree of ripeness. Freshness can usually be ascertained by a quick visual examination: for example, plump fresh berries are easily distinguished from limp ones, and wizened peaches obviously are not fresh. For eye appeal it is always desirable to select fruit completely free of blemishes and bruises, but for maximum keeping quality there must be no bruised areas, since this is where spoilage occurs most quickly.

Some fruit may be available in two or more sizes and the consumer must decide between the larger, higher-priced size and the smaller, less-expensive size. If strawberries were to be used whole as a garnish on a fruit plate, there would be some merit in buying the more attractive large berries, but small strawberries could well be used for a jelly-roll filling.

Grade standards have been established by the Consumer and Marketing Service of the U. S. Department of Agriculture. The actual standards are specified for the many different fruits labeled on the basis of grade standards. For the various fruits, there are two or more grades described, with the top grade being designated as either U. S. Fancy or U. S. No. 1. Some fruits packaged for consumers are packed under continuous inspection, a fact that is noted by a label bearing the official USDA grade shield or a statement "Packed under Continuous Inspection of the U. S. Department of Agriculture" (or alternately, "Packed by — — — — Under Continuous Federal-State Inspection").

The selection of individual fruits, although not difficult, can be described more accurately by a brief summary of the characteristics of interest to consumers, as provided in Table 5.3.

Table 5.3. A Guide to the Selection of Fresh Fruits

Fruit	Desirable Qualities	Characteristics To Avoid
Apples	Firm; crisp; good color for the variety of apple	Overripe; soft and mealy; bruises
Apricots	Uniform, golden color; plump; juicy; barely soft	Soft or mushy; hard; pale yellow or green color
Avocados	Firm if to be used later, slightly soft for immediate use	Dark patches; cracked surfaces
Bananas	Firm; bright color; free from bruises	Bruises; discolored skin
Blueberries	Dark blue with silver bloom; plump; firm; uniform size	Soft, spoiled berries; stems and leaves
Cherries	Dark color in sweet cherries; bright red in pie cherries; glossy; plump	Shrivelling; dull appearance; soft, leaking fruit; mold

Table 5.3. A Guide to the Selection of Fresh Fruits (continued)

Fruit	Desirable Qualities	Characteristics to Avoid
Cranberries	Plump and firm; lustrous; red color	Soft and spongy; leaking
Grapefruit	Firm; well-shaped; heavy for size; thin skin indicates juiciness	Soft and discolored areas; mold
Grapes	Plump; yellowish cast for white or green grapes; red color predominating for red grapes; stems green and pliable	Soft, wrinkled; bleached area around stem; leaking
Lemons	Rich yellow color (pale or greenish yellow for higher acid content); firm; heavy	Hard or shrivelling; soft spots; mold; dark yellow
Limes	Glossy skin; heavy	Dry skin; decay
Melons		
Cantaloupes	Smooth area where stem grew; bold netting; yellowish cast to the skin	Soft rind; bruises
Casaba	Yellow rind; slight softening at blossom end	Decayed spots
Crenshaw	Deep golden rind; very slight softening of rind; good aroma	Decayed spots
Honeydew	Faint odor; yellow to creamy rind; slight softening at blossom end	Greenish white rind; hard and smooth skin
Persian	Same as cantaloupe	Same as cantaloupe
Watermelon	Slightly dull rind; creamy color on the underside	Cracks; dull rind

Table 5.3. A Guide to the Selection of Fresh Fruits (continued)

Fruit	Desirable Qualities	Characteristics to Avoid
Nectarines	Slight softening; rich color; plump	Hard or shriveled; soft
Oranges	Firm and heavy; bright, fresh skin either orange or green tint	Light weight; dull skin; mold
Peaches	Slightly soft; yellow color between the red areas	Very firm, hard; green ground color; very soft; decay
Pears	Firm, but beginning to soften; good color for variety (Bartlett, yellow; Anjou or Comice, light green to yellow green; Bosc, greenish yellow with skin russeting; Winter Nellis, medium to light green)	Weakening around the stem; shriveled; spcts
Pineapples	Good pineapple odor; green to yellow color; spike leaves easily removed; heavy for size	Bruises; poor odor; sunken or slightly pointed pips
Plums	Good color for variety; fairly firm	Hard or shriveled; poor color; leaking
Raspberries	Good color for kind; plump; clean; no caps	Mold; leaking
Strawberries	Good red color; lustrous; clean; cap stem attached	Mold; leaking; large seeds
Tangerines	Bright lustrous skin	Mold; soft spots

When buying some fresh fruits, more than one variety may be available in the market at a given time. Wise selection of variety then becomes significant in achieving the best end products possible. For example, both Bing cherries and sour cherries may be available at the same time. The choice of Bing cherries for a fruit salad would be excellent, but the sour cherries are

FIGURE 5.4   Muskmelons in this display are (lower right to upper left) cantaloupe, Casaba, and honeydew. Watermelon is a separate type of melon.

the variety of choice for cherry pie. Tangerines are another type of fruit where several varieties may confront the consumer at a given time. Choices may need to be made among the Mandarins (including Satsuma, Kinnow, Wilking, and Kara), the Algerian, the Temple, the Dancy, and the Orlando or Minneola Tangelos. If the fruit were being selected for packing in a child's lunch box, the easy peeling of the loose rind and the few seeds in Satsuma Mandarin would make this an ideal choice. In contrast, the difficulty of peeling the Orlando Tangelo and its many seeds would make this variety less desirable. The Dancy Tangerine probably is the most available of the tangerines; its ease of peeling and somewhat tart flavor help to offset the annoyance of many seeds.

Perhaps more than any other fruit, apples require a special knowledge of varieties if the best one is to be selected for a particular end use. The apple is an extremely versatile fruit, with various varieties being well suited to making apple sauce, coddled apples, baked apples, pies, salads, or for simply eating them raw. Table 5.4 summarizes the appropriate uses for several of the more common varieties.

Table 5.4. Suggested Uses for Selected Varieties of Apples

Variety	Use			
	Fresh and Salads	Pie	Sauce and Coddling	Baking
Delicious				
Red	Excellent			
Golden	Excellent	Excellent	Good	Good
Gravenstein	Good	Good	Good	Good
Grimes				
golden		Good		
Jonathan	Good	Good	Excellent	Good
McIntosh	Excellent	Excellent	Good	
Newtown				
pippin	Good	Excellent	Good	Good
Northern				
spy				Good
Rhode Island				
greening		Excellent	Excellent	Good
Rome				
beauty	Good	Good	Excellent	Excellent
Wealthy	Good	Good	Good	
Winesap	Excellent	Good	Excellent	Good
Yellow				
transparent		Excellent	Good	

Apples are available all through the year, but many of the fruits have a relatively short period when they are available in large quantities. At the time when a fruit is in season, its quality generally will be highest and its price the lowest for the entire year. Table 5.5 provides a guide to the seasonal availability of fresh fruits. Of course, the consumer also has the option of buying frozen, canned, or dried fruits for use in food preparation. However, extensive use of fruits in season is a nutrition bonus that pleases many people.

Table 5.5. A Guide to Average Monthly Availability of Fresh Fruits[a]

Fruit	Jan. (%)	Feb. (%)	Mar. (%)	Apr. (%)	May (%)	June (%)	July (%)	Aug. (%)	Sept. (%)	Oct. (%)	Nov. (%)	Dec. (%)	Total (million lbs)
Apples	10	10	10	8	7	4	2	3	10	13	11	11	3284
Apricots					2	55	37	5					40
Avocados	10	9	10	9	9	8	7	7	7	7	8	9	119
Bananas	8	8	9	9	9	9	8	7	8	9	8	9	3650
Blueberries					3	29	38	26	4				43
Cantaloupes			1	4	9	21	22	25	11	4	1		1563
Cherries					6	44	43	7					79
Coconuts	7	8	9	5	4	4	4	5	9	13	16	17	27
Cranberries									8	19	52	21	40
Grapefruit	12	11	13	11	9	5	3	2	3	10	11	11	1500
Grapes	5	3	4	3	2	4	11	17	19	15	11	7	733
Honeydews			6	12	7	4	12	10	19	20	10	2	244
Lemons	7	6	8	8	10	12	12	10	8	7	6	7	495
Limes	5	4	5	5	8	16	16	13	8	7	6	9	28
Mangoes			4	9	17	31	24	12	2				10
Nectarines	1	4				11	33	38	13				129
Oranges	12	12	13	11	10	6	4	4	4	5	8	12	2909
Papayas	8	8	7	9	11	10	9	7	7	9	9	7	7
Peaches					3	24	33	27	12	1			1326
Pears	7	6	7	6	5	2	5	13	17	15	11	7	426
Persimmons	6	1							1	27		23	6
Pineapples	6	8	13	14	14	10	6	5	4	5	7	6	137
Plums-prunes	1	1	1			16	30	31	19	2			295
Pomegranates									5	60	33	2	6
Strawberries	2	3	7	16	27	24	9	4	3	2	1	1	287
Tangerines (including Tangelos)	18	4	2	1						4	31	41	399
Watermelons					2	14	29	30	19	5			3027

[a]Adapted from *Guide to Average Monthly Availability of Fresh Fruits and Vegetables.* United Fresh Fruit and Vegetable Association. 777 14th St., N. W. Washington, D. C. 20005. 7th rev. ed. 1969.

Canned and Frozen Fruits

Canned and frozen fruits may be graded according to federal standards established by the United States Department of Agriculture's Consumer and Marketing Service. U. S. Grade A or Fancy, the top grade, is characterized by fruit of excellent color, uniform size, optimum ripeness, and few or no blemishes. This grade is desirable for use in fruit plates, as a single fruit dessert, or for service as a baked or broiled accompaniment to a meat entree. U. S. Grade B or Choice, the second grade, is comprised of fruit somewhat less perfect than Grade A. Grade B fruit is a suitable quality for use in molded gelatin products, in fruit cups, compotes, and as a topping. U. S. Grade C or Standard, the lowest grade available to consumers, may contain broken and uneven pieces with occasional blemishes. The average quality in U. S. Grade C is good. This grade is well suited to the preparation of sauces, fruit-containing desserts such as cobblers, and jams.

Labels on the packages or cans must include the following:

1. Common or usual name of the fruit.
2. Form (whole, slices, halves, pitted) if not visible in the container.
3. Some fruits must indicate variety or color.
4. Syrups, sugar, or liquid used in packing. Canned fruits may be packed in heavy syrup, light syrup, or water pack. Frozen fruits usually are packed in sugar.
5. Net weight of contents of can in ounces (also in pounds and ounces or pounds and fractions of pounds for containers between one and four pounds).
6. Ingredients, including spices, flavoring, coloring, and any other additives.
7. Any special type of treatment.
8. Packer's or distributor's name and place of business.

Additionally, label information may provide an indication of the grade, size, and cooking directions, recipes, or serving suggestions. The USDA grade shield can be imprinted on cans and packages that have been packed under continuous inspection by the United States Department of Agriculture.

Specific requirements for the labeling of selected products may be expected to increase as a result of the consumer movement in the United States. One such regulation went into effect late in 1972. The labeling requirement is designed to clarify the content of various orange beverages. Under the legislation, these categories are defined:

Orange juice drink blend, containing between 70 and 95 percent orange juice.

Orange juice drink, containing between 35 and 70 percent orange juice.

Orange drink, containing between 10 and 35 percent orange juice.
Orange flavored drink, containing more than 0, but less than 10 percent
orange juice.

The label on these products must specify the percentage of orange juice
rounded to the nearest 5 percent for all of these beverages except the orange
flavored drink, which must be labeled to the nearest 2 percent. Fruits identified as being enriched with vitamin C (or any other nutrition statement)
will need to conform to the nutrition labeling requirements by the end of
1974, as described in Chapter 4.

Dried Fruits

Although the federal government has established grades for dried
fruits, there actually is very little use made of the grades. Quality can be
judged by color and appearance. Dried fruits that have a bright color for
their type and that are firm, but flexible, are generally of high quality. Dried
apples have a rather creamy color, dried pears are somewhat more yellow,
while prunes and raisins are a deep brown. Apricots and golden seedless
raisins maintain their attractive golden to orange color as a result of being
treated with harmless sulfur dioxide fumes, which subsequently are evaporated during the cooking of the fruit. Sulfur dioxide treatment may also be
used in preparing dried peaches, although this fruit frequently is dried to a
brown that carries a hint of the golden yellow of the fresh fruit. Dried fruits
often are separated by size and marketed as small, medium, large, and extra
large, with the price increasing along with the size of the fruit.

Perhaps the most popular of the dried fruits are raisins. By far the
largest selling raisin is the natural seedless, a sun-dried raisin made from
Thompson seedless grapes. This dark-colored raisin is to be compared with
the golden seedless raisins, for the latter also are made from Thompson
seedless. The difference in the two products is due to the sulfur dioxide
treatment given to the golden seedless. Although they are not nearly as
plentiful as the natural seedless raisins, seeded muscats, sun-dried from
muscat grapes, are another popular dark raisin particularly well suited for
use in baked products. Zante currants, frequently identified simply as currants, are sun dried to a dark color from Black Zante grapes. These are the
dried fruit that should be used in traditional hot cross buns.

STORAGE IN THE HOME

Some fruits are quite perishable and will be in the kitchen only a short
time whereas others may be able to be stored for long periods. Ripe fruits,

of course, should be used as soon as possible. Berries will likely be served fairly soon, but regardless of their intended storage duration they should be sorted before being stored. This must be done gently to avoid bruising the fragile fruit. No washing is done prior to storage for water encourages spoilage of berries. Most other fruits will be inspected by the consumer during the selection process in the store, so they may be stored without further examination.

Some fruits are poorly suited to refrigerated storage. Bananas, avocados, pineapples, and melons retain their quality better when stored in a cool room rather than in the refrigerator, but they may be chilled before they are served. Temperatures below 56°F cause a rather startling brown color to develop on the skin of bananas. Long-term storage of citrus fruits is best in an environment just slightly warmer than refrigerator temperature.

If fruits such as peaches, pears, and plums are slightly green when purchased, they may be ripened at room temperature and then stored in the refrigerator. Many common fruits may be suitably stored in the refrigerator. The hydrator drawers in the refrigerator are useful storage areas for fruit since they retard loss of moisture. Dried fruits are usually stored at room temperature in a cupboard, but in humid weather it is wise to place them in the open section of the refrigerator to prevent the absorption of excess moisture from the damp room air.

PREPARATION

Raw Fruits

Most fruits are highly palatable when served raw. The preparation of raw fruits may be as simple as merely washing the fruits thoroughly in cool running water.

Conservation of ascorbic acid is an important aspect to be considered in the preparation of fruits. To minimize loss of water-soluble ascorbic acid through cuts and breaks in the surface, strawberries are usually hulled after washing. Citrus fruits will contain more ascorbic acid if they are served in uncut sections. Cutting fruits shortly before serving minimizes the oxidative loss of ascorbic acid.

It is important to equate nutritive and esthetic values when planning fruit service. Artistically served fruits are certainly more likely to be consumed than carelessly prepared fruits. Attractive slices of fruit are slightly less nourishing than uncut fruit, but may be more acceptable to the diner. Cut fruits that have been prepared long before a meal is served, however, will discolor and be unappealing as well as less nutritious. More specific suggestions regarding the use of fruits in salads are considered in Chapter 6.

The primary color problem with fruits is browning or discoloration. During preparation, this problem may be minimized by preparing fruits just before serving them. If the fruit must be prepared ahead of time, a dip in an acidic fruit juice such as citrus or pineapple prior to refrigerated storage is effective in delaying browning. A sugar coating or sugar solution also is a practical means of reducing the amount of oxygen that comes in contact with the fruit, thus delaying the onset of browning. Of course, heating fruit also stops enzymatic browning because the enzyme action is destroyed as the proteinaceous enzyme becomes denatured.

Simmered Fruits

Various fruits may be prepared in a number of ways in addition to serving them raw. Stewing or simmering softens the cellulose in fruits and alters the flavor, but a cover should be used to help retain the volatile flavoring substances. Rhubarb and berries are easily reduced to indistinct shapes and may tend to become watery when cooked. This tendency is minimized by adding a very small amount of water and using a low heat. Slow heating retards the loss of shape, but the agitation resulting from rapid boiling hastens disintegration.

Dried fruits are prepared by simmering them in water until the fruit is tender and rehydrated. Prunes are done when the pit may be removed easily; other dried fruits are ready when they may be cut easily. The simmering time for dried fruits depends on the amount of soaking, the size of the pieces of fruit, and the amount of exposed cut surface. A somewhat shorter simmering time is required if the fruit is soaked in warm water for an hour prior to heating. Overnight soaking is not necessary to soften the fruit. As would be expected, small dried fruits become tender in a shorter time than larger fruits. It also can be easily demonstrated that dried fruits with cut surfaces are more quickly rehydrated than are those with intact skins.

When fruits are simmered, osmotic pressure develops, depending upon the conditions outside the fruit cells. During the simmering period, water diffuses through the cell walls in an attempt to equalize the concentration of solute on both sides of the semipermeable membrane (the cell wall). Water will flow toward the point of highest solute concentration.

Apples effectively illustrate the changes that may be achieved by simmering fruits. By altering extracellular conditions, osmotic pressure is controlled to yield diverse products from the same fruit. If water can be made to flow into a cell, the cell will become so plump with water that the cell wall will yield to the increased pressure and will rupture. Conversely, water may be drawn from the cells to produce a shriveled and limp product.

Applesauce preparation utilizes the former technique, that is, causing water to go into the cells. This is accomplished by heating the apples in

FIGURE 5.5a To section citrus fruits, the rind and membrane are peeled with a sharp knife to reveal the juicy sections. Subsequently, the individual sections are freed by cutting along the membrane on one side of the section and then flipping out the section with a turn of the knife.*(b)*

water to which no sugar has been added. Some water is thus drawn into the cells, causing them to swell and eventually rupture. The rupturing of the cells gives the desired texture to the sauce. After the cooking period is completed, sugar is then stirred into the sauce for flavoring.

Coddled or glazed apples may be made under conditions illustrating the reverse process. In theory, coddled apples are cooked in a sugar syrup that has a sugar/water ratio similar to that found in the cells. This ratio is approximately one part sugar to two parts water. When the proper ratio is maintained, a small plumping of the apple rings occurs. If the water that evaporates during the coddling of the rings is not replaced, however, a highly

(b)

concentrated sugar solution forms and the apples begin to shrivel as water is drawn out of the cells into the sugar syrup.

Additional Procedures

Fruits such as apples, pears, avocados, and bananas are excellent when baked. Apples retain their shape best during baking if a narrow strip of skin is removed around the middle of the apple perpendicular to the core. This narrow belt allows space for the apple to expand as steam forms inside. Baked avocado is suggested as a base for a hot salad.

Some fruits may be broiled or fried. Broiled grapefruit with a sprinkling of brown sugar are very quick to prepare and may serve equally well as a special breakfast treat or a light dessert after a heavy dinner. Broiled peach halves, either fresh or canned, are eye-catching garnishes for a meat platter. Fried apple rings are a tasty complement to pork chops.

FIGURE 5.6 Fruits add interest to many baked products; apples in this Dutch apple pancake provide a tempting example.

Occasionally, fruits are fried in deep fat. For example, fruit fritters are made with apples, bananas, figs, pears, oranges, or pineapple. The sliced fruits are dipped in medium batter, fried briefly at 375°F until golden brown, and served hot with powdered sugar or syrup. Fresh fruits dipped into melted chocolate are popular among fondue fanciers.

A variety of baked products incorporates fruits. Many quick breads gain their distinctiveness from a particular fruit. Cranberry, blueberry, orange, date, prune, apple, fig, and lemon muffins are some of the variations possible with a basic muffin recipe. Special breads may use mashed, stewed, canned, frozen, fresh, grated, or candied fruits.

Pies may have a sweetened filling made from fresh, canned, or frozen fruits thickened with starch. Grated citrus rinds are excellent flavoring substances for chiffon pies if none of the bitter albedo is grated with the flavedo. Cream pies are often made with a layer of various fruits such as bananas, peaches, or strawberries.

Sherbets and ice creams made with fruit are a particularly pleasing summer creation. More exotic fruit desserts include cherries jubilee, peach melba, fruit tortes, fruit-filled angel food cakes, and fruit soufflés.

SUMMARY

Fruits are attractive and appetizing foods that are particularly important as sources of ascorbic acid and vitamin A. Raw fruits are consumed as appetizers, salads, and desserts; in addition, fruits may be simmered, baked, fried, or used to make elaborate desserts or baked products. The commercial fruit industry processes fruits as canned sauces, pickles, juices, jams, and jellies, and also markets large quantities of frozen, dried, and candied fruits.

Careful selection, storage, and preparation are essential if one is to serve fruit of optimum palatability. Of particular concern in the preparation of raw, cut fruit is the problem of oxidation, which causes a reduction in the ascorbic acid content and a browning of some fruits. Problems of discoloration of the pigments are also created by enzyme activity in the raw fruit.

During the simmering of fruit, the external environment surrounding the fruit can be controlled to create the desired osmotic pressure. Heating fruit in water causes water to flow into the cells and rupture them, as is done when preparing applesauce. In a thin sugar syrup there is little flow of water into the cells and the outline of the fruit remains distinct. A concentrated sugar syrup surrounding the fruit causes a reversal and water passes from the fruit into the sugar syrup, thus creating a shriveled fruit product.

BIBLIOGRAPHY

Anonymous. *Conserving the Nutritive Values in Foods.* Consumer and Food Economics Research Division, Agricultural Research Service. Home and Garden Bulletin No. 90. U. S. Department of Agriculture, Washington, D. C. Rev. ed. 1971.

Anonymous. *Diluted orange juice beverages. Consumer Register* 2, No. 1, April 1, 1972.

Anonymous. Story of the amazin' raisin. *Forecast for Home Economics.* December 1969.

Biale, J. B. Postharvest biochemistry of tropical and subtropical fruits. *Adv. Food Res. 10*:293–347, 1960.

Charley, H. *Food Science.* Ronald. New York, N. Y. 1970.

Consumer and Food Economics Research Division. *Fruits in Family Meals.* Home and Garden Bulletin No. 125. U. S. Department of Agriculture, Washington, D. C. Rev. ed. 1970.

Corse, J., and K. P. Dimick. Volatile flavors of strawberry. In *Flavor Research and Food Acceptance.* Arthur D. Little, Inc. (Research Co.), Reinhold Publishing Corp., New York, N. Y. 1958.

Greeley, E. T. *How to Buy Canned and Frozen Fruit.* Home and Garden Bulletin No. 191. Consumer and Marketing Service. Washington, D. C. 1971.

Griswold, R. M. *Experimental Study of Foods.* Houghton Mifflin. New York, N. Y. 1962.

Hulme, A. C. Biochemistry of apple and pear fruits. *Adv. Food Res. 8*:297–395. 1958.

Joslyn, M. A., and J. B. S. Braverman. Chemistry and technology of pretreatment and preservation of fruit and vegetable products with sulfur dioxide and sulfites. *Adv. Food Res. 5*:97–146. 1955.

Joslyn, M. A., and J. D. Ponting. Enzyme-catalyzed oxidative browning of fruit products. *Adv. Food Res. 3*:1–46. 1951.

Kirchner, J. G. Chemistry of fruit and vegetable flavors. *Adv. Food Res. 2*:259–290. 1949.

Lee, F. A. Fruits and nuts. Chapter 28 in *Chemistry and Technology of Food and Food Products,* ed. by M. B. Jacobs, Vol. *2,* 2nd ed. Interscience Publishers, New York, N. Y. 1951.

Moyer, W. C. *The Buying Guide.* Blue Goose. Fullerton, Calif. 1971.

Redstrom, R. Storing perishable foods at home. *Food, Yearbook of Agriculture, 1959.* U. S. Department of Agriculture, Washington, D. C. 1959.

Seelig, R. A. Conserving nutrients in handling, storing and preparing fresh fruits and vegetables. In *Fruit and Vegetable Facts and Pointers.* United Fresh Fruit and Vegetable Assoc., 777 14th St., N. W., Washington 5, D. C.

Smith, M. E. *How to Buy Fresh Fruits.* Home and Garden Bulletin No. 141. Consumer and Marketing Service., U. S. Department of Agriculture, Washington, D. C. 1967.

Stadtman, E. R., Nonenzymatic browning in fruit products. *Adv. Food Res. 1*:325–369. 1948.

Stanley, W. L., Citrus flavors. In *Flavor Research and Food Acceptance*. Arthur D. Little, Inc. (Research Co.), Reinhold Publishing Corp., New York, N. Y. 1958.

Sunkist Growers. *Tangerines*. Sunkist. Los Angeles. 1968.

Tellus, B. *Clean Western Produce*. Western Growers. Los Angeles.

Western Ways with Fresh Vegetables and Melons, ed. by B. Tellus. Western Growers Association, Consumer Service Division, 3091 Wilshire, Los Angeles, Calif., 90005. 1963.

SUGGESTIONS FOR STUDY

1. Visit a grocery store to determine what fresh fruits are available. Compare the cost of the fresh fruits with their frozen and/or canned counterparts.
2. Classify each of these fruits: orange, avocado, strawberry, plum, apple, nectarine, tangerine, Thompson seedless grape, cranberry, kumquat, apricot, pear, Casaba melon, quince, pomegranate, currant, Tokay grape, banana, pineapple. During what periods of the year are they usually available?
3. What are the important nutritional contributions of fruits?
4. Explain why processing in a vacuum lowers the boiling point of orange juice. Why is this technique desirable?
5. Using a diagram, show how osmotic pressure is used to advantage in making applesauce and coddled apples.
6. What is the purpose of adding ascorbic acid to some fruits that are to be frozen?

CHAPTER 6

Salads and Salad Dressings

Danes are noted for their sandwiches. Scandinavians for their smorgasbords, Italians for their pizza, and Americans are emerging as a nation of salad lovers. Salads have gradually been developing into a specialty item which the American people relish at home or in a restaurant. Crisp, light salads are the favorite for summer, but these yield to hearty salads for cold winter evenings. There are salad variations to suit any occasion; a person's imagination may take the reins when salads are being planned. Cookbooks may provide suggestions, but salad time may well be adventure time to experienced or inexperienced cooks alike.

The notion that men do not like salads is becoming happily obsolete. It is not unusual for men with desk jobs to select a luncheon salad in a restaurant rather than the more traditional meat, potatoes, and gravy. Salads now have gained a prominence they richly deserve for salad ingredients are highly nourishing foods.

Salads may be planned to include representative foods from all four of the groups in the Basic Four Food Plan:

From milk and dairy products: cheeses of many types and some use of whipping cream.

From meats and meat alternatives: beef, pork, ham, chicken, turkey, eggs, and legumes.

From fruits and vegetables: practically all fruits and vegetables.

From breads and cereals: croutons and macaroni.

In addition, salad dressings are an excellent source of linoleic acid, the essential fatty acid. Dressings also are a concentrated source of calories.

SALAD PLANNING

Role in the Meal

The first step in planning a salad is to decide the role the salad will play in the meal. Will the salad be an appetizer course? Will it accompany the entree as a part of the main course? Will it be a separate salad course? Will it be the main course for a luncheon? Or will it serve as the dessert? Its intended use will determine the size of the salad and will likely help to establish some of the ingredients that might be used.

An appetizer salad ideally is a conservative size to whet rather than sate the appetite, whereas a salad that is to provide most of the nourishment of a meal should be much larger and have a satiety value far in excess of any of the other types of salads. The accompaniment salad may vary somewhat

FIGURE 6.1   Thin slices of ham combine with cheese, citrus fruits, and dried figs in this hearty main dish salad.

in size to balance the rest of the meal. A light meal could suitably have a hearty accompanying salad, but a large dinner is more appropriately complemented with a small salad. Once the role of the salad has been established for a meal, other considerations such as arrangement, color, flavor, and texture may be explored.

Arrangement and Shape

Care may well be given to the attractive arrangement of salads. A salad with asparagus spears loses its appeal when the stalks are jumbled like a game of pick-up-sticks. These spears become a unit when they are aligned neatly as a center of interest for a vegetable salad. A salad, whether on a large platter for buffet service or on a salad plate, should be arranged in a pleasing fashion. A balance between the various areas of a salad, coupled with a center of interest, will create a tempting salad. Any variety of salad greens may serve as a unifying component in the background to frame the salad into an artistic whole.

The salad plate should be adequate for the size of the salad and the

FIGURE 6.2 A buffet salad with its individual components attractively arranged invites the diner to assemble a salad suited to his own design.

ingredients should be arranged so that they are easy to eat. When one must be concerned with the kinetic energies that may develop as a salad is dismantled, some of the pleasure is lost.

Salad arrangement has been the subject of some controversy. One school faithfully attempts to make salads that accurately depict some subject in nature, such as a rabbit, a flower, or even some type of hat. This naturalist school is opposed by the individuals who feel that the salad ingredients are beautiful in themselves and need not use the excuse of representing something else to be worthy of inclusion in a meal. Children may occasionally enjoy a pictorial salad for a special celebration, but this is one of the rare times when such a salad is appropriate.

Color

The nature of the ingredients ordinarily dictates that a salad will be the color highlight of a meal, but even salads may be drab if the planner does not consider color. Most of the colors found in nature blend into a pleasing color combination. It may be necessary to add only a bright color accent to a salad. In some salads the use of several types of salad greens will furnish the range of color needed to create an intriguing salad, or perhaps a small garnish might be used to provide a touch of color. The simple device of leaving the skin on apples and pears adds important color touches to fruit salads in which these fruits are used.

Flavor

Salad flavors not only should be coordinated with each other, but also should complement the other foods in a meal. An accompaniment salad may add some zest to a meal or it may be used to soothe the taste buds. A bland salad containing avocados presents a welcome contrast to a spicy curry. A dinner of baked ham may gain distinction when a fruit salad is used to offset the saltiness of the meat.

Within a salad, flavors should enhance each other rather than compete. Cauliflower does little for a cabbage salad, but green pepper adds a refreshing touch. A dull potato salad achieves considerable sparkle when celery seed and chopped onion are added.

Texture

Crisp and soft textures may be combined to good advantage in a salad. Tuna salad gains textural interest when some crisp celery or green pepper is added. The softness of a tomato wedge is a pleasing contrast to the crispness of a tossed salad.

Salad texture should also be integrated with the rest of the meal. Sliced avocado and baked fish are monotonous because of the similarity of texture. A raw vegetable combination salad would provide a better contrast of texture. Crisp fried chicken may be paired with a gelatin fruit salad for a shift in texture.

TYPES OF SALADS

The total number of salad combinations appears to be almost infinite, but some order can be pulled out of this array for discussion purposes by classifying salads into garnishes, fruit salads, vegetable salads, high-protein salads, and gelatin salads.

Garnishes

A bright touch of color or a bit of a taste tantalizer will greatly increase the eye appeal of a meal. Some vegetables may be prepared in shapes that add interest and variety. By crisping thinly cut carrots, celery, and radishes in ice water, it is possible to make them curl and open up into a variety of shapes. Celery stalks, green pepper rings, or carrot circles may be stuffed with cheese. Hollow dill pickle rings serve as a holder for thin carrot sticks, or this may be reversed by using a hollow carrot circle to encompass sweet or dill pickle sticks. Crisp cucumber slices, onion rings, or tomato wedges offer additional garnishing possibilities.

Cranberries, corn, or green tomatoes may be used to make relishes that not only add color to appeal to the eye, but also add a flavor to excite the appetite. Fruit garnishes may consist of a small serving of fresh fruit or a spiced crab apple, spiced peach, watermelon pickle, or some other spiced fruit. The pleasing flavor touch that pickles add to a meal may be varied with cauliflower pickles, bread-and-butter pickles, beet pickles, green pickles, or other vegetable pickles.

Vegetable Salads

Mastery of salad making includes a knowledge of the different types of greens that may suitably be used either as the liner for a salad or as an integral part of the salad. Many different kinds of leaves are of merit in adding color to a salad. Carefully washed leaves from grapes, oranges, lemons, avocados, mint, ivy, or nasturtiums may be used effectively to highlight fruits, but are not commonly used as actual salad ingredients.

A number of greens may be utilized to frame a salad or as an ingredient to give some variety. Raw spinach, endive, leaf lettuce, romaine, red leaf

FIGURE 6.3   Greens for salads or garnishes include spinach (top), parsley, watercress, and chives.

lettuce, Chinese cabbage, escarole, watercress, and Boston or bibb lettuce
provide flavor differences as well as color and textural contrasts.

Tossed, mixed green, and combination salads may include a large
variety of vegetables. In addition to the greens already suggested, cucumbers,
cabbage, carrots, celery, cauliflower, red cabbage, and fresh mushrooms
provide variety. Occasionally mandarin oranges, pineapple, apples, and
other fruits are combined with greens.

Variations of bean salads are useful when a hearty salad is desired.
Baked beans, string beans, wax beans, and kidney beans are all potential
ingredients. A particularly nutritious salad utilizes kidney beans and hard-
cooked eggs combined with pickle relish, onion, and mayonnaise. Baked
beans with celery and onion are another tasty combination, or string, wax,
and kidney beans may be marinated in a highly seasoned oil-and-vinegar
marinade.

Potato salad is as American as apple pie. Recipes for this type of salad
are quite varied, and often include hard-cooked eggs, chopped onions, celery
or celery seed, mayonnaise, chopped pickles or pickle relish, mustard, and
green pepper. This potato salad is served cold. A somewhat different potato
salad is the hot potato salad which contains crisp bacon, onion, and a thickened dressing of vinegar and bacon drippings.

The vegetable salads previously discussed utilize vegetables in small
pieces, either grated, chopped, or sliced. Other vegetable salads make use

FIGURE 6.4 Onion rings serve as a rhythmic accent in this vegetable salad.

of the whole vegetable and are more formal in arrangement. Asparagus stalks neatly arranged on a bed of bibb lettuce with a strip of pimiento for garnish is an example of a salad with a definite arrangement. Tomatoes in slices or wedges also may be arranged suitably in a formal fashion. Another attractive use for tomatoes is a stuffed tomato salad in which the tomato is cut into a stylized flower and stuffed with a vegetable or meat salad.

Fruit Salads

Fruits are used for dessert salads, as well as in other courses of a meal, for their natural sweetness is appropriate at the conclusion of a dinner.

Fruit salads may be spectacular arrangements of beautiful fruits for a large buffet dinner or they may be scaled to enhance a small family dinner.

A potpourri of fruits cut into pieces and combined with a sweet fruit dressing is always enjoyable. Excellent fruit combinations are possible any time of year although the available fruits will vary with the season. Preparation for cut fruit salads of excellent quality requires careful washing and a judicious cutting of the fruits. When fruits are cut in very small pieces they begin to lose their identity and also their appeal. A variety of fruits in a salad presents the possibility of cutting the assorted fruits in different simple harmonious shapes to create a prettier salad.

A mixed fruit salad may be jauntily served in a natural fruit container such as a scooped out half of a pineapple, grapefruit, or melon. Another edible salad boat is a peeled avocado half which can hold mixed fruits, vegetables, or sea foods.

Fruits are particularly appealing in summer when arranged in a fruit plate featuring an ice made with fruit. Homemade ices and ice creams may contain a number of fresh fruits to give a variety of flavors not commonly

FIGURE 6.5 Avocado halves make attractive and edible containers for these individual salads, served in a buffet setting.

available commercially. These products are delicious when served with a fruit salad or as a dessert.

Frozen salads incorporating fruits are always popular. These salads are made with a base of whipped cream, mayonnaise, sugar, and cream cheese into which a number of cut up fruits are folded. Excessive quantities of sugar in a frozen salad may make it difficult to serve, especially in hot weather, because the high sugar content lowers the freezing point and causes the salad to soften quickly at room temperature. A salad of this type with just enough sugar to sweeten the cream base, however, will not melt too quickly.

High-Protein Salads

Tasteful combinations of meats with vegetables are popular with men as well as with women for a luncheon plate. Ground ham or ground roast beef may be combined with pickles, mayonnaise, and suitable seasonings to be served as a salad or sandwich filling. Cooked poultry is an excellent meat for hot or cold salads when it is diced and combined with other ingredients; crab, shrimp, and lobster are popular in seafood salads. Julienne ham, beef, and poultry are nutritious additions to vegetable salads.

The addition of eggs to a salad is an inexpensive way of boosting the protein content. Eggs are customarily hard cooked when used in a salad, but Caesar salad employs an uncooked egg in the dressing.

Several cheeses are particularly well suited to salad preparation. A scoop of cottage cheese blends well with fruits. Cream cheese softened with fruit juice may be whipped and used as a dressing. Strips of process cheese, longhorn, cheddar, jack, or American cheese enhance the appearance as well as the nutritive value of vegetable salads. Blue cheese, Roquefort, or Gorgonzola are flavorful additions to tossed salads.

Gelatin Salads

Gelatin salads are made in the home from commercially colored and flavored gelatin mixes or from plain gelatin. Plain gelatin is selected for salads needing only the structural qualities of gelatin. Aspics are made from unflavored gelatin, for they contain other ingredients that will give the salad the desired flavor. Flavored gelatin products have been available to the public for many years, but the variety of flavors has been increased considerably recently. The fruit flavors may be used with practically any food to create a tasteful salad.

Preparation of gelatin products is a two-step process requiring (1) complete dispersion of the gelatin to form a sol (see Chapter 17 for a discussion of sols and gel structure), and (2) chilling to form the desired gel. Unflavored

FIGURE 6.6 Carefully prepared and skillfully unmolded gelatin salads have a sparkling appearance and a distinct outline.

gelatin is coarser than the flavored product and must be hydrated by soaking the powdered gelatin in a small amount of cold water. Following this preliminary step, both the hydrated, unflavored and flavored gelatin may be prepared by adding a measured amount of boiling liquid and then stirring slowly to facilitate dispersion of the gelatin granules. An undisturbed chilling period aids in the formation of the desired random structural network in the finished gel. A good gelatin product will be clear, will hold its shape when cut, and yet will be tender. There will be no rubbery areas or small gelatinous particles in the gel.

Deviations from the desired product include too thin a product or a gel that is tough. A less than optimum concentration is responsible for the former; too much protein causes the latter. Careless hydration or dispersion procedures will produce the undesired rubbery areas.

Tenderness of Gelatin Gels. The tenderness of a gelatin gel is of great importance not only for palatability, but also because of its influence on the ease of serving. Considerable inconvenience can result when a gelatin product fails to reach the desired firmness. Several factors may be responsible for such a culinary problem. The concentration of gelatin in a food is important in determining the tenderness or firmness of the product; a minimum concentration necessary for gel formation produces a very tender gel in contrast to the somewhat tenacious gel produced with a much greater concentration of the protein. When few gelatin molecules are present in a system, there is little likelihood of the molecules uniting to form even a very fragile gel. A system with large numbers of gelatin molecules, however, has many potential linkage sites and a continuous, interlinking network of a tenacious character can result.

The concentration of gelatin required for adequate gelation varies with the acidity of the mixture. Less gelatin is needed for gelatin to occur at pH 5 (the isoelectric point of gelatin) than if the pH of the gel is shifted to either a more alkaline or acidic pH.

The amount of sugar in a gelatin product influences the tenderness of the product since the addition of sugar, in effect, reduces the concentration of the gelatin and produces a more tender gel. Too much sugar will prevent gelation.

Additional factors affecting the tenderness of a gelatin product include the age and temperature of the gel. As aging occurs, water is gradually lost from the gel, causing a change to an almost rubbery consistency with distinct loss of tenderness. In essence, the concentration of the gelatin has been increased as a result of the water loss. The other factor, temperature, can be observed easily, for gelatin mixtures become so tender on a warm day that it is not unusual for them to gradually revert to a sol. Gels are distinctly more firm when held at a cooler temperature until just before serving. The change in state with variability in temperature is utilized when a gelatin salad is to be unmolded. A brief dip of the mold in warm water melts the gelatin in contact with the metal mold without melting the internal unwarmed portions; a brief shake and the gelatin then slips out easily.

Although most fruits may be used in gelatin mixtures either fresh, frozen or canned, pineapple is an exception. Fresh pineapple contains a protein-digesting enzyme called bromelin. If either fresh or frozen pineapple is added to gelatin, this enzyme breaks down the gelatin, which is a protein. As a result, the gelling capability of gelatin is lost. Heating, as is done in the canning of pineapple, destroys the enzyme, making it possible to use cooked pineapple in gelatin products.

Setting Time for the Gel. Occasionally the setting time required for a gelatin salad may be of considerable interest because of a need to serve the product within half a day of when it is prepared. Then the concentration of the gelatin and the rate at which the sol is cooled are extremely critical. A high concentration of gelatin promotes gel formation and reduces the time required for gelation to occur. Although one should always drain canned fruit and count any of the juice used as part of the total liquid, this procedure is even more critical when the setting time available is limited. An additional amount of juice dilutes the concentration of the protein and delays gelation.

Gelatin gels can be formed quite rapidly by dispersing the gelatin in a small amount of boiling water and then stirring in ice, which melts to provide the remaining liquid needed for a tender gel. The ice-gelatin mixture should be stirred slowly until the gel begins to form, at which time any remaining pieces of ice are removed. When a gelatin is set quickly by using ice, the gel will soften more readily than a comparable gelatin mixture that has been set at a more moderate temperature. This variation between methods of preparation will only be a handicap on an unusually hot day or when the salad is to be served at a buffet where it may be left out at room temperature for a relatively long period of time. For most purposes, the addition of ice is a useful timesaver. One precaution must be noted in this practice, however: all gelatin particles must be dispersed in the boiling water so that they are invisible to the naked eye before any ice is added. Failure to completely dissolve the gelatin produces a less rigid product interspersed with rubber-like fragments.

The presence of sugar in a gelatin mixture also influences the setting time. A very small amount of sugar increases the setting time of a gel, but greater concentrations of sugar decrease the setting time. In fact, gelatin sols high in sugar set faster than the gelatins that contain no sugar.

GENERAL SUGGESTIONS FOR PREPARING SALADS

The following suggestions for making any salad are designed to promote preparation of a salad that is fresh, attractive, and flavorful.

Freshness of fruits and vegetables is of paramount importance for the optimum texture and color of a salad. Ideally, the fresh fruits or vegetables should be completely free from blemishes and canned foods should be of top quality. All fresh produce should be washed thoroughly to remove dirt and possible insecticides.

The handling of greens is particularly important in preparing salads. To prepare lettuce cups for lining a salad, the head is cored, either by using a knife or by hitting the core firmly against the sink. After the core is removed, cold water can be run with some force into the cavity, a procedure which loosens the leaves for easy removal. Lettuce cups, like all other greens used in salads, need to be carefully and thoroughly drained, so that the water on greens will not collect in the bottom of the plate and dilute the dressing. Salad greens may be prepared in advance if they are tightly covered and stored in the refrigerator to maintain crispness. When preparing greens, more attractive shapes will be achieved by tearing rather than by cutting with a knife.

FIGURE 6.7 For maximum crispness of vegetable salads, add dressing just prior to serving to minimize the loss of water in the cells due to osmosis.

Salads will have the most appeal when they are served with careful attention. Cold salads assume greater importance in the meal when the ingredients, the plates, and the salad fork have all been thoroughly chilled in the refrigerator. Dressings should be added just before serving to avoid the wilting that occurs when dressing is allowed to come in contact with greens for a period of time. This wilting is the result of osmosis, wherein the water from the cells of the greens is drawn out into the dressing in an attempt to balance the salt content of the liquid within and outside the cell. As the cells lose water, the fragile structure of succulents begins to collapse and wilting begins.

SALAD DRESSINGS

Uncooked salad dressings are emulsions in which a liquid is suspended in droplets in another liquid, the two liquids being immiscible with each other. Anyone who has ever attempted to mix oil and water together is cognizant of the lack of affinity between these two media. Vigorous stirring or shaking is necessary to mix the two and then they quickly separate again.

Salad dressings are classic examples of oil in water emulsions, in which droplets of oil are suspended in an aqueous medium. Some salad dressings separate very quickly, others rather slowly, and some seemingly do not separate at all. These are classified as temporary, semipermanent, and permanent emulsions. (See Chapter 17 for a more complete discussion of emulsions in foods.)

Temporary Emulsions

French and Italian dressings are favorites on tossed and mixed green salads. These are representatives of the class of emulsions known as temporary emulsions. The ingredients consist of vinegar (the aqueous medium), an oil, and some dry ingredients that vary from one recipe to another. The vinegar is the continuous phase, the oil is the dispersed phase, and the insoluble seasonings, such as mustard and paprika, collect at the oil-water interface to give a very slight degree of stability to the emulsion. Such dressings are characteristically of a thin viscosity. Because of their instability, temporary emulsions need to be reformed by vigorous shaking each time before the dressing is used.

Although the ingredients required for preparing this type of salad dressing are very simple, there are two important ingredients that need to be selected carefully for their flavor. The vinegar used in dressing may be wine vinegar, tarragon, white, or other type of vinegar with a flavor that pleases. Oil for dressings also requires consideration. Olive oil is a popular oil for

FIGURE 6.8   Italian dressing is an example of a temporary emulsion, which begins to separate into layers of oil and vinegar soon after it is shaken or stirred.

use in dressings because of its distinctive flavor. However, olive oil becomes rancid and develops a strong flavor if it is stored on the shelf for a period of time. Oils suitable for salad dressings and that have a longer shelf life include cottonseed, corn, soybean, peanut, and safflower. French dressings made commercially must contain a minimum of 35 percent vegetable oil. The acid ingredients may be a vinegar, lemon, or lime juice. A small amount of an emulsifying agent and seasonings help to add some stability to the dressing. Home-prepared French, oil and vinegar, or Italian dressings ordinarily contain two or three parts of oil to one part of vinegar.

Semipermanent Emulsions

A wide variety of salad dressings may be considered to be semipermanent emulsions. These emulsions, in contrast to the relatively thin temporary emulsions, are characterized as being approximately the viscosity of thick cream. This increased viscosity retards the separation of semipermanent emulsions.

A comparison of recipes for semipermanent emulsions and temporary emulsions will reveal the ingredients responsible for the difference in the viscosity and stability of the two types. Home recipes for semipermanent emulsions will contain one or more of the following: a cooked sugar syrup, honey, a starch-thickened base, a condensed soup base, or an unusually large quantity of dry ingredients.

Commercial dressings of this type may contain any of the aforementioned thickening substances or such commercial stabilizers as gelatin, gum tragacanth, gum arabic, or pectin. In small quantities these substances yield semipermanent emulsions; in larger amounts they will produce permanent emulsions.

Permanent Emulsions

The classic example of a permanent oil in water emulsion is mayonnaise. The stability of either homemade or commercially prepared mayonnaise has long been appreciated in the home for the dressing is always ready to use and the emulsion does not need to be reformed at the time of use. By legal definition, commercial mayonnaise must contain either egg yolk or whole egg and must have oil content of not less than 65 percent. The egg yolk serves as an emulsifier, while the rather high percentage of oil contributes significantly to the viscosity of the dressing. Although this definition permits manufacturers to omit identifying ingredients on the label, more informative labeling is a move being supported by the Food and Drug Administration and manufacturers. Ingredients are listed in order by descending weight on the labels.

Permanent emulsions are quite viscous; in fact, it is possible to make mayonnaise so thick that it may be sliced and still retain its exact shape. This great viscosity makes it difficult for the oil droplets to touch and coalesce. The high viscosity, the distribution of the oil in many very small globules, and the presence of efficient emulsifying agents all contribute to the stability of a permanent emulsion.

Egg yolk is an unusually effective emulsifying agent in food work and is the stabilizing agent most often used in the home. Apparently the fact that egg yolk is itself an emulsion explains at least in part why it is such an outstanding agent. Whole egg and gelatin are other proteins frequently employed to stabilize emulsions. Dry mustard, paprika, and any other insoluble dry ingredients also make a small contribution toward the stability of mayonnaise.

Selection of a high-quality oil is essential to the preparation of mayonnaise for the presence of even a slight degree of rancidity will impair its flavor and shelf life. Winterized oils (Chapter 19) are preferred in mayonnaise because crystallization of the oil in the refrigerator will cause the emulsion to break. Vinegar or lemon juice contribute to the flavor of mayonnaise. In addition, the acid of either of these liquids helps to prevent spoilage during storage.

Mayonnaise preparation in the home is basically the simple process of making an oil in water emulsion, utilizing egg yolk and dry seasonings as the emulsifying agents. The addition of part of the vinegar to the emulsifying agents at the beginning of beating gives a larger volume of liquid and makes it somewhat easier to use the beaters effectively in the mayonnaise.

Oil must be added a teaspoon at a time with thorough mixing after each addition. Agitation helps to distribute the oil in the very small globules needed to form a stable emulsion. As the volume of mayonnaise becomes larger it is possible to begin to add the oil somewhat faster. Care must be exercised, however, to emulsify one addition of oil before adding the next portion. When there is no oil visible, it has been emulsified and more oil may be added.

As oil is added to mayonnaise, the product becomes increasingly thicker until finally so much oil may be added that the continuous phase can no longer separate the many droplets of oil, and the oil will coalesce and separate from the mayonnaise. Recipes for mayonnaise do not approach this quantity of oil because the dressing is too thick for practical use long before the emulsion contains this critical amount of oil. Customarily mayonnaise contains 70–80 percent oil by weight.

A broken emulsion, wherein oil separates from the other ingredients, during mayonnaise preparation is far from a culinary disaster. The broken mayonnaise emulsion should simply be considered as oil. The reformation of the dressing can then be accomplished by beating a yolk or whole egg and then slowly adding the broken emulsion to it.

Separation of mayonnaise may occur as a result of long storage, warm temperatures, freezing, or considerable shaking or agitation during shipping. This problem is controlled commercially by fine division of the oil droplets, use of an adequate stabilizer, and cool storage temperatures. When an emulsion breaks, the oil coalesces into a continuous phase and forms a layer of oil.

Cooked Salad Dressings

Cooked salad dressings may be made in the home; they also are available commercially identified simply as "salad dressing." The home product and the commercial dressings may be distinctly different in their formulation. The home-prepared cooked salad dressings customarily are thickened with starch and/or egg. Very little, if any, oil is used in these dressings. However, the commercial salad dressings are required to contain, at least, 30 percent oil. Although these salad dressings often are very similar in appearance to mayonnaise, they cannot be labeled mayonnaise because of the lower oil content plus the fact that these products may not contain egg yolk and may be thickened with a range of suitable stabilizers. Because of the reduced use of oil and egg in these commercial dressings, the cost of production is lower,

FIGURE 6.9 Cooked salad dressings with special touches, such as poppy seed and coriander, are a welcome and economical change from commercial dressings.

a fact reflected in a lower retail price as well. The reduced oil content has the additional advantage of being lower in calories than mayonnaise. Various low calorie commercial salad dressings now are available for the diet conscious. Restricting the quantity of dressing on salads is another obvious way of reducing caloric intake.

Home preparation of cooked salad dressings may involve both starch cookery and protein cookery. When starch is used in a recipe, care should be taken to mix the dry ingredients together carefully and to blend them well with the liquid before applying direct heat. Starch mixtures should be brought to a boil while being stirred constantly. Dressings containing eggs should be heated over hot water after the egg is added in order to obtain maximum thickening from the protein. If a recipe includes both starch and egg, the starch mixture should be boiled over direct heat and then placed over hot water when the egg is added.

Fruit juices or other acids should be added after the dressing is thickened and removed from the heat if maximum thickening of the product is to be achieved. More complete explanations of thickening with starch and eggs are included in Chapters 7 and 10.

Variations of Salad Dressings

Basic salad dressings are useful because they may be used as they are or altered by the addition of other ingredients. Sour cream, cream, milk, cream cheese, diced cheddar cheese, or Roquefort-type cheeses blend well with a variety of dressings. Pickles, olives, grated onions, pickle relish, and chopped egg are flavorful additions for vegetable or meat salads. Fruit juices blend well into dressings for fruit salads.

Evaluation of Salad Dressings

Salad dressings are easily prepared by making basic dressings at home or by buying commercial dressings and varying them to suit the salad. A good dressing has a pleasing flavor that blends well with the salad ingredients. The dressing should be thin enough to blend easily with the salad, but should not be so thin that it drains readily to the bottom of the dish. For optimum flavor the ingredients of a dressing should be well blended when poured on the salad. No oil should be in evidence on mayonnaise, nor should there be any trace of rancidity. Cooked salad dressings should be free of lumps.

SUMMARY

Salads are appropriate for any course of a meal and present an appetizing means of serving fruits and vegetables. Meat, cereal, and dairy products offer additional variety as salad ingredients. When a salad is planned, consideration should be given to its role in the meal, arrangement, color, flavor, and texture. Artistic salads are enhanced with a well-chosen dressing. Dressings may be temporary, semipermanent, or permanent emulsions.

An emulsion is a suspension formed by blending two immiscible liquids. The stability of the emulsion is determined by the viscosity of the mixture and the presence of emulsifying agents. Thin dressings with only a few dry ingredients to coat the interface around the drops of oil will separate quickly, whereas a thick dressing with egg yolk as the emulsifying agent will be stable.

BIBLIOGRAPHY

Ames, W. M. The viscosity of gelatin solutions. *Chem. Ind.* 567, May 1954.

Boedtker, H., and P. Doty. A study of gelatin molecules, aggregates and gels. *J. Phys. Chem. 58*:968–983. 1954.

Ferry, J. D. Protein gels. *Adv. Prot. Chem. 4*:8–47. 1948.

Ferry, J. D. Mechanical properties of substances of high molecular weight, IV: Rigidities of gelatin gels; dependence on concentration, temperature, and molecular weight. *J. Am. Chem. Soc. 70*:2244. 1948.

Grass, J. Collagen. *Scient. Am. 204, 5*:121–130. 1961.

Harrington, W. F. The structure of collagen and gelatin. *Adv. Prot. Chem. 16*:1–138. 1961.

Idson, B., and E. Braswell. Gelatin. *Adv. Food Res. 7*:236–328. 1957.

Olsen, A. G. Evidence of structure in gelatin gels. *J. Phys. Chem. 36*:529–533. 1934.

Robinson, C. *Nature and structure of collagen,* ed. by J. T. Randall. Academic Press, New York, N. Y. 1953.

Urbain, W. Meat and meat products. Chapter 46 in *Chemistry and technology of food and food products,* ed. by M. B. Jacobs, Vol. *3,* 2nd ed. Interscience Publishers, New York, N. Y. 1951.

Ward, A. G. A recent advance in gelatin research. *Chem. Ind.* 502–503. May 1954.

Western ways with fresh vegetables and melons, ed. by B. Tellus. Western Growers Association, Consumer Service Division, 3091 Wilshire, Los Angeles, Calif. 90005. 1963.

Worrell, L. Flavors, spices, condiments and essential oils. Chapter 32 in *Chemistry and technology of food and food products,* ed. by M. B. Jacobs, Vol. *2,* 2nd ed. Interscience Publishers, New York, N. Y. 1951.

SUGGESTIONS FOR STUDY

1. Compare the cost of commercial and homemade salad dressings. Calculate the amount of time required to prepare the dressings at home. Under what circumstances would you select: (a) commercial dressings, (b) homemade dressings?

2. Plan a salad for: the main course of a luncheon, an appetizer, an accompaniment to the main course, and a dessert.
3. Why does the viscosity of a salad dressing influence the stability of an emulsion?
4. Classify several salad-dressing recipes as temporary, semipermanent, or permanent emulsions. Identify the ingredients in the individual recipes which contribute to the stability of the emulsion.
5. Identify and explain the factors that influence the tenderness of a gelatin gel.
6. Prepare two gelatin salads, one using fresh pineapple and one using fresh papaya. Explain the effect of fresh pineapple on a gelatin product. Does fresh papaya have a similar effect? Why?

CHAPTER 7

Cereals and Starch Cookery

Cereal grains and their products add considerable variety to the diet along with meaningful quantities of nutrients. Although many of the forms in which cereals are marketed today are the results of technological developments, cereal grains in various forms have occupied a prominent place in man's diet for centuries. Archaeologists have discovered evidence of the use of cereals in many cultures. The Chinese grew wheat 27 centuries before the birth of Christ; in 4800 B.C. the people living in what is now Iraq were using wheat. The grains were named cereals after the Roman goddess Ceres, Goddess of Grain. A list of the cereal grains includes barley, corn, rice, oats, millet, rye, sorghum, and wheat.

Of the grains grown around the world, those in highest production and contributing most significantly to meeting world nutrition problems are wheat and rice. Almost twice as much land area is dedicated to raising wheat as is utilized for rice, although the total supply of calories available from these two grains is about equal. When all of the grains are considered together, more than 70 percent of the earth's cultivated land is devoted to raising grain crops.

In some regions of the world, heavy reliance is placed on grains, usually wheat or rice, to provide the bulk of the calories in the local diet. However, although products made from grains are still used in large amounts as inexpensive sources of energy, the patterns of cereal consumption have changed in the last half-century as the United States has become a more affluent nation. There has been a distinct downward trend in cereal usage with an increase in income. This probably reflects the decreased activity and consequent decreased caloric needs of the general public as well as the change in income. There also has been a gradual shift in the forms of cereal consumed: a decrease in purchase of flour, but an increase in the purchase of baked products; a decrease in cooked cereals, but an increase in ready-to-eat cereals.

Corn is considered to be a rather special American crop for, unlike many of our foods that originated in other areas of the world, maize was found growing in the Western Hemisphere when Columbus arrived, and subsequently was introduced into Europe. A large percentage of the corn consumed in the United States is grown in the Midwestern Corn Belt. The three types of corn produced commercially are: sweet, field, and popcorn. Sweet corn is raised for human consumption, and field corn is grown for feeding livestock. Popcorn is popular as a snack item in the United States.

Rice has been the principal food in China, Japan, and India as well as other smaller Far Eastern countries for centuries. It has been considered a

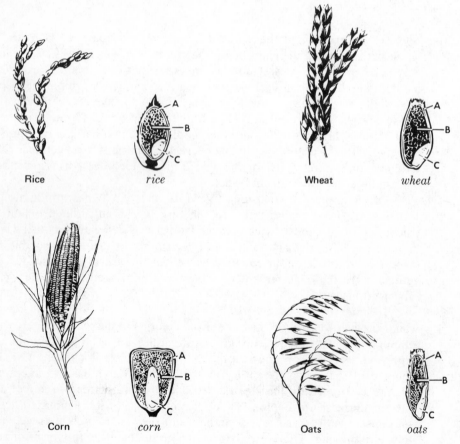

Rice   *rice*   Wheat   *wheat*

Corn   *corn*   Oats   *oats*

FIGURE 7.1 Popular cereal grains include rice, wheat, corn, and oats. In the cross-sectional diagrams: *(a)* bran, *(b)* endosperm, *(c)* germ.

less important grain in the diet in the United States, but apparently it is becoming somewhat more popular. Rice is classified as long, medium, or short grain. Long-grain rice is preferred by the majority of consumers in this country. Rice is grown in the south-central region of the United States (including Missouri, Arkansas, Mississippi, Louisiana, and Texas) and in California.

Four types of wheat are available in the United States: hard red spring, hard red winter, soft red winter, and white. The hard wheats are grown primarily in the area circumscribed by Montana, Nebraska, Minnesota, and Texas. Soft wheat generally is grown south and east of Illinois. White wheat is predominant in the Pacific region.

Durum wheat, a different species, is an amber-colored wheat used for macaroni, spaghetti, lasagna noodles, and other alimentary pastes. This type is the hardest known variety of wheat. Following its import from the Crimea in the middle of the 19th century, this crop has been bred for high protein content and resistance to disease. Thirteen counties in northeastern North Dakota raise approximately 85 percent of the durum wheat grown in the United States, with most of the remainder being produced in Minnesota and Montana.

Oats are grown along the northern tiers of states, from Nebraska and the Dakotas to Pennsylvania and New York, and also in Texas. Barley is raised in the northernmost states from Washington to Minnesota and in California. These grains are used primarily in breakfast cereals, with limited use in baked products. Another of the cereal grains, rye, has protein with the potential for developing some structure in baked products. Consequently, rye has some use in bread formulations, where it generally is combined with wheat flour for greater strength.

GRAIN STRUCTURE

Cereal grains are comprised of three parts: the bran, the endosperm, and the germ. The bran portion actually consists of the several outer protective layers covering the endosperm and germ. These bran layers are high in cellulose, but also contain several of the B vitamins and some protein (see Table 7.1). The endosperm is the region of the kernel where starch is deposited in a protein matrix. This area, comprising the large majority of the kernel, is a source of both starch and protein plus limited amounts of several of the B vitamins. This is the fraction that is utilized primarily in the milling of wheat flours. By far the smallest, but of considerable interest, is the germ or embryo, which constitutes only about $2\frac{1}{2}$ percent of the kernel. The germ is the viable sprouting portion of the kernel. This fraction is unique in that only the germ contains fat. Although this portion is rich in thiamin, the germ usually is removed because the fat limits the storage life of the grain products.

Table 7.1. Distribution of Nutrients in the Kernel of Wheat[a]

Nutrient	Bran (percent)	Endosperm (percent)	Germ (percent)
Protein	19	70–75	8
B vitamins			
Thiamin	33	3	64
Riboflavin	42	32	26
Niacin	86	12	2
Pyridoxine	73	6	21
Pantothenic acid	50	43	7

[a]Adapted from *From Wheat to Flour.* Wheat Flour Institute. Chicago, Ill. 1966. Page 38.

NUTRITIONAL CONTRIBUTION

Since cereal grains are utilized and prepared in so many different ways, general statements regarding nutritive value are difficult to make. Protein content in cereals typically is not high, but the large intake of cereals in some diets may mean that cereals are a significant source of protein for these consumers. As an example, one slice of bread contains two grams of protein; six slices would provide 20 percent of the protein needed daily by an adult man. Another way of providing 20 percent of the day's protein need is by consuming three cups of cooked rice or four cups of cooked corn grits. Cereal proteins are classified as incomplete proteins which are useful to the body, but which need to be supplemented with other proteins providing the amino acids that are inadequate in the specific cereal protein.

All cereals are rich sources of starch, making them not only good sources of energy, but also inexpensive. A slice of bread contributes 60 kilocalories, a cup of cooked corn grits yields 120 kilocalories, and a cup of cooked rice provides 185 kilocalories. Much of the caloric content of these cereals is derived from carbohydrates; the protein content is modest, and the fat content generally is nil as a result of the removal of the germ.

Blanket statements regarding the B vitamin content of different cereal products simply cannot be made. A large assortment of cereals and cereal products confronts the shopper, and the actual nutritive value of them varies considerably, depending on the part of the kernel used and the enrichment that may have been a part of the processing. Fortunately, the nutritive content of cereals is listed on the package for the benefit of consumers who are interested in learning more about the actual nutritional value of the products they eat. Some cereals are sources of little but energy, whereas others have been enriched with some of the B vitamins and iron. The cereal products, such as those described in Table 7.2, that are enriched are termed enriched cereals. In some instances, cereal products are made from a portion of the grain, but have had the level of nutrients contained in the original grain added back into the cereal product. Such products are identified as restored cereals. Whole grain cereals contain the nutrients that are present at the beginning of processing because the germ, endosperm, and bran are retained in their original proportions. Fortified cereals have gained popularity in the breakfast cereal market. When products are labeled as being fortified, extra nutrients not normally present in the food have been added.

COMMERCIAL PROCESSING OF GRAINS

In addition to enrichment, several other technological developments have been engineered to modify cereals into a wide range of products. Perhaps no other section of the modern supermarket affords as many consumer choices as are found in the cereal and pasta sections. Most whole grain cereals are broken up by various means so that they are more functional for cooking purposes. The exception to this is brown rice, which is not subdivided before being marketed. Cracked wheat and oatmeal are examples of whole grain cereals that are broken mechanically into smaller pieces so that the cellulose and starch will be modified more quickly during cooking. Oats are not only cut for the preparation of quick cooking rolled oats, but they are also rolled to make them considerably thinner for quicker heat penetration.

Table 7.2. Federal Standards for Enriched Rice and Enriched Macaroni Products

Nutrient	Macaroni Products Ingredients per Pound of Flour	Rice Ingredients per Pound
Required	(in milligrams)	(in milligrams)
Thiamin	4.0– 5.0	2.0– 4.0
Riboflavin	1.7– 2.2	1.2– 2.4
Niacin	27.0– 34.0	16.0–32.0
Iron	13.0– 16.5	13.0–26.0
Optional		
Calcium	500.0–625.0	
Vitamin D	250 –1000 USP units[a]	

[a]One USP unit equals one International Unit (IU).

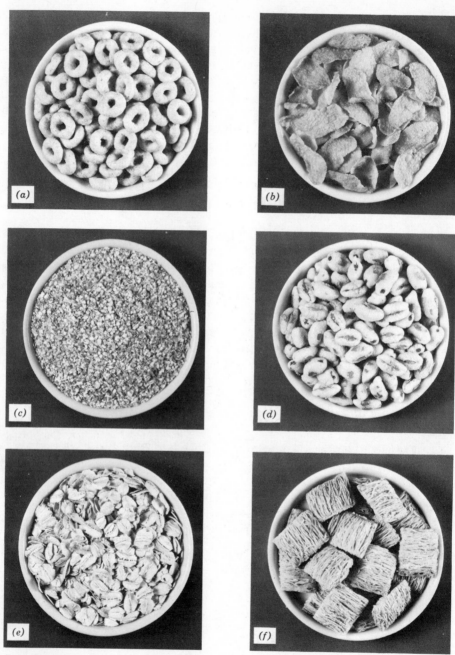

FIGURE 7.2 Commercial processing techniques utilized today produce a variety of cereal products: (a) extruded, (b) flaked, (c) granulated, (d) puffed, (e) rolled, (f) shredded.

Fractionation of the kernel is done frequently in cereal processing. By removing one or more portions of the kernel, specific storage or cooking properties may be achieved. For example, the hull is removed from popcorn, thus facilitating the popping action. Both the bran and germ are removed when wheat is milled into flour. Rice often is polished to remove the outer bran layers and the germ, thus, decreasing cooking time, lengthening storage life, and modifying the appearance. The above examples represent the three types of fractionation that are used: hulling, milling, and polishing.

Removal of the bran layers produces white cereal products. Since lipases present in wheat, rye, and barley cause undesirable changes in the flavor of the fat, the germ is often removed to increase storage life. Another

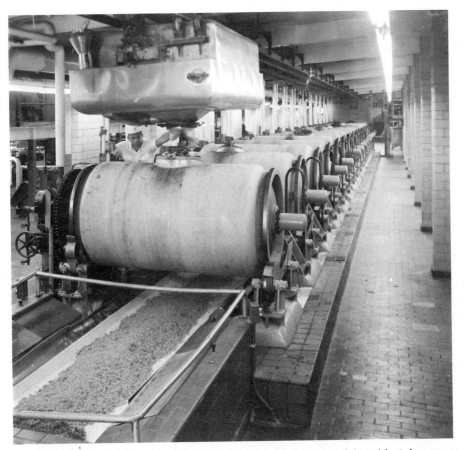

FIGURE 7.3 Ready-to-eat cereals are an important part of breakfast for many people. Through fortification and enrichment, these products are a good source of nutrients, particularly when eaten with milk.

means of controlling spoilage during storage is the maintenance of a dry atmosphere tailored to keep the moisture content low in the grain. Storage of grains with a moisture content above 14 percent is detrimental to grain quality since higher moisture content hastens deteriorative changes and mold growth.

New breakfast cereals, both ready-to-eat and hot, are constantly entering the market today. It is apparent from a quick inspection of the packages that considerable thought and effort have gone into the expansion within this field of food processing. The ready-to-eat cereals afford a wide range of textures, flavors, and shapes. There are six basic kinds of processed cereals: extruded, flaked, granulated, puffed, rolled, and shredded. Even more variety is available by mixing the different cereal grains (corn, wheat, oats, and rice) to provide products to suit any palate. Different flavorings used to broaden the varieties include cocoa, honey, sugar, and freeze-dried fruits. The shopper is confronted with all of these choices, and in addition, must decide between various sized packages.

Several cereal products now may be purchased as quick cooking or instant products. These types of cereals have had additional processing during their manufacture. The quick-cooking cereals and rices have disodium phosphate added to reduce the amount of cooking time required to soften the product. This is accomplished because the disodium phosphate decreases the amount of heat energy needed for water to penetrate the granule. The resulting product has greater viscosity but, unfortunately, is also more gummy and sticky. Instant hot cereal products have been heat treated so that the starch is pregelatinized during the manufacture of the various items. The pregelatinized starch is then dehydrated. All that remains for the consumer is to rehydrate the starch by adding boiling water.

Corn and Barley

Among the cereals and cereal products requiring at least token preparation are various items prepared from corn, rice, oats, and wheat. The most common products from corn are hominy, grits, and cornmeal. Hominy is made by removing the bran and germ of the corn kernel. Grits are hominy broken into uniform, small particles. These two corn products may be made from either white or yellow corn, the latter being more common in the northern part of the United States and the white being traditional in the South. Cornmeal, which is simply finely ground corn, also is made from either white or yellow corn. Cornmeal and hominy grits ordinarily are marketed as the enriched product.

Barley occupies a very small fraction of the cereal market in the United States. The customary form in which it is marketed is as pearl barley, which is the portion remaining after the bran has been removed.

ice

With the increased emphasis on gourmet foods, rice is being recognized for its value as a food on a somewhat higher plane than it previously occupied. Exotic recipes may use'rice as a base for creamed foods, or the rice itself may be prepared as a separate food and seasoned with unusual herbs. Several types of rice are available and these merit some comment.

Brown rice may now be purchased in the instant or in the regular form. In either instance the rice consists of an outer bran layer (pericarp) plus the seed (inner bran layer, endosperm, and germ). Such rice, called brown or unpolished rice, is high in nutrients as compared with polished rice and consequently has gained a certain degree of fame as a "health food." Brown rice is a light brown color and has a distinctive nutty flavor.

Polished rice is preferred by many people because of its fluffy white appearance and very mild flavor. Since polishing removes the bran and germ and leaves the endosperm, polished rice has little food value except for calories. Removal of the germ is tantamount to removing the fat, and removal of the fat reduces the development of rancid flavors. Polished rice originally gained its popularity because of its excellent keeping qualities and it is the type of rice commonly used throughout the world.

It is possible to greatly increase the nutritive value of polished rice. Prior to polishing, rice is soaked and steamed under pressure and then dried. This parboiling treatment draws the vitamins into the endosperm portion where they are retained in the milling process. The nutritive losses are greatly reduced by this conversion: thiamin retention is about 92 percent, riboflavin is 70.8 percent, and niacin is 77.6 percent. No nutrients have been added in this process; it is designed merely to retain the natural vitamins of the rice. The market name for this product is parboiled rice.

Rice may be enriched effectively by artificial means, as it was in a nutrition research project conducted on Bataan Peninsula in the Philippine Islands. A vitamin premix is applied to the rice with a protective coating. This protective coating helps to reduce vitamin loss during washing and boiling. Rice that has had vitamins and iron added will be identified as enriched rice.

Wild rice is not actually a rice, but is a wild grass from the lake country of Minnesota and Canada. Harvesting of this crop is restricted by the United States government to the Indians who live in this area. The grass grows in marshy areas or shallow water. The Indians harvest the crop by pushing canoes through the grass, bending the grass into the canoe and then shaking off the grains. This process is repeated two or three times during September. Since this crop is the chief source of income for these Indians, the harvesting restrictions have been maintained by the federal authorities despite the fact that this causes the price of wild rice to remain extremely high. The nutritive value of wild rice is considerably higher than that of brown or polished rice. The distinctive, rather strong flavor of wild rice makes it a favorite stuffing for game birds.

Wheat

Wheat is an extremely versatile cereal grain that can be adapted to many uses. One of the hot cereals that has been popular for many years is farina, which is the granulated endosperm of wheat with no bran present and no more than 3 percent flour. Rolled wheat can be purchased for use as a breakfast cereal or as an ingredient in baked products and casseroles.

Bulgur is a wheat product with a flavor reminiscent of nuts and a distinctly chewy texture. This very old form of wheat processing has been gaining in popularity as a substitute for rice. This distinctive wheat product is available as the whole kernel or cracked. The manufacturing steps are parboiling, drying, and partial removal of the bran layer.

Durum wheat products present a whole new range of cereal products in the form of pastas. The three basic forms of pastas are spaghetti, mararoni, and noodles. These products are made from doughs containing a large amount of semolina (a granular product obtained from the milling of durum wheat, containing no more than 3 percent flour) and/or granulars (milled durum containing more flour than semolina). Macaroni and spaghetti and their variations are extruded from doughs composed of the durum product and water. Noodles also are made from durum flour, but have more than 5 percent egg solids or yolk added to the dough. A new type of mararoni product is undergoing test marketing and appears to have some possibility of competing in the pasta market. This item is identified as enriched yellow corn-soy-wheat-macaroni.

STORING CEREALS AND PASTAS

To prolong shelf life and avoid the development of off flavors, cereals and pastas should be stored away from strong smelling items and in a cool, dry cupboard. By keeping their packages closed securely and refolding inner wrappings when they are a part of the package, these products should be of good quality up until the storage period indicated in Table 7.3. If humidity is high and cereals begin to lose their crisp texture, they may be heated until they lose the excess moisture in a 350°F oven.

PREPARATION OF CEREALS

The wide variety of cereal treatments makes it impossible to outline specific procedures for preparing all cereals, but the objectives for the prepa-

Table 7.3. Approximate Storage Time for Cereals and Pastas[a]

Product	Maximum Storage Period for Maintaining Best Quality
	(months)
Breakfast cereals	2–3
Bulgur	6
Cornmeal and hominy grits	4–6
Pasta	
Macaroni and spaghetti products	12
Egg noodles	6
Rice	
White, parboiled, packaged and precooked	12
Brown and wild	6

[a]Adapted from Cereals and Pasta in Family Meals. Home and Garden Bulletin No. 150. U. S. Department of Agriculture. Washington, D. C. 1968.

ration of various cereals may be generalized as follows: (1) to soften the cellulose, and (2) to gelatinize the starch. A well-prepared hot cereal will have a pleasing flavor with no suggestion of a raw starch flavor, will be free of lumps, will be light on the tongue rather than pasty, and will pile softly when hot. The directions for preparation that are listed on the cereal package are the best guide to follow for a specific cereal. Frequently, these packages also suggest variations that will help to increase interest in cereals when they are served. For instance, milk may be used as the cooking medium rather than water. This changes the flavor as well as increasing the nutritive value of the cereal. Various fruits and toppings also add variety and nutrients.

In all cereals the basic problem is gelatinization of the starch. To avoid lumps, fine cereals such as corn meal should be mixed with some cold water before being added to boiling water. Other cereals may be stirred directly into the boiling, salted water. During gelatinization, slow stirring prevents lumps without creating a sticky cereal.

Cooked cereal is done when it is thickened and the raw starch flavor is gone. The actual length of time needed to reach this point is determined by the size of the cereal particles, the amount of cellulose, previous treatment, and elevation. Small cereal granules, of course, are gelatinized and softened more quickly than large ones since the distance of heat penetration is less. Rice illustrates the influence of cellulose: brown rice is high in cellulose and therefore must be boiled twice as long as polished rice to soften the cellulose. Previous gelatinization or the addition of disodium phosphate significantly

FIGURE 7.4 The starch in instant hot cereals has been gelatinized during manufacturing so that home preparation requires merely rehydration with boiling water.

shorten the preparation time of cereals. When the starch in a cereal has been gelatinized previously, the preparation involves primarily a simple rehydration of the cereal. Disodium phosphate shortens the boiling time by reducing the amount of energy needed to enable water to enter the starch granules. From the discussion of boiling points in Chapter 2, it is apparent that cereals boiled at a high elevation will require more time than at sea level because of a lower actual temperature.

The amount of water to use for cereals is generally stated on the package for a particular product. The figures in Table 7.4 are helpful, however, if such specific information is lacking.

Table 7.4. Suggested Amounts of Water To Use for Preparing Various Hot Cereals[a]

Type of Cereal	Quantity of Cereal	Quantity of Water
Rolled, flaked	1 cup	2 to 3 cups
Coarse or cracked	1 cup	3 to 4 cups
Fine granules	1 cup	4 to 5 cups

[a]Package directions are a better guide to preparing specific cereals. This table is a general guide to cereal cookery.

Rice Cookery

Unless otherwise specified on the package, polished rice should be boiled in 2 to $2\frac{1}{4}$ cups of salted water per cup of rice. Ideally, all of the water will have been absorbed at just the time that the rice is done, but there will be enough water present to allow the rice to soften to the desired end point. If the rice begins to stick and is still too firm, more water may need to be added to finish gelatinizing the starch. The average boiling time for polished rice, cooked until a grain rubbed between the fingers reveals no hard spots, is 20 minutes; brown rice requires approximately 40 minutes. Minute rice and minute brown rice require a much shorter time than their conventional counterparts. In addition, there is a difference in the appearance of the conventional and minute rices. Brown rice, parboiled rice, and enriched rice are all good sources of water-soluble B vitamins. Therefore, they should not be washed, either before or after boiling. If desired, rice may be fluffed by spreading the hot rice in a thin layer on a large flat pan, covering with cheese cloth, and heating briefly in the oven. Rice also may be prepared very easily simply by pouring the boiling water over the measured amount of salt and rice, covering tightly, and baking in a 350°F oven for 35 minutes.

Wild rice is cooked most successfully by pouring boiling water on the rice at intervals and letting the rice soak in the hot water. Tepid water is drained off, boiling water is added, and this process is repeated until the rice is tender. When wild rice is done, it will curl open at the ends. This technique is prolonged, but it produces a relatively mild-flavored rice. Wild rice may also be boiled, but the product is slightly less desirable.

The finished characteristics of cooked rices are influenced appreciably by the type of rice used as well as by preparation techniques. These qualities are related to the amylose content of the particular variety of rice selected. Since individual taste for rice is varied, it is impossible to classify one type of rice as superior to another, but it is possible to predict the characteristics

FIGURE 7.5 Rice may be incorporated in desserts, as in this molded dessert with mandarin oranges.

of the finished product prepared from different varieties of rice. The long-grain rices generally are high in amylose. During boiling the long-grain rices absorb more water, lose less starch into the water, and gelatinize at a higher temperature than the medium- and short-grain rices. Properly prepared long-grain rice retains its shape well as it swells, whereas the short and medium grains may split on the ends and become less distinct in outline. The fluffiness of long-grain rice is preferred by many Americans although the more cohesive, sticky short grain rice is in demand in the South. Short-grain, sticky rice is useful when preparing a rice mold and also is the choice of many Orientals and others who may choose to eat rice with chopsticks.

Bulgur

The preparation of bulgur is similar to that of polished enriched rice. Since this type of wheat cereal is a source of the water-soluble B vitamins, the bulgur is not washed at all, either before or after preparation. As is done with rice, the bulgur is stirred into boiling, salted water, covered tightly, and held at a slow boil for 20 minutes. Bulgur also may be prepared by heating the boiling water-salt-bulgur mixture for 30 minutes or until tender in a 350°F oven.

Hominy Grits

Hominy requires five cups of boiling, salted water for each cup of grits to be prepared. The mixture is maintained at a slow boil for 15 minutes, until thickened. Unlike rice and bulgur, which swell approximately three times in volume as they cook, one cup of grits will expand to a volume of four cups.

Pasta

Pasta products generally are packaged with the directions for preparation clearly spelled out on the container. In the event that directions for the specific pasta are not available, most pastas are boiled satisfactorily by using six cups of boiling water (containing one teaspoon of salt and one teaspoon of oil to reduce sticking and foaming) for each one-half pound of pasta. The pasta is added slowly to the boiling water so that boiling is continuous and to enable long pastas to soften slowly as they are pushed into the pan. All of the pasta must be covered by boiling water to insure uniform heating of the pasta. The time required to reach the desired "al dente" stage of doneness varies with the type of pasta, but the time indicated on the package usually is fairly close. The al dente stage is reached when the pasta can be cut rather easily by pressing with a fork against the side of the pan or by actually tasting to be sure that the pasta feels firm and chewy, yet has just the tiniest suggestion of a hard core. Pasta needs to be drained thoroughly by placing in a colander or strainer.

STARCHES

Starches are valued in food preparation as a thickening agent for four reasons: (1) a small amount of starch will thicken a relatively large amount of liquid, (2) the various starches have little flavor, (3) dry starches keep well, and (4) they are inexpensive. Starches for commercial and home food use may be from cereal grains, root sources, or from trees. Edible starches from roots include arrowroot, tapioca (from cassava root), and potato. Sago, a tree starch, is a common commercial starch. In many regions, pure corn starch and wheat starch in the form of flour are the most commonly used cereal starches. These starches each have their own characteristics. For example,

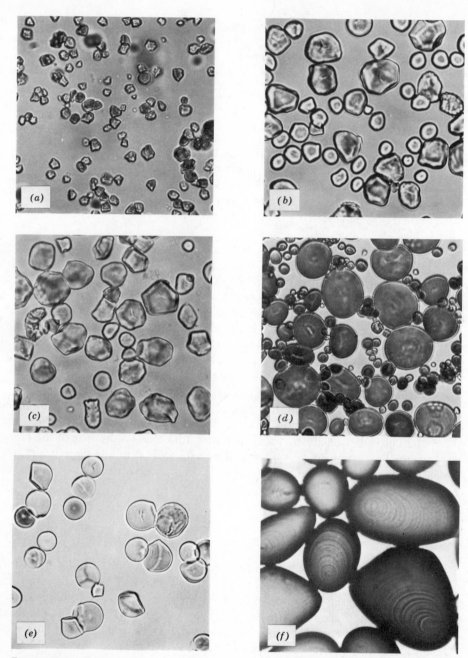

FIGURE 7.6 Photomicrographs of starches (magnification 500X). Cereal starches: (a) rice, (b) corn, (c) waxy corn, (d) wheat. Root starches: (e) tapioca, (f) potato.

wheat starch granules are the largest of the cereal starches, and those of rice starch are the smallest. Cornstarch granules are intermediate.

The appearance of the starch granule, as seen under a microscope, varies according to the particular type of starch. The shape may be spherical, oval, disc, or oyster-shaped depending on the type of starch. Potato starch is a large round granule in comparison to the typically small and angular rice granules. Wheat starch has some large lentil-shaped granules and some smaller spherical granules.

PRINCIPLES OF STARCH COOKERY

Dextrinization

The phenomena that occur when starch is subjected to moist or dry heat are frequently utilized in food preparation. These changes will be more clearly understood if they are related to the chemistry of starch, as discussed in Chapter 18.

Dextrinization is the change effected when starch is subjected to dry heat. In this process the starch chain itself is reduced in length to shorter molecules called dextrins, which are more soluble and possess less thickening ability than starch. The actual extent of the breakdown of starch molecules to dextrins is determined by the intensity and duration of heating. Longer times and higher temperatures cause increasingly greater breakdown of the molecule. Illustrations of this process may be seen when bread is toasted or flour is browned for a brown sauce. If browned flour is used for thickening a sauce, it will be noted that additional flour must be used to thicken the product, because the shorter chain dextrins in the browned flour have less thickening ability than the original starch had.

Gelatinization

Swelling in Cold Water. Swelling is a physical phenomenon occurring within the starch granule when it is placed in water. The actual amount of swelling in cold water is limited, but depends on the kind of starch and the previous treatment. The weak forces within the granules of root starches permit greater swelling at lower temperatures than is permitted by the relatively stronger internal bonding of the cereal starches. At room temperature some water will penetrate the starch granule, causing a swelling of the particle. Damaged cells swell considerably at room temperature because the break in the granule offers a relatively large vulnerable surface to the water surrounding the granule.

As water is imbibed, a pressure develops within the starch granule and heat is released. This heat, called the heat of hydration, is unnoticeable in small quantities of dough, but is significant when large commercial batches of dough are prepared.

Swelling during Heating. When mixtures of starch and water are heated, water penetrates the granule with increased ease and considerable swelling results. This irreversible change is termed gelatinization. As water gradually penetrates the interior of the granule during gelatinization, an internal pressure develops. If the pressure due to swelling becomes too great, the starch granule ruptures and starch fragments are released, disrupting the organized starch grain structure. Corn and wheat will burst when 100 grams of the starch have absorbed about 40 grams of water, but potato starch will hold its equivalent weight of water.

Properties of the Hot Paste. The imbibition of water within the starch granule greatly increases its diameter. When this happens to many starch granules, the increase in the volume of the starch is quite apparent and is manifest as a distinct increase in the viscosity of the mixture. The change in viscosity is due not only to the greater volume of the starch that inhibits the flow of the water, but also is caused by the fact that less water is actually mobile since a significant amount is now bound internally within the starch granules.

The temperature at which maximum swelling of the starch granule occurs depends on the source of the starch and on the previous treatment. In root starches swelling begins at 65–70°C, with gelatinization being completed at temperatures considerably below 100°C. Cereal starches are more resistant to water penetration and must be heated to temperatures ranging between 95° and 100°C for gelatinization to be completed.

Starch that has been gelatinized and then dehydrated will rehydrate at room temperature to become a very viscous mixture. Such starch is well adapted to use in instant pudding mixes.

Root starches subjected to prolonged heating or boiling temperatures disintegrate into fragments, but cereal starches are much more resistant to rupturing. Mechanical agitation or the agitation from boiling also can cause fragmentation because the swollen starch granules are rather fragile. Fragmentation, whether by heating or agitation, causes the starch mixture to be sticky and less viscous.

Gelatinization not only causes an increase in viscosity but also causes the suspension to change from an opaque, milky appearance to a more translucent mixture. The milky appearance of ungelatinized starch mixtures is caused by the organized crystalline arrangement within the starch granules as well as by the presence of amylose. As water enters the starch granule, opacity begins to change to translucency partially because of the solution of some of the amylose and partially because of the disruption of the crystalline arrangement of amylose within the starch granule. Cereal starches form less translucent pastes than root starches. In practical terms, it can be summarized that the increases in viscosity and translucency that accompany gelatinization are useful changes that improve the appearance of the mixture and prevent the starch particles from settling. Table 7.5 lists some commonly used starches and their characteristics.

Factors Influencing Viscosity. Several factors determine the viscosity of a gel. The most obvious one is the concentration of starch. The source or kind of starch, the final temperature to which it is heated, the addition of acid or sugar, the extent of dextrinization, and thoroughness of dispersion are the other factors to be considered.

Since starch does gelatinize, its presence in a heated mixture is responsible for much, if not all, of the thickening that occurs. Obviously, the higher the starch concentration, the greater will be the potential viscosity of the sauce. Increasing the liquid (or decreasing the starch) in a recipe reduces the concentration of starch and results in a thinner mixture, whereas decreasing the liquid (or increasing the starch) produces a thicker product.

Cereal starches have greater thickening ability than root starches, but there is also variation in viscosity within these groups. For example, cornstarch is capable of producing a distinctly viscous gel, whereas rice starch produces a more tender gel than those made with either corn or wheat starch. If flour is substituted for cornstarch in a recipe, the measure of flour should

Table 7.5. Commonly Used Starches and Their Characteristics

Starch	Classification	Comparative Thickening Ability	Characteristics of the Paste
Cornstarch	Cereal starch	Great	Optimum thickening achieved by heating to 95–100°C; moderately translucent
Flour (contains wheat starch)	Cereal starch	½ as great as cornstarch	Optimum thickening achieved by heating to 95–100°C; more opaque than cornstarch
Rice starch	Cereal starch	Moderate	Optimum thickening achieved by heating to 95–100°C; moderately translucent
Potato starch	Root starch	Less than cereal starches	Thins when boiled; tendency to become gummy; quite translucent
Tapioca	Root starch	Less than cereal starches	Thins when boiled; tendency to become gummy; quite translucent

be increased to twice the amount of cornstarch indicated. Conversely, half as much cornstarch can replace the amount of flour indicated as the thickening agent in a recipe. The ratio does not indicate that cornstarch has twice the thickening capability of wheat starch, but rather recognizes that flour is not pure starch. Potato and arrowroot, representing the root starches, yield even more tender gels than rice starch.

The temperature to which a starch paste is heated is an important factor in determining viscosity. Gelatinization begins at moderate temperatures, but will be completed only when temperatures approaching boiling are achieved. It can be definitively stated that a starch mixture that is not heated to a sufficiently high temperature for complete gelatinization to occur will naturally be thinner than a comparable one that has been heated adequately.

To eliminate raw starch flavor and ensure complete gelatinization, it is practical to bring cornstarch or flour mixtures to the boiling point. Tapioca is an exception, for gelatinization and maximum viscosity are reached at a lower temperature, and heating to boiling causes a thinning to occur.

It should be noted that cookbooks frequently advocate cooking a starch mixture in a double boiler. At sea level it is possible to reach temperatures above 95°C in the upper portion of a double boiler, although more time is required than would be needed if the sauce were placed over direct heat. At higher elevations, however, the starch will not gelatinize completely when heated over boiling water because the temperature of the boiling water, and hence the temperature of the mixture in the upper portion of the double boiler, will be too low. Therefore, it is preferable to boil the mixture over direct heat and then, if the recipe includes a protein food such as cheese or eggs, place the starch and protein over hot water to coagulate the protein.

Sugar influences starch pastes and gels because it successfully competes with starch for the water in the mixture, with the result that less water is available for the gelatinization of the starch. Therefore the following statements are true for starch mixtures containing sugar:

1. The temperature at which the initial rise in swelling and the maximum swelling occur is higher for the sugar-starch mixture than it is for starch alone.

2. The maximum viscosity of the starch paste is reduced when sugar is present because of a decrease in water imbibition into the starch.

3. Less disintegration of the starch grains occurs when sugar is present since there is less swelling.

4. The resulting gel is less rigid because the minimized disruption of the starch granules also means that less amylose will be released into the liquid to form the gel network.

5. Syneresis (separation of the liquid from the gel) is increased as more sugar is added to a starch mixture.
6. Translucency increases with an increase in sugar.

These effects are much more pronounced when the concentration of sugar exceeds 20 percent.

Adding acid prior to heating a starch mixture will result in a thinner product. As the mixture is heated, acid will cause hydrolysis of some of the starch molecules. Hydrolysis is the cleavage of the starch chain at various intervals to produce smaller molecules. As the cooking time is extended, as the temperature is raised, or as the concentration of acid is increased, the rate of hydrolysis will increase. The shorter chains produced by hydrolysis are more soluble than the original starch molecules and hence have less thickening ability. For this reason acids should not be added until gelatinization has been completed. This principle is applied in the preparation of lemon meringue pies; maximum thickening is achieved by adding the lemon juice after the filling has been cooked. A more complete discussion of the effect of acid and sugar is given in Chapter 18.

If dextrinized flour is used, the viscosity of the product will be reduced unless certain compensations are made. The darker the flour, the greater is the extent of dextrinization. As more dextrinization occurs there is an accompanying increase in solubility. Therefore more starch will be needed to achieve the correct viscosity. It is common practice to supplement dextrinized flour with white flour for a brown sauce. This enables one to make a sauce with a pleasing flavor and color while achieving the correct viscosity.

Lumping in starch pastes not only reduces the viscosity, but also has an adverse effect on appearance and texture. Lumps occur when starch starts to swell before it has been thoroughly dispersed in fine particles throughout a mixture. When many starch granules are clumped together, the outside ones will begin to swell as the suspension is heated. This prevents water from reaching the granules in the center of these groups and results in lumps with dry flour in the center. Since no liquid reaches the starch in the middle of such lumps, the trapped starch cannot gelatinize and, in essence, the effective concentration of starch is reduced. Therefore the sauce will be less viscous than one would expect.

Three techniques are useful in preparing starch products that are free from lumps. In many instances all three will not be used in preparing a food, but using more than one increases the possibility of avoiding lumps. The three techniques are: (1) separation of the starch granules by mixing starch thoroughly with other dry ingredients; (2) complete separation by mixing the starch with melted or liquid fats before, adding liquids; and (3) addition of some cold liquid with thorough stirring prior to the addition of hot liquids to the starch. As illustrations, the first and third methods are used when making cornstarch or cream puddings and the second is used when preparing white sauce.

Gelation

If a gelatinized starch mixture contains sufficient starch, the hot paste changes from a pourable sol into a gel that will not flow. A random structure resembling a brush pile is established as the swollen starch granules become enmeshed in a network of amylose molecules which have become insoluble as the mixture cools. These amylose molecules are attracted to the starch granules. The network thus established traps the water that previously had been mobile. Such a solid or semisolid material is called a gel; the formation of the gel is called gelation. The actual firmness of the gel will be determined by the concentration of the starch granules, the quantity of amylose free in the paste, and the time and temperature of heating.

Syneresis

Liquid slowly drains from a gel structure when a cut is made through the starch network. This release of moisture from a gel is called syneresis or "weeping." This phenomenon may be observed by cutting a starch gel and letting it stand for a period of time. Syneresis occurs in starch puddings as well as in certain other foods.

EXAMPLES OF STARCH COOKERY

White Sauces

Since white sauces are so widely used in cookery, knowledge of their preparation is important. The appropriate type of white sauce for a specific purpose is essential for preparing food products of high quality. The viscosities of white sauces and their suggested uses are: (1) thin sauce—cream soups; (2) medium sauce—creamed vegetables, base for a cheese sauce, and gravy; (3) thick sauce—soufflés; and (4) very thick sauces—binding agent for croquettes. White sauces are made according to the proportions in Table 7.6.

All white sauces are made by melting fat and then thoroughly blending in the flour. Cold milk is then added and blended thoroughly with the starch. When making two or more cups of white sauce, time may be saved by scalding three-fourths of the milk and reserving the remainder to be used cold during the initial blending of the ingredients. Constant stirring is necessary while the sauce is coming to a boil if lumps are to be avoided. Otherwise

Table 7.6. Proportions for White Sauces

Type of Sauce	Flour	Fat	Milk	Salt
Thin	1 Tbsp	1 Tbsp	1 c	$\frac{1}{4}$ tsp
Medium	2 Tbsp	2 Tbsp	1 c	$\frac{1}{4}$ tsp
Thick	3 Tbsp	3 Tbsp	1 c	$\frac{1}{4}$ tsp
Very thick	4 Tbsp	4 Tbsp	1 c	$\frac{1}{4}$ tsp

gelatinization occurs quickly on the sides and bottom of the pan where the mixture is hotter, and when these areas are stirred, some of the thickened portions are scraped free to become lumps in the sauce. A well-prepared white sauce will be smooth, well seasoned, free of a fat film, and of the appropriate viscosity for the type being prepared. Accurate judgment of the viscosity of a sauce can be made only when a sauce is hot, because the sauce thickens as it cools.

The most common deviations in a white sauce are lumps or a fat film.

FIGURE 7.7   A medium white sauce is utilized in this casserole dish. Sauces of medium viscosity also are used for gravies, vegetables, and dessert sauces.

FIGURE 7.8 Timbales utilize a very thick white sauce as a binding agent. The medium sauce being poured over the timbales contains bits of celery for added texture.

Lumps may be caused by incomplete dispersion of the starch or from inadequate stirring.

One cause of a fat film, particularly in a thin sauce, is incomplete gelatinization of the starch due to insufficient heating. This situation will be recognized by the thinness of the sauce as well as by the fat film. The remedy for this problem is simply to reheat the sauce to the boiling point. It is not unusual for the fat to separate from a very thick white sauce as it is boiled. This separation is more likely to occur if the sauce is heated very slowly because excessive evaporation will occur and there will then be too much fat in proportion to the milk. This fat film may be eliminated by stirring in a little additional liquid.

Gravies

Gravy preparation varies according to the type of drippings to be used. After meat has been fried or roasted, the fat that accumulates should be removed from the pan and measured. Two tablespoons of the drippings for each cup of gravy desired are then measured and returned to the pan. Flour is then stirred directly into the drippings until the mixture is smooth. Salt and the measured amount of cold liquid are mixed in carefully and the gravy is stirred constantly as it is brought to a boil. The proportions and the procedure are the same as those used for making a medium white sauce. This is the roux method for making gravies.

Fats from meats to which liquid has been added as they were cooked present a different problem in gravy making. If flour is added directly to this hot liquid mixture, lumps will form because of the hot water present. A smooth gravy can be prepared, however, by vigorously shaking the necessary flour with a small amount of cold water in a tightly covered container until all the lumps are gone. This flour suspension can then be stirred into the drippings without forming lumps. Again it is necessary to stir constantly as the gravy is heated to boiling. Trimbo and Miller (1971) found that this "kettle" method produces a somewhat thinner product than does the roux method.

Gravy is evaluated on the basis of smoothness, flavor, and absence of a fat film. Its viscosity should be that of a medium white sauce.

Cream Soups

Cream soups utilize as the base a thin white sauce, prepared as previously described. In most cream soups one tablespoon of flour is used for each cup of milk. Cream of potato soup, however, is prepared with less flour since the starch in the potatoes provides additional thickening for the soup.

The amount of vegetable added usually varies between two and four tablespoons per cup of soup. The exact amount of vegetable is dictated by the appearance and flavor of the soup. Spinach, for instance, is used in the smaller measure because large amounts result in a soup that has an objectionable green color and too strong a flavor. Celery, since it has a mild flavor and subtle color, may be used in larger amounts.

According to the strict definition of a cream of vegetable soup, the vegetables should be puréed. Finely diced vegetables are frequently used, however. This practice results in a soup that is somewhat higher in ascorbic acid, since puréeing causes some destruction of that vitamin. The diced vegetables also furnish a contrast in texture.

Cream of tomato soup presents a particular problem not encountered in the other cream soups. The acidity of the tomatoes is likely to cause curdling of the milk when the milk and vegetable are combined. The possibility of curdling is kept to a minimum by using very fresh milk and by combining the tomato and white sauce in the following manner. By adding hot tomato to the white sauce, the soup is always maintained at as alkaline a pH as possible. Reversing this procedure, that is, pouring the white sauce into the

FIGURE 7.9 Cream soups utilize a thin sauce as their base.

tomatoes, causes the first portion of milk to be in a distinctly acid medium. With this procedure, curdling always occurs. Extended heating of the soup increases the tendency toward curdling because the heating period causes the soup to become slightly more acidic. Therefore the tomato purée should be added to the white sauce just before the soup is to be quickly heated for serving.

The color of cream of tomato soup is important for palatability. A soup prepared from canned tomatoes which includes a large proportion of the juice will be rather orange in color, whereas a pleasing reddish color is achieved by using more of the pulp of the tomato and less juice.

Well-prepared cream soups should be smooth, free of a fat film, well seasoned, and an appropriate color. All cream soups should have the viscosity of a thin sauce.

Cornstarch Puddings

Whether it is elegantly called blancmange or more simply named vanilla pudding, a cornstarch pudding is a nourishing, simply prepared dessert that can be served in a variety of ways or with different flavorings.

Cornstarch puddings utilize two means of incorporating starch into a product: the first step requires careful mixing of the cornstarch, sugar, and any other dry ingredients; the second device for dispersion of the starch is thorough mixing of cold milk with the dry ingredients. After this step, hot milk may be added without forming lumps. Scalding three-fourths of the milk while the dry ingredients and the remaining quarter of cold milk are being mixed reduces the preparation time appreciably.

Careful, thorough stirring is necessary as the starch is gelatinizing to prevent the formation of large lumps. Since such lumps appear when a pudding is stirred inadequately, some people tend to stir very briskly all during the heating period. Vigorous stirring damages the starch granules and causes them to be sticky. The result is a gummy, heavy pudding. Gumminess can also result from the extensive stirring required when a pudding is heated very slowly.

The small lumps sometimes found in puddings are due to carelessness in mixing the dry ingredients and in adding the cold liquid. Care in initial mixing and conscientious stirring at a medium rate of speed will result in smooth, light pudding.

The pudding not only should be smooth, but also should be appropriately firm when cold. Accurate measurements, of course, are important in achieving the desired firmness, but it is also important to boil the mixture to the correct end point. The pudding needs to be boiled until a spoon pulled slowly broadside through the pudding leaves a distinct path. If the pudding is not thick enough to give this test, it should be heated longer or the pudding will be too thin. After the pudding is removed from the heat, vanilla and butter are added and the pudding is cooled in tightly covered dishes to control scum formation.

In summary, a standard cornstarch pudding will look smooth and feel delicate and light on the tongue. There will be no hint of gumminess or stickiness. When the pudding is cut, there should be a slight softening of the outline of the cut portion. The flavor should be mild and pleasing.

Pudding mixes are widely used because they save the time required for measuring ingredients. Instant puddings effect the greatest saving of time, but the flavors generally are considered to be less desirable than the fresh puddings. As artificial flavorings are more accurately developed, however, it is not unreasonable to expect that the flavor of instant puddings may approach the flavor of a homemade pudding.

SUMMARY

Cereals such as corn, wheat, and rice are important, relatively inexpensive sources of carbohydrates unless they have been modified extensively during production. Processing procedures permit fractionation of the cereal grain by polishing, milling, or hulling. Whole-grain cereals are marketed as the intact grain or in subdivided particles. The preparation of cereals requires gelatinization of the starch and softening of the cellulose.

Starch from various plant sources commonly is used as a thickening agent in food preparation. Two important changes can occur when starch is

FIGURE 7.10 Cornmeal muffins are yet another means of incorporating a variety of cereals in the diet.

subjected to heat. Dextrinization, the change effected by heating the dry starch, results in a loss of thickening power as well as a change in color. Gelatinization or a swelling of starch occurs when aqueous starch suspensions are heated. To ensure uniform gelatinization rather than lumping, starch may be combined with dry ingredients, melted shortenings, and/or cold liquids. Factors influencing final viscosity of a hot starch paste include concentration of the starch, type of starch, temperature to which it is heated, adequacy of dispersion of the starch, and the presence of an acid or sugar. Starch pastes increase in viscosity as they cool and in many instances will form a gel. Starch gels will exhibit syneresis. Familiar examples of starch-thickened products are puddings, cream soups, white sauce, and gravy.

BIBLIOGRAPHY

American Association of Cereal Chemists. *Approved Methods.* 7th ed. AACC, 1955 University Ave., St. Paul 4, Minn. 1962.

Cereal Institute. *Cereal Glossary.* Cereal Institute, Inc. 135 S. LaSalle St., Chicago, Ill. 60603. 1969.

Durum Wheat Institute. Durum definitions. *Durum Wheat Notes,* March 1970.

Elbert, E. M. Starch: changes during heating in the presence of moisture. *J. Home Econ. 57*:197–200. 1965.

Elliott, J. S. and C. M. McPherson. Nutrient values of and consumer preference for grain sorghum wafers. *J.A.D.A. 58*:225. 1971.

Food Industry Staff Writer, Instant rice. *Food Ind.* 86–91, Aug. 1947.

Geddes. W. F. Technology of cereal grains. In *Chemistry and Technology of Food and Food Products,* ed. by M. V. Jacobs, Vol. *3,* 2nd ed. Interscience Publishers, New York. 1951.

Geddes, W. F. Recent developments in foods from cereals. *J. Agr. Food Chem. 7, 9*:605–610. 1959.

Halick, J. V., and K. K. Keneaster. The use of a starch-iodine-blue test as a quality indicator of white milled rice. *Cereal Chem. 33*:315–319. 1956.

Human Nutrition Research Division. *Cereals and Pasta in Family Meals.* Home and Garden Bulletin No. 150. U. S. Department of Agriculture, Washington, D. C. 1968.

Matthews, R. H., and E. A. Bechtel. Viscosity of white sauces made with wheat flours from different U. S. regions. *J. Home Econ. 58*:392. 1966.

Montgomery, R., and F. Smith. Review of carbohydrates of wheat and other cereal grains. *J. Agr. Food Chem. 4, 8*:716–720. 1956.

Quaker Oats. *Quaker Quotes,* No. 9–57. Chicago.

Reitz, L. P. and M. A. Barmore. The quality of cereal grains. In *Food, the Yearbook of Agriculture, 1959.* U.S. Department of Agriculture, Washington, D.C. 1959.

Sandstedt, R. M. et al. Effect of salts on the gelatinization of wheat starch. *Die Starke 12*:333. 1960.

Trimbo, H. B. and B. S. Miller. Factors affecting the quality of sauces (gravies). *J. Home Econ. 63*:48. 1971.

Wheat Flour Institute. *From Wheat to Flour.* Chicago. 1966.

Williams, V. R., W. Wu, H. Y. Tasi, and H. B. Bates. Varietal differences in amylose content of rice starch. *J. Agr. Food Chem.* 6:57–58. 1958.

SUGGESTIONS FOR STUDY

1. Compare the ease of preparation, cost, and palatability of regular and quick cooking cereals.
2. Prepare and view slides of starch dispersions to illustrate the variation in shape of the various types of starch.
3. Prepare starch pastes from wheat, corn, rice, and potato starch, using 2 Tbsp. starch per cup of water. Boil the pastes for one minute. Compare the viscosity and the translucency of the various pastes.
4. Prepare thin, medium, thick, and very thick white sauces. Observe the difference in viscosity. What sauce would be appropriate to use for: creamed vegetables, soufflés, cream soups, croquettes?
5. What processing techniques are used to produce the instant hot cereals that are now found in the market?
6. Identify the advantages and disadvantages of the various rices.

CHAPTER 8

Milk and Cheese

MILK PRODUCTS

Fresh Whole Milks

Whole milk is cow's milk that contains a minimum of 3.25 percent milkfat and 8.25 percent nonfat milk solids. This milk ordinarily is prepared for marketing by inspecting, homogenizing, and pasteurizing. Milk that is transported across state lines must be inspected under provisions of the Cooperative State-United States Public Health Service Program for Certification of Interstate Milk Shippers. To receive the designation of Grade A, the milk must contain a maximum bacterial count of 20,000 per milliliter. Vitamin D fortification frequently is done at the rate of 400 International Units per quart. If vitamin D has been added, this will be indicated on the label.

Although most of the fresh whole milk sold today is Grade A, vitamin D fortified, pasteurized, and homogenized, some milk may be available as cream-line. This designation simply means that the fat has not been broken up into smaller globules and, therefore, will rise to the top of the milk. Some people prefer cream-line milk because they like to pour off the cream for their cereal and coffee and use the remainder for drinking and cooking. Fresh milk also is available on a limited basis as concentrated milk, a type of milk in which two-thirds of the water has been removed.

In a few areas, raw milk is still available as certified raw milk. This type of milk presents a potential health hazard despite the fact that the cows are inspected and the bacterial count is held very low (in fact, lower than is required for Grade A milk that is to be pasteurized). Since the raw milk does not undergo any heat treatment, bacteria or other microorganisms that are

175

FIGURE 8.1   Milk and cheese add considerable variety as well as excellent nutritive content to the diet for people of all ages.

in the milk will still be viable if the milk is consumed without its being heated in the home. The use of this milk can lead to human illnesses that can be avoided simply by using only pasteurized milk.

Skim Milks

Varying amounts of milkfat may be removed from whole milk to make products that appeal to various consumers. The richest of these milks is 2 percent skim milk. This type of milk has a fat content of 2 percent and a content of nonfat milk solids of 10 percent. The removal of this amount of fat is useful in reducing the number of calories available from milk while still boasting the flavor benefits of the milkfat.

Lowfat milk is the designation given to milk containing between 0.5 and 2.0 percent milkfat. This milk represents yet another consumer choice for those who wish to reduce fat intake without completely sacrificing the flavor contributed by the milkfat. There has been much confusion among consumers regarding the difference between lowfat and nonfat milk. Many have considered these two terms synonymous, but actually they are not. Nonfat or skim milk must contain no more than 0.5 percent milkfat and, at least, 8.25 percent nonfat milk solids, according to legislation in many states. Actually, the milkfat level usually is 0.1 percent or less.

One of the concerns about the nutritive value of nonfat milk has been that vitamin A is removed along with the milkfat. This problem is solved by the use of fortified skim milk. Vitamin D is added at the level of 400 International Units per quart, vitamin A is included at the rate of 2000 International Units per quart, and the nonfat milk solids level is at least 10 percent. Thus the nutritive value of fortified skim milk is excellent, and yet people who wish to reduce caloric intake or to eliminate animal fats from their diets can procure the nutritional benefits of milk.

Flavored Milks

Chocolate is the usual flavor added to vary fresh-milk taste. Chocolate milk is simply whole milk flavored with chocolate and a sweetener, whereas chocolate-flavored milk is identical except that cocoa is used in place of chocolate. Chocolate drink is made by using skim or lowfat milk, chocolate, and a sweetener. The addition of nonfat milk solids is optional. Chocolate-flavored drink is comparable to chocolate drink, with cocoa being substituted for the chocolate. Flavored milks also may be made by flavoring whole milk with strawberry, coffee, maple or other flavoring. When skim or lowfat milk is used in preparing these beverages, the product is identified as a flavored drink.

Cultured Milks

Acidophilus milk has had the bacterium *Lactobacillus acidophilus* added to it. As a result of the growth of this culture, the milk becomes more acidic as lactic acid is formed from lactose. The nutritive value is comparable to pasteurized nonfat milk, the milk used in making acidophilus milk. Commercial distribution of this product is distinctly limited.

Cultured buttermilk is a popular product made by adding a lactic-acid bacterial culture to either fresh, pasteurized fluid nonfat milk, whole milk, concentrated fluid milk, or reconstituted nonfat dry milk. Most commonly skim milk is used to make buttermilk. To add to the palatability of this flavorful and smooth type of milk, granules of butter are sometimes added, bringing the fat content to a maximum of one percent.

Yogurt is perhaps the most popular of the cultured milk products presently on the market. This custardlike product is made from either whole or skim milk which is fermented with a mixture of *Streptococcus thermophilus, Bacterium bulgaricus,* and *Plocamo-bacterium yoghourti.* Fruits and other flavorings are often added to provide a variety of yogurt flavors. These products are very pleasing dressings for fruit salads and have also found a prominent place in many weight control diets.

Canned Milks

Evaporated milk is usually made from fresh whole milk. During processing, the milk is concentrated by removing more than one-half of the water under vacuum prior to canning. Homogenization and fortification with vitamin D are done and then the can is sealed and heat sterilized to kill bacteria, thus making it possible to store unopened cans without refrigeration. Evaporated milk as it comes from the can contains a minimum of 7.9 percent milkfat and 25.9 percent total milk solids. When reconstituted with an equal volume of water, evaporated milk often is used as the milk component of infant formulas. Other uses are in the preparation of meat loaf

FIGURE 8.2 Sweetened condensed milk, when combined with acid, thickens to the viscosity of a cream pie filling without heating.

and casseroles, puddings, and desserts. The cooked flavor of evaporated milk is masked in these foods if the other ingredients have distinctive flavors. Undiluted evaporated milk, when chilled until ice crystals begin to form, can be whipped.

Sweetened condensed milk is also a milk prepared for canning by evaporating approximately one-half of the water from the milk. However, this product is very different from evaporated milk because of the high sugar content added to make sweetened condensed milk. The high percentage of sucrose and/or dextrose (44 percent) is an effective deterrent to bacterial growth, so the sealed cans do not require heat treatment for safe storage. Sweetened condensed milk is a smooth, very sweet milk product that may be used effectively without dilution to make a variety of desserts. When acid, such as lemon juice, is added to sweetened condensed milk, the milk will thicken without heating to the consistency of a pudding or pie filling. A browning reaction will take place between the sugar and the milk protein if sweetened condensed milk is heated. The result of this process is a very viscous product resembling a caramel pudding.

Dry Milks

The most common dry milk product is nonfat dry milk. This type of milk is prepared by evaporating part of the water under vacuum from pasteurized skim milk. This concentrated milk then is sprayed into a drying chamber to evaporate the water. The solids are collected and then instantized by moistening the dried milk with steam so that it clumps into aggregates that disperse readily when reconstituted in water. Nonfat dry milk may have vitamins A and D added to enhance nutritive value. The low cost and good shelf life without refrigeration (until it is reconstituted) make this a particularly valuable milk buy. In addition, the solids may be partially reconstituted and then whipped to provide a low calorie, low cost "whipping cream."

Whole dry milk also is manufactured, but the original milk used is whole milk rather than skim. The shelf life of dry whole milk is somewhat shorter than the nonfat counterpart because of the presence of fat. The major use of this type of milk is in infant feeding and commercial chocolate and candy manufacturing.

Creams

Several different weights of cream are usually available in the market. The lightest of the creams, that is, the one with the lowest fat content is called half-and-half. This mixture of milk and cream has a milkfat content of, at least, 10 to 12 percent. This type of cream is often used on cereals.

Table cream, also frequently called coffee cream, contains at least 18 percent milkfat. Still higher in fat content is light cream, with a minimum of 30 percent milkfat. The largest percentage, at least 36 percent milkfat, is found in heavy whipping cream. Pressurized whipped creams are marketed in aerosol cans. These types of whipped cream may be made by using table or whipping cream, plus sugar, stabilizer, and an emulsifier.

Sour cream is a dairy product containing, at least, 18 percent milkfat. This product has grown greatly in popularity for use in various baked products, as a salad dressing base, and as a base for chip dips. Sour cream is pasteurized for 30 minutes at temperatures ranging from 165 to 180°F, a procedure that kills bacteria and promotes the desired firm body of the sour cream. A controlled culture of lactic acid bacteria is added to develop the desired acid tang in the finished product. Since sour cream curdles readily when heated in food preparation, optimum food quality is achieved by adding the cream near the end of the baking period.

Butter

Butter, another important milk product, contains a minimum of 80 percent milkfat. It may be made from sweet or sour cream. Before the cream is churned, lactic acid bacteria are allowed to work in the pasteurized cream for three to four hours to develop aroma and flavor. Then the vigorous churning action causes a change from an oil in water emulsion to a water in oil emulsion. Subsequently, the buttermilk is drained off, the butter is washed, salt is added, the finished product is worked, and then the butter is cut into one pound packages. Legislation is playing an important role in the regulations concerning the production of butter and its competitor, margarine.

Unsalted butter, labeled as either sweet butter or unsalted butter, is available for special types of food preparation and for use in salt-free diets. Whipped butter is simply butter whipped to incorporate air. This increases volume and promotes spreadability. If substituted for butter in a recipe, whipped butter should be substituted by weight rather than volume.

Ice Cream

Ice cream and its associated products have become a big industry. Most large markets today carry several qualities of ice cream or ice milk. The price of the product varies directly with the fat content. Dieters' specials are made from skim milk and catering-quality ice cream is made using whipping cream. The milkfat content of ice cream varies usually within the range of 10 to 20 percent, with the average value being 10 to 12 percent; ice milks range from 2 to 7 percent milkfat; and sherbets contain between 1 and 2 percent milk fat. In addition to the fat, ice creams and related products contain varying amounts of sugar, stabilizers, milk solids, flavorings, and coloring.

After mixing and pasteurizing, the ice cream is frozen in either a batch or continuous freezer. Agitation in the batch freezer permits incorporation of air, whereas the continuous freezer introduces fixed amounts of air as the ice cream proceeds through the freezer. Either method increases the volume through the addition of air. It may be of interest to the consumer to permit a comparable amount of several qualities of ice cream to melt and then compare the products. Ice cream with a very low cream content is stabilized with additives, such as gelatin, and will still retain a foam structure as liquid drains from the melting ice cream. High-quality ice creams will contain less stabilizer.

In a few states, mellorine and parevine are available alongside ice cream. These products are frozen desserts similar to ice cream except that vegetable fat replaces milkfat in the formulation. These two foods are fortified to be nutritionally equivalent to ice cream. They also bear the distinction of being the first product for which standards have been proposed under the Food and Drug Administration's "Imitation Foods" regulation. Their labels must carry full nutrition labeling, but must not refer to ice cream or imitation.

"Imitation" Products

Some new products appearing in the markets have caused consumer confusion and merit clarification here. Filled milk, although it has been defined on a federal level since 1923, is a type of milk product that had received little attention until the end of the 1960s. Congress defined filled milk as:

> "any milk, cream, or skimmed milk whether or not condensed, evaporated, concentrated, powdered, dried, or desiccated, to which has been added or which has been blended or compounded with any fat or oil other than milk fat, so that the resulting product is an imitation or semblance of milk, cream, or skimmed milk whether or not condensed, evaporated, concentrated, powdered, dried, or dessiccated."[1]

Coconut oil, a vegetable oil with more than 90 percent of its fatty acids being saturated, has been used as the replacement for milkfat. This substitution appears to be of no advantage over the milkfat, which contains approximately 60 percent saturated fatty acids. Recently, partially hydrogenated soybean and corn oils are being used more, and coconut oil is being used less frequently as an ingredient in filled milks. Filled milk cannot enter interstate or foreign commerce.

[1]Filled Milk Act, Public No. 513, 67th Congress, RR 8086, approved March 4, 1923.

Imitation milks are products made to resemble milk, but they contain no complete milk ingredients. Sodium caseinate frequently is the protein used; vegetable fat rather than milk fat is an ingredient; dextrose or corn syrup replaces lactose in the formulation. Artificial color, flavor, and emulsifiers round out these products. The actual formulas for imitation milks are quite variable, since no federal definitions have yet been established. An attempt was made to develop standards, but the flurry of interest in imitation milks was so brief that the proposal was dropped. At the present time, imitation milks may be entered in interstate commerce, but they must be identified as "imitation milk."

Coffee whiteners or lighteners are unique products that have considerable commercial interest because they have a storage life of six months at temperatures of 100°F or two years at 70°F. Such longevity obviously is a distinct advantage to persons who only desire cream for use in their coffee. These whiteners are somewhat varied in ingredients, but generally are a combination of a vegetable fat, a protein (sodium caseinate), corn syrup or other sweetener, emulsifiers, stabilizers, coloring, and flavoring.

QUALITY DESIGNATION OF DAIRY PRODUCTS

Milk and other dairy products inspected under the supervision of the United States Department of Agriculture (USDA) will be identified with an appropriate shield imprinted on the container. This inspection is maintained continuously under the surveillance of the Agricultural Marketing Service of the USDA. Inspection includes monitoring of the plant and surrounding areas to insure clean, orderly, and well maintained physical facilities for production. Incoming raw materials are checked regularly for safety, and products made and packaged in the plant must be subjected to a regular laboratory testing program to assure safe quality control.

FIGURE 8.3 Grade shields used to designate USDA-inspected dairy products: U. S. Grade AA is the highest quality of butter and cheddar cheese; U. S. Extra Grade signifies quality instant nonfat dry milk that mixes instantly with water; Quality Approved assures good quality and sanitary processing of cottage cheese and process cheese.

Butter is graded according to U. S. grade standards as U. S. Grade AA (highest quality), U. S. Grade A, or U. S. Grade B. U. S. Grade B usually is made from sour cream and has a slightly acid, but generally acceptable flavor.

Instant nonfat dry milk may be identified with a shield stating "USDA Quality Approved." This designation indicates that the product is of good quality and was processed under sanitary conditions. If the shield says "U. S. Extra Grade," the product is stipulated to be an instant nonfat dry milk with a sweet and pleasing flavor, a natural color, and the ability to dissolve immediately in water.

Cheeses may also carry USDA labeling. The USDA shield stating "Quality Approved" on cottage cheese and pasteurized process cheese indicates good quality and production under USDA supervision. Cheddar cheese may be identified with grades, with AA being the top federal grade, and A being just slightly lower in quality.

NUTRITIONAL VALUE

One of the food groups in the Basic Four Food Plan is milk and its related products. The importance of milk in the diet has long been recognized — in fact, its nutritive value has been magnified so unrealistically in the eyes of some people that they feel they are getting all the necessary nutrients if they just drink milk. Milk does contain important amounts of most nutrients, but it is very low in iron and ascorbic acid, and it is rather low in niacin.

Calcium and phosphorus levels in milk are very high, hence milk is important as a daily source of these minerals. Without milk in the diet, it is difficult for adults as well as children to meet the body's need for calcium. Both calcium and phosphorus from milk are well utilized by the body. A quart of irradiated milk meets the child's daily vitamin D requirement of 400 International Units. Vitamin A levels are high in whole milk, but this fat-soluble vitamin is removed when the cream is removed in the production of skim milk. Riboflavin, a B vitamin, is present in significant quantities in milk unless the milk has been exposed to light. Since riboflavin is extremely unstable in light, milk should not be left outside very long after it is delivered. The use of tinted brown glass bottles and milk cartons has helped to reduce this problem.

The composition of whole milk is approximately 4.9 percent carbohydrate, 3.5 percent fat, 3.5 percent protein, and 87 percent water. Lactose, or milk sugar as it is sometimes called, is the main carbohydrate in milk. The most abundant fatty acids in milk are oleic, palmitic, and stearic acids. Milk is a complete protein food containing several protein complexes; the chief protein fraction in cow's milk is casein. Whey protein complexes include lactalbumin, lactoglobulin, and lactomucin.

DISEASES TRANSMITTED VIA MILK

Milk is an excellent medium for the growth of microorganisms, but the safety of milk as a food is virtually assured when pasteurization, refrigeration, and handling are controlled during production and marketing as well as in the home. The sanitary handling of milk is extremely important because of the serious nature of some diseases that may be carried by milk. These diseases include tuberculosis, undulant fever, scarlet fever, septic sore throat, typhoid fever, gastroenteritis, and diphtheria. Some of these diseases are transmitted by the cow and some may be introduced by persons handling the milk.

Certain precautions in milk production significantly reduce the possibility of contamination in the milk. All dairy cows are now tested for bovine tuberculosis and many are tested for *Brucella abortus,* which causes undulant fever in man. The test for *Brucella abortus* is extremely important if the milk is to be sold raw. Adequate housing for the animals and high sanitation standards are essential to maintain the dairy herd in good health. All equipment that is to come in contact with the milk must be kept absolutely clean.

Immediate cooling of milk by mechanical refrigeration avoids the excessive growth of microorganisms occurring in warm milk. Insulated tank trucks or insulated railroad tank cars are essential for shipping to the pasteurizing point. All these precautions are necessary because warm milk is an excellent medium for growth of microorganisms.

PROCESSING OF MILK

It seems a curious quirk of fate that a man from a country that is noted for its wines rather than its milk production should have been the one to consider and solve the important problem of safeguarding milk for human consumption. Louis Pasteur, the French scientist after whom the process is named, is credited with developing the heat treatment of milk as a method for inactivating disease-producing microorganisms.

To ensure safety, most milk is pasteurized by either the hold method or the high-temperature, short-time method. Holding is done by heating milk to 145°F, holding it at this temperature for 30 minutes, and then rapidly cooling to 45°F or cooler. In the second method, milk is heated to 161°F, held for a minimum of 15 seconds at this temperature, and quickly cooled to 50°F or lower. After pasteurization, milk is centrifuged to separate any fine sediment and cattle leucocytes from the milk and then it is bottled automatically and sealed in hygienically clean bottles.

Whole milk today is homogenized by being forced through a small opening under pressure of 3000 pounds per square inch to break the fat into particles so small that they remain distributed uniformly throughout the milk rather than floating to the top of the bottle. During homogenization a change is effected in the casein which causes this protein to precipitate more readily and to form a softer, more digestible curd than that formed from non-homogenized milk. Because of this alteration in the protein, homogenized milk is particularly useful in feeding babies.

Milk is commonly fortified with vitamin D (400 IU/quart) in any one of three ways: feeding irradiated yeast to the cows, which is most expensive; irradiating milk by letting a thin stream of milk run under an ultraviolet light prior to pasteurizing; and adding a vitamin D concentrate to milk prior to pasteurization, which is a simple, inexpensive method.

STORAGE OF MILK AND CREAM

Since dairy products are rather perishable, careful attention to proper storage is warranted. For those products requiring refrigerated storage, the time standing on the counter at room temperature should be kept to an absolute minimum. Table 8.1 is a guide to the safe home storage of dairy products.

Table 8.1. Home Storage of Dairy Products[a]

Product	Storage Conditions	Duration of Safe Storage
Fresh whole milk	Covered, refrigerator	3 – 5 days
Fresh skim milk	Covered, refrigerator	3 – 5 days
Reconstituted nonfat dry milk	Covered, refrigerator	3 – 5 days
Evaporated milk		
Unopened can	Room temperature	6 months
Opened can	Covered, refrigerator	3 – 5 days
Sweetened condensed milk		
Unopened can	Room temperature	Several months
Opened can	Covered, refrigerator	3 – 5 days
Dry milks		
Whole	Refrigerator	Few weeks
Nonfat	Room temperature	Few months
Cream, table and whipping	Covered, refrigerator	3 – 5 days
Whipped cream in aerosol can	Refrigerator	Few weeks

[a]Adapted from *Milk in Family Meals*. Home and Garden Bulletin No. 127. U. S. Department of Agriculture, Washington, D. C. Rev. 1972. Page 5.

MILK IN FOOD PREPARATION

Milk is valued in food preparation for its solvent capacity and its nutritive contribution. In many recipes milk, because of its high water content, is the dispersing medium. For example, milk is used in a pudding to disperse the starch and to dissolve the sugar. In scalloped potatoes the liquid portion of milk is necessary for gelatinization of the potato starch.

Two main problems occurring when milk is heated are scum formation and curdling. Both of these phenomena are due to the proteins present in milk, and both are undesirable because they detract from the attractiveness of food products.

Scum Formation

Scum forms as the milk proteins coagulate. Longer heating and higher temperatures will cause a gradual increase in the quantity and toughness of the scum. This scum may be removed by moving a spoon across the milk, but the surface will soon be covered again. Because of this protein scum, care must be taken so that milk does not boil over when it is heated. A slow rate of heating reduces this hazard and helps to prevent scorching the milk.

A scum can be minimized by heating milk for short periods at temperatures below boiling. A white sauce or a gravy made with milk will have less scum formation if a cover is placed over the completed product until it is served. Milk-containing puddings should be tightly covered as soon as they are removed from the heat to prevent the formation of a thick scum while the product is cooling.

Curdling

Vegetables that are acidic or high in polyphenols are likely to cause milk to curdle. Adding acid foods such as tomatoes brings milk closer to its isoelectric point, hence the proteins are less soluble and precipitate as curds. Tomato soup and the problems of curdling associated with it are discussed in the chapter on starch cookery (Chapter 7).

Curdling of milk in the presence of meats may be controlled by several practices. Since salts tend to increase the possibility of curdling, the use of fresh rather than salted or cured meats will give better results. The milk in scalloped potatoes containing ham always curdles because of the salts in the ham. Over-baking increases this problem. Adding a little fresh milk from time to time aids in decreasing the tendency to curdle.

Some recipes require buttermilk or sour milk. When these do not happen to be available, a suitable substitute can be made by putting a tablespoon of either lemon juice or vinegar in a liquid measuring cup and then filling the cup to the cup measure with sweet milk. After this mixture has stood for approximately five minutes, the milk protein will have started to precipitate and the desired curdled, sharp-tasting milk is ready for use.

WHIPPING CREAM AND MILK

Whipped cream is used as a topping or in a number of dessert recipes. For best results, whipping cream is the dairy product of choice because its high fat content promotes stability of the whipped foam, but chilled light cream (at least 30 percent fat) can be used. Optimum conditions for whipping are provided by chilling the cream to a temperature between 35 and 40°F and chilling the bowl and beaters. An electric mixer is useful, but not absolutely essential. Whipped cream, when whipped to the recommended point where it mounds and holds its shape, will just about double in volume as a result of incorporating air. Overbeating can cause the whipped cream to suddenly transform into a water in oil emulsion, namely, butter. When this change begins, the whipped product is no longer satisfactory for its intended use as whipped cream. Sugar can be added to whipped cream to sweeten the flavor, but adding sugar before beating is done delays foam formation. Chilled cream is more viscous than somewhat warmer cream that has been allowed to sit at room temperature for awhile. The viscous nature of the chilled cream makes it possible for air to be trapped in the developing foam as the beater blades pull air into the cream.

Evaporated milk foams can be made by whipping undiluted evaporated milk that has been chilled in an ice tray until ice crystals begin to form. The milk protein in evaporated milk is sufficiently concentrated to enable a foam to form; the protein facilitates foam formation by lowering the surface tension of the milk. Acid, ordinarily in the form of lemon juice, can be added to help bring the milk proteins closer to their isoelectric point, thus aiding in increasing the viscosity of the milk and promoting formation of the foam. Unless evaporated milk foams are stabilized with gelatin or some other additive, the foams are relatively unstable. However, they will hold for almost an hour if they are refrigerated.

Yet another foam can be made from partially reconstituted nonfat dry milk solids. This type of foam gains its stability from the high concentration of protein comprising the walls of the air cells. During beating, some of the protein molecules are denatured, thus providing some rigidity to the cells. The addition of lemon juice also promotes the formation of a more stable foam. As is true with evaporated milk foams, the addition of gelatin aids in foam stability. The texture of nonfat dry-milk foams is distinctly more porous than the fine texture characteristic of both the evaporated milk foam and whipped cream. One of the obvious advantages of the nonfat dry-milk foam is its lower caloric content because of the absence of fat.

FIGURE 8.4 Partially reconstituted nonfat dry milk solids will whip to a fine foam with good volume. By adding gelatin, the foam is given added stability.

CHEESES

Although the origin of cheesemaking is unknown, cheese may have been used as long ago as 9000 B.C. Apparently cheese production began in Arabia, and it flourished in Europe during the Middle Ages, especially in the monasteries. Until the idea of a cheese factory was developed in New York state in the middle of the nineteenth century, cheesemaking in the United States was done on individual farms. Wisconsin has since become a state famous for cheese production; in fact, Swiss cheese production in this country was started there. Today many types of cheese are produced in various areas of the United States.

Cheese is a highly nourishing, concentrated, complete protein food that contains important amounts of calcium, phosphorus, and vitamin A. Lactose is the carbohydrate used by bacteria as the source of food in the production of cheese. With the exception of cottage cheese and a few other cheeses made with skim milk, cheese is high in fat and calories.

The great versatility of cheese is partially responsible for its wide acceptance. Cheeses are used to good advantage in any course of a meal from the appetizer to the dessert. They are also a nourishing snacktime food. Cheese may be served hot or cold, alone, as the main ingredient, or as a flavor highlight in a recipe. Specific uses include utilizing cheese in a main

FIGURE 8.5 Cheeses suitable for dessert include (clockwise from the top) cheddar, process cheese roll, cream cheese, Camembert, blue, and Gouda, with Neufchatel in the center. These cheeses range from the firmness of cheddar to the fluidity of ripened Camembert.

dish such as a fondue, in a salad or in salad dressings, as a dessert with crackers or fruit, in baked products such as cheese biscuits and cheese cake, in dips, as a sandwich filling, or as a garnish such as grated Parmesan in French onion soup.

Types of Cheese

There are two basic categories of cheese: natural and process. Natural cheeses may be classified on the basis of the following criteria: means of clotting (lactic acid or rennin), amount of ripening (uncured or cured), firmness, and source of the milk (cow, goat, or sheep). Process cheese products are differentiated into categories on the basis of moisture and fat content.

Natural Cheeses

Natural cheese production involves the basic steps of clotting the protein in milk to form a curd. This curd then is cut and manipulated and ultimately drained to remove the liquid whey. In most cheeses, the curd is pressed into a compact mass. Treatment of the curd mass varies. Coloring may be added. Bacteria and molds may be introduced to modify the flavor and texture of the cheese. Some cheeses are marketed at this point as unripened cheese.

Often natural cheeses are submitted to a storage period to ripen. Ripening, an important step in producing many natural cheeses, causes changes that enhance the quality of cheese as food. The cheese loses some of its tough and rubbery characteristics, enabling it to be more readily blended into other foods. Textural changes are varied: some cheeses become very soft, whereas others become harder and even slightly crumbly during ripening; some become distinctly more porous. In addition, fuller flavors are developed during storage; the actual extent of these changes depends on

FIGURE 8.6 Some of the cheeses available in the United States: (top row) Provolone, Mozzarella, cheddar cheese spread, cheddar pineapple, Camembert, cheese spread, Liederkranz, grated Parmesan, Limburger spread, cottage cheese; (middle row) blue, brick, Gouda, Swiss, cheddar, Port du Salut, Parmesan, process American; (bottom row) packaged cheddar wedge, Edam, Mozarella, sliced packaged process cheeses, spreadable cheese food, cream cheese, Muenster.

storage time and temperature, with warm storage temperatures accelerating flavor development.

Identification and use of several of the more popular natural cheeses, both ripened and unripened, are reviewed in Table 8.2. The discussion of a few of the cheeses, divided on the basis of their firmness, provides additional background on natural cheeses.

Soft Cheeses. Cottage cheese is made commercially or at home from skim milk that is clotted by rennin and/or lactic acid. When milk is allowed to stand, lactic-acid-producing bacteria (*Streptococcus lactic*) begin to convert lactose to lactic acid and the milk becomes increasingly acidic. As the pH approaches the isoelectric point of casein, the casein becomes less soluble and begins to precipitate. The calcium of the milk remains in the whey in the form of soluble calcium salts (calcium lactate). Therefore lactic-acid-clotted cottage cheese is lower in calcium than was the milk from which it was made.

Rennin is a proteolytic enzyme prepared commercially from the stomach lining of calves and lambs. When this enzyme is used to clot the milk, cottage cheese will retain more calcium in the curd because the calcium in milk forms an insoluble salt with the protein, casein. Cottage cheese is marketed as creamed (4% fat) and uncreamed. The uncreamed contains slightly fewer calories and slightly more protein than the creamed product.

Cream cheese is made from whole milk with some cream added. Lactic acid is the means used for curd formation. Neufchâtel is similar to cream cheese, but is made with less cream.

Camembert is a soft cheese, clotted with rennin, then cured with *Penicillium camemberti*. Characteristically the center of this cheese should be somewhat liquid when fully ripened. Brie is similar to Camembert, but is firmer. Limburger and Liederkranz are the other soft cheeses frequently used as dessert cheeses.

Semisoft cheeses. Gorgonzola, Roquefort, and blue cheese are rennin-clotted cheeses with a characteristic blue-green color and pronounced flavor, which is caused by *Penicillium roqueforti* or a similar mold during a 2 to 12 month ripening period. Unlike Gorgonzola and blue, which are made from cow's milk, Roquefort is produced from sheep's milk. Roquefort cheese was named after Roquefort, France, the town close to the caves where the cheese is ripened.

The characteristics of Muenster cheese vary with their site of production; Muenster cheese from the United States is mild in flavor as compared with Muenster from Europe, where the cheese is ripened more.

Brick is a semihard, yet mild and sweet-flavored cheese which derives its name from its shape.

Hard Cheeses. Cheddar cheese derives its name from the town in England where it was first made, but in this country this kind is called either

Table 8.2. Characteristics of Some Popular Varieties of Natural Cheeses[a]

Kind or Name Place of Origin	Kind of Milk Used in Manufacture	Ripening or Curing Time	Flavor	Body and Texture	Uses
		Soft, Unripened Varieties			
Cottage, plain or creamed. (Unknown)	Cow's milk skimmed; plain curd, or plain curd with cream added.	Unripened	Mild, acid	Soft, curd particles of varying size.	Salads, with fruits, vegetables, sandwiches, dips, cheese cake.
Cream, plain (U.S.A.)	Cream from cow's milk.	Unripened	Mild, acid	Soft and smooth	Salads, dips, sandwiches, snacks, cheese cake, desserts.
Neufchatel (Nü-shä-těl'). (France)	Cow's milk	Unripened	Mild, acid	Soft, smooth similar to cream cheese but lower in milkfat.	Salads, dips, sandwiches, snacks. cheese cake, desserts.
Ricotta (Rĭ-cŏ'-ta) (Italy)	Cow's milk, whole or partly skimmed, or whey from cow's milk with whole or skim milk added. In Italy, whey from sheep's milk.	Unripened	Sweet, nut-like.	Soft, moist or dry	Appetizers, salads, snacks, lasagne, ravioli, noodles and other cooked dishes, grating, desserts.

[a]Adapted from Fenton, F. E. How to Buy Cheese. Home and Garden Bulletin No. 193. U. S. Department of Agriculture, Washington, D. C. 1971. Pages 8–17.

Firm, Unripened Varieties

Name (Origin)	Kind of Milk	Ripening	Flavor	Texture	Uses
Mysost (Müs-ôst) also called Primost (Prēm'-ôst). (Norway)	Whey from cow's milk	Unripened	Sweetish, caramel	Firm, buttery consistency	Snacks, desserts, served with dark bread
Mozzarella (Italy)	Whole or partly skimmed cow's milk	Unripened	Delicate, mild	Slightly firm, plastic	Snacks, pizza, lasagne, casseroles

Soft, Ripened Varieties

Name (Origin)	Kind of Milk	Ripening	Flavor	Texture	Uses
Brie (Brē) (France)	Cow's milk	4–8 weeks.	Mild to pungent.	Soft, smooth when ripened.	Appetizers, sandwiches, snacks, good with crackers and fruit, dessert.
Camembert (Kăm'ĕm-bâr). (France)	Cow's milk	4–8 weeks.	Mild to pungent.	Soft, smooth; very soft when fully ripened.	Appetizers, sandwiches, snacks, good with crackers, and fruit such as pears and apples, dessert.
Limburger (Belgium)	Cow's milk	4–8 weeks.	Highly pungent, very strong.	Soft, smooth when ripened; usually contains small irregular openings.	Appetizers, snacks, good with crackers, rye or other dark breads, dessert.

Table 8.2., continued

Kind or Name Place of Origin	Kind of Milk Used in Manufacture	Ripening or Curing Time	Flavor	Body and Texture	Uses
Semisoft, Ripened Varieties					
Muenster (Mün'stēr). (Germany)	Cow's milk	1–8 weeks	Mild to mellow.	Semisoft, numerous small mechanical openings. Contains more moisture than brick.	Appetizers, sandwiches, snacks, dessert.
Firm Ripened Varieties					
Cheddar (England)	Cow's milk	1–12 months or more.	Mild to very sharp.	Firm, smooth, some mechanical openings.	Appetizers, sandwiches, sauces, on vegetables, in hot dishes, toasted sandwiches, grating, cheeseburgers, dessert.
Edam (Ē'dăm) (Netherlands.)	Cow's milk, partly skimmed	2–3 months.	Mellow, nutlike.	Semisoft to firm, smooth; small irregularly shaped or round holes; lower milkfat than Gouda.	Appetizers, snacks, salads, sandwiches, seafood sauces, dessert.

194

Name (Origin)	Kind of Milk	Ripening Time	Flavor	Body and Texture	Uses
Swiss, also called Emmentaler. (Switzerland)	Cow's milk	3–9 months.	Sweet, nut-like.	Firm, smooth with large round eyes.	Sandwiches, snacks, sauces, fondue, cheeseburgers.

Very Hard Ripened Varieties

Name (Origin)	Kind of Milk	Ripening Time	Flavor	Body and Texture	Uses
Parmesan (Pärˈmē-zăn) also called Reggiano. (Italy)	Partly skimmed cow's milk	14 months to 2 years.	Sharp, piquant.	Very hard, granular, lower moisture and milkfat than Romano.	Grated for seasoning in soups, or vegetables, spaghetti, ravioli, breads, popcorn, used extensively in pizza and lasagne.
Romano (Rŏ-māˈ-nō) also called Sardo Romano Pecorino Romano. (Italy)	Cow's milk. In Italy, sheep's milk (Italian law).	5–12 months.	Sharp, piquant.	Very hard granular	Seasoning in soups, casserole dishes, ravioli, sauces, breads, suitable for grating when cured for about one year.

Blue-Vein Mold Ripened Varieties

Name (Origin)	Kind of Milk	Ripening Time	Flavor	Body and Texture	Uses
Blue, spelled Bleu on imported cheese. (France)	Cow's milk	2–6 months.	Tangy, peppery.	Semisoft, pasty, sometimes crumbly.	Appetizers, salads, dips, salad dressing, sandwich spreads, good with crackers, dessert.

Table 8.2., continued

Kind or Name Place of Origin	Kind of Milk Used in Manufacture	Ripening or Curing Time	Flavor	Body and Texture	Uses
Gorgonzola (Gôr-gŏn-zō'-lä). (Italy)	Cow's milk. In Italy, cow's milk or goat's milk or mixtures of these.	3–12 months.	Tangy, peppery.	Semisoft, pasty, sometimes crumbly, lower moisture than Blue.	Appetizers, snacks, salads, dips, sandwich spread, good with crackers, dessert.
Roquefort (Rŏk'-fērt) or (Rōk-fôr'). (France).	Sheep's milk	2–5 months or more.	Sharp, slightly peppery.	Semisoft, pasty sometimes crumbly.	Appetizers, snacks, salads, dips, sandwich spreads, good with crackers, dessert.
Stilton[b] (England).	Cow's milk	2–6 months.	Piquant, milder than Gorgonzola or Roquefort.	Semisoft, flaky; slightly more crumbly than Blue.	Appetizers, snacks, salads, dessert.

[b]Imported only.

FIGURE 8.7   A rarebit featuring cheddar cheese provides an unusual, but appealing highlight for apple slices.

cheddar or American cheese. The production of cheddar cheese is initiated by introducing lactic-acid-producing bacteria in order to acidify the milk sufficiently for optimum rennin coagulation. If a yellow cheese is desired, a yellow food coloring substance, anatto (extracted from seed pods of a tree in Central America), is added and then the cheese is allowed to set while it forms a curd. Completion of the manufacture of this cheese involves repeated cutting of the curd and draining of the whey followed by salting and ripening.

Edam and Gouda cheeses are hard cheeses recognized by their bright red wax coatings. These dessert cheeses originated in Holland.

Swiss or Emmentaler cheese is prepared by using lactic-acid-producing bacteria (*Streptoccus thermophilus* and *Lactobacillus bulgaricus*) and rennin to produce the curd. During ripening, gas is produced by the action of *Propionibacterium shermanii* which causes the large holes characteristic of

Swiss cheese. This versatile cheese is used in many recipes, in sandwiches, or as a dessert cheese.

Parmesan is a very hard cheese of Italian origin which is particularly well suited to grating. Several times during the 16 months to several years of the ripening process, Parmesan cheeses are rubbed with an oily mixture which causes a dark green to black exterior.

Process Cheese

Process cheese is preferred by some people when the cheese is to be used in hot foods because it will not become stringy or tough as do the other cheeses just mentioned. The manufacturing of process cheese involves: selection of natural cheeses with the desired characteristics; the grating or shredding of these cheeses; the addition of an emulsifier, such as sodium citrate or disodium phosphate, and water; and the heating and stirring of this mixture at temperatures between 145 and 165°F until the cheese becomes homogeneous. The heating of process cheese halts bacterial and enzyme action so that ripening does not occur. Therefore process cheese has excellent keeping qualities and usually has a bland flavor.

In addition to pasteurized process cheese, two other types of process cheese products are marketed. Pasteurized process cheese food has more moisture and lower fat content than process cheese as a result of the inclusion of somewhat less cheese, the use of nonfat dry milk or whey solids, and water. Different flavors are created by introducing various flavoring substances, such as meats and pimiento. Pasteurized process cheese spread usually contains even more moisture than is found in process cheese food, and a stabilizer is added to prevent separation. These spreads are versatile in use and varied in flavor, depending on the flavoring substances added.

Coldpack cheese, also called Club cheese, is formulated in the same way as process cheese. However, there is one distinction in its preparation. Unlike process cheeses, coldpack cheese is not heated. Its flavor is very similar to the cheeses that may be used to produce specific coldpack cheeses, but the spreading qualities are superior to natural cheeses.

CHEESE COOKERY

When cheese is included in a food product, the selection of a reasonably well-ripened cheese is of paramount importance, for green or slightly ripened cheese will not blend well in a product. The two cardinal rules for heating cheese are to maintain the cheese at a relatively low temperature and to avoid prolonged heating periods. The low temperature and short heating are dictated by the large amount of protein in cheese, for these pro-

FIGURE 8.8   A smooth cheese fondue sets the stage for a simple, informal dinner.

teins become tough and stringy when heated too long or at too high a temperature. These conditions also may cause the fat to separate and drain from the cheese. Anyone who has eaten a cheese pizza is well aware of these changes.

Cheese soup, cheese sauce, rarebit, and fondue require that the cheese be added after the starch in the white sauce has been gelatinized and just before serving. After the cheese is added, the product should be heated only enough to melt the cheese and should then be served as soon as possible. At no time should a mixture containing cheese be boiled because high heats or long heating will cause sauces containing natural cheeses to become grainy and stringy and will cause the fat to separate. In fact, if fondue is heated a long time it may become so stringy that the cheese is almost impossible to chew.

Any sauce utilizing cheese should be of the appropriate viscosity for its intended use, should be very smooth with no layer of fat, and should be flavorful.

Cheese frequently is used in foods such as macaroni and cheese or a cheese soufflé. Since it is impossible to add the cheese near the end of the baking period, it is necessary to take other precautions to avoid overheating the cheese. Overbaking should be avoided to reduce the likelihood of over-heating the cheese. Low oven temperatures should be used when feasible, but cheese can be protected from more intense oven heat by placing the baking dish in a pan of hot water or by placing some insulating food such as buttered crumbs on the top. If cheese is to be used as a garnish on the top of a casserole, it should be added just long enough before the end of the baking period to permit the cheese to melt.

Casserole dishes may pose another problem in addition to those caused by the presence of cheese. Any casserole containing a carbohydrate such as noodles or macaroni must be made using a fully gelatinized pasta. Unless the gelatinization is complete, the starch will take liquid from the rest of the

FIGURE 8.9 Buttered crumbs on cheese-containing casseroles are one means of protecting natural cheeses from the intense oven heat that will cause the protein to become tough.

casserole to complete the gelatinization process. This results in a gummy, doughy mixture that is unrelated to any problems that might have arisen from the use of cheese.

Pizza or other cheese-containing foods that must be baked at high temperatures will be improved by putting the cheese under the sauce, by limiting the baking period to as short a time as practical, and by sprinkling a small amount of cheese on top just before the baking period is completed.

SUMMARY

Milk and milk products are important in the diets of people of all ages. Valuable dietary contributions of milk include vitamin A, riboflavin, vitamin D, calcium, and phosphorus; the nutrients notably low in quantity are iron and ascorbic acid. Because of these inadequacies, milk should not be considered as the only necessary food in the diet. The food value of milk is often altered during the processing of the various kinds of milk that are now being marketed.

The chief difficulties encountered in the use of milk in food preparation are scum formation and curdling. These conditions occur when the protein in milk becomes insoluble due to changes wrought by heat or a change in the pH of the milk. The use of low temperatures and short heating periods is an aid in reducing scum formation. Curdling is less likely to occur if the acidity of milk or milk-containing foods is minimized. Long heating periods, the use of milk that is beginning to lose its freshness, the addition of acid foods, and the use of salted and cured meats in milk products will increase the probability of curdling.

Foams may be whipped from whipping cream, light cream, very cold nondiluted evaporated milk, and nonfat dry milk diluted with an equal part of water. These foams vary in their stability and ease of formation, but all are useful in food preparation.

The many different cheeses marketed today are categorized as natural or process cheese, depending on the production procedures and ingredients used. All ripened natural cheeses respond favorably to heating when the temperature is kept low and the period of heating is of reasonable duration. Violation of these conditions, however, may result in drastic changes in the cheese. Process cheese can be heated without such concern for dire consequences, but the flavor of this type of cheese is generally more mild than that found in the various ripened cheeses.

BIBLIOGRAPHY

Agricultural Marketing Service. *How to Buy Dairy Products*. Home and Garden Bulletin No. 201. U. S. D. A. Washington, D. C. 1972.

Andrews, J., and A. W. Fuchs. Pasteurization and its relation to health. *J. Am. Med. Assn. 138*:128. 1948.

Carash, P. Milk and milk products. Chapter 5 in *Chemistry and technology of food and food products,* ed. by M. B. Jacobs. Interscience Publishers, New York, 1951.

Consumer and Food Economics Research Division. *Milk in Family Meals.* Home and Garden Bulletin No. 127. U. S. Department of Agriculture, Washington, D. C. Rev. 1972.

Council on Foods and Nutrition. Substitutes for whole milk. *JAMA 208,* No. 9. June 2, 1969.

Fenton, F. E. *How to Buy Cheese.* Home and Garden Marketing Service. Bulletin No. 193. U. S. Department of Agriculture, Washington, D. C. 1971.

Food and Drug Administration. Milk and milk-type products. *FDA Fact Sheet.* April 1972.

Food and Drug Administration. Mellorine and parevine. Facts from FDA. DHEW Publication No. (FDA) 73–2036. April 1973.

Jacobs, M. B. Milk, cream, and dairy products. Chapter 20 in *Chemistry and technology of food and food products,* ed. by M. B. Jacobs. Interscience Publishers. New York. 1951.

McIntire, J. M. New dairy and related products. *AJPH 61,* No. 1: 157. 1971.

McWilliams, M. *Illustrated Guide to Food Preparation.* Plycon Press. Fullerton, CA. 1972.

Mrak, E. M., and G. Mackinney. The dehydration of foods. Chapter 33 in *Chemistry and technology of food and food products,* ed. by M. B. Jacobs. Interscience Publishers, New York. 1951.

National Dairy Council. Composition and nutritive value of dairy foods. *Dairy Council Digest 42,* No. 1:1. 1971.

Newer knowledge of cheese. National Dairy Council, Chicago, 1964.

Newer knowledge of milk. National Dairy Council, Chicago, 1965.

Patton, M. Milk. *Scientific American 221,* No. 1:58. 1969.

SUGGESTIONS FOR STUDY

1. Taste whole milk, filled milk, and imitation milk. Compare their palatability, nutritive value, and cost.

2. What useful changes occur in milk as a result of the homogenization process?

3. Compare the ease of formation and stability of foams made from whipping cream, coffee cream, half and half, evaporated milk, and nonfat dried milk solids. What constituents contribute stability to each of the foams?

4. Why is the calcium content of cottage cheese clotted with acid lower than that clotted with rennin?

CHAPTER 9

Meats, Poultry, and Fish

MEATS

If one type of food were to be singled out as the cornerstone of American food habits, the obvious type mentioned would be meat. Even more specifically, the preference runs strongly for beef. As reported in 1969, the average American ate 109 pounds of beef, 66 pounds of pork, 37 pounds of chicken, 8 pounds of turkey, 4 pounds of veal, and 4 pounds of lamb. During the 1950s and 1960s, beef consumption rose almost 70 percent, chicken just about doubled, turkey increased, pork remained the same, and lamb consumption decreased. This preference for meats makes selection of the meat, fish, or poultry a logical starting point for planning a menu. The purchase, storage, preparation, and service of meat deserve very careful attention, because meat not only is the focal point of many meals but also frequently is the most expensive single item in the menu. A thorough understanding of these aspects of meat in the menu will enable the consumer to spend his food dollar with maximum effectiveness and to derive great satisfaction from preparing and eating tender, flavorful, and juicy meats.

This chapter is designed to acquaint the student with the composition of meat, the various types and cuts of meat, and basic meat-cookery principles. The term "meat" will be used herein to include beef, veal, pork, lamb, and other red meats.

MUSCLE

Structure

Muscle is composed of approximately 75 percent water and 20 percent protein with the remaining 5 percent comprised of fat, carbohydrate, and

203

FIGURE 9.1   Beef continues to be the most popular food in the United States despite its high cost. Standing rib roast is a glamorous meat when carved with skill at the table.

minerals. The percentage of water in meat varies; the actual amount of water in meat, termed its water-holding capacity, varies with the kind of meat, the type of muscle, the season of the year, and the pH of the meat.

Muscle is a more complex structure than it at first appears to the naked eye. The smallest structural unit is the fiber. The individual fibers consist of muscle proteins and bound water which are contained by the sarcolemma. Apparently the number of fibers does not increase after birth of the animal, but rather growth occurs as a result of the growth of the existing fibers. Several of these fibers are joined by connective tissue (endomysium) into bundles called fasciculi. The fasciculi and some fatty deposits are sheathed as a muscle by the perimysium.

When viewed under a microscope, muscle does not appear to be a homogeneous material. Striations of alternating bands with different refractive indices are visible in skeletal muscle.

Muscle Proteins

The chemical composition of proteins is being studied extensively, but considerable work remains to be done in the area of meat proteins. Myosin, the most abundant muscle protein, is a relatively large globular protein with a molecular weight of approximately 382,000. This globular protein forms a gel when heated. Another protein, tropomyosin, is considerably smaller (molecular weight, 50,000), but has properties similar to myosin. Actin is a water-soluble protein with a molecular weight of approximately 70,000. Actomyosin, theorized to be a complex of actin and myosin, is the protein responsible for muscle contraction.

Myoglobin, important because of its influence on the color of meats, is a protein similar to hemoglobin and is capable of combining with oxygen, carbon monoxide, or nitric oxide. When myoglobin undergoes oxidation with chlorates or nitrates, the iron in the heme portion is changed to a different valence state (from ferrous to ferric) and the color changes from the desired red color of myoglobin to the brown pigment of metmyoglobin. Oxidized iron in meats also may cause a gray or green color. Such oxidation occurs more readily in meat that is heated, frozen, treated with acid, or exposed to ultraviolet light. When molecular oxygen reacts with heme, a green color forms. It is apparent that these color changes are a problem to meat retailers.

Discoloration can be retarded by wrapping meat cuts in relatively airtight packages and storing away from sunlight or incandescent lights. Ascorbic acid or niacin may be added to help maintain the desired red color. Ordinarily discoloration should be slight for up to three days when the meat is being stored in a refrigerated case. Freezing causes some fading, although changes are minimized when a good wrapping is applied.

CONNECTIVE TISSUE

The two proteins of connective tissue are collagen and elastin. Collagen, the structural protein of connective tissue, is sometimes referred to as "white connective tissue." Collagenous fibers may be arranged parallel to each other or may run randomly in any direction. Each collagen molecule consists of three fibrous strands of gelatin molecules. The gelatin molecules contain approximately 1000 amino acid residues and collagen has roughly 3000.

In the presence of heat and water the three strands of collagen will be separated to individual gelatin strands. Considerable time is required for this conversion to take place; the actual time depends on thickness of the tissue, acidity of the solution, temperature, and size of the piece of meat. It is this conversion to gelatin that causes less tender cuts of meat to increase in tenderness.

Elastin is made of very strong and elastic branched fibers. A mass of elastin, such as is found parallel to the muscle in a standing rib roast, is yellow. Since elastin is extremely resistant to change by heat or acid, no significant changes occur in elastin when meat is cooked.

FAT

Fat deposits in animals consist of many fat cells grouped together. Fat is first laid down subcutaneously as a protective layer around the organs. Then fat is accumulated around and between muscles. The last deposition occurs within the muscle and is known as marbling. The various fat cells increase in size as the animal becomes fatter. Marbling is desirable, for the amount of fat and the water-holding capacity of the meat greatly influence its juiciness.

NUTRITIONAL COMPOSITION

Meat contributes many valuable nutrients to the diet. Since meat is a complete protein and contains 9–19 percent protein, it is a very useful source of protein in the diet. Normal heating has little influence on protein quality. Severe protein heating, however, reduces the protein quality because amino acids and bonding forces within the protein are altered.

Beef contains a somewhat higher proportion of protein than pork, whereas pork is higher in fat. The amount of fat contributed by a serving of meat depends not only on the kind of meat, but also on the amount of trimming and the method of cookery.

The minerals occurring in meats in significant amounts are phosphorus, copper, and iron. Of particular interest is the quantity of iron and copper contained in liver. Pork liver contains considerably more iron than beef liver, but beef liver is also an excellent source of iron.

The vitamin content of different meat varies. The B vitamins, thiamin, riboflavin, and niacin, occur in significant amounts in all meats. Pork is particularly high in thiamin. Since these vitamins are water soluble, loss of these nutrients from the meat is greater in moist-heat than in dry-heat cookery, although a large percentage of this loss will be retained in the cooking liquid. Liver usually contains a useful amount of vitamin A.

DEVELOPMENTS IN MEAT PRODUCTION

Large-Scale Feedlot Operations

Meat production is frequently a large-scale operation in which feeders operate very large feed lots designed to mature and fatten stock as efficiently and economically as possible. To ensure maximum gain by ready access to food and restricted activity, the animals are confined to a small area. A large beef-feeding operation in southern California is designed to function constantly with 22,500 feeders on hand, and an area 5 by 7 feet or a total of 35 square feet is allotted for each animal.

Tenderizing by Enzyme

Reportedly, Mexicans in the sixteenth century tenderized their meats by wrapping them in papaya leaves, but this knowledge seems to have remained dormant until an enzyme derived from papaya was introduced in the last few years to tenderize beef. This enzyme, namely papain, is presently available for commercial and home use.

A large meat-packing company is now using a patented process utilizing papain in some of its meat. A solution of papain is injected into the beef selected for tenderizing shortly before slaughter. The enzyme, since it is injected into the blood stream, theoretically circulates through the entire body prior to slaughter. By this means the complete muscles, not just the surface, contain the enzyme. The enzyme remains inactive in the meat until it is heated to 55°C (130°F), at which time the enzyme becomes active and begins to digest the protein. This tenderizing action stops when the enzyme is inactivated at 71°C (160°F). Some cuts of meat that usually are classified as less tender may be sufficiently tenderized by the enzyme to permit use of dry-heat methods. There is a slight increase in the price per pound for meat treated in this manner.

If papain is purchased for home use, it is sprinkled on the surface of the meat where it will penetrate a depth of approximately one millimeter per hour. Penetration is somewhat improved if the papain-treated surface is pricked in many places with a fork. Meat treated on the surface with papain is likely to be tenderized so much in some places that some areas will become powdery, for it is difficult to spread the desired quantity uniformly.

Although papain is the most common plant enzyme used to tenderize meats, bromelin and ficin also can be used. Preparations of proteolytic enzymes of animal origin suitable for tenderizing meats include trypsin, chymotrypsin, pepsin, and pancreatin. Rhozyme P-11 is a protease from bacteria or fungi.

Hormones

The first interest in using sex hormones in animal production was generated by the observation that these hormones accelerated cattle growth. The male hormone testosterone was shown early to have no deleterious effect on palatability of cattle receiving the hormone. Interest then shifted to synthetic female hormones. Diethylstilbestrol (DES) was found to hasten the growth of cattle and produce meat with a higher meat-to-bone ratio. Similar effects were noted in lambs, although occasionally the carcasses were watery and soft. Pigs apparently do not respond to diethylstilbestrol. Chickens showed increased fat deposition, which increased palatability. Turkeys reached market maturity about three weeks faster and in better condition because of a temperament change resulting in fewer fights. On the negative side, the skin of both turkeys and chickens tore more easily when DES had been implanted.

Hormones may be administered by a pellet implant, injection, or feeding. When administered orally, they should be withdrawn from the animal at least 48 hours before slaughter. Pellet implants should be made in inedible areas of the body because residue levels are highest in the immediate vicinity of the pellet. Regardless of the form of the hormone or its method of administration, it is important that the residual level of hormone in the meat be essentially nonexistent. Carelessness by producers in regard to the implantation of the hormone in chickens has led to the banning of the use of this hormone in poultry production. Residues have not been found in cattle, however, when stilbestrol is administered by the recommended procedures. Because of the growth and feed utilization advantages, stilbestrol has been used widely. It has been estimated that 75 percent of the beef cattle produced in the United States in 1961 had received stilbestrol. However the use of DES in cattle feed still is subject to question. Legislation in 1975 reinstated use of DES previously banned briefly in cattle feed up to two weeks before slaughter.

Postmortem Changes

After the animal is slaughtered, certain changes occurring in meats cause a stiffening called rigor mortis. Adenosine triphosphate continues to be synthesized from glycogen after the death of the animal until the glycogen supply is depleted or the pH is lowered to approximately 5.3. The lactic acid that is produced concurrently with the formation of adenosine triphosphate (ATP) causes the lowering of the pH, with the exact pH being determined by the amount of glycogen in the body at the time of death. Actual pH of the animal varies according to the portion of the animal being tested.

As rigor mortis approaches, there appears to be some association of myosin and actin to form actomyosin, which characteristically is found in contracted muscle. Stiffening then occurs. With the onset of rigor, ammonia begins to be liberated as a result of the ultimate breakdown of adenosine triphosphate.

Since the ultimate pH of the animal is so closely related to meat quality, factors influencing this level are the subject of some study. A high glycogen level produces the desired low pH. Practices such as adequate feeding and resting, followed by a calm dispatching operation optimize the likelihood of a high glycogen level in the carcass. Fasting, exercise, nervous exhaustion, or insulin injections prior to slaughter cause a low glycogen level in the body. This in turn causes a relatively high pH in the carcass during rigor. Such meat will characteristically be an undesirable dark color and will have poor flavor and texture. A long period of stress before slaughter produces more adrenaline in the animals and this results in meat with a sticky, gummy feel and a dark color. Rigor mortis usually reaches a peak in about 24 hours, followed by a gradual softening of the muscle tissue.

METHODS OF SHORT AND LONG-TERM STORAGE

Cold Storage

Control of spoilage is an important problem during storage of meats. Meat spoilage is retarded by preventing fatigue, hunger, and thirst in animals that are to be slaughtered. Many other factors, however, also need to be controlled. The introduction of microorganisms during the slaughtering, skinning, and eviscerating can be a serious source of contamination. When the carcasses are washed and cut, additional microorganisms may be introduced. The sawdust used on the floor of the chilling room may cling to the carcass. Obviously, considerable attention should be given to maintaining high standards of sanitation during these operations. In addition, spoilage will be reduced if the meat is left in as large a piece as is practical to handle, for organisms will not flourish on the intact carcass. The fat and connective tissue on the surface of a carcass do not provide a favorable environment for active growth of microorganisms, but cut surfaces do.

Regardless of the future intended use of meat, at least a short period of cold storage will be necessary while the carcass passes through rigor. The water-holding capacity of meat drops rapidly after slaughter and then begins to rise slowly as rigor passes. Because of this increase in water-holding capacity after rigor passes, meat that is to be frozen will have less drip loss when frozen after, rather than during, rigor mortis.

Since packing-house beef may be held as long as five to ten days before shipping, all storage conditions should be aimed at preventing growth of microorganisms. Rapid cooling of carcasses, achieved by carefully maintaining a low relative humidity and constant low temperature in the chilling rooms, promotes optimum storage of the meat and minimum growth of microorganisms. Storage in an atmosphere containing either ozone or carbon dioxide has been of benefit in aiding the inhibition of microorganisms. Under proper storage conditions, carcasses may be kept safely about three weeks. Meat that is cut into retail cuts, however, because of the increased surface exposure, will not keep for an extended period.

Maintenance of quality in fish is difficult. Ocean fish often must be kept several days on shipboard before the fishing vessel puts into port. Immediate storage in crushed ice slows deteriorative changes, but some fish still may spoil if the ship is far from shore. It has been observed that contamination of fish begins in the slime of the skin. The flesh easily loses its firmness and the colors begin to fade. Trimethylamine, a substance that contributes substantially to the strong odor of fish, is formed as fish lose their freshness during storage.

Various means have been devised to improve the retention of quality during storage of fish. Fish keep reasonably well when stored at a constant temperature just above the freezing point of the fish in an atmosphere saturated with water vapor to prevent drying. The elimination of oxidizers retards spoilage also. Chlorides may be added as an aid in keeping large tuna. Sodium nitrite is another fairly effective additive. Of particular interest currently are studies of the use of antibiotics such as aureomycin and the influence of storing in an atmosphere of carbon dioxide. The antibiotics are proving to be quite effective.

Aging

All red meats are aged at least briefly before reaching retail outlets. Some prime beef, however, is selected to be aged or ripened for a period of time ranging from 15 to 40 days. Prime sides of beef are suitable for this ripening process because a heavy layer of fat surrounds the meat and protects it from microbiological contamination. Although mold does grow on the surface of the fat layer, this covering is so thick that the mold can be removed by simply trimming off the outer portion of fat. Lower-quality beef does not have enough external fat to permit aging without causing deleterious changes in the meat. Veal also is unsuitable for aging for this same reason. Pork, although it may have relatively thick fat deposited around the carcass, cannot be aged since rancidity develops in the fat.

A 10- to 20-day storage period for aging beef has been shown to increase tenderness of the muscle. The fibrous proteins in the meat are attacked by proteolytic enzymes to effect this change. There is also increased hydration of the protein during ripening. No evidence of changes in connective tissue by aging has been found, so the increased tenderness appears to be solely the result of changes in the muscle proteins.

The fresh color or bloom of the meat is gradually lost with increased aging time. As a result the red color of the meat changes to a gray brown at a lower internal temperature when it is heated. Aged meat also is noticeably darker than unripened meat when the two are compared before they are heated. The flavor develops and becomes more intense as the meat is ripened. Flavor is considered to be better with 20 to 40 days of storage.

Although changes during ripening occur more slowly at low temperatures than at higher ones, temperatures just above freezing are generally used for storing the ripening meat in order to retard bacterial spoilage.

Curing

Curing is a means of preserving beef and pork. Beef cured in a cold brine solution is the familiar corned beef. Pork becomes known as ham when it is cured. The characteristic changes in color and flavor are achieved by treatment with a combination of salt, sodium nitrate, and heat. During the brining period the nitrate is reduced to nitrite; the reaction of nitrite with the myoglobin in the meat produces the familiar red color of cured meats. At the time of this writing, the safety of nitrites is being debated and studied. Occasionally a brownish pigment called hemichromogen forms in the meats as a result of long storage, heat, and light. The presence of molecular oxygen then causes a color change to a green or gray.

The normal pH of meat ranges from 5.2 to 6.6. Curing agents penetrate best in meat at the more acidic end of this range. Cured meats with a higher pH are more susceptible to spoilage than more acid meats, but the chance of spoilage is reduced by heating the more alkaline meats. Heating improves penetration of the curing agents. Sage, black pepper, and salt hasten rancidity at the surface, whereas other spices retard this development.

Smoking

Ham frequently is processed by smoking and fish are smoked occasionally. Smoking is not only a means of preserving, but also a means of enhancing the flavor and coagulating the proteins. The best fuel for smoking is sawdust from hard woods. Slow smoking is preferable since the extended period enables more drying to occur. Drying is responsible for much of the preservative action from smoking, although smoking also aids in retarding rancidity. As a further deterrent to the development of rancidity, ascorbic acid can be added to smoked pork sausage.

In many areas of Asia, fish are the chief protein foods available for the general populace. The economic conditions dictate that methods less expensive than freezing, canning, or icing be used to preserve the fish. Fish sauces having a high salt content similar to soy sauce are prepared by kneading small fish by hand, salting them, and then burying them in pottery pots for several months. Fish pastes also are prepared. Either of these types of fish preparations is intended as a strong-flavored condiment to complement the bland flavor of rice.

Salting and drying of fish is a common preservation method in Asia, but some spoilage occurs as a result of undersalting. Another disadvantage is the necessity of redrying occasionally because moisture is drawn into the fish by the hygroscopic salt.

Freezing

Freezing, as a storage method for meats, has gained widespread acceptance. The two freezing methods employed are sharp freezing and quick freezing. Sharp freezing utilizes a storage room that is maintained at −23°C (−10°F). Air may be moved rapidly through the room to speed the freezing.

Quick freezing may be done by any combination of three basic methods: immersion, indirect contact, and convection. The immersion method is sometimes used for fish. Fish frozen in this manner will be somewhat salty since they are frozen by immersion in a brine solution. Recently, fish are more commonly frozen by placing them in closed metal containers which are then immersed in a refrigerated brine solution, a technique that eliminates the salty flavor. Various mechanical systems such as the Birdseye multiplate freezer are specially designed for quick freezing by indirect contact. Convection freezing is done by placing the product in a blast of cold air.

Quick freezing is preferred over sharp freezing for two reasons: (1) the ice crystals formed in quick freezing are smaller, and (2) bacterial, yeast, and mold growths are less since the meat is cooled rapidly below the optimum temperature for growth. Carefully considered sanitation procedures are important during the freezing of all meats, but are particularly crucial for chickens and fish.

Tenderness is promoted in meat during frozen storage. The chief drawback to frozen storage is that freezing has an adverse effect on the amount of drip from meat. The degree of this disadvantage, however, is influenced by the rate of freezing. When meat is frozen slowly, water will leave the fibers and be frozen between fibers, whereas a rapid rate of freezing traps the water within the fibers. The latter placement results in less drip loss. Rapid freezing is accomplished with small cuts of meat and very cold temperatures. Another factor affecting drip loss during frozen storage is the length of time that elapses between slaughtering and freezing. In contrast with pork, lamb, and veal, which need twenty-four hours of chilling, beef should be chilled at least two days before freezing.

Storage temperatures of −18°C (0°F) permit longer frozen storage than higher temperatures. Commercially, meats are held in storage rooms at −23 to −18°C (−10°F to 0°F). Air flow during storage is retarded as much as possible since movement of air increases desiccation or drying of the meats.

Packaging materials for freezing meat are important. In the home, heavyweight aluminum foil is particularly convenient. Heavy, specially treated wrapping paper is an excellent covering, but is less convenient to keep in the home. Commercially, various polymeric materials have been adapted to overcome frozen storage problems. Packaging needs to be tight to prevent air from reaching the meat. When tears occur in packages, desiccation results, leaving a dried, rather tough area of freezer burn on the meat.

Freeze Drying

Drying has long been a means of preserving meat. Dried beef and dried fish are still sold in markets, but with technological advances the potential use of dried meats has expanded. Some technical advances in food preservation have been made as a direct result of research keyed to solving food-supply problems of the Army. A practical illustration is the freeze drying of meats.

There are two basic methods of freeze drying: prefreezing can be done before the food is dried under vacuum; and evaporative freezing is done by placing the food in a vacuum and then evaporating the moisture as cooling occurs. This latter method is somewhat undesirable for meat since it causes some hardening of the tissue. Dehydration of cooked ground meat may be done effectively at high temperatures, but rather large pieces of meat acquire a hard outer surface and a burned flavor when treated in this manner. Radiant heating is particularly well suited to freeze drying of thin pieces of meat. Chicken dehydrated by this technique is used in commercial dehydrated soups.

INSPECTION

Inspection of meat dates back more than 80 years to the Meat Inspection Act of 1890, which authorized inspection of bacon, salted pork, and live animals being exported to European markets. The Cattle Inspection Act of 1891 provided inspection of cattle for export and voluntary inspection for cattle being slaughtered for interstate commerce. The measure was so weak that sanitation in meat plants was bombasted by Upton Sinclair. The one-year Meat Inspection Act of 1906 was followed quickly by the Meat Inspection Act of 1907, which extended the provisions of the 1906 legislation requiring all meat entering interstate commerce to be inspected and specifying sanitation standards for packing houses. In 1926 the United States Department of Agriculture began inspection of live poultry, on the invitation of individual states. Mandatory inspection of meat in interstate commerce was extended to also cover poultry in 1957. The Wholesome Meat Act of 1967 and the Wholesome Poultry Products Act of 1968 mandated that meats and poultry, respectively, involved in intrastate commerce must be inspected under state programs deemed to be, at least, equal to the federal inspection required for meat and poultry inspected under the interstate regulations. Such inspection can be conducted under either state or federal inspection.

Inspection is done by state or federal inspectors who ascertain the healthiness of the animal before slaughter and monitor the conditions that prevail in the packing houses during slaughtering and packing. Rigid standards of cleanliness and sanitation must be maintained throughout the entire operation in the packing plant to fulfill the requirements that are monitored by the government inspectors. The purpose of this inspection is solely to safeguard the consumer's health. In no other way does federal inspection indicate the eating quality of the meat. It simply signifies that the meat was safe for consumption at the time of inspection: subsequent sanitary handling is not guaranteed by the inspection stamp.

Inspected meat is identified with a stamp to signify that federal inspection has occurred and to identify the packer by number. This stamping is done with a safe yellow or red vegetable dye on each wholesale cut. Since this mark is relatively small, it is not unusual to buy a retail cut that has been inspected, but which has no identifying mark. Poultry is tagged with the inspection stamp because it is impractical to attempt to stamp the skin.

The one hazardous organism that may occur in meat, but is not revealed by inspection is *Trichinella spiralis*. This is a worm that infects less than

FIGURE 9.2 A federal inspector examines carcasses to assure the wholesomeness and safety of the meat. The round stamp is placed at selected intervals so that primal cut will bear the stamp.

FIGURE 9.3 This stamp on a primal cut indicates that inspection has been conducted by federal inspectors.

0.2 percent of the hogs raised on grain, and very few of those who are infected present a hazard to humans. Since hogs fed on uncooked garbage present a much greater likelihood of carrying the trichinae, all states require garbage being fed to swine to be cooked so that the trichinae will be killed. Despite the greatly reduced likelihood of contracting trichinosis from pork (see Chapter 15), fresh pork and cured picnic shoulders should be heated to an internal temperature of 77°C (170°F), and heat-cured hams (labeled "cook before eating") should be heated to 71°C (160°F) to be certain the trichinae that might be present are dead. On a commercial basis, trichinae also may be killed by holding frozen meats at temperatures no higher than −15°C (5°F) for 20 days, processing to 58°C (137°F), or curing in a large amount of salt for 20 to 25 days under controlled temperatures.

DEFINITION OF MEATS

Various terms are used to designate a particular type of animal. Veal is the meat from cattle slaughtered 3 to 14 weeks after birth. The practice of feeding the young on cow's milk has led to the advertising of veal as milk-fed veal in some instances. From 14 to 52 weeks the slaughtered animal is classed as a calf. This type of meat is beyond the stage for good veal, but has not achieved the characteristics of beef. Because there is less expense involved in raising cattle to this stage than to maturity, occasionally calves are slaughtered and marketed as baby beef or calf. Calf liver is preferred by many people over beef liver because of the milder flavor, but the other portions of a calf are less desirable than mature fattened beef because of the weak flavor and high proportion of connective tissue to muscle. The term "beef" is applied to cattle over one year old. The classes of beef are defined according to the sex, age, and sex condition of the animal as follows.

1. Steer: male castrated at a very young age.
2. Heifer: female that has never borne a calf.
3. Cow: female that has borne a calf.
4. Bull: male.
5. Stag: male castrated after reaching maturity.

Swine are usually marketed between the ages of 5 and 12 months before the amount of fat becomes excessive. The meat is sold, without sex distinction, as pork. Swine are still classified, however, in the livestock market.

1. Barrows: young males.
2. Gilts: young females.
3. Sows: females that have borne young.
4. Boars: mature uncastrated males.
5. Stags: mature castrated males.

Sheep, up to the age of a year, are marketed as lambs; when one year old, they are termed yearlings; and the older sheep are called mutton. As sheep age the delicate flavor of lamb slowly changes to the stronger flavor characteristic of mutton. Tenderness also decreases with age. With proper preparation, however, either lamb or mutton will be acceptable to most people. In the United States, lamb is generally preferred, whereas many citizens of countries in the United Kingdom prefer the more mature mutton.

GRADING

Since no law requires the grading of meat, packers may elect one of three options: (1) federal grading, (2) packer grading, or (3) no grading of meat. Federal graders are hired by many packers to classify the meat according to government specifications into the appropriate federal grade. Some packers prefer to have graders classify the carcasses according to the company's own grading system, whereas still others may elect the third alternative, that is, no grading. The chief value of grading for the consumer is that inexperienced shoppers have a guide to meat quality. The range of quality within a grade is evaluated by the more knowledgeable buyer, but grading is a definite aid to the novice.

Beef

Two primary factors determine the value of a beef carcass: the quality of the lean (palatability, tenderness, juiciness, and flavor) and the amount of salable meat. The former, that is the quality of the lean, is indicated on fed-

FIGURE 9.4 Federally graded meat is identified by a continuous marking of the carcass with the grade shield.

erally graded beef carcasses by a shield-shaped stamp stating USDA Choice (or other appropriate grade). The yield factor is indicated by a USDA yield stamp bearing the number indicating the yield grade. For steers and heifers there are eight quality grades: USDA Prime, Choice, Good, Standard, Commercial, Utility, Cutter, and Canner. The five yield grades are simply numbered, with number one representing the highest yield.

Quality is evaluated on the basis of the firmness of the lean, the amount of marbling, and the maturity of the animal. Marbling is the fat that is deposited in flecks throughout the muscle. In beef, marbling may range from abundant to almost nonexistent. This deposition occurs as the animal matures and, therefore, is present in only small amounts in immature animals, even though the meat may be of high quality in every other respect. In mature beef, marbling is considered to be a sign of high quality. The conformation of the animal also is considered in establishing a grade for quality. Particular attention is given to the muscling in the round and loin regions, since these portions are highly valued. A carcass rating high in conformation is moderately plump and thickly muscled, that is, the muscles are thick in relation to the length and depth of the carcass.

Maturity is judged by examining the bones of the animal. The appearance of both cartilage and bone are carefully defined in grade requirements established by the United States Department of Agriculture. Progressive

FIGURE 9.5   The shield used to designate the quality of meat, according to United States Department of Agriculture standards. Prime is the top grade for beef.

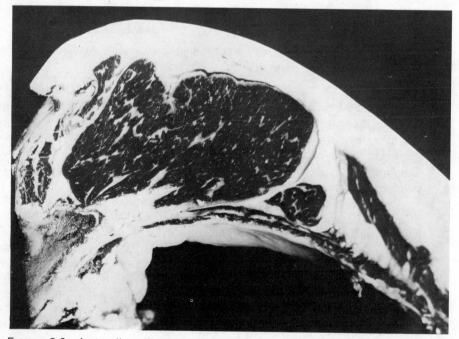

FIGURE 9.6   A standing rib roast bearing the grade of USDA prime. Note the abundance of marbling in this grade of beef.

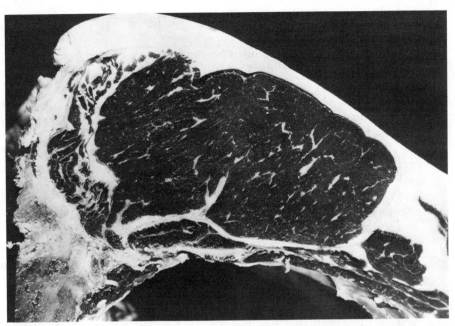

FIGURE 9.7   Note the difference in fat deposition both around and within the muscle of this USDA choice beef in comparison with USDA prime beef (Figure 9.6)

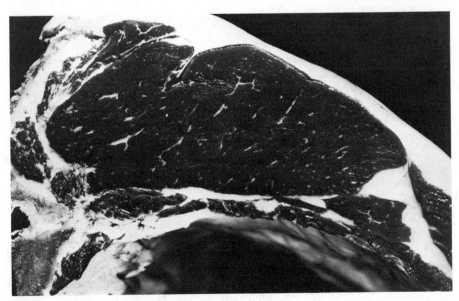

FIGURE 9.8   USDA good beef has a high ratio of meat in proportion to waste because of the lesser amount of fat, a fact of interest to the thrifty and the weight conscious.

changes in degree of ossification and shape of these structural elements occur as the animal matures. Prime, choice, good, and standard grades can be assigned only to the younger beef cattle; commercial grade is given only to cattle that are too mature to qualify for the first four grades; utility, cutter, and canner grades may include animals of all ages.

Textural changes from fine to coarse accompany the maturation of the animal. Finer grain generally is preferred in meats and therefore will receive a higher rating than coarse-textured meat from a mature animal.

Color of beef and lamb changes with increasing maturation. Beef progresses from a light red to a dark red; lamb also darkens as the animal matures, and will actually be a darker color than beef.

"Dark cutting beef" (see the section on post-mortem changes in this chapter), although quite palatable, is generally less acceptable to the consumer and therefore is classified one grade below the expected rating.

Although there are several grades of beef, only the upper ones are commonly found in the grocery stores. The top grade, prime, constitutes only a small fraction of the total beef production and, since restaurants buy most of this grade, little is available in retail stores. Choice grade, usually available in markets, embraces a rather wide range of quality from meat that is almost prime to that which is just slightly better than good grade. Good grade is commonly available. The lower grades—standard, commercial, and utility—are not found in most retail stores. These, combined with cutter and canner, are used for processed meats.

When purchasing meat, it is important to evaluate the range of meat within a grade. The knowledgeable consumer will be able to select the better meat from a grade and thus get slightly higher quality for the money than will someone who selects a cut at random.

The yield grade is determined by assessing the (1) thickness of the fat over the ribeye, (2) the ribeye area, (3) the quantity of kidney, pelvic, and heart fat, and (4) the carcass weight. Excessively fat or thinly muscled carcasses are relegated to the lowest grade, grade 5. The criteria for Yield Grade 1 provide that a carcass thus graded will yield 79.8 percent or more in retail cuts, in contrast to Yield Grade 5 with its predicted yield of 65.9 percent or less.

Pork

The grading of pork basically is on the basis of acceptable and unacceptable. The acceptable pork is graded from the high U. S. No. 1 to U. S. No. 4. These grades actually are an indication of yield rather than of quality, and they are provided only to indicate carcass yield differences for the four major lean cuts. The consumer will not be able to find any grade designation on pork in the retail store. Pork that is rated as unacceptable receives a grade designation of U. S. Utility. Soft and watery pork will receive this grade rating.

Lamb

The quality of lamb varies far more than does pork despite the fact that both species generally are marketed at quite a young age. Lamb has five quality grades (USDA Prime, Choice, Good, Utility, and Cull); yearling mutton and mutton have their top grade designated as USDA Choice, with the lower grades corresponding to those used for lamb. These grade designations are imprinted on the carcass from a roller inked with an edible red vegetable dye, just as it is on beef and veal. Yield grades for lamb range from USDA Yield Grades 1 to 5, with the chief difference being determined by the amount of fat covering the outside of the carcass and the fat deposited inside. The USDA grades for meats are summarized in Table 9.1.

SELECTION OF MEAT

Since such a significant fraction of the food dollar is spent on meat, it is important for the shopper to be able to select meat wisely. Selection of a meat cut should be made on the basis of a comparison of the price per pound of a tender versus a less tender cut, use for which it is intended, time available for preparation, quality of a particular cut as compared with other similar pieces of meat available at the meat counter, and ratio of meat to bone.

Meats are classified into tender and less tender cuts, the tender cuts generally being more expensive than those that are less tender. The classi-

Table 9.1. USDA Grades for Beef, Veal, Lamb, and Pork

Beef		Veal	Lamb	Pork
Quality	Cutability			
Prime	1	Prime	Prime	U. S. No. 1
Choice	2	Choice	Choice	U. S. No. 2
Good	3	Good	Good	U. S. No. 3
Standard	4	Standard	Utility	U. S. No. 4
Commercial	5	Utility	Cull	Utility
Utility		Cull		
Cutter				
Canner				

fication of a particular cut of meat depends on the grade, the position on the animal, and the type of meat. Some cuts of meat, for instance a beef rump roast, may be considered as tender from a very high-quality animal and less tender from a lower-grade animal. Cuts from portions of the carcass that are exercised little will be more tender than those from muscles that are used extensively by the animal. The tenderloin muscle receives almost no exercise and is much more tender than the shoulder, even when the tenderloin is from an animal of low quality. Cuts from the shoulder, rump, and belly are classified as less tender as compared with the tender rib and loin sections.

Veal, although young, is generally only moderately tender because of the relatively high ratio of connective tissue to muscle. Deposition of fat within the muscle of veal is minimal. Lamb generally is tender, with the exception of the neck, shoulder, breast, and shank. Pork usually is classified as tender, regardless of the cut.

A woman who has the dual role of working outside the home and homemaking will frequently be limited for time in the kitchen. As a result she may need to buy meats that require little preparation time, but which cost more than some other cuts. If she has an oven that may be turned on by a clock, the selection of meat available to suit her needs is immediately broadened. With this device it is possible for her to buy meats that must be started long before the meal will be served. She must be careful, however, not to leave meat in the oven long enough to cause spoilage. The problem is magnified in a gas oven because of the heat created by the pilot light.

Meat that has been in the grocer's case long enough to discolor only slightly is safe if consumed that day, and frequently can be purchased at a reduced price. The wise shopper will also select carefully from the cuts available at the regular price, for there will be quality differences among cuts from different carcasses even though they may be the same grade.

By careful examination one can select packages of meat with a minimum of bone in proportion to the meat. Usually types of cuts that are characteristically high in bone are less expensive than those containing little bone.

Once the type of meat has been selected, the decision on the amount to buy must be made. Boneless meat purchases are suitably based on the value of one-fourth pound of meat per serving. Amounts to buy vary for bone-in cuts in proportion to the amount of bone. If a cut contains a small amount of bone, one-third pound per serving will be adequate; for an average amount of bone, one-half pound of uncooked meat per serving is generous; for very bony meats such as spare ribs or duck, however, approximately three-fourths to one pound per serving is appropriate.

Identification of Cuts

To identify a cut of meat, the animal source and the particular cut of meat should be ascertained. Beef cuts are the largest, followed in decreasing

FIGURE 9.9   Sides of beef are cut into front and hind quarters between the twelfth and thirteenth ribs to make the carcasses easier to handle.

size by veal, pork, and lamb. The color of the muscle varies: beef is red, veal is a light pink, pork is a grayed pink, and lamb is a dark red. Fat also is a means of identification. Pork fat is soft and slightly pink, lamb fat is very hard, veal has very little fat, and beef fat is hard and white to yellowish white.

Primal cuts of beef are made by first cutting the carcass into halves (sides) lengthwise and then making a cut between the twelfth and thirteenth rib to yield the fore and hind quarters. These quarters are divided into the primal cuts (Figures 9.10–9.13). In turn, these primal cuts are divided by retailers into the various cuts available to the consumer. Veal, pork, and lamb are cut into slightly different wholesale cuts because their smaller size enables butchers to easily handle a larger fraction of the carcass in one piece. The retail cuts for the various animals are shown in Figures 9.10–9.13. The identification of meat cuts has been a matter of growing consumer concern because of the common practice of generating names for cuts seemingly to tempt the consumer. A cut in New York might have a totally different name from that of the same cut in Oregon. Even within a narrow geographic range,

BEEF CHART

RETAIL CUTS OF BEEF — WHERE THEY COME FROM AND HOW TO COOK THEM

CHUCK
Braise. Cook in Liquid

② Boneless Chuck Roll

③④ Chuck Short Ribs

② Blade
Pot-roast or Steak

③ Arm
Pot-roast or Steak

③ Boneless Shoulder
Pot-roast or Steak

④ Boston Cut

① Beef for Stew

① Ground Beef**

RIB
Roast, Broil, Panbroil, Pantry

② Standing Rib Roast

② Rib Steak

② Rib Steak, Boneless

② Rib Eye (Delmonico) Roast or Steak

SHORT LOIN
Roast, Broil, Panbroil, Pantry

① Club Steak

② T-Bone Steak

③ Porterhouse Steak

①②③ Top Loin Steak

②③ Tenderloin (Filet Mignon) Steak or Roast (also from Sirloin 1a)

SIRLOIN
Roast, Broil, Panbroil, Pantry

① Pin Bone Sirloin Steak

② Flat Bone Sirloin Steak

③ Wedge Bone Sirloin Steak

①②③ Boneless Sirloin Steak

ROUND
Braise, Cook in Liquid

④ Heel of Round

① Rolled Rump*

③ Cube Steak*

** Ground Beef**

③ Round Steak

③ Top Round Steak*

③ Bottom Round Steak or Pot-roast

③ Eye of Round*

TIP
Braise

④② Sirloin Tip*

④② Tip Steak*   ④② Sirloin Tip Kabobs*

FLANK
Braise, Cook in Liquid

① Flank Steak*

① Flank Steak Fillets*

Ground Beef**

Beef Patties**

SHORT PLATE
Braise, Cook in Liquid

①② Skirt Steak Fillets*

① Short Ribs

①② Beef for Stew (also from other cuts)   Ground Beef**

BRISKET
Braise, Cook in Liquid

③ Fresh Brisket

③ Corned Brisket

FORE SHANK
Braise, Cook in Liquid

① Shank Cross Cuts

② Beef for Stew (also from other cuts)

*May be Roasted, Broiled, Panbroiled or Panfried from high quality beef.
**May be Roasted, (Baked), Broiled, Panbroiled or Panfried.

This chart approved by
National Live Stock and Meat Board

FIGURE 9.10   Primal and retail beef cuts.

VEAL CHART

RETAIL CUTS OF VEAL — WHERE THEY COME FROM AND HOW TO COOK THEM

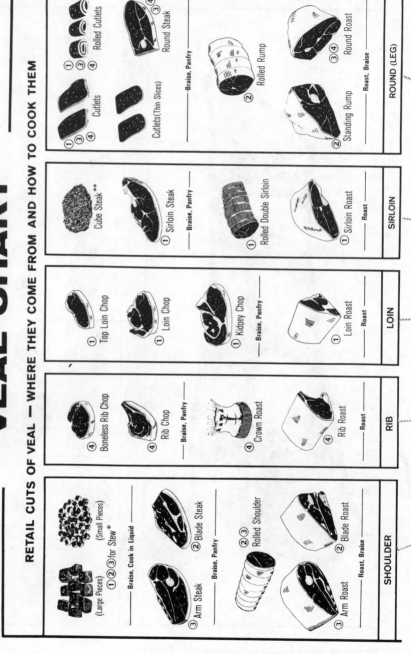

SHOULDER

(Large Pieces) (Small Pieces)
① ② ③ for Stew *
— Braise, Cook in Liquid —

② Blade Steak
③ Arm Steak
— Braise, Panfry —

② ③ Rolled Shoulder

② Blade Roast
③ Arm Roast
— Roast, Braise —

RIB

④ Boneless Rib Chop
④ Rib Chop
— Braise, Panfry —

④ Crown Roast

④ Rib Roast
— Roast —

LOIN

① Top Loin Chop
① Loin Chop
① Kidney Chop
— Braise, Panfry —

① Loin Roast
— Roast —

SIRLOIN

① Cube Steak **
① Sirloin. Steak
— Braise, Panfry —

① Rolled Double Sirloin

① Sirloin Roast
— Roast —

ROUND (LEG)

① ③ ④ Cutlets
① ③ ④ Rolled Cutlets
④ Cutlets(Thin Slices)
③ ④ Round Steak
— Braise, Panfry —

② Rolled Rump
② Standing Rump
③ ④ Round Roast
— Roast, Braise —

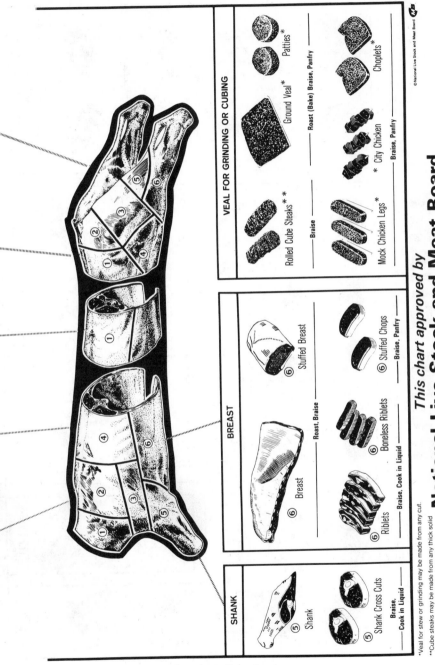

VEAL FOR GRINDING OR CUBING

Ground Veal*

Patties*

Roast (Bake) Braise, Panfry

Choplets*

Rolled Cube Steaks**

City Chicken*

Braise

Braise, Panfry

Mock Chicken Legs*

BREAST

Stuffed Breast

⑥ Stuffed Chops

Roast, Braise

Braise, Panfry

⑥ Breast

⑥ Boneless Riblets

⑥ Riblets

Braise, Cook in Liquid

This chart approved by

National Live Stock and Meat Board

SHANK

⑤ Shank

⑤ Shank Cross Cuts

Braise,
Cook in Liquid

*Veal for stew or grinding may be made from any cut.
**Cube steaks may be made from any thick solid
piece of boneless veal.

FIGURE 9.11   Primal and retail veal cuts.

PORK CHART

RETAIL CUTS OF PORK—WHERE THEY COME FROM AND HOW TO COOK THEM

LEG (FRESH OR SMOKED HAM)

1 ② ③ Rolled Leg (Fresh Ham) — Roast —
① ② ③ Sliced Cooked "Boiled" Ham — Heat or Serve Cold —
① ② Canned Ham
① Boneless Smoked Ham — Roast (Bake) —
② Center Smoked Ham Slice Broil, Panbroil, Panfry
① ② ③ Boneless Smoked Ham Slices — Broil, Panbroil, Panfry —
③ Smoked Ham, Shank Portion
① ② Smoked Ham, Sirloin (Butt) Portion — Roast (Bake), Cook in Liquid

LOIN

① Blade Chop
② Rib Chop
② Loin Chop
② ③ Butterfly Chop — Braise, Broil, Panbroil, Panfry —
② Top Loin Chop
③ Sirloin Chop
③ Sirloin Cutlet
① Porklet* (Cube Steak)
① Country Ribs — Roast (Bake), Braise, Cook in Liquid —
① ② ③ Back Ribs — Braise, Cook in Liquid
② Smoked Loin Chop — Roast (Bake), Broil, Panbroil, Panfry —
① ② ③ Canadian-Style Bacon — Roast (Bake), Braise, Panfry —
① ② ③ Rolled Loin
① ② ③ Rolled Double Loin — Roast —
② ③ ④ Tenderloin — Roast (Bake), Braise, Panfry —
① Blade Loin
② Center Loin — Roast —
③ Sirloin

BOSTON SHOULDER

② Porklet* (Cube Steak) — Braise, Panfry —
② Blade Steak — Braise, Panfry —
Pork Cubes — Braise, Cook in Liquid, Broil —
② Smoked Shoulder Roll — Roast (Bake), Cook in Liquid
② Rolled Boston Roast
② Boston Roast — Roast —

① CLEAR PLATE ④ FAT BACK

④ Fat Back — Panfry, Cook in Liquid —
① ④ Lard — Pastry, Cookies, Quick Breads, Cakes, Frying

① SPARERIBS   ② BACON (SIDE PORK)

② Slab Bacon

② Sliced Bacon
— Bake, Broil, Panbroil, Panfry —

① Spareribs

① Salt Pork
Bake, Broil, Panbroil, — Panfry, Cook in Liquid

PICNIC SHOULDER

Ground Pork*
— Roast (Bake), Panbroil, Panfry

③ Arm Roast
———— Roast ————

③ Arm Steak
— Braise, Panfry —

Link

Sausage*
— Panfry, Braise, Bake —

Roll

④ Smoked Picnic
③ ④ — Roast (Bake), Cook in Liquid —

② ③ Neck Bones
——— Cook in Liquid ———

④ Fresh Picnic
——— Roast ———

Smoked Hock

Fresh Hock
③ — Braise, Cook in Liquid —

This chart approved by

National Live Stock and Meat Board

National Live Stock and Meat Board

Printed in U.S.A.

JOWL

① Bacon Square
Cook in Liquid, Broil, — Panbroil, Panfry —

① Pig's Feet
— Cook in Liquid, Braise —

*May be made from Boston Shoulder, Picnic Shoulder, Loin or Leg.

FIGURE 9.12   Primal and retail pork cuts.

LAMB CHART

RETAIL CUTS OF LAMB — WHERE THEY COME FROM AND HOW TO COOK THEM

SHOULDER

② Saratoga Chops

② Blade Chop

③ Arm Chop

—Broil, Panbroil, Panfry—

Cubes for Kabobs***

—— Broil ——

②③ Rolled Shoulder

②③ Cushion Shoulder

②③ Square Shoulder

—— Roast ——

SHOULDER

NECK

① Neck Slices

—— Braise ——

NECK

RIB

① Frenched Rib Chops

① Rib Chops

—Broil, Panbroil, Panfry—

① Crown Roast

① Rib Roast

—— Roast ——

RIB

LOIN

① Loin Chops

① English Chop

—Broil, Panbroil, Panfry—

① Rolled Double Loin

① Loin Roast

—— Roast ——

LOIN

SIRLOIN

① Sirloin Chop

—Broil, Panbroil, Panfry—

① Rolled Double Sirloin

① Sirloin Roast

—— Roast ——

SIRLOIN

LEG

②③ Leg Chop (Steak)

—Broil, Panbroil, Panfry—

②③ Center Leg

②③④ American Leg

③④ Shank Half of Leg

②③④ Leg, Sirloin off

①②④ Combination Leg

①②③④ Rolled Leg

①② Sirloin Half of Leg

①②③④ Leg, Sirloin on

—— Roast ——

LEG

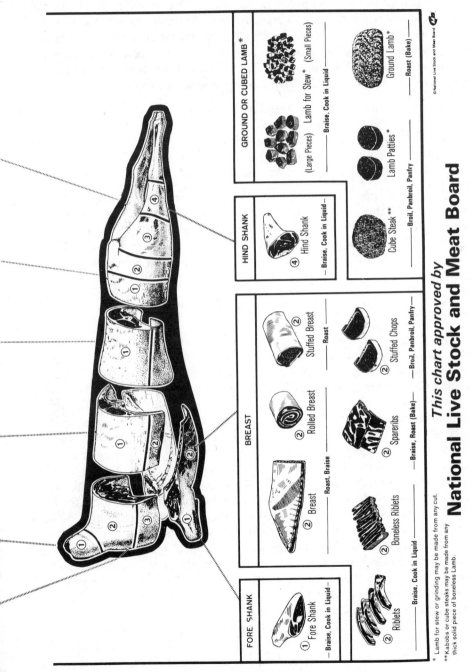

FIGURE 9.13   Primal and retail lamb cuts.

meat nomenclature has been confusing. In 1972 and 1973 the National Live Stock and Meat Board developed a list of primal and retail cuts (Appendix E) for use in labeling retail cuts of meat. By labeling cuts of meat according to the primal designation, consumers across the country can have a reasonable understanding of the portion of the carcass from which the cut originated. The primal cuts the Board designated were as follows:

Beef	Chuck, rib, loin, tenderloin, sirloin, round, tip, shank, brisket, plate, and flank
Pork	Shoulder, loin, leg, side (belly)
Lamb	Shoulder, rib, loin, leg, sirloin, breast, shank
Veal	Shoulder, rib, loin, leg, sirloin, breast, shank

Since beef, pork, lamb, and veal all have comparable bone structure, much can be determined about a cut of meat simply by identifying the bone(s). Of course, there are many different bones in the carcass, but seven basic bone shapes can serve as a guide to the location of a specific cut. These bones are identified in Table 9.2 by the name, shape, and cuts in which they are found.

Storage

Meat, poultry, and fish are highly perishable food items requiring refrigeration at all time. The period of time between removal from the meat counter and storage in the refrigerator at home should be kept to an absolute minimum to reduce microbiological growth. When meat is stored at home, the store's plastic wrap should be removed or, at least, loosened to allow some air to enter during storage. A loose covering is ample to keep the surface from becoming excessively dry in the refrigerator. In fact, brief storage without a cover is appropriate. The slight drying of the surface that does occur serves as a deterrent to microbiological growth. Meats that come in a ready-to-eat form (cured, smoked, cold cuts) prepackaged from the meat processor can be left unopened in their original packages. Although the can should not be opened for storage, canned hams require refrigerator storage unless package directions indicate that this is not required.

The coldest part of the refrigerator is the ideal place for storing fresh meats. Some refrigerators have a special meat compartment set aside in the appropriate section. The temperature in this part of the refrigerator should be maintained between 2 and 4°C (35 and 40°F) for optimum storage. Freezer storage at temperatures no warmer than −18°C (0°F) is a very satisfactory way of prolonging the storage period for meats. Meats to be used more than a couple of days after purchase may be placed in the ice cube or freezing section of the refrigerator to increase storage life. However, the ice cube section does not maintain a sufficiently cold environment for regular frozen

Table 9.2. Identification of Retail Cuts by Bone Shape[a]

Name	Bone Shape	Cuts
Arm bone		Shoulder, arm cuts
Blade bone	(Near neck)　(Center)　(Near rib)	Shoulder blade cuts
Back bone and rib bone		Rib cuts
Back bone (T-bone)		Short loin cuts
Hip bone	(Pin bone) (Flat bone)[b] (Wedge bone)[c]	Hip (sirloin) cuts
Leg or round bone		Leg or round cuts
Breast and rib bones		Breast or brisket cuts

[a]Adapted from *Lessons on Meat*. National Live Stock and Meat Board. Chicago, Ill. 2nd ed. 1968. Page 35.
[b]Formerly part of "double bone" but today the back bone is usually removed leaving only the "flat bone" (sometimes called "pin bone") in the sirloin steak.
[c]Wedge bone, which is near the round, may be wedge shaped on one side of sirloin steak while on the other side the same bone may be round.

storage; meat storage in this section should be limited to approximately one week. The storage times suggested for maintaining meat at optimum quality are indicated in Table 9.3.

PREPARATION METHODS

The two basic types of meat preparation are moist and dry heat. The selection of the procedure to use for a meat cut is based on its classification as a tender or a less tender cut. Less tender cuts become more tender when prepared by moist heat since moist-heat methods provide the proper conditions for converting collagen to gelatin. Moist-heat methods for meats are braising and boiling or stewing. Tender cuts do not require additional tenderizing, hence dry heat is appropriate. Roasting, broiling, pan broiling, pan frying, and deep-fat frying are dry-heat methods.

Table 9.3. Storage Guide for Fresh, Processed, and Cooked Meats[a]

Product	Storage Period (To Maintain Its Quality)	
	Refrigerator 35° to 40° F (Days)	Freezer 0° F (Months)
Fresh Meats		
Roasts (beef and lamb)	3– 5	8–12
Roasts (pork and veal)	3– 5	4– 8
Steaks (beef)	3– 5	8–12
Chops (lamb and pork)	3– 5	3– 4
Ground and stew meats	1– 2	2– 3
Variety meats	1– 2	3– 4
Sausage (pork)	1– 2	1– 2
Processed Meats		
Bacon	7	1
Frankfurters	7	½
Ham (whole)	7	1– 2
Ham (half)	3– 5	1– 2
Ham (slices)	3	1– 2
Luncheon meats	3– 5	Freezing not recommended
Sausage (smoked)	7	
Sausage (dry and semidry)	14–21	
Cooked Meats		
Cooked meats and meat dishes	1– 2	2– 3
Gravy and meat broth	1– 2	2– 3

[a]Adapted from *Meat and Poultry Care Tips for You.* Home and Garden Bulletin No. 174. U. S. Department of Agriculture, Washington, D. C. 1970. Page 7.

After the method of preparation is selected, an appropriate oven or fat temperature must be chosen. Studies have illustrated that a lower oven temperature (149–177°C or 300–350°F), as contrasted with a higher temperature (219–232°C or 425–450°F), results in less drip loss, less shrinkage, increased juiciness, and more uniform color throughout a cut. Slightly higher temperatures are appropriate for deep-fat frying to avoid excessive fat absorption.

Testing for doneness is certainly vital in meat preparation. Tender cuts of meat are most accurately tested by the use of a meat thermometer. Recommended final temperatures in the center of the cut of beef are: rare,

60°C (140°F); medium, 71°C (160°F); and well done, 77°C (170°F). Lamb is medium at 79°C (175°F) and well done at 82°C (180°F). Fresh pork is heated to well done (77°C or 170°F) to ensure safety from *Trichinella spiralis*. Cured pork is required by federal law to be treated in a manner that will destroy this organism, hence all government-inspected ham should be safe. Tenderized hams are partially heated and ready-to-eat hams are heated to doneness during processing. All hams may be heated to a temperature palatable to the consumer, but an internal temperature of 74–77°C (165–170°F) is suggested for hams that have not been heated during processing.

Timetables are helpful as a guide in planning how long a piece of meat will require to reach the desired degree of doneness. Variations in time due to differences in oven temperature, amount of bone, amount of fat, and amount of aging, however, make the use of a thermometer mandatory for optimum palatability of the tender cuts. (See Tables 9.4 to 9.8.)

Moist-heat methods will produce well-done meats in every instance. Less tender cuts are done when a fork may be inserted and removed from the meat easily. It is not necessary to use a thermometer in these cuts.

FIGURE 9.14   Crown roast is a specially cut rib roast that may be prepared from either pork or lamb. This tender cut is roasted, a dry-heat cooking method.

Table 9.4. Timetable for Roasting[a]

Cut	Approximate Weight (kg[b])	Oven Temperature (°C[c])	Interior Temperature When Removed from Oven (°C[c])		Approximate Cooking Time (min/kg[d])
Beef					
Standing rib	2.7–3.6 (6–8)	150–160 (300–325)	60	rare (140)	51–55 (23–25)
			71	medium (160)	60–66 (27–30)
			77	well (170)	70–77 (32–35)
	1.8–2.7 (4–6)	150–160 (300–325)	60	rare (140)	57–70 (26–32)
			71	medium (160)	75–84 (34–38)
			77	well (170)	88–92 (40–42)
Rolled rib	2.3–3.2 (5–7)	150–160 (300–325)	60	rare (140)	71 (32)
			71	medium (160)	84 (38)
			77	well (170)	106 (48)
Rib eye	1.8–2.7 (4–6)	175 (350)	60	rare (140)	40–44 (18–20)
			71	medium (160)	44–49 (20–22)
			77	well (170)	49–53 (22–24)
Tenderloin, whole	1.8–2.7 (4–6)	220 (425)	60	rare (140)	45–60 total
Tenderloin,	0.9–1.4	220 (425)	60	rare (140)	45–50 total
Rolled rump (high quality)	1.8–2.7 (4–6)	150–160 (300–325)	66–77	(150–170)	55–66 (25–30)
Sirloin tip (high quality)	1.6–1.8 (3-1/2–4)	150–160 (300–325)	66–77	(150–170)	77–88 (35–40)
Veal					
Leg	2.3–3.6 (5–8)	150–160 (300–325)	77	(170)	55–77 (25–35)
Loin	1.8–2.7 (4–6)	150–160 (300–325)	77	(170)	66–77 · (30–35)
Rib (rack)	1.4–2.3 (3–5)	150–160 (300–325)	77	(170)	77–88 (35–40)
Rolled shoulder	1.8–2.7 (4–6)	150–160 (300–325)	77	(170)	88–99 (40–45)

Table 9.4 continued

Cut	Approximate Weight (kg[b])	Oven Temperature (°C[c])	Interior Temperature When Removed from Oven (°C[c])	Approximate Cooking Time (min/kg[d])
Pork, fresh				
Loin				
Center	1.4–2.3 *(5–8)*	160–175 *(325–350)*	77 *(170)*	66–77 *(30–35)*
Half	2.3–3.2 *(5–7)*	160–175 *(325–350)*	77 *(170)*	77–88 *(35–40)*
Blade loin or sirloin	1.4–1.8 *(3–4)*	160–175 *(325–350)*	77 *(170)*	88–99 *(40–45)*
Roll	1.4–2.3 *(3–5)*	160–175 *(325–350)*	77 *(170)*	77–99 *(35–45)*
Picnic shoulder	2.3–3.6 *(5–8)*	160–175 *(325–350)*	77 *(170)*	66–77 *(30–35)*
Rolled	1.4–2.3 *(3–5)*	160–175 *(325–350)*	77 *(170)*	88–99 *(40–45)*
Cushion style	1.4–2.3 *(3–5)*	160–175 *(325–350)*	77 *(170)*	77–88 *(35–40)*
Boston shoulder	1.8–2.7 *(4–6)*	160–175 *(325–350)*	77 *(170)*	99–110 *(45–50)*
Leg (fresh ham)				
Whole (bone in)	4.5–6.4 *(10–14)*	160–175 *(325–350)*	77 *(170)*	55–66 *(25–30)*
Whole (boneless)	3.2–4.5 *(7–10)*	160–175 *(325–350)*	77 *(170)*	77–88 *(35–40)*
Half (bone in)	2.3–3.2 *(5–7)*	160–175 *(325–350)*	77 *(170)*	88–99 *(40–45)*
Pork, smoked				
Ham (cook before eating)				
Whole	4.5–6.4 *(10–14)*	150–160 *(300–325)*	71 *(160)*	40–44 *(18–20)*
Half	2.3–3.2 *(5–7)*	150–160 *(300–325)*	71 *(160)*	49–55 *(22–25)*
Shank or butt portion	1.4–1.8 *(3–4)*	150–160 *(300–325)*	71 *(160)*	77–88 *(35–40)*
Ham (fully cooked)				
Whole	4.5–6.4 *(10–14)*	160 *(325)*	54 *(130)*	33 *(15)*
Half	2.3–3.2 *(5–7)*	160 *(325)*	54 *(130)*	40–53 *(18–24)*
Picnic shoulder	2.3–3.6 *(5–8)*	150–160 *(300–325)*	71 *(160)*	77 *(35)*
Shoulder roll	0.9–1.4 *(2–3)*	150–160 *(300–325)*	71 *(160)*	77–88 *(35–40)*
Canadian style bacon	0.9–1.8 *(2–4)*	150–160 *(300–325)*	71 *(160)*	77–88 *(35–40)*

Table 9.4 continued

Cut	Approximate Weight (kg[b])	Oven Temperature (°C[c])	Interior Temperature When Removed from Oven (°C[c])	Approximate Cooking Time (min/kg[d])
Lamb				
Leg	2.3–3.6 *(5–8)*	150–160 *(300–325)*	79–82 *(175–180)*	66–77 *(30–35)*
Shoulder	1.8–2.7 *(4–6)*	150–160 *(300–325)*	79–82 *(175–180)*	66–77 *(30–35)*
Rolled	1.4–2.3 *(3–5)*	150–160 *(300–325)*	79–82 *(175–180)*	88–99 *(40–45)*
Cushion	1.4–2.3 *(3–5)*	150–160 *(300–325)*	79–82 *(175–180)*	66-77 *(30–35)*

[a]Adapted from *Lessons on Meat*. National Live Stock and Meat Board. Chicago. 2nd ed. 1968. Page 67.
[b]Figures in italics are weight in pounds.
[c]Figures in italics are for temperature in Fahrenheit degrees.
[d]Figures in italics are minutes per pound.

Table 9.5. Timetable for Broiling[a]

Cut	Weight (kg[b])	Approximate Total Cooking Time in Minutes	
		Rare	Medium
Beef			
Chuck steak (high quality)			
1 in.	0.7–1.1 *(1.5–2.5)*	24	30
1-1/2 in.	0.9–1.8 *(2.0–4.0)*	40	45
Rib steak			
1 in.	0.4–0.7 *(1.0–1.5)*	15	20
1-1/2 in.	0.7–0.9 *(1.5–2.0)*	25	30
2 in.	0.9–1.1 *(2.0–2.5)*	35	45
Rib eye steak			
1 in.	0.2 *(0.5)*	15	20
1-1/2 in.	0.3 *(0.7)*	25	30
2 in.	0.4 *(1.0)*	35	45
Club steak			
1 in.	0.4–0.7 *(1.0–1.5)*	15	20
1-1/2 in.	0.7–0.9 *(1.5–2.0)*	25	30
2 in.	0.9–1.1 *(2.0–2.5)*	35	45
Sirloin steak			
1 in.	0.7–1.4 *(1.5–3.0)*	20	25
1-1/2 in.	1.0–1.8 *(2.2–4.0)*	30	35
2 in.	1.4–2.3 *(3.0–5.0)*	40	45

Table 9.5 continued

Cut	Weight (kg[b])	Approximate Total Cooking Time in Minutes	
		Rare	Medium
Porterhouse steak			
1 in.	0.6–0.9 *(1.2–2.0)*	20	25
1-1/2 in.	0.9–1.4 *(2.0–3.0)*	30	35
2 in.	1.4–2.3 *(3.0–5.0)*	40	45
Ground beef patties			
1 in. thick × 3 in.	0.1 *(0.2)*	15	25
Pork—smoked			
Ham slice			
1/2 in.	0.3–0.4 *(0.7–1.0)*	Always well	10–12
1 in.	0.7–0.9 *(1.5–2.0)*	done	16–20
Canadian style bacon			
1/4 in. slices			6– 8
1/2 in. slices			8–10
Bacon			4– 5
Pork—fresh			
Rib or loin chop	3/4–1 in.	Always cooked	20–25
Shoulder steaks	1/2–3/4 in.	well done	20–22
Lamb			
Shoulder chops			
1 in.	0.1–0.2 *(0.3–0.5)*	Not usually	12
1-1/2 in.	0.2–0.3 *(0.5–0.7)*	served rare	18
2 in.	0.3–0.4 *(0.7–1.0)*		22
Rib chops			
1 in.	0.1–0.2 *(0.2–0.3)*		12
1-1/2 in.	0.1–0.2 *(0.2–0.4)*		18
2 in.	0.1–0.3 *(0.2–0.7)*		22
Loin chops			
1 in.	0.1–0.2 *(0.2–0.5)*		12
1-1/2 in.	0.2–0.3 *(0.4–0.7)*		18
2 in.	0.2–0.4 *(0.5–0.9)*		22
Ground lamb patties			
1 in. × 3 in.	0.1 *(0.2)*		18

[a]Adapted from *Lessons on Meat*. National Live Stock and Meat Board. Chicago, Ill. 2nd ed. 1968. Page 68.
[b]Figures in italics are weight in pounds.

Table 9.6. Timetable for Braising[a]

Cut	Average Weight (kg[b]) or Thickness (in.)	Approximate Total Cooking Time (hr)
Beef		
Pot roast	1.4–2.3 *(3–5)*	3–4
Swiss steak	1-1/2 to 2-1/2 in.	2–3
Fricassee	2-in. cubes	1-1/2–2-1/2
Beef birds	1/2 in. (×2 in. × 4 in.)	1-1/2–2-1/2
Short ribs	Pieces (2 in. × 2 in. × 4 in.)	1-1/2–2-1/2
Round steak	3/4 in.	1–1-1/2
Stuffed steak	1/2–3/4 in.	1-1/2
Pork		
Chops	3/4–1-1/2 in.	3/4–1
Spareribs	0.9–1.4 *(2–3)*	1-1/2
Tenderloin		
Whole	0.3–0.4 *(0.7–1)*	3/4–1
Fillets	1/2 in.	1/2
Shoulder steaks	3/4 in.	3/4–1
Lamb		
Breast, stuffed	0.9–1.4 *(2–3)*	1-1/2–2
Breast, rolled	0.7–0.9 *(1-1/2–2)*	1-1/2–2
Neck slices	3/4 in.	1
Shanks	0.3–0.4 *(0.7–1)*	1–1-1/2
Shoulder chops	3/4–1 in.	3/4–1
Veal		
Breast, stuffed	1.4–1.8 *(3–4)*	1-1/2–2-1/2
Breast, rolled	0.9–1.4 *(2–3)*	1-1/2–2-1/2
Veal birds	1/2 inch (×2 in. × 4 in.)	3/4–1
Chops	1/2–3/4 in.	3/4–1
Steaks or cutlet	1/2–3/4 in.	3/4–1
Shoulder chops	1/2–3/4 in.	3/4–1
Shoulder cubes	1–2 in.	3/4–1

[a]Adapted from *Lessons on Meat*. National Live Stock and Meat Board. Chicago, Ill. 2nd ed. 1968. Page 71.
[b]Figures in italics are weight in pounds.

Table 9.7. Timetable for Cooking in Liquid[a]

Cut	Average weight (kg[b])		Minutes per Kilogram[c]		Approximate Total Cooking Time (Hours)
Smoked ham (old style and country cured)					
Large	5.5–7.3	*(12–16)*	44	*(20)*	4–5.4
Small	4.5–5.5	*(10–12)*	55	*(25)*	4.1–5.0
Half	2.3–3.6	*(5– 8)*	66	*(30)*	2.5–4.0
Smoked ham (tendered)					
Shank or butt half	2.3–3.6	*(5– 8)*	44–55	*(20–25)*	1.7–3.3
Smoked picnic shoulder	2.3–3.6	*(5– 8)*	99	*(45)*	3.8–6.0
Fresh or corned beef	1.8–2.7	*(4– 6)*	88–110	*(40–50)*	2.6–5.0
Beef for stew					2.5–3.5
Veal for stew					2.0–3.0
Lamb for stew					1.5–2.0

[a]Adapted from *Lessons on Meat*. National Live Stock and Meat Board. Chicago, Ill. 2nd ed. 1968. Page 73.
[b]Figures in italics are weight in pounds.
[c]Figures in italics are minutes per pound.

Table 9.8. Timetable for Cooking Variety Meats[a]

Type	Broiled		Braised[b]		Cooked in Liquid	
	Total Time	Minutes	Minutes	Hours	Hours	Minutes
Liver						
Beef						
3–4 lb piece				2–2-1/2		
Sliced			20–25			
Veal (calf)						
Sliced		8–10				
Pork						
Whole (3–3-1/2 lb)				1-1/2–2		
Sliced			20–25			
Lamb						
Sliced		8–10				

Table 9.8 continued

Type	Broiled Total Time	Broiled Minutes	Braised[b] Minutes	Braised[b] Hours	Cooked in Liquid Hours	Cooked in Liquid Minutes
Kidney						
Beef					1–1-1/2	
Veal (calf)		10–12			3/4–1	
Pork		10–12			3/4–1	
Lamb		10–12			3/4–1	
Heart						
Beef						
Whole				3–4	3–4	
Sliced				1-1/2–2		
Veal (calf)						
Whole				2-1/2–3	2-1/2–3	
Pork				2-1/2–3	2-1/2–3	
Lamb				2-1/2–3	2-1/2–3	
Tongue						
Beef					3–4	
Veal (calf)					2–3	
Pork ⎱ Usually sold						
Lamb ⎰ ready-to-serve						
Tripe						
Beef		10–15[c]			1–1-1/2	
Sweetbreads						
Beef		10–15[c]	20–25			15–20
Veal (calf)		10–15[c]	20–25			15–20
Lamb		10–15[c]	20–25			15–20
Brains						
Beef		10–15[c]	20–25			15–20
Veal (calf)		10–15[c]	20–25			15–20
Pork		10–15[c]	20–25			15–20
Lamb		10–15[c]	20–25			15–20

[a]By permission of National Live Stock and Meat Board.
[b]On top of range or in a 300°F oven.
[c]Time required after precooking in water.

Dry-Heat Methods

Roasting. Today roasting is most commonly done by the constant-oven-temperature method. With the exception of bone-in rib roasts, an oven roast is placed uncovered on a rack in a shallow pan to keep the meat out of the drippings. The rib roast furnishes its own rack because of its bone structure so no additional rack is needed. The oven thermostat should be set at 149 or 163°C (300 or 325°F). The lower temperature is suggested for large roasts so that there will be an opportunity for more uniform heat penetration of the mass. In small roasts the heat does not need to diffuse as far and a somewhat hotter oven is satisfactory. These temperatures promote retention of juices and also ease oven-cleaning problems because less splattering and burning result as compared with using very high oven temperatures.

A thermometer should be inserted carefully in the center of the largest muscle so that the tip is not touching bone or resting in a layer of fat. Since flavorings will not penetrate very far into the meat, it is not necessary to salt the meat before roasting. The uncovered meat is roasted until the desired internal temperature is indicated on the meat thermometer. If desired, the meat may be basted during the roasting period. Oven roasts carve better if they are removed from the oven about 20 minutes before serving. Meat roasted in a hot oven has a greater temperature rise after removal than meat from a cooler oven. A large roast contains more residual heat than does a small roast removed from the oven at the same internal temperature and therefore has a greater temperature rise as the result of residual heat than

FIGURE 9.15 Rack of lamb or pork roast are carved by placing them flat on the carving board. Their dimensions do not allow them to rest on end, as is done with standing rib of beef (see Figure 9.1)

FIGURE 9.16 A butt half of a ham is roasted (baked) by dry heat and then is carved in this manner.

the small one. Ham, pork loin roast, crown roast of pork or lamb, standing rib of beef and very fine, choice rump are all well suited to roasting.

The other method of oven roasting requires use of a hot 260°C (500°F) oven to brown or sear the roast, after which the temperature is reduced to 150°C (300°F). This method apparently has no advantage but rather has the disadvantages of high drip and evaporative losses and greater fuel consumption. Consequently, this method is not commonly used.

Broiling. Broiling is the only preparation method that utilizes direct heat. In charcoal broiling the heat comes from below whereas in oven broiling the heat comes from above. Broiling is suited to tender meats that are at least one inch thick. Thinner cuts will be too dry if broiled. Ranges generally include specific directions for operating the broiler unit and also the rotisserie if one is included. Meat should be broiled on a specially designed pan that allows the fat to collect in a tray beneath the meat rack. Such an arrangement protects the fat from the intense broiler heat and results in cleaner broiling and a sharply reduced fire hazard.

Porterhouse, T-bone, club, and rib steaks of beef, ham slices, lamb chops, veal and lamb liver, sweetbreads, brains, and bacon are suited to broiling. Meat to be broiled should first be scored by making cuts just through the fat and connective tissue at intervals of about one inch and then placed so that the top surface of the meat is about three inches from the heating element. Scoring prevents curling of the cut, thereby promoting uniform heat penetration. When thickness of the meat permits, a thermometer should be used to determine more accurately the temperature of the meat. The meat should be turned when it is about half done and the exposed side is browned. Just before turning, salt should be sprinkled on the upper surface. The second side should then be broiled without turning until the desired final internal temperature is reached. Broiled meats are desired by many people because fat melts and drains from the meat constantly as it broils.

Unusual flavors can be obtained by marinating meats in some types of salad dressings or juices for at least an hour before broiling. This treatment also permits some hydrolysis of protein to occur and thus produces a small increase in tenderness.

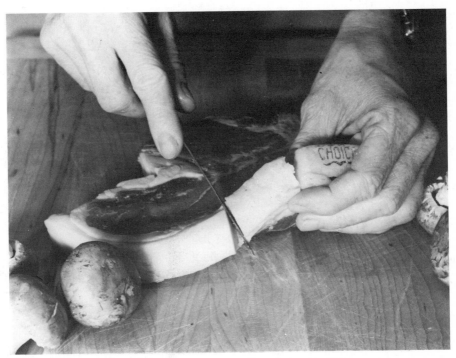

FIGURE 9.17   Scoring of steaks prevents curling during broiling.

Pan Broiling. Pan broiling also results in meat with a reduced amount of fat. Cuts suitable for broiling are equally well suited to pan broiling. In addition, tender cuts of meat less than one inch thick may suitably be pan broiled. Meat prepared by this method will seem more juicy than it will if it is broiled. Meat to be pan broiled is slowly heated in an ungreased heavy skillet. As fat collects, it is removed from the pan. At no time should fat be allowed to accumulate. The low temperature is sufficient to brown the meat. Pan-broiled meats should be turned occasionally to assure uniform heat penetration.

Pan Frying. Pan frying is another commonly used dry-heat method. In this method some fat is added to the skillet to keep the meat from sticking. In addition, as the meat fries, the fat is allowed to accumulate in the pan. As with pan broiling, it may be necessary to turn the meat occasionally to develop an even color on the meat, but turning should be kept to a minimum. Careful control of the burner temperature is necessary in both pan broiling and pan frying. Meat quickly develops a burned flavor and dryness if the temperature is too high. High temperatures break the fat to a product called acrolein which not only impairs the flavor of the meat, but also causes a smarting of the eyes.

FIGURE 9.18   Porterhouse steak is carved so that each diner receives part of the loin and part of the tenderloin. Note the back (T-) bone.

Pan frying and pan broiling are suitable methods for preparing thin (half inch thick) pork chops. Such pork chops are thin enough to allow the interior of the meat to become well done before the exterior becomes too brown. These methods are also appropriate for preparing steaks, lamb chops, bacon, ham slices, chicken, and fish. Thick steaks may be broiled, pan broiled, or pan fried, but steaks less than an inch thick will be more palatable if they are pan broiled or pan fried.

Deep-Fat Frying. A dry-heat method particularly well suited to quick preparation of chicken fryers and fish is deep-fat frying. The most important consideration in deep-fat frying is temperature control (150–180°C or 300–350°F), for too high a temperature not only causes the fat to smoke, but also causes the meat to be underdone in the middle when the outside is a pleasing color. A temperature that is too low will lengthen the frying time and result in a greasier product. Choice of an appropriate oil or fat is important for the preparation of fried foods of high quality. A well-prepared deep-fried product will have a pleasing brown exterior and will be done in the center.

Summary of Dry-Heat Methods. Dry-heat methods for preparing meats include roasting, broiling, pan broiling, pan frying, and deep-fat frying. Tender cuts of beef, pork, and lamb may be prepared by these methods. Use of dry heat permits selection of the desired final interior temperature for the meat. Beef may thus be heated to rare, medium, or well done, depending on individual preference.

Moist-Heat Methods

Moist heat is used for less tender cuts of meat. The combination of moisture, heat, and a long preparation period causes the meat to become more tender as gelatin gradually is formed from collagen. This change in the connective tissue is responsible for the tenderizing of meat that occurs during extended heating in the presence of moisture.

Braising. Braising is a popular moist-heat method in which the meat is first carefully but thoroughly browned on all sides. Then a small amount of liquid is added and the meat is tightly covered for a long (usually two to three hours) period of time until the meat becomes tender. The liquid should be maintained at simmering during the covered heating period. This relatively low temperature keeps toughening of protein at a minimum, but still permits conversion of the connective tissue.

Although water is commonly used as the liquid, many flavors may be introduced into braised meats by the use of other liquids. Various soup concentrates are excellent additions to braised meats. Tomatoes and fruit juices have a triple function in braising and are used frequently. Tomatoes or tomato derivatives are commonly used in the preparation of Swiss steak and similar products; lemon juice or other fruit juices are also useful as liquids for braising. Both the tomato and the fruit juices not only furnish liquid for softening the collagen, but they also afford a variety of flavors, and may hydrolyze the protein because of their acidity. Cuts particularly well suited to braising include round steak, flank steak, and pot roasts of beef; all cuts of veal; pork chops and steaks; breast of lamb; and heart, sweetbreads, and brains.

Stewing. Stewing, boiling, or cooking in liquid are terms used for the same process. Since the high protein content dictates that meats should never be exposed to a boiling temperature, the second term is actually a misnomer. Meats that are to be stewed may be browned if desired or they may simply be simmered in water with no preliminary browning at all. An example of the latter is the stewing of a hen. Ordinarily, the other commonly stewed meats are browned as the initial step in their preparation. Then a large amount of water is added and the meat is simmered until tender.

FIGURE 9.19   Blade pot roasts are identified by the blade (7-) bone. This cut requires moist heat (braising) until fork tender. The individual muscles are carved across the grain by turning them on edge.

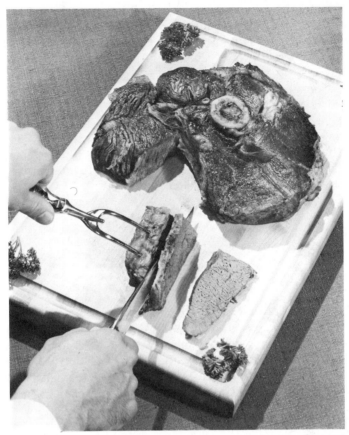

FIGURE 9.20   A beef arm roast (also called an O-bone roast) is best when it is prepared by braising.

All stew meats, corned beef, and variety meats (except liver) are suitable for this preparation method.

Summary of Moist-Heat Methods. In both braising and stewing, liquid
may be added as needed. The necessity of adding water is determined to a
large extent by the tightness of the lid used to cover the meat and by the
intensity of the heat input. Frequently, braised meats may be placed in the
oven to continue simmering after they are browned. This technique usually
causes the water to evaporate from the pan rather slowly.

Meats prepared by either of these methods will, of necessity, be well
done. The connective tissue softens so slowly that almost no conversion to
gelatin occurs until the interior temperature of the meat is well past the rare
stage. When a fork may be easily inserted and extracted from the braised or
stewed meat, the meat is ready to be served.

The palatability of veal cuts definitely may be enhanced by braising the veal. The relatively high proportion of connective tissue and the mild flavor of veal favor the selection of a moist-heat method. The slow moist heating converts the collagen, and the addition of a flavorful liquid enhances the flavor.

Thick, uncured pork such as pork chops one inch or more in thickness should always be heated to an internal temperature of 77°C (170°F) to ensure safety against trichinosis. The high interior temperature required to kill trichinae is most satisfactorily achieved in pork chops over an inch in thickness by using moist-heat methods, that is, braising. Extreme drying or even burning of the outer surfaces may occur if one attempts to fry thick pork chops to the necessary internal temperature.

POULTRY

KINDS OF POULTRY

Poultry is an inclusive term for several kinds of fowl that usually are served as the entree in meals. Chicken has been famous in times past as being the star for Sunday dinners in the United States. Turkey has been featured at Thanksgiving since the first festive celebration of the holiday. Although not served as frequently nor so readily available, duck and goose also are found in meals occasionally today. Chicken (and turkey) have gained in popularity as many consumers have been steering away from beef fat toward the lesser quantity of fat and the unsaturated fatty acids of chicken. Another important motivation toward greater use of poultry is the normal market situation where poultry is distinctly less costly than beef.

Each type of poultry available on the retail market is divided into classes according to distinct definitions. The designation of the class of fowl is an aid to the consumer in knowing how to prepare the bird. The classes defined for each of the fowl under discussion are listed below.

Chickens
1. Cornish game hen or Rock Cornish game hen: young chicken (either Cornish chicken or a cross between a Cornish and another breed) usually 5–7 weeks old and weighing a maximum of 2 pounds.
2. Broiler or fryer: usually 9–12 weeks old.
3. Roaster: 3–5 months old.
4. Capon: castrated male, usually under 8 months old.
5. Stag: male under 10 months old.
6. Hen or stewing chicken: mature female less than 10 months old.
7. Cock: mature male having coarse skin and toughened, darkened meat.

Turkeys

1. Fryer-roaster turkey: usually under 16 weeks old.
2. Young hen turkey: female, usually 5–7 months old.
3. Young tom turkey: male, usually 5–7 months old.
4. Yearling hen turkey: female under 15 months old.
5. Yearling tom turkey: male under 15 months old.
6. Mature or old turkey: more than 15 months old.

Ducks

1. Broiler or fryer duckling: usually under 8 weeks old.
2. Roaster duckling: usually under 16 weeks old.
3. Mature or old duck: usually over 6 months old.

Geese

1. Young goose: tender flesh, windpipe easily dented.
2. Mature or old goose: toughened flesh, hardened windpipe.

CONSUMER NOTES

Poultry, like the meats discussed earlier in this chapter, is inspected

FIGURE 9.21   Turkey graded U. S. Grade A will have a plump breast and legs and the skin will be virtually free of defects.

for wholesomeness by the United States Department of Agriculture if it is to enter interstate commerce or by a state inspector on the basis of criteria at least equal to the federal criteria if the fowl will be marketed intrastate. Provision for such inspection is made by the Wholesome Poultry Products Act of 1968. After a fowl has passed inspection, it may be graded according to federal or federal-state programs. The USDA grades for all poultry, that is, for chicken, turkey, duck, goose, and guinea, are U. S. Grade A, U. S. Grade B, and U. S. Grade C. The consumer ordinarily sees only the USDA Grade A designation. Birds receiving this grade are characterized by having a good overall appearance denoting good conformation and meatiness, a well-developed layer of fat in the skin, and skin virtually free of defects. The lower two grades may be sold on the retail market, but usually the grade mark is not in evidence. These lower grades also are utilized in making processed foods.

FIGURE 9.22 Half a chicken barbecues well and satisfies large appetites economically.

In addition to noting the grade, the wise shopper will need to decide just what poultry buy will best suit individual needs. For example, a family of two may wish to buy a 14-pound tom turkey for a company dinner, but might grow very tired of turkey if forced to eat it without assistance. For the small family, a roasting chicken or Rock Cornish game hen or, perhaps, a duck may be a much more appropriate choice. Of course, turkeys are available in parts, quartered, and halved as well as whole. Chickens also are available in a variety of packages. They may be sold whole, split, cut into pieces, or the pieces may be separated and marketed as packages of legs, packages of breasts, and so on. Sometimes the shopper may be faced with the question of deciding to buy a whole fryer or pieces. As a guide, if a fryer costs 39 cents per pound, then the following are comparable in price: breast halves at 55 cents per pound, thighs at 52, drumsticks at 48, and wings at 31 (see p. A41).

Poultry may also present considerable question regarding the amount to buy because of the bone. For barbecuing chickens or broiling them, allow one-fourth chicken per person if appetites are small or the chickens are more than $2\frac{1}{2}$ pounds. For smaller chickens or larger appetites, one-half a chicken should suffice. For whole fryers, approximately one-half pound should be allowed for adults. Turkeys also will provide just over two servings per pound. Duckling and goose provide only two servings per pound.

STORAGE

Fresh poultry is quite susceptible to spoilage because of rapid microbiological growth, especially in the body cavity. Therefore, refrigeration just as soon as possible after purchase is essential. Table 9.9 outlines satisfactory refrigerator and freezer storage periods for fresh and cooked poultry.

Much of the poultry that is purchased today is marketed in the frozen form. Ideally, this poultry will be thawed completely just at the time the bird is to be prepared. For a small bird, this may seem to be an insignificant matter, but larger ones require foresight if they are to be thawed at the proper time. A choice of thawing methods is available. These include thawing in the refrigerator, in cold water, or in a cool room. If individual pieces can be separated and the giblets removed, thawing will be somewhat faster than is indicated in Table 9.10. Thawing in the refrigerator or in a cool room will require the use of a tray to catch the drippings that may escape from the packaging.

POULTRY COOKERY

Although all kinds of poultry can be roasted, turkey is perhaps the most common choice for this method of preparation. The first step requires a

Table 9.9. Refrigerator and Freezer Storage Periods for Poultry[a]

Type of Poultry	Storage Period	
	Refrigerator 2–5°C (35–40°F) Days	Freezer −18°C (0°F) Months
Fresh poultry		
Chicken	1–2	12
Turkey	1–2	12
Duck	1–2	6
Goose	1–2	6
Giblets	1–2	3
Cooked poultry		
Pieces covered with broth	1–2	6
Pieces not covered	1–2	1
Cooked poultry dishes	1–2	6
Fried chicken	1–2	4

[a]Adapted from *Inspection, Labeling, and Care of Meat and Poultry.* Agriculture Handbook 416. U. S. Department of Agriculture, Washington, D. C. 1971.

Table 9.10. Estimated Thawing Time for Chicken and Turkey[a]

Frozen Poultry To Be Thawed	Time Required		
	Refrigerator[b]	Cold Water[c]	Cool Room[d]
Chickens			
Less than 4 pounds	12–16 hours	1–1½ hours	8–10 hours
Four pounds or more	1–1½ days	2 hours	12 hours
Turkeys			
4–12 pounds	1–2 days	4– 6 hours	12–15 hours
12–20 pounds	2–3 days	6– 8 hours	15–17 hours
20–24 pounds	3–4 days	8–12 hours	17–20 hours

[a]Based on *Poultry in Family Meals.* Home and Garden Bulletin No. 110. U. S. Department of Agriculture, Washington, D. C. Rev. 1971. Page 7.
[b]Leave in original wrapping with poultry sitting on a tray.
[c]Cover poultry, wrapped in watertight bag, with cold water. Change water frequently.
[d]Wrap bird in at least two thicknesses of heavy paper or two sacks and let thaw in a room no warmer than 21°C (70°F).

careful preparation of the bird, including a thorough scrubbing of the interior after the giblets and neck have been removed from the cavity and also complete removal of any pinfeathers and other feathers that may be found. If a stuffing is desired, the bird should be stuffed immediately before roasting begins. The practice of stuffing a turkey the night before and then roasting it in the morning is distinctly dangerous because warm dressing and the interior of a turkey provide an optimum circumstance for growth of microorganisms in sufficient quantities to cause food poisoning. The stuffing is placed into the body cavity and at the neck opening without packing so that there will be a little room for the dressing to expand during roasting. The neck flap is skewered over the dressing to the back skin and the legs are tied together prior to inverting the turkey to place it breast down in a V-shaped rack. This rack needs to be placed in a pan large enough to catch the drippings. Then the turkey assembly is placed in the oven with the rack at a position sufficiently low to allow the turkey to be centered in the oven. A meat thermometer should be placed in the dressing if the bird is stuffed or in the interior thigh muscle. The turkey can be left untended throughout the roasting period, or it may be basted occasionally. This clearly is a dry-heat method of meat cookery because no cover is used and no water is added during the roasting period. The turkey is roasted until the thermometer in

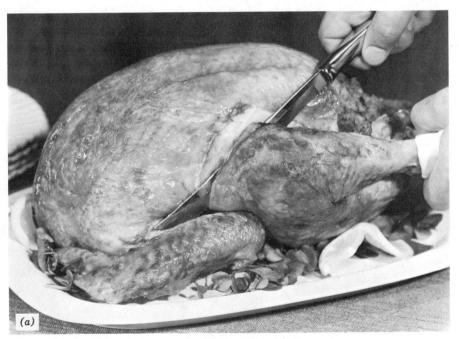

FIGURE 9.23a   The first step in carving roast turkey is to remove the leg and thigh. Place these on a separate plate to carve for those desiring dark meat.

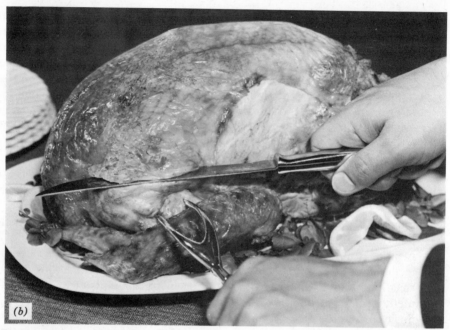

FIGURE 9.23*b*   Next, a cut is made above the wing joint to the bone, and the wing is placed on the platter.

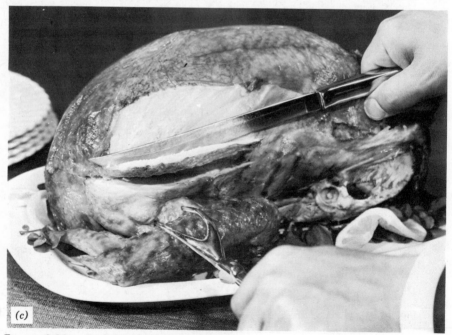

FIGURE 9.23*c*   Parallel slices are made to carve the breast meat.

the dressing indicates a temperature of 74°C (165°F) or the thigh temperature reaches 82–85°C (180–185°F). Roasting times indicated in Table 9.11 are approximate, since the rate of heat penetration does vary. The weight of a stuffed bird is approximately the weight indicated on the original package because the stuffing weight is similar to the weight of the neck and giblets that have been weighed in the original purchase weight.

Other dry-heat meat cookery methods may also be used successfully in preparing poultry unless it is definitely mature. Methods that are suitable include deep-fat frying, broiling, and frying. The preparation by each of these methods is as described earlier in this chapter. However, one useful variation of frying deserves mention because of its usefulness in busy schedules, and

Table 9.11. Timetable for Roasting Poultry[a]

Kind	Ready-to-Roast Weight (kg[b])	Approximate Total Roasting Time at 163°C (325°F) (hrs)
Chickens, whole		
Broilers, fryers, or roasters	0.7–1.1 *(1.5–2.5)*	1–2
	1.1–2.0 *(2.5–4.5)*	2–3½
Capons	2.3–3.6 *(5.0–8.0)*	2½–3½
Ducks	1.8–2.7 *(4.0–6.0)*	2–3
Geese	2.7–3.6 *(6.0–8.0)*	3–3½
	3.6–5.5 *(8.0–12.0)*	3½–4½
Turkeys		
Whole	2.7–3.6 *(6.0–8.0)*	3–3½
	3.6–5.5 *(8.0–12.0)*	3½–4½
	5.5–7.3 *(12.0–16.0)*	4½–5½
	7.3–9.1 *(16.0–20.0)*	5½–6½
	9.1–11.0 *(20.0–24.0)*	6½–7
Halves, quarters, pieces	1.4–3.6 *(3.0–8.0)*	2–3
	3.6–5.5 *(8.0–12.0)*	3–4
Boneless roasts	1.4–4.5 *(3.0–10.0)*	3–4

[a]Adapted from *Poultry in Family Meals.* Home and Garden Bulletin No. 110. U. S. Department of Agriculture, Washington, D. C. Rev. 1971. Page 10.
[b]Figures in italics are weight in pounds.

FIGURE 9.24 Oven frying is a convenient method of preparing chicken. Cereal crumbs may be used as a coating to add variety.

that method is oven frying. Chicken or other poultry are prepared by rolling the washed pieces in flour or crumbs, followed by a coating in oil or melted fat. The pieces are placed in a shallow baking dish and baked at 205°C (400°F) for an hour; the pieces are turned once to promote uniform browning.

Moist-heat methods are necessary to tenderize mature poultry. Although braising can be done, the more common method is stewing. Poultry to be stewed may be left whole if a container of sufficient size is available, or it may be cut into pieces for greater convenience. A pressure cooker or pressure saucepan provides a variation in stewing. Stewed hens and other poultry should be simmered until a fork penetrates the flesh easily, a tenderizing process that usually requires approximately two hours.

FISH

Nutritionists generally agree that fish are a highly nourishing, yet sadly under-utilized part of the nation's larder. They are an excellent source of protein and generally are much lower in fat content, and consequently lower in calories, than other meats used commonly in the diet. From the standpoint of food preparation, fish also have considerable merit in crowded schedules because they are prepared quickly and easily.

KINDS OF FISH

Fish offer far more variety to the consumer than do the poultry and meats discussed previously, for more than 240 varieties of fish and shellfish are sold in the United States. These include freshwater, saltwater, and anadromous fish. First, there is a division between fish and shellfish. A fish is a cold-blooded aquatic animal equipped with fins, a backbone, a skull, and gills for removing air from the water. Shellfish also are aquatic, but they lack the fins, skull, and backbone. In their stead, the shellfish is equipped with a shell, in the case of mollusks (oysters, scallops, mussels), or with a horny outer covering, as is typical of the crustacea (shrimp, lobsters, and crab).

For the convenience of consumers who may be seeking fish as a low-calorie protein source or for those who value fish as a pleasing source of polyunsaturated oils, a listing of some of the more common fish according to their fat content is helpful (Table 9.12).

Table 9.12. Approximate Fat Content of Selected Common Fish[a]

Oily Species (6–20% Oil or More)	Intermediate (2–6% Oil)	Nonoily Species Less than 2% Oil
Chub, lake	Bass	Clams
Herring, Sea	Buffalo fish	Cod
Mackerel	Carp	Haddock
Salmon, King	Crab	Halibut
Salmon, silver (medium red)	Oysters	Lobster
Salmon, sockeye (red)	Salmon, chum	Mullet
Sardines	Salmon, pink	Ocean perch
Smelt	Shrimp	Pike, lake
Tuna, canned		Perch, lake
Whitefish, Lake		Pollock
		Rockfish
		Scallops
		Sole and flounder
		Whiting

[a]Fisheries Marketing Bulletin. Bureau of Commercial Fisheries. FMB35-20M-61. Page 8.

INSPECTION AND GRADING

The inspection and grading of fish are under the direction of the United States Department of the Interior, rather than under the United States Department of Agriculture as is true for the other types of meat discussed in this chapter. Grade standards have been developed for a number of different fishery products, with the grade designations being: Grade A for top or best quality; Grade B for good quality, but with more toleration of size variation and blemishes than allowed in Grade A; and Grade C denoting nourishing and wholesome food, but of somewhat lower quality than the other grades. Fish monitored and graded under this system will bear a shield stating U. S. Grade A or a shield announcing that the fish was packed under continuous inspection of the United States Department of the Interior. The raw materials and the condition of the plant are under constant surveillance under this program. Considerable care must be taken because fish are very susceptible to spoilage.

SELECTION

The price of fish of different types usually covers a broad range, from inexpensive ocean perch to live lobsters air freighted to market. In many markets there will be a choice between frozen fish and some varieties of fresh fish. If frozen fish is selected, the fish should have a plump look rather than a spongy, somewhat desiccated appearance, the wrapping should be intact, and the package should be frozen solidly. Fresh fish of desirable quality will have a mild odor, the skin should be shiny and unfaded, the gills should be red and the eyes clear, and the flesh of cut fish should look fresh and not dry.

Sometimes fish may be bought dressed only with the scales and entrails removed and the head and tail gone. More commonly fish are available as fillets, which are the sides of the fish stripped lengthwise from the backbone. Steaks are simply cross-sectional slices from a large dressed fish such as salmon. When one is purchasing fish, the following information will describe the amounts to buy for an average serving:

Dressed	1/2 lb
Fillet or steaks	1/3 lb
Sticks	1/4 lb
Canned	1/6 lb

Fish should be refrigerated or frozen immediately after purchasing. If they are stored in the refrigerator in the coldest part, fish may be kept as long as four days; in the freezer, storage should be limited to six months.

FISH COOKERY

Fish have a limited amount of connective tissue, and it is more tender than that found in land animals. Therefore, fish cookery basically becomes a problem of heating the fish to a desirable serving temperature to coagulate the protein and then serving immediately. Longer cooking by any method will begin to toughen the muscle proteins in fish and the product becomes increasingly tougher. For optimum juiciness and tenderness, fish cookery should be brief.

Either dry-heat methods or moist-heat methods may be used satisfactorily in preparing fish. Baking, broiling, deep-fat frying, oven frying, and panfrying are very satisfactory ways of preparing fish. Of these methods, baking requires the longest time (up to an hour for a three-pound fish). Broiling and oven frying (at 260°C or 500°F) require approximately 15 minutes. Pan frying is slightly faster, usually being completed within 10 minutes, and the three to five minutes used for deep-fat frying are certainly minimal. Poaching and steaming are the moist-heat methods for preparing

FIGURE 9.25   Whether prepared by moist- or dry-heat methods, fish will be most tender and juicy when cooked only briefly.

fish. Fish are poached by placing a single layer in a large frying pan and barely covering them with a liquid such as milk, water, or white wine. The fish are simmered until the fish flakes part easily with a fork, usually a period of 5 to 10 minutes. Fish to be steamed are placed on a rack above boiling water, and the pan then is tightly covered so that steam surrounds the fish. Usually between 5 and 10 minutes steaming time will be sufficient for the fish to flake easily.

SUMMARY

Meat production, distribution, and preparation have grown from arts to sciences. Various scientific fields have combined forces to improve the

FIGURE 9.26 Chicken and other poultry gain added interest when glazed with fruit juices or other flavored sauces.

health and meat of animals. With technological changes, it is now possible to get high-quality fresh, frozen, or dried meat to the consumer.

Meat cuts are identified as tender and less tender. The dry-heat methods suitable for tender cuts include broiling, roasting, pan broiling, pan frying, and deep-fat frying. Less tender cuts become more tender with moist heat and long simmering times which promote the formation of gelatin from collagen. Stewing and braising are the two basic moist-heat methods.

Poultry and fish are important additions to menu planning because of the variety they afford and their help with the budget. In addition, their low-fat content and the presence of polyunsaturated fatty acids add to their nutritive assets. Poultry most commonly are prepared by dry-heat cookery methods, although mature birds require the tenderizing action of moist heat. Fish may be prepared very satisfactorily by a variety of dry-heat and moist-heat methods. The key to successful fish cookery is to avoid overcooking.

BIBLIOGRAPHY

American Meat Institute. *Questions and Answers on the Wholesome Meat Act of 1967.* American Meat Institute. Chicago. 1968.

Animal Disease and ·Parasite Research Division. *Trichinosis.* Leaflet No. 428. U. S. Department of Agriculture, Washington, D. C. Rev. 1966.

Ayres, J. C. Microbiological implications in the handling, slaughtering, and dressing of meat animals. *Adv. Food Res.* 6:110–154. 1955.

Beck, S. A. *Inspection, Labeling, and Care of Meat and Poultry.* Agriculture Handbook 416. U. S. Department of Agriculture, Washington, D. C. 1971.

Bird, H. R. Additives and residues in foods of animal origin. *Am. J. Clin. Nut. 9:* 260–268. 1961.

Borgstrom, G. Microbiological problems of frozen food products. *Adv. Food Res.* 6:163–211. 1955.

Bramblett, V. D. et al. Effect of temperature and cut on quality of pork roast. *J.A.D.A.* 57:132. 1970.

Bureau of Commercial Fisheries. *Special Fisheries Marketing Bulletin.* U. S. Department of the Interior. Washington, D. C. 1961.

Bureau of Commercial Fisheries. *Fishery Product Inspection.* Circular 218. U. S. Department of the Interior. Washington, D. C. 1965.

Bureau of Commercial Fisheries. *Let's Cook Fish.* Fishery Market Development Series No. 8. U. S. Department of the Interior. Washington, D. C. n.d.

Burtis, J. and R. G. Kerr. *How to Cook Shrimp.* Test Kitchen Series No. 7. U. S. Department of the Interior. Washington, D. C. 1961.

Burtis, J. et al. *How to Cook Lobsters.* Test Kitchen Series No. 11. U. S. Department of the Interior. Washington, D. C. 1964.

Carlin, A. F., D. M. Bloemer, and D. K. Hotchkiss. Relation of oven temperature and final internal temperature to quality of pork loin roasts. *J. Home Econ.* 57:442–446. 1965.

Consumer News. Meat names to be standardized. *Consumer News 2,* No. 9:1. 1972.

Consumer and Marketing Service. *How to Buy Meat for Your Freezer.* Home and Garden Bulletin No. 166. U. S. Department of Agriculture. Washington, D. C. 1969.

Consumer and Marketing Service. *How to Buy Poultry.* Home and Garden Bulletin No. 157. U. S. Department of Agriculture. Washington, D. C. 1968.

Consumer and Marketing Service. *Meat and Poultry Care Tips for You.* Home and Garden Bulletin No. 174. U. S. Department of Agriculture. Washington, D. C. 1970.

Consumer and Marketing Service. *Poultry in Family Meals.* Home and Garden Bulletin No. 110. U. S. Department of Agriculture. Washington, D. C. Rev. 1971.

Cover, S., and R. L. Hostetler. *Beef Tenderness by New Methods.* Texas Agr. Expt. Sta. Bull. No. 947. 1960.

Feeney, R. E., and R. M. Hill. Protein chemistry and food research. *Adv. Food Res. 10:*23–67. 1960.

Hamm, R. Biochemistry of meat hydration. *Adv. Food Res. 10:*355–443. 1960.

Harper, J. C., and A. L. Tappel. Freeze-drying of food products. *Adv. Food Res. 7:*172–220. 1957.

Keller, D. M. et al. *How to Cook Scallops.* Test Kitchen Series No. 13. U. S. Department of the Interior. Washington, D. C. 1964.

Livestock Division. *U. S. Grades for Beef Carcasses.* U. S. Department of the Interior. Washington, D. C. 1970.

Law, H. M. et al. Ground beef quality at the retail level. *J.A.D.A. 58:*230. 1971.

National Live Stock and Meat Board. *Lessons on Meat.* National Live Stock and Meat Board. Chicago. 2nd ed. 1968.

Osterhaug, K. L., and R. G. Kerr. *How to Cook Clams.* Test Kitchen Series No. 8. U. S. Department of the Interior. Washington, D. C. 1964.

Rice, E. E., and J. F. Benk. Effects of heat upon the nutritive value of protein. *Adv. Food Res. 4:*233–271. 1953.

Robey, D. M., and R. G. Kerr. *How to Cook Crabs.* Test Kitchen Series No. 10. U. S. Department of the Interior. Washington, D. C. 1964.

Scott, W. J. Water relation of food spoilage microorganisms. *Adv. Food Res. 7:* 84–123. 1957.

Simone, M., F. Carroll, E. Hinreiner, and M. T. Clegg. Effect of corn, barley, stilbestrol, and degree of finish upon quality of beef. *Food Res. 20:*521–529. 1955.

Todhunter, E. N. *Chicken Talk.* National Broiler Council. Washington, D. C. n.d.

Tomiyasu, Y., and B. Zenitani. Spoilage of fish and its preservation by chemical agents. *Adv. Food Res. 7:*42–74. 1957.

Wang, H., and N. Maynard. Enzymatic meat tenderization. *Food Res. 20:*587–597. 1955.

Watts, B. M. Oxidative rancidity and discoloration in meat. *Adv. Food Res. 5:*1–42. 1954.

Whitaker, J. R. Chemical changes associated with the aging of meat with emphasis on proteins. *Adv. Food Res. 9:*1–47. 1959.

SUGGESTIONS FOR STUDY

1. What federal departments are responsible for inspecting the following foods when they enter interstate commerce: (a) beef, (b) pork, (c) lamb, (d) veal, (e) poultry, (f) fish, and (g) shellfish?
2. What are the two types of connective tissue? What means can be employed for tenderizing meat cuts containing a high percentage of connective tissue?
3. What criteria determine the suitability of meat for aging?
4. Discuss the value of federal inspection and grading programs from the standpoint of the consumer.
5. Suggest several retail cuts of meat that are suitable for each of these preparation methods: (a) broiling, (b) braising, (c) frying, (d) roasting, (e) pan broiling, (f) stewing, (g) deep-fat frying.
6. Poach one fillet of fish 8 minutes and another one of comparable size for 20 minutes. Describe the differences. What caused them?

CHAPTER 10

Eggs

Because of their great versatility, eggs are frequently used in food preparation for any meal. They are often fried, poached, scrambled, or soft cooked for breakfast. For luncheon or a light supper, omelets, and soufflés are popular. An airy, sweet fruit soufflé, fluffy baked Alaska, or poached meringues topped with a smooth, stirred custard and plump, fresh strawberries are exotic egg desserts suitable for even the most formal dinner. In addition, eggs are important ingredients in many different types of recipes.

The thickening power and foam-forming ability are two extremely useful properties. Custards are thickened by coagulation of the egg proteins (see Chapter 20). Angel cakes, sponge cakes, soufflés, and meringues utilize egg foams. Another use of eggs is as an emulsifier and binding agent.

NUTRITIVE VALUE

Nutritionally, eggs provide a significant amount of complete protein at a reasonable cost to the consumer. The quality of egg protein is comparable to that of meat, and the cost of eggs is certainly lower.

The yolk is a particularly important source of iron and it also contributes vitamin A. The actual quantity of vitamin A depends on the diet of the hen. The vitamin D level may vary with the season because hens exposed to sunlight lay eggs containing more vitamin D than do hens exposed to less sunshine. This factor is becoming less significant with the increased incidence of large-scale, egg-producing units based on indoor production. The white contains a significant quantity of riboflavin.

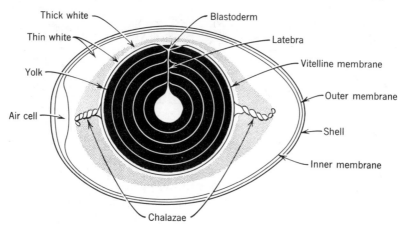

FIGURE 10.1 Diagram of the cross section of an egg.

STRUCTURE OF THE EGG

The shell, made up predominantly of calcium carbonate, is covered with a protective coating that aids in maintaining the freshness of the egg by covering the many small holes in the shell. If this mucin layer or "bloom" is removed by washing or buffing, the holes are exposed for bacterial penetration and dehydration, thus hastening deterioration of quality.

Within the shell are an inner and outer membrane that also protect the quality of the egg. The white of the egg consists of three layers: two areas of thin white encompassing one area of thick white. The yolk is encased in the vitelline membrane and suspended in the white by two chalazae. The indistinct spot on the yolk is the germ spot or blastoderm, beneath which extends a white column called the latebra. The yolk itself is layered into sections of white and yellow yolk.

The composition of the white is quite different from that of the yolk. Of importance is the large amount of water (87 percent) and the absence of fat in the white, as contrasted with the reduced amount of water (49.5 percent) and large quantity of fat (33.3 percent) in the yolk.

GRADING

Several states require that eggs be graded if they are to be sold on a retail basis. A grading program, referred to as the Federal-State Grading Program, is administered by the United States Department of Agriculture. Under this impartial grading program, eggs for the retail market are classed into three consumer grades: U. S. Grade AA or Fresh Fancy Quality, U. S. Grade A, and U. S. Grade B.

FIGURE 10.2   USDA grade designations for eggs.

Fresh Fancy Quality was initiated in the grading system in 1959 for use in grading eggs produced in large laying flocks. In such large commercial operations eggs of relatively uniform quality are produced by controlling age of the flock, environmental conditions of humidity and temperature, and efficiency of marketing. By testing only five or ten eggs weekly from such flocks, the general quality of the eggs can be ascertained objectively. Eggs of Fresh Fancy Quality must be marketed with this grade identification within ten days from the testing date.

The United States grading system for shell eggs requires a clean, unbroken shell, an air cell less than one-eighth inch deep, and a yolk that is well-centered and free of defects if the egg is to be classed as Grade AA.

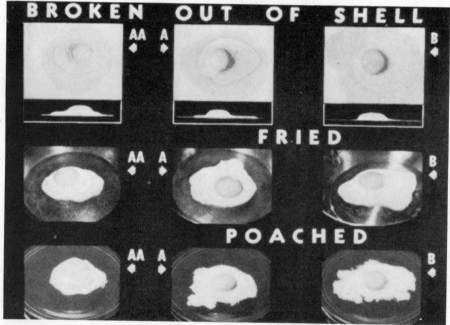

FIGURE 10.3   Quality guide to USDA egg grades.

Eggs of A quality meet slightly less rigid standards, that is, the air cell may be one-fourth inch deep. The yolk is fairly well centered and is practically free of defects. The lowest consumer grade, Grade B, is assigned to an egg that has a clean to slightly stained shell, a somewhat more mobile yolk with a flattened appearance, and an air space up to three-eighths of an inch deep. These grades are assigned at the time of grading and are not an absolute guarantee of the quality at the time of purchase.

Out of the Shell

In commercial situations, such as freezing and drying of bulk eggs, where it is feasible to grade egg quality out of the shell, the appearance of the shelled egg is an excellent indication of freshness. One objective means

FIGURE 10.4   Grader using micrometer to measure the height of the thick albumen, a means of grading eggs out of the shell.

of ascertaining quality is a measurement of the yolk index, a figure derived by dividing the height of the yolk by the diameter of the yolk. The other objective measurement is determination of the height of the thick albumen (thick white), expressed in arbitrary units called Haugh units. In this system Grade AA whites have a minimum value of 72 Haugh units; Grade A, 60–71; and Grade B, 31–59 Haugh units. Contrary to popular belief, color of the yolk is not an indication of quality, but simply is a reflection of the hen's diet.

In the Shell

Grading of eggs in the shell for retail marketing is most commonly done by candling. This process employs a simple device consisting of a metal container enclosing a 30-watt light bulb. The egg is held tightly against a hole in the device, which dully illuminates the interior as the candler rotates the egg. By this technique the size of the air space, position and mobility of the yolk, and the possible presence of foreign substances such as rots, molds, and blood spots in the white can be ascertained. A blood spot on the yolk is not graded down for it can easily be removed, but blood in the white is not acceptable, since this condition causes rapid spoilage. Since deterioration occurs more readily in eggs with large pores, a porous shell is graded lower than a shell with fine pores. Color of the shell, a characteristic determined by heredity, in no way influences the quality of the egg and consequently is not graded.

Deterioration is a steady process from the time the egg is laid. Proper storage conditions retard this process, but do not completely halt it. Eggs slowly become more alkaline as carbon dioxide escapes through the pores. This gas loss causes the air cell at the end of the egg to grow larger; in addition, loss of quality may be accompanied by a shifting of this air space from the end to the side of the egg.

Certain deteriorative changes are noticeable when eggs are broken out of the shell. A fresh egg, for example, will have a high yolk with the opalescent white coming up well around it. There will be a large proportion of thick white. With loss of freshness, the yolk will begin to flatten, the white will not pile well around the yolk, and the white will become more transparent. The amount of thick white decreases, causing a resulting increase in the thin white and an increased mobility of the yolk. In addition, the vitelline membrane surrounding the yolk gradually weakens and the yolk is more easily broken.

WEIGHT CLASSES

The United States Department of Agriculture has established six official weight classes based on the minimum weight of a dozen eggs. They are: jumbo, 30 ounces; extra large, 27 ounces; large, 24 ounces; medium, 21 ounces; small, 18 ounces; and peewee, 15 ounces. Within a box of eggs the individual eggs may show some variation in size. The weight classes apply only to the total weight of a dozen eggs and not to the size of a single egg in the package. Sometimes consumers falsely equate size with quality. The size designation does not reflect the quality at all, just as the grade designation is not an indication of size.

STORAGE

The storage conditions used today are aimed at keeping bacterial growth and the increase in alkalinity to a minimum. By carefully controlling the storage atmosphere of carbon dioxide, the change in the pH of eggs is minimized. Since enzymatic activity is greater at warmer temperatures, eggs should be stored in a cool environment to retard deterioration. Temperatures between -1 and $-2°C$ (29°F and 31°F) are optimum for long-term storage; storage conditions must also ensure that the shells remain dry to avoid mold and bacterial growth. Under controlled conditions, it is possible to store eggs satisfactorily for periods in excess of six months.

One means of slowing deteriorative changes is the coating of shells. Originally this term meant dipping the eggs in some fat. Water glass has also been used. Today mineral oil is widely used. The oil covers the pores of the egg, hence reduces mold penetration and retards spoilage. This process is most effective when the eggs are dipped and then stored at temperatures just below freezing.

The processing of eggs with mineral oil is done with the oil bath maintained at $43°C$ (110°F). This temperature is high enough to keep the oil from being drawn into the egg. Oil colder than the egg may cause contraction of the air cell, which allows the oil and any microbiological contamination in the oil to penetrate the pores. The eggs are dipped for a few seconds, drained briefly and then packed and refrigerated. It is important that the oil be kept clean at all times during dipping if the egg flavor is to be unimpaired.

The importance of adequate refrigeration of eggs during transport and marketing cannot be overemphasized. Eggs that are exposed to warm temperatures will deteriorate rather quickly. Therefore it is essential that the marketing and transporting temperatures be maintained below the absolute maximum temperature of $16°C$ (60°F) at all times. Unless eggs are shipped and marketed under refrigeration, their quality will be something less than their grade classification indicates. When a consumer buys eggs that are not marketed in refrigerated cases, quality lower than that indicated on the carton should be expected. Unfortunately, there is no way for the consumer to know the temperatures to which the eggs may have been subjected in transit.

PROCESSING OF EGGS

Freezing

Frozen eggs have been incorporated into many foods, such as baked products, which are produced commercially. Since egg production and quality are high in the early spring, most freezing of eggs is done in the spring. As a result, the composition of frozen eggs is relatively constant. This constancy of composition is of particular value in commercial baking formulas.

One of the important problems in freezing is the control of microorganisms. To reduce contamination, the shells are usually washed before the eggs are broken from the shell. Freezing as quickly as possible, after washing and breaking, is effective in keeping contamination at a minimum. Extremely careful control of sanitary conditions during breaking and mixing is exercised, since these steps offer the opportunity for considerable contamination of the frozen egg mixture. Pasteurization of the white, yolk, or whole egg is also an aid in reducing microorganism count. The baked products made from pasteurized eggs are only slightly altered by the heat treatment.

Frozen whole egg and egg white are more satisfactory than frozen yolks since a few weeks' storage causes some thickening of the yolk. Adding salt or sugar to the yolks prior to freezing reduces this tendency, however, thus making it easier to incorporate the yolks into a batter.

Drying

Dried eggs have been in use for a number of years. Originally, drying was done in the United States. Then the belt-drying process used in the United States after the first World War was adopted by the Chinese, who soon produced a large percentage of the world market. Concurrently, spray drying was developed and is now the most common method employed for drying eggs. In spray drying, the liquid egg is forced through an atomizer as a fine spray which is quickly dried, cooled, and packaged. As with freezing, bacterial control is vital to the production of a high-quality food.

Eggs may be dried as the yolk, the white, or the whole egg. Objectionable changes in color, flavor, odor, and solubility occur when either dried yolks or whole eggs are held at temperatures higher than 5°C (40°F). A lower temperature retards the undesirable changes, until at −18°C (0°F) very little change occurs. Reconstituted dried eggs are acceptable for use by commercial bakers if the eggs are freshly dried or have been stored properly. Commercial preparation of baked products containing dried eggs requires that the ingredients be combined and mixed at elevated temperatures (68 to 80°C or 154 to 176°F).

PROTEINS IN EGGS

The white contains seven proteins that have been studied extensively and also several proteins that have received less attention. Of particular interest is ovalbumin, which occurs in much larger quantities (over half of the total solids) than any of the other proteins. This protein can be coagulated readily simply by mechanical agitation. Ovomucin is the protein credited with providing the structure of the thick white. About four times as much ovomucin is found in the thick as in the thin white.

The water-soluble protein fraction in egg yolk is called livetin. The two lipoprotein fractions (lipid-protein compounds) occurring in egg yolk are identified as lipovitellin and lipovitellinin. These lipoproteins are important emulsifying agents.

FACTORS INFLUENCING COAGULATION

Since the various proteins coagulate at different temperatures, the coagulation temperatures of undiluted protein foods will be determined by the combinations of proteins in the food. The coagulation of the proteins in egg white begins as low as 52°C if the heating conditions are carefully controlled. When the white is heated more quickly, coagulation begins around 60°C and is completed around 65°C. At approximately 65°C, egg yolk begins to thicken and at 70°C it is firm.

A slow rate of heating permits coagulation to be completed at the lower end of the temperature range, whereas a rapid rate raises the coagulation temperature to the upper end of the range.

The foregoing temperatures are for eggs to which nothing has been added. Eggs frequently are combined with other ingredients, however, so these figures would change. Diluting the egg protein by adding other substances, such as milk, raises the temperature for coagulation.

Sugar in an egg mixture elevates the coagulation temperature. At least a partial explanation of this is that the addition of sugar also serves to reduce the concentration of protein. It appears, however, that other factors also may be involved.

Acids such as cream of tartar or lemon juice lower the coagulation temperature of the egg protein as the pH of the egg mixture approaches the isoelectric point. The isoelectric point of a protein is the pH at which the positive and negative charges on a protein are equal. In this state the protein molecules can approach each other more readily and thus show a greater tendency to precipitate or coagulate. If sufficient acid is added to lower the pH of the protein mixture below the isoelectric point, the coagulation temperature again begins to rise.

Salts must be present for egg mixtures to coagulate. Various chlorides and other mineral salts that aid coagulation are found in liquids used in food preparation. Therefore one need not be concerned about the presence of salts in regular food preparation. The need for salts may be illustrated, however, by baking a custard made with distilled water. The mixture remains liquid until salts are added to the custard. The salts cause coagulation to occur because the charges on these ions neutralize the protein molecules. Milk, the liquid customarily used for baked custard, already contains the necessary salts to cause coagulation to proceed.

EGG PRODUCTS

Eggs are used in food preparation to thicken, to emulsify, to improve color and flavor, to bind ingredients, and to form foams. This versatility has given eggs an important role in many phases of food preparation.

Eggs Prepared in the Shell

Hard-cooked eggs, contrary to common practice, should be heated at a simmering temperature to avoid toughening the protein. Hence the name hard-boiled eggs is actually a misnomer. Many times a green color is observed at the yolk-white interface when an egg is hard cooked. This compound is ferrous sulfide and is formed by the union of iron in the yolk with sulfur in the white. As the egg is heated, iron and sulfur combine to form ferrous sulfide where they come in contact at the interface. The use of stale eggs, prolonged heating period, or a slow rate of cooling will increase the amount of ferrous sulfide formed. By carefully timing the simmering period and by rapidly cooling the hot eggs in very cold water, it is possible to eliminate or, at least, significantly reduce the formation of ferrous sulfide.

A standard hard-cooked egg is tender, the well-centered yolk is completely coagulated, and there is no ferrous-sulfide ring surrounding the yolk. The outline of a high-quality egg that has been hard cooked has only a small indentation revealing the size and position of the air space.

Soft-cooked eggs also are prepared in simmering water to promote tenderness of the product. The criteria for evaluating a soft-cooked egg are: the white should be firm but tender, and the yolk should be slightly thickened, yet not firm at the edges.

Hard- or soft-cooked eggs may be most accurately timed by placing the eggs in boiling water and then maintaining a simmering temperature. If enough water is used to cover the eggs, a hard-cooked egg should be simmered 20 minutes and a soft-cooked egg requires approximately 5 minutes.

Eggs Prepared Out of the Shell

Fried Eggs. Eggs prepared in very simple ways are included frequently in the diet, especially at breakfast time. Fried eggs, an American breakfast favorite, may be satisfactorily prepared in either of two ways. In one method eggs may be slowly fried in an excess amount of fat with the upper surface coagulated by basting with hot fat. In the other method just enough fat is used to keep the eggs from sticking. By adding a small amount of water and then covering the pan, steam is formed and trapped to coagulate the upper portion of the eggs. Either method should result in an egg that has a tender white and a slightly thickened, unbroken yolk. The white should be coagu-

FIGURE 10.5 Poached eggs may be incorporated into special sandwiches for brunch, lunch, or supper fare.

lated across the upper surface of the yolk and there should be no evidence of crisp browning around the edges of the white. To prepare an excellent fried egg, it is essential to use a high-quality egg and to maintain a controlled low heat.

Poached Eggs. Poached eggs are popular today because of the dietary emphasis on low consumption of fat. They are prepared by breaking the egg into a bowl and then carefully slipping it into a pan of simmering water. Directing the egg toward the edge of the pan as it is poured into the water helps to keep the egg from spreading too much in the water. It is also important that the water be at simmering before the egg is added if spreading is to be minimized, for the water is then hot enough to quickly begin to coagulate the egg.

An extremely important factor in controlling the appearance of a poached egg is the use of a high-quality egg. Eggs of high quality have a large amount of thick white and consequently have little tendency to spread in the simmering water; low-quality eggs are difficult to manage because the large quantity of thin white causes them to cover a large area.

The use of simmering water in preference to boiling water is dictated by two factors: (1) the egg proteins will be more tender and (2) the egg will hold its shape better. The turbulence of boiling water tends to cause some disintegration of the egg-white mass. When the white is completely coagulated, the egg should be quickly removed from the water.

A well-prepared poached egg has a firm, tender white surrounding the slightly thickened, unbroken yolk.

Scrambled Eggs. Scrambled eggs are an excellent way to serve eggs that may be of somewhat lower quality than Grade AA. Broken yolks and a large quantity of thin white are not a problem since the eggs are beaten to a homogeneous mixture. Scrambled eggs should be beaten only until the mixture is thoroughly blended, but not foamy. Scrambled eggs are customarily prepared by adding a small amount of milk to dilute the protein and produce a more tender product. Again, a low temperature is desirable for coagulating the eggs. It is recommended that the eggs be stirred occasionally rather than continuously to coagulate the eggs in moderate-sized pieces. Heating should cease when the eggs are just slightly moist. There should be no flecks of white in scrambled eggs. Other points to judge are tenderness, degree of doneness, and size of the pieces. The tender, slightly moist eggs should have no brown on them.

French Omelet. A French omelet is prepared from the same recipe as scrambled eggs, but the procedure results in a product with quite a different appearance. It is not mandatory that high-quality eggs be used in a French omelet, although the flavor of very fresh eggs is superior to older eggs.

FIGURE 10.6   Western omelet, a variation of a French omelet, being folded for immediate serving.

The eggs and milk for a French omelet are beaten just until they form a homogeneous mixture. Then, when the fat is just bubbling in a skillet, the beaten mixture is poured in and allowed to begin to coagulate undisturbed. With a narrow spatula, small areas of the coagulated portion are raised to allow the uncoagulated egg to collect on the bottom of the pan. As this procedure continues, the pan must be tipped to get the last liquid portion to drain down to the bottom of the pan. Manipulation of the omelet should cease just before there is no fluid egg remaining. Thus the omelet will be a continuous disc of coagulated egg that is slightly moist on the upper surface. A brief period of heating at a slightly increased temperature will develop a pleasing brown color on the bottom of the omelet. If desired, crumbled bacon, grated cheese, jelly, or some other filling may be spread over half of the omelet. The omelet is then folded into a semicircle and served.

French omelets have a pleasing browned, unbroken exterior and a homogeneous, yellow-colored interior. The controlled low heat produces a tender product.

Baked Eggs. Eggs are sometimes baked in the oven in individual ramekins. As with other methods of egg preparation, a low temperature of 163°C (325°F) helps to produce a tender, completely coagulated white and a slightly thickened yolk. It is easier to avoid breaking the yolk if high-quality eggs are used, but it is possible to bake eggs of Grade A quality if considerable care is taken.

Eggs as Thickening Agents

As egg proteins coagulate in a product, the entire mixture becomes more viscous. This fact is utilized in a number of products such as custards and cream pie fillings. Proper control of the coagulation process is largely responsible for determining the final quality of the food. Slow coagulation with lower temperatures produces more palatable products than very hot temperatures.

Stirred Custard. A stirred custard effectively illustrates the use of eggs as thickening agents since the thickening that occurs in a stirred custard is due largely to the coagulation of the egg protein. A stirred custard is a nutritious and pleasing dessert sauce sometimes served over cake or fruit. It is

FIGURE 10.7   A stirred custard is a nourishing sauce to serve on gingerbread, unfrosted cakes, or over fruit.

prepared by beating and straining whole eggs, milk, and sugar, and then stirring the custard as it coagulates over hot water. When coagulation reaches the point at which the mixture evenly coats a silver spoon, the custard should be quickly poured into a shallow dish placed in ice water. This procedure ensures rapid cooling and minimizes the tendency to curdle.

A slow rate of heating is essential to the preparation of a smooth, viscous stirred custard. The cooking time is somewhat longer than the time required if a faster rate of heating is used, but this slower rate of coagulation permits more even coagulation of the protein as a result of the longer time available for stirring the custard uniformly. The slower heating causes the custard to thicken visibly before it curdles. Hence the custard can safely be removed from the heat and cooled without curdling. In custard that is heated very quickly, there is almost no time lapse between the stage of adequate thickening and the point of curdling. The custard may be smooth when removed from the heat, but will likely curdle because of the residual heat in the custard.

Egg protein in a custard will coagulate into a smooth, creamy liquid. Additional heating, however, causes the protein to draw up more tightly and squeeze out some of the liquid that was formerly part of the homogeneous mixture. The resulting curdled custard is attractive neither to the eye nor the tongue.

A stirred custard should have the viscosity of heavy cream and should be very smooth, with no suggestion of curdling. The practice of straining the beaten eggs is good because this removes the chalazae and thus results in a smoother custard. Stirring the custard actively during the coagulation period and using high-quality eggs will help to produce a thicker product.

✓ *Baked Custard.* Baked custards are made from the same recipe used for stirred custards. Again the ingredients are beaten together to form a homogeneous mixture and the chalazae are removed by straining. If a foam is formed during the mixing, it is necessary to let the custard mixture sit until all the bubbles break in order to avoid a porous texture in the finished product.

Baking results are best when the custards are placed in a pan of hot water in a 177°C (350°F) oven. The water acts as an insulator to slow the rate of heat penetration, thus helping to keep the outside of the custard from becoming overbaked before the interior is set.

Baked custards should be removed from the oven when a knife inserted halfway between the edge and the center comes out clean; the residual heat in the custard will be adequate to finish coagulating the center of the custard. If the custard remains in the oven until the center is coagulated, the custard will be overbaked and will exhibit excessive syneresis (separation of liquid from the custard). Underbaking results in a custard that is too soft, and may even be liquid in the center.

A baked custard should be firm, yet tender; the texture should be smooth rather than porous. When cut, no syneresis or weeping should be apparent. The color should be uniform with no flecks of yellow or white, and the flavor should be mild with perhaps a small amount of a spice such as nutmeg to brighten the flavor. A particularly pleasing baked custard is made by sprinkling brown sugar on a baked custard and broiling the sugar briefly. This is an excellent dessert to serve alone or with fresh fruit.

The filling for a custard pie is baked custard. Because the custard is fluid for quite a long time in the baking pie shell, custard pies frequently have a soggy bottom crust. This may be avoided by baking the crust and the filling in separate pie pans. The cooled filling can then be slipped into the baked crust.

Two other custard-type pie fillings, pumpkin and pecan, deserve some mention. Since these pies are basically custards, they should be tested for doneness by the same test used for baked custards, that is, by inserting a knife halfway between the edge and the center of the pie. This practice will prevent the rather watery pumpkin and pecan fillings that result when they are overbaked.

Cream Puddings and Pies. Cream pies and cream puddings are nourishing foods that may be particularly useful to families in which milk and egg consumption present a problem. The term cream pudding is rather surprising since it is egg yolk that is added to a cornstarch pudding rather than cream.

The procedure and problems are the same for cream pudding as for cornstarch pudding until the egg is added, that is, the starch mixture is boiled over direct heat until the broad side of a spoon leaves a path through the pudding. Then it is removed from the heat and a spoonful of the hot pudding is carefully stirred into the beaten yolks. This process is repeated until three or four tablespoons have been blended in, at which time the yolk mixture is stirred into the pudding and the entire mixture is placed over simmering water for about five minutes. Slow stirring during this period is necessary to coagulate the egg yolk evenly.

The foregoing procedure prevents the lumps that would form if the yolks were stirred directly into the hot pudding. The addition of a small amount of hot pudding to the yolks gradually warms the yolks, thus preventing the immediate coagulation that would occur if the egg yolk protein were to come in direct contact with a large quantity of very hot pudding. In addition, diluting the egg yolk with some pudding raises the coagulation temperature of the yolks slightly, which means that there will be time to stir the yolk mixture into the bulk of the pudding before the yolks become hot enough to coagulate. It is imperative that the pudding then be heated long enough to ensure complete coagulation of the yolks. If coagulation is incomplete, the pudding will become quite thin when it cools.

The procedure just described will result in a smooth pudding with no suggestion of curdling. Many cookbooks state that the yolks should be combined with the other ingredients and boiled with the entire mixture. This causes curdling of the yolks and results in a somewhat thinner product with a grainy texture. The preferred technique of boiling the starch yields maximum thickening from the starch, and the heating of the yolk over hot water results in maximum thickening of the yolk.

Preparation of lemon meringue pie presents the opportunity to apply theories of protein coagulation, gelatinization of starch, and the effect of acids. The hydrolytic effect of acid on hot starch mixtures and the resultant decrease in viscosity were considered in Chapter 7. From this discussion it is apparent that maximum thickening will be obtained if the starch is gelatinized before any acid is added. Therefore the starch mixture should be boiled and the egg yolks coagulated before the lemon juice is added in order to avoid acid hydrolysis.

In summary, cream puddings and pie fillings are of optimum viscosity when the starch, sugar, salt, and water are boiled together until very thick. This mixture is removed from the heat and some of it is stirred carefully into the beaten egg yolks. After the egg yolk mixture is blended with the starch mixture, the filling is slowly stirred over simmering water for five minutes to coagulate the protein. Acids, flavorings, and butter are stirred in after all heating has been completed. The crust of lemon meringue or any other cream pie will remain crisp longer if the filling is cooled slightly and poured in the baked shell when the meringue is ready. It is necessary, however, to cool

FIGURE 10.8 Fillings in cream pies should soften slightly when cut. If a filling is very fluid when cooled, the mixture was not heated sufficiently to coagulate the egg yolk.

the filling for a banana cream pie before it is poured over the fruit in the shell to avoid a cooked flavor in the bananas.

The various cream puddings and pie fillings should be smooth and feel light on the tongue with no suggestion of gumminess or stickiness. When cut, the pie filling should soften slightly but not flow. The filling should have the pleasing flavor typical for the type of pie.

Egg Foams

Factors Influencing Foam Formation and Stability. Eggs can be used effectively to produce foams sufficiently stable to be incorporated in various food mixtures or to be baked alone. Whites form foams much more readily than do yolks, but yolk foams can be produced with some effort. Egg white foams are utilized in meringues, souffles, puffy omelets, angel cakes, sponge cakes, and chiffon cakes as well as various other recipes. Egg yolk foam is a component of sponge cake. Whole egg foams are used occasionally to make sauces, but their use is much more limited than is the use of egg white foams. These various foams aid in producing an increased volume when they are incorporated in a recipe. The proteins in egg can be stretched into films in which air bubbles are encased. These films are sufficiently stable so that the foam can be blended gently with other ingredients while still retaining many of the air bubbles. When these foam-containing products are baked, the air trapped in the foam will expand as the temperature of the mixture rises in the oven. The expansion can continue until the protein in the film surrounding the air is coagulated during baking or until the film is stretched so thin that it breaks. Ideally, cell walls will be stretched very thin to give maximum volume, but they will coagulate before the cell wall collapses. If coagulation does not occur soon enough, the cells break and the sponge cake (or other foam-containing product) will collapse and have a very poor volume. The volume that develops as a result of the use of a foam is of value not only for eye appeal of the product but also for tenderness. As cell walls stretch thinner, they become more and more tender, and tenderness is generally viewed as a highly desirable quality in foam-containing foods.

The qualities of a foam that are of special interest are its volume, texture, and stability. The ability of eggs to foam is of great interest. Whites foam readily to a large volume, with thin whites foaming even more voluminously than thick whites. The difference in foaming ability appears to be related to a difference in the proportions of specific egg white proteins in the two types of white. The presence of fat is a strong deterrent to formation of an egg white foam. If even a small amount of the yolk is present in egg whites, the whites will not foam well because of the presence of the fat contained in the yolk. For this reason, beater blades and bowls must be completely free of fat if they are being used to make an egg white foam. Egg yolks do foam, but the volume change is much less dramatic than is true for either thick or thin whites. The volume of egg white foams is greater when the whites are at room temperature when beaten than when they are beaten immediately after being removed from the refrigerator. In a few instances, such as in a puffy omelet, liquid is added during the preparation of a foam. This dilution of the egg protein results in an increased volume of foam.

However, volume is not the only important criterion in foam formation. Ultimately, a foam needs to be stable if it is to be useful in food preparation. Stability is an extremely significant consideration and even overrides volume in importance. Some of the factors that increase volume have a distinctly detrimental result on stability. Perhaps the best illustration of this is the addition of water to an egg white foam to increase the volume of a puffy omelet. Unless considerable speed is used in preparing and heating this omelet, the foam will not hold up satisfactorily and a heavy layer will collect on the bottom. This product illustrates the importance of the concentration of protein in promoting stability of a foam.

Several other factors also are essential in promoting stability of egg foams: quality of the egg, pH, temperature, presence of sugar, and extent of beating. A high-quality egg, because it has more thick white, will yield a more stable foam than does a lower quality egg. Eggs warmer than room temperature can be whipped to a foam, but this foam will be less stable than cooler foams. Of course, heating foams to coagulate the protein in the walls encasing the air is a very important step in achieving foam stability. When foams are underbaked and some of the protein is not coagulated, the foam will tend to drain and will not hold up well. Still another factor of considerable significance in achieving a stable foam is the presence of sugar. One apparent explanation for the ability of sugar to increase stability of a foam is that sugar is hygroscopic and thus attracts liquid that otherwise would tend to drain from the foam.

Egg whites are naturally very alkaline in comparison with other foods. The addition of an acid such as cream of tartar or lemon juice brings the pH of the whites closer to the isoelectric point of egg-white protein and thus facilitates coagulation of some of the protein. When enough acid is added to decrease the pH to approximately the isoelectric point, the foam achieves maximum stability. The addition of enough acid to bring the pH of the whites below the isoelectric point, however, causes some hydrolysis or breakdown of the protein, thus delaying foam formation and reducing stability.

The extent of beating has a distinct influence on the stability of a foam. However, this factor is related to the ingredients that may be added to a foam. For instance, the addition of acid and/or sugar delays formation of the foam. Therefore, considerably more beating will need to be done in these foams to achieve the desired end point than is done when nothing is added to the egg white. There is an optimum amount of beating that should be done for any given foam to achieve maximum stability. This end point should be sought in preparing egg foams even though a longer period of beating is required to reach this end point when sugar or acid may be used.

Since the texture of a foam ultimately influences the texture of any product in which it may be incorporated, there is merit in determining what modifies a foam from a coarse texture with large and uneven cells to one with a fine and uniform texture. Sugar greatly influences the texture of a foam. As a result of the long period of beating required to reach the correct end point when sugar is added to a foam, a considerable amount of manipulation of the foam occurs. This prolonged beating continually stretches out the protein more and more and keeps breaking the bubbles into smaller and smaller, but more numerous bubbles. Thus, sugar helps to achieve a very fine foam structure. Acid has somewhat the same influence on foam texture.

Stages in Foam Formation. Recognition of the various stages in the beating of egg-white foams is essential. At the foamy stage, when the white

FIGURE 10.9   Egg whites beaten until the peaks just bend over are ready to blend with a gelatin mixture (chilled to a syruplike consistency) to complete a chiffon pie filling.

is beaten briefly, bubbles form on the surface but a bit of liquid remains in the bottom of the bowl. At this stage, in which the bubbles are coarse and opalescent and the foam is very unstable, acid and the first sugar are introduced. When sugar is added gradually, commencing at the foamy stage, a fine-textured, stable foam results. The addition of sugar at the beginning of beating delays foam formation unnecessarily, but if sugar is not added until after the foamy stage, it may not be possible to dissolve all of the sugar. This causes decreased stability, increased drainage, and the foam is coarser in texture and may feel gritty on the tongue.

As beating is continued beyond the foamy stage, more air is beaten into the whites, causing a white, more opaque appearance. The bubbles grow increasingly smaller as agitation continues. When the peaks will just bend over as the beater is slowly pulled out of the foam, the egg whites are suitable for folding into a batter. The foam is reasonably stable. This soft-peak stage is appropriate for the beating of soft meringues.

Further beating causes the peaks to stand up straight as the beater is withdrawn. Stability is at a maximum at this point, but the foam requires excessive manipulation to fold it in with other ingredients. Hard meringues are beaten to this stiff-peak stage.

Continued beating produces a dry foam that breaks into pieces when an attempt is made to blend it with other ingredients. Stability of the foam is decreased. At this dry stage the whites are definitely overbeaten and have little utility in food preparation.

Hard and Soft Meringues. Hard and soft meringues are simply egg white foams with some acid and sugar added. A fine-textured, soft meringue for a pie results when two tablespoons of sugar per egg white are added as outlined in the preceding section. The use of dessert sugar is helpful because the fine crystals dissolve readily. Meringues beaten until the peaks just bend over are sufficiently stable and yet have enough elasticity to permit some expansion during baking. For maximum volume and minimum drainage, a meringue should be placed immediately on a warm filling, carefully sealed to the edges, and then baked in a preheated oven. Since no foam is completely stable, the volume will be greatest if the meringue is baked immediately to coagulate the protein films.

A meringue shaped with one or two long swirls around the surface will brown nicely, in contrast to one with high peaks that brown or even burn before the main body of the foam is heated enough to coagulate the protein. A meringue is done when a pleasing medium brown color develops on the ridges of the meringue. If the meringue is underbaked, the structure will not be set and the foam will break down and leak onto the surface of the filling. A meringue that is allowed to brown too much is tough at the surface and does not cut easily.

A well-prepared soft meringue is a pleasing study in brown and white with no burned peaks. The texture is fine and uniform; the foam is light and high. The meringue remains sealed to the edge of the pie and is easy to cut. Beads of moisture, due to overcoagulation of the protein, are not present.

Usually soft meringues are baked at 177°C (350°F) to permit the heat to coagulate the protein in the center of the meringue before the exterior is overbaked, but one recipe is an exception to this. A baked Alaska uses a layer of cake on the bottom with egg whites on the top and sides to insulate ice cream against the oven heat while the meringue is baking. Needless to say, speed is important in all phases of this preparation. Everything should be ready to be assembled and the oven should be preheated to 232°C (450°F) before the ice cream is removed from the freezer. The high oven temperature causes the meringue to brown before the heat penetrates sufficiently to begin melting the ice cream. With these precautions this seemingly elaborate dessert actually is not difficult to prepare.

Hard meringues are made with two times as much sugar (four table-spoons per egg white) as is used in soft meringues. The large amount of sugar

FIGURE 10.10 Hard meringue shells are an example of a very sweet meringue baked at a low oven temperature for a period long enough to dry them through-out. Various fillings and sauces may be served in them.

significantly delays foam formation. Therefore it is practical to gradually add half the sugar to form a soft meringue. Very slow addition of the last half of the sugar promotes the desired stiffness, that is, the peaks stand up very straight. Hard meringues may be formed into meringue shells or cookies which are then baked at 93–121°C (200–250°F) to dry out the meringues without browning them.

A desirable hard meringue is white, is an appropriate size, and is easy to cut without being brittle. Sticky meringues are due to underbaking or underbeating. Hard, tough meringues are the result of overbaking. Brown meringues are caused by too high an oven temperature.

Fluffy Omelets. Fluffy or puffy omelets are made by beating the yolks and whites separately, folding them together, and then baking in a skillet. First the yolks must be beaten until they are very thick and will pile; then the whites are beaten until the peaks just bend over. At this point the yolks and whites are carefully folded together until no streaks of color show. Meanwhile the oven is preheated to 163°C (325°F) and butter is melted to bubbling in a heavy skillet. The omelet is immediately heated over direct heat briefly to brown the bottom surface and subsequently is baked in the oven until the surface is dry and the protein is coagulated. The omelet is folded in half and served with or without a sauce.

The egg white foam in fluffy omelets is relatively unstable because of the added liquid that dilutes the protein in the foam. As a result, there is a strong tendency for liquid to collect in the bottom of the pan and form a heavy layer. Therefore, a fast worker is capable of producing a better fluffy omelet than a person who moves slowly. In addition, this tendency to drain can be minimized by using an acidic liquid, by thoroughly beating the yolks until they are very thick, by beating the whites to just the right point, by completely blending the yolks and whites, and by starting the coagulation process immediately and at a relatively high temperature. Acidic liquids, such as tomato or lemon juice, help to stabilize the foam and reduce drainage. Underbeating the yolks results in more fluid which will drain out easily. Underbeaten and overbeaten whites are unstable and allow drainage. Slow heating and delays in initiating the heating allow more time for the yolk to drain before the structure is set.

Maximum volume is achieved by beating the yolks and whites to just the right stage, efficiently but carefully folding in the yolks, baking immediately, and avoiding over- or underbaking. Foams of underbeaten yolks or whites are not stable and do not hold a maximum amount of air. Overbeaten whites cause poor volume in a fluffy omelet because extra folding is required to blend the yolks with the whites. In addition, the overbeaten foam is not as elastic and extensible in the oven. Overbaking causes the protein to shrink; underbaking causes the omelet to fall because the protein has not coagulated sufficiently to give rigidity to the structure.

FIGURE 10.11   Puffy omelets may be served with a variety of sauces or ingredients folded into them.

When well prepared, a fluffy omelet is light, tender, and nicely browned on the outside. There is no suggestion of a layer in the omelet and no streaks of white show. The omelet shrinks only slightly when it is removed from the oven.

Soufflés. Soufflé preparation is somewhat similar to making a fluffy omelet. The chief difference is that a thick white sauce is prepared and the yolks are added to it in the same fashion described for adding yolks to cream puddings. The whites are beaten as they are for fluffy omelets and then the sauce containing the yolks is folded in just until no streaks of color show.

The yolk sauce is thick, but not so thick that it cannot be spread over the whites as the two are folded together. If a sauce is too viscous to be folded into the whites, a little liquid should be added so excessive folding is not required. Sometimes excessive evaporation of liquid occurs during the preparation of a thick chocolate or cheese sauce for a soufflé. When a certain critical moisture level is reached, the oil will separate from the sauce, making the sauce totally unusable in that form. However, the emulsion can be reformed satisfactorily into a smooth and uniform sauce by very gradually adding either water or milk and stirring until all of the oil disappears back into emulsified form. In this manner a sauce that appears to be disastrous can be salvaged with absolutely no detrimental affect.

Immediate baking forestalls the development of a layer on the bottom of the dish. By setting the dish in a pan of hot water and using moderate oven temperatures, the structure can be set in a reasonable time without unduly

FIGURE 10.12 Souffles can carry the image of unbelievable lightness if they are baked in souffle dish that is slightly too small for the souffle. A removable foil collar confines the souffle during baking.

toughening the soufflé. In contrast to baked custards, soufflés must be baked until a knife inserted in the center comes out clean, because it is essential that the structure be set in the center of the soufflé before removal from the oven or this delicate structure will collapse. Since slight shrinking is expected even when the structure is set in the center, a soufflé will be more attractive if it is served as soon as it is done. The discussion of layer formation and volume as outlined in the section on fluffy omelets is applicable to soufflé preparation.

Soufflés should be light, pleasingly browned, and well blended, with no layer on the bottom. A good soufflé is tender and flavorful. The impression of having prepared an unusually light soufflé may be created by baking the soufflé in a small dish and putting a paper collar around the top to contain the soufflé as it rises. When the soufflé is baked, the paper is removed and the soufflé is high above the rim of the dish. Such a soufflé always seems lighter and better than one of comparable quality which has been baked in a dish large enough to accommodate it. The use of such psychological techniques helps to create dramatic impressions with foods. Soufflés may be the main course for a luncheon or they may be desserts, depending on the type of soufflé. When served with butter, spoon bread, which is actually a corn-meal soufflé, makes an attractive potato substitute at a meal.

Sponge Cakes. Sponge cakes are somewhat similar to fluffy omelets in their preparation. A very thick egg yolk foam is prepared by first thoroughly beating the yolks with lemon juice and sugar. True sponge cakes utilize the separated whole egg, but contain no chemical leavening agent or shortening. Since air is an important leavening agent in sponge cake, the cake will be appreciably lighter if considerable air is beaten into the yolks. In addition, beating increases the viscosity of the yolks and makes it improbable that the yolks will drain from the whites to form a layer at the bottom of the cake pan. The addition of water to the yolks dilutes the protein, raises the coagulation temperature of the cake structure, and results in a more tender cake.

The folding of the cake flour into the yolks is a crucial step. This operation should be done thoroughly, yet efficiently. Streaks of flour are offensive in a cake, but excessive folding overdevelops the gluten in the flour and also releases some of the air. The result is a less tender cake with a decreased volume.

Egg whites must be beaten until the peaks just bend over if maximum volume and tenderness are to be achieved. The elasticity remaining in the protein at this stage permits the cell walls of the cake to extend as the air in the cells expands during baking, thus increasing the volume of the cake. Tenderness is also increased since the distended cell wall is thinner. Beating part of the sugar into the egg whites produces a finer texture and increases the volume of the cake. The increased volume is due to the greater stability of the sugar and egg white foam during folding and baking.

A good sponge cake has fairly fine, uniform cells and thin cell walls. The interior is homogeneous and does not reveal flecks of egg white, streaks of yellow, or the beginnings of a layer. The exterior is a pleasing golden brown. The cake is tender and of good volume. Maximum volume of a sponge cake is maintained by cooling the cake in an inverted position so that the cell walls are stretched out by the weight of the cake. A tube pan with legs is excellent for sponge cakes.

Angel Cake. An angel cake is basically an egg white foam with a little flour added to strengthen the structure. Neither shortening nor baking powder is used. The factors influencing volume, formation, and stability of egg white foams are discussed earlier in this chapter. Since egg whites are such a vital ingredient in this cake, high-quality eggs should be used because they produce more stable foams. Warming the whites to room temperature facilitates the formation but not the stability of the foam. Angel cakes are most satisfactorily made by mixing part of the sugar with the cake flour to reduce the tendency of the flour to roll into little balls that are difficult to fold into the whites. The flour mixture is carefully folded into whites beaten with sugar until the peaks just bend over. When the batter is in the pan it is wise to cut around the batter with a knife to break large air pockets and produce a more uniform texture. Angel cakes should be baked until the top springs back when the surface is lightly touched. Underbaking results in a compact cake that likely will fall from the pan as it cools. Overbaking causes the cake to be less moist and tender.

The structure of angel and sponge cakes is quite delicate when the cakes are hot. A tube pan gives a center surface to help pull up the cake to maximum volume in the oven. The narrower diameter of the cake also contributes to the greater volume by promoting rapid heating and coagulation of the structural proteins before the foam begins to lose volume. These tender cakes will settle and become somewhat compact if cooled in a normal position, hence they are inverted to keep the cells stretched as the structure cools and becomes firmer. Tube pans with legs allow air to circulate under the cake and keep the surface from becoming damp.

Excellent angel cakes may be prepared from mixes. These mixes are less expensive than angel cakes from fresh eggs during certain seasons of the year. In addition, one is not confronted with the necessity of finding ingenious ways to use twelve egg yolks. After the dried egg whites are reconstituted, the procedure for preparing an angel cake from a mix is basically the same as for the fresh angel cake. Experience has shown, however, that better volume is obtained from the angel cake mixes if the whites are beaten until they pull up in very stiff peaks. This stage of beating exceeds considerably the amount of beating done when fresh egg whites are used.

A good angel cake is light, moist, and very tender. The air cells are rather uniform, though not fine in size, and the cell walls are thin. The exterior is a pleasing brown.

Eggs as Emulsifying Agents

The emulsifying properties of eggs definitely are significant in salad dressings (see Chapter 6). Various baked products, however, rely on eggs as the emulsifier. In a cheese soufflé, egg yolks prevent a separation of the fat in the cheese from the soufflé. Cream puffs exhibit considerable exudation of oil unless an adequate amount of yolk is present as an emulsifier. Eggs promote formation of an emulsion in a conventional cake batter, thus producing a cake of fine texture.

SUMMARY

Eggs are one of the most versatile and nourishing foods in the American diet. Nutritionally, eggs are valued as a complete protein which can be afforded by nearly all people. The yolk provides a significant proportion of the iron intake in many diets.

Chickens are being encouraged to be less seasonal in their laying habits, but there are still peaks and depressions in egg production during the year. Cold storage, drying, and freezing are current methods of distributing the egg supply throughout the year. The quality of eggs may be maintained during cold storage if the conditions are satisfactorily controlled.

Grading of eggs according to federal specifications may be done by candling in the shell or evaluation out of the shell. High-quality eggs are preferred for culinary uses because the flavor and performance are at their peak. Scrambled eggs, French omelets, and some casseroles, however, are satisfactory ways to use eggs of slightly lower quality.

Egg preparation is based on the need for reasonably low temperatures to avoid toughening of the protein. When egg is used as a thickening agent, it is necessary to avoid the direct addition of egg to any hot mixture. Best results are obtained when a small portion of the hot liquid is stirred into the egg before the egg is added to the other ingredients. Continuous stirring is necessary while the egg is coagulating. These two precautions produce a smoothly thickened rather than a lumpy product. Maximum thickening from egg proteins is achieved by maintaining the food at temperatures just under boiling until coagulation is completed.

The success of any product containing an egg foam depends on the character of the foam itself. Egg yolk foams for fluffy omelets and sponge cakes must be beaten until they are quite viscous, otherwise they tend to drain from the whites and form an undesirable layer at the bottom. Egg white foams change in character with the extent of beating, the quality of the eggs, and the presence of other substances. When whites are beaten to the foamy stage, it is time to begin adding sugar, liquid, or acids that may be a part of the ingredients. Egg white foams to be used for soft meringues or for folding into other ingredients should be beaten to the soft-peak stage, that is, the peaks bend over slightly. Hard meringues are beaten still more until the peaks stand up straight, the stiff-peak stage. Continued beating beyond the stiff-peak stage results in a dry, rather brittle foam that has no functional use. Soufflés, fluffy omelets, angel and sponge cakes, as well as hard and soft meringues utilize egg foams.

BIBLIOGRAPHY

Consumer and Marketing Service. *USDA Egg Products Inspection.* U. S. Department of Agriculture. Washington, D. C. 1968.

Fresh fancy or grade AA eggs. *Marketing Bulletin No. 26.* U. S. Department of Agriculture, Agricultural Marketing Service, Poultry Division. Washington, D. C. 1963.

Grange, G. R. *Regulations Governing the Grading and Inspection of Egg Products.* U. S. Department of Agriculture, Agricultural Marketing Service, Poultry Division. Washington, D.C. 1964.

Grange, G. R. *Regulations Governing the Grading of Shell Eggs and United States Standards, Grades, and Weight Classes for Shell Eggs.* U. S. Department of Agriculture, Agricultural Marketing Service, Poultry Division, Washington, D. C. 1965.

Griswold, R. *Experimental Study of Food.* Houghton Mifflin, Boston, Mass. 1962.

Hester, E. E., and C. J. Personius. Factors affecting the beading and leakage of soft meringues. *Food Tech. 3:236.* 1964.

How to buy eggs by USDA grades and weight classes. *Leaflet No. 442,* U. S. Department of Agriculture, Agricultural Marketing Service. Washington, D. C. 1964.

Kenneth, H. C., Jr., and J. C. Fitzgerald. Shell egg grading and inspection of egg products. *Marketing Bulletin No. 30.* U. S. Department of Agriculture, Agricultural Marketing Service, Poultry Division. Washington, D. C. 1964.

Know the eggs you buy. U. S. Department of Agriculture, Agricultural Marketing Service, Poultry Division. Washington, D. C. 1956.

Lowe, B., *Experimental Cookery.* 3rd ed. Wiley. New York, N.Y. 1953.

USDA Acceptance Service for Poultry and Eggs. U. S. Department of Agriculture, Agricultural Marketing Service, Poultry Division. Washington, D. C. 1964.

SUGGESTIONS FOR STUDY

1. Compare the time and ease of preparation, cost, and palatability of an angel cake made with fresh eggs with an angel cake prepared from a mix.
2. Outline the bases for evaluation of egg quality in the shell and out of the shell.

3. What factors determine the coagulation temperature of an egg mixture?
4. What are the causes of a layer in the bottom of a soufflé?
5. What are the characteristics of an overbaked custard?
6. Why is a soufflé tested in the center and a custard in the region halfway between the center and the edge of the dish?

CHAPTER 11
Leavening Agents

Many batters and doughs undergo impressive changes in volume during the baking period. This expansion is caused by gases generated within the cells pressing outward against cell walls as the oven heat causes these gases to expand and develop pressure. Controlled increases in volume are essential in the production of high-quality baked products. The leavening agents, used in various combinations, are air, steam, and carbon dioxide produced by yeast or chemical reactions.

AIR

Air is one leavening agent present in all batters and doughs. Its contribution toward leavening of the finished product, however, varies considerably. Air incorporated during mixing begins to expand as it is warmed in the oven and causes some increase in the volume of the baked product. The amount of air contained in a batter is determined by the amount of manipulation, the viscosity of the batter, the nature of the ingredients, and the length of time elapsing before baking.

Amount of manipulation

The amount of manipulation is a factor requiring some explanation for, although increased mixing generally encases more air in a product, it cannot be stated flatly that this is always true. The beating of egg whites is an outstanding example of the use of manipulation to incorporate more air, with increased manipulation to an optimum point causing a greater volume in the finished product. Beyond this point, however, the cell walls in the foam become less elastic and either increased beating or folding will cause loss of

295

air and reduced volume. When egg white foams are folded into a batter, minimal manipulation is an aid in avoiding loss of air from the foam.

Viscosity of the Batter

The extensive creaming of fat and sugar is done to produce a foam of gas in a solid. Although this is a heavy foam compared to an egg white foam, it is very important because fine-textured cakes result when the fat-sugar-air foam has been beaten sufficiently to produce many tiny air pockets. The air in such a foam contributes a proportionately small, but highly significant leavening action.

The viscosity of the unbaked mixture varies with the temperature and the proportion of the ingredients. It is certainly more difficult to cream a chilled fat than to cream a fat at room temperature. The increased viscosity of the colder fat makes it more difficult to encase air in the mixture so that, with the same amount of work, less air actually is in the creamed mixture. This situation is analogous to the beating of a cold batter as contrasted with one in which the ingredients are at room temperature. On the other hand, a very warm, fluid batter is less able to trap the air in the mixture than is a somewhat cooler, less fluid mixture. Also, the proportions of ingredients influence the viscosity of a batter or dough. An extremely fluid mixture with a high proportion of liquid is incapable of holding a large amount of air for a long period of time, although the decreased viscosity permits rapid beating. Popovers are a classic example of this type of batter. A thicker batter with less liquid in proportion to the dry ingredients requires considerable effort to beat in air, but it is difficult for the air to escape.

Nature of the Ingredients

An example of the influence of the nature of ingredients on the quantity of air is that of an oil versus a plastic shortening. Air creamed into a plastic fat is held within the batter more effectively than that beaten into a product using oil.

Egg foams present a more striking example. When the egg in a formula is incorporated as an egg white foam, the large amount of air held in the foam contributes appreciable leavening, as in an angel cake. Certainly a lesser amount of air will be contained in an egg yolk or a whole egg foam. Although some leavening is achieved by yolk or whole egg foams, their contribution is appreciably less significant than that of an egg white foam.

Bench Time

The length of time elapsing during preparation of a product prior to baking (generally referred to as bench time) also determines the amount of

FIGURE 11.1   Air is an effective leavening agent when trapped in an egg-white foam used to prepare a souffle.

air available for leavening. It is true that the loss is greater in some batters than others, but some loss occurs in any batter with the passage of time. Hence, the greatest amount of leavening from air is attained by working rapidly and initiating baking as soon as possible.

STEAM

Steam, like air, is an ever-present leavening agent. Even a small amount of water in a batter or dough causes an appreciable leavening action because a volume of water expands 1600 times when it is converted to steam during baking. Therefore, even in a typical cooky dough, water accomplishes some leavening through its conversion to steam. In a highly fluid popover batter, the larger quantity of water is converted by the intense oven heat to steam, which rapidly achieves a dramatic increase in volume.

FIGURE 11.2 The high oven temperature and fluid batter work together to generate steam, the primary leavening agent of popovers.

In summary, it may be stated that both steam and air effect some leavening in all baked products. The actual amount of such leavening is related directly to the amount of air or water in the batter or dough. In certain products these two sources of gas are sufficient, but in others an additional substance is needed to complement their influence.

YEAST

The leavening of some products is due primarily to the production of carbon dioxide by a one-celled plant called a yeast. The study of yeasts and their life cycle dates back to 1680 when Leeuwenhoek studied a yeast under a microscope; and in 1838 Meyer studied the process of fermentation by yeast. Considerable sophistication marks the current research efforts, but a strain of yeast used in early studies is the type of yeast still in common use in the modern kitchen.

Saccharomyces cerevisiae, the particular strain of yeast used in baked products today, multiplies rapidly under controlled conditions to release large quantities of carbon dioxide. The yeast plants feed on simple sugars and metabolize them ultimately to carbon dioxide, water, and alcohol. In 1897 Buchner gave the name zymase to the enzyme complex necessary for this conversion.

In yeast-containing batters and doughs, the sugar required by the yeast is available from three sources: sugar added in the mixing period, sugar present as such in flour, and sugar released from wheat starch by enzymatic action. The sugar (sucrose) added during mixing is necessary to ensure adequate gas for leavening. The yeast itself contains sucrase, the enzyme needed to split sucrose to glucose and fructose. Flour naturally contains 1 to 2 percent of the monosaccharide glucose that is immediately available to the yeast. In addition, the starch in wheat flour can be broken down by several enzymes, including β-amylase, which systematically breaks off units of the disaccharide, maltose. Subsequently, maltose is split to glucose to provide food for the yeast. Other enzymes participating in the release of glucose from starch include R-enzyme, Z-enzyme, and limit dextrinase.

Growth of yeast, and hence carbon dioxide production, is governed by temperature as well as available dietary sugar. Yeast activity begins at 10°C (50°F) and multiplies rapidly at temperatures of 29–35°C (85–95°F), whereas cooler temperatures are less effective in promoting multiplication and the accompanying release of carbon dioxide. The rise in temperature of a yeast dough as it warms in the oven is accompanied by an accelerated release of carbon dioxide until the dough approaches the temperature at which the yeast are killed. According to Hart, yeast are killed in five minutes at 60°C (140°F) and in one hour at 43°C (110°F). Obviously, the killing of the yeast, either by excessively hot liquid during mixing or by oven heat, eliminates the possibility of further gas formation.

The fermentation process with its ultimate release of alcohol, carbon dioxide, and water must be controlled to achieve the desired texture and

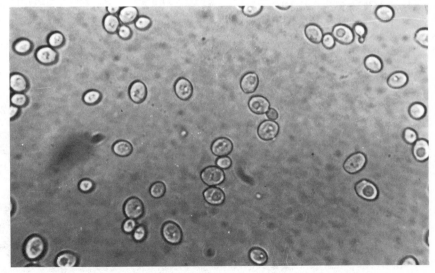

FIGURE 11.3   *Saccharomyces cerevisiae* as seen under a microscope.

flavor. Providing sugar as a food for the yeast and maintaining suitable temperatures encourages fermentation. A desirable rate of gas production is achieved by adding salt to slightly retard gas formation. Fermentation must be halted by baking before the dough becomes too porous from excessive amounts of carbon dioxide.

Yeast is marketed as compressed or active dry yeast. Compressed yeast is formed into cornstarch-containing cakes which are preferred by some people because of their rapid action. The moisture content of the compressed cakes is approximately 72 percent. The chief drawbacks to compressed yeast are that (1) it must be stored at cool temperatures, that is, 1–3°C (34–38°F), and (2) even at this storage temperature the shelf life is only approximately five weeks.

The production of active dry yeast involves a propagation period in dilute molasses at 30°C (86°F), followed by recovery of the yeast and compression into press cake. This press cake then undergoes extrusion and dehydration to about 8 percent moisture at approximately 43°C (110°F). The final step is grinding to produce the familiar granular active dry yeast. When this type of yeast is packaged by a vacuum process or in a nitrogen-containing environment, storage life is greatly increased, which counterbalances the inconvenience of rehydrating the active dry yeast. Rehydration is most effectively accomplished at temperatures between 38 and 46°C (100 and 115°F).

The actual effective shelf life of active dry yeast is related to the storage temperature. According to Peppler, active dry yeast stored at 5°C (40°F) will still be an effective leavening agent after two years, whereas six months is a reasonable storage period for active dry yeast held at 32°C (90°F). This type of yeast can also be frozen without destroying its activity. The expiration date is stamped on each package of either type of yeast and should not be ignored if optimum results are to be expected.

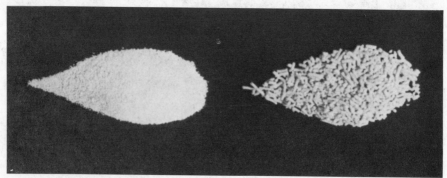

FIGURE 11.4   Active dry yeast after dehydration process (left) and following coarse granulation process.

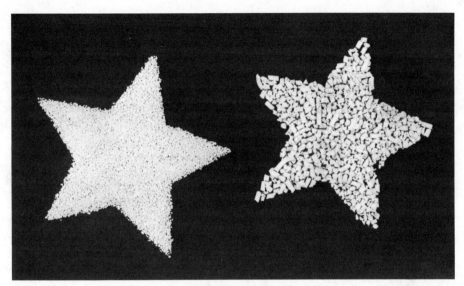

FIGURE 11.5   Fine granular active dry yeast is tailored for institutional and consumer use; coarse granules are used by wholesale bakers.

CHEMICAL LEAVENING AGENTS

The chemical leaveners so often used today to produce carbon dioxide were developed originally in Europe in the nineteenth century. Liebig, the nineteenth-century German chemist, introduced and manufactured baking powder in Europe more than 100 years ago. A baking powder containing 60 parts cream of tartar, 30 parts baking soda, and 10 parts of potato starch was marketed by Dr. Price in Illinois in 1858. Phosphate-type powders appeared in 1861, followed by a tartrate powder in 1868 and sodium aluminum sulfate in 1892.

These basic types of powders are still available for home use, although the leavening agents available to commercial bakers have become more diverse through research. Today the commercial baker has the choice of several leavening agents, some of which are specifically designed to be used in a particular food such as doughnuts and others that are intended for more general use.

Criteria for Evaluating Baking Powders

Five factors are important when a baking powder is being considered for home use.

1. Since the can probably will be emptied rather slowly, it is important for the powder to have a long shelf life and not proceed to react

FIGURE 11.6   The volume of conventional cakes is due largely to the release of carbon dioxide from baking powder during mixing and baking.

slowly in the can. If use of baking powder is quite limited in home food preparation, the smallest can available will be the wisest selection because any baking powder will deteriorate over an extended storage period.

2. From the gustatory standpoint it is necessary that an ideal baking powder have no unpleasant residue flavor in the baked product and that the residue be harmless to humans. The latter aspect is controlled by the Food and Drug Administration.

3. Ideally, the baking powder is inexpensive.

4. A perfect baking powder gives little gas at room temperature during the mixing period, but releases it during the initial phase of baking before the structure of the baked product has set completely. This circumstance achieves maximum leavening without rupturing the product.

5. It is also suggested that a baking powder should give the most gas possible for the least volume and weight of the material. However, the baking powders for home use today are required by law to give not less than 12 percent carbon dioxide. As a safety margin for their own protection, most baking-powder manufacturers produce a pow-

der designed to give approximately 14 percent carbon dioxide. This standardization of the amount of gas given off by the various baking powders is a boon to the homemaker since it makes it possible for various powders to be used interchangeably in a formula.

Ingredients

Soda (sodium bicarbonate) is the alkaline ingredient common to all baking powders. This is the only substance that has ever been used in baking powders to neutralize the various acid ingredients found in the powders. Baking powders commonly contain 28–30 percent soda in their formulas.

Various acid ingredients are used in baking powders either singly or in combination with another acid to react with soda and produce carbon dioxide. The nomenclature of baking powders is based on the acid ingredient used in the powder. The acids are considered in the next section.

Soda and the acid salt are the active ingredients in baking powder. When the baking powder is moistened, as is true when the leavening agent is added to batters and doughs, these substances react to produce carbon dioxide according to the following general formula:

$$NaHCO_3 + HX \longrightarrow CO_2 \uparrow + H_2O + NaX$$
$$\text{(soda)} \quad \text{(acid)}$$

Starch serves two functions in a baking powder: (1) it keeps the reaction of the acid and soda in the can to a minimum by separating the granules and absorbing moisture that would cause some reaction of the powder during storage; (2) it is used as a filler to standardize the amount of gas to be released from a measured amount of the powder. Although potato starch was used in Dr. Price's baking powder, cornstarch is commonly used today.

Egg albumen is dried and ground to a powder when it is used as an optional ingredient in baking powders. In cold water it dissolves and increases the viscosity of the dough. This helps to hold the gas bubbles in the dough, thus increasing the effectiveness of the baking powder. When albumen is used, it is added in a very small quantity (0.15 percent).

Acid Ingredients

Tartrates. Tartrate baking powders, desirable because of their virtually tasteless residue, often are the choice of experienced cooks. They are unsatisfactory, however, for slow workers because they have the disadvantage of being able to release most of their gas at room temperature. Other factors to be considered when selecting a tartrate powder are its slightly higher price and its limited shelf life due to the ease of reaction in the can.

The residues of all baking powders act as cathartics and diuretics, but tartrate residues are more potent than those from the sodium aluminum sulfate powders. The Food and Drug Administration, however, considers all these substances safe in their normal usage. This is true even of powder containing cream of tartar, which has a substantially higher residue level than other powders.

Tartaric acid, one of the tartrate salts commonly used, reacts with soda as follows:

$$2NaHCO_3 + H_2C_4H_4O_6 \longrightarrow Na_2C_4H_4O_6 + 2H_2O + 2CO_2 \uparrow$$

Acid potassium tartrate, commonly called cream of tartar, is the other tartrate salt used in tartrate powders. Its reaction is:

$$NaHCO_3 + KHC_4H_4O_6 \longrightarrow NaKC_4H_4O_6 + H_2O + CO_2 \uparrow$$

Royal baking powder is a familiar example of a tartrate baking powder.

Phosphates. The phosphate powders react somewhat more slowly at room temperature than do the tartrates, but they still may lose a high percentage of their gas prior to baking. In 1920 sodium acid pyrophosphate (SAPP) and/or monocalcium phosphate (MCP) were used in combination as the two acid ingredients in a phosphate baking powder. Calcium acid phosphate, from phosphate rocks and bones, was chosen because of its keeping qualities, and sodium acid pyrophosphate was a logical choice because of its lower cost. The reaction of monocalcium phosphate, also called calcium acid phosphate, is:

$$8NaHCO_3 + 3CaH_4(PO_4)_2 \longrightarrow Ca_3(PO_4)_2 + 4Na_2HPO_4 + 8H_2O + 8CO_2 \uparrow$$

Rumford represents this type of baking powder.

Both the tartrates and phosphates produce so much of their potential gas at room temperatures that there is some possibility that products made with these will fall because of insufficient carbon dioxide content to maintain the maximum volume until the structure sets. The ready release of gas at mixing temperatures does aid in developing a fine uniform texture because many small gas bubbles are present in the batter.

Sodium Aluminum Sulfate. The reaction of sodium aluminum sulfate with soda, occurring primarily at oven temperatures, is:

$$2NaAl(SO_4)_2 + 6NaHCO_3 \longrightarrow 2Al(OH)_3 + 4Na_2SO_4 + 6CO_2 \uparrow$$

Although the keeping qualities of this sulfate baking powder are excellent, other shortcomings have been noted. The residue of sodium sulfate has a distinctly penetrating, bitter flavor objectionable to many people.

Also sodium aluminum sulfate, or SAS as it is usually termed, is unsuitable as a single leavening acid because the crust of a baked product will set before a sufficient quantity of gas has been generated to produce the desired volume.

Sulfate-phosphate. Because of the limitations of the types of powders just described, SAS has been combined with calcium acid phosphate to produce the familiar double-acting baking powders such as Calumet. In double-acting (sulfate-phosphate) powders the phosphate releases some gas at room temperature during mixing and continues to work during the initial phase of the baking. As the temperature of the product rises, the SAS begins to react and continues the leavening process. The customary ratio is four parts phosphate to one part SAS. The primary disadvantage of this type of powder is the bitter residue flavor. The large quantity of gas released only at oven temperatures makes this a particularly suitable leavening agent for those who work at moderate or slow speeds.

Chemical Leavening Agents for Commercial Use

A variety of acid ingredients is presently being marketed for commercial bakers. These acids are sold as separate ingredients to be combined with soda in the dough, rather than being combined with soda at the factory and marketed as a complete leavening agent. The obvious advantage of this system is that the shelf life of the acids is extended since there is no alkaline ingredient present for reaction. The disadvantage is the increased possibility of error in the baking formula.

Phosphates. Phosphates have received considerable attention in the pursuit of suitable acid ingredients for leavening purposes. Several variations in sodium acid pyrophosphate (SAPP), monocalcium phosphate (MCP), and sodium aluminum phosphate (SAP) are currently available for commercial utilization.

Monocalcium phosphate, an example of which is marketed as V-90, releases about 60 percent of its carbon dioxide at room temperature during mixing. Its rapid activity limits its usefulness as a single acid ingredient, but it has found acceptance when used in combination with other acids. Monocalcium phosphate is useful in helping to create and expand gas cells during mixing. An anhydrous substance can be coated onto the monocalcium phosphate to slow its reaction at room temperature.

Sodium acid pyrophosphate (SAPP) is manufactured in granules of varying sizes to provide a baking powder with the desired reaction speed. SAPP powders of very fine granules react more slowly than do the powders with larger granule size. The reaction rate varies somewhat depending on the age of the flour and the presence of milk. The calcium ions in milk or milk

solids apparently form a coating around the granules of SAPP which dissolves with the passage of time and/or increase in temperature. If a dough
is allowed to stand for a period prior to baking, enzymes in the flour cause
the dough to become more acidic and carbon dioxide is lost.

Sodium aluminum phosphate is appreciated commercially for its relatively consistent behavior with various flours. This characteristic aids in
producing cakes with sufficiently firm cell walls to minimize the tendency
to fall. This acid also is available in forms varying in reactivity. More research with this acid may be anticipated.

Dicalcium phosphate is an acid ingredient used for leavening in combination with other acids. When used alone it is unsatisfactory for it releases
carbon dioxide so late in the baking period that the structure is almost set
before leavening action begins. This acid is suitable as a partner with other
acids, primarily in products with relatively long baking times.

Glucono-delta-lactone. Glucono-delta-lactone is a different type of compound from the commercial acids just mentioned for it is a carbohydrate-
like substance with the structure

$$
\begin{array}{l}
O{=}C \\
H{-}C{-}OH \\
HO{-}C{-}H \quad O \\
H{-}C{-}OH \\
H{-}C \\
\quad CH_2OH
\end{array}
$$

Considerable interest has been generated in it because of its effective leavening action and its tasteless, harmless residue. Reports regarding its use
indicate that it promotes the development of a structure similar to that
found in yeast-leavened products. It is reasonable to expect extensive use
of this relatively new acid ingredient in commercial baked products.

SUMMARY

Air and steam are leavening agents of universal occurrence but of
varying significance in different baked products. Yeast may be added as a
means of providing a source of carbon dioxide in some doughs. All chemical
baking powders contain soda, a standardizing agent (cornstarch), and an
acid ingredient. The acid may be a tartrate, phosphate, or sodium aluminum
sulfate salt or a combination of these. No one of these types of powders
is ideal.

Advances have been made in the acid salts available to commercial bakers, but they are frequently tailormade to a specific use rather than to the general use required of home baking powder. With the rapid expansion in the marketing of mixes and both frozen and fresh bakery products, it is not surprising that research has centered in the industrial rather than in the home market. Some of the new acids, however, have characteristics that could be adapted readily to home use.

BIBLIOGRAPHY

Actif-8 technical data. Stauffer Chemical Co. Victor Chemical Division. 380 Madison Ave. New York, N.Y. 1962.

Atkinson, T. G. *Baking powder.* Commonwealth Press. Chicago, Ill. 1915.

Baking acids. Stauffer Chemical Co. Victor Chemical Division. 155 N. Wacker Drive. Chicago 6, Ill. 1964.

Baking powder, the chemical leavening for cakes, biscuits, and cookies. *Bulletin No. 173.* American Society of Bakery Engineers. Room 1354. LaSalle Wacker Building. 121 W. Wacker Drive. Chicago, Ill. November 1963.

Byers, H. G. *The difference in baking powders.* Commonwealth Press. Chicago, Ill. 1928.

Darral, J. E. *Modern baking powders.* Commonwealth Press, Chicago, Ill. 1927.

Feldberg, C. Instant bakery specialties. *Food Processing.* October 1960.

Feldberg, C. Glucono-delta-lactone in baked goods. *Food in Canada 22:* 44. 1962.

Foot, F. N., *Baking powder and other leavening agents.* Spice Mill Publishing Co. 521 Washington St. New York, N.Y. 1906.

Geddes, W. F. Role of enzymes in milling and baking technology *Food Tech. 4:* 441–446. 1950.

Glucono-delta-lactone in food products. *Technical Bulletin No. 93.* Chas. Pfizer and Co. 235 E. 42nd St. New York 17, N.Y. 1961.

Handbook of Food Preparation. American Home Economics Association. 1600 20th St., N.W. Washington 9, D.C. 1959.

Hart, R. N. *Leavening Agents.* Chemical Publishing Co. Easton, Pa. 1914.

Improved Leavening with Sodium Aluminum Phosphate. Stauffer Chemical Co. Victor Chemical Division. 380 Madison Ave. New York, N.Y. 1964.

Lowe, B., *Experimental Cookery.* 3rd ed. Wiley. New York, 1953.

Meyer, L. H. *Introductory Chemistry.* Macmillan, New York, N.Y. 1951.

Peppler, H. J. Yeast. Chapter 2 in *Bakery technology and engineering,* ed. by S. A. Matz, Avi Publishing Co. Westport, Conn. 1960.

Pfizer products for the food industry. Chas. Pfizer and Co. Chemical Sales Division. 235 E. 42nd St., New York 17, N.Y. 1963.

Properties and uses of leavening acids. Stauffer Chemical Co. Victor Chemical Division. 380 Madison Ave. New York, N.Y. 1964.

Schoch, T. J. Starches and enzymes. *Am. Soc. Brewing Chemists Proc.* 1961. Pages 83–92.

Strauss, M. *Effect of Ingredient Variation on Chemically Leavened Batter and Dough Products.* M. S. thesis. Oregon State College. 1954.

Tucker, J. Fundamentals and applications of chemical leavenings. *Am. Miller and Processor.* December 1959. Pages 12–14.

SUGGESTIONS FOR STUDY

1. Explain the factors that influence the leavening contribution of air in batters and doughs.
2. What are the sources of food for yeast in a dough? How will the availability of sugar influence the yeast plants? What will be the observable result on the baked product of decreasing the amount of sugar in the recipe?
3. What is the function of each of the ingredients in a baking powder?
4. What are the advantages and disadvantages of *(a)* tartrate, *(b)* phosphate, *(c)* sodium aluminum sulfate, *(d)* sulfate-phosphate baking powders?

CHAPTER 12

Baked Products

Baked products have long been an important part of daily fare throughout the world, although the actual products may take many different forms. Throughout history evidence has indicated the existence of breads of different types. As far back as 50 centuries ago, Egyptians apparently had discovered the secrets of making leavened bread. Modifications of breads developed throughout the world to utilize available foodstuffs and equipment; whether baked in primitive ovens or steamed, the fundamental ingredient was wheat flour. The flours that were ground from wheat had the unique ability to form a cohesive mixture when liquid was added, and this simple discovery set the stage for the development of the many yeast breads, quick breads, pastries, cakes, cookies, and other baked products that are so popular today.

If people were asked to describe their favorite baked product today, doubtless there would be a tremendous range of answers. This variety would be due, in part, to the many different types of items that are considered to be batters and doughs. However, the descriptions would range from the frozen ready-to-eat baked products, off-the-shelf items, and foods prepared from mixes, to freshly baked goods made in the kitchen by using individually measured and mixed ingredients. Many people enjoy baking in the home and are anxious to know how to evaluate their products and make them even better the next time. Others probably will buy most of the baked products consumed by their families, while many others will use mixes extensively while buying a few products already baked and making a few from the beginning at home. Regardless of the actual products selected, the wise consumer will study the formulation and final products so that he will have a better understanding of the standards for evaluation and the contributions that the various ingredients and their proportions make to the finished products.

FIGURE 12.1   Yeast breads and other baked products afford a wide range of flavors and textures.

INGREDIENTS AND THEIR FUNCTIONS

Eggs, sugar, salt, a leavening agent, a liquid, shortening, and flour are ingredients common to most baked products. In addition, various other ingredients such as chocolate, nuts, spices, or fruits are used to add interest to the foods. The basic ingredients fulfill certain important structural and leavening functions in batters and doughs.

FLOUR

Baked products all rely on flour for their basic structure. Among the cereal grains, rye has limited potential for making cohesive baked products, and the flour made from wheat has a far greater capacity for binding ingredients together into baked products with the integrity of structure that generally is considered desirable. When a piece of cake is served, for example, one expects the cake to have sufficient structural strength to remain intact when a serving is removed from the pan. A slice of bread is expected to hold together so that a sandwich will not disintegrate in the hands. Presumably, a wedge of pie will have sufficient strength in the crust so that the piece can be transferred to a serving plate without falling apart. Procedures and formulations for baked products are based on the ability of wheat flour to develop a structure that can be served and eaten easily, yet one that is not tough. The unique component of wheat that contributes this special structural quality is a protein complex, gluten.

Wheat Proteins

The protein content of wheat varies from 6 percent in weak wheats to more than 18 percent in a few varieties; the protein content of wheat flour ranges from 10 to 17 percent. The variation in the quantity and quality of protein in flour is useful, for bread of superior quality can be made with flour containing a strong protein ranging in level from 11.5 to 14 percent, whereas a flour with less protein and of a less cohesive nature is preferable

FIGURE 12.2   The protein in wheat flour plays a major role in the structure of baked products, including breads, cakes, and pastries.

for cakes. The distribution of protein in the various portions of the wheat grain is as follows: endosperm, 72 percent; aleurone, 16 percent; testa and pericarp, 4 percent; and scutellum and embryo, 8 percent. Within the endosperm the protein content decreases from the outer portion of the endosperm to the interior. From the nutritional standpoint, lysine is the essential amino acid present in the least adequate quantity in wheat flour, and the proportion of this amino acid to the total protein decreases with an increase in the level of total protein.

Protein Fractions of Wheat Flour. The proteins of wheat may be divided into two groups on the basis of water solubility. The water-soluble proteins are albumins and globulins (see Table 12.1). Researchers have identified eleven albumins and three globulins in wheat flour. Approximately 10 percent of the total proteins are albumins and 7 percent are globulins.

Of particular interest is the water-insoluble fraction, gluten, which is divided into two subfractions: gliadin, with a molecular weight of approximately 50,000, is soluble in 60 percent aqueous alcohol; and glutenin comprises the remaining water-insoluble proteins. The molecular weight of glutenin is two to three million. Present theory states that glutenin is a protein built from a basic polypeptide unit with a molecular weight of 20,000 and that these units are then linked into the larger molecule called glutenin.

Milling

The milling process begins with selection of the wheat to be milled and a blending of the wheats, followed by cleaning and tempering. The tempering process, wherein the bran is toughened by exposure to steam, simplifies the problem of separating the bran layers from the more friable endosperm after milling. The germ also is separable because its high oil content causes the germ to be pressed into flakes rather than becoming pulverized like the endosperm. The tempering process is critical since too little tempering causes difficulty in separating the bran and endosperm, and too much tempering causes the germ and endosperm to flake together.

Table 12.1. Protein Composition of Wheat Flour

Type of Protein	Solubility in Water	Approximate % of Total Flour Protein
Albumins (11 known)	Yes	10
Globulins (3 known)	Yes	7
Gluten	No	80–85
Gliadin	No	
Glutenin	No	

Breaking, a combination of shearing and crushing action, pulverizes the endosperm and enables it to be separated from the other fractions. The material from the first break is bolted to separate the small amount of flour and then is purified to remove extraneous material from the coarse middlings. The middlings are further crushed between smooth reduction rolls and the bolting and purifying are repeated until the desired degree of grinding has been achieved. The sifted material resulting from each bolting operation is called a stream. These streams can be blended or separated, depending on the grade of flour desired.

Bleaching and maturing agents are now used to achieve artificially the whiter color and improved baking performance that formerly were gained by storing flour. Nitrogen peroxide and benzoyl peroxide are bleaching agents; chlorine, nitrosyl chloride, and chlorine dioxide are maturing agents. Enrichment programs included as part of the milling increase the riboflavin, thiamin, niacin, and iron content of many of the highly refined flours as follows (all figures are in milligrams per pound of flour): thiamin, 2.0–2.5; riboflavin, 1.2–1.5; niacin, 16.0–20.0; and iron, 13.0–16.5.

Grades of Flour

Grade is an indication of the potential baking quality of a flour. In mills where the streams are separated, patent indicates the percentage of streams used: family patent is 70–75 percent of all the streams; short patent is 78–80 percent of all streams; medium patent is 80–85 percent; and long or standard patent is 90–95 percent.

A very short patent (30 percent) cake flour containing less than 8 percent protein is made from soft red and soft white wheat. Chlorine also is added to this flour to adjust the pH to 5.1–5.3 to further weaken the gluten of the flour.

After the patent flours have been packaged, the remaining streams are used to produce the fancy clear, first clear, and second clear. Red dog is the lowest grade; straight flour is a blend of all the streams of flour in a mill. All of these nonpatent grades are poor for baking white bread, for they are higher in bran and germ than are the patent flours. One reason for their inferiority is the excess enzymes contributed by the bran in the clear flours.

Types of Flour

There are several kinds of flour available to the consumer, and each is tailored to meet specific baking requirements. The flours differ in the quantity and the strength of the protein complex. They also vary in their capacity to absorb liquids. For individuals who do a considerable amount of baking, the purchase of more than one type of flour will yield the best results.

FIGURE 12.3 The baked gluten ball on the left was made with cake flour. The one on the right was made from a comparable amount of all-purpose flour.

Cake flour, made from soft wheats, is particularly well suited for cakes because of the slightly higher carbohydrate content and lower protein content in comparison to all-purpose flour. The protein content of cake flour is approximately 7.5 percent, and the protein in this type of flour is less strong and tenacious than the gluten complex occurring in all-purpose flour. Hence cake flour is particularly adapted to use in a variety of cake recipes.

Self-rising flour is made from hard and soft wheats blended to contain a moderate amount of protein (approximately 9.3 percent). This type of flour has salt, sodium bicarbonate, and monocalcium phosphate or some other acid ingredient, with the amounts being equal to $1\frac{1}{2}$ teaspoon of baking powder and $\frac{1}{2}$ teaspoon of salt per cup of self-rising flour. Since the leavening ingredients are already present, additional leavening in the form of a chemical leavener or yeast should not be included in batters and doughs made with this type of flour.

All-purpose flour is made from hard wheat or a blend of hard and soft wheats and has an average protein content of approximately 10.5 percent. All-purpose flour, also called family flour, is suitable for use in yeast and quick breads, cookies, pastries, and in some very rich cake recipes. The bleached all-purpose flour is characterized as having a gluten (protein complex) sufficiently strong to provide a satisfactory structure for breads, yet one that could be kneaded satisfactorily by hand. A variation of this flour is available as "instantized, instant blending, or quick-mixing." This is a granular flour produced by an agglomeration or clumping process.

Pastry flour is a low-protein flour (about 7.5 percent) prepared from soft wheat for use in cookies and pastries. Although this flour is popular with commercial bakers, it is not commonly available for home use.

The absorption of liquid by various flours varies considerably from one part of the country and from one type of flour to another. In general, hard wheat has a high rate of water absorption. On the other hand, soft wheats tend to absorb less water. This variation will cause a dough prepared from flour purchased in one part of the country to have a different dough-handling character than will a dough prepared with exactly the same proportions but with flour from a distant place. For example, a pastry dough made in the South may be stickier and more difficult to handle than it would be if a flour made from a hard winter wheat had been used.

Gluten

The structural role of wheat flour is due to the presence of gluten. Gluten is the water-insoluble gliadin-glutenin complex that forms when flour and water are worked together. Gluten is significant for its abundance (80–85 percent of the total protein in flour) and its ability to form the primary cohesive and elastic structural network of baked products. Glutenin appar-

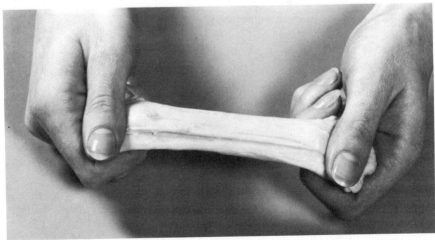

FIGURE 12.4   Gluten has a rubberlike quality which is important to the structure of baked products.

ently absorbs water and forms the continuous protein network in gluten, and gliadin then adheres to this network.

Lipids play an important role in gluten development. Considerably more mixing is required to develop the gluten in a dough made with flour from which the lipids have been extracted than from unaltered flour. Also, doughs made with flour containing rancid fat have poor flow properties.

The gluten in wheat flour is the only protein complex in cereal flours possessing the attenuating qualities necessary for production of a satisfactory structural network for baked products. The proteins in other cereal flours do not form a strong, continuous structural network and, as a result, the products from these flours are so crumbly that they disintegrate when handled.

Both agitation and liquid are necessary for gluten development, and an optimum amount of gluten development must occur during mixing if the finished product is to have some cohesiveness. More than optimum development, however, decreases volume and tenderness.

The amount of flour in a formula in relation to the other ingredients influences the finished product both in volume and tenderness. During mixing, ratios of liquid to flour which yield a sticky batter, such as a muffin batter, require a minimum of stirring to develop a gluten of an appropriate strength. Mixing beyond that point decreases both volume and tenderness because of excessive gluten development. Increasing the amount of flour in a given formula beyond the optimum amount causes the baked product to be less tender and more compact. The increased level of protein introduced with the addition of more flour lowers the coagulation temperature and hence allows less time for expansion prior to coagulation and setting of the structure. Too little flour in a product causes reduced volume since the structural network of gluten is inadequate, the actual volume of the product being directly related to the insufficiency.

The contributions of flour in baked products include not only structure, but also color and flavor. During baking, some color change occurs on the surfaces as a result of dextrinization of the starch in the flour. A somewhat less important function of white flour is flavor, but whole-wheat or rye flours certainly alter both the color and flavor of baked products.

EGGS

Eggs, depending on the quantity used and the treatment prior to inclusion in the batter, may fulfill a variety of important functions in addition to adding to the nutritive value of the product. During the mixing of a batter or dough, eggs act as a liquid in helping to moisten dry ingredients and develop gluten. The coagulation of egg proteins during baking is partially responsible for the stable structure of a baked product, the actual importance of this contribution depending on the amount of egg used. When the proportion of egg in a formula is small, the strengthening of the structure due to the presence of egg protein is small, but when several eggs are used, they assume an important structural role in the product. In addition, eggs contribute flavor and, when the yolks are used, color.

When eggs are incorporated in a batter as yolk or white foams, they enclose a large amount of air which becomes an effective means of leavening during baking. The leavening occurring in sponge cakes is an excellent illustration of the value of yolk foams and white foams. The excellent emulsifying properties of yolks aid in the formation of emulsions in some baked products, such as cake batters. The emulsifying ability of yolks is perhaps most significant in the preparation of cream puffs. In summary, eggs are important for their nutritive value, structural contribution, color, flavor, leavening action due to their foaming ability, and their emulsifying properties.

SUGAR

Certainly it is obvious that sugar contributes significantly to the flavor of a baked product. One has only to sample a cake made with an inadequate amount of sugar to become fully cognizant of the importance of sugar for flavor.

Sugar also has an important influence on the browning of sugar-containing foods as they are baking. The golden brown color that develops on the surface is partially due to caramelization of the sugar wrought by the dry heat of the oven.

The tenderness and volume of baked products is influenced by the amount of sugar in the formula. Sugar is hygroscopic, that is, it has a high affinity for water. When sugar is added to a batter or dough, some of the liquid is attracted to the sugar and becomes unavailable to aid in gluten development. Gluten development is therefore definitely retarded so that more manipulation is necessary to develop the gluten network in batters and doughs high in sugar than those with no sugar. The presence of sugar permits adequate mixing of the ingredients without causing the undue toughening that results from excessive gluten development.

The strength of the gluten network developed during mixing is an important factor in determining the volume of the baked product. During the baking period, gases in the batter or dough begin to expand and the cell walls begin to stretch. Weaker, less well-developed gluten offers somewhat less resistance to the pressure of the expanding gas. The gluten in doughs with little or no sugar generally is well developed during mixing and offers appreciable resistance to expansion of the warming gas. The difference in the strength of the gluten network developed in batters made with and without sugar partially explains the larger volume for the baked product containing sugar, and the smaller volume in a similar product prepared without sugar.

A further explanation of the influence of sugar on volume is related to coagulation of the proteins in the product. When sugar is added to any food containing protein, the coagulation temperature is raised. A partial explanation of this effect is that adding sugar is tantamount to reducing the concentration of protein. When the concentration of protein is decreased, the coagulation temperature is elevated. In baked foods a product containing sugar has a higher coagulation temperature than a similar product made without sugar. Since the product containing sugar must reach a higher temperature before coagulation occurs, there is a longer time for expansion in the oven before the proteins coagulate and the structure is finally set. The ultimate result of this longer period for expansion prior to coagulation is a larger volume for the product with sugar, as contrasted with the product made without sugar. This point may be clarified if it is borne in mind that cell walls (which contain protein) are elastic and may be stretched until the protein coagulates.

The characteristic tenderizing effect of sugar in a baked product is closely related to the influence that sugar has on volume. The larger volume resulting from the sugar causes the cell walls to be thinner because more volume has to be enclosed in the same amount of materials. This fact may seem more lucid if a balloon is used as an illustration of a cell. When a balloon is inflated slightly, the volume is small and the walls of the balloon are thick. This same balloon may be inflated until the volume is distinctly larger. If the walls of the balloon are again examined, it is apparent to the observer that the walls are stretched thinner to encompass the larger volume. Cell walls in a baked product act in the same way as the rubber in a balloon and, just as in a balloon, when the containing surface is stretched thinner, the wall becomes more tender and fragile.

An extension of the relationship of sugar in batters and doughs to the volume and tenderness of the baked product should be made. As the amount of sugar is increased, the volume and tenderness also increase until a certain critical level is reached. At that time the coagulation temperature is elevated to a point at which the protein structure is not coagulated until after the cell walls are stretched so thin that they break. When the cell walls break, the structure collapses, as seen in a cake that has fallen. To avoid this problem, the ingredients in baked products must balance each other appropriately.

SALT

Salt is used mainly for flavoring. In yeast breads, however, the salt has a regulating (inhibiting) influence on the yeast growth.

LEAVENING AGENTS

The sole purpose for using leavening agents is to manufacture gas in the food as it bakes and thus to stretch out the cells to achieve a thin cell wall, increased volume, and increased tenderness. To be effective, a leavening agent should provide an adequate amount of gas during baking to stretch the structure of the baking batter or dough and to maintain that volume until the extended protein structure coagulates. A discussion of the various leavening agents is given in Chapter 11.

LIQUIDS

Liquids used in batters and doughs usually are water, milk, sour milk, or sour cream. An important function of liquid is to aid in the development of gluten, for gluten is not developed until liquid is added to a flour mixture. Because liquid is present, some gelatinization of starch occurs during baking. Milk and other liquids act as solvents for dry ingredients such as sugar and salt, and are particularly important as a solvent for the reaction of chemical leavening agents. As previously mentioned, some leavening also occurs as a result of the formation of steam from liquid during baking.

FATS AND OILS

Fats and oils have a tenderizing effect whenever they are used in flour mixtures. Fat retards gluten development, thus making it possible to manipulate the mixture more before the gluten is developed to the point where a tough product results. Fat apparently coats the gluten strands so that they slide over each other rather than sticking together. The consistency of the fat also influences the appearance of the baked foods. For example, firm fats produce a very flaky and tender pastry, whereas an oil also yields a tender pastry, but one that is distinctly compact rather than flaky.

Additionally, fats contribute to the flavor of baked products, giving a subtle richness. When used in bread products, fats make a softer crumb and crust. This softening effect is observed by comparing French bread with a conventional bread made at home. Butter and margarine also add some color, although this contribution depends on the quantity used.

QUICK BREADS

Quick breads are aptly named because they are made quickly and are usually baked immediately after mixing. The viscosity of the various quick breads ranges from very thin popover batter to soft doughs.

Comparison of Quick Breads

Table 12.2 shows a comparison of the ingredients in various quick breads. An examination of the flour/liquid ratio and the content of other ingredients reveals why the various quick breads exhibit such diverse characteristics. Biscuits contain a solid fat that is cut in to aid in giving the desired flakiness. All the others, with the possible exception of a few fruit and nut breads, utilize a liquid shortening or a melted fat.

Popovers and cream puffs undergo an impressive increase in volume although they are the only quick breads without a chemical leavening agent. This is explained by the large amount of liquid and the steam that is produced from it at a very high baking temperature.

The relatively large amount of sugar in doughnuts and the very small amount of liquid are a deterrent to gluten formation, but it still is necessary to keep manipulation to a minimum. The formulas for muffins and biscuits contain similar quantities of liquid. This ratio of approximately twice as much flour as liquid is quite different from the one-to-one ratio of most of the other quick breads. The proportions in muffins and biscuits produce a viscous mixture in which the gluten is readily developed.

The desirable characteristics inherent in the various quick breads can be optimized when one realizes the nature of the formula and judiciously uses this knowledge. Since there is such a variation in the proportions of ingredients, the shortening used, and the manner of mixing, a discussion of each type of quick bread is presented.

Muffins

Muffins include the basic ingredients for all the quick breads, namely milk, flour, salt, and shortening. The additional ingredients are egg, baking powder, and sugar.

Table 12.2. Typical Formulas for Quick Breads

Type	Flour, cups	Milk, Tbsp.	Shortening Amount Tbsp.	State	Egg	Sugar, tsp.	Baking Powder, tsp.
Muffins	1	7	3	Liquid	1/2	4	1-1/2
Biscuits	1	5-1/2–6	2	Solid	–	–	1-1/2
Popovers	1	16	1/2	Liquid	1	–	–
Cream puffs	1	16[a]	8	Liquid	4	–	–
Waffles	1	11-1/2	4-1/2	Liquid	1+	–	1-3/4
Pancakes	1	13	1-2/3	Liquid	1	2-1/2	2-1/2
Doughnuts	1	3-1/2	1	Liquid	1	10-1/2	1-1/2

[a]Liquid is water.

FIGURE 12.5 The amount of mixing determines the characteristics of muffins. Undermixed muffins (left) have a rough surface, some specks of dry flour, poor volume, and are crumbly. Muffins mixed correctly will be slightly rounded, have a good volume, and will not crumble readily. Overmixed muffins (right) are distinguished by their peaked appearance and interior tunnels directed toward that peak.

Mixing of muffins is definitely a quick method. Ingredients are divided into two groups, liquid and dry, the fat being classified as a liquid since an oil or melted fat is used. In the muffin method of mixing, the dry ingredients are sifted together into a bowl and a depression is made in them. The liquid ingredients are prepared by first vigorously beating the egg and subsequently beating the milk and liquid shortening with the egg. The liquids are poured all at once into the well in the dry ingredients. By careful stirring, it is possible to moisten all of the dry ingredients before the batter loses its lumpy appearance.

When spooning the muffins into the muffin pans, care should be exercised to remove enough batter for one muffin with each dip of the spoon. This must be done with a minimum of stirring to avoid overmixing the remaining batter.

The amount of mixing has a marked influence on the surface and silhouette of muffins. Muffins baked from an undermixed batter have rough points on the surface, reduced volume, and a rather flat top. The poor volume is the result of incomplete reaction of the baking powder, a problem arising from not moistening all of the powder. These muffins are very crumbly and an occasional white spot of flour is observed. Muffin batter mixed the correct amount results in baked muffins that have a cauliflower-like surface and a curved rather than a flat top. The interior is rather coarse and the muffins are less crumbly. Overmixing of the batter produces muffins with a smooth surface that rises into a hump, the general outline of which is very similar to a kind of grass hut. The interior reveals tunnels where the gas has collected and risen toward the top of the muffin. The general direction of such tunnels is vertical, usually terminating in the vicinity of the peak of the muffin. The cells between the tunnels will be fairly fine, but not very uniform. The muffin becomes progressively less tender as the amount of overmixing is increased. Desirable muffins have a rounded, cauliflower-like top that is a pleasing golden brown. The interior is coarse, but only slightly crumbly.

Sometimes the time plan for a particular meal necessitates the preparation of muffins early in the schedule. In such a situation one has the option of baking the muffins then and warming them at meal time or spooning the batter into the pans and letting it sit a short time before baking. The latter is possible only when a double-acting baking powder is used.

Many recipes may be found for chemically leavened fruit and nut breads. These are most commonly made using the muffin method. The principles just reviewed in relation to muffins are generally applicable to these breads. Humped loaves may result if the batter is overmixed or baked in too small a pan. If the formulas have a larger amount of fat, the plastic fat frequently is creamed with sugar. These richer breads are a hybrid between muffins and cakes; their keeping quality is good and the texture is fairly fine.

Nut and fruit breads should be baked until a toothpick inserted in the center comes out clean. Overbaking dries the bread excessively, which is particularly detrimental to the crust. In general the expected staling time is shortened in relation to the degree of overbaking. Underbaking causes the loaf to fall because the structure does not coagulate sufficiently. Lacking the strength of the coagulated protein, the cell walls are unable to bear the load when the cooling gas contracts within the loaf; thus the center portion collapses. These fruit and nut quick breads slice more easily the day after baking rather than when they are very fresh.

Biscuits

Biscuits and their variations offer variety in the menu with a minimum amount of time required for preparation and baking. To prepare biscuits, firm fat is cut into the dry ingredients with a pastry blender until the fat is in pieces about the size of split peas. These fat particles remain intact until they are melted during baking. Since gluten does not penetrate these particles, there is no structural material in these areas and the finished product will peel off in layers when stroked horizontally with the finger, a characteristic termed flakiness. When the fat is cut into the proper size, all the milk is poured in at once and the dough is stirred with a fork just until all the flour is stirred in. Most biscuit recipes suggest a variable quantity of milk. The larger amount gives a slightly crisper product and may cause the biscuits to curl up a bit on the edges. This curling is considered undesirable even though the product appears to be slightly more tender. The dough is turned out onto a lightly floured board after mixing is completed.

After mixing, the dough is kneaded on a lightly floured board by folding the far edge of the dough over to the front edge and giving a light push with the fingertips. The dough is then rotated a quarter of a turn, folded forward and again pushed with the fingertips. This rotation and kneading procedure is done approximately ten times. During kneading, the dough is mixed more uniformly, gluten is developed to a greater extent, and the desired layered structure is promoted. Kneading must be done lightly and for a brief period or the biscuits will become tough.

After kneading, the biscuit dough is rolled to the desired thickness; a rule of thumb to serve as a guide in rolling is that the biscuits will just about double in height during baking. Thin biscuits will be crusty and dry, thicker biscuits will have a pleasing crispness on the surface and will be breadlike in the center. Most people seem to prefer biscuits made from dough that is rolled about one-half inch thick. Cutters should be reasonably sharp and should be pressed down as evenly as possible. These precautions help to keep the biscuits from being lopsided. Another aid is to place the biscuits on the baking sheet so their sides touch and thus help to hold each other straight. This also produces biscuits with soft rather than crusty sides. The arrangement on the baking sheet, either with the biscuits touching or separated, is strictly a matter of personal preference. Lightly brushing the tops

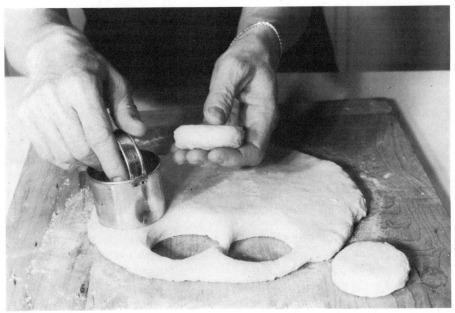

FIGURE 12.6   Biscuits are cut with a sharp cutter from dough rolled to a uniform thickness of approximately one-half inch.

FIGURE 12.7 Well prepared biscuits have a flat top, straight sides, and a flaky interior.

of the biscuits with milk before baking will dissolve baking powder at the surface of the biscuit and prevent the brown freckles of baking powder. As with muffins, biscuits may stand a while before they are baked if they are cut and placed on the sheet ready for baking. This sometimes makes the preparation of a meal less hectic.

Well-prepared biscuits have a flat top and straight sides. Their color is a pleasing medium brown. The crumb is tender and the interior is flaky. Horizontal cracks around the sides provide a visual indication of flakiness.

Popovers

Popovers represent a distinctly different type of quick bread for they contain no chemical leavening agent. The hollow center is achieved by baking at a high oven temperature to rapidly form a considerable volume of steam in the popovers. As the steam expands it exerts a pressure against the structural components. Actually, expansion is confined essentially to an upward cylindrical shape above the sides of the pan because the very hot oven temperature quickly coagulates the flour and egg proteins at the edge of the popovers. A somewhat distorted top results from the pressure of the steam which pushes against the partially set upper surface.

The preparation of popovers is a simple, quick process. All the ingredients (milk, flour, unbeaten eggs, and salt) are placed in a bowl and beaten vigorously until the batter is smooth. The fluidity of the batter causes the gluten development to proceed more slowly than it does in a more viscous batter such as muffin batter. When the batter is smooth, the gluten is sufficiently developed to be useful in the structure of the popovers, when supplemented with the relatively large proportion of egg protein. Overmixed popovers do not pop readily because the gluten is so developed that is resists the pressure exerted by the steam.

The best popovers are prepared when the freshly mixed batter is quickly poured into a well-oiled, preheated pan and immediately placed in a preheated oven. Popovers require a high initial baking temperature of 219–232°C (425–450°F) to produce a large volume of steam before the structure is set. These high temperatures, particularly 232°C (450°F), cause excessive browning before the interior is dried out. Therefore it is common practice to turn the oven temperature 55°C (100°F) lower after 15 minutes at the higher temperature. This alteration slows browning and permits some drying of the interior. This type of quick bread may be left in the oven after the heat is turned off so that some additional drying of the interior will occur. Popovers are particularly well suited to a meal that requires much last-minute attention because they are mixed and in the oven 45 minutes to an hour before serving time.

Well-prepared popovers are crisp and have medium golden brown exteriors. They are large in volume with a large cavity and reasonably thin walls. These walls should be slightly moist to rather dry, depending on personal preference.

FIGURE 12.8 When popovers are broken open, the large cavity created by the steam generated during baking is revealed.

Cream Puffs

Although cream puffs are considered a dessert item, they are sufficiently similar in appearance to popovers to merit discussion together for purposes of comparison. Both popovers and cream puffs are leavened by steam. They also contain as much liquid as flour, although water is the liquid used in the cream puffs. The differences are found in the amount of fat and the number of eggs used. Popovers contain only the fat required to keep them from sticking to the pan. However, cream puffs are made with half as much butter as water, and the butter is melted, which clearly will lead to a distinctly unstable situation. The puffs are made by stirring all of the flour into a boiling mixture of water and butter. The flour becomes coated with the butter as it is stirred into the liquid mixture. The entire mixture then is heated until it forms into a ball when the starch is gelatinized. At this point, one of the eggs is beaten in to begin to form an emulsion; subsequently the remaining eggs are added, one at a time. When done properly, a smooth paste results. However, if too much water is evaporated during the preparation of the paste, butter will ooze from the paste. This situation is remedied in the same way that a broken emulsion is remedied in making the sauce for a chocolate or cheese souffle, that is, by gradually stirring in just enough water to allow the fat to be reemulsified.

Cream puffs, like popovers are baked in a preheated, hot oven to begin to generate steam for leavening before the structure is set. The steam creates sufficient pressure to force up the paste, and the characteristic cavity is formed.

Cream puffs should have a good volume with a large interior cavity. The surface should be a pleasing brown and somewhat crisp. Failure to puff may be the result of either too little or too much water, too little butter, or too cool an oven.

Waffles and Pancakes

Another group of quick breads includes waffles, pancakes, and their variations. These batters are sufficiently fluid to permit more mixing of the liquid and dry ingredients than can be satisfactorily done on more viscous batters. Because of the proportions of ingredients used, pancakes or waffles may be beaten until there are no more flour lumps in the batter. Even though these products contain baking powder as an effective leavening agent, still lighter waffles may be made by beating the whites separately and folding them in carefully for the final mixing step.

Thermostatically controlled griddles and waffle irons are an important aid in baking either of these food products since the temperature remains relatively constant at the selected temperature. With some care, however, it is possible to make excellent pancakes without a thermostatically controlled griddle.

Before the batter is poured, the griddle or waffle iron should be hot enough to cause drops of cold water to dance when they are dropped on the surface. Pancakes should be turned when the bubbles formed during baking have popped and the bottom is a pleasing brown. The second side is then browned. Pancakes and waffles should be a golden brown color; they should be light and tender and are most appetizing when served hot.

Crepes are very thin pancakes made by pouring a fluid pancake-like batter into a heated crepe pan and pouring out the excess batter before continuing to brown the crepe on both sides. These are used in many ways: in desserts such as crepes Suzette, and in main dishes which involve rolling cubed chicken or other items in crepes and serving with a sauce.

Cake Doughnuts

Coffee and doughnuts are a common midmorning snack for many Americans, but good homemade doughnuts are a rare item. The making of doughnuts is not difficult if care is taken to avoid working excess flour into the dough and to keep manipulation at a minimum. Extra flour and over-enthusiastic mixing cause a toughening of the doughnuts. Chilling the dough adequately makes it possible to roll out the dough without excessive gluten development.

The fat temperature for deep-fat frying must be controlled. Too high a temperature causes excessive breakdown of the fat. The strong-smelling and eye-stinging fumes that result not only are annoying, but also impair the flavor. In addition, the doughnuts will brown too much before the centers are done, and the doughnuts will be doughy and underdone. Too low a temperature results in inadequately browned doughnuts that are quite greasy.

YEAST BREADS

The other classification for breads is yeast breads. In contrast to the quick breads, the making of yeast breads is a lengthy process due to the fermentation periods required for carbon dioxide production by the yeast. The use of yeast as a leavening agent is discussed in Chapter 11. Salt is used not only for flavor, but also to control the rate of yeast growth. Although the addition of sugar has an accelerating influence, salt retards yeast growth to give controlled fermentation and the desired, moderately fine texture in bread. Too much salt, however, produces a heavy bread because of its excessive inhibition of yeast growth.

Yeast breads are usually prepared by softening the yeast in lukewarm liquid while scalded milk is mixed with the sugar, salt, shortening, egg (if used), and a small amount of flour. The addition of a hot liquid actually serves two purposes: (1) it melts the shortening and aids in uniformly distributing the fat; and (2) it causes more rapid rising because it warms the dough. Yeast should be added only when this mixture has been cooled to lukewarm, for high temperatures kill yeast. The addition of yeast to hot liquids is probably the most common cause of yeast bread failure. A vigorous beating after about one-third of the flour is added helps to improve the structure of the bread by developing a good network of gluten. Sufficient flour is then blended in to make a soft dough but one that can be kneaded without becoming too sticky. Kneading is done to help mix the ingredients together more thoroughly and to further develop the gluten.

The kneading of rolls should be a vigorous process utilizing the heel of the hand. After the dough is folded in half, a firm push with the heel of both hands is given to the dough; the dough is then rotated a quarter of a turn and kneaded again in the manner just described. Kneading is continued until blisters show in the dough when it is folded over. This is a much more vigorous process than is the kneading of biscuits.

FIGURE 12.9   Kneading of yeast dough is a vigorous process in which the heel of the hands is used to develop a strong network of gluten.

FIGURE 12.10   Irish soda bread is an old-fashioned yeast bread that can be made using the rapidmix method.

The surface of the kneaded dough is oiled and the dough is allowed to rise until the volume is doubled. After a downward push with the fist, the dough is ready to be shaped into loaves or rolls. A second rising period will again double the volume. The dough is then baked until a pleasing brown color develops. During the initial baking period the dough will continue to rise quickly until the yeast is killed. The process just described is the straight dough method of mixing yeast breads. This process is preferred by many because of the relatively short mixing time. Its chief drawback is that the mixing requires more vigor.

A method, known as the rapidmix method, has been developed. The rapidmix method is begun by thoroughly mixing the undissolved yeast with two cups of flour to distribute the yeast throughout the flour. Then very hot water from the tap or warm milk is added with margarine or butter and the mixture is beaten vigorously by hand or at medium speed with an electric mixer to develop the gluten. The remaining flour is then stirred in, and the dough is subsequently handled in the same manner as in the straight dough

FIGURE 12.11 Adequate kneading, followed by properly controlled fermentation and baking, results in a loaf with good volume and a uniform, breadlike texture.

method. The very warm liquid used in the rapidmix method does not harm the yeast because the mixture cools to a safe temperature for the yeast before the yeast is rehydrated.

An older method, which is still used occasionally, is the sponge method. In this method the salt and part of the flour are omitted during an initial fermentation period. Then these ingredients are added and the process continues as in the straight dough method, that is, kneading, rising, shaping, rising, and baking. This method was used originally when the dried yeast was not activated and hence required some time to become really active. Most dough formulas today are based on the straight dough method.

Aside from the control of temperature to avoid killing the yeast, the chief problem in yeast breads is the fermentation period. It must be kept in mind that the yeast can produce gas only as long as there is sugar available in the dough. Omission or reduction of sugar is a limiting factor in the production of a light product.

Excessive fermentation should be avoided because it produces rather strong flavor and a distinctly porous texture. When rolls more than double their volume before baking, the cell walls become so thin that some of these walls will break and an uneven texture results. If fermentation is allowed to continue too long, so many of the cells will rupture that the rolls will fall and be compact. Over-fermentation also presents the possibility that all of the sugar may be used by the yeast before the structure of the rolls is set during baking. If this occurs, there will not be enough gas present to maintain the extended structure until it sets. Again, this will cause the rolls to fall and be heavy. Careful mixing, fermentation, and baking produce breads or rolls that are light, golden brown, uniform in texture, and pleasing in flavor.

FIGURE 12.12   Yeast breads may be modified by varying ingredients in the dough, shaping in different forms, and by adding flavorful touches before or after baking. These rolls gain added interest as a result of the rye flour and molasses incorporated in the dough and the caraway seeds sprinkled on top.

These products are similar to quick breads in that the crusts are more pleasing if they are removed from the baking pans as soon as they are done. The one exception to this is rolls baked with a syrup in the bottom of the pan—pecan rolls, for example. These rolls should be cooled in the pan until the syrup thickens a bit. Then the pans are inverted and allowed to sit upside down briefly while the syrup drops onto the rolls. This procedure is the most successful way of getting a maximum amount of syrup out of the pan and onto the rolls.

Many people feel that they do not have time to make rolls because of the long rising time involved. This problem may be circumvented by mixing and kneading roll dough in the evening and placing it covered in the refrigerator for the night. The next morning the dough has doubled and is ready to

FIGURE 12.13   A sour dough starter is the secret to these slightly sharp-flavored sour dough breads, which are made by the sponge method.

be shaped. Another way is to process the rolls through the first rising and through the shaping the evening before and then place the freshly shaped rolls in the refrigerator. In the morning they will be ready to be baked. Because the dough is chilled, a slightly longer baking time will be needed. The main problem with the second solution is the large amount of refrigerator space needed to store the rolls when they are already shaped.

A pleasing variation from the yeast breads and rolls ordinarily prepared is provided by the use of a sour dough starter, which is a somewhat acidic yeast-containing sponge. The making of sourdough is a strong blend of legend interspersed with the same precautions that are applicable to the making of other yeast-leavened products. There are many recipes for sourdough including bread, pancakes, waffles, biscuits, muffins, and cakes. These are all based on the use of an on-going sponge or starter containing viable yeast. The starter is made with flour, sugar, yeast, and water and is stored at room temperature. This sponge is perpetuated by always saving some of the starter and adding more flour and water to replenish the starter pot for subsequent use.

CAKES

Comparison of Sponge, Angel, Chiffon, and Conventional Cakes

Although sponge cakes and angel cakes have been discussed in the chapter on eggs, it seems appropriate to compare these cakes with chiffon cakes and conventional cakes. Table 12.3 quickly reveals the important differences. Angel and sponge cakes achieve their light character by incorporating air into a foam. Their tenderness is due in part to the thin cell walls that accompany the large volume. No fat of any type is present. This is contrasted with chiffon and conventional cakes which have liquid and plastic shortening, respectively, to aid in producing a tender cake. Stable egg foams enclose a large volume of air that is responsible for much of the leavening in angel and sponge cake batters. Cream of tartar, because of its acidity, promotes the development of a stable foam. Sugar also contributes stability to the foam. Stability is an important factor since the foam must not collapse before the structure is set during baking if maximum volume is to be achieved. Foams do play a part in leavening chiffon and some conventional cakes, but the chief leavening is accomplished with baking powder.

Chiffon Cakes

Chiffon cakes are prepared by combining all of the ingredients except the egg white and cream of tartar in a large bowl, and then beating until the batter is smooth. Since this batter is quite fluid, extensive beating can be

Table 12.3. A Comparison of Four Basic Types of Cakes

| Cake | Flour | Liquid | Eggs | | Fat | | Leavening Agent |
			Number, Part Used	Manner of Adding	Type	Amount	
Angel	1 c	—	12 whites	Foam, folded in	—	—	Air (egg white foam stabilized with sugar and cream of tartar), steam
Sponge	1 c	5 Tbsp	4 yolks and whites	Foams, folded in	—	—	Air (egg white and yolk foam stabilized with cream of tartar and sugar), steam
Chiffon	1⅛ c	6 Tbsp water	2 yolks, 4 whites	Yolks added with liquid, white foam folded in	Oil	¼ c	Baking powder (1½ tsp), air, steam
Conventional	1 c	½ c milk	1 whole	Creamed with fat and sugar	Plastic fat	¼ c	Baking powder (¾ tsp), air, steam

done without excessively developing the gluten. The whites are then beaten with the cream of tartar (added at the foamy stage) until the peaks just bend over. The batter is carefully but thoroughly folded into the beaten whites. Unless this folding is adequate, a large layer of the batter will drain toward the bottom of the pan, causing a nonhomogeneous texture in the finished cake.

A few chiffon cake recipes have unusually fluid batters that drain readily from the egg white foam. Usually such recipes can be modified by adding half the sugar to the batter and by gradually adding the other half to the egg whites as they are beaten. This technique not only is effective in eliminating the problem of layering in a chiffon cake, but also produces a somewhat finer-textured cake because of the fine egg white foam resulting from the addition of sugar. A well-prepared chiffon cake is tender, slightly moist, uniform in texture, and high in volume. The cells characteristically are of moderate size. There should be no indication of layering when the cake is viewed in cross section.

Conventional Cakes

Conventional cakes vary widely in proportions and kinds of ingredients used. Variations in conventional cake formulas are found in the type of liquid used, portion of egg used, and in flavoring substances. Two variations very frequently made are white cakes and chocolate or devil's food. White cakes are white in color because the egg yolk is not used; the whites are beaten and folded in at the end of mixing.

Chocolate cakes contain cocoa or chocolate. Many chocolate or devil's food cake recipes contain sour cream or sour milk. The acid is counteracted by adding baking soda to produce some carbon dioxide. Since the acid and soda will react at room temperature, speed in mixing is helpful in achieving maximum volume. The final volume of such a cake is inversely related to the time elapsing between the addition of soda to acid and the beginning of baking. The inclusion of hot water further accentuates the need for speed in mixing because gas production is accelerated when the water is hot. The addition of a small amount of baking powder increases the volume of such a cake. For more consistent results, recipes using baking powder are recommended.

Several methods are available for combining the ingredients in a conventional cake. The methods, their advantages, and disadvantages merit some discussion.

Conventional Method. Mention already has been made of the leavening due to baking powder in conventional cakes. Another source of leavening is from air that is incorporated during the creaming of sugar and fat. Thorough creaming of sugar and shortening, the first step in making a cake by the conventional method, is an extremely important procedure. As sugar is mixed with the fat, air is trapped in the plastic mixture. This trapped air helps to increase the volume and to produce a fine, uniform texture. It should be explained that the term "plastic" in reference to fats means that the fat is neither liquid nor hard but of a malleable consistency.

The flavoring substances should be creamed with the sugar and fat. Fat carries flavors far better than any other ingredient. Hence thorough mixing of the flavoring in the creamed mixture guarantees uniform distribution of flavor throughout the batter.

By blending the beaten eggs with the creamed mixture, an emulsion is established which aids in the production of a fine-grained cake. If beating is continued, however, until the shortening becomes extremely soft, the

FIGURE 12.14   The conventional method, with its creaming of sugar and fat, promotes the desired fine texture in cakes. Note the uniformly small cells and relatively thin cell walls. Contrast this structure with the stronger structure required in bread (see Figure 12.11).

egg-fat emulsion may break. When this curdling is observed in a cake batter, the finished product is coarser in texture and is somewhat less desirable.

Dry ingredients should be sifted together before the creaming process is begun in order to avoid delays during mixing which might cause some loss of air and a smaller finished product. One-third of the sifted dry ingredients is mixed into the creamed mixture. This practice usually prevents curdling the batter when one-half of the liquid is added. The alternate additions of the second third of flour, last half of liquid, and last third of flour are continued with some mixing after each. Best results are obtained when a formula has been standardized for the optimum amount of mixing. This may be expressed either as the number of strokes when mixed by hand or as minutes at a specified speed on a mixer.

Cakes made by the conventional method are noted for their excellent keeping qualities and their fine texture. Their chief disadvantages are the somewhat longer preparation time and the energy required.

Modified Conventional Method. As in the conventional method, the process starts with careful creaming of the fat and additional creaming with the sugar. The beaten egg yolks are then added gradually. After the dry and liquid ingredients have been added in the conventional manner, the beaten egg whites are folded in. This process is more laborious than the conventional method, but it produces an excellent cake that keeps well.

Conventional Sponge Method. The conventional sponge method is similar to the modified conventional method and is particularly adaptable to a cake that is low in fat. In this method half the sugar is creamed with the fat and the other half is beaten with the whites to form a meringue. The meringue is folded in during the last 50 strokes of mixing. This method produces a cake of good volume and fine texture with good keeping quality.

Muffin Method. As the name implies, cakes may be prepared in the same way in which muffins are mixed. The dry ingredients are placed in one bowl and the liquid ingredients are mixed together in another bowl. This method, of course, requires the use of an oil or melted shortening. The liquids are then poured into the dry ingredients and blended together.

Muffin method cakes are quickly prepared since no creaming is required. This advantage is perhaps counterbalanced by the disadvantages of the finished product, that is, a coarse texture and distinctly limited keeping qualities. The decision to use this method is feasible when the cake will be consumed quickly.

Single-Stage Method. The single-stage method was developed as the answer to the need for a very quick way of making cakes. This basically is the method that has evolved for making cakes from mixes. One requisite for this method is that the fat be at room temperature so that it will be quite plastic. The dry ingredients are sifted together and then, when the shortening and most or all of the milk have been added, the mixture is blended a set length of time, preferably on the mixer. Then the egg and any remaining liquid are added, mixing again is done for a specified length of time, and the batter is finished. The advantages of speed and ease of preparation by this method should be weighed against the coarser texture and the more rapid rate of staling found in the cake that results. The differences in these five methods are summarized in Table 12.4.

Baking

All cakes should be poured into the baking pans as soon as they are mixed and should then be baked in a preheated oven. The pan is prepared before the mixing begins. Chiffon cakes, like angel and sponge cakes, are suitably baked in an ungreased tube pan of two-part construction for easy removal of the cake. The use of an ungreased pan is advantageous because the cake can cling to the sides more readily for support. For a conventional cake it is convenient to line the bottom of the pan with waxed paper so that the cake can be removed easily, but the sides do not need to be greased. When waxed paper is used, the cake should be turned out of the pan while the cake is still warm enough for the wax on the paper to be slightly soft. The cake structure will be set by then, but the wax will not have glued the paper

Table 12.4. Comparison of Methods for Making Conventional Cakes

Method	Method of Adding		
	Eggs	Fat	Liquid and Flour
Conventional	Whole, beaten, blended into creamed mixture	Creamed with sugar	Alternately (1/3 flour, 1/2 liquid, 1/3 flour, 1/2 liquid, 1/3 flour)
Modified conventional	Yolks, beaten and blended with creamed mixture Whites, beaten without sugar and folded in at end	Same as conventional method	Same as conventional method
Conventional sponge	Same as modified conventional except half of sugar used to make egg white foam	Same as conventional method	Same as conventional method
Muffin	Whole, beaten and added with liquid ingredients	Oil or melted shortening added with liquid ingredients	All of liquid and dry ingredients combined at one time
Single stage	Whole, near end of mixing when last liquid added	With all dry ingredients and most of liquid	Dry ingredients and most of liquid added at same time as shortening. Remainder of liquid added with egg after initial mixing period

to the pan. Cakes that are to be left in the pan do not need a waxed paper lining, but require only a light greasing of the bottom of the pan. Again, the sides are ungreased.

Baking of conventional cakes is completed when a toothpick inserted in the center comes out clean. Removal from the oven at this stage prevents the dryness resulting from the overbaking that occurs when a cake is baked until it pulls away from the sides of the pan. A good conventional cake has fine cell walls, a uniform texture, and a velvety crumb. The volume is good, the cake is tender, and it has a pleasing flavor. The nicely browned surfaces are moist, not crusty.

Causes of Variation in Cake Quality

Various deviations from the foregoing description may be caused by improper proportions of ingredients.

Baking Powder. Varying the amount of baking powder in a recipe has a distinct influence on the volume of a cake. Decreasing the amount of baking powder decreases the volume of a cake, whereas increasing the amount increases the volume. The latter statement must be qualified by saying that the volume will increase until so much baking powder is added that the cake falls. When too much gas is released in a cake, the pressure may stretch the cell walls until they rupture and the cake falls. Tenderness of a cake is increased with an increase in baking powder since the cell walls are thinner. If a double-acting baking powder is used, the strong residue flavor that results from a large quantity of baking powder is objectionable.

Sugar. Sugar has a tenderizing effect on a cake. The cake volume increases progressively in proportion to the increase of sugar until the struc-

FIGURE 12.15 Cake pans should be positioned on the rack so that air can flow easily around each pan, resulting in uniform baking. If one pan is placed directly under another, the lower cake will fail to brown well because of restricted circulation of air.

ture becomes so tender that it falls. The factors influencing the effect of sugar on volume have been discussed in detail earlier in this chapter. An increase in the proportion of sugar in a cake necessitates more agitation to achieve optimum gluten development.

The surface of a cake changes in appearance with an increase in sugar, because sugar causes the cake surface to brown more readily. When a formula has an excess of sugar, the cake surface will brown excessively and become mottled with white areas that have a crystalline appearance. Another obvious change due to an increase in the level of sugar in a cake formula is the increased sweetness of the product.

FIGURE 12.16 Too small a baking pan (top) results in an unattractive cake with batter running over the edge. Proper pan size (center) allows the cake to reach its maximum volume and to brown uniformly. Cake baked in too large a pan (bottom) fails to brown well because the layer is spread too thinly to rise high in the pan.

FIGURE 12.17   Correct baking temperature is needed. (a) Too low a temperature results in a coarse-textured, heavy cake with a poor volume and a pitted surface. (b) The results of too high a baking temperature; the cracking and humping in this cake are caused by very rapid setting of the structure in the exterior portions while gases continue to expand the uncoagulated central region.

Fat. Increasing the fat increases the tenderness of a cake until so much fat is added that the cake falls. The increase in fat, however, is accompanied by a corresponding increase in the greasiness of the crumb and a greater ease of browning.

Flour. Since flour makes a highly significant contribution to the protein content of a cake, altering the concentration of flour changes the tenderness of a cake. Increasing the flour not only reduces the tenderness, but also makes the cake drier and more compact. The type of flour, as well as the quantity, influences the characteristics of a cake. Due to its lower protein content and weaker gluten, cake flour is a more suitable choice than all-purpose flour for most cakes.

Eggs. Eggs also are high in protein. Exceeding the optimum amount of egg in a recipe produces a less tender cake with a somewhat waxy crumb.

Extent of Mixing. The extent of mixing also causes variations in the texture, volume, and tenderness of the baked cake. Inadequate creaming of the sugar and shortening results in a more porous texture. Mixing of all the ingredients must be sufficient to develop an adequate gluten network, but not so much that the cake becomes tough. Undermixing produces a smaller cake as a result of inadequate gluten development. Overmixing produces a tenacious gluten that will be manifest in a rather tough crumb, slightly reduced volume, and occasional tunnels in the cake.

COOKIES

Cookies are yet another baked product, but they vary so greatly that they are difficult to categorize. However, the majority of cookies may be classified as drop, bar, or refrigerator cookies. Their preparation is usually done by the same general method as is employed in making conventional cakes. The ingredients also are similar to those in cakes, although the proportions and supplementary items such as raisins, nuts, and chocolate chips frequently are modified from those in cakes.

Drop cookies generally are somewhat richer, and the dough is stiffer than a cake batter. These cookies are either dropped from a spoon onto a cooky sheet or are pressed through a cooky press in preparation for baking. They are baked, usually in a 190°C (375°F) oven for 10 to 15 minutes until nicely browned. Appearance is the criterion for determining doneness of these cookies.

Bar cookies, also known as sheet cookies, are very similar to drop cookies in their consistency, although some bar cooky doughs are a little softer than drop cooky doughs. These cookies are baked by spreading the

FIGURE 12.18 Drop cookies (top), bar cookies (center), and rolled refrigerator cookies may be served when baked or frozen for later use.

mixture in a shallow pan. The individual bars are cut after baking. Unlike cakes, these cookies may be cut satisfactorily before they are completely cool because the structure is less delicate than that of a cake.

Refrigerator cookies are made by refrigerating a stiff dough until thoroughly chilled. The individual cookies then may be sliced from the dough log or rolled and cut into various shapes and baked when needed. These doughs may be frozen and baked at a much later date. Of course, virtually all cookies may be frozen very satisfactorily after baking.

PASTRY

Ingredients

The four ingredients in pastry—flour, salt, fat, and water—function in these ways: flour is the structural element; salt adds flavor; fat contributes flakiness and tenderness; water gives the mixture cohesiveness. The ratio of these ingredients is vital to production of a tender pie crust. A practical ratio to use is six parts flour to two parts fat to one part water. Translating this into actual measurements gives the following formula for a two-crust pie: one and a half cups flour, one-half cup shortening, one-fourth cup water, and three-fourths teaspoon salt. These proportions produce a dough that will be tender when handled a reasonable amount.

Some people prefer a somewhat less rich crust, that is, a fat: flour ratio of 1:4. This means that the product will have four times as much flour as fat instead of the richer three parts flour to one part of fat suggested above. With this decreased amount of shortening, it is necessary to handle the crust very carefully to produce a tender crust.

Preparation

Various methods of mixing have been tried: whipping fat into boiling water before adding the dry ingredients results in a tender, uniform pastry; combining a small quantity of dry ingredients with water before the water is added to the dough promotes tenderness, for the water is then less available to combine with the rest of the flour. Any technique that develops definite strands or clumps of gluten produces a correspondingly less tender pastry.

In the usual mode of pastry preparation the first step is the mixing of the flour and salt, after which the fat is cut into the flour until the particles are the size of rice kernels. The cutting in is done most efficiently and quickly by using a pastry blender with a light tossing motion. A relaxed flick of the wrist helps to avoid pressing the dough mixture together.

Water is added drop by drop with the left hand while the mixture is lightly and quickly tossed with a fork held in the right hand. The water should be distributed as uniformly as possible throughout the bowl. When all the water has been added, the dough should be stirred quickly with a fork to moisten the ingredients and help them cling together. The entire mixture is then picked up in the hands and quickly, but gently, worked into a ball.

For a two-crust pie, the dough is divided into two parts: half the dough then is flattened quickly into a circular shape with smooth edges. This procedure prepares the dough so that it may be easily rolled on a lightly floured pastry cloth into a uniform circular shape. A more uniform thickness is achieved if rolling is initiated in the center of the crust with a rather firm pressure which is lightened as the far edge of the dough is approached. The dough is rolled until the entire area is thin enough that the pressure of a finger leaves only a slight imprint.

The easiest way to transfer the crust from the cloth to the pan is to gently fold the dough in half and then in half again, lightly place it in the pie pan, and then unfold it. To avoid making a crust that shrinks excessively,

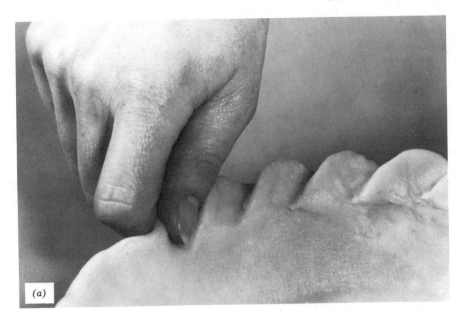

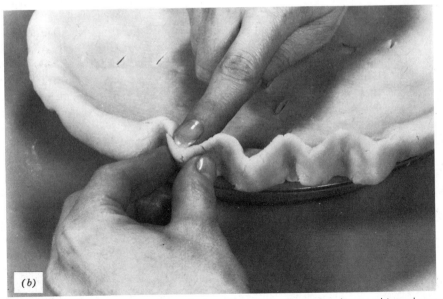

FIGURE 12.19   Various edging techniques such as these may be used to enhance the appearance of a pie.

fit the pastry to the sides of the pan by letting the weight of the crust pull it down to the junction between the side and bottom of the pan.

A one-crust pie shell that is to be baked before the filling is put in should have a number of holes pricked in the crust before it is baked. This pricking, done quickly with a fork, prevents the formation of large blisters and air pockets in the crust. A crust baked without a filling sometimes falls away from the top of the pie pan and creates a problem when the filling is added. If the crust is not rolled too thin and if the edge of the crust is finished so that it extends across the rim of the pan, this circumstance usually is avoided. Adequate pricking of the crust may help, too. These crusts should be baked until they are a pleasing light brown color.

Factors Influencing Tenderness

Tender pastry results when the flour is thoroughly coated with fat before any liquid is introduced. A fat that is moderately soft during blending and that contains a reasonably high percentage of unsaturated fatty acids is a good choice for making pastry. Soft, warm fat is blended more easily and more completely with the flour, and gluten development is minimized to produce a very tender pastry. Oil reduces cohesiveness of dough, thus producing a more tender pastry than is made with a comparable quantity of a hydrogenated fat.

Thorough blending of the fat and flour before the water is added permits enough stirring to achieve a relatively uniform distribution of this water without causing appreciable toughening of the pastry. Extended mixing after the water is added, however, permits greater gluten hydration and development, causing the baked pastry to be less tender.

The proportions as well as the kinds of flour, fat, and liquid are significant in determining the tenderness of pastry. Increasing the amount of flour decreases the tenderness, particularly if some of the flour is added when water is already present, as occurs when extra flour is incorporated into the pastry during rolling. A hard-wheat or a high-protein flour such as bread flour decreases the tenderness of a pastry. A decrease in the amount of fat causes a corresponding decrease in the tenderness of the finished pastry. Pastries with excess fat brown easily, but unevenly. When comparable amounts of margarine or butter are substituted for lard or vegetable shortenings in a pastry, the pastry is less tender, for not only is the actual amount of fat reduced 15.5 percent, but also the amount of water is substantially increased because of the water content of these two fats.

Flakiness in Pastry

Flakiness is due to the expansion that occurs when water in the dough is converted to steam in the oven. Thorough distribution of water and small

FIGURE 12.20   The flakiness of this pastry is evident when viewed in cross section. Note also the slight flow of the filling, a desirable characteristic in fruit pies.

pieces of fat throughout a pastry produce cavities between the protein framework of the pastry. The size and frequency of the areas of moisture within the pastry determine the flaky nature of a pastry. The protein network is coagulated in the oven and retains its extended form after the steam is gone.

A flaky, tender pastry has many small air pockets surrounded by thin sheets of gluten encased in very thin layers of fat. Oil or pastry flour reduces flakiness and a hard-wheat flour increases flakiness of pastries made from the same formula.

Evaluation of Pies

Two-crust pies sometimes have a soggy bottom crust. If the filling is reasonably cool when it is placed in the bottom crust, if the bottom crust is not rolled too thin, and if baking begins immediately after the pie is assembled, the soaking of the crust is held to a minimum. Some soaking may also be avoided by having the top crust rolled out and ready to put on the pie before the filling is placed in the shell. Ventilation of the top crust is necessary to let the steam escape from the filling during baking.

Two-crust pies are judged on both crust and filling. The top and bottom crusts should have no suggestion of sogginess. The crust should be about one-eighth inch thick. It should be flaky and tender. The flavor should be pleasing and the crust should be a medium brown. There should not be a

FIGURE 12.21 Close packing of the apple slices and adequate venting of the upper crust resulted in a crisp upper crust that conformed to the filling.

wide space between the top crust and the filling. This gap is avoided in fresh-fruit pies by packing the fruit in snugly before putting on the top crust, and by providing adequate steam vents in the upper crust. The fruit fillings should be softly gelled, not runny or rigid.

One-crust pies generally include three types: custard, chiffon, and meringue or cream pies. The chiffon and cream pie crusts are baked before the filling is added. These crusts should conform well to the shape of the pan and should have an even edging. The problems involved in preparation and the evaluation of cream fillings and meringues are discussed in Chapter 10.

Chiffon pies present problems in thickening egg yolk protein, in beating whites, and also in gelation. To avoid lumping, gelatin must be softened in cold water before being dissolved in the egg yolk mixture while the egg yolk is being coagulated over hot water. This gelatin and egg yolk mixture is then cooled until the gelatin is partially congealed, at which time it is ready to be folded into the beaten whites. Chiffon fillings should be rigid when they are cut, that is, they must hold a straight line along the cut edge. The fillings should be light, airy, and tender, with no rubbery bits of gelatin.

Custard pies are evaluated according to the criteria discussed in Chapter 10. Perhaps the greatest difficulty in preparing a custard pie is the avoidance of a soggy bottom crust. If a custard filling is baked in the crust, a fairly long time passes before the liquid filling coagulates. This time lapse permits the liquid to soak into the crust. A workable solution to this situation is to bake the filling and pastry in separate pie pans and then slide the cooled filling into the baked pastry. Avoiding overbaking of the filling also reduces sogginess of the crust because less syneresis occurs when a custard is baked only until it is set.

All pies are best when served the same day they are made. Meringues become sticky and difficult to cut the second day. Chiffon fillings get slightly rubbery, and all bottom crusts become somewhat soggy.

THE USE OF MIXES

Numerous food companies have invested considerable time and money in the development of mixes and convenience foods. Impressive strides have been made in developing an extremely broad range of products to aid consumers today. The choices cover the broad spectrum from frozen bread doughs, mixes for quick breads and cakes, to frozen cakes that are baked and

FIGURE 12.22   Meringues need to be pushed against the edge of the baked crust to form a seal. Swirling of the surface, without actually forming high peaks, provides the opportunity for a pleasing variation in color to develop during baking.

FIGURE 12.23 Chiffon pies, noteworthy for their high volume and airy fillings, hold a sharp edge when cut because the foam is stabilized with gelatin. Variation in pies also is possible through the use of cereals, coconut, and crumbs to prepare unique pie shells.

frosted. Some products, such as pizza mix, offer only a limited saving of time while other items, such as frozen puff patty shells, are tremendous time-savers. An angel cake mix saves the time involved in separating a dozen eggs and has the additional advantage of not presenting the cook with the dilemma of utilizing a dozen yolks. Refrigerated biscuit doughs and cooky doughs afford very quick solutions to the problem of preparing something with a minimum of effort when unexpected company materializes.

Foods that have been at least partially prepared are a part of the contemporary scene that shows every indication of remaining in vogue. The increasing numbers of employed women are adding to the buying power of today's families so that the additional expense involved in buying some of the convenience items is offset. However, the time required for preparing food is a very real problem faced by most women who work outside the home. The products developed by the food industry offer some saving of time to these women. Their use in the family menu is based on the acceptance of a particular food product and the satisfaction it affords to the person preparing it and to those who eat it. In quite a few instances now, the quality of the convenience foods is highly satisfactory; generalizations regarding expense simply cannot be made because of the tremendous variation. For those who miss the opportunity for creativity in baking, many unusual variations can be developed utilizing mixes and convenience foods. The decision on the use of these foods actually is a highly individual matter that can best be made in relation to a specific situation.

FIGURE 12.24 Custard pies and their variations are done when a knife inserted halfway between the center and edge comes out clean. Whipped cream, piped on when the filling cooled, was used to garnish this prune custard pie.

SUMMARY

Baked products generally may be grouped into quick breads, yeast breads, cookies, cakes, and pastries and pies. Flour, liquid, and salt are basic to all these foods. Many of the batters and doughs also contain leavening agents, eggs, shortening, and sugar.

The proportion of the various ingredients in the formula, the method of incorporation of the ingredients, and the manner of heating the product cause large variations in batter and dough products. Care must be exercised when making any batter or dough if optimum results are to be achieved.

BIBLIOGRAPHY

Arlin, M. L., M. M. Nielsen, and F. T. Hall. The effect of different methods of flour measurement on the quality of plain two-egg cakes. *J. Home Econ. 56*:399–401. 1964.

Block, R. J., and R. H. Mandl. A comparative study of the amino-acid composition of commercial samples of a high-protein and a low-protein wheat flour. *Boyce Thompson Institute 18*:477–482. 1957.

Bloksma, A. H. Influence of extract of lipids from flour on gluten development and breakdown. *Chem. Ind. 21*:253–254. 1959.

Bottomley, R. A., B. R. McAuslan, and A. D. G. Powell. Lipid-protein complex of wheat flour. *Chem. Ind. 28*:1476–1477. 1958.

Carlson, W. A., and E. M. Ziegenfuss. Functional properties of vital gluten. *Food Tech. 12*:629–632. 1958.

Cereal Laboratory Methods, 7th ed. Committee on Revision. American Association of Cereal Chemists. 1955 University Ave. St. Paul 4, Minn. 1962.

Cereal Science Today, Staff Writer, White flour in the U. S. A. *Cereal Sci. Today 3, 9*:229. 1963.

Chemistry and Engineering News Staff Writer, Wheat gluten surrenders four more proteins. *Chem. Eng. News 39*:44–45. June 5, 1961.

Consumer and Food Economics Research Division. *Breads, Cakes, and Pies in Family Meals*. Home and Garden Bulletin No. 186. U. S. Department of Agriculture. Washington, D. C. 1971.

Cunningham, D. K., W. F. Geddes, and J. A. Anderson. Preparation and chemical characteristics of cohesive proteins of wheat, barley, rye, and oats. *Cereal Chem. 32*:91–106. 1955.

Food Engineering Staff Writer, Latest milling techniques make new production strides. *Food Eng. 33, 7*:76–78. 1961.

Food, Yearbook of Agriculture, 1959. U.S. Department of Agriculture. Washington, D. C. 1959.

Geddes, W. F. The role of enzymes in milling and baking technology. *Food Tech. 4*:441–446. 1950.

Griswold, R. *Experimental Study of Food*. Houghton Mifflin. Boston, Mass. 1962.

Hess, K. Protein, gluten, and lipids in wheat grains and flour. *Koll.-Zeit. 136*:84–99. 1954. A translation by M. Burnett and J. Cluskey. Northern Utilization Research Branch, U. S. Department of Agriculture. Peoria, Ill. 1955.

Matthews, R. H., and O. M. Batcher. Sifted versus unsifted flour: weight variations and results of some baking tests. *J. Home Econ. 55*:123–124. 1963.

Olcott, H. S., and D. K. Mecham. Characterization of wheat gluten, I. Protein-lipid complex formation during doughing of flours. *Cereal Chem. 24*:407–414. 1947.

Pence, J. W., D. K. Mecham, and H. S. Olcott. Review of proteins of wheat flour. *J. Agr. Food Chem. 4,* 8:712–716. 1956.

Pomeranz, Y. et al. Molecular approach to breadmaking. *Science 167*:944. 1970.

Sullivan, B. Proteins in flour: Review of the physical characteristics of gluten and reactive groups involved in change in oxidation. *J. Agr. Food Chem. 2*:1231–1234. 1954.

Sword, J. Flour, what it was, is, and may be. *Chem. Ind.,* pp. 1972–1979, December 9, 1961.

Watt, B. K., and A. L. Merrill, Composition of foods. *Agriculture Handbook No. 8.,* U. S. Department of Agriculture, Agricultural Research Service, Washington, D. C. 1963.

Wheat Flour Institute. *From Wheat to Flour.* Wheat Flour Institute. Chicago, Ill. 1966.

Woychik, J. H., J. A. Boundy, and R. J. Dimler. Amino acid composition of proteins in wheat gluten. *J. Agr. Food Chem. 9*:307–310. 1961.

SUGGESTIONS FOR STUDY

1. Prepare similar cakes from mixes and from recipes. Compare the time of preparation, cost, and palatability. When is a mix the best choice? When is a homemade cake preferred?

2. Prepare one gluten ball from all-purpose flour and one from cake flour by adding just enough water to a cup of the flour to make a stiff dough. Knead the dough vigorously for five minutes. Then place the ball of dough in a linen cloth under cold running water. Squeeze and manipulate the dough inside the linen until the water runs clear and the protein is free of starch. Roll the gluten into a ball, weigh it, and bake it on a baking sheet in a 450°F oven for 15 minutes and then a 300°F oven for 30 minutes. Compare *(a)* the weight of the unbaked ball made from cake flour with the ball made with all-purpose flour; *(b)* the volume of the two baked gluten balls; *(c)* the appearance of the interior of the baked balls. Explain the reasons for these differences. Why is cake flour chosen for cakes?

3. Outline the milling of wheat.

4. In baked products, what functions are fulfilled by *(a)* eggs, *(b)* sugar, *(c)* shortenings, *(d)* liquids, *(e)* flour?

5. What differences might you expect to observe between a cake made

with one cup of sugar and one made with one and one-fourth cups of sugar?

6. Explain the differences that may be observed between a cake and muffins.

7. What is the probable cause of yeast rolls losing volume in the oven?

8. What is the procedure for making cakes by the conventional method? Contrast this method with the conventional sponge method.

9. Compare pastry made with oil with (a) one made with hydrogenated shortening and (b) one made with butter. Use exactly the same proportions for each, changing only the type of fat used. Compare the baked pastries.

CHAPTER 13
Crystallization: Sugar Cookery and Frozen Desserts

Crystal formation and control of crystal growth are key factors in sugar cookery and in making frozen desserts. In the case of candy making, the crystals being formed are those of various sugars; ice crystals are the primary concern in frozen dessert preparation. For both types of products, crystals are an essential component of their structure. However, the size of the crystals is of great importance because of the impact on texture. Small crystals feel smooth on the tongue and give an impression of velvety smoothness without hinting of the actual presence of the crystals. In contrast, large crystals can be detected on the tongue, creating a coarse sensation which is generally considered undesirable in foods. The central focus of this chapter is control of crystallization to achieve the desirable texture and consistency.

SUGAR COOKERY

Sugar as we know it today has undergone significant changes in quality, quantity, and price since it was first used in the Near East. Although sugar was once a rare item which only kings could afford, today it is an accepted staple item. The history of sugar begins sometime between A.D. 300 and 600 when various techniques were developed in the Near East to refine and crystallize sugar. News of this remarkable food was carried to Europe by the returning Crusaders and eventually reached the Western Hemisphere when Columbus introduced sugar to Santo Domingo in 1493.

Of course, changes in sugar production took place through the centuries, but perhaps the single most important discovery was the realization

355

by a nineteenth-century German chemist that the sugar beet was an out-standing source of sugar. By the beginning of the twentieth century the sugar beet was becoming as important as sugarcane in sugar production. Levels of consumption of cane versus beet sugar vary in different sections of the country. Logically, where sugar beet production is high, beet sugar consumption will be higher than cane sugar, but the picture reverses where cane is raised.

SUGAR PRODUCTION

Sugarcane

The sugarcane crop in Hawaii has been adjusted so that production is on a year-round basis with each field being replanted every four to eight years. Crops are scientifically fertilized and, in many instances, irrigated during the 18 to 24 months required for the crop to reach maturity. Just before harvesting, the dramatic "burning off" of the fields is done to clear the field of everything except the cane stalks.

Raw sugar is prepared from the washed cane stalks by squeezing the cane through a series of rollers to extract the juice. After the juice is heated in the presence of lime, the lime and many adhering impurities are allowed to settle out. The resulting medium brown juice is then evaporated to a mixture of highly viscous syrup and raw sugar crystals. Centrifugation is used to isolate the raw sugar crystals that will be the starting material for the refining process.

Much of the raw sugar is shipped to the United States mainland for refinement and distribution. The coarse, yellow, sticky raw sugar is transformed into white fine sugar crystals during refining. This change is effected by decolorizing a syrup of raw sugar and water with charcoal, recrystallizing the sugar from the syrup, and ultimately drying and separating the crystals according to granule size.

Sugar Beets

The sugar beet crop reaches maturity in approximately nine months, at which time the beets are pulled from the ground by a spiked wheel device. Sugar beets are sliced into long strips, called cossettes, which are soaked in hot water to release the sugar by diffusion. The resultant blue-black juice containing the sugar undergoes treatment with lime and carbon dioxide in a process comparable to the clarification of cane sugar with lime and charcoal. The clear juice is then processed in sequence through the following steps: evaporation, crystallization under controlled conditions, centrifugation, air drying, screening, and packaging. An interesting sidelight is that a by-product of this production process is used to make the flavor enhancer, monosodium glutamate.

The United States government has established annual import quotas for raw sugar, subject to fluctuations in the political climate of trading nations. The bulk of the sugar consumed in the United States is raised in Hawaii, continental United States, Puerto Rico, and the Virgin Islands; approximately 30 percent is imported.

SWEETENING SUBSTANCES

By taking advantage of particular properties of the various forms of sugar available for use in food preparation, one can achieve desirable variations in food products. Some forms are liquids and others are crystalline solids; some have more sweetening power than others; some crystalline sugars are coarse and others are very fine textured; some sugars are highly refined, and some have many flavorful impurities. The comparative sweetness of these various substances has been analyzed as follows when the sweetness of sucrose is arbitrarily set at 100: corn syrup, 30; maple syrup, 64; molasses, 74; and honey, 97.

Granulated Sugar

Between 50 and 85 percent of factory sugar production is devoted to granulated sugar because its sweetness, color, and solubility are well suited for wide use in food preparation. The words cane sugar or beet sugar appear on the package label to identify the source of the sugar although the two sugars are identical chemically.

White granulated sugar may be purchased in different granule sizes ranging from superfine to regular granulated sugar. The name dessert sugar, a synonym for superfine, suggests the group of foods in which the very fine crystals are used to best advantage. Superfine crystals are readily soluble because of their petite dimensions, hence are particularly useful for making hard and soft meringues. Regular granulated sugar is suitable for most uses and has the advantage of being less expensive than dessert sugar.

Cube sugar is actually granulated sugar which has been moistened with a white syrup, molded into cubes, and then dried in that shape. The plain cubes are convenient for sweetening tea and coffee.

Frosting Sugar

One of the newer sugar products, frosting sugar, is manufactured in round, easily dissolved bubbles particularly adapted for use in uncooked icings. Unlike powdered sugar, this product contains no cornstarch.

Powdered Sugar

Powdered or confectioner's sugar, frequently used for preparing un-cooked icings and for sweetening fruits, is made by pulverizing granulated sugar and adding 3 percent cornstarch. The cornstarch is added to absorb moisture and thus to prevent caking of the powdered sugar.

Brown Sugar

Because of its pleasing and distinctive flavor, brown sugar frequently is used in baked products. The color and flavor of brown sugar are corre-lated with its state of refinement; a dark, strong-flavored brown sugar has undergone less purification than has a light, mild-flavored brown sugar. A brown sugar that will pour from the box is industry's latest solution to the problem of the lumping that occurs during shelf storage.

Molasses

Molasses is a product made from sugarcane and may be marketed as unsulphured molasses, sulphured molasses, or blackstrap molasses. Sul-phured molasses, ranges in color from a rather light color to a somewhat darker brown, depending on whether it is prepared by centrifuging from the first boiling of the sugarcane juice (the lighter color) or from the second boiling. Sulphured molasses is a by-product that is available after the sugar has been crystallized and removed from the cane juice. Unsulphured molas-ses is made from ripe sugarcane and is not subjected to sulphur fumes, as is the custom when sugar is the principal product and molasses is merely a by-product. The unsulphured product is a full flavored, reddish brown liquid that has been aged to enhance its flavor. Blackstrap molasses is the material remaining after commercial extraction of sugar has been completed. Much of its use is as an animal food.

Maple Sugar and Syrup

The tapping of sugar maple trees and the boiling of the collected sap to make maple syrup and maple sugar date back to the early colonial days in the eastern United States. It is still possible to buy maple syrup and sugar but limitations in the production process have hampered output and have caused prices to remain relatively high.

Several syrups on the market have artificial maple flavoring and are considerably less expensive than genuine maple syrup, but the true maple syrup is still preferred by many people. This type of syrup is most fre-quently used for sweetening pancakes or waffles, but occasionally it is used to add flavor and sweetness to baked products.

Corn Syrup

The other sugars discussed are produced from sugar naturally occurring in plants, but corn syrup is made from starch. During the processing of corn syrup, starch is treated with hydrochloric or sulfuric acids in the presence of heat and pressure to produce a mixture of sugars. The predominant sugar formed is glucose, but maltose is also found and an intermediate breakdown product, dextrin, is present in small quantities. Corn syrup, as the name indicates, is a liquid.

Honey

Honey, another sweetening substance used in the home, is produced by the honey bee, which uses nectar from flowering plants. The source of the nectar determines the flavor quality of the honey; honey from weeds has a strong and objectionable flavor as contrasted with the sweet honey made from clover and alfalfa. Clover honey is the most common honey on the market. Recently, specialty honeys made from orange blossoms, sage, and exotic Hawaiian plants have been promoted and accepted. Honey is unique in that it contains a large amount of fructose.

REACTIONS OF SUGAR

Caramelization

When sugar (sucrose) is heated by itself or in highly concentrated solutions, it undergoes a change called caramelization. As dry sugar is heated it melts to a colorless liquid that soon begins to develop a brown color. Then as the liquid sugar darkens, the pleasing characteristic aroma subtly changes to that of burning sugar. Caramelization should be halted by the addition of some water when the desired color and flavor have developed. Extreme care needs to be taken when adding water to caramelizing sugar. Because of the large difference in temperature between the very hot molten sugar and the boiling water, considerable splattering will take place. For blending into foods, caramelized sugar, or burnt sugar as it is often called in recipes, should be diluted with liquid because the caramelized sugar alone becomes very hard and brittle as it cools. The caramelization of sugar may also be observed when caramels and other candies requiring high final temperatures are made. As the sugar syrup becomes more concentrated with continued cooking, the candy begins to darken and to emit the characteristic odor of caramelizing sugar.

The breakdown products during caramelization are quite varied and are not yet fully classified, but it is apparent that organic acids are formed. The presence of organic acids is illustrated when soda is added to hot peanut brittle. The addition of this alkaline ingredient to the caramelized candy product causes a sudden release of gas as the organic acids in the candy react with the soda to make carbon dioxide. This reaction is responsible for the porous texture of brittle.

Hydrolysis

Hot acid solutions cause a cleavage of disaccharides into monosaccharides by a chemical reaction termed acid hydrolysis. In sugar cookery an acid such as cream of tartar is frequently heated with a sugar solution. The following equation illustrates the hydrolytic reaction that occurs in candy preparation.

$$C_{12}H_{22}O_{11} + H_2O \xrightarrow{\text{acid}} C_6H_{12}O_6 + C_6H_{12}O_6$$

$$\underset{\text{Sucrose}}{} \qquad \underset{\text{Glucose} \quad \text{Fructose}}{}$$

$$\text{Invert sugar}$$

The extent of hydrolysis depends on the length of time that the sugar solution is held at a high temperature. Therefore, sucrose in a candy that is cooked slowly will undergo more acid hydrolysis than in a candy that is rapidly heated to its final temperature. Extensive hydrolysis produces a softer candy than one might expect. The reason for this is discussed in the section on crystallization in this chapter.

Hydrolysis of the sugar molecule also will be effected by the addition of the enzyme invertase. Invertase, found in yeasts and fungi, will act on sucrose to form the same products as those resulting from acid hydrolysis, namely a mixture of fructose and glucose. Heat facilitates acid hydrolysis, but halts the action of invertase. Therefore, invertase should be added after the candy has cooled if the enzyme is to be used. More extensive information on the chemistry of sugars is presented in Chapter 18.

TYPES OF CANDIES

The Arabs call it khandi, the British call it sweets, we call it candy; but regardless of the name, candy making is undergoing a transition from a little understood art to a science. Many people still trust to luck when they make confections, not realizing that a basic understanding of solutions would remove much of the mysticism surrounding candy making.

Before considering the steps involved in preparing confections, it is helpful to study the two basic types of candies. Amorphous candies possess a heterogeneous structure that reveals no evidence of a formal crystal

FIGURE 13.1 Fudge and cream-centered candies have a crystalline structure; the caramels featured in the center of the lower dish are examples of amorphous candies.

arrangement. These candies always feel smooth on the tongue since there is no possibility of large, coarse crystals forming. In contrast to the crystalline candies, most amorphous candies, such as toffees and brittles, are very hard and are cracked into pieces, rather than being cut with a knife. Caramels, however, the softest of the amorphous candies, may be cut with a knife.

Crystalline candies are the fondant-type candies having a definite crystal structure that is evident when viewed under a microscope. These candies are easily chewed and may be cut with a knife. Examples of crystalline candies are fondant, cream centers in chocolate dipped candies, fudge,

and panocha. Considerable care must be taken in the preparation of crystalline candies if the finished product is to have a smooth, velvety texture.

Amorphous Candies

Amorphous candies are somewhat easier to make than crystalline
ones since crystallization is not a factor. Accurate final temperature, however, is important in making noncrystalline candies if they are to have the
expected characteristics. The other problem relates to flavor and color, for
the high temperatures necessary for making these candies may permit considerable scorching unless the mixture is carefully stirred throughout the
boiling period. Scorched candy will have an undesirable flavor and a very
dark color.

The consistency of amorphous candies varies as a result of the wide
range of ingredients and temperatures used in making these confections.
Each candy should be judged according to the firmness or brittleness appropriate for the product, that is, true taffy is quite hard, toffee is brittle, and
caramels are chewy and somewhat elastic. The other criterion for these
candies, flavor, is determined by the ingredients and the presence or absence of scorching during boiling.

Crystalline Candies

The procedures involved in making crystalline candies are designed
to produce a smooth-textured and soft, yet firm, candy. Achieving the desired firmness is most easily accomplished by using a thermometer carefully. Boiling the candy to the appropriate temperature for the particular
candy assures the desired firmness unless the boiling time is unusually long
or the weather is very humid. Excessive acid hydrolysis during very slow
boiling may produce a candy that is too soft because too much invert sugar
forms. On a very humid day the cooling sugar solution will take up moisture
from the air and decrease the sugar concentration sufficiently to produce a
softer, somewhat sticky candy. Under normal conditions the only variations from desired consistency will be the soft product resulting from failure
to boil the candy to a high enough final temperature or the extra firm candy
attributed to boiling to too high a temperature.

Crystalline candies are judged on their consistency, texture, and flavor.
A good crystalline candy will be firm but not hard and it will have a very
smooth feel on the tongue. The flavor will be pleasing and will have no
suggestion of a scorched taste.

If an unsatisfactory crystalline candy is prepared, it may be rectified
by adding water, reheating to the proper temperature, cooling, and then
beating it. A grainy candy may result from incomplete solution of the sugar,

from use of a recipe that does not contain substances helpful in inhibiting crystallization, from disturbance during cooling, or from inadequate agitation. To achieve a better understanding of the problems encountered in crystalline sugar products, it is essential to consider supersaturated solutions and also the factors influencing crystallization.

SATURATED AND SUPERSATURATED SOLUTIONS

In sugar cookery, a true solution is made with water as the solvent and sugar as the solute. This true solution is a homogeneous mixture in which there is no variation in the content of samples taken from different portions of the mixture. Water is capable of dissolving just so much sugar at a given temperature. When this maximum amount of sugar is in solution, the solution is said to be saturated. Any additional sugar will reach an equilibrium with the sugar that is already in solution, that is, undissolved sugar will go into solution as some of the dissolved sugar precipitates out of solution. The total quantity of sugar in solution at a specific temperature, however, remains fixed.

As the temperature rises, the solvent can hold more of the solute in solution, so additional solute that may be present will begin to go into solution. This is a fundamental principle utilized in sugar cookery. A candy recipe requires a finite amount of sugar in a finite amount of aqueous liquid. The quantity of sugar required is too much to go into solution at room temperature no matter how much it is stirred. Therefore the candy must be heated to get all of the sugar in true solution.

A fundamental principle in sugar cookery is that the greater the proportion of sugar to water in the finished candy, the harder will be the final product. The final suggested boiling temperatures for various candies are based on this fact. Crystalline candies, since they are softer than amorphous candies, are heated to relatively low temperatures; and amorphous candies are heated to very high temperatures to achieve a very hard consistency. Typical candies, their ingredients, and final temperatures are listed in Table 13.1.

The quantity of sugar in a candy is determined when it is measured into the pan, but the quantity of water is altered through evaporation while the candy is boiling. Therefore the greater the evaporative loss, the greater will be the proportion of sugar to liquid in the finished candy.

Sugar solutions that reach a high ratio of sugar to liquid are very viscous and rather brown because caramelization occurs during the long period of boiling required to concentrate the sugar solution. The viscosity of the concentrated solution is used in crude determinations for doneness of a candy. Colorful descriptive words such as hard ball, soft ball, and hard

Table 13.1. Ingredients and Final Temperatures for Some Typical Candies

Candy	Basic Ingredients	Final Temperature
Crystalline		
Fondant	Granulated sugar, corn syrup or cream of tartar, water	114°C (238°F)
Fudge	Granulated sugar, cocoa or chocolate, milk, corn syrup, butter	112°C (234°F)
Panocha	Brown sugar, granulated sugar, milk, corn syrup, butter	112°C (234°F)
Amorphous		
Caramels	Granulated sugar, corn syrup, butter, cream	118°C (245°F)
Taffy	Granulated sugar, corn syrup, water	127°C (260°F)
Toffee	Granulated sugar, butter, water, corn syrup	149°C (300°F)

crack are household words to describe the viscosity achieved in candy making, but these stages are impossible to judge accurately.

The use of a candy thermometer is the only reliable means of telling the temperature and, ultimately, the adequacy of the sugar concentration. Slight inaccuracies in factory calibration of thermometers make it imperative that the boiling temperature of water be checked on the thermometer to permit adjustment of the final registered temperature. In this way calibration errors can be corrected. For instance, a candy that should be boiled to 112°C would be taken to a final temperature of 110°C if the thermometer showed that water boiled at 98°C. This is very important, for an undercooked candy will be too soft and an overcooked one too hard.

It should be emphasized that candies are saturated solutions while they are boiling, but as soon as they are removed from the heat the temperature of the solution begins to drop. As the mixture cools, all of the sugar may remain in solution if circumstances are carefully controlled. Thus the solution actually is holding more solute than could a solution of sugar and water, at the same temperature, which had not been previously heated to a higher temperature. Such a solution is said to be supersaturated; the cooler the candy becomes, the greater the degree of supersaturation.

Supersaturated solutions are very unstable and become increasingly unstable as the degree of supersaturation increases. Amorphous candies change abruptly from this supersaturated condition and become hard with no opportunity for crystal growth. Crystals do form ultimately in crystalline candies, however, and it is the size of these crystals that determines the texture of the product. Very large crystals sometimes found in carelessly made crystalline candies have a grainy, almost sandy feel on the tongue. Since such texture is not considered desirable, the factors influencing crystal growth need to be understood and controlled when preparing crystalline candies.

FACTORS INFLUENCING CRYSTAL GROWTH

The size of the crystals in crystalline candies is influenced by the degree of supersaturation at the time crystallization commences, the time at which agitation or beating begins, the duration of beating, the presence of substances to act as nuclei for crystal growth, and the inclusion of substances inhibiting crystallization.

A high degree of supersaturation is essential if very small crystals are to be formed. Crystal growth occurs rather slowly if candy is only slightly supersaturated when crystallization begins. Since only a few nuclei are present under this circumstance, the sugar that crystallizes as the mixture gradually cools will be deposited on the existing crystals rather than forming new small crystals.

This condition contrasts with the crystallization of a cooler solution

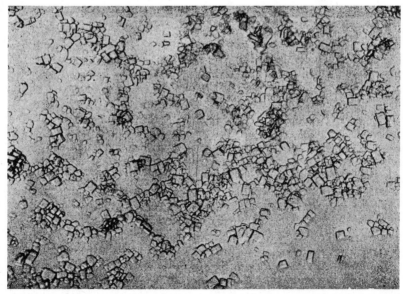

FIGURE 13.2   Crystals from fondant cooked to 113°C, cooled to 40°C, and then beaten until the mass was stiff and kneadable (magnification 200X).

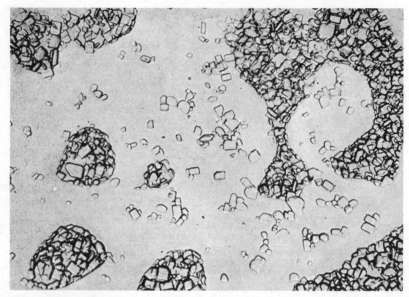

FIGURE 13.3 Crystals from fondant in Figure 13.2 after 40 days of storage. Note the crystal growth (magnification 200X).

that has reached a higher degree of supersaturation before crystallization begins. In the latter instance, many nuclei will be available for crystal growth and the sugar will be precipitated quickly in very small crystals.

Many people have the misconception that beating causes a candy to get hard, when actually extensive beating will not harden a candy that has been undercooked. The reason candy needs to be beaten is that agitation aids in developing small crystals. As the candy is beaten the sugar crystals bump against each other, preventing the formation of large aggregates. Ideally, crystallization will be delayed until the candy has cooled to 43°C (110°F), at which time beating is initiated. At this temperature the candy is highly viscous and has achieved a high degree of supersaturation. The disturbance of the supersaturated solution as beating begins immediately starts crystallization of a great number of nuclei and a fine-textured product quickly results. Constant agitation is necessary until crystallization is virtually completed if a fine-textured product is to be the result. If beating ceases too soon, the sugar that continues to precipitate will build on the existing nuclei and the crystals will be large.

Crystallization may be started accidentally by a number of different circumstances before the candy has cooled to 43°C. Situations such as the following are typical occurrences that trigger the crystallization process: disturbance of the surface by an object; movement of the candy which causes rippling on the surface; particles of dust that might fall on the surface and act as nuclei; or undissolved sugar crystals that serve as nuclei for the growth of large crystals as the candy cools. Anything that disturbs the candy in any way while it is cooling will start crystallization.

Agitation must be begun as soon as crystallization is initiated. Otherwise the few nuclei present will seed the solution and the sugar will grow on these existing nuclei as it precipitates, causing a very granular candy. Beating helps to minimize the size of the crystals since it constantly disturbs the formation of larger crystals. Unfortunately, even with rapid, constant beating until the candy stiffens, such candy will not be quite as fine grained as it would have been if it had cooled properly. Prolonged beating from the onset of crystallization, however, is far preferable to waiting to begin beating until the crystallizing candy reaches 43°C (110°F). Undisturbed crystallization produces a distinctly grainy candy.

It is possible to partially control the size of crystals in crystalline candies by adding substances that inhibit crystal growth. When more than one sugar is present, crystals form less readily. Therefore the addition of corn syrup to a crystalline candy recipe is useful because it is a mixture of glucose, maltose, and dextrins, the combination of which inhibits crystallization.

Acid ingredients cause a hydrolytic reaction that breaks some of the

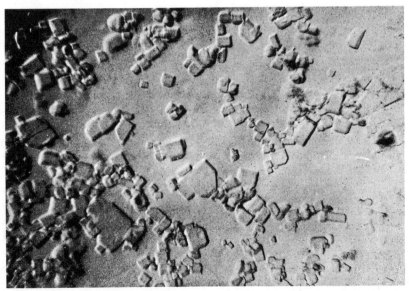

FIGURE 13.4 Crystals from fondant cooked to 113°C and then beaten immediately and continuously until the mass was stiff and kneadable (magnification 200X).

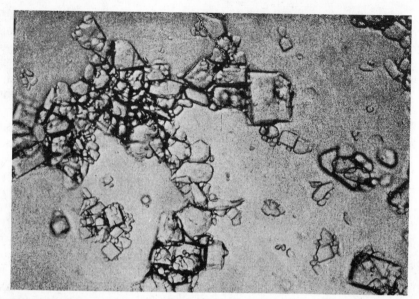

FIGURE 13.5 Frozen desserts require careful control of crystallization factors if a smooth, creamy texture is to be achieved.

sucrose in the candy into invert sugar. The mixture of the sucrose and invert sugar in the candy causes crystallization to occur less readily and a finer-grained candy results. The extent of acid hydrolysis is related to the time that the candy is boiled. A very slow rate of heating may cause so much inversion of the sucrose that crystallization may be too greatly inhibited and the candy may not become firm. This effect can be demonstrated by making a fondant with cream of tartar, using a low heat.

Fats are useful inhibiting substances because they coat the sugar crystals and make it difficult for additional sugar to precipitate onto an existing crystal. This is an important factor in making velvety smooth crystalline candies. Butter and/or cream are the customary fat-containing substances used in candy making.

The heat of crystallization is an interesting physical phenomenon which is observable as a slight softening just as the candy mass changes from a very viscous liquid to a solid. In small quantity work this softening due to the release of heat is difficult to see, but is more easily observed in large, commercial batches. Abruptly after this heat is released, the candy will become too stiff to spread. A gentle, kneading motion with the fingers is then effective in working the crumbly mass into a malleable product.

A 24-hour ripening period in a tightly covered container softens a crystalline candy slightly and promotes smoothness. Crystal growth, however, is an important consideration during longer storage of candy as well as during its preparation, for the structure of candy is constantly undergoing change. Small sugar crystals dissolve into the mother liquor (the liquid medium between the crystals) and subsequently recrystallize from the mother liquor onto existing nuclei. Since the small crystals are more soluble than the larger ones, there is a gradual transition from the original small crystals of the freshly made candy to larger crystals during prolonged storage. The presence of more than one type of sugar and/or an abundance of fat in a candy are useful aids in inhibiting crystallization, thus helping to maintain the fine grain desired in crystalline candy during storage.

COMMERCIAL CANDY PREPARATION

Commercially, candies are divided into three categories according to the ingredients they contain: candies made entirely of sugar with or without flavor and color include hard candies, creams, and stick candies; pectin jellies, marshmallows, and nougats are classified as candies containing 95 percent or more sugar and 5 percent or less of nonsugar ingredients; and the candies containing nonsugar ingredients in the proportion of 5–25 percent include fudge, caramels, starch jellies, and chocolates.

Commercial Additives

The problems encountered in the commercial confectionery industry are a composite of the problems in making homemade candies plus storage and shipping hazards. To successfully produce candy of high quality, the candy industry has found it helpful to utilize some substances not used in the home.

Glycerol and large quantities of corn syrup are helpful in maintaining the moisture in candy and in retarding the development of a gritty texture in creams and mints. Various emulsifiers including monoglycerides are helpful in retarding staling and toughening of candies having a starch jelly base.

Cream of tartar is used commercially as well as in the home to promote the conversion of sucrose to invert sugar. The acidic character of cream of tartar is responsible for its hydrolytic effect in candy.

The enzyme invertase is added to cream centers because of its ability to convert sucrose to invert sugar. As the conversion takes place the cream center of the candy begins to soften to the desired consistency. This conversion takes some time, however, and it is because of this time lapse that invertase is so useful. Manufacturers are able to make firm centers containing invertase which are easily handled during the chocolate-dipping operation. Then the delayed action of the invertase commences the conversion that ultimately gives the desired consistency to the centers of the candy.

Gums are added to give the appropriate gelling properties to various candies. Gums are defined as any material that will dissolve or disperse in water to give a viscous or sticky mixture. This sticky mixture may be either highly viscous or have definite gelling properties as the material cools. Most gums used commercially in candy production are carbohydrates derived from seaweed, plant seeds, or tree exudates. The seaweed extracts such as agar and Irish moss have been commonly used for a long time commercially, but they are now often replaced by starch and pectin. Carrageenan (Irish moss) is used to prevent the "oiling off" that occurs in caramels, toffees, and nougats in hot weather. Two tree exudates, gum arabic and gum tragacanth, have the dual function of preventing crystal growth and emulsifying fat to avoid fat separation in candies.

FROZEN DESSERTS

Frozen desserts may be prepared in the home by using a variety of ingredients, including sugar, liquids of various types, and a wide assortment of flavoring substances. The texture and serving consistency are important quality criteria in these products, and the ingredients included in the mixture play a significant role in achieving a desirable product. The definitions of commercial frozen desserts are given in the identification of dairy products enumerated in Chapter 8.

Ingredients and Their Influence

Sugar. As anyone who has ever tasted ice cream knows, sugar is an important ingredient for improving the flavor of ice cream and other frozen desserts. The sweetness of the sugar is essential to the flavor impact of the product. However, sugar has an effect on the freezing point of the mixture as well as a role to play in the flavor. Sugar impedes the formation of ice crystals as the product is being frozen. This phenomenon may be caused by sugar molecules attracting water molecules in a manner that interferes with the formation of the ice crystals. Each cup of sugar lowers the temperature at which one liter of water freezes by approximately 1°C. To illustrate, a frozen dessert made with one-half liter of water and two cups of sugar would have a freezing point four Celsius degrees lower than the freezing point of pure water, that is, the freezing point of the frozen dessert would be approximately −4°C.

Although this effect of sugar may seem to be rather small, this can become an important matter in formulating recipes for frozen desserts and frozen salads. A very sweet mixture will require a longer time to freeze. It also will melt at a lower temperature, making very sweet products more difficult to serve without being too soft. This negative contribution of sugar is somewhat offset by the fact that sugar helps to inhibit the growth of large ice crystals. Consequently, sugar promotes a smooth texture.

Dairy Products. Cream is commonly used as the liquid in making ice cream. Of course, the fat in cream contributes to the full, rich flavor sought in such desserts. The fat also is a boon because of its influence on crystal formation. An ice cream made with cream will have a smoother texture than will one made with milk. This difference is due to the action of fat as an interfering agent to inhibit crystal growth. When the fat has been broken into smaller globules by homogenization, the effect is even greater than it is with the nonhomogenized cream. The addition of milk solids is an aid in promoting the desired fine texture. This is due partially to the increased viscosity of the mixture and also to the greater foaming property of the mixture when more milk protein is present. Evaporated milk, when used without reconstituting to its regular concentration, helps to achieve a smooth texture because of the greater concentration of milk solids. If too large an amount of nonfat dry milk solids is used, the texture may be just a bit sandy as the result of the extra lactose contained in the solids. Lactose is less soluble than sucrose and may precipitate into crystals sufficiently large to be noticed in the ice cream.

Fruit Juices. Fruit juices are often used in making ices. Their flavors add significantly to the finished product. However, fruit juices are acidic, a fact which necessitates the inclusion of more sugar to offset the acidity. Mixtures made with fruit juices, but with controlled amounts of sugar, will freeze satisfactorily and have a smooth texture. If milk is used as well as acid, the mixture may curdle. Prompt freezing of the mixture should avoid curdling. The viscosity of the mixture before freezing will be increased a bit by the effect of the acid on the milk protein. This increased viscosity helps to promote a smooth texture in the frozen product.

Freezing the Mixture

With Agitation. Frozen desserts may be frozen either with or without agitation. Those in which agitation is employed are frozen in an ice cream freezer which is equipped with a dasher suspended in a covered metal container, with the entire assembly mounted in a larger bucket of wood. The ice cream mixture is poured into the metal container, which is then assembled and placed in the bucket with the crank firmly attached. The bucket is packed with a mixture of rock salt and ice. Rock salt is a very coarse salt that suits this purpose well because the particles have less tendency to cake than is true of finer salts.

The ice cream mixture must be chilled to the freezing temperature of the product, a process which requires that heat be removed. The metal

FIGURE 13.6 Frozen desserts require careful control of crystallization factors if a smooth, creamy texture is to be achieved.

container housing the mixture facilitates removal of heat because of its conducting qualities. This heat goes into the ice and salt mix which is slowly melting to form a brine. The ice is used to lower the freezing point of the brine. The actual temperature of the brine solution is regulated by the amount of salt that is used in proportion to the ice. The minimum temperature that can be reached is achieved by using a 29 percent salt to 71 percent ice mixture. With this blend, a temperature of $-21°C$ ($-6°F$) is reached, and this temperature is much colder than is necessary for freezing ice cream. A good rate of chilling and crystallization is achieved by using approximately one part rock salt for eight parts of ice for freezing ice creams and a ratio of one to six for reaching the colder temperatures needed for freezing ices.

During the first part of the freezing process, the ice cream mixture should be cranked rather slowly to enable the mixture to cool quite uniformly throughout rather than becoming appreciably colder at the edge of the container than in the center. As the mixture begins to freeze, agitation needs to be increased to a rapid rate to help maintain small crystals of ice rather than developing coarse ones that give a rough texture to the finished product. As more and more ice crystals form, the mixture becomes increasingly viscous, and it will be necessary to crank more slowly until cranking is too difficult to maintain. The ice cream then is no longer cranked, but is allowed to chill undisturbed in the cold brine-ice mixture to continue crystallizing for about half an hour, or long enough for the ice cream to firm up to a serving consistency.

The key to successful preparation of frozen desserts that are cranked is to maintain the agitation at the appropriate rate throughout the freezing process. Very rapid cranking before crystallization begins may cause the butterfat to clump together and contribute to a curdled appearance in the finished product. Insufficient agitation during the period of active ice crystal formation contributes to the development of ice crystals that are larger than desired; the finished product will feel rather grainy in the mouth.

Proper control of the temperature of the ice-brine mixture is also important in achieving the best possible finished product. If the ice-salt ratio is unbalanced in favor of too much salt, the temperature of the brine will be unduly cold. This causes the ice cream to chill very rapidly, with the result that the mixture freezes into a very heavy, solid mixture; there had been too little time for air to be whipped in during the cranking operation before the ice crystals had formed throughout the mixture. Actually, the incorporation of air during freezing is considered desirable. This causes an increase in volume, known as overrun, and an accompanying characteristic of lightness in the product. Of course, excessive overrun is not desirable, since this gives a frothy quality.

Without Agitation. Frozen desserts may be frozen in the freezer compartment of the refrigerator simply by placing them in a metal tray and leaving them alone while the product chills and ice crystals form. Many of these recipes will include interfering substances to inhibit the formation of large ice crystals. The inclusion of a fairly high amount of cream in the recipe impedes crystal formation because of the increased viscosity of the original mixture and also the inhibiting effect of the many fat droplets. The problem of lightness is solved, in part, by incorporating some type of foam in the original mixture to be frozen. Foams might be whipped cream, whipped undiluted evaporated milk, egg whites, and gelatin. These foams not only help the structure of the ice cream, but also inhibit the formation of large crystals. With frozen desserts that are not cranked during freezing, the amount of sugar is of particular significance in determining texture. A very sweet product will require longer to freeze.

Evaluation

Well-prepared frozen desserts will have a rather light feel on the tongue and will seem to be very smooth when eaten. The ice cream should be neither frothy nor gritty feeling. The product will be free of any curdling. The flavor should be distinctive, yet pleasing, and the color should be tempting, but not garish. Ice creams should be sufficiently hard to be able to remain firm during the serving period.

SUMMARY

Candies are classified as crystalline or amorphous on the basis of their internal organization. Achievement of a highly supersaturated solution and careful control of crystal growth are essential when preparing crystalline candies. Amorphous candies require careful heat control and some agitation to ensure even heat distribution in the product while boiling to the high final temperatures required. In the preparation of these candies, hydrolysis occurs during the boiling period. Hydrolysis may be due to the presence of acid and will result in the formation of invert sugar from sucrose. Enzyme hydrolysis, effected by the addition of invertase to crystalline candies after they are cooled, is another means of producing invert sugar to promote a smoother texture. During the boiling of amorphous candies, another degradative reaction begins to take place. This process, known as caramelization, results in a change in flavor and color as organic acids are formed from sucrose.

The control of the crystallization process in crystalline candies and in frozen desserts is essential to the quality of both types of products. In the case of the candies, the crystals are sugar crystals that form following the formation of a highly supersaturated solution. Beating is used to help prevent the formation of large crystal aggregates that would create an undesirable texture in the finished product. The firmness of the candy is influenced by the rate of heating, the ingredients, and the final temperature to which the mixture was boiled.

Frozen desserts require careful control of the formation of ice crystals so that a smooth texture will be the result. Crystal formation is modified by agitating the mixture as it freezes, which continually breaks the aggregates into smaller crystals to provide the velvetiness considered desirable in ice creams. The rate of agitation needs to be regulated during the preliminary cooling period to prevent the clumping of the butterfat. Frozen desserts that are not agitated during the crystallization process will have a more desirable consistency when the recipe includes ingredients such as whipped cream or whipped undiluted evaporated milk. These foams increase the viscosity of the mixture to inhibit the formation of large crystals of ice and also add the airy quality needed to avoid too solid a feeling on the tongue. In cranked frozen desserts, the dasher effectively incorporates air to increase the volume (overrun) and achieve the desired lightness.

BIBLIOGRAPHY

Charm, S. E. Nature and role of fluid consistency in food engineering applications. *Adv. Food Res. 11:* 356–432. 1962.

Martin, L. F. Applications of research to problems of candy manufacture. *Adv. Food Res. 6:*1–55. 1955.

Meade, G. P. Sugar and sirups. Chapter 41 in *Chemistry and Technology of Food Products,* ed. by M. B. Jacobs, Vol. 3, 2nd ed. Interscience Publishers, New York, N.Y. 1951.

Meyer, L. H. *Introductory Chemistry;* 2nd ed. Macmillan. New York, N.Y. 1959.

Schoen, M. Confectionery and cacao products. Chapter 42 in *Chemistry and Technology of Food Products,* ed. by M. B. Jacobs, Vol. 3, 2nd ed. Interscience Publishers, New York, N.Y. 1951.

Sherman, P. Texture of ice cream. *J. Food Sci. 30:*201. 1965.

SUGGESTIONS FOR STUDY

1. What is the result of a very slow rate of heating on a crystalline candy? Explain the reaction that occurs.
2. What influence does the amount of beating have on a crystalline candy?
3. Does the time of initiation of beating influence the quality of a crystalline candy? How?
4. What is the purpose of adding the following ingredients to a basic fondant recipe: cream of tartar, corn syrup, chocolate, butter?
5. Why does the temperature of boiling candy gradually rise?
6. Compare an ice cream mixture that is frozen without agitation with one that was made by using the same recipe but with agitation during freezing. Explain the differences.
7. Why is ice cream that is cranked in an ice cream freezer agitated slowly during the initial part of the freezing process? What may happen if the cranking is much more rapid?

PART II
Food Management

CHAPTER 14

Food Preservation

Patterns of food preservation have been undergoing considerable change during this century as the country has undergone societal changes in response to today's urbanized technological framework. The former pattern of family units that raised and preserved a large fraction of their food supply for use throughout the year has largely been replaced with the consumer who relies almost entirely on the local supermarket for his daily bread. Advances in the transportation and distribution of foodstuffs have made it possible to provide fresh foods throughout a large fraction of the year in most localities, but still many preserved foods remain in the diet. These foods ordinarily have been preserved by commercial processors, with only a limited amount of preservation actually being done in the home. However, some consumers are deriving economies and pleasures from making jams and jellies, canning, or freezing homegrown or seasonal produce.

The underlying purpose in all preservation techniques is to restrict spoilage of the food so that it may be consumed safely in a palatable form at a later time. Preservation methods are designed to kill microorganisms, to greatly restrict the growth of microorganisms, to halt or greatly restrict enzyme action, and/or to prevent or delay sprouting. Control of these problems is essential to securing a long shelf life and to achieving a food that will be appetizing and safe. Very high temperatures during processing may be used to kill microorganisms and inactivate enzymes so that spoilage will not occur during normal storage periods. Frozen storage is an effective device for retarding the growth of microorganisms and the activity of enzymes. Drying to achieve a very low moisture content results in a medium unfavorable to the growth of microorganisms. The use of heavy salt, or high sugar concentrations kills microorganisms.

379

COMMERCIAL METHODS OF FOOD PRESERVATION

Some of the processing techniques for commercial preservation have undergone little change in recent years. For example, many fruits and vegetables are still canned in a fashion very similar to that being used 30 years ago. However, the strong consumer acceptance of frozen foods has opened the way to this means of preserving foods, too. In the frozen food field there have been many changes in products to include a far broader range than was first available in the frozen foods section. Such additions as frozen vegetables with various sauces packaged in bags that serve as the pan within a pan are readily accepted by consumers despite their relatively high cost. Frozen dinners, frozen baked products, frozen foods ready to pop into the oven, and frozen concentrated fruit juices are other examples of food products that are typical of the ways in which foods are preserved commercially today for later use.

Frozen orange juice and other fruit drinks have gained an important share of the citrus market. Other frozen fruit products have been marketed with varying degrees of success. Fresh pineapple and cherries freeze particularly well. Berries are somewhat limited in use after they have been frozen, since the rupturing of the cell walls that takes place when water freezes in the cells causes them to lose their shape when they are thawed. This problem can be minimized by using nitrogen spray to freeze the berries. The very low temperature results in very rapid freezing so that the ice crystals that form are extremely small and thus cause less damage to the cell wall. Frozen melon balls become soft and slippery when completely thawed; palatability is much higher when they are served with a suggestion of ice crystals still remaining than when they are thawed completely. Sprayed liquid nitrogen is an aid in minimizing this structural change in frozen melons.

Although canning and freezing are the two preservation methods that are utilized most frequently, other methods have been developed and are significant in the total food plan. Freeze-drying is a preservation method that is seemingly still developing its potential. In this process, foods are frozen and then the frozen food is dehydrated under a high vacuum. In this high vacuum, the ice that has formed in the frozen food sublimes rather than melting before evaporating.

Freeze-dried foods have a porous structure with a very low content of water. This limited water content makes it possible to store the freeze-dried food at room temperature rather than having to hold it in frozen storage to prevent spoilage. Since frozen storage is considerably more expensive and also more restrictive than is room temperature storage, freeze-dried foods have received considerable attention. They have been incorporated effectively as freeze-dried fruits in some breakfast cereals, as meats in dehydrated soups, and have found wide acceptance among campers who face serious food spoilage problems because of inadequate refrigeration facilities for food storage. The foods also are extremely light because of the very limited amount of water remaining, thus making them particularly popular among hikers. Freeze-dried coffee has gained a large market.

Irradiation has been used as a means of preserving foods. By subjecting the food to gamma rays from cobalt[60] or cesium[137], microorganisms and insects can be killed, thus enhancing the storage qualities of the food. For example, wheat and other grains can be stored for long periods of time when they have been irradiated. However, the safety of irradiation as a means of food preservation has been undergoing extensive review. Some irradiated foods have been found to be potentially unsafe for human consumption. Hence, this method of preservation does not appear to have future potential if the present concerns are perpetuated.

Drying is a very, very old and distinctly unsophisticated way of preserving food, and yet the popularity of foods such as raisins and dried beans

FIGURE 14.1   Raisins are produced by sun drying the grapes for 10–28 days.

seems never to wane. Sun-drying is an effective, yet unfortunately slow way of drying foods. Therefore, some liquids, notably milk and eggs, are dried by spraying the liquid in a very fine spray into a stream of hot air. Other foods are placed on conveyor belts running through a controlled environment designed for drying the food. Foam matting is yet another variation, in which liquids are concentrated and then foamed for drying. Puff-drying is a variation which begins with partial drying of the food, followed by the injection of super-heated steam.

PRESERVING FOOD AT HOME

Although food preservation in the home is done much less now than in the past, some canning is done. Freezing of fresh produce apparently is done on a small scale, and some people make their own jams, jellies, and preserves. If fresh produce is available from a home garden or at a very reasonable price in season, home preservation can be a distinct economy. When the food for preservation must be purchased at ordinary retail prices, the decision becomes one based more on satisfaction than on economy.

CANNING

For foods to be canned and stored successfully, the processing must be done in a manner that guarantees destruction of molds, yeast, and bacteria and the jars or cans must be sealed tightly to insure no contamination during storage. Molds, bacteria, and yeast are destroyed readily at 100°C (212°F), a temperature that can be reached without special equipment. The spores of bacteria, however, are viable above the temperature of boiling water; pressure must be utilized to reach the high temperature (116°C or 240°F) necessary to insure their destruction. Foods that have a relatively high acidity, that is a low pH, do not provide a good medium for the growth of bacteria. As a result, the matter of spores and their resistance to heat is not a serious consideration in canning such acid foods as fruits and tomatoes. However, other vegetables have a higher pH. This reduced acidity favors bacterial growth, and the higher processing temperature is imperative to avoid the hazard of viable spores. The danger from faulty processing of vegetables is due to the toxin produced by *Clostridium botulinum,* a topic discussed in more detail in Chapter 15. Since two different temperatures are required for processing fruits (and tomatoes) and vegetables, two methods are required. These are the boiling water bath and the pressure cooker.

Boiling Water Bath

The boiling water bath method is suitable only for fruits, pickles, and tomatoes because the temperature is too low to destroy bacterial spores which may be present in foods lower in acidity. In this method, the equipment needed includes a large kettle, a cover for the kettle, a rack that will fit inside the kettle, and canning jars with appropriate closures for the design of the jar. The kettle must be deep enough to allow at least an inch and a half above the top of the jars. The rack to hold the jars needs to keep the jars about half an inch above the bottom of the pan so the water can circulate readily.

The first step in canning by the boiling water bath method is to fill the kettle with sufficient water to rise one inch above the jars when the kettle is filled with jars. This water is heated with a cover so that it will be boiling when the food is ready to be processed. Next, the jars are prepared by washing both jars and covers in hot, soapy water, rinsing thoroughly with scalding water, and inverting the jars to drain while preparing the food. The covers are covered with boiling water and allowed to stand by without further heating until they are needed.

Fruits and tomatoes are prepared for canning as indicated in Table 14.1. The food is placed carefully in the jar and then a knife or narrow rubber spatula is moved gently through the jar to release any pockets of air that may be trapped. Fruit should be no higher in the jar than within one-half inch of the top. Boiling syrup, juice, or water then is poured to within $1\frac{1}{2}$ inches of the top if the fruit has been placed in the jars without heating, or to within $\frac{1}{2}$ inch of the top of the jar if the fruit is packed hot. The syrup may be thin, medium, or heavy, according to individual preference. These are made by boiling the following amounts of sugar with a quart of water for five minutes:

Thin syrup	2 cups of sugar
Medium syrup	3 cups of sugar
Heavy syrup	$4\frac{3}{4}$ cups of sugar

The lid is then fastened on the jar as firmly as can be done by hand. The jars are placed in the boiling water bath and processed for the period of time indicated in the table. When the processing period is over, the jars are removed from the kettle and cooled upright on several thicknesses of cloth. The following day the seal should be checked for tightness. Two-piece closures are checked by pressing the center of the lid to see that it is down and that the lid does not move. Zinc closures are checked by turning the jars around on their sides and watching for leakage. If the seal is not good, the food should be reprocessed or else eaten right away.

1. Check jars. Be sure there are no nicks, cracks, or sharp edges. Use new lids.

2. Wash and rinse jars and caps. Leave jars in hot water until ready to use.

5. Cut peaches into halves, pit, and peel. Drop halves into salt-vinegar water (2 tablespoons each to 1 gallon cold water). Rinse before packing.

6. Stand hot jar on rubber tray, wood, or cloth. Pack peaches, cavity-side down, layers overlapping. Leave ½-inch head space.

9. Wipe top and threads of jar with clean, damp cloth. Put lid on, screw band tight to hold red rubber sealing compound against top of jar.

10. As each jar is filled, stand it on rack in canner. Water should be hot, but not boiling. If needed, add more water to cover jars to 1 to 2 inches. Put cover on canner.

FIGURE 14.2 Peaches and other fruits are safely canned using the boiling water bath method outlined in this series.

3. Sort, wash, and drain only enough firm-ripe peaches for one canner load. Fill water bath canner half full with hot water. Put canner on to heat. Prepare sugar syrup.

4. Put peaches in wire basket or cheese-cloth. Dip peaches into boiling water ½ to 1 minute to loosen skins. Dip into cold water. Drain.

7. Cover peaches with boiling hot syrup, leaving ½-inch head space. It will take 1 to 1½ cups syrup for each quart jar.

8. Run rubber bottle scraper or similar non-metal utensil between fruit and jar to release air bubbles. Add more syrup, if needed.

11. Bring water to a boil. At altitudes less than 1,000 feet above sea level, process pints 25 minutes, quarts 30 minutes, at a gentle, but steady boil (longer period required for higher altitudes).

12. Remove jars from canner. Let cool for about 12 hours. Remove bands. Test for seal. Store without bands.

Table 14.1. Canning Recommendations for Selected Fruits and Tomatoes[a]

Food	Preparation Instructions	Time in Boiling Water Bath (min)[b]	
		Pints	Quarts
Apples	Wash, pare, core, cut in pieces. Drop in slightly salted water. Drain. Boil 3 to 5 minutes in syrup	20	25
Apricots	Wash, halve, and pit	20	25
Berries	Wash, stem	15	20
Cherries	Wash, stem, and pit	20	20
Cranberries	Wash, remove stems, boil 3 minutes in heavy syrup	10	10
Peaches	Peel after immersing in boiling water, add syrup and boil 3 minutes	20	25
Pears	Using not overripe pears, pare, halve, and boil in syrup 3 to 5 minutes	25	30
Plums	Wash, prick skins	20	25
Tomatoes	Scald ½ minute. Cold dip, peel, core, and quarter	35	45

[a]Adapted from Kerr Home Canning Book. Page 8. Kerr Glass Manufacturing Corp. Sand Springs, Okla. 1971.
[b]At altitudes above sea level, add one minute for each 1000 feet if the time indicated above is less than 20 minutes; add two minutes for each 1000 feet if more than 20 minutes are recommended.

Pressure Canning

A pressure cooker may be used satisfactorily for canning vegetables and meats, although the latter rarely are canned in the home today. The operating instructions for the pressure cooker are the best guide to follow, but the suggestions included here are generally applicable. The jars and covers are prepared as they are for the boiling water bath. The food is handled as indicated in Table 14.2. While the food is being placed in the first jar, two inches of boiling water should be poured into a large pressure cooker and maintained at a boil, with each jar being placed in the cooker as it is filled. Vegetables are packed only to within an inch of the top. One inch headspace should be maintained. Then boiling water is added to within one-half inch of the top of the jar. The lids are fastened as before, and the jars are placed in the pressure cooker. When the cooker is full of jars, the cover of the cooker is securely fastened and the petcock is left open for 7 to 10 minutes to exhaust the cooker. The petcock is closed then, and the pressure is allowed to build to 10 pounds (or more if at a higher elevation, as indicated in Table 14.2). The heat is adjusted to maintain the proper pressure and the processing time begins. At the end of the processing time, the pressure cooker is removed from the heat and allowed to cool at room temperature until the pressure gauge reaches zero. The petcock then is opened gradually. When steam no longer escapes, the cover of the cooker can be removed, but the jars should be left in the cooker until the liquid in them stops boiling. At this time, they can be removed from the cooker safely. The cooling and checking for sealing are done the same as for the boiling water bath method.

Table 14.2. Canning recommendations for selected vegetables[a]

Food	Preparation Instructions	Time at 10 Pounds Pressure[b]	
		Pints	Quarts
Asparagus	Wash, pack raw or boil 3 minutes.	25	30
Beans (wax or green)	Wash, string, cut, and pack raw or boil 5 minutes	20	25
Beets	Wash, boil 15 minutes, and skin	30	40
Corn	Remove shucks, cut from cob, pack raw or bring to boil	55	85
Okra	Wash, boil 1 minute	25	40
Peas	Shell, wash and grade for tenderness. Pack raw or bring to boil	40	40
Spinach	Wash, steam or boil to wilt	70	90

[a]Adapted from Kerr Home Canning Book. Kerr Glass Manufacturing Corp. Sand Springs, Okla. 1971. Page. 9.
[b]At altitudes above 2000 feet, the pressure must be increased one pound for each 2000 feet.

1. Check jars for nicks, cracks, and sharp edges. Wash jars and caps in hot soapy water; rinse. Leave jars in hot water until ready to use. Use new lids and good bands.

2. Thoroughly wash freshly gathered beans, which are young, tender, and crisp, using several changes of water. Lift beans out of water and drain.

5. Stand hot jar on wood or cloth. Add 1 teaspoon salt per quart; cover beans with boiling water, leaving 1-inch head space.

6. Wipe top and threads of jar with clean, damp cloth. Put lid on with the red rubber sealing compound next to the jar. Screw band down evenly and tightly.

9. Leave vent open until steam escapes steadily for 10 minutes. Close vent. At altitudes less than 2,000 feet above sea level, bring pressure to 10 pounds. Keep pressure steady for 20 minutes for pints, 25 minutes for quarts.

10. Remove canner from heat. Let pressure fall to zero. Wait 2 minutes. Slowly open vent. Open canner and remove jars. Do not tighten bands.

FIGURE 14.3 Vegetables and other low-acid foods require pressure processing to reach high enough temperatures for safe preservation, as outlined in this series.

3. Trim ends, removing any strings. Cut or break into pieces. Prepare only enough for one canner load.

4. Cover beans with boiling water and boil for 5 minutes or pack raw.

7. Put jars into steam pressure canner containing 2 to 3 inches of hot water or the amount recommended by the canner manufacturer.

8. Place canner over heat. Lock cover according to the manufacturer's instructions.

11.Stand jars several inches apart, out of drafts, to cool for about 12 hours. Remove bands.

12. Test the seal by pressing center of lid. If dome is down (or stays down when pressed), jar is sealed. Store without bands in dry, dark, reasonably cool place.

An important precaution should always be observed when preparing home canned vegetables and meats. Since the possibility exists that the processing may not have been done accurately enough to eliminate the possibility of toxin production in the canned food, all vegetables and meats canned at home should be boiled actively for 15 minutes before even being tasted. Any jars with bulging lids should be discarded without opening them.

FREEZING

Freezing has become the most popular method of food preservation because of its ease and its fine results in the freezer section of the refrigerator or in separate home freezers. No complex, special equipment is necessary to freeze foods. Containers used for freezing include glass jars, plastic containers of either rigid or flexible plastic, and cardboard containers. Glass jars are reasonably satisfactory if the jar has a wide mouth that will permit the entire contents of the jar to slide out while the food is still frozen. Any container for freezing should fit snugly. Dehydration in the freezer is slowed appreciably when the container is reasonably airtight.

Vegetables

Vegetables may be frozen quickly and easily, and the quality of the product, when ultimately served, generally is high. Green vegetables will be a bright green color when properly prepared, the flavors will be excellent, and the texture of vegetables with rather rigid cell walls will be very satisfactory. Loss of integrity of the cell walls during freezing is caused by ice crystals forming in the cells, expanding and ultimately rupturing some of the cell walls. When thawed, such vegetables are limp, so it is impractical to freeze chopped onion or green pepper to be used in a salad. High-quality peas, string beans, corn, fresh lima beans, asparagus, and spinach are particularly well suited to freezing. These should be washed well and examined carefully for any bruised or spoiled areas.

Blanching, a short heating period in boiling water or steam, is necessary to slightly reduce the volume of the vegetable and to inactivate the enzymes, thereby halting deteriorative changes caused by enzyme activity. Hanson et al., have tested a short blanching period as compared with completely precooking a vegetable before freezing to determine the best prefreezing treatment and have found that blanched vegetables have a better texture than the precooked ones. Blanching for optimum quality should be done quickly but completely so that the vegetable is heated throughout. A small quantity should be blanched at a time since small loads will heat quickly and thus avoid overcooking the exterior portions. Blanching can be done by steaming or by immersing briefly in boiling water. The hot, blanched vegetable should be cooled quickly by immersing in ice water or by running cold water over it.

Sometimes vegetables are frozen in a salt solution, but there seems to be no particular advantage in this as compared with vegetables frozen in a plain pack. The plain pack is a bit less trouble since it is done by simply draining and packing the vegetables. Rapid packing and immediate placement in the freezer help to maintain quality. Table 14.3 outlines suggested procedures for preparing selected vegetables for freezing.

Tests done at storage temperatures from $-10°F$ to $40°F$ have revealed a time-temperature relationship in maintaining the quality of frozen cauliflower, that is, the higher the storage temperature the shorter the acceptable period of storage. Vegetables stored at $-10°F$ maintained their quality during

Table 14.3. Procedures for Preparing Selected Vegetables for Freezing[a]

Vegetable	Preparation Procedures	Scalding Time[b] (min)
Asparagus	Wash, drain, and trim	3
Beans, lima	Shell, wash, and drain	3
Beans, green, and wax	Wash, drain, and cut if desired	3
Broccoli	Cut into sections, wash and drain	3–4
Brussels sprouts	Trim, wash, and drain	3–4
Cauliflower	Cut into sections, wash, and drain	3–4
Peas	Shell, wash, and drain	2–3
Spinach	Wash, drain	2–3
Corn	Boil 3 to 4 minutes, dip in cold water, cut from cob, and rinse in cold water. Drain	Done in preparation

[a]Adapted from *Home Canning and Freezing Sketch Book*. Ball Brothers. Muncie, Indiana. 1966. Page 14.
[b]For altitudes above 5000 feet, increase the scalding time one minute.

the six month period of the study; those stored at 10°F were acceptable but not of high quality at six months; at 20°F quality had deteriorated by five weeks in some cases.

Fruits

Fruits are frozen easily at home without dedicating a day to the job, and it is actually better to freeze fruits in small quantities. A home freezer can quickly freeze a few containers whereas a large number of containers will freeze slowly because of the greater volume to be cooled. Larger crystals form in fruit during slow freezing and this causes more damage to the cell structure. The net result is a less distinct shape and a softer fruit as contrasted with one that is frozen quickly.

Quite a large number of fruits, including grapes, pineapple, plums, raspberries, rhubarb, strawberries, blackberries, blueberries, cranberries, currants, figs and gooseberries, may be frozen by simply cleaning them thoroughly, packaging them in an appropriate container, and placing them in the freezer. It is not even mandatory that sugar be added, although many people prefer to use a sugar or syrup pack. To sugar pack fruits, simply sprinkle three-fourths cup sugar on each quart of tart fruit or one-half cup sugar on each quart of sweet fruits. Better color will be retained in fruits subject to browning reactions if a solution of one-fourth teaspoon ascorbic acid and one-fourth cup water is combined with the fruit.

A syrup pack is prepared in the same manner as the sugar pack except that the fruit is covered with a cooled sugar syrup rather than the dry sugar. This syrup, containing three cups of sugar for four cups of water, is appropriate for all fruits except the very tart ones which need to have four and three-fourths cups of sugar for one quart of water. Table 14.4 summarizes appropriate procedures for freezing fruits in the home.

Fruits packed by any of these methods will keep well for periods up to a year if the freezer is maintained at a temperature of −18°C (0°F) or colder. The plastic containers or freezer jars used for the fruit should bear a label identifying the contents of the package and the storage date.

Other Foods

In addition to fruits and vegetables, many other foods may be frozen satisfactorily either before or after cooking. Meats, poultry, and fish freeze very satisfactorily when they are wrapped tightly in an airtight package. As with fruits and vegetables, meats will be of better quality after freezing if they are frozen very rapidly so that small ice crystals form. This quick freezing is an aid in minimizing drip loss upon thawing and in achieving the

Table 14.4. Procedures for Freezing Fruits

Fruit	Preparation	Type of Pack	Addition of Ascorbic Acid
Apricots	Scald apricot halves 30 seconds, chill in ice water	Syrup pack or dry sugar pack	Yes
Blackberries	Sort, wash, drain	Syrup pack, dry sugar, or no sugar	No
Cherries	Sort and wash	Syrup pack or dry sugar pack	Yes
Peaches	Wash and peel, halve or slice	Syrup pack or dry sugar pack	Yes
Raspberries	Sort, wash, drain	Syrup pack, dry sugar, or no sugar	No
Rhubarb	Wash, cut into short pieces, and blanch 1 minute, cool in ice water	Syrup pack	No
Strawberries	Sort, wash, remove cap, drain	Syrup pack, dry sugar, or no sugar	No

desired juiciness in meats. Various casseroles and stews may be prepared and then frozen. The primary difficulty occurs as a result of syneresis after thawing. Better texture of sauces in casseroles will be maintained by substituting waxy rice flour for flour or cornstarch if it is available.

Baked products typically freeze well. Rolls and breads of all types may be baked, cooled, and then frozen in a plastic or other airtight wrap. Cakes, cookies, cream puffs, and doughnuts also are baked and cooled before being frozen. Powdered sugar icings will freeze satisfactorily, but more elaborate icings on cakes do not survive frozen storage universally well. Pies are of better quality when they are frozen before baking. Soft meringues should be added after frozen storage, but hard meringues may be frozen following baking.

JAMS, JELLIES, AND PRESERVES

A number of different types of spreads are gelled from various parts of fruits. These spreads are yet another means of preserving fruits for later use. Their keeping qualities are due to the high sugar content, which discourages microbiological growth. The gelling occurs because of the presence of a carbohydrate, pectin, which is found in varying amounts in fruits. Acid is also required for the formation of the desired gel structure. The colloidal nature of these gels is explained in Chapter 17; the chemistry of pectin and the other pectic substances is considered in Chapter 18.

Specific nomenclature is used to designate the various spreads that may be prepared from fruits. Jelly is the gelled fruit-juice product that contains little or no solid material and is quite clear. The terms jam and preserves are virtually synonymous in that both products contain pieces of the fruit. Preserves are considered to have slightly larger pieces than jam, but there is no clear line of demarcation. Conserves are preserves with nuts added. Marmalades are citrus preserves. Fruit butters are semisolid rather than firm and contain puréed fruit to which spices usually have been added.

Selection of Fruit for Jellies

Fruits ideally suited to jelly making have two factors in common: (1) a high pectin content and (2) a relatively low (acidic) pH. It should be pointed out that, during the maturation of a fruit, there is a continuous conversion of protopectin in the green fruit to pectin in ripe fruit, and ultimately to pectic acid in overripe fruit. The pectin level in a fruit is definitely a far from static value. Any very green fruit is unsuitable for jellies because of the low pectin content. Although it is true that some of the protopectin in the very green fruit is converted to pectin as the jelly is boiled, this conversion is inadequate to form enough pectin for optimum gelation.

As fruit ripens, a natural conversion of protopectin to pectin is catalyzed by enzymes, and the pectin content is elevated as the protopectin level drops. The pectin, in turn, is gradually transformed into pectic acid as the fruit becomes very mature. This increase in pectic acid reduces the gelling ability of a fruit. Fruit is optimum for making jelly when it is barely ripe because the pectin content is at its peak and the levels of protopectin and pectic acid are low. Even when pectin content is at its peak in a fruit, some types of fruits contain inadequate quantities of pectin for successful gelation. Familiar examples of fruits low in pectin include strawberries, raspberries, peaches, and apricots. Some fruits are naturally low in acid, hence are less well suited to jelly preparation. A familiar example of a low-acid fruit is the banana. Another common fruit in this class is ripened sweet apples. Tart apples, berries, citrus fruits, and grapes are appropriately acidic for jelly making.

This discussion of the importance of adequate acid and pectin in fruits is a guide in fruit selection. Some of the fruits that are low in acid or pectin can, indeed, be made into excellent jelly or jam. If jelly is to be made using a fruit inadequate in the content of either acid or pectin, the missing substance is added during preparation of the jelly. Acid may easily be increased in a fruit juice by the addition of lemon juice or other acid fruits. Commercial pectins, prepared from the skins and cores of apples or the albedo (white portion) of the skin of citrus fruits, are readily available in liquid or powdered form to supplement the pectin in the fruit. Powdered pectin is preferred by some people who make small quantities of jelly infrequently, for the powdered pectins have a long shelf life. Liquid pectins are very convenient to use, but an open bottle must be used soon before the pectin begins to break down.

Gelation of Jellies

Solutions containing pectin, sugar, and acid will gel under the right conditions. Ideally, the pH of the liquid will be approximately 3.3, although some fruit pectins will gel at a considerably more acidic pH value. At an appropriately acidic pH, the charges on the pectin molecules are at a minimum and there is little hydration of the pectin. These two factors make the

FIGURE 14.4   Jellies, jams, and preserves are preserved by the high sugar content. For good gelation, a balance of acid, pectin, and sugar is needed.

pectin more susceptible to precipitation. In addition, because of its hygroscopic nature, sugar attracts the water that otherwise would be available to hydrate the pectin. The result is that pectin molecules precipitate and form a continuous fibrous network that traps the liquid. Precipitation of enough pectin molecules to form a continuous network produces a firm gel.

Preparation of Jelly

To cause gelation of jelly the ingredients are boiled rapidly to quickly bring the sugar to a concentration of 60–65 percent. Two changes may occur in the sugar during the heating period: (1) some inversion of sucrose takes place because of the hydrolytic action of the acid, and (2) some of the sugar may caramelize. Inversion is desirable because the formation of invert sugar inhibits crystallization of the sugar in the jelly as it stands on the shelf. Caramelization, since it produces a darker color and a flavor that masks the natural flavor of the jelly, should be avoided. Rapid heating and the preparation of jelly in small quantities are precautions that will prevent this problem. For both maximum yield and general desirability of the jelly, an adequate amount of sugar should be used so that long boiling will not be required to concentrate the sugar sufficiently to gel the product. Obviously, a short period of boiling will cause less evaporative loss and maximize final volume. This short boiling period also avoids darkening of the color and excessive concentration of the pectin. Unnecessary loss of volatile flavors is circumvented by a short boiling time. An excess of pectin causes the jelly to be elastic and to lose its normal spreading characteristics.

Heating effects a detrimental change in pectin as well as in sugar in a jelly. When pectin and acid are heated together, a hydrolytic reaction causes a reduction in the size of the pectin molecules and an accompanying reduction in gel strength. The presence of sugar retards this hydrolytic action, but does not prevent it. Clearly, hydrolysis of pectin should be minimized in jelly making. This argument again points to the need for a short boiling period.

Various tests for doneness are suggested for making jellies. The use of a thermometer is an excellent way of estimating the concentration of sugar. A temperature 5°C (8.7°F) higher than the boiling point of water indicates a sugar concentration of about 65 percent. The hot jelly will be viscous enough to drop from the spoon in sheets when it reaches this concentration. A hydrometer may also serve to measure the progress of the boiling jelly. This device measures the specific gravity of the jelly. Commercial jelly producers may determine doneness by measuring the refractive index of the boiling liquid.

As soon as jelly is removed from the heat, it should be poured into glasses. Pouring after gelation begins disrupts the gel structure and weakens the jelly. A good jelly should be strong enough to retain the outline of the glass when it is unmolded, yet should be flexible enough to sway when

moved. When spread with a knife, jelly breaks easily into pieces that retain their shape, except under pressure. The flavor should be fresh and characteristic of the fruit, and the color should be bright. There should be no sugar crystals in the jelly, and it should be free of mold.

Improving Jellies

A jelly that is too soft or even runny may be the result of an imbalance in the ratio of pectin, sugar, or acid to the liquid or of inadequate heating of the liquid jelly. If fruits low in pectin are used, commercial pectin should be added to increase the pectin content. Citric or tartaric acids may be added to lower the pH to a point suitable for easy precipitation of the pectin. Adequate sugar may be added to aid in the precipitation of the pectin and to minimize hydrolysis of the pectin. Inadequate heating will not concentrate the sugar sufficiently to give a jelly of good strength.

Jellies sometimes contain rough sugar granules if the jelly is boiled to too high a temperature. Excessive boiling will concentrate the sugar too much and some of the sugar will crystallize as the jelly cools and becomes supersaturated. A thermometer can be used effectively to avoid this complication. Poor color in jelly is due to the selection of fruit of poor color or excessively slow or unnecessarily long heating periods. Rubbery jellies result when too much pectin is used, when too little sugar is added, or when the jelly is boiled too long. Sugar is an effective preservative that is useful in preventing mold growth in jellies. Very low concentrations of sugar permit molds to flourish, but the concentration of sugar in good jelly is too high to encourage mold growth.

Syneresis or weeping of a jelly is undesirable. Very acidic jellies exhibit this tendency more than jellies at a pH of about 3.3. Cranberry pectin produces a gel that weeps more excessively than do jellies made with pectin from other sources.

SUMMARY

Foods may be preserved by canning, freezing, drying, freeze-drying, adding preservatives such as salt and sugar, and by irradiation. In the home, food preservation has been declining as a result of greater availability of fresh produce and commercially processed foods throughout the year. All preservation techniques are directed toward preventing the growth of yeasts, molds, and bacteria that will cause destruction of the food or illness. Canning utilizes high temperatures to kill microorganisms. Freezing significantly retards the growth of microorganisms. Drying promotes long storage life because microorganisms fail to thrive in an extremely low moisture environment. Irradiation kills microorganisms, and high concentrations of salt or sugar prevent their growth. Whether preservation is done commercially or in the home, processing must be conscientiously controlled to insure safety and long storage life of the food.

Although all canning needs to be done carefully, particular attention must be given to the processing of vegetables and meats because of their low acid content. These foods must be canned in a pressure cooker so that the food will reach a high enough temperature to inactivate spores of *Clostridium botulinum*. The toxin that this bacterium can produce in these foods is lethal to humans even in infinitesimal amounts. If such foods are boiled for 15 minutes, they will be safe to eat.

BIBLIOGRAPHY

Animal Husbandry Research Division. *Freezing Meat and Fish in the Home.* Home and Garden Bulletin No. 93. U. S. Department of Agriculture. Washington, D. C. Rev. 1970.

Baker, G. L. High-polymer pectins and their deesterification. *Adv. Food Res. 1*: 395–422. 1948.

Ball Blue Book, 27th ed. Ball Brothers Co., Inc., 1966.

Blair, G. W. *Foodstuffs: their Plasticity, Fluidity, and Consistency.* Interscience Publishers. New York, N. Y. 1953.

Consumer and Food Economics Research Division. *Home Care of Purchased Frozen Foods.* Home and Garden Bulletin No. 69. U. S. Department of Agriculture. Washington, D. C. Rev. 1971.

Food Protection Committee. *Evaluation of Public Health Hazards from Microbiological Contamination of Foods.* Food and Nutrition Board, National Academy of Sciences—National Research Council. Pub. 1195. Washington, D. C. 1964.

Gilpin, G. L. Freezing food at home. *Food, Yearbook of Agriculture,* 1959. U. S. Department of Agriculture. Washington, D. C. 1959.

Harper, J. C., and A. L. Tappel. Freeze-drying of food products. *Adv. Food Res. 7*:171–234. 1957.

Hollis, J. What everyone should know about botulism. *California's Health 30,* No. 3:12. 1972.

Human Nutrition Research Division. *Home Canning of Fruits and Vegetables.* Home and Garden Bulletin No. 8. U. S. Department of Agriculture. Washington, D. C. Rev. 1965.

Human Nutrition Research Division. *How to Make Jellies, Jams, and Preserves at Home.* Home and Garden Bulletin No. 56. U. S. Department of Agriculture. Washington, D. C. Rev. 1965.

Human Nutrition Research Division. *Making Pickles and Relishes at Home.* Home and Garden Bulletin No. 92. U. S. Department of Agriculture. Washington, D. C. Rev. 1966.

Human Nutrition Research Division. *Home Freezing of Poultry.* Home and Garden Bulletin No. 70. U. S. Department of Agriculture. Washington, D. C. Rev. 1970.

Joslyn, M. A. Chemistry of protopectin: a critical review of historical data and recent developments. *Adv. Food Res. 11*:2–94. 1962.

Joslyn, M. A., and J. B. S. Braverman, Chemistry and technology of pretreatment and preservation of fruit and vegetable products with sulfur dioxide and sulfites. *Adv. Food Res. 5*:97–146. 1955.

Joslyn, M. A., and J. D. Ponting. Enzyme-catalyzed oxidative browning of fruit products. *Adv. Food Res. 3*:1–46. 1951.

Kerr, R. *Kerr Home Canning Book and How to Freeze Foods.* Kerr Glass Manufacturing Corp. Sand Springs, Olka. 1971.

Kertesz, Z. I. *Pectic Substances.* Interscience Publishers, New York, N. Y. 1951.

Neubert, A. M., and J. L. St. John. Fruit juice, jams, jellies, and preserves. Chapter 44 in *Chemistry and Technology of Food and Food Products,* ed. by M. B. Jacobs, Vol. 3, 2nd ed. Interscience Publishers. New York, N. Y. 1951.

U. S. Atomic Energy Commission. *Radiation Preservation of Foods.* Proceedings of International Conference on Radiation Preservation of Foods. National Academy of Sciences – National Research Council. Washington, D. C. 1964.

SUGGESTIONS FOR STUDY

1. Outline the steps in canning by the boiling water bath method. What foods may suitably be canned by this method?
2. Why is the boiling water bath method unsatisfactory for some foods?
3. What breads and desserts may be frozen satisfactorily after baking? Which ones should be frozen without being baked?
4. What changes occur in pectic substances as a fruit ripens? In what way is the transition from protopectin to pectin to pectic acid manifest in the fruit itself?
5. What is the role of pectin in jelly?
6. What contributions do sugar and acid make to gel formation in a jelly?

CHAPTER 15

Food Sanitation Problems

Problems of food safety have been a part of life throughout history, but the diagnosis and prevention of food-borne illnesses have been achieved with only limited success even today. One of the primary difficulties has been the reporting of these illnesses. Apparently only a small fraction of the people who become ill from eating specific, contaminated foods are diagnosed and reported. The usual pattern for such illnesses, when they are not threatening to life, is to suffer with the discomfort at home and simply diagnose the problem as being caused by "something I ate." Reporting problems are further complicated by the mobility of today's citizens and by the increasing pattern of consuming food away from home. Persons eating a restaurant meal, particularly in airport dining facilities, may be dispersed to cities thousands of miles apart before noting any symptoms of food-borne illness. Single individuals at such diverse points are not likely to be traced to the common point where the contaminated food was eaten. Even in restaurants within a city, many of the diners may come from many parts of the city or may be visitors from other cities. Unless the problem is quite severe, illnesses of this kind are not likely to be reported and traced.

The contamination and subsequent growth of microorganisms in foods can occur at several points along the chain between harvest and consumption. Contamination may occur as the result of human interaction during harvest, slaughter, or primary handling and processing. Packaging provides an additional opportunity for contamination. These microorganisms and other contaminants that have managed to get into food to this point then are able to begin to proliferate during storage unless storage conditions are ideal. The problems of safe storage are magnified by the shipping and retail storage that must take place before the food reaches the consumer. Quantity food production for group feeding and storage in vending machines add additional dimensions to the problem. When food enters the home, there are other opportunities for contamination and growth of microorganisms. In other words, at every point along the chain, keen awareness of the potential hazard of various types of food contamination should be maintained, and every step should be taken to insure an absolute minimum of risk to the eventual consumer. The careful attention of all food handlers is essential to all consumers as a result of the highly complex operations involved in getting food to the ultimate consumer today.

The possibility of contaminants or poisonous substances in foods is not pleasurable, but it is one that should be considered by anyone who is to be involved in the preparation of food. The many diagnosed cases of food poisoning that occur each year, in addition to the unreported cases, attest to the widespread incidence of the problem. Estimates of the actual number of gastrointestinal upsets due to food poisoning of various types range from several hundred thousand to more than a million cases per year in the United States. Generally these upsets are a source of considerable discomfort; in rare instances, they may lead to death.

One approach to reducing poisons in foods is through the use of additives designed to inhibit spoilage. Additives may also serve other purposes,

FIGURE 15.1   Attention to maintenance and sanitation are essential not only to food processing plants, but also in kitchens and restaurants—in short, in any situation where food is handled or stored.

such as improving palatability of manufactured foods. Federal regulations and legislation have been developed to regulate the use of additives, and the Food and Drug Administration often serves as the agency for enforcement.

FOOD ADDITIVES

Food additives may be classified as intentional and incidental. Intentional additives are known to be added to foods during processing to prolong shelf life or to perform some other useful function in foods. Intentional additives are only permitted when they are shown to be of definitive value. In contrast, incidental additives are unintentionally incorporated in foods. In some instances they may have only limited influence on the quality of the food, but some contaminants, such as certain poisonous molds and toxin-producing bacteria, may be quite dangerous to the consumer.

Intentional Additives

Intentional additives may be incorporated in foods or in their packaging for a variety of reasons. Nutritional additives are permitted in specified foods because of their value in increasing the intake of nutrients that are recognized to be essential but, generally, are not consumed in sufficient amounts. Illustrations of nutritional additives include potassium iodide in salt and the B vitamins and iron added to flour and cereal products. Standards for such fortification are established on a national basis. Of course, these additives are viewed as advantageous to the consumer on the basis of health.

Other intentional additives are incorporated in food products as a means of increasing shelf life of foods. A familiar example of this type of additive is calcium propionate to retard the spoilage of bread. Shortenings may have butylated hydroxyanisole (BHA) or other antioxidants added to retard the onset of rancidity and extend the shelf life. Some packaging materials are impregnated with antioxidants to aid in extending shelf life. Fruits may be dipped in wax to retard their deterioration during marketing. Many examples of such additives are found in the numerous processed foods available in the markets today.

Other additives are utilized to enhance the appeal of a food product. The addition of food coloring to a number of different kinds of food is an outstanding example of this type of additive. Red food coloring agents frequently are used to enhance the red color of foods, which tends to fade during processing. Yellow coloring agents are added to margarines and some cheeses to increase their eye appeal. Other additives may be used to improve or strengthen the flavor of foods. Although flavor enhancers are not effective in attracting the first purchase of the food, they may be of considerable importance in promoting continuing purchases. Monosodium glutamate is an outstanding example of a flavor enhancer that has gained widespread usage. Artificial sweeteners also may be considered as additives that are flavor enhancers.

The Food Additive Amendment of 1958 was passed to provide greater protection for consumers by changing certain provisions of the Food, Drug, and Cosmetic Act of 1938. Under the earlier law the Food and Drug Administration was required to prove that food additives were poisonous or deleterious before it was possible to require that they be omitted from foods produced commercially. This provision not only was costly and time consuming for the government, but it also became extremely unwieldy as the introduction of various chemicals mushroomed with the increased interest in food technology.

To cope with this rapidly expanding field it became necessary to have the company desiring to use a chemical additive assume the responsibility for proving that the additive was safe. Such proof is considered to be satisfactory when two years of minimal feeding tests fail to show any harmful effects caused by the compound under scrutiny. Chemicals that were approved before passage of the amendment in 1958 (named on the list Generally Recognized as Safe or "GRAS" list), pesticides for agricultural use, and accidental contaminants are exempted from the provision requiring proof of safety, although testing of GRAS chemicals is now in progress. For example, saccharine is on the GRAS list but is being tested and may be banned on the basis of the Delaney clause. This clause, which bans the use of any chemical shown to cause cancer at any level of use, caused cyclamates to be banned earlier.

Any food containing an additive that has not been sanctioned by the Food and Drug Administration is considered to be adulterated. Foods also are classified as adulterated if the additives are not used in accordance with any specifications that may have qualified the quantity or use of a particular substance.

Incidental Contaminants

Incidental contaminants are varied in food products. Such items as a leaf from a bean plant or part of a pea pod are classified as incidental contaminants in processed foods. The author knows of one instance in which a portion of a rubber glove was unintentionally canned with some corn in a commercial cannery. Although such items are not palatable or desirable, they are not generally harmful for they have gone through the general canning process and have thus been heat treated. In addition, the size of such contaminants makes them readily apparent to anyone working with the food, and they can be removed.

Grain products are particularly susceptible to infestation with various insects during storage. The detection of such contaminants presents a difficult problem, although various techniques have proved to be reasonably effective in solving this difficulty. Visual observation tests have been used with only reasonable success, for the eggs of insects may be buried within the kernels. A staining technique has been devised, however, to stain the plugs covering the holes where insects have laid eggs. Flotation tests, density differences, and X-ray radiography are other tests used to show the presence of foreign substances.

Insects create problems in the larva, pupa, and adult stages as well as in the previously mentioned egg phase. An extreme illustration of such contamination is that caused by the presence of molting beetles who have been known to shed more than ten skins. Not all insects found in foods are as large as the beetle or the cockroach. Mites so small that they are barely visible can be found in some grain products. It has been observed that when one insect begins to invade a food, the environment may become favorable for further infestation.

Obviously, economic losses result from the presence of insects in food. Entire carloads of grain may be declared to be filthy and unfit for human use. The original contamination can be controlled to some extent by avoiding storing any infested grains and by thorough cleaning of commercial storage areas so that no grain is allowed to collect in any crevices of the storage bins. Storage in a cool, dry environment retards the life cycle and reproduction of many of the pests. The presence of these uninvited guests also may be observed in grain products stored in the home for an extended period. Storage in metal or glass containers prevents the entrance of insects into uncontaminated foods.

FOOD POISONING

Bacterial Poisoning

To many persons food poisoning and botulism are virtually synonymous. In reality food poisoning can occur from a variety of sources and is not confined simply to cases of botulism, which is only one example of poisoning wrought by a toxin-producing microorganism. There are certain other microorganisms which, by their presence, produce illness, but they do not produce toxin. Animal parasites can become active in a person ingesting them. Environmental conditions also can cause people to react to certain foods. Chemical additives are controlled by legislation, but some unapproved ones may be an unintentional ingredient of some foods. These potential hazards may well be examined in more detail.

Poison from Toxins

The two types of food poisoning caused by toxin-producing microorganisms are botulism and that due to staphylococci.

Botulism. Botulism is caused by the toxin produced by any of several strains of the bacteria, *Clostridium botulinum.* In many instances, botulism seemingly can be traced to soil containing the offending microorganisms. Preserved fish and marine life, however, are also potential sources of contamination.

The toxin responsible for the physiological reaction in humans is produced only in anaerobic conditions such as are found in canned products. Ingestion of the toxin is not always fatal; the approximate statistic is that one out of three will survive. An idea of the potency of the toxin will be gained when one realizes that 0.35 micrograms of toxin will kill a man, or that 1 gram is sufficient to kill three million people. With such statistics one wonders how anyone might be expected to survive.

It is reassuring to know that an antitoxin has been developed to combat the poison. Unfortunately the antitoxin is most effective before the toxin begins to cause obvious symptoms, and therefore is somewhat limited in its use.

The symptoms of botulism generally are related to the functioning of the nervous system. The most severe reaction is experienced in the respiratory system, with death ultimately being caused by the paralysis of the respiratory muscles. The initial symptoms are observed 12 to 36 hours after ingestion of the offending food. If a patient survives until the ninth day, the prognosis for recovery is good, although the recuperative process may be quite extended.

Occasional instances of food poisoning diagnosed as botulism are reported and usually are traced to a home-canned food in which the *Cl. botulinum* flourished and produced the toxin. Generally, commercial operations are carefully controlled to avoid the possibility of food poisoning. However, commercial canning operations on rare occasions have not controlled the temperatures used during processing carefully enough to destroy the contaminant. A widely publicized episode occurred in 1971 when a now defunct processing organization failed to can gourmet soups properly and botulism was the result.

During frozen storage, *Cl. botulinum* survives but does not grow. Hence frozen foods do not present the hazard of this type of poisoning as compared with canned foods, particularly those foods processed and canned in the home. Of particular concern in home canning are the nonacid vegetables because these foods require a high temperature to inactivate the toxin-producing bacteria. The actual required processing time varies with the temperature to which the food is subjected. Food canned at 109°C

(228°F) must be processed 45 times as long as food at 127°C (260°F). Such temperatures are reached only by heating under pressure. Home-canned vegetables can definitely present a hazard because of the toxin that can be produced in the food during shelf storage if all the toxin-producing *Cl. botulinum* have not been destroyed during the canning operation. Fruits and tomatoes are distinctly more acidic than vegetables such as peas and beans and therefore may be canned safely at 100°C (212°F). As a further precaution, home-canned foods should be boiled at least 20 minutes before serving.

Staphylococcus Poisoning. Staphylococcus poisoning is claimed to be the cause of 75–80 percent of the proven food poisoning in the United States. The difficulty of actually diagnosing and accounting for the many types of food poisoning may invalidate this percentage, but it is apparent that this type of poisoning is relatively abundant. Poisoning of this nature is due to ingestion of enterotoxin produced by staphylococci in food stored at temperatures ranging between 4° and 49°C (40° and 120°F), temperatures at which staphylococci flourish. Foods that are highly suspect as potential sources of this type of poisoning are baked ham, creamed foods, poultry, cream pies, and milk and cheese products. The suggestion has been presented that dairy products may be more of a problem now than in the past because the widespread use of antibiotics may have led to the development of more highly resistant strains of staphylococci.

Other Bacterial Poisonings

Salmonellosis is the illness caused by the ingestion of live salmonellae in foods. The name is derived from its discoverer, D. E. Salmon, rather than from the name of the fish. This type of poisoning is manifest anywhere from 6 to 72 hours after ingestion of the infected food, with 12 hours being the customary period prior to development of the symptoms. Abdominal cramps, fever, nausea, and diarrhea are present in this type of poisoning. Sick people and infants are more susceptible. The diagnosed cases of salmonellosis are increasing, but whether this increase is a reflection of a higher incidence or improved diagnosis is difficult to establish.

Salmonellae are ubiquitous, but they are more numerous in foods such as pork, poultry, and eggs, and any products containing these foods. Storage at room temperature (70–80°F), which encourages the activity of salmonellae, should be kept to a minimum period for the foods just mentioned. Acids and heat tend to destroy the microorganisms. As is true with staphylococci, it cannot be assumed that frozen storage kills salmonella, for at −18°C (0°F) both types are still viable after six months of storage.

The various dysenteriae found in foods may present problems of food poisoning, but are not nearly as abundant as the salmonellae. *Clostridium perfringens* is a potential source of poisoning in cooked, cold, or leftover meats that have been subsequently warmed. Diagnosis is difficult since the symptoms are general abdominal cramps and pain accompanied by diarrhea, but with no fever or vomiting. Onset occurs approximately 10 to 12 hours after eating and a half to a full day completes the recovery period. Diseases such as typhoid fever and brucellosis are contracted via ingestion of foods containing the appropriate bacteria.

Streptococcal infections may be transmitted in poultry, and to a lesser extent in other meats, and baked products. The stuffing of poultry has been pinpointed as a particular hazard, especially in turkeys weighing more than 18 pounds. It is important that the stuffing reach a minimum temperature of 74°C (165°F) in order that the staphylococci, streptococci, and salmonellae that may be present will be killed. The timetables for roasting large turkeys have little safety margin allowed, but the use of a thermometer in the center of the stuffing will aid in eliminating this possible source of trouble. It should also be realized that the incubation period for microorganisms in the dressing of large fowl is rather extended, since the large bulk requires a rather long time to reach the critical temperature of 74°C (165°F).

Poultry are more likely to be infected than many other meats because of the correspondingly larger number of hand operations required in the dressing of fowl. The chance for contamination is increased as more workers come in contact with the meat, as would be the case in commercially prepared products such as chicken, turkey, or beef pies. A summary of bacterial food poisoning and means of prevention is given in Table 15.1.

Diseases Resulting from Animal Parasites

The most familiar disease caused by an animal parasite is trichinosis Larvae of *Trichinella spiralis* are sometimes consumed in meat, especially in pork. Actually, the incidence of these worms is rather low in swine fed on grain or in the pasture, but is appreciably higher for those fed uncooked garbage. Government inspection of pork does not involve detection of trichinae, hence no pork can be assumed to be free of them.

The larvae are first confined to the intestinal area, but soon they mature and produce larvae within the host before they die. Ultimately these larvae invade the muscular areas of the body, only to become encapsulated in cystlike formations that may survive as long as 10 years in the host. Symptoms in severe infestation may include diarrhea, nausea, and vomiting, but such reactions are not always present. Over a period of weeks intermittent fever and muscular pains accompany the migration of larvae within the body.

Table 15.1 Foodborne Illnesses from Bacteria[a]

Name of illness	What Causes It	Symptoms	Characteristics of Illness	Control Measures
Salmonellosis	Salmonellae. Bacteria widespread in nature, live and grow in intestinal tracts of human beings and animals. About 1200 species are known; 1 species causes typhoid fever. Bacteria grow and multiply at temperatures between 44° and 115°F.	Severe headache, followed by vomiting, diarrhea, abdominal cramps, and fever. Infants, elderly, and persons with low resistance are most susceptible. Severe infections cause high fever and may even cause death.	Transmitted by eating contaminated food, or by contact with infected persons or carriers of the infection. Also transmitted by insects, rodents, and pets. Onset: usually within 12 to 36 hours. Duration: 2 to 7 days.	Salmonellae in food are destroyed by heating the food to a temperature of 140°F. and holding for 10 minutes or to higher temperatures for less time. Refrigeration at 45°F. inhibits the increase of Salmonellae, but they remain alive in the refrigerator or freezer, and even in dried foods.
Perfringens poisoning	*Clostridium perfringens.* Spore-forming bacteria that grow in the absence of oxygen. Spores can withstand temperatures usually reached in cooking most foods. Surviving bacteria continue to grow in cooked meats, gravies, and meat dishes held without proper refrigeration.	Nausea without vomiting, diarrhea, acute inflammation of stomach and intestines.	Transmitted by eating food contaminated with abnormally large numbers of the bacteria. Onset: usually within 8 to 20 hours. Duration: may persist for 24 hours.	To control growth of surviving bacteria on cooked meats that are to be eaten later, cool meats rapidly and refrigerate promptly at 40°F. or below.

Staphylococcal poisoning (frequently called staph)	*Staphylococcus aureus.* Bacteria fairly resistant to heat. Bacteria growing in food produce a toxin that is extremely resistant to heat. Bacteria grow profusely with production of toxin at temperatures between 44° and 115°F.	Transmitted by food handlers who carry the bacteria and by eating food containing the toxin. Onset: usually within 3 to 8 hours. Duration: 1 or 2 days.	Growth of bacteria that produce toxin is inhibited by keeping hot foods above 140°F. and cold foods at or below 40°F. Toxin is destroyed by boiling for several hours or heating the food in pressure cooker at 240°F. for 30 minutes.
Botulism	*Clostridium botulinum.* Spore-forming organisms that grow and produce toxin in the absence of oxygen, such as in a sealed container. The bacteria can produce a toxin in low-acid foods that have been held in the refrigerator for 2 weeks or longer. Spores are extremely heat resistant. Spores are harmless, but the toxin is a deadly poison.	Transmitted by eating food containing the toxin. Onset: usually within 12 to 36 hours or longer. Duration: 3 to 6 days.	Bacterial spores in food are destroyed by high temperatures obtained only in the pressure canner. More than 6 hours is needed to kill the spores at boiling temperature (212°F). The toxin is destroyed by boiling for 10 or 20 minutes; time required depends on kind of food.

aFrom U.S. Department of Agriculture Home and Garden Bulletin No. 162. 1969. Pages 10–11.

Only rarely does death result from trichinosis. Persons infected with the organism have been treated by the use of thibenzole to aid in controlling the course of the illness.

Usually the source of this infection is insufficiently heated pork. Heating pork to an internal temperature of 77°C (170°F) is a suitable, convenient means of killing the trichinae that may be present.[1] A meat thermometer is a convenient tool for measuring the degree of doneness in the center of a piece of pork. Freezing at 0°F for a minimum of one day or at 5°F for at least 20 days provides another means of destruction.

In 1969 a new method for detecting trichinosis in hogs was developed by using a small sample from the diaphragms of 20 hogs. From this sample, microscopic examination will reveal the presence of any trichinae and the contaminated animal can be identified and eradicated. Although this test promises the potential for eliminating the concern for trichinosis, the consumer presently needs to continue to prepare fresh pork by using sufficient heat to kill any parasites that still might be present.

Other parasites can and do cause illness in humans. These generally are introduced into the body via impure water or foods prepared under poor conditions of sanitation in which the workers failed to keep their hands and the food clean of contaminants. The use of a safe water supply and thorough washing of fresh fruits and vegetables are the most effective means of controlling parasitic invasion other than that of *Trichinella spiralis.*

Chemicals as a Source of Poison

Reactions to chemicals vary, but they are often observed much sooner than those attributed to harmful microorganisms in food. Sodium nitrite has been found to produce disturbances within an hour and a half. Heavy metals cause intensive vomiting soon after they are consumed. Niacin, customarily present in meat in concentrations of approximately three milligrams per 100 grams of meat, can cause itching and a rash when the vitamin occurs at a level of 50 milligrams per 100 grams of meat.

Numerous reports of various accidental chemical additives have occurred over the years and doubtless will continue. Perhaps the greatest source of accidental contamination in the kitchen occurs when plated equipment becomes so worn that the core metal of the utensil is exposed and comes in contact with foods. Such equipment should be discarded as a protection to the consumer. Also, care should be taken to keep all pesticides well labeled and away from food.

[1]Actually, the parasites are killed when the internal temperature of a cut of pork reaches at least 60°C (140°F), but the higher temperature of 77°C is recommended to insure a suitable margin of safety without impairing the acceptability of the meat.

Environmental Causes of Poisoning

Many persons are aware of the adage that oysters should be eaten only in months with an R in their names. Apparently this axiom originated when it was observed that in the summer months oysters sometimes caused persons to become ill. The illness, called shellfish poisoning, is transmitted through clams and mussels as well as oysters at certain times of the year.

During the summer months and early fall, a one-celled organism, *Gonyaulax catanella,* is an abundant food for shellfish. In extremely large concentrations, this organism actually causes the fluorescence and reddish coloring of the water known familiarly as "red tide." Less obvious concentrations of *Gonyaulax catanella,* however, are capable of causing shellfish to be toxic to man. The substance produced by the organisms has been identified as saxitoxin. Strangely enough, there appears to be no harm to the shellfish even when they have consumed and built up concentrations of saxitoxin that are great enough to cause death in man.

The poison is accumulated in the digestive gland of the shellfish and may rapidly change from a barely detectable quantity to a toxic level within three or four days of its appearance. Saxitoxin is relatively quickly dissipated by the oyster, is removed somewhat more slowly by mussels, and is reluctantly eliminated by the butter clam. A holding period in clear water is effective in lowering the hazard to humans, since the shellfish will eliminate some of the poison.

The poison acts with startling rapidity, for death can ensue in as little as two hours after consumption; a loss of strength in the extremities and the neck is followed by failure of the respiratory system. The quantity of poison ingested is a factor in determining whether or not the patient will die. It appears that the poison is less effective if the shellfish has been fried in oil and eaten as part of a large meal. Artificial respiration is an aid in treating cases in which the respiratory system is affected.

The most obvious means of avoiding poisoning of this nature is to avoid consuming shellfish during the period of possible contamination. Since the effectiveness of the poison is reduced by high temperatures and the leaching action of water, frying destroys a large proportion of the poison, and steaming or boiling reduces the concentration of the poison by about 70 percent because of the water solubility of the poison. Cooking liquid should be discarded if the poison is to be minimal. Commercial canneries heat shellfish in steam and thus are able to greatly reduce the amount of poison that might be present. They also use chemical tests to determine the possible presence of poison. The commercial harvesting of clams and mussels is done under government control to further reduce the hazard.

Particular attention must be given to the sanitation of all types of fish.

Control of water pollution is necessary to ensure healthy fish for market. This is particularly important for fish such as oysters, which are sometimes consumed raw, and shrimp, which may be consumed in their entirety including their digestive tract. Once they are caught, fish should be maintained at cool temperatures. This is even more important for fish than for other types of meat; the enzyme systems of fish are active at somewhat lower temperatures than those of land animals.

MAINTAINING FOOD SAFETY IN THE HOME

Even when food is safe from harmful levels of microorganisms when it is brought into the home, the potential for food-borne illnesses still exists. In the home, standards of hygiene need to be maintained in all aspects of food preparation. Personal hygiene, good kitchen sanitation practices, and appropriate storage for the various types of food all must be maintained with high standards to avoid food-borne illnesses.

One key aspect of avoiding the transmission of illness through food is to be aware of and to eliminate habits that transport microorganisms from the food handler to the food. Although the requirements are remarkably simple, many food handlers fail to observe appropriate precautions. As a starting point, all persons handling food should wash their hands thoroughly with soap and water before beginning work with food and at any time that the hands become soiled during the preparation period. Clean clothing and nails are important, too. Only clean silverware should be used for tasting food. After a tasting spoon has been used, the spoon should be placed in dishwater. A tasting spoon is never used twice by persons who are following good standards of sanitation. Similarly, fingers are not licked. Food handlers also need to develop the habit of avoiding touching their hair, mouth, and nose to minimize contamination. If a person must sneeze or blow his nose, he should use disposable tissues and be sure to wash his hands thoroughly with soap and water before handling food again. Appropriate habits can be established rather quickly if food handlers concentrate on these suggestions until the behavior occurs unconsciously.

Clean food can be prepared only in a clean kitchen. Dishes need to be scrubbed thoroughly, washed in soap or detergent, and rinsed thoroughly in very hot water. All surfaces in the food preparation area should be washed carefully with soap and water after each use, with particular attention being given to such difficult to clean areas as the rim around the sink.

Storage temperatures require careful control. Refrigerators should maintain a temperature lower than 4°C (40°F) so that food will be below the optimum range for growth of microorganisms. The temperature range between 4° and 60°C (40° and 140°F) is particularly favorable for growth and

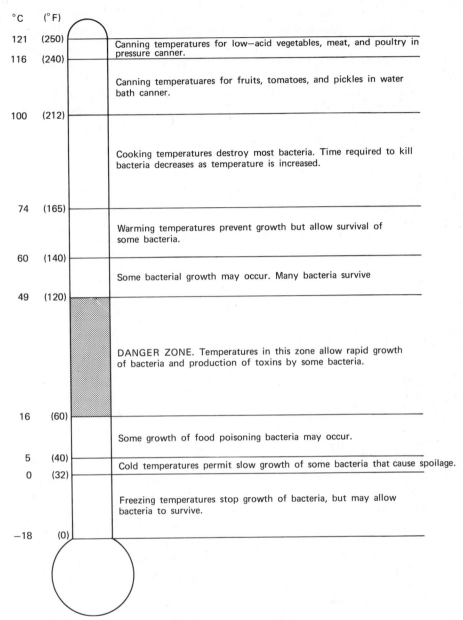

°C   (°F)

121 (250) — Canning temperatures for low—acid vegetables, meat, and poultry in
116 (240) — pressure canner.

Canning temperatuares for fruits, tomatoes, and pickles in water
bath canner.

100 (212) —

Cooking temperatures destroy most bacteria. Time required to kill
bacteria decreases as temperature is increased.

74   (165) —

Warming temperatures prevent growth but allow survival of
some bacteria.

60   (140) —

Some bacterial growth may occur. Many bacteria survive

49   (120) —

DANGER ZONE. Temperatures in this zone allow rapid growth
of bacteria and production of toxins by some bacteria.

16   (60) —

Some growth of food poisoning bacteria may occur.

5   (40) —
0   (32) — Cold temperatures permit slow growth of some bacteria that cause spoilage.

Freezing temperatures stop growth of bacteria, but may allow
bacteria to survive.

−18 (0) —

FIGURE 15.2   Storage temperatures for controlling bacterial growth.

should be avoided when handling meats, milk, eggs, creamed foods, egg-containing products such as meringue pies and cream fillings, fish, gravies, poultry, stuffings, and salads with mayonnaise dressings (see Figure 15.2). A simple rule to remember is to keep cold foods cold (colder than 4°C) and hot foods hot (warmer than 60°C). In practice, this means that room temperatures should be avoided just as much as possible. Cold foods require refrigerator storage. Hot foods can be held safely in warming ovens that maintain a temperature above 60°C. When storing leftovers, food should be cared for promptly after the meal. Hot foods should be cooled as quickly as possible to the point where they can be placed in the refrigerator without raising the refrigerator above 7°C (45°F). By stripping the flesh from the bones of turkeys and scooping the dressing out of the cavity, this bulky and potentially hazardous type of leftover can be cooled and refrigerated very quickly after roasting. Meringue and custard pies should be refrigerated when they have cooled sufficiently to be held comfortably in the hand. Cakes with cream fillings can be refrigerated as soon as the icing task is completed. Potato salad should be kept refrigerated at all times except when it is removed for service.

SUMMARY

The number of food handlers involved in the route from harvest to the table continues to increase as more and more food is being processed commercially and in restaurants. The growing remoteness of the consumer from the source of his food supply necessitates ever-increasing vigilance if food is to be safe to eat. During commercial operations, both incidental and intentional additives may be incorporated in the food. Intentional additives are monitored by the Food and Drug Administration, which supervises the use of additives on the GRAS list and also adjudicates the incorporation of additives tested by commercial laboratories and demonstrated to be safe for use in foods. Intentional additives may be included for the following reasons: (1) to improve the nutritive value of certain foods, (2) to enhance the flavor of certain foods, (3) to maintain appearance, palatability, and wholesomeness, (4) to maintain and acquire desired consistency, (5) to control acidity and alkalinity, (6) to impart desired and characteristic color, and (7) to impart desired characteristics of color, flavor, or baking quality.

Despite the fact that the consumer is protected by the Food and Drug Administration from many practices that might cause contamination or poisoning in foods, many episodes of food poisoning occur each year. The incidence of food poisoning can be reduced by careful sanitary controls throughout the food marketing chain and also in the home. All persons handling food need to be aware of the importance of their personal habits of hygiene. They also need to know the potential hazards of holding protein foods at temperatures ranging between 4° and 60°C and to avoid any storage time within this range. Food poisoning may be the result of the consumption of: (1) toxins produced by microorganisms; (2) the microorganisms themselves; (3) parasitic organisms; (4) harmful chemicals; and (5) food exposed to unfavorable environmental conditions.

Properly controlled pressurized canning of nonacid vegetables and a long boiling before serving are safeguards against botulism, which is frequently fatal. Although other types of food poisoning, with the exception of shellfish poisoning, are rarely fatal, considerable discomfort is always present. It is therefore important that all food handlers observe care in sanitation procedures. Controlled temperature storage is an extremely important aspect in the control of the growth of microorganisms. Adequate heating of pork is essential if trichinosis is to be avoided. Finally, organization of materials in the kitchen is important so that there is no possibility of accidentally substituting a harmful chemical for the intended ingredient in a product. The foregoing precautions should be taken wherever food preparation is involved.

BIBLIOGRAPHY

Abrahamson, A. E. Frozen foods: their impact on health. *Assn. Food Drug Off. U.S. Quart. Bull. 22:* 7–16, 1958.

Beeson, P. B. Salmonella infections. Pp. 201–210 in *Textbook of Medicine,* ed. by Cecil and Loeb, 10th ed. W. B. Saunders Co., Philadelphia, Pa. 1959.

Borgstrom, G. Microbiological problems of frozen food products. *Adv. Food Res. 6:* 163–211, 1955.

Castellani, A. G., Q. R. Clarke, M. I. Gibson, and D. F. Meisner. Roasting time and temperatures required to kill food poisoning microorganisms introduced experimentally into stuffing in turkeys. *Food Res. 18:* 131–138, 1953.

Coon, J. M. Protecting our internal environment. *Nutrition Today 5,* No. 2: 14. 1970.

Dack, G. M. *Food Poisoning.* University of Chicago Press, Chicago, Ill. 1955.

Dack, G. M. Food poisoning. Pp. 521–526 in *Textbook of Medicine,* ed. by Cecil and Loeb, 10th ed. W. B. Saunders Co. Philadelphia, Pa. 1959.

Daughters, G. T. Food additive amendment to the Food, Drug, and Cosmetic Act. *Assn. Food Drug Off. U.S. Quart. Bull. 23,* 2: 73–76. 1959.

Feig, M. Diarrhea, dysentery, food poisoning and gastroenteritis. *Am. J. Pub. Health 40:* 1372. 1950.

Food Protection Committee. *Evaluation of Public Health Hazards from Microbiological Contamination of Foods.* Publication No. 1195. National Academy of Sciences—National Research Council. Washington, D.C. 1964

Harrell, G. T. Trichinosis. Pp. 390–393 In *Textbook of Medicine,* ed. by Cecil and Loeb, 10th ed. W. B. Saunders Co., Philadelphia. 1959.

Hoshull, E. M. Preservation of food without heat. *Assn. Food Drug Off. U.S. Quart. Bull. 21:* 200–210. 1957.

Human Nutrition Research Division. *Keeping Food Safe to Eat.* Home and Garden Bulletin No. 162. U. S. Department of Agriculture. Washington, D.C. 1969.

Jensen, E. T. Why and how of shellfish sanitation program. *Assn. Food Drug Off. U. S. Quart. Bull. 23,* 1; 11–18. 1959.

Johnson, S. Problems in connection with convenience foods. *Assn. Food Drug Off. U. S. Quart. Bull. 24,* 4: 184–189. 1960.

Korff, F. A. Salmonellae infections: an ubiquitous hazard. *Assn. Food Drug Off. U. S. Quart. Bull. 26,* 3: 130–135. 1962.

Lehman, A. J. Food packaging materials. *Assn. Food Drug Off. U. S. Quart. Bull. 20:* 159–168. 1956.

Lehman, A. J. Botulism. *Assn. Food Drug Off. U. S. Quart. Bull. 24:* 3: 147–149. 1960.

MacLennan, J. D. Clostridium infections, revised by H. M. Rose. Pp. 191–194 in *Textbook of Medicine,* ed. by Cecil and Loeb, 10th ed. W. B. Saunders Co. Philadelphia, Pa. 1959.

Manufacturing Chemists' Association. *Food Additives.* Washington, D.C. 1971.

McFarren, E. F., M. L. Schafer, J. E. Campbell, K. H. Lewis, E. T. Jensen, and E. J. Schantz. Public health significance of paralytic shellfish poison. *Adv. Food Res. 10:* 136–173. 1960.

Michelbacher, A. E. Insects attacking stored products. *Adv. Food Res. 4:* 281–349. 1953.

Milner, M. New methods to detect and eliminate insect-infested grain. *Adv. Food Res. 8:* 111–129. 1958.

Slocum, G. G. Food sanitation and food poisoning. *Assn. Food Drug Off. U. S. Quart. Bull. 23,* 1: 3–10. 1959.

Stone, O. J., C. T. Stone, Jr., and J. F. Mullins. Probable cure for trichinosis. *J. Am. Med. Assn. 187,* 7: 536–538. February 15, 1964.

Williams-Walls. *Clostridium botulinum* Type F: isolation from crabs. *Science 162:* 375. 1968.

Werrin, M. Chemical food poisoning. *Assn. Food Drug Off. U. S. Quart. Bull. 27,* 1:38–45. 1963.

SUGGESTIONS FOR STUDY

1.   What precautions should be taken in the home to avoid food poisoning?
2.   Why are home-canned vegetables a more likely source of food poisoning than home-canned fruits? What type of poisoning may result from the consumption of home-canned vegetables? How may this hazard be controlled?
3.   Which foods are likely causes of food poisoning?
     What is the GRAS list? What agency enforces the Food, Drug, and Cosmetic Act?
5.   State five reasons for the addition of intentional additives in food processing.
6.   What is the Delaney clause?

CHAPTER 16

Meal Management

Meal management in today's families is a responsibility requiring a combination of skills that include time and money management, goal setting, decision making, food preparation, and artistry. The goal for meal management may be to serve a nourishing and appetizing meal in a relaxed and attractive setting at a cost consistent with the family's resources of money and time. Even to state this goal in a single sentence is somewhat frustrating because of the many qualifying statements and explanations that need to be added to tailor the goal to an individual family.

The responsibility of meal preparation is a demanding one that is met in most American families, at least, two times a day with varying degrees of success. The degree to which a family moves toward the goal of excellent meal management is important to all family members because of the role that meals can play in contributing to an involved and harmonious family group, and also because of the financial implications of food costs in relation to the budget.

The successful management of any meal requires a blending of managerial skills, a knowledge of basic nutrition, an understanding of the principles of food preparation, the touch of an artist, and the thoughtfulness of a gracious hostess. This sounds like a tremendous task for the novice and, indeed, may seem impossible at times. Even in this contemporary world of prepared foods, mixes, and automatic range controls, there are times when a servant, or at least a third hand, would be invaluable. Since neither of these is usually available, however, the best alternative is to improve one's own managerial ability. This chapter provides a brief guide to the subject.

FIGURE 16.1   Nourishing meals, attractively prepared and served, are a meaningful contribution to a family's health and well-being.

NUTRITIONAL ASPECTS

Meal management requires a functional understanding of nutrition so that daily menu plans can be reviewed accurately and modified, if necessary, to provide all the nutrients an individual needs each day. All the nutrients needed for maintaining good health are available in the grocery store, but wise planning and selection are necessary ingredients, too. To cope successfully with the problems of pricing, nutrient labeling, and quality selection, the shopper needs a basic knowledge of what nutrients are needed and which foods are important sources of the nutrients. An understanding of the foods that may be exchanged in a menu to provide certain nutrients will facilitate wise selection nutritionally while enabling the shopper to take advantage of good food buys.

Only a very brief overview of nutrition can be given here. Readers wishing more detailed information are referred to any basic nutrition text such as those listed at the end of this chapter.

Protein

Proteins are nitrogen-containing molecules made up of many amino acids linked together. There are approximately 20 amino acids found in the proteins that are commonly consumed as food. Of these amino acids, eight are required by adult man (nine are needed by children) to maintain tissues in the body, to form hormones and enzymes, and to be available as a potential source of energy. These amino acids, which must be eaten in the diet to maintain life in adults and to provide for growth and maintenance in children, are termed "essential amino acids." The essential amino acids are all present in animal foods such as milk, eggs, cheese, meats of all types, poultry, and fish. Gelatin is the sole exception to the statement that foods of animal origin are sources of complete protein. When a protein is said to be "complete," this means that the protein contains all of the essential amino acids.

Some plant foods, notably legumes and cereals, also contain useful amounts of protein. Although their protein does not contain all of the essential amino acids, nevertheless, the various plants are good sources of many

FIGURE 16.2 Poultry, as well as other animal sources, legumes, and cereals all contribute to meeting the body's need for protein.

of the essential amino acids as well as of the nonessential amino acids. Excellent protein intake can be achieved by consuming a mixture of plant and animal protein foods. The fact that a high quality protein intake is possible without extensive use of meat is important when meal planning possibilities are curtailed by budget limitations. Contrary to the popular notion that meat must be served every meal, meat substitutes and milk can be used judiciously to cut food costs without reducing a meal's nutritive quality.

Carbohydrate

Carbohydrates have been maligned by many people recently, but the fact remains that carbohydrates are important in the diet. They are valued as a source of energy and for their role in helping to metabolize fats. They also are useful because of their contributions to the flavor of foods and to the consistency of various products such as soups and gravies. Sugars contribute in an important way to the flavor of foods, making them more tempting and enjoyable to eat. Surely it is a rare person who eats waffles without syrup, toast without occasionally spreading it with jam, or cereal without a bit of sugar on top. Starch-containing foods such as rice and potatoes are valuable as inexpensive sources of energy that contribute to the satisfaction of a meal. Another type of carbohydrate, cellulose, is significant as a source of roughage to help promote motility of food through the intestinal tract. Clearly, carbohydrates have functions to perform in the human body; the problem that overweight people need to consider is that of consuming a reasonable amount of carbohydrate rather than an excessive quantity. This problem is also true for them in regulating the amount of fat and protein that is eaten. Carbohydrate alone is not the culprit in weight control problems.

Fat

Fats are needed in the diet not only as a concentrated source of energy but also as a source of an essential fatty acid (linoleic acid) and a carrier of fat soluble vitamins (vitamins A, D, E, and K). In contrast to proteins and carbohydrates, which provide approximately four kilocalories for each gram of the pure substance, fats contribute nine kilocalories per gram. Butter and margarine are good sources of vitamin A as well as fat. Salad oils also are concentrated sources of lipids in the diet and are valued for their content of linoleic acid.

Although fats are required in the diet, the typical American actually consumes more fat than is essential for good health. With the widespread consumption of many fried foods and rich desserts, the intake of energy from fat typically is in the vicinity of 40 percent. Nutritionists recommend reducing fat intake to approximately 30 percent of the calories in the diet, or even less if possible.

Minerals

Carbohydrates, proteins, and fats all contribute energy to the body. In contrast, the next two groups of substances, that is, minerals and vitamins, do not provide calories when food is used in the body. However, they do perform other very unique functions that are vital to good health and life itself. Minerals are inorganic elements frequently occurring as salts in foods. There are many minerals in foods, but some of them have been shown to perform unique roles in the body. As a general group, minerals help to maintain proper osmotic pressure and regulate acid-base balance. Specific roles have been identified for calcium, phosphorus, magnesium, and fluoride as components of bones and teeth, a clearly significant structural role. Calcium also plays a vital role in maintaining the heart beat and transmitting nerve impulses. Milk and milk products are particularly rich sources of calcium and phosphorus; green, leafy vegetables are good sources of calcium; and cereals and protein-rich foods are valuable for their phosphorus content. Fluoride is available in fluoridated water in controlled amounts to optimize the formation of strong teeth and bones.

Hemoglobin is the compound in blood responsible for transmitting oxygen to the tissues. This essential substance is formed in the presence of copper and must have iron available for incorporation in the heme portion of the molecule. With an inadequate intake of iron, iron-deficiency anemia may result, and this is one of the key nutritional problems in the United States today. Particular attention in meal planning should be given to the inclusion of meats, eggs, whole-grain or enriched cereals, leafy green vegetables, dried fruits, and legumes to help insure an adequate intake of iron and copper.

Specific minerals are needed for the formation of one of the vitamins in the body and also for making certain hormones. Cobalt is required to form vitamin B_{12} in the intestinal tract. Actually, the intake of cobalt does not need to be planned for in the diet because consumption of animal foods insures a sufficient intake of vitamin B_{12} from these sources. Insulin is a hormone required for metabolism of carbohydrates. This hormone is formed in the body and requires zinc for completion of the molecule. Another key hormone in the body is thyroxine, the hormone produced in the thyroid gland to regulate basal metabolic rate. Thyroxine has four atoms of iodine incorporated in it as a structural part of the molecule. With insufficient iodine in the diet, inadequate levels of thyroxine will be generated and goiter develops. This problem has been diagnosed in many regions of the United States. Its eradication is possible simply by always using iodized salt.

Care must be taken when one shops to be sure that the salt that is purchased is iodized; both iodized and uniodized salt are available side by side at the same price. Of course, salt itself is composed of sodium and chlorine, two minerals of importance in regulating fluid balance in the body.

FIGURE 16.3 A simple meal consisting of representatives of each of the four food groups.

While we are mentioning the need for iodized salt, there is also merit in remembering that salt levels in the preparation of food should be kept at modest amounts to avoid the possible complication of high blood pressure from excessive salt intake.

This is but a quick overview of minerals and their roles in the body. From the standpoint of menu planning, the important guides to insuring adequate mineral intake are as follows:

1. Milk and milk products should be included daily as outlined in the Basic Four Food Plan.
2. A wide variety of fruits and vegetables should be a part of the plan rather than concentrating on only two or three favorites. Variety helps to insure inclusion of the many trace minerals.

3. One should always buy iodized salt.
4. Some animal foods as well as plants should be included on a daily basis.

Vitamins

Vitamins are chemical compounds essential to life and needed in the diet in very, very small quantities. These substances are categorized as water soluble or fat soluble. The fat-soluble vitamins are vitamins A, D, E, and K: the B vitamins and ascorbic acid are water soluble. All of these vitamins are available in the food supply if a varied and appropriately selected diet is eaten. Vitamin supplements are not required for good health by the normal individual who eats a good diet.

Each vitamin performs certain essential functions in the body. Vitamin A is noted for its role in enabling people to adapt to changes in light intensity and to see in a dim light. Insufficient vitamin A leads to a condition known as night blindness. More severe deficiencies of vitamin A, particularly in childhood, can lead to blindness because of pinching of the optic nerve due to impaired skeletal growth. This vitamin also helps to maintain healthy mucous membranes, and in this manner is an aid in preventing colds and other infections. Vitamin A is available from butter, eggs, and liver; pro-vitamin A (precursors of vitamin A that can be converted to vitamin A in the body) is contained in dark green, leafy and yellow (orange) vegetables. Sufficient vitamin A intake is assured by planning a dark green, leafy vegetable or a deep yellow one such as carrots or sweet potatoes, at least, every other day.

The B vitamins include many different substances that are important in various ways to the maintenance of a healthy body and nerves. Three of the B vitamins—thiamin, riboflavin, and niacin—are particularly well known for their related roles in metabolizing carbohydrates, fats, and proteins to release energy. An inadequate intake of thiamin results in the development of beriberi; too little riboflavin causes ariboflavinosis; and a deficiency of niacin causes pellagra. All three of these conditions have been observed in the United States, but their occurrence is not common at the present time. One of the important ways of helping to insure adequate intakes of these three B vitamins has been through the practice of fortifying or enriching bread and other cereal products with these three vitamins (as well as with iron). Milk is a particularly good source of riboflavin and is also a useful source of thiamin. Meats, eggs, and legumes are excellent sources of all three of these vitamins.

Although the remaining B vitamins may not be quite so well known, they nevertheless are essential to normal body functioning. Pyridoxine is required to convert the amino acid tryptophan into niacin as well as to assist in other amino acid reactions in the body. Folic acid is valued for its role in promoting the maturation of red blood cells. Another of the B vitamins, vitamin B_{12}, also is required for normal blood formation. Without vitamin B_{12}, people will develop pernicious anemia. Pantothenic acid is the B vitamin needed for coenzyme A to be available for normal lipid metabolism. These B vitamins are available in adequate amounts when one regularly eats a wide variety of vegetables and meats.

Ascorbic acid is the water-soluble vitamin that is needed for formation of connective tissue. The deficiency condition known as scurvy was a common problem before Lind discovered that an unidentified nutrient in citrus fruits could prevent this disease which posed such a threat to sailors. The quantity of ascorbic acid (or vitamin C) needed for maintaining healthy gums and for forming necessary connective tissue is available simply by including orange juice or other ascorbic acid-rich foods in the diet each day.

Vitamin D is the fat-soluble vitamin that promotes utilization of calcium and phosphorus in the body by enhancing absorption of these two minerals from the intestine. With inadequate vitamin D, a child may develop rickets due to poor calcification of the bones. This vitamin is somewhat unique in that it can be formed in the skin when the skin is exposed to sunlight. For children living in climates where frequent exposure to the sun is not possible, a dietary source of vitamin D is necessary. A quart of milk fortified with vitamin D will provide the amount of vitamin D needed by children and pregnant and lactating women.

Vitamin E is noted for its antioxidant properties in the body. Its apparent role in the human body is to protect ascorbic acid and vitamin A against oxidation. Although this vitamin has been shown to be of importance in the reproductive cycle of rats, evidence of this role in humans has not been found. Vitamin E is found in vegetable oils.

The last vitamin is vitamin K. This vitamin is needed for normal clotting of the blood. The normal individual probably can synthesize and absorb all the vitamin K he needs. There ordinarily is no reason to be concerned about dietary sources of this vitamin.

These nutrients are all known to be important in maintaining a healthy body and in promoting optimum growth of children. The actual ingestion of the appropriate quantities of these nutrients by all family members is the nutritional goal of persons responsible for meal management. Adequate nutrition can be accomplished only when appropriate planning is teamed successfully with acceptance of a wide variety of foods and with ultimate consumption of the foods prepared. Good nutrition is achieved only when a well-balanced diet is consumed. A well-planned meal that is only partially eaten provides less nourishment to the individual. For this reason the homemaker is concerned that her meals be accepted by the family. Just serving nourishing food is not always sufficient in itself; the food needs to be attractive and appealing. When applied to the preparation and service of food, art principles are an important factor in food acceptance. The combination of well-prepared, well-planned, and attractive meals served in an amicable setting aids greatly in the building and maintenance of well-nourished bodies.

PLANNING FOR GOOD NUTRITION

Recommended Daily Allowances

Menu planning in a family situation implies the consideration of the total food intake for the day, as well as the menu for a particular meal. The National Research Council has established a table of recommended allowances to indicate the dietary needs of individuals of various ages. These are given in Table 16.1. Such specific figures are invaluable for those who are working professionally in diet planning. A less cumbersome, albeit less accurate method of ascertaining the nutritional adequacy of a diet, however, is the use of the Basic Four Food Plan.

The Basic Four Food Plan

The Basic Four Food Plan has been carefully devised to facilitate planning menus that will supply the necessary nutrients for good nutrition. This plan, based on four food groups, has rather generally replaced the Basic Seven since the reduced number of categories makes it somewhat easier to use. In fact, because of its simplicity, one will find that little time is required to compare the entire day's menu with the suggested list to determine inadequacies. The four food groups and the suggested daily servings in each group are:

Meat group: Two or more servings. Included in this group are beef, veal, pork, lamb, poultry, fish, and eggs. Alternate foods are dried beans, dried peas, and nuts.

Milk group: Three to four cups for children; four or more cups for teenagers. Two or more cups for adults; four or more cups for pregnant women; and six or more cups for lactating women. Included in this group are milk and other dairy products such as ice cream and cheese.

Vegetable and fruit group: Four or more servings including one serving of citrus fruit or other high-ascorbic-acid food daily and one serving of a dark green or yellow vegetable every other day. Foods in this group include those just mentioned plus any other fruits and vegetables, including potatoes.

Bread and cereal group: Four or more servings. Whole grain or enriched cereal products are included here.

Table 16.1 Recommended Daily Dietary Allowances[2] Revised 1973. Designed for the maintenance of good nutrition of practically all healthy people in the U.S.A.

	(years) From Up to	Weight (kg)	Weight (lbs)	Height (cm)	Height (in)	Energy (kcal)[3]	Protein (g)	Vitamin A Activity (RE)[4]	Vitamin A Activity (IU)	Vita-min D (IU)	Vita-min E Activity[6] (IU)
Infants	0.0–0.5	6	14	60	24	kg×117	kg×2.2	420[5]	1,400	400	4
	0.5–1.0	9	20	71	28	kg×108	kg×2.0	400	2,000	400	5
Children	1–3	13	28	86	34	1300	23	400	2,000	400	7
	4–6	20	44	110	44	1800	30	500	2,500	400	9
	7–10	30	66	135	54	2400	36	700	3,300	400	10
Males	11–14	44	97	158	63	2800	44	1,000	5,000	400	12
	15–18	61	134	172	69	3000	54	1,000	5,000	400	15
	19–22	67	147	172	69	3000	54	1,000	5,000	400	15
	23–50	70	154	172	69	2700	56	1,000	5,000		15
	51+	70	154	172	69	2400	56	1,000	5,000		15
Females	11–14	44	97	155	62	2400	44	800	4,000	400	10
	15–18	54	119	162	65	2100	48	800	4,000	400	11
	19–22	58	128	162	65	2100	46	800	4,000	400	12
	23–50	58	128	162	65	2000	46	800	4,000		12
	51+	58	128	162	65	1800	46	800	4,000		12
Pregnant						+300	+30	1,000	5,000	400	15
Lactating						+500	+20	1,200	6,000	400	15

Fat-Soluble Vitamins

[1]Reproduced by permission of the Food and Nutrition Board, National Academy of Sciences— National Research Council.

[2]The allowances are intended to provide for individual variations among most normal persons as they live in the United States under usual environmental stresses. Diets should be based on a variety of common foods in order to provide other nutrients for which human requirements have been less well defined. See text for more-detailed discussion of allowances and of nutrients not tabulated.

[3]Kilojoules (KJ) =4.2 × kcal

[4]Retinol equivalents

[5]Assumed to be all as retinol in milk during the first six months of life. All subsequent intakes

Additional servings of any of these groups may be added to fulfill the body's need for calories. One particular group not mentioned in the four food groups is fats and oils. The body has a specific need for fats and oils; therefore these substances should be included daily in the diet. The plan outlined here presupposes that an individual will eat either margarine or butter on bread and that some fat will be used in cooking. With these suggested additions the four food groups make a sound nutritional pattern for planning a day's meals. It should be understood that the suggested numbers of servings are for a day and need not be met in each meal.

Nutritional needs are the first consideration in menu planning. Since protein is better utilized by the body when it is ingested at various intervals

| Water-Soluble Vitamins | | | | | | | Minerals | | | | | |
Ascorbic Acid (mg)	Folacin[7] (µg)	Niacin[8] (mg)	Riboflavin (mg)	Thiamin (mg)	Vitamin B_6 (mg)	Vitamin B_{12} (µg)	Calcium (mg)	Phosphorus (mg)	Iodine (µg)	Iron (mg)	Magnesium (mg)	Zinc (mg)
35	50	5	0.4	0.3	0.3	0.3	360	240	35	10	60	3
35	50	8	0.6	0.5	0.4	0.3	540	400	45	15	70	5
40	100	9	0.8	0.7	0.6	1.0	800	800	60	15	150	10
40	200	12	1.1	0.9	0.9	1.5	800	800	80	10	200	10
40	300	16	1.2	1.2	1.2	2.0	800	800	110	10	250	10
45	400	18	1.5	1.4	1.6	3.0	1200	1200	130	18	350	15
45	400	20	1.8	1.5	1.8	3.0	1200	1200	150	18	400	15
45	400	20	1.8	1.5	2.0	3.0	800	800	140	10	350	15
45	400	18	1.6	1.4	2.0	3.0	800	800	130	10	350	15
45	400	16	1.5	1.2	2.0	3.0	800	800	110	10	350	15
45	400	16	1.3	1.2	1.6	3.0	1200	1200	115	18	300	15
45	400	14	1.4	1.1	2.0	3.0	1200	1200	115	18	300	15
45	400	14	1.4	1.1	2.0	3.0	800	800	100	18	300	15
45	400	13	1.2	1.0	2.0	3.0	800	800	100	18	300	15
45	400	12	1.1	1.0	2.0	3.0	800	800	80	10	300	15
60	800	+2	+0.3	+0.3	2.5	4.0	1200	1200	125	18+[9]	450	20
60	600	+4	+0.5	+0.3	2.5	4.0	1200	1200	150	18	450	25

are assumed to be one-half as retinol and one-half as β-carotene when calculated from international units. As retinol equivalents, three-fourths are retinol and one-fourth as β-carotene.
[6]Total vitamin E activity, estimated to be 80 percent as α-tocopherol and 20 percent other tocopherols. See text for variation in allowances.
[7]The folacin allowances refer to dietary sources as determined by *Lactobacillus casei* assay. Pure forms of folacin may be effective in doses less than one-fourth of the RDA.
[8]Although allowances are expressed as niacin, it is recognized that on the average 1 mg of niacin is derived from each 60 mg of dietary tryptophan.
[9]This increased requirement cannot be met by ordinary diets; therefore, the use of supplemental iron is recommended.

rather than in one meal during the day, it is wise to include a food rich in protein at each meal. This food may be a plant protein, such as navy beans, or an animal protein. The animal proteins include eggs, cheese and other dairy products, and all types of meats. Vegetable proteins are generally less expensive than those from animals, hence they are a good value for the budget conscious. Some animal protein, however, should be served each day to supply the body with all the essential amino acids in adequate quantities.

Dairy products should be recognized as sources of calcium and phosphorus as well as most of the other important nutrients. Milk is often termed nature's most perfect food, but it is notably low in iron and ascorbic acid. This deficiency is particularly important in the nutrition of children, for some mothers show little concern for the dietary needs of their children if milk is ingested in large quantities. They fail to realize that milk must be supplemented with other foods that supply the missing nutrients. Other menu planners experience problems in their meals because they do not recognize the importance of dairy products for adults. It is true that the quantity of milk needed is reduced as the individual reaches maturity, but the nutritional status of adults, including senior citizens, will be better if milk or milk products are included daily in the diet.

The selection of fruits and vegetables can be done somewhat at the discretion of the individual, with the realization that a good source of ascorbic acid should be served each day and a food high in vitamin A should be served at least every other day. Particularly useful sources of ascorbic acid are the citrus fruits and strawberries, and vitamin A is obtained by consuming dark green leafy vegetables or yellow-orange ones such as carrots or sweet potatoes. Vegetables sometimes are not well accepted by prejudiced individuals, so they may present a particular challenge to the menu planner. By serving a wide variety of fruits and vegetables from day to day and by preparing them in tasteful ways, acceptance of these foods probably will be high.

MENU PLANNING

When the nutritional aspects of meal management are well understood, this knowledge can be applied skillfully in the actual planning of menus that will be accepted by the consumers and that will meet the nutritional needs and budgetary restrictions of the family. Although one may wish to start occasionally with a new recipe as the initial planning point for a menu, frequently meat selection or a main dish is the most practical point at which to begin structuring a menu. The flavor of the meat may suggest the foods that complement this flavor. The method of preparation sometimes influences the other foods to be included in a meal. As illustrations, an oven roast, since it necessitates the heating of the oven, frequently may be accompanied by vegetables that may be baked in the oven, or by a baked dessert; steamed vegetables may be prepared by steaming them in the same pan with a pot roast. The color of the meat also influences the choice of other foods in a meal. White fish and cauliflower certainly do little for each other from an esthetic standpoint.

The choice of the meat, as well as the other foods in a meal, frequently is influenced by the price of the particular commodity. Seasonal foods usually are less expensive, and may be of higher quality, than those that are more difficult to obtain. The quality of the food also is instrumental in determining the price, so there is economic merit in deciding what quality is actually necessary for a particular use.

The overall considerations for successful meal planning include a pleasing combination of colors, shapes, flavors, and textures. For example, the bland flavor of rice is a suitable complement to a flavorful sweet-sour pork dish. Color accents or attractive combinations add important eye appeal to a meal. Broiled salmon with a bright yellow twist of lemon, French cut green beans with toasted almonds, and a stuffed baked potato present a tempting appearance on the plate in contrast to a white fish served with mashed potatoes and cauliflower. Texture contrasts may be provided by such touches as the almonds just mentioned, by crisp frying of an item, or by using stir-fried vegetables or other types of food that contrast with the soft textures that often are the predominant feature of a menu. The menu for a meal should be reviewed carefully in the mind's eye to insure that the appearance, texture, and flavor of the total meal will be pleasing and tempting to those who will be eating the food.

Another factor that must be considered is the satiety value of a meal. A meal may be beautiful to view and appealing to the palate, but it may fail to provide a feeling of satisfaction when it is consumed. The inclusion of fat and protein in the meal is an aid in this regard. Adequate serving portions also are necessary for the nutritional needs of the various persons who will consume the meal. No exact rule of thumb can be given in regard to the size of the portions, for the activity and metabolism of individuals vary. Therefore experience with the particular group to be fed is the best indication of serving size.

Meal planning becomes more exciting and less routine if an attempt is made to include new foods and recipes as time and interest dictate. Many magazines and newspapers constantly suggest new ideas, and cookbooks abound in libraries and book stores. Ideas may range from the very exotic and expensive to simply the use of a different seasoning in a familiar food. Not only do such explorations in the field of foods help to relieve the possible monotony of meal preparation three times a day, but they also aid in broadening the tastes of family members.

Good meal planning takes into consideration the available time, energy, and experience of the homemaker as well as the family's financial resources and personal preferences. It is particularly important that the resource of energy be considered, for a beautiful meal loses much of its charm when it is served by a fatigued hostess. A warm welcome in a relaxed atmosphere is an appropriate setting for fine food and friendship. A harried hostess only succeeds in making others uncomfortable. Although the quality of the food in a meal has been stressed throughout this book, it should not be obtained at the expense of the gracious atmosphere that enhances the meal.

With the large number of working homemakers today, the problems of meal management assume a still more complicated aspect. Time limitations may make long-cooking items inappropriate for menus during the week. Foods that can be prepared ahead and held for later use may be very valu-

FIGURE 16.4 Considerable time can be saved by preparing less tender cuts of meat in a pressure saucepan, this equipment is of particular value to home-makers working outside the home.

able additions in these circumstances. Meats with short-cooking times and vegetables and salads requiring only minimal preparation time also work well in meals that must be prepared and served quickly. In some instances, meals may be placed in the oven and the timer set to turn on the heat at an appropriate hour. However, such a practice needs to be reviewed because of the potential for food spoilage if meat is held in the oven for several hours before being heated. Frozen meats and casseroles have a potential for this type of meal preparation because of the time required to warm the meat or other items to the temperature where microbiological growth begins to flourish. Electric ovens are cooler than gas ovens because they do not have the heat of the pilot light to hasten the thawing of the meat; hence, a somewhat longer period of time in the oven prior to actual heating is possible.

MARKETING

For optimum efficiency in planning and shopping, meals should be planned for a week at a time so that shopping can be done at one time. This procedure has the advantage of saving time going to and from the store as well as time saved waiting in line and walking through the store. Another advantage is that weekly buying generally keeps impulse buying to a minimum. The shopper is rare who does not yield to at least one tempting item in the store that he had not planned to purchase ahead of time. By planning menus for a week, a clear plan can be developed for the handling of leftovers or for utilizing the other half of an ingredient that is needed in a special recipe.

Usually the best food buys are available under the weekend specials advertised by the grocer. The day that the weekend advertisements come out is the ideal time to plan the week's menus. This arrangement makes it possible to work the special items into the planning, thus eliminating the need for drastic revision of menus at the store. Some people like to shop in several stores to take advantage of the buys available in each. However, such a practice may not always be the most economical. Costs for driving to the store must be considered as well as the value of the shopper's time.

When the menus for the week are final, special items needed for the recipes should be checked to be sure that they are available at home or else are on the shopping list. Staple items also need to be checked. The list should be arranged in a logical sequence with the canned and heavier items first, followed by the lighter packaged items, the frozen goods and, finally, the fresh produce. By structuring the list in this manner, the heavy items will be in the bottom of the cart and the perishable, more easily damaged foods will be at the top.

The quantities of food needed will vary considerably from family to family depending on the number in the family, the age of the family members, and the ordinary food consumption patterns. The amounts needed for a week will gradually be known to the person doing the family's weekly shopping. However, Table 16.2 provides a guide to the amounts needed by average people of various ages. When shopping for food for a week, the storage facilities that are available must be considered. There is little merit in buying more frozen foods than can be stored in the freezer or the frozen food section of the refrigerator. Fresh produce often requires hydrator storage, or at least refrigerator space. To exceed the storage capacity of the freezer and refrigerator is an unwise shopping practice. For families, the purchase of milk may require more storage space than is available. In such a situation, home delivery, the use of dried nonfat milk solids, or a midweek purchase of milk may be suitable alternatives to purchasing fresh milk in the grocery store.

Table 16.2. Suggested Quantities[a] of Food To Buy for One Week for Persons of Various Ages[b]

Kinds of Food	For Children 1 to 6 Years	For Children 7 to 12 Years	For Girls 13 to 19 Years	For Boys 13 to 19 Years	For Women All Ages	For Women Pregnant and Nursing	For Men, All Ages	Total Suggested for Your Family
Milk, cheese, ice cream (milk equivalent)[c]	6 qts	6-6-1/2 qts	7 qts	7 qts	3-1/2 qts	7-10 qts	3-1/2 qts	
Meat, poultry, fish[d]	1-1/2-2 lb	3-4 lb	4-1/2 lb	5-5-1/2 lb	4-4-1/2 lb	4-5 lb	5-5-1/2 lb	
Eggs	6 eggs	7 eggs	7 eggs	7 eggs	6 eggs	7 eggs	7 eggs	
Dry beans and peas, nuts	1 oz	2-4 oz	2 oz	4-6 oz	2 oz	2 oz	2-4 oz	
Grain products (flour equivalent)[e] Whole-grain, enriched, or restored	1-1-1/2 lb	2-3 lb	2-1/2-3 lb[f]	4-5 lb	2-2-1/2 lb	2-3 lb	3-4 lb	
Citrus fruits, tomatoes	1-1/2-2 lb	2-1/2 lb	2-1/2 lb	3 lb	2-1/2 lb	3-1/2-5 lb	2-1/2-3 lb	
Dark-green and deep-yellow vegetables	1/4 lb	1/2-3/4 lb	3/4 lb	3/4 lb	3/4 lb	1-1/2 lb	3/4 lb	
Potatoes	1/2-1 lb	1-1/2-2-1/2 lb	2 lb	3-4 lb	1-1-1/2 lb	1-1/2-3 lb	2-3 lb	
Other vegetables and fruits	3-1/2 lb	5-1/2 lb	6 lb	7 lb	4-6 lb	6-6-1/2 lb	5-7 lb	
Fats, oils	1/4-1/3 lb	1/2-3/4 lb	3/4 lb	1-1-1/4 lb	1/2 lb	1/2-3/4 lb	3/4-1 lb	
Sugars, sweets	1/4-2/3 lb	3/4 lb	3/4 lb	1-1-1/4 lb	1/2-1 lb	3/4 lb	1-1-1/2 lb	

[a]When a range is given, unless otherwise noted the smaller quantity is for younger children, adults over 55, or pregnant women.
[b]Adapted from *Family Fare.* Home and Garden Bulletin No. 1. U. S. Department of Agriculture. Washington, D. C. 1960. Pages 14–15.
[c]Milk equivalents: process cheddar-type cheese, 1-1/3 oz.; cream cottage cheese, l lb.; creamed cottage cheese, 3/4 lb.; ice cream, 1 pt.
[d]To meet the iron allowance needed by children 1 to 6, girls 13 to 19, and pregnant and lactating women, include 1 large or 2 small servings of liver or other organ meats weekly.
[e]Multiply 3/2 to determine the weight of bread and other baked products needed.
[f]The larger quantity is for the younger girl.

Appropriate food selections are discussed in the various chapters and need not be reviewed here. However, the shopper does need to become a wise person who reads labels and takes the time to compare ingredients and serving costs when appropriate. Labels list the ingredients in the order of decreasing weight from the most abundant ingredient to the item used in the smallest amount. Thus, a product listing chicken ahead of noodles on the label will likely be a more nourishing choice than an item comparable in price that lists noodles ahead of chicken. Label reading also requires attention to details such as the indication of whether or not cherries are pitted, what size the shrimp is, and whether or not salt is iodized.

The price per serving and the number of servings per container are also significant. If a very large container size holds significantly more food than a family might be expected to eat, this choice might prove to be more expensive than a somewhat smaller container that costs slightly more per serving. Of course, this typs of choice is also related to the adequacy of storage facilities and a family's willingness to eat leftovers.

TIME PLANNING

Perhaps the most difficult phase of meal preparation is the management of time. Time planning begins with the selection of a menu, for the meal should be one that can be prepared within the time limitations imposed. For instance, a working wife should plan meals using meats that may be prepared in a short time rather than those requiring an afternoon of careful tending. The less experienced person should plan relatively simple meals at first rather than attempting several items that require attention at the same time. Careful consideration of this problem during the planning of a meal can greatly facilitate the time plan for the actual preparation.

As one gains experience in the preparation of an entire meal, formal time planning becomes less essential. Gradually it becomes possible to develop a workable plan and carry it through without sitting down and planning all the details. A rather carefully constructed time plan, however, is invaluable to the novice.

Probably the easiest way to develop a time plan is to first establish the serving time and then calculate the time required for each food on the menu. From these figures the starting time of each can be quickly calculated. Then comes the problem of estimating how much time is needed to do any preparation or mixing. This time is highly variable and depends on the experience of the individual and the speed at which she can work comfortably. People with small children and telephones need to allow for unexpected interruptions, too. Considerable frustration in the kitchen can be avoided by allowing a realistic length of time for the various steps that must be performed by hand.

It is also necessary to allow time to set the table, plan the serving dishes, and arrange the centerpiece, as well as a period for serving the food and placing it on the table. For a family meal, the time required may be minimal, but a meal for guests may involve a more complicated decoration and the assembling of dishes not regularly used by the family. These various tasks may be done before the food preparation is begun or as time permits during the preparation period.

It is a good plan to first write down the scheduling of the actual preparation times, followed by a listing of the various extra tasks that must be accomplished for the meal under consideration. For the inexperienced person, this listing should be as complete as possible and might well include a supplementary list of the pieces that are to be placed on the table before the meal begins, the silver to be used at each cover, and the serving dishes and silver. Details such as icing the water and the arrangement of salads require valuable time, yet may be overlooked in a hastily drawn schedule.

One aspect of meal management and time planning too often is ignored; a gracious, attractively groomed and attired hostess is appreciated by all the people at the table. This picture presents a pleasing contrast to the chef who is disheveled and unable to find the time to visit with the guests. A good time plan includes an opportunity to check one's appearance.

A brief evaluation of the time plan sometime after the meal is a valuable learning experience and enables the individual to ascertain the strengths and weaknesses of the plan. This review facilitates the formulation of subsequent plans. After some experience has been gained, many of the rudiments of meal management become semiautomatic and do not require such extensive plans. Many people, however, continue to plan the details of large dinners with considerable care.

TABLE APPOINTMENTS

Linens

Even with today's informal living, certain suggestions regarding the setting of a gracious table are generally followed. The first consideration is the use of table linens. Not too many years ago tablecloths were classified as a necessity in most homes. It may seem slightly incongruous that, although laundry facilities are greatly improved, the use of tablecloths is apparently on the decline and the acceptance of place mats is on the increase. A cloth, however, is considered desirable for more formal dinners even when it is not generally used for family meals.

Simplicity in table linens is always tasteful. For a picnic or patio party a gay cloth may be appropriate, but even then the pattern should not detract

FIGURE 16.5   Place mats are easy to care for, yet attractive for family meals.

from the food itself. Often a textured fabric provides ample interest in a cloth for luncheon or an informal dinner. Cutwork or lace cloths such as those made in Italy or Belgium, respectively, provide a beautiful background for more formal dinners. Plain linen or damask cloths are always appropriate for dinners.

The chief questions to be considered when selecting a cloth are: (1) will the color or pattern detract from the food or will it enhance its appearance, (2) is the cloth appropriate for the formality or informality of the occasion, (3) will it be possible to maintain it easily under the laundering conditions available, and (4) is the cloth of an appropriate size for the table?

Many women today not only do their own housework, but also have positions outside the home to demand their time and energy. For such women or for women with small children it seems an unnecessary expenditure of time and energy to select table linens requiring special care and attention. The wide variety of fabrics containing blends of synthetics has greatly expanded the selection of table linens available to most homemakers. Machine-washable cloths that require little pressing even with a steam iron can be attractive from the esthetic as well as the practical point of view. When tablecloths are laundered, they are pressed with a crease running the

FIGURE 16.6   Fine linens still are the appropriate table covering for receptions and other formal occasions.

length of the cloth. Additional folds may be made to store the cloth, but these are kept to a minimum and are not pressed in.

The size of the cloth may vary somewhat, but a rule of thumb is that the cloth for a formal dinner should be long enough to extend approximately 10 inches beyond the ends and sides of the table. This length is important for it provides an attractive setting, but does not inconvenience the diners. Beneath the cloth itself is placed a silence cloth or pad which not only protects the surface of the table but also eliminates the sound of dishes against a hard surface. The cloth is placed with the long crease extending lengthwise along the center of the table and the surface is smoothed. The cloth should be centered so that it extends the same distance over the edge at both ends and at both sides.

Since a lace cloth reveals the surface of the table in a number of places, it is used to advantage only when the table top is a well-kept wooden surface. Because the wooden table surface actually becomes a part of the picture when a lace cloth is used, a silence cloth is omitted from this type of setting.

Cloths for lunch, breakfast, or a late snack are frequently a bit smaller than the more formal-size cloths just discussed. These cloths vary in size from those that just fit the table to almost the size of the formal cloths.

Place mats have become particularly popular table linens because of their easy care and attractive appearance. A convenient size for the individual mat is a rectangle approximately twenty-two inches long and fifteen inches deep, but slightly smaller sizes may be used when necessary. Round or oval mats may well be used on a circular table. In addition to the mats for each individual who is to be served, a center doily that matches the mats is used in the middle of the table as a base for the centerpiece.

An attractive table is essential when place mats are used, for the table is barren between the mats and the center doily. Suggestions for the selection of place mats are similar to those for tablecloths. Generally, place mats seem

FIGURE 16.7   Fine place mats on a well finished table are appropriate for any but the most formal of dinners.

less formal than cloths, but fine place mats may well be used for formal dinners. Place mats should be stored flat with no creased in them.

Frequently, napkins are sold in sets with the place mats or tablecloths, but they may also be purchased separately in contrasting materials. Napkins for luncheon or breakfast are usually twelve- or fifteen-inch squares, whereas dinner napkins are approximately eighteen inches square. After napkins are laundered, they are ironed with a crease when they are folded in half and again as they are folded over to form the desired square or rectangle. For family and patio meals, paper napkins of excellent quality may be convenient, but cloth napkins are used for more formal meals.

Centerpieces

The planning of a centerpiece is somewhat simplified when one considers the type of meal and the amount of space available for the display. Flowers are always good materials for a center arrangement, but a bit of imagination may be very rewarding also. An edible arrangement of fruits may fulfill the dual function of decoration and dessert course. A meal centered around foreign foods may suggest the use of unusual candles or decorative pieces depicting the theme of the meal.

A centerpiece should be planned so that it is an appropriate size for the table. For instance, a table set for twelve guests would require a large decoration compared with a table set for two. In either case the arrangement should leave adequate surface area for an uncrowded appearance when all the dishes are on the table.

Anyone who has ever sat behind a tall centerpiece and attempted to conduct a conversation with someone hidden behind it will surely be aware of the necessity for a low centerpiece. Flowers can be floated in a bowl or placed in a simple, low-lying, or airy arrangement. Often a few flowers can be used more effectively for a table display than can a larger bouquet.

A buffet or tea table offers the opportunity for more dramatic displays since it is not necessary to keep the arrangement low. The table also may be less crowded and thus provides ample space for a lovely creation. Candles may be used in conjunction with a center arrangement, but they should always be lighted if they are on the table.

Flatware

The choice of flatware usually is made among sterling silver, silver plate, and stainless steel. Each material has certain advantages and disadvantages that should be considered.

Sterling silver is surprisingly durable when one considers the fact that

FIGURE 16.8 A buffet table is an ideal opportunity for a rather dramatic center-piece, since dinner conversation will not need to flow around or across it to others.

silver is actually a fairly soft metal. It is not uncommon for this type of flat-ware to be handed down from one generation to the next. Silver does become scratched during use, but the shininess of new silver is replaced with a soft sheen called patina. This patina, the result of the many light scratches in-curred during service, enhances the appearance of the pieces.

Silver requires some care since a disfiguring tarnish gradually collects, particularly when the silver is in contact with egg yolk. This may be removed easily with silver polish. The pitting caused by prolonged contact of salt and silver cannot be removed, hence this circumstance is to be avoided. In con-sidering the purchase of silver, one must compare its initial high cost with the pleasure it gives and its expected longevity of service.

Silver plate is less expensive than sterling silver because this flatware contains simply a silver coating over a less expensive metal. This difference in price is an obvious advantage to the person faced with buying the many necessities of a beginning household.

Silver plate is now fashioned in many attractive designs and frequently

FIGURE 16.9 Whether the selection made is silver, silver plate, or stainless steel, the pattern chosen needs to be compatible with the other table appointments. Note the pleasing rhythm of the silverware and china patterns.

is well made. Silver plate, however, does not have the life expectancy that sterling silver does since the plating gradually will wear off to reveal the core metal. In silver plate of high quality this is a very slow process because the points of maximum wear are reinforced with silver. Plate, like sterling silver, will tarnish.

Stainless steel varies greatly in quality from the very inexpensive light-weight type available in dime stores to carefully crafted, very heavy flatware. The big advantage of stainless steel is that it will not tarnish and thus eliminates the need for polishing. Some persons do not care for the dulled appearance of the stainless-steel flatware as compared with the more shiny silver.

Once the decision has been made in regard to the material, attention focuses on design. A wide variety of design may be found in any of the three types of flatware. Some people prefer the contemporary simple patterns, whereas others select more ornate designs. It is advisable to consider the appearance of all the pieces in a particular pattern and not to make a decision based only on the appearance of a fork or spoon. The design of the blade of the butter spreader or perhaps the tines of the salad fork may be objectionable to a person even though the other pieces are attractive.

It is also wise to handle the pieces to see just how they would feel when they are being used. Some less expensive flatware is poorly balanced and therefore is more difficult to manipulate. If possible, it is desirable to arrange the flatware with the dishes selected to be certain of harmony in design.

Dishes

When selecting dishes, one is confronted with a multitude of decisions. Because of their fragility, dishes are not likely to be as permanent a posses-

FIGURE 16.10   The elaborate design of the china and silverware harmonize with the formality of the table setting and damask cloth.

sion as flatware. The choice of material for dishes often is determined by price as well as the needs of the family. Pottery is less expensive than china, but probably will need to be replaced more frequently because of its tendency to chip and break. The durability of china often is related to price also for there are some less expensive chinas that are more susceptible to breakage than some of the harder bone chinas. A family with small children may find the breakage of pottery and china to be prohibitive and thus may select a plastic material.

Many of the china patterns are quite formal and lend themselves well to a formal dinner, whereas pottery designs are often more informal in nature and highly appropriate for breakfast or luncheon. Plastic dishes are usually quite informal. By careful selection it is possible to choose a pattern that can be used appropriately for almost any occasion. A person with adequate storage space and funds, however, may enjoy having a choice of dishes for a particular occasion. In this case it is appropriate to select a pattern that definitely conveys a particular mood.

Regardless of the type of dish to be selected, it is important to remember that the dishes will be used with food. A design that is busy and involved tends to detract from the appearance of the food; a stylized design is often preferable to a realistic one. The colors of the design or the background should be harmonious and complementary to the colors found in foods.

Before a final selection is made, it is essential to note the shape of the serving pieces as well as the various pieces in a place setting, for designers sometimes add surprising touches. A particularly important piece to check is the cup. A rectangular cup is difficult to use gracefully because of the necessity of rotating the cup in order to drink from the corner. Some cups have beautifully designed handles which are very easy to hold, whereas others create a gross feeling of insecurity when they are used. A properly designed cup has a handle that is comfortable to both men and women. A cup is more functional when its shape is relatively deep rather than shallow. Such a design not only keeps beverages hotter, but also reduces the likelihood of spilling.

Dishes with a platinum trim are inappropriate for people who plan to use a dishwasher regularly. Also, some of the less expensive plastic dishes do not respond well to the very high temperatures in a dishwasher.

Glassware

The selection of glassware should first be based on the decision between crystal and less expensive glassware. Crystal goblets and other pieces are lovely and make a handsome contribution to any table setting. There is always the possibility of breakage, however, and the replacement may be difficult and expensive. The availability of patterns in less expensive glassware has increased appreciably in recent years until it is now possible to purchase such stemware and glasses to suit many tastes.

Practical considerations should be combined with the esthetic when glasses are being considered. Most hostesses will concur with the idea that it is important that glasses be stable as well as beautiful. Stability in goblets and other stemware can be achieved by the use of a broad base, a weighted stem, or a combination of these. These same devices are utilized effectively in the design of other glasses, too. Glasses to be used by rather small children should be of fairly heavy glass since youngsters have been known to imprudently sample the glass or crystal along with the beverage. Relatively heavy glass presents a sufficiently hard obstacle to deter all but the most persistent child.

Table Settings

Linens are placed carefully on the table as the first step in table setting. A silence cloth or pad is placed under damask or linen cloths for a formal dinner, but is omitted if a lace cloth or place mats are used.

The silver is then placed with the ends of the handles approximately one inch from the edge of the table. The menu determines the pieces of silverware that are placed at each cover. The knife (or knives) is placed immediately to the right of the plate with the sharp side of the blade directed toward the plate. Spoons are arranged in order of use, with the first piece to be used placed farthest away from the plate. Customarily a maximum of three pieces of silverware is placed on either side of the plate, and it looks more balanced if approximately the same number of pieces is used on both sides.

By placing the butter spreader on the bread and butter plate parallel to the edge of the table, it becomes easier to follow these suggestions. The handle of the butter spreader is placed toward the right of the diner and the sharper edge of the blade is directed toward the diner. The placement of the cocktail fork or soup spoon on the liner used for the service of the first course offers an additional possibility for avoiding excessive amounts of silverware on the table. Often it is convenient to place the dessert silverware when the dessert course is served.

It should also be pointed out that other options exist. If a knife or other piece of silverware is not needed at a meal, there is no need to place it on the table. If only a spoon and fork are needed, the two pieces may be set in their customary positions or they may be arranged at the right of the plate with the fork nearer the plate. The objective in placing silver is to place the pieces in a balanced fashion in which the intended use for each piece is clear to the users.

Napkins usually are placed just to the left of the forks with the edge

FIGURE 16.11 These place settings have been arranged carefully so that the handles of the silverware are a uniform distance from the edge of the table, the sharper edge of the knife blade is directed toward the plate, and the butter spreader is parallel to the edge of the table. The water glass is at the tip of the knife, the butter plate is above the fork, and the napkin is to the left of the fork. The placement of the two forks tells the diner that the inner fork will be used for dessert.

approximately one inch from the edge of the table. The most convenient placement is that in which the open corner of the rectangle is on the right of the napkin and closest to the edge of the table. This arrangement makes it easy for a diner to unfold the napkin to half its full size and unobtrusively place it on his lap. An optional arrangement has the open corner on the left rather than on the right side of the napkin. In either case this corner is next to the edge of the table.

The water glass is placed just above the tip of the knife and any additional beverage glasses are arranged to the right of the water glass and slightly closer to the edge of the table. The salad plate is placed to the left of the fork; the bread and butter plate is located just above the fork. If the napkin is large enough to interfere with the placing of the salad plate, the salad plate may be placed farther back from the edge of the table and the bread and butter plate shifted slightly to the right of the tip of the fork.

MEAL SERVICE

The type of service to be used for a meal needs to be adapted to the group and to the formality of the occasion. When time permits and the occasion is somewhat formal, families may wish to use English style service. In this type of service, the serving dishes and serving silver are arranged conveniently around the host's (or hostess') place and the dinner plates are placed in front of the host. When the first plate has been served, it is passed to the hostess along the left side of the table. The persons sitting to the host's left then are served in order from the hostess back to the host. The process is repeated on the second side of the table, with the host serving himself last.

An alternative to the English service is that of family service. In this arrangement, a plate is set at each place and the food is placed in the center of the table. The serving dishes are passed, usually from left to right, with each person helping himself as the food is passed. The important thing in family service is to be certain that all food is passed the same direction. Of course, the food needs to be sliced or arranged for easy service with one hand, since the other hand is required to hold the dish while the food is being served.

Yet a third alternative that fits well into the life-style of families today is blue-plate service. In this style, the plates are served in the kitchen and placed at the individual covers before people are seated at the table. If desired, additional food may be placed in the center of the table or on a serving cart or table adjacent to the dining table.

The goals in serving food are to make all diners feel comfortable and to have the hot foods served hot and the cold foods well chilled. The type of service should be selected which will most likely insure that these goals are met. The practice of warming the dinner plates and chilling salad plates will help to hold the food at the desired temperature until all are served.

Etiquette requires that the hostess begin to eat first, with the others joining her immediately. She has the responsibility of seeing to it that all people have their needs satisfied and that all feel welcome. So that nobody feels rushed, she should try to time her meal so that she does not finish until the others finish. To signify that one is finished, the silverware should be positioned on the liner if soup or an appetizer has been served; silverware for the main course should be placed parallel from the right, with the tip of the knife at the edge of the recessed portion of the plate. By positioning the silverware in this manner, dishes may be removed easily without the problem of silverware balancing precariously or falling from the plates.

Despite the fact that very few families today have help in serving a meal, the practice of clearing the table after each course is commonly followed. After the main course, the serving dishes are removed first, followed by the salt and pepper and other auxiliary items, and finally the individual plates are removed. Ideally, plates are carried to the kitchen without any stacking in the dining area. Although individual practice may vary, the customary procedure is to serve and remove any plates from the left and to serve and replenish beverages from the right. Sometimes seating arrangements may make this pattern awkward, in which case suitable sensible adjustments should be made to fit the situation. The emphasis in service today is toward common sense and convenience. Informality tends to be the style, and warm hospitality is the keynote.

Buffet Service

Buffet service is a convenient and attractive way to serve a group of people. The buffet table is arranged for the convenience of the guests. The plates are stacked at the end of the table where service is to begin. The meat or main dish is placed next to the plates. The other foods are arranged along the table so that they are easy to reach. If the service of any of the foods is difficult to manage while holding a plate, it is appropriate to have the hostess or a friend serve the food. The silverware and napkins are placed at the far end of the table. When many guests are present, service is expedited by the use of duplicate service on both sides of the table.

It is usually convenient to have the beverage served to the guest after he is seated, rather than requiring him to juggle so many items. The dessert course may be served from the buffet table or may be carried to the guests where they are seated. This decision will be based on the type of dessert and the available assistance.

Teas and Coffees

In America a coffee is generally an informal morning party. The refreshments for such an affair are simple and the emphasis is on hospitality. Coffee is the beverage customarily served, although hot chocolate or other beverages are sometimes offered. A hot bread is frequently the only other item on the menu. Occasionally fresh fruit is also served.

Service may be from a table or cart in the living room. In this instance appropriate linen is used on either the table or the cart. A small decoration such as a rose bowl adds a pleasing touch of color. The cups are arranged on the left with the handles toward the hostess. If several people are to be served, the cups may be stacked in groups of two to conserve space. The coffee pot preferably is placed on the right side of a tray. The hostess or a friend can then place the cup on the tray to pour the beverage and ultimately place the filled cup on the plate to serve the guest. The stack of plates should be near the hostess so that she can reach them easily. After the guest receives the beverage and plate, she serves herself from the platter of refreshments and takes a napkin and any necessary silver.

A tea is generally a rather formal type of afternoon entertainment in which a buffet service commonly is used. Fine linens and a formal centerpiece form the background for gracious hospitality. The food may be relatively simple or quite elaborate.

The type of food served at a tea is often varied, but all of it is artistically arranged and dainty in size. The menu for a tea may include a choice of two beverages, a variety of tea sandwiches, tarts, small cookies and cakes. candies, and nuts. These foods are most easily served by using buffet service in which the sandwiches are arranged on platters placed just after the beverage. The dessert foods are next, and the candies and nuts are placed just before the silver and napkins.

SUMMARY

Effective meal management is becoming ever more challenging despite the many convenience foods and supplementary pieces of equipment that are available for preparing special items. Many families have employed homemakers as the person responsible for managing meal service for the family. In addition, schedules of various family members may make the timing of meals quite complex. Despite scheduling problems, good meal management is an important aspect of family functioning. Meals must be planned to provide adequate nutrition for each person, and they should be prepared and served in a manner that will insure the consumption of an appropriate amount of food.

Good menu planning builds in a suitable variety of foods in an interesting and tempting combination of colors, shapes, flavors, and textures. The overall plans for the day will provide for all of the nutrients needed daily for good nutrition. Planning and shopping on a weekly basis are recommended as a good approach to managing both time and money. However, suitable storage facilities must be teamed with this approach to shopping. Another important aspect of planning is that of timing. The original menu plans need to take into consideration the time available for both pre-preparation and for the preparation just preceding the meal. For the beginning manager, a written time plan is a valuable asset in learning to manage time, energy, and resources.

The final phase of meal management is the actual service of the meal. Suggestions for selecting the table accessories and for comfortable and practical service have been outlined. Since few people today have help available for serving meals, English service, family service, or blue-plate service are all suitable solutions. Buffet service is very functional as well as attractive when large groups are being served. In all types of food service, the important accompaniment is gracious hospitality.

BIBLIOGRAPHY

Bogert, J. et al. *Nutrition and Physical Fitness.* 9th ed. Saunders. Philadelphia, Pa. 1973.

Fleck, H. *Introduction to Nutrition.* 2nd ed. Macmillan. New York, N. Y. 1971.

Guthrie, H. *Introductory Nutrition.* 2nd ed. Mosby. St. Louis, Mo. 1971.

Kramer, M. and M. Spader. *Contemporary Meal Management.* Wiley. New York, N. Y. 1972.

Kinder, F. *Meal Management.* 3rd ed. Macmillan. New York, N. Y. 1973.

McWilliams, M. *Meatless Cookbook.* Plycon. Fullerton, Calif. 1973.

Stare, F. and M. McWilliams. *Living Nutrition.* Wiley. New York, N. Y. 1973.

SUGGESTIONS FOR STUDY

1. Plan a day's menu for an adult woman. How might this menu be altered to fit the needs of her *(a)* husband, *(b)* 16-year-old son, *(c)* 10-year-old daughter?

2. Prepare a time plan for preparation of a specific dinner menu. Plan the table setting and service for this meal. Prepare and serve the meal and evaluate the meal on the basis of the planning and execution of the project.

3. Plan a table setting for *(a)* breakfast, *(b)* family dinner, *(c)* buffet dinner for twelve, *(d)* holiday dinner.

PART III
Food Science

CHAPTER 17

Colloids

Colloidal systems are commonly found in foods. These systems consist of a substance with a particle size ranging between one and 100 millimicrons[1] dispersed in a continuous phase. Colloidal particles are somewhat larger in size than simple molecules, but are still much too small to be visible to the eye even with the aid of the ordinary microscope. These particles are too large to pass through parchment and other semipermeable membranes. However, they may be studied with an ultramicroscope.

Since colloids may be either gas, liquid, or solid, there are several different ways in which colloidal dispersions occur. In all colloidal systems, there will be a continuous phase (also referred to as the dispersion medium) and a discontinuous phase. Foams in foods are useful examples of a colloidal system in which the liquid colloid is the dispersing medium for a gas. Whipped cream is illustrative of this colloidal dispersion. Emulsions provide illustrations of foods that are liquid in liquid colloidal dispersions. For example, a salad dressing has colloidal-size droplets of oil dispersed in vinegar. Jams and jellies, with their content of pectin, are illustrations of a colloidal system comprised of a liquid and a solid. A colloidal dispersion involving a liquid and a solid may be either a gel or a sol. When the liquid is the continuous phase, the dispersion will flow. This is a sol. When the solid is the continuous phase, the flow property is lost, and the dispersion is a gel. Some foods such as gelatin and pectin dispersions have the capacity for becoming either a gel or a sol, depending on conditions. In their initial state these mixtures are classified as sols because they may be poured. But when their properties are altered by heating and subsequent cooling so that the mixture no longer can be poured in a continuous stream, these foods are classified as gels.

[1] One millimicron equals one-millionth of a millimeter.

SOLS

A colloidal sol characteristically will exhibit the Tyndall effect. With the aid of a microscope, this may be demonstrated by directing a bright beam of polarized light through a sol. The observer will note specks of light in the microscope. The colloidal particles in the sol scatter the light of the polarized light beam when it is passed through a sol, causing the phenomenon known as the Tyndall effect. Another physical characteristic of sols is that they have a low osmotic pressure. Colloidal particles in a sol are constantly in motion (termed Brownian movement). If distribution of the particles were determined solely by Brownian movement, the concentration of particles would be uniform throughout the sol. This movement is competing with gravitational pull, however, so there is a tendency for a slightly greater concentration of the dispersed particles toward the bottom of a sol.

Viscosity is resistance to flow and is altered when other particles are dispersed in a liquid. The viscosity of a colloidal sol is due to the friction between the dispersed and the continuous phase. This characteristic of a sol depends on the shape of the molecules because elongated molecules create friction and cause a liquid to be more viscous. Viscosity is measured by timing the flow of a liquid through a viscometer.

GELS

A gel is a colloidal system that has some rigidity. Different theories of gel formation, or gelation, have been advanced by various researchers. The following sequence appears to be a reasonable explanation of the gelling phenomenon: portions of two colloidal molecules in a sol associate to form a pair; these pairs are then crystallized into bundles termed crystallites; the crystallites continue to grow in size and gradually are united with other crystallites to form a gel. This gel structure may be pictured as a brush heap of many molecules of the dispersed phase, tangled and intertwined in a relatively tight network which then traps water between the molecules. When this happens, the sol loses its fluidity and becomes a gel. Several loci, or points of attraction, are needed on a molecule in order for molecules to link together in a gel structure. Different colloidal substances have differing numbers of loci, hence the characteristics of the gel vary. The associations between molecules in a gel generally are random rather than orderly and precise in nature.

Factors Influencing Gel Formation

Gel formation is favored by lower temperatures, a minimum of agitation, and a greater concentration of the dispersed phase. A cooler temperature reduces the mobility of the colloidal molecules in a sol and increases the viscosity. This condition facilitates the association of molecules as they pass near each other, causing the initiation of gel formation. When the proposed theory of gel formation is borne in mind, it is not difficult to appreciate that agitation of a dispersion that is beginning to gel will disrupt some of the associations occurring and will thus retard gelation. The probability of molecules being attracted to each other is certainly enhanced when more molecules are present in a given volume of sol.

Acid and salts influence gel formation adversely or favorably depending on their concentrations. Colloidal particles characteristically carry a charge, which creates a repulsion between the particles and favors continued suspension rather than precipitation or association of the particles. When the pH of a pectin and sugar suspension is brought near the isoelectric point, the charges on the pectin molecules are at a minimum and the molecules can associate more readily to form the gel network. Salts, because of their charges, can also enhance or discourage gel formation.

At variable concentrations, sugar will influence ease of gel formation.

Physical Characteristics of a Gel

A gel is considerably more viscous than a sol and exhibits rigidity in varying degrees. This property, measured by a penetrometer, increases with age of the gel. A gel that has just set is usually quite soft, but it begins to become more rigid as the molecules within the gel form more associations. With increased storage time, a gel becomes firmer and may eventually begin to assume a rubbery quality. This change can be crudely observed simply by preparing a jelly and observing it regularly over a period of several days. The observed changes are due to increased associations between the molecules and also to some loss of water. The nonstatic nature of gel structure is important when the rigidity of a gel is to be tested. Researchers customarily will maintain gels at the selected testing temperature for five or six hours prior to performing penetrometer tests in order to allow the gel to reach a relatively constant rigidity. The tenderness and turbidity of a gel may be subjectively evaluated by a taste panel.

A gel is smaller in volume than the equivalent sol due to shrinkage during gelation. This shrinkage results from the closer packing of the dispersed phase as the molecules join together. The shrinkage is too small, however, to be of concern in home food preparation.

Syneresis, another characteristic of gels, may be defined as the drainage of liquid from a gel. When one considers that the fluid in a gel structure is simply trapped by the random network of the colloidal molecules, it is not difficult to realize that a cut through this network will release fluid from many little pockets. The amount of liquid that drains from a gel varies with the type of gel and the conditions under which it was prepared. Cranberry gels

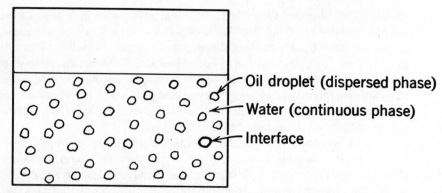

FIGURE 17.1 Diagram of an oil in water (o/w) emulsion.

are noteworthy for the amount of fluid that will drain from them. Syneresis is troublesome, for a gel is less attractive and more difficult to serve when considerable drainage occurs.

EMULSIONS

Emulsions are colloidal dispersions in which a liquid is dispersed in colloidal-size droplets in another immiscible liquid, the continuous phase. Actually, an emulsion is a contradiction to the familiar saying that "oil and water do not mix." In a number of food systems, oil and water (or their equivalents) do mix with a bit of assistance from mechanical agitation or interfering substances. The suspension of droplets of one liquid in another is basically an unstable arrangement; the use of emulsifiers to provide a protective coating of the droplets at the interface between the two media is important in promoting stability.

There are two types of emulsions found in foods. In the more common one, the continuous phase is water and the discontinuous phase is oil. This type of emulsion, known as oil in water, is found in milk and salad dressings, for example. Another way of designating an oil in water emulsion is by using the symbols o/w. The reverse type of emulsion, namely the water in oil emulsion, is represented by butter. In a water in oil emulsion (w/o), oil is the continuous phase and water is dispersed as the discontinuous phase.

All liquids, whether oil or water, exhibit surface tension. This surface tension is the tendency of a liquid to pull in or be attracted to itself and to present the smallest possible surface area. One large sphere represents significantly less surface area than does an equal volume of liquid broken up into many tiny spheres. Thus, if a droplet of liquid in the dispersed phase of an emulsion comes in contact with another droplet, there is a strong tendency for the two droplets to unite into one larger droplet with a reduced total surface area. When this process is repeated many times in an emulsion, the emulsion will begin to break and the two liquids will separate into two distinct layers, with the oil rising to the top because of its lower specific gravity. Droplets will coalesce quickly, and the emulsion will break if there are no interfering substances to prevent the liquid in the droplets from coming in contact with each other.

An emulsion can be formed rather easily by agitating an oil and some water with a rotary beater or even simply by shaking. This is demonstrated when making a French dressing. The energy available from this mechanical agitation is sufficient to permit the oil to break up into small droplets. However, the fluidity of such a mixture enables the droplets to move about freely, and they quickly bump into other oil droplets and coalesce. Such highly fluid and simple systems are termed "temporary emulsions" because of their instability. They must be reformed each time the mixture is used.

Emulsifying agents can be added to emulsions to enhance the stability of the system and to promote better storage of the emulsion. Surface active agents, to be effective, must have a portion of the molecule that is attracted to the water medium and another portion attracted to the oil. Molecules of this type will orient themselves at the interface where the oil and water come in contact at the surface of the dispersed spheres. In effect, the emulsifying agents form a layer surrounding the spheres and help to keep the spheres from actually touching and coalescing. These agents also operate by decreasing the surface tension of the dispersed phase more than they influence the surface tension of the continuous phase. This difference also impedes the formation of larger spheres from smaller ones because the emulsion is not basically so energetically unstable. Proteins are capable of acting as emulsifiers. However, the most effective emulsifying agent naturally occurring in foods is lecithin, a phospholipid in egg yolk. Lecithin is credited

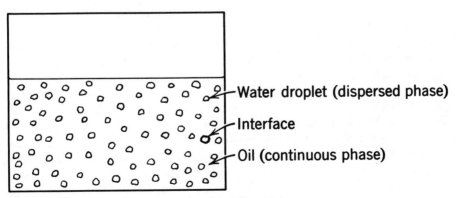

FIGURE 17.2   Diagram of a water in oil (w/o) emulsion.

with being the compound in egg yolk that accounts for its remarkable effectiveness as a stabilizer. When egg yolk is utilized in recipes such as mayonnaise, a permanent emulsion is formed because of the ability of lecithin to orient along the interface and enhance stability. Another factor contributing to stability is viscosity. When various gums and thickeners are used in emulsions, they increase the viscosity, thus impeding movement of the discontinuous phase and reducing the frequency of impacts between droplets.

Emulsions need to be stable when they are a part of a food product if top quality is to be achieved. When the emulsion in a cake batter is broken, the cake will be coarse in texture. The inclusion of emulsifying agents in commercial shortenings helps to increase the stability of the emulsion, thereby promoting finer texture in cakes. Emulsifiers in margarine help to make it possible to warm margarine without excessive splattering from the water that also is present. Success in cream puffs and also in souffles demands that the emulsions be stable during preparation of these products.

FOAMS

Factors Influencing Foam Formation and Stability

A foam may be defined as bubbles of a gas encased by thin layers of a liquid. Several examples may be cited in food preparation, namely egg foams, milk and cream foams, and gelatin foams. Formation of a foam is possible when a substance with a reasonably low surface tension and a low vapor pressure is vigorously agitated. Low surface tension of the liquid allows the liquid to increase its surface area around the gas bubbles without squeezing out the gas too quickly. Low vapor pressure of the liquid is important because then there is little tendency for evaporation to occur; with a high vapor pressure the thin layers of liquid evaporate quickly and thus destroy the foam.

The stability of a foam is determined not only by the vapor pressure and surface tension, but also by any substance that helps give rigidity at the interface of the gas and liquid. Some of the proteins in food foams are denatured by mechanical agitation, thus giving some rigidity and stability to the foam.

Foams can be formed by using a rotary hand beater, electric mixer, or a wire whip, all of which are designed to incorporate air and cause some mechanical coagulation of the protein in the food. This coagulation helps give some rigidity to the cell walls of an egg white foam, but increased stability is achieved by heating the foam to effect further denaturation of the egg white proteins in the thin films of the foam structure.

Egg Foams

Stability of egg foams is determined by several factors: quality of the egg, concentration of the protein, pH, temperature, presence of sugar, and extent of beating. The relation of these factors to egg white foam stability merits consideration. Thick whites form more stable foams than thin whites, although thin whites may initially yield a larger volume of foam. A high concentration of protein is important for a stable foam. Egg yolks or whites to which some water has been added are less stable than the undiluted egg. The original volume of a foam is increased by adding liquid, but this advantage is counteracted by the decreased stability of the foam.

Gelatin Foams

Gelatin is another proteinaceous material capable of forming stable foams. When gelatin is dispersed in some liquid at room temperature, the product can readily be whipped into a foam because of the relatively low surface tension. If this foam is chilled, the gelatin will set into the foam to give stability to the walls of the cells in the foam. Such foams are quite stable, in fact distinctly firm, as long as the gelatin is chilled. The stability will be lost gradually when gelatin foams are allowed to stand at room temperature. Gelatin forms foams readily when beaten with a rotary beater. Beating should be initiated when the melted gelatin has been cooled to the viscosity of whipping cream. At this point the foam is formed quickly with a minimum of effort. A successful product can be formed if beating begins while the gelatin is more fluid, but a longer time and more effort will be required to beat the gelatin to a stiff foam. It is better to start beating too early rather than too late, however, for after the gelatin begins to set, agitation causes it to break into small particles that will be detected on the tongue. These particles also detract from the appearance if a colored gelatin is used because they are more highly colored than the surrounding foam.

A good gelatin foam will be medium fine and uniform in texture with no gelatinous particles evident, the flavor will be pleasing, the volume will be approximately three times its original volume, and the amount of drainage should be insignificant. Inadequate beating decreases the volume and increases drainage. To have a good flavor, gelatin foams require more flavoring than other gelatin products because of the greatly increased volume of the final product and the resultant decrease in concentration of the flavoring substances.

Dairy Foams

Nonfat dry milk solids may be used to form rather unstable, but high-volume foams. The protein in the milk solids has a low surface tension, thus promoting the formation of the foam. A dilution of equal volumes of dry solids and water works well to develop the foam. Gelatin may be added to provide stability in desserts such as Bavarian cream. In a similar fashion, very cold evaporated milk that has not been diluted also will form foams of large volume. The protein in these two types of milk foams is not sufficient to give permanent stability to these products, but they can be frozen in ice creams or stabilized with a gum or other types of material capable of gelling.

In contrast to the two dairy foams noted above, whipping cream can be whipped to a moderately stable foam as long as the cream content is high enough and the fat is cold enough to give rigidity to the foam's cell walls. If the fat is not well chilled, the butterfat becomes too fluid, and the foam will be difficult to form and quite unstable. Whipped cream is dependent on refrigeration for prolonging its stability. Freezing gives considerable rigidity to such a foam, thus making it possible to hold the frozen foam for some time without loss of volume.

BIBLIOGRAPHY

Griswold, R. M. *Experimental Study of Foods*. Houghton Mifflin. Boston, Mass. 1962.

Jacobs, M. E. *Chemistry and Technology of Foods and Food Products*. Interscience. New York, N.Y. 2nd ed. 1951.

Knightly, W. H. Surfactants in food manufacturing. 2. Applications and modes of action. *Food Mfg. 38:* 661. 1963.

Lowe, B. *Experimental Cookery*. Wiley. New York, N.Y. 4th ed. 1955.

Meyer, L. H. *Introductory Chemistry*. Macmillan. New York, N.Y. 1959.

SUGGESTIONS FOR STUDY

1. Define a colloid.
2. What is the difference between a gel and a sol? Explain a possible theory of gel structure.
3. Why is mayonnaise more stable than the emulsion in a French dressing?
4. What are two factors that influence the stability of a foam?

CHAPTER 18

Carbohydrates

Carbohydrates are a group of chemically related substances that are important in the diet for the energy they provide. Carbon, hydrogen, and oxygen, the only elements contained in the compounds of this food group, are arranged in molecules of varying size to form the various sugars, dextrins, pectic substances, starch, and cellulose found in nature.

SUGARS

Monosaccharides

The simplest carbohydrates are the monosaccharides or simple sugars. These consist of a chain containing three or more carbon atoms to which hydrogen and oxygen are attached. Several monosaccharides are known to exist naturally, but the pentoses (five carbons) and hexoses (six carbons) are the most common. Arabinose is an example of a pentose, and glucose, sometimes referred to as dextrose, is the hexose occurring most frequently. Other hexoses commonly found in foods are galactose and fructose. An examination of their structures reveals the similarity among these three hexoses (Haworth structure shown).

Glucose   Fructose   Galactose

459

These compounds are shown in one form. Chemists frequently use two other forms for showing the structures of sugars. These structures are shown here, using glucose as the sugar. The form on the left is that of a pyranose and that on the right is a Fischer structure.

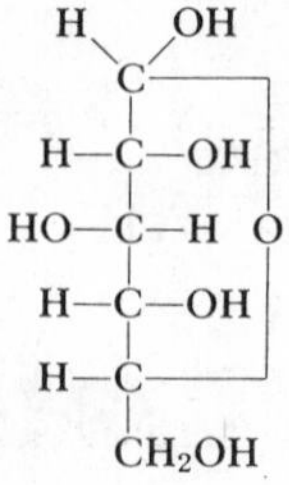

Glucose
(Pyranose structure)

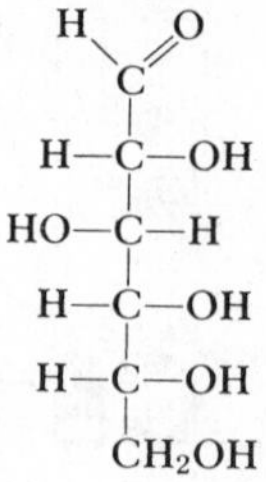

Glucose
(Fischer structure)

Disaccharides

Monosaccharides or simple sugars are the building blocks for other sugars called disaccharides. Two units of glucose linked together form the disaccharide, maltose; a unit of glucose and one of fructose form the most common disaccharide, sucrose; lactose, the sugar found in milk, is a disaccharide containing one glucose and one galactose group.

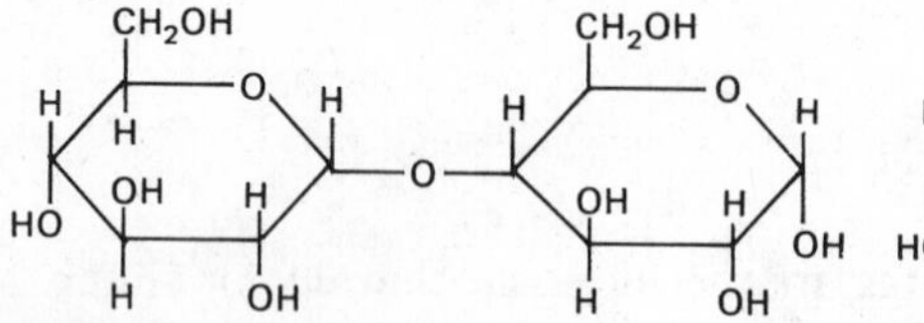

Maltose

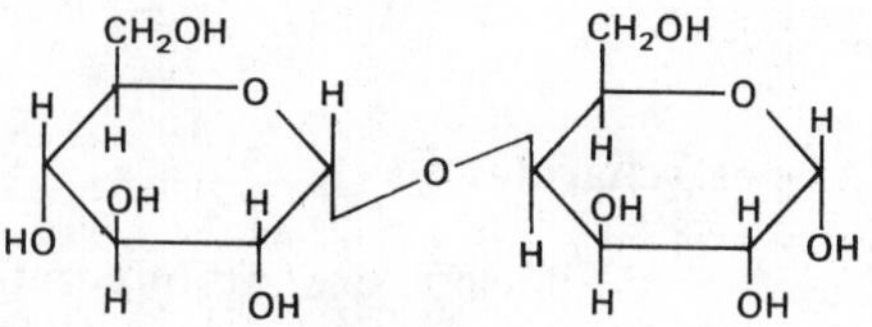

Lactose

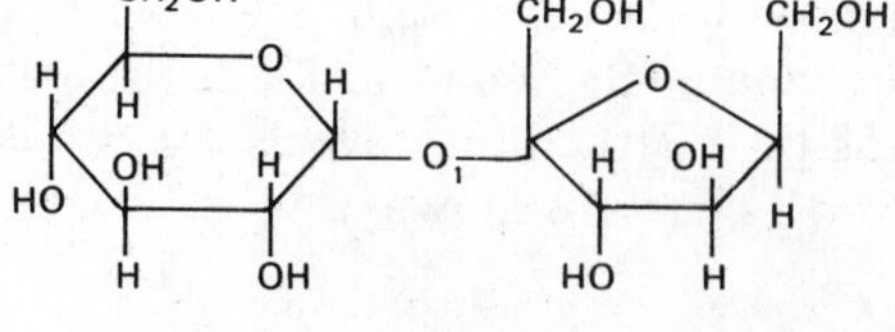

Sucrose

Maltose is a sugar formed when starch, another carbohydrate, is broken down to a simpler substance. Maltose, in turn, may be broken down to two glucose molecules. This chemical breakdown is the basis for the production of corn syrup. Sucrose occurs naturally in all plants but is found in particularly high concentrations in sugar beets and in sugarcane. Sucrose is extracted from these sources and refined into white granulated sugar. Lactose, as such, is not ordinarily used in the home. This is sometimes called "milk sugar," since the natural sugar in milk is in the form of lactose.

Mono- and disaccharides are important for their sweetening ability. This characteristic is related to their solubility and to the hydroxyl (–OH) groups which they contain. Sugars are noted for their solubility. The hygroscopic (water-attracting) character in sugars is responsible for the lumping of sugar that occurs during storage in a humid environment. In contrast to some members of the carbohydrate group, sugars have no thickening ability. Sugar cookery and the chemical reactions occurring during the heating of sugar solutions are discussed in Chapter 13. Table 18.1 lists the relative sweetness of several types of sugars.

Table 18.1 Sweetness Values of Selected Sugars[a]

Sugar	Sweetness value
Fructose	140–175
Invert sugar	100–130
Sucrose	100
Glucose, monohydrate	60– 75
Maltose	30
Lactose	15
Galactose (estimated)	58

[a]Adapted from Eisenberg, S. Uses of sugars and other carbohydrates in the food industry. In *Advances in Chemistry,* Series 12, p. 78. 1955.

DEXTRINS

Dextrins are polysaccharides intermediate in molecular size between starch and sugars. Several glucose units are linked together to form these substances. The actual molecular weight of dextrins shows considerable variability, from weights approaching those of starch to those almost as small as maltose. The properties of dextrins are related to the size of the dextrin under consideration. Those of high molecular weight are only slightly soluble and will swell slightly in the presence of water and high temperatures, whereas those of lower molecular weight are quite soluble and have little thickening ability.

Dextrins are formed in food preparation when bread is toasted or when flour is browned. In the latter instance, the reduction in thickening ability of the dextrins is apparent if browned flour is used as a thickening agent. The starch in flour that has browned only slightly has been converted to the large dextrins, hence exhibits appreciable thickening ability. Prolonged browning, however, permits breakdown of the starch to the more soluble, smaller dextrin molecules. These shorter dextrins have lost much of the thickening ability characteristic of starch but have begun to show slightly the increased solubility and sweetness of the sugars.

STARCH

Starch is a polysaccharide composed of many glucose units linked together with a maltose α linkage. This α linkage explains the difference between starch and cellulose. The β linkage of cellulose, although only slightly different from the α linkage in starch, is not susceptible to enzymatic action in the human body, whereas the body has the appropriate enzymes needed for the digestion and ultimate utilization of starch. Some animals, notably ruminants, have enzymes capable of breaking the β linkage of cellulose and therefore can use grass and other materials high in cellulose content as food.

α Linkage (starch)

β Linkage (cellulose)

Starch is formed by the plant and is deposited in the amyloplast of the cells of the endosperm portion of the grain. The amyloplast is the sac in the cytoplasm which holds the materials necessary for production of starch. As the glucose chains are formed they precipitate and form the granules of starch within the amyloplasts. A large quantity of starch in the granules will swell the amyloplast until the sacs eventually may break.

Amylose

There are actually two fractions of starch, each with distinctly different properties; their differences are explained by examining the linkage between the glucose units. Amylose is generally pictured as a long, unbranched chain consisting of more than 600 glucose units joined in the α linkage between the first carbon on one glucose unit and the fourth carbon of the next unit. Amylose is soluble in hot water, gives a blue iodine test, and forms the

Amylose

crystalline structure observed in the starch granule. Apparently the large amylose chains actually have a small amount of branching on them, hence these molecules of amylose begin to assume some of the properties of the other starch fraction, amylopectin. The very large amylose molecules are less soluble than the smaller ones.

Amylopectin

Amylopectin, the less-soluble fraction of starch, is composed of chains twenty to twenty-five glucose units in length which are linked by the 1,4 α-glucosidic linkage. These chains in turn are fastened to each other in a branched fashion by linking the first carbon on the end glucose unit of one chain with the sixth carbon on a glucose unit of another chain. These 1,6 carbon unions produce the highly branched structure that characterizes amylopectin. Varying numbers of the 1,4-linked chains may be joined together to form relatively larger or smaller amylopectin molecules. When fewer branches are joined to form a molecule, the molecular size is smaller and will begin to approach those of the slightly branched larger molecules of amylose. Generally short amylose chains are approximately 600 glucose units in length; very slightly branched amylose contains more than 600 units; minimally branched amylopectin has about 1000 glucose units; and more complex branching incorporates up to 1500 glucose units in one amylopectin molecule.

The Starch Granule

When viewed under an ordinary microscope, the individual amylose and amylopectin molecules are invisible. What is seen is a much more complex structure containing many starch molecules and which will be referred to herein as the starch granule. The proportions of amylopectin to amylose which occur in the starch granule vary, but in most of the starches used in

Amylopectin

the home the ratio is approximately four amylopectin molecules to each amylose molecule.

Some starches are classified as waxy starches because their properties are distinctly different from the regular starches. These differences are due to the very high percentage of amylopectin and the dearth of amylose in waxy starches. The influence of this compositional difference will be discussed later.

Translucency of starch pastes varies because of differences in the molecular weight of amylose from different sources: cereal starches such as cornstarch have a high-molecular-weight amylose that makes a cloudy paste because of the poor solubility of the large amylose molecules; in contrast, the lower-molecular-weight arrowroot and other root starches contain small amylose molecules that are more soluble and hence produce a more translucent paste.

Effect of Acid

Commercial Preparation of Starch. The commercial preparation of starch influences the properties of the starches to be used in the home. Cornstarch prepared at an alkaline pH has an enhanced swelling capacity in a starch mixture heated to 70°C; cornstarch prepared in an acid medium has a marked increase in swelling when heated to 90°C. Chlorine treatment has been observed to produce a starch with decreased swell unless acid is used in the preparation of the starch.

Gelatinization. In general, when acid and starch are heated together, acid reduces the viscosity of the resulting starch paste because the acid causes fragmentation of the starch, which may be interpreted as meaning that the starch granules not only release more amylose but also are broken into smaller fragments that physically offer less obstruction to the flow of liquid in the gelatinized mixture. The free amylose in the gelatinized paste is hydrolyzed by the acid into shorter, more soluble chains, which partially explains the decrease in viscosity due to the presence of acid.

A very small amount of acid causes increased swell of the starch granules and releases just enough amylose to effectively bind the gel, whereas a larger quantity of acid hydrolyzes the amylose into chains that are too short to bridge and hold the swollen starch grains. The combination of the presence of sugar and acid in a starch mixture such as may be made in the home will produce a less viscous product. The actual characteristics of the product, however, depend not only on the presence of acid, but also on the concentration of starch and sugar. The influence of the latter is discussed in Chapter 7.

Enzymes

The breakdown of the straight starch chains in both amylose and amylopectin may be accomplished by α- or β-amylase. β-Amylase splits off maltose units at alternate 1,4 linkages. α-Amylase also acts on the 1,4 linkage, but in a random fashion anywhere along the chains so that a variety of short-chain carbohydrates is formed.

R-enzyme attacks the 1,6 branching linkage in amylopectin. Z-enzyme and limit dextrinase have been postulated to break this same linkage.

Enzymes are more effective as the starch mixture is being heated, although the presence of fat delays enzyme action. Enzymatic action is stopped when the enzymes are deactivated by high temperatures. Enzymatic breakdown in starch is of importance because this action, if extensive, completely alters the properties of the mixture. As the chains are shortened through enzymatic breakdown, they become more soluble, and their swelling or thickening power becomes progressively lessened.

Retrogradation

Retrogradation may be described as the attempt of the starch granule to return to its original organized crystalline structure after it has been heated. The success of this attempt if influenced by the quantity of swollen amylose granules and free amylose in the mixture. Retrogradation occurs in any cooked starch mixture.

When surface active agents such as POEMS (polyoxyethylmonostearate), glycerol monostearate, glycerol monopalmitate, and lecithin are used, the leaching of amylose during baking is retarded so there is less free amylose in the baked product to retrograde and stale.

The staling of bread offers an interesting example of retrogradation, for amylose will precipitate as bread stales. This precipitation may be reversed by heating the bread without loss of moisture, and thus increasing the solubility of the amylose. Unless the bread is served warm, however, the amylose will once again precipitate and the bread will seem stale. Retrogradation of amylose is retarded by freezing bread because water is immobilized in the form of ice crystals.

Staling is a rather rapid process in bread because retrogradation occurs most readily at the normal moisture content of this product. Since the moisture content of crackers is below that range, their staling is somewhat slower. It should be noted that the hygroscopic character of salt on crackers tends to increase the moisture content to the more susceptible range and then the starch in the crackers will retrograde and the crackers will stale.

Commercial Starch Products

Frozen Products. Fragile starch sponges can be produced by gelatinizing a 5 percent starch paste, cooling, and then freezing it. These sponges may be used as a crunchy candy when dried and dipped in chocolate, as an emergency ration, and as a carrier for vitamins.

Frozen puddings and pie fillings have been successfully prepared using waxy rice flour to replace eggs or cornstarch as the thickening agent. The combination of waxy rice flour and gelatin results in a frozen pudding that assumes its original consistency upon thawing and does not exhibit marked syneresis such as occurs in puddings made with cornstarch, egg, or starch-containing additives (chocolate). Puddings using the waxy or glutinous rice can be stored at $0°F$ for six to nine months and custards at the same temperature are satisfactory after two to four months. The chief objection to the use of waxy rice flour is its raw cereal taste.

Syneresis is a definite problem in frozen white sauces, although reheating above $50°F$ helps to reverse this instability. Reheating reverses the retrogradation that has occurred during frozen storage, which is thought to be the prime cause of the syneresis. A specially prepared starch with phosphate cross linkages is now manufactured for use in frozen foods that have sauces thickened with starch. The starch does not retrograde as readily as the normal starch so syneresis is minimized.

Special Starches

By selective breeding it has been possible to produce varieties of plants with starches possessing unusual ratios of amylopectin and amylose.

Starches containing an unusually high percentage of amylopectin are termed waxy starches. Amioca, the starch from a carefully bred corn, is such a product. The usual amylopectin percentage of 72–80 percent has been altered to 100 percent amylopectin in amioca. Pastes made with this starch are thick and clear and have little tendency to gel owing to the absence of amylose. In low concentrations at high temperatures, amioca produces pastes comparable in viscosity to potato starch, but at high concentration and with longer cooking times the paste from amioca will be slightly thicker than tapioca and distinctly less viscous than a comparable potato starch paste. Amioca is particularly well suited to pie fillings, candies, salad dressings, and instant puddings. Because no amylose is present to precipitate, amioca does not form a skin on the surface of the pudding.

The linear molecules of amylose are suitable for casting thin films for use in a variety of industries. Research in this direction has been the reverse of the development of waxy corn starches. In 1957 a corn was produced containing starch with more than 80 percent amylose and less than 20 percent amylopectin. Since films made from high-amylose starch are edible, the possibilities of the uses for these films are extensive. Packaging in materials that can be dropped into hot water and dissolved in one possibility; another application could be casings for various meat products.

Precooked Starches

After much research dating from 1941, instant rice was satisfactorily produced and marketed in 1946. This long-grain rice undergoes heating until it is 60 percent cooked and is then dried. Minute tapioca is another precooked starch product presently available; instant puddings also contain pregelatinized starch. These products require only rehydration before they are ready to serve.

Precooked potatoes have gained widespread acceptance for they are less bulky, keep far better than fresh potatoes, and save preparation time. The potatoes are cooked in small cubes, frozen at $-23°C$, thawed at $4.5°C$, and then dehydrated to 8 percent moisture. These environmental conditions during processing of the dehydrated mashed potatoes are vital to quality.

At the factory, cooking of the potatoes softens the cellulose and hydrolyzes the intercellular pectic substances so that the cells are easy to separate during mashing, but overcooking causes considerable rupturing of the starch granules and increased fragility. This combination plus the possibility of overbeating during final preparation in the home can cause mashed dehydrated potatoes to be sticky and gummy. Quick freezing and controlled thawing are helpful in achieving a high degree of porosity and minimum horniness or harshness in precooked potatoes. Whiteness of the finished product increases with the incorporation of air.

CELLULOSE

Cellulose, one of the important structural substances of plants, is a carbohydrate closely related to starch. Although the β linkage of cellulose is not readily attacked by enzymes in man, cellulose-containing vegetables or fruits are useful in the diet as sources of roughage to promote motility in the intestinal tract. Since cellulose is not altered readily by customary food-preparation procedures, it is sufficient for the purposes of this book to simply note the existence of cellulose in foods.

PECTIC SUBSTANCES

The cells of plants are cemented together by a group of substances called the pectic substances. These are considered to be polysaccharides composed of units of derivatives of galactose, that is, galacturonic acid and its methyl esters. The chemistry of the pectic substances has been a subject of much research since 1917 when Ehrlich first reported the relationship of the pectic substances.

Galacturonic acid is the basic unit in all the pectic substances, and is repeated in varying amounts depending on the particular substance. More accurately, it may be stated that pectic substances are composed of many anhydrogalacturonic-acid units. In other words, many galacturonic-acid units have been combined together with the loss of a molecule of water between each unit.

Galacturonic acid is a six-carbon acid that differs from the simple sugar, galactose, in that is has an acid radical ($-COOH$) at the sixth carbon. The similarity of structure is shown here in the ring or Haworth structure of each compound.

Galactose   Galacturonic acid

Nomenclature

Pectic substances have been the subject of much confusion in nomenclature. Part of the reason is due to the heterogeneity of the group, for some other compounds such as galactose and arabinose occur in these substances.

In addition, there is much variation in the length of the chains, which has raised the question of when a pectic substance ceases to be a pectic substance, or how long must a polygalacturonic-acid chain be in order to be classified as a pectic substance. The frequency of methyl ($-CH_3$) groups on the galacturonic-acid units has also complicated the classification of these compounds. As if these factors were not enough, different researchers used their own systems of classification during the initial phases of research on these substances so that several names were being used for the same material in some cases.

Order was brought out of confusion when an official, revised system of nomenclature was adopted for the pectic substances in 1944. The terms used in this discussion will be those defined at that time. The substances included in this discussion are defined as follows. The use of pectins in jelly making is discussed in Chapter 14.

Pectic substances are the complex carbohydrate derivatives containing a large proportion of anhydrogalacturonic-acid units. These substances must be of colloidal size and they may contain methyl groups and some bases. This is a group term that includes protopectin, pectinic acids, pectin, and pectic acids.

Protopectin is the parent compound of pectin. These large molecules do not exhibit gel-forming properties. Unripe fruits contain appreciable quantities of protopectin.

Pectin is a term used to include any and all of the pectic substances that are capable of forming a gel. Pectinic acids and/or pectinates therefore are implied when the term pectin is used. These substances can be extracted from plants by heat and pressure. The molecular weight of pectin varies with the source; apple pectin is estimated to have a molecular weight of approximately 280,000, and citrus-fruit pectin is about 220,000. The concentration of pectin is greatest in fast-growing surface tissues. Formation of pectin from protopectin is enzyme-catalyzed by polygalacturonase and pectin esterases. Enzymatic activity is accelerated by high temperatures and/or injury to the surface of the fruit.

Pectinic acids are polygalacturonic-acid chains of colloidal size. In addition, they have methyl groups ($-CH_3$) esterified at varying intervals along the chain. Pectinic acids are formed from protopectin as it breaks down to smaller molecules in the ripening fruit. These acids have gel-forming properties.

Pectinates are salts of pectinic acid which occur in fruits. These substances, like their related acids, are of value because they can form gels.

Pectic acids are also of colloidal size, but have essentially no gel-forming ability as compared to pectinic acids. This loss of capability apparently is due to the lesser number of methyl groups in pectic acids.

SUMMARY

Mono-, di-, and polysaccharides constitute the group of substances known as carbohydrates. The sugars are relatively small, water-soluble molecules; the dextrins are intermediate in size between sugar and starch; starch is composed of two types of molecules, amylose and amylopectin, which are of a high molecular weight. When heated in an aqueous medium, starch gelatinizes and causes a thickening of the product. Acids and/or enzymes break the starch into smaller molecules, thus reducing the thickening power. Sugar also decreases the viscosity of a gelatinized starch mixture. Recent research has utilized the properties of starch to produce a variety of new products and convenience foods.

Pectic substances are polysaccharide derivatives of galacturonic acid. Protopectin and pectic acids are impractical as gel-forming substances, but pectinic acid and pectinates are useful in making jelly and related foods.

BIBLIOGRAPHY

Bear, R. S., and E. G. Samsa. Gelatinization mechanism of starch granules. *Ind. Eng. Chem. 35*:721–726. 1943.

Campbell, A. M., and A. M. Briant. Wheat starch pastes and gels containing citric acid and sucrose. *Food Res. 22*:358–366. 1957.

Dux, E. F. W. Recent advances in starch chemistry and manufacture. *Food Manuf. 30*:492–498. 1955.

Geissman, T. A. *Principles of organic chemistry.* Freeman, San Francisco, Calif. 1962.

Hanson, H. L., K. D. Nisheta, and H. Lineweaver. Preparation of frozen puddings. *Food Tech. 7*:462–465. 1953.

Hellman, N. N., B. Fairchild, and F. R. Senti. The bread staling problem. *Cereal Chem. 31*:495–505. 1954.

Hester, E. E., A. M. Briant, and C. J. Personius. The effect of sucrose on the properties of some starches and flours. *Cereal Chem. 33*:91–101. 1956.

Hilbert, G. E. et al. Starch sponge – a promising new ingredient. *Food Ind.* pp. 72–76. August 1945.

Instant rice. *Food Ind.* pp. 86–91. August 1947.

Leach, H. W., L. D. McCowne, and T. J. Schoch. Structure of the starch granule, I. Swelling and solubility patterns of various starches. *Cereal Chem. 36*:534–544. 1959.

Leach, H. W., and T. J. Schoch. Structure of the starch granule, II. Action of various amylases on granular starches. *Cereal Chem. 38*:34–46. 1961.

Lehninger, A. L. *Biochemistry.* Worth. New York, N. Y. 1970.

Meyer, K. H. The past and present of starch chemistry. *Experentia 8*:405–420. 1952.

Meyer, L. H. *Introductory Chemistry.* Macmillan, New York, N. Y. 1961.

Osman, E., and M. R. Dix. Effects of fats and non-ionic surface-active agents on starch pastes. *Cereal Chem. 37*:464–475. 1960.

Osman, E., and P. D. Cummisford. Some factors affecting the stability of frozen white sauces. *Food Res. 24*:595–604. 1959.

Schoch, T. M. Starches and enzymes. *Am. Soc. Brewing Chem. Proc.* pp. 83–92. 1961.

Schopymeyer, H. H. Amioca—the starch from waxy corn. *Food Ind.* pp. 106–109. May 1945.

Sjöström, O. A. Microscopy of starches and their modification. *Ind. Eng. Chem. 28*: 63–74. 1936.

Waldt, L. M. Pregelatinized starches for the food processor. *Food Tech. 14*:50–53. 1960.

White, A., P. Handler, and E. L. Smith. *Principles of Biochemistry,* 3rd ed. McGraw-Hill, New York, N. Y. 1964.

SUGGESTIONS FOR STUDY

1. Cite examples of monosaccharides, disaccharides, and polysaccharides.
2. What is the relationship between glucose and starch?
3. Although cellulose, starch, and pectin are polysaccharides, their behaviorial characteristics are quite different. What structural features and behavioral characteristics do starch, pectin, and cellulose have in common? What differences exist?
4. Explain the phenomena of gelatinization, dextrinization, and retrogradation.
5. What is the relationship of the pectic substances to each other?

CHAPTER 19

Fats

Fats are important in many types of recipes. They are used as the medium of heat transfer when foods are fried. Some fats contribute flavor to foods. One of the most frequent uses of fats is as a shortening or tenderizing agent in various baked products. Lard and butter have long been used in food preparation in these various capacities, but today a much wider selection of fats and oils is available in retail stores. Manufacturers have used various techniques to alter the characteristics of different fats. As a result, it is possible to buy fats uniquely tailored for use in particular products. To more readily understand how these changes are effected, it is first necessary to examine the composition of fats.

CHEMISTRY OF FATS

Glycerol

Fats are composed of two substances, glycerol and fatty acids. Glycerol is a three-carbon alcohol containing three hydroxyl (–OH) groups. Fatty acids are organic acids that contain a chain of carbon atoms linked to a terminal organic-acid radical or carboxyl group $\left(-C\begin{smallmatrix}O\\\\OH\end{smallmatrix}\right)$. A variety of fatty acids occurs in the various common fats and oils.

Glycerol   Fatty acid

When fatty acids esterify with the hydroxyl (−OH) groups of glycerol, a fat is formed. The compound formed when one hydroxyl group is esterified with a fatty acid is termed a monoglyceride; two hydroxyl groups combined with two fatty acids is a diglyceride; and all three hydroxyl groups reacting with three fatty acids form a triglyceride. In the equation, which illustrates the formation of a monoglyceride, the R represents the carbon chain of the fatty acid. Actually, esterification can occur on any of the three carbons of glycerol, and therefore other permutations occur in addition to those shown. The general formulas for diglycerides and triglycerides are:

Glycerol   Fatty acid   Monoglyceride

Fatty Acids

The chemical composition of the fatty acids is responsible for the variable characteristics of fats. Fatty acids naturally occurring in foods usually contain an even number of carbon atoms ranging in chain length from four to twenty-two carbon atoms, and they may either be saturated with hydrogen or contain a varying number of double bonds capable of adding hydrogen, in which case they are known as unsaturated fatty acids. These double bonds are located in positions that are characteristic for each particular unsaturated fatty acid. When a fatty acid has more than one double bond, it is said to be polyunsaturated.

The backbone carbon chain of the fatty acid is a linear configuration except where a double bond occurs. At a double bond the chain may continue in its same configuration *(trans)* or the next portion of the chain may proceed at a different angle, as illustrated. When the chain proceeds in an altered direction, the configuration is classified as *cis*. The significance of this change in angle will be discussed later in the section on factors influencing melting points. In nature the most commonly occurring unsaturated fatty acid is oleic (18 carbons), and the most common saturated fatty acid is palmitic (16 carbons).

Trans   *Cis*

Laboratory Tests

Literature reporting research in the area of fats regularly refers to values for certain common chemical tests. The following tests are used in the laboratory to gain information about characteristics of a particular fat.

1. The free fatty acids in a fat are determined by measuring the number of milligrams of potassium hydroxide required to neutralize the free fatty acids in one gram of fat. This information tells the amount of fatty acids present in a free form rather than esterified with glycerol.

2. The saponification number is determined by measuring the milligrams of fat. This is a measure of the molecular weight.

3. The iodine number is the number of grams of iodine absorbed by 100 grams of fat, which is a measure of the unsaturation (number of double bonds) in a fat.

4. The peroxide value is an estimate of the number of millimoles of peroxide per kilogram of oxidized fat. The hydroperoxide determination is another means of determining the amount of breakdown occurring in a fat.

PHYSICAL PROPERTIES OF FATS

Before discussing the use of fat in food preparation, it is helpful to consider the physical nature of fats and how the physical characteristics may be altered by various processes. Fats exist as a liquid or a solid. The solid form of fats requires further explanation, for the so-called solid fat is actually a mixture of liquid fat trapped within a network of fat crystals. This state was first recognized by Chevreul in 1814 when he determined that lard contained a solid which he called stearine and a liquid he named elaine.

Melting Point

Whether a fat will exist as a solid or as a liquid at a given temperature is influenced by the length of the fatty-acid chains, the degree of saturation, the configuration (*cis* or *trans*) of the unsaturated fatty acids, and the position of the double bonds. Information regarding the melting point of selected fats and fatty acids occurring in food fats is given in Table 19.1.

Fatty acids with long carbon chains have higher melting points than do those with shorter carbon chains. This can readily be seen when butyric acid (four carbons) is compared with stearic acid (eighteen carbons), for butyric acid is a liquid at room temperature (melting point, −7.9°C) and stearic acid is a solid at room temperature with a melting point of 69.6°C.

The number of double bonds in a fatty acid is an important factor in determining the melting point of a fat because each double bond lowers the

Table 19.1 Characteristics of Selected Fatty Acids and Fats Occurring in Foods[a]

Type	Structure and Configuration	Chain Length	No. of Double Bonds	Melting Point, °C	Appearance	Source
Fatty Acid						
Butyric	$CH_3CH_2CH_2COOH$	4	0	−4.7 to −7.9	Colorless liquid	Milk fat
Stearic	$CH_3(CH_2)_{16}COOH$	18	0	69.6	Colorless, waxy solid	Animals, plants
Oleic	$CH_3(CH_2)_7CH=CH(CH_2)_7COOH$ *(Cis)*	18	1	16.3	Yellow liquid	Animals, plants
Elaidic	$CH_3(CH_2)_7CH=CH(CH_2)_7COOH$ *(Trans)*	18	1	43.7	Solid	
Linolenic	$CH_3(CH_2CH=CH)_3(CH_2)_7COOH$	18	3	−11	Colorless liquid	Soy
Fats						
Tripalmitin		16	0	65.5	White crystalline solid	
Tristearin		18	0	71.6	White crystalline solid	
Triolein		18	1	−4	Yellow liquid	

[a]Selected from *Biochemists' Handbook,* ed. by C. D. Long, Van Nostrand, Princeton, N.J., 1961.

melting point. The saturated, 18-carbon fatty acid, stearic acid, has a melting point of 69.6°C, but the fatty acid of the same carbon-chain length with three double bonds, linolenic, melts at −11°C.

The *cis* or *trans* form at a double bond is another factor in determining the melting point of an unsaturated fatty acid: the *trans* form has a significantly higher melting point than does the *cis* form of the comparable acid. For example, elaidic acid is a *trans* fatty acid with a melting point of 43.7°C. The *cis* form of the comparable fatty acid is oleic acid whose melting point is 16.3°C.

Commonly used food fats consist of a mixture of saturated mono-, di-, and triglycerides and unsaturated triglycerides. Such mixtures melt over a wide temperature range, whereas a simple triglyceride containing only one kind of fatty acid has a sharp melting point.

Plasticity

Plasticity of fats may be defined as the ability of a fat to retain its shape under slight pressure, but to yield to increased pressure such as that encountered in mixing or spreading. With today's technological capabilities the range of temperatures at which a fat is plastic can be extended.

The incorporation of some triglycerides containing only fatty acids with low melting points and of others containing fatty acids with high melting points produces a fat with a wide plastic range. Control of the degree of saturation and of the isomeric products resulting from partial hydrogenation, coupled with regulation of the molecular weight of the fat molecule, will result in the production of a fat that will be plastic over a wide temperature range. Rearrangement of the fatty acids to different positions on glycerol is another means of increasing the plastic range of a fat.

Acetin, a fat that contains acetic acid (CH_3COOH) esterified on the glycerol, is a practical addition to mixed fats for its lower melting point gives a wider plastic range to the fat. Acetin is of value because it can be added to fats such as beef tallow which otherwise would be too hard for optimum baking performance. Acetoolein can be used to produce such a wide plastic range that margarine containing this fat remains plastic over the range of temperatures found at both the equator and the poles.

Crystal Formation

Although Chevreul commented on the two-phase system 150 years ago, it has been only within approximately the last 20 years that the crys-

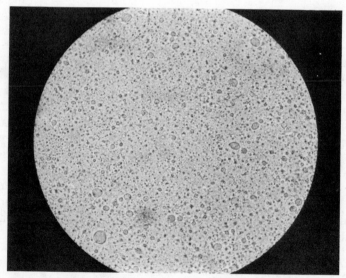

FIGURE 19.1 Microphotograph of margarine (500X) showing the various size droplets of the dispersed phase of the emulsion, as seen under ordinary light. The liquid and crystalline fat are now shown in detail.

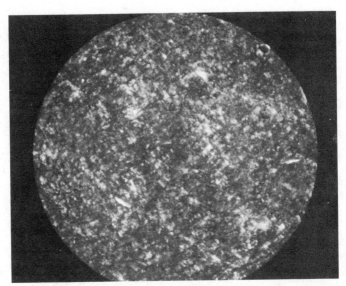

FIGURE 19.2 Microphotograph of margarine (500X) showing the crystalline portions (light areas) as seen under polarized light. Liquid portions do not show
in the picture.

talline structure of fats has been studied in careful detail. It has been found
that, in a solid fat, a network of fat crystals exists which will trap the liquid
phase. This continuous network of crystals is formed more easily by fats of
the *trans* configuration than by the *cis* fats because the *cis* form cannot
approach another molecule closely enough to bond tightly with it.

The crystals in a fat can exist in any one of four forms: α, β', intermediate, and β. The α crystals are very tiny, translucent, and relatively unstable. Crystals in the β' form are relatively small and are distinctly more
stable than the α form. This crystal form is desirable for use in baked products. Gradually a transition from β' crystals to the intermediate form takes
place, accompanied by a loss of desirability in baked products. Finally the
transition to the very stable, coarse β crystals takes place. These crystals
are so large that the fat has a grainy appearance and is unsuited for use in
food products.

The rapid conversion of lard crystals to the undesirable β form has
been one of the chief blocks to its use in the natural state. Industry's answer
to this problem has been the rearrangement of the fatty acids on the glycerol
portion of the fat molecules in lard. By putting the fatty acids in different
positions on the glycerol, the shape of the molecules is varied and crystal
transformation to the β form is retarded. Such lard is marketed as rearranged
lard.

Another means of altering crystal structure is to introduce flakes of a

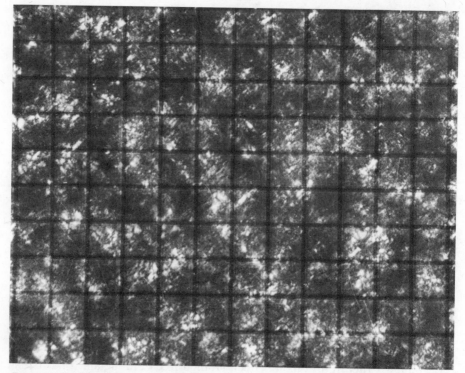

FIGURE 19.3 Photomicrograph of β' fat crystals in polarized light (200X). Grid lines represent 18 microns.

different fat into a fat with less desirable crystal characteristics. Curiously, the introduction of the crystals causes the fat to crystallize in the form commonly assumed by the flakes, rather than in the form that the unaltered fat would characteristically assume. By this means, it is possible to alter some fats that are inexpensive, but less desirable, into fats that have culinary advantages.

To maintain fats in α or β' crystals during storage, it is important to avoid fluctuations in temperature. Partially hydrogenated vegetable oils and rearranged lard are best when stored at 60–65°F, whereas natural lard retains a better crystalline form for a long period if it is stored at 40–45°F in the refrigerator.

Variations in Fats Due to Origin

Fats from milk contain a variety of fatty acids ranging in chain length from four to twenty-six carbons; nine saturated and seven unsaturated fatty acids are in abundance, in contrast to the usual occurrence of three saturated and two unsaturated fatty acids as the chief components in fats from other sources.

Body fats vary greatly depending on the species, location within the animal, and sometimes on the diet. Characteristically, sheep fat is highest in polyunsaturated fatty acids; cattle fat is harder than fat from pigs or poultry. In any animal the fats near the surface of the animal are softer and higher in unsaturated fatty acids than the leaf fat surrounding the internal organs.

The metabolic processes of each species result in differences in the fat composition of the various kinds of animals. Nonruminants deposit some dietary fats unchanged so it is possible to influence the fatty-acid composition of such animals fats by altering the type of fat in the diet. Cattle, however, have bacteria in the rumen which alter dietary fats; therefore it is impossible to produce appreciable changes in their body fat.

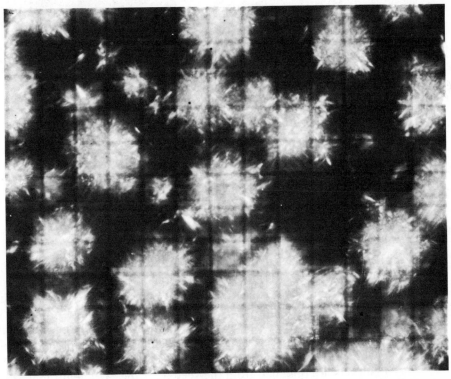

FIGURE 19.4 Photomicrograph of intermediate fat crystals in polarized light (200X). Grid lines represent 18 microns.

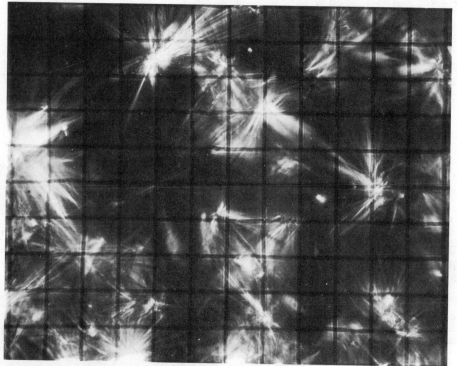

FIGURE 19.5 Photomicrograph of β fat crystals in polarized light (200X). Grid lines represent 18 microns.

TECHNOLOGY OF FATS

Rendering

The basic steps in the production of fats are rendering, refining, hydrogenating, blending, and tempering. The process of extracting fats and oils from animal tissues is termed "rendering." Steam rendering, wherein the finely chopped fatty tissues are heated with 40 to 60 pounds of steam pressure, is the most commonly used method for the preparation of animal fats today; dry rendered lard cooked in an open kettle is available, however, for people who prefer a lard with a cooked flavor.

Plant oils are obtained from the seed after the extraneous materials are removed by pressing or by extraction with a solvent. Any proteins that may be present in the oil are then coagulated by a cooking period in steam.

Refining

The crude fats and oils contain not only the desired fat, but also free fatty acids and other miscellaneous materials that contribute undesirable qualities to the finished product. An alkali is added to form a water and oil emulsion which is then heated, broken, and separated. Additional washings and centrifugal separations in a continuous process purify the fats to a free fatty-acid content of only 0.01 to 0.05 percent, a degree of purity necessary for the production of fat with a reasonable shelf life. Bleaching and deodorizing complete the refining process.

Hydrogenating

Under controlled conditions (100–200°C and less than 15 atmospheres of pressure) and in the presence of a nickel catalyst, hydrogen can be intro-

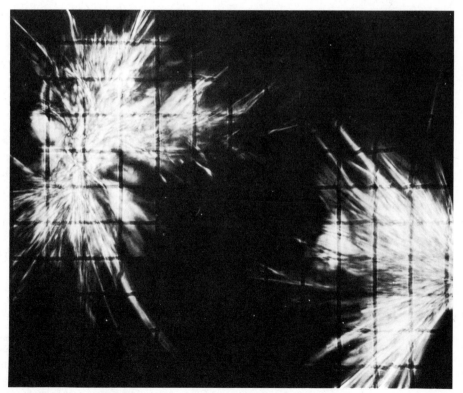

FIGURE 19.5 Photomicrograph of β fat crystals in polarized light (200X). Grid lines represent 18 microns.

duced into an oil at the double bonds in the fatty-acid moieties. The addition of hydrogen results in a less fluid material; oils, such as corn and soybean, can be modified from their fluid state to a plastic fat.

Blending and Tempering

A desirable, rather wide temperature range of plasticity is achieved when an appropriate blend of fats is supercooled rapidly and then crystallized with agitation to achieve a matrix of fine fat crystals (α or β' crystals) enclosing the oil. Practically, this is achieved by cooling the fat to 65°F in 30 seconds in a closed system containing nitrogen, and then working the fat inside the system for one to four minutes to produce fine crystals. A period of tempering (controlled temperature storage) for one to two days completes the manufacture of a shortening.

Winterizing

Cottonseed, corn, and soybean oils are winterized by cooling to 7°C and then filtering to remove the crystals that form at the reduced temperature. This winterizing process produces an oil that may be stored in a refrigerator and still remain clear, since the fatty acids with the highest melting points have been removed.

Other Modifications of Shortenings

The other technological changes responsible for changed characteristics of the fat, mentioned in other sections but suitably grouped together here, include; rearrangement of the fatty acids on the glycerol molecule (as in lard) to form a fat that stays in the desired β' crystal form longer; the introduction of emulsifying agents such as the mono- and diglycerides to make the superglycerinated shortenings tailored for use in cakes; the introduction of fats or fat flakes with desired characteristics which makes less desirable fats more functional; and the addition of antioxidants for longer shelf life.

SHORTENING VALUE OF FATS

Shortening power may be defined as the ability of a fat to produce tenderness, that is, structural weakness, in a baked product. When the fat is mixed with flour, it is gradually extended into thinner layers and the flour becomes separated into smaller masses which are protected by the fat from the liquid when it is added. The layers of fat inhibit gluten development not only because of the protective coating formed around the flour, but also because the fat reduces the friction of the dough during mixing.

Plasticity of the Fat

Fats that are soft at mixing temperatures are good shortening agents, but fats that are too soft do not give maximum shortening because they tend to run out of the dough. Hard fats are less effective shortening agents because they resist efforts to spread them into thin layers during mixing.

Fats that are plastic over the range of temperatures commonly encountered in mixing are particularly useful as shortenings. It is apparent that mixing at a warm enough temperature to facilitate spreading of the shortening without permitting it to run out of the dough ensures that maximum shortening value is derived from the fat.

Surface Area Covered by a Fat

The effectiveness of the various shortenings is determined by the amount of surface area that a fat can cover, as well as by the plastic character of the shortening during blending. In fats the —C=C— of the unsaturated fatty-acid chains and the —COO$^-$ portions of the fat molecule are polar, hence are attracted to water and increase the cohesion of the fat and water at their interface; the remaining portions of the fatty-acid chains, because of their nonpolar character, are attracted toward the oil portion as indicated in the following diagram. The carbon chains between double bonds are pulled up into the oil rather than stretched out along the interface.

Saturated fatty acid

One double bond

Two double bonds

Three double bonds

Unsaturated fats containing one double bond cover twice as much surface area at the interface as do saturated fats; fats with two double bonds cover approximately the same area as the single unsaturated fatty acids because the fat molecule is unable to bend back sharply enough for the second double bond to reach the interface; with three double bonds in the chain the fatty-acid chain can effectively cover a large surface area at the interface.

Monoglycerides are effective as emulsifiers in fats, for the two —OH groups of the glycerol plus the —COO⁻ of the one fatty acid cover considerable area at the water-fat interface. These emulsifiers are particularly well suited for cake making.

CHANGES EFFECTED IN FATS BY HEAT

Polymerization

Heating fats causes three possible basic changes in fats: polymerization, oxidation, and hydrolysis. Polymerization is the formation of larger fat molecules through condensation of simple fat molecules. This increase in the molecular weight of a fat can occur at any of the temperatures to which fat would be subjected for culinary purposes. One manifestation of polymerization is an increase in the viscosity of the fat. Nutritive value is impaired when polymerization occurs.

Oxidation

Oxidation, a chemical change leading to rancidity in fats, is greatly accelerated at the high temperatures used for frying foods. The length of time the fat is exposed to heat and oxygen determines in large part the nutritive value of the fat. Oxidation is considered in greater detail in the section on oxidative rancidity. The addition of antioxidants to the cooking fat is an aid in retarding oxidation, but the antioxidant properties of some substances are rapidly lost at elevated temperatures. The ability of an antioxidant to retain its unique properties during heating is termed its carry-through property.

Hydrolysis

Acrolein formation. Hydrolysis, the reaction of water and fat to form free fatty acids and glycerol, occurs when hot fats are used to fry food. Subsequently, additional heating causes smoking as free glycerol breaks down to the volatile, eye-irritating compound called acrolein. Changes accompanying acrolein formation include foaming of the fat, darkening of the color, and gradual development of a strong flavor. The hydrolysis of the fat and the subsequent dehydration of the glycerol may be illustrated by the following equations.

$$\begin{matrix} H & O \\ H-\overset{|}{C}-O-\overset{\parallel}{C}-R \\ & O \\ H-\overset{|}{C}-O-\overset{\parallel}{C}-R \ + \ 3H_2O \ \xrightarrow{\Delta} \\ & O \\ H-\overset{|}{C}-O-\overset{\parallel}{C}-R \end{matrix} \qquad \begin{matrix} H \\ H-\overset{|}{C}-OH \\ H-\overset{|}{C}-OH \ + \ 3R-C \overset{\displaystyle O}{\underset{\displaystyle OH}{}} \\ H-\overset{|}{C}-OH \\ H \end{matrix}$$

Fat Glycerol Free fatty acids

$$\begin{matrix} H \\ H-\overset{|}{C}-OH \\ H-\overset{|}{C}-OH \ \xrightarrow[\Delta]{(-H_2O)} \\ H-\overset{|}{C}-OH \\ H \end{matrix} \qquad \begin{matrix} H \\ \overset{|}{C}-H \\ \parallel \\ \overset{|}{C}-H \\ H-C=O \end{matrix}$$

Glycerol Acrolein

Smoke Point. The temperature at which fat begins to smoke is called the smoke point of the fat. With prolonged heating or higher temperatures more acrolein is produced and the smoke point of the fat is progressively decreased. Because of the undesirable characteristics that develop in a fat that smokes at the temperature needed for frying, it is imperative that a fat with a satisfactorily high smoke point be selected for frying. The use of a superglycerinated shortening (a shortening with a high monoglyceride content) provides a graphic illustration. Heating of superglycerinated fats results in a rapid breakdown of the monoglycerides and an accompanying reduction in the smoke point. It is hypothesized that this effect of superglycerinated fats may be explained by the fact that it is less difficult to remove the one fatty acid of a monoglyceride than it is to remove all three fatty acids on a triglyceride to free glycerol for ultimate acrolein production.

The selection of an appropriate shortening or oil for frying is only one means of controlling the smoke point. Other factors that help to prevent smoking during frying in shallow or deep fat are: the frequent use of fresh fat, the use of recommended frying temperatures rather than overheating the fat, removal of fragments of food from the fat, and reducing the surface area. The presence or absence of antioxidants does not alter the smoke point.

RANCIDITY AND ANTIOXIDANTS

Rancidity

Rancidity is the presence of an undesirable odor or flavor caused by the oxidation or hydrolysis of fats. In hydrogenated fats a preliminary change called reversion causes highly unsaturated fats to develop a slightly fishy flavor before true rancidity occurs. Actual rancidity is classified as oxidative or hydrolytic.

Oxidative Rancidity. Oxidative rancidity begins with the removal of a hydrogen atom from a point of unsaturation in a fatty acid and the subsequent addition of oxygen. Heat and light can provide the energy needed for this to proceed, but they are not necessary to continue the oxidation of fat once the reaction is initiated, that is, the reaction is autocatalytic. The short-chain fatty acids which are the ultimate products of the oxidation reaction are largely responsible for the objectionable flavors and odors characteristic of rancid fats. Metals such as copper, iron, and nickel catalyze oxidation reactions so that less heat and/or light is needed for the reactions to proceed. Hematin, an iron-containing substance in meat, serves as a catalyst for oxidative reactions in the fatty tissues of meat. So little energy is required for this reaction that even freezing does not completely halt the process. This type of oxidative rancidity is important when meat is stored. Lipoxidases, enzymes found in vegetables, also can cause oxidative rancidity by catalyzing oxidation of particular triglycerides and/or unsaturated fatty acids. Very little energy is needed for lipoxidases to work, but freezing halts this type of oxidative change.

Oxidative rancidity is curtailed by hydrogenation of unsaturated fats, the addition of antioxidants and synergists, storage at a low, relatively uniform temperature away from light, elimination of any contact with catalytic metals, and careful processing.

Hydrolytic Rancidity. Hydrolytic rancidity is the reaction whereby water effects a splitting of the fatty acids from the glycerol portion of the fat molecule. Such reactions are catalyzed by lipases (enzymes that act on fats) and certain other enzymes.

Enzymatic reactions are slowed by cold temperatures, but the exact temperatures needed to adequately slow the reaction rates of particular enzymes vary with different species. In liver, hydrolytic rancidity develops rapidly at 37°C, but at −10°C the enzymes needed for the reaction are less effective and the changes proceed very slowly. In contrast, poor flavor can be caused in fish by hydrolytic changes even in storage at −14°C, but storage at −22°C greatly retards these reactions.

The presence of water naturally encourages hydrolytic rancidity, but this type of rancidity can occur even at the moisture level of dehydrated foods. When hydrolysis produces free fatty acids with a chain length of twelve or fewer carbons, a rancid flavor is apparent.

Antioxidants

Role in Fats. Antioxidants are either naturally occurring substances or additives that help to minimize the development of oxidative rancidity in fats. Some antioxidants retard oxidation by donating hydrogen to an unsaturated fatty acid and thus prevent the formation of the compounds capable of adding oxygen. Others prevent metals from catalyzing the oxidation reaction.

Natural Antioxidants. The various tocopherols naturally occurring in plant oils are useful antioxidants. Delta (δ) tocopherol is the most effective antioxidant whereas alpha (α) tocopherol, the most effective vitamin form, is the least active antioxidant of this group.

Several organic compounds, including some amino acids and phenols, have valuable antioxidant properties. Citric acid retards oxidative rancidity by combining with iron and nickel, and ascorbic acid sequesters (ties up) copper. Ascorbic acid, an antioxidant used in many foods, is difficult to incorporate into shortenings so is not frequently used in fats.

Altering the body-fat composition of animals by changing dietary intake is one means of controlling rancidity in meat, for nonruminants will deposit fat of varying degrees of saturation, depending on the ration fed. It is also possible to feed antioxidants and cause some of them to be deposited in the fat of nonruminants, but the practicality of the technique is questionable.

Technological Applications. The value of the various compounds as antioxidants is based on their promotion of shelf life of fats, their carry-through ability if the fats are to be heated, and the possible toxic effect they might have on humans. Certain additive antioxidants have been approved by the U.S. Government (Food and Drug Administration) and are presently widely used.

Frequently a synergist is added to a fat in addition to the primary antioxidant. Synergists are compounds that alone may have little antioxidant value, but when added to an antioxidant will enhance the antioxidant ability above that of either substance alone. Propyl gallate is an effective synergist with butylated hydroxyanisole (BHA), for it reduces BHA and thus extends or prolongs its antioxidative action.

Studies have shown that the levels of antioxidants and synergists are critical. At a level exceeding the optimum, the antioxidant action of a compound may suddenly be reversed to that of a prooxidant and hasten rancidity.

Butylated hydroxyanisole, when used in concentrations above 0.2 percent, has good carry-through properties during heating. It is an effective primary antioxidant and is particularly effective when propyl gallate is added as a synergist with it to increase shelf life. Citric acid, butylated hydroxyanisole, and propyl gallate are a common and highly effective antioxidant combination used in cereals, olives, nuts, meat pies, lard, and other shortenings. Butylated hydroxyanisole and butylated hydroxytoluene (BHT) are also a useful team. Butylated hydroxyanisole and propyl gallate are somewhat more effective than butylated hydroxytoluene combined with propyl gallate. Propyl gallate has poor carry-through properties so it is more effective if added after all heat processing is completed. Nordihydroguaiaretic acid (NDGA) has poor carry-through properties, but is useful for increasing the shelf life of fat-containing foods when added after heating is completed. Development of rancidity in some instances may be controlled effectively by coating packaging materials with a suitable antioxidant.

SUMMARY

Fats are the class of food composed of the various fatty acid esters of glycerol. The melting point, plasticity, and crystalline form of a fat are important factors in determining the suitability of a fat for a particular use. Through research efforts it is now possible to modify natural fats to improve their characteristics for various culinary purposes.

Deteriorative changes in fat, through both storage and heating, present problems. During storage, fats may undergo changes in their crystal form to a less desirable crystal size. Rancidity may also develop and impair the flavor and odor of the fat. Undesirable changes during heating include polymerization, oxidation, and hydrolysis. Various antioxidants and synergists presently are used to prolong the useful life of a fat.

BIBLIOGRAPHY

Baur, F. J. Acetin fats, I. Products made from mixed acetin fats. *J. Am. Oil Chem. Soc. 31:* 147–151. 1954.

Carlin, G. T., R. P. Hopper, and B. P. Rockwood. Some factors affecting the decomposition of frying fats. *Food Tech. 8:* 161–165. 1954.

Deuel, H. J. *The lipids,* Vol. I, *Chemistry.* Interscience Publishers, Inc., New York, N.Y. 1951.

Dugan, L. R. Development and inhibition of oxidative rancidity in foods. *Food Tech. 15:* 10–18. 1961.

Feuge, R. O. Aceto-glycerides—new fat products of potential value to the food industry. *Food Tech. 9:* 314–318. 1955.

Hawley, H. K., and G. W. Holman. Directed interesterification as a new processing tool for lard. *J. Am. Oil Chem. Soc. 33:* 29–35. 1956.

Hilditch, T. P., and P. N. Williams. *The Chemical Constitution of Natural Fats,* 4th ed., Wiley, New York, N.Y. 1964.

Hoerr, C. W., and D. F. Waugh. Some physical characteristics of rearranged lard. *J. Am. Oil Chem. Soc. 32:* 37–41. 1955.

Hoerr, C. W. Morphology of fats, oils, and shortenings. *J. Am. Oil Chem. Soc. 37:* 539–546. 1960.

Hoerr, C. W. X-ray diffraction of fats. *J. Am. Oil Chem. Soc. 41,* 7: 4, 22, 32, 34. 1964.

Hornstein, L. R., F. B. King, and F. Benedict. Comparative shortening value of some commercial fats. *Food Res. 8:* 1–12. 1943.

Kraybill, H. R., and L. R. Dugan, Jr. Antioxidants: new developments for food use. *J. Agr. Food Chem. 2:* 81–84. 1954.

Noble, I. T., H. McLaughlin, and E. G. Halliday. Factors influencing the apparent shortening value of a fat. *Cereal Chem. 11:* 343–346. 1934.

Perkins, E. G. Nutritional and chemical changes occurring in heated fats. *Food Tech. 14:* 508–514. 1960.

Privett, O. S., and F. W. Quackenbush. The relation of synergist to antioxidant in fats. *J. Am. Oil Chem. Soc. 31:* 321–323. 1954.

Sair, L., and L. A. Hall. The use of antioxidants in deep fat frying. *Food Tech. 5:* 69–73. 1951.

Sanders, J. H. Processing of food fats. *Food Tech. 13:* 41–45. 1959.

SUGGESTIONS FOR STUDY

1. Heat butter in a small pan. Note the temperature at which it smokes. Repeat this procedure using other types of fats and oils. Which fat would be best for deep fat frying?
2. What factors influence the fluidity of a fat?
3. What is the practical significance of the information that a fat can exist, under varying conditions, in as many as four different crystal forms?
4. What changes occur in a fat during prolonged heating?
5. From the consumer's viewpoint, why is it important that antioxidants be included in some food products?

CHAPTER 20

Proteins

Proteins are unique among organic compounds in foods because they contain nitrogen as well as carbon, hydrogen, and oxygen. Plant foods, with the exception of legumes, contain rather small amounts of proteins, but the animal tissues used as foods are excellent sources of them. Various qualities of the different proteins are utilized in the production of a wide variety of food products. For instance, the foaming quality of the proteins found in gelatin, milk, and eggs is important in producing light and airy products such as angel cakes, Bavarian cream, and whipped evaporated milk desserts. Under controlled conditions, some proteins are capable of forming gels, of aiding in the formation of emulsions, of binding water in food mixtures, and even of enzymatic activity. Milk proteins precipitate to provide the basis for cheese production, and the protein in wheat flour strengthens the cell walls of baked products. This wide range of action in food mixtures makes proteins extremely important in food preparation. The behavior of these compounds must be considered carefully in developing procedures for preparing food products containing significant amounts of protein-containing ingredients.

In some instances, as when invertase is added to a candy or papain is used to tenderize meats, the enzyme must not be heated at all or the enzymatic activity will be lost because of changes occurring in the enzyme structure. In other cases, the protein must be heated gently to inactivate the enzyme and prevent its normal action. An example of this situation is found when pineapple is added to gelatin. Fresh pineapple will prevent gelation of the mixture because of the proteolytic action of its enzyme, bromelin, on the gelatin molecules. However, the heating that is done during the canning of pineapple modifies the configuration of the bromelin and destroys its proteolytic ability.

Heating modifies the characteristics of many foods because of the changes in protein molecules that occur during the cooking process. Muscle proteins in meat undergo configurational changes that make the meat somewhat less tender. On the other hand, collagenous connective tissue slowly converts to gelatin, thus resulting in a contradictory tenderizing effect. When eggs are heated, their proteins become less soluble, and the flow properties of both the egg and the yolk gradually are lost. Gluten, the protein complex that is developed during the mixing of flour-containing batters and doughs, undergoes a transformation from a highly extensible material to one that is rigid. These changes in protein can be used to advantage when heating conditions are controlled properly.

The modification of protein caused by heating changes the spatial configuration of protein molecules. Prior to heating, the protein is referred to as native protein because it has not been modified from the way it occurred naturally. As a result of heating, the properties of the molecule are changed, and the protein is then referred to as a denatured protein. Solubility and flow properties are modified significantly in denatured proteins. Denaturation of proteins also can be caused during food preparation as a result of beating, as is the case when egg whites are beaten to a foam. These changes are more meaningful when considered in the context of the chemical composition and physical shape of protein molecules.

COMPOSITION OF PROTEINS

Proteins are composed of varying numbers of amino acids linked together to form very large molecules. Amino acids are organic acids containing an amino group ($-NH_2$) on the carbon adjacent to the acid radical ($-COOH$). The basic formula for an amino acid, R representing the variable remaining portion of the molecule, is:

$$R-\underset{\underset{NH_2}{|}}{C}-C\overset{\displaystyle O}{\underset{\displaystyle OH}{\diagup}}$$

Twenty amino acids commonly occur in proteins, and it is from this group that various combinations of amino acids are united to form the proteins occurring in plants and animals. Different proteins vary greatly in the number of amino acids constituting a molecule, hence their molecular weights show a wide variation. The molecules of a particular protein, however, will have the same basic composition. It has also been observed that there often is a definite repeating pattern in the sequence and/or occurrence of certain amino acids along the backbone chain of a protein molecule.

Certain characteristics of amino acids are of great significance in determining the behavior of proteins in food preparation. The amino acids are amphoteric in dispersions, that is, they may behave both as acids or as bases, depending on the environmental circumstance. In strong acids, the carboxyl group will ionize to $-COO^-$; in strong alkalis, the amino group ionizes to $-NH_3^+$. In the pH range common in foods, pH 4 to 9, both groups will ionize and form zwitterions. These dipolar ions have both a positive and a negative charge.

The R group is the part of the amino acid responsible for differing characteristics of the molecule. Some amino acids possess R groups that are primarily short carbon chains, some R groups contain sulfur, others are characterized by the possession of a carboxyl group, an amide, or a cyclic structure. Since each of these R groups requires some space and introduces the potential for attraction or repulsion on the basis of charge, the influence of an R group on the protein molecule actually is much greater than one might conclude from simply seeing an R represented in a formula. A cyclic structure, such as is found in tryptophan (Table 20.1), introduces much greater impedance to convolutions in a protein molecule than is caused by the single atom of hydrogen which is the R group for glycine. The sulfur atoms found in the R groups of cysteine, cystine, and methionine introduce the possibility for bonding between amino acids, thus adding a new dimension to the potential for modifying protein configuration. R groups composed of carbon and hydrogen are nonpolar and influence the shape of protein molecules because of their repulsion from water. In contrast, oxygen-containing amino acid R groups are attracted to water.

Table 20.1 R Groups of Selected Amino Acids

Name	Formula of R Group
Glycine	$-H$
Alanine	$-CH_3$
Phenylalanine	$-CH_2-$
Cystine	$-CH_2-S$
	$\quad\quad\;\;\mid$
	$-CH_2-S$
Methionine	$-CH_2-CH_2-S-CH_3$
Lysine	$-CH_2-CH_2-CH_2-CH_2-NH_2$
Histidine	$-CH_2-C{=}CH$
Tryptophan	

STRUCTURE OF PROTEINS

Proteins are highly complicated molecules in which intramolecular relationships are important in determining spatial conformation. The organization of all proteins includes a chemical linking of the amino acids, known as the primary structure. In addition, proteins form a secondary structure; a further complication is found in proteins capable of forming a tertiary structure and in those very large molecules that have a quaternary structure. An appreciation of these structures will make the changes occurring in proteins during food preparation considerably more comprehensible.

Primary Structure

Amino acids are linked by a peptide linkage to form the basic backbone chain of all protein molecules. To form this backbone, the carboxyl group of one amino acid is covalently bonded to the amino group of another amino acid with the loss of a molecule of water.

When many amino acids have been linked together in sequence via the formation of peptide linkages, a protein molecule is formed. The repeating backbone chain forms a strong chain because of the relative strength of covalent bonds that comprise the chain. Actually, steric considerations cause the backbone chain to exist in a zigzag fashion, as shown below.

Basic backbone chain of proteins

This chain is the same in all proteins; specific proteins are the result of the various R groups of the amino acids that protrude from the chain. The basic backbone chain formed by uniting the amino acids often is referred to as the primary structure of a protein. This primary structure of protein is very resistant to chemical change, although enzymes are capable of splitting the chain to form smaller peptide units or even to release individual amino acids.

Secondary Structure

Most proteins in foods assume a helical form, which is comparable to a slightly extended, coiled spring (Figure 20.1). This coiled configuration is found in many fibrous and also in globular proteins. Pauling and Corey

FIGURE 20.1   Secondary structure of protein is oriented into a helical configuration.

discovered that the backbone of amino acids did not occur in nature as an extended chain but, instead, assumed a coiled form. The backbone chain is held into the coiled shape by hydrogen bonding between the hydrogen (attached to nitrogen in the backbone chain) of one amino acid and the oxygen of the carbonyl (—C=O) of the fourth amino acid down the chain. This hydrogen bonding occurs along the coiled chain at regular intervals, thus giving some stability to the coiled structure. In the coiled secondary structure, the energy requirements are at a minimum. The various R groups generally are accommodated by only minor perturbations of the coiled α-helix. The usual arrangement of the α-helix is in a right-handed helix, the more stable form. Hydrogen bonding, disulfide bridges, and van der Waal's forces are the forces that hold the primary structure in the coiled secondary structure. The additional bonding made possible by attractive forces between R groups lends increased stability to the coiled orientation.

Some fibrous proteins assume a pleated sheet structure in which the rather tightly coiled α-helix is distinctly extended into a zig-zag extension known as the β-conformation. The pleated sheet structure is of importance in wool and hair and may be characterized as having some degree of stretch.

Collagen is still different than these other forms that may be assumed to form secondary structures. This connective tissue protein lacks the highly extensible quality that may be achieved in the other types of secondary structure. The frequent repetition of proline and hydroxyproline in the backbone chain of collagen impedes the formation of the anticipated α-helix. This disruption of the helical structure is explained by looking at the structure of these amino acids.

Proline

Hydrozyproline

Since the linkage of these two amino acids must involve the restricted ring structure, the backbone chain is more rigid and less able to assume the coiled structure required in the α-helix.

Tertiary Structure

In some proteins the helically coiled backbone chain is contorted into various shapes and held by weak bonding forces. This tertiary structure can be illustrated effectively by twisting and squeezing the spiral binding from a notebook into random shapes.

In the tertiary configuration, many of the R groups of the component amino acids are folded into the inner portion of the molecule and thus are not available to interact or influence the behavior of the individual protein molecule in relation to any other molecules in a dispersion. In the native state, protein molecules will tend to bend or convolute at points of minimum stability of the α-helix. For example, a proline moiety in the chain generally results in a distinct bend in the backbone chain. When sulfur-containing residues approach each other, there will be disulfide bonding which will help to stabilize the tertiary structure. Many of the hydrophobic R groups will be trapped within the molecule. This tertiary structure may represent some areas of stress where bulkiness of an R group is accommodated with difficulty. Such points may be vulnerable to change with only a minimal change in environmental conditions, such as heating. The changes that occur in the spatial configuration of the tertiary structure during food preparation are of great importance in modifying the qualities of foods containing globular proteins.

FIGURE 20.2 Tertiary structure of globular proteins is a distortion and twisting of the helically-coiled protein molecules.

Quaternary Structure

Very large proteins (molecular weights exceeding 50,000) may consist of more than one peptide chain. The orientation and association between these peptide chains that results in the final configuration of a molecule such as hemoglobin is known as the quaternary structure. This structure, as is true also in the secondary and tertiary structures, is formed by hydrogen and other secondary bonding forces.

TYPES OF PROTEINS

Fibrous Proteins

The two main classifications of pure proteins, based on their structural shape, are fibrous and globular proteins. Fibrous proteins are elongated protein molecules existing in the helical structure in nature. Fibroin in silk, keratin in hair, and fibrinogen in blood are characteristic examples of this group. Atypical examples of the fibrous proteins in food are collagen and gelatin.

Globular Proteins

The globular proteins are complex ellipsoidal structures that present many problems to scientists attempting to elucidate the structures. Portions of the globular proteins exist in the helical form, but other areas of the molecule are straight, perhaps due to strain where the chain bends back sharply on itself; in other areas there are complex convolutions of the amino acid chain. The myoglobin molecule, for example, has been shown to be approximately 70 percent in the helical configuration and 30 percent in a straight chain; approximately half of the molecule of zein, a protein found in corn, exists in the helical structure; and it happens that gluten from wheat flour is only about 35 percent helical.

REACTIONS OF PROTEINS

Denaturation

Denaturation is the process wherein a native protein molecule is changed in shape without cleaving the backbone chain. Generally denaturation is characterized as a two-step sequence; first, an unfolding of the tertiary structure of the protein molecule occurs as some of the hydrogen and other weaker bonds are broken by the addition of energy; next there is a clumping together or agglomeration of several molecules. The unfolding in the first step changes some of the properties of the protein, for the increased surface area exposes many of the reactive groups of the amino acids which were previously trapped within the molecule and hence were unavailable for reactions. It is suggested that the decreased solubility of proteins is due to the exposure of hydrophobic groups which had previously been hidden within the molecule.

The actual degree of denaturation may vary from a very slight alteration to a major change in the structural outline of the molecule. Some pro-

FIGURE 20.3   Protein from soybeans can be modified and extruded into fibers used to develop textured protein foods.

teins undergo reversible denaturation, but the majority of the denaturation reactions are permanent.

In the home, heat is the most common means of effecting denaturation. A small increase in the temperature of a protein at certain critical temperature ranges greatly accelerates the rate of denaturation, for the heat provides the energy needed to break the bonds that hold the protein in the helical shape.

Freezing also causes denaturation of protein, particularly at freezing temperatures of −15°C to 0°C. One explanation for this effect of freezing is that the ice crystals rupture the cell membranes and thus expose protein surfaces to possible denaturation. It is also possible that the dehydration which can occur in frozen foods causes denaturation as the bound water is removed from the food.

Both commercially and in the home, denaturation often occurs when protein films are formed, as when egg whites are beaten. Denaturation, in this instance, is due to the mechanical agitation and the greatly increased surface area.

The salts naturally occurring in milk and other foods are important in denaturation reactions for they may cause some weakening of the forces maintaining the secondary and tertiary structure of the protein molecules. Dilute solutions of proteins are somewhat more subject to denaturation than are very concentrated solutions, seemingly because more of the surface of the protein is subject to surface reactions in the dilute concentration. Ultraviolet light, extremely high pressure, and ultrasonic waves are other means used by industry to denature proteins.

It is interesting that some water must be present to aid in the breaking of the secondary bonds so that denaturation may occur. Commercially dehydrated foods, however, have sufficient water retained in them to enable denaturation to take place.

Coagulation is the process in which partially denatured protein molecules aggregate and form a precipitate or a gel. The changes that an egg undergoes during heating are generally considered to be twofold: the assumption of an altered shape by the protein molecule, and second, the coagulation or precipitation of masses of protein molecules.

Hydrolysis

Hydrolysis is a cleavage of the backbone chain of a protein molecule into shorter chains with the uptake of a molecule of water. Solubility of protein is increased with hydrolysis. Conversely, the thickening power is reduced. Acid hydrolysis occurs when an acid and a protein are mixed together, but an increase in temperature greatly accelerates the breakdown. This type of reaction occurs when meat is simmered with an acidic liquid such as lemon juice or tomato. Enzymatic hydrolysis of proteins is utilized in the meat industry today both in the form of meat tenderizers for home use and as an injection into the live animal just before slaughter.

Browning Reaction

The Maillard or browning reaction is a change in which the amino $(-NH_2)$ group from a protein reacts with the aldehyde $\left(-C\diagup^{O}_{\diagdown H}\right)$ group of a sugar to produce a brown color in the food product. This browning may not be objectionable in stored baked products for the color change may be only slightly noticeable in comparison with the already browned crust. Many commercial products including various mixes, however, have been plagued by this reaction when stored for a long period of time. Browning at room temperature is a lengthy process, but the change is drastically accelerated at simmering temperatures.

During normal periods of storage in the home, this browning does not occur, but the reaction may be observed by heating a can of sweetened condensed milk in a boiling water bath for at least an hour. The milk becomes distinctly caramel-like in appearance because of the Maillard reaction.

Reactions with Metals

A reaction that may be troublesome is the production of a pink color caused by the reaction of the exposed iron in a worn egg beater with conalbumin, an egg-white protein. There is also a tendency for ferrous sulfide to form when the sulfur present in egg yolks comes in contact with a cast-iron skillet.

Copper oxides may form toxic complexes with proteins, thus suggesting the need to discourage the excessive use of uncoated copper utensils in the kitchen.

Isoelectric Point

Proteins, like amino acids, are amphoteric, that is, they have the ability to carry either a negative or a positive charge under certain conditions. When the protein possesses neither a positive nor a negative charge, the molecule is said to be at its isoelectric point. At this pH the protein will not migrate in an electric field because of its neutral state. The pH at which this occurs is different for the various proteins. The isoelectric point of a protein is of significance in food preparation, since the solubility of proteins is notably reduced when the pH of the medium is at or near the isoelectric point. A familiar example of this phenomenon is the curdling or flocculation that occurs when milk becomes sufficiently acidic to approach the isoelectric point of casein.

SUMMARY

Proteins are highly organized and complex molecules composed of amino acids linked together by peptide linkages. This organization forms the primary structure. The covalent bonding that is the basis of the primary structure results in molecules that are resistant to changes during food preparation, although some enzymes can cleave these chains at the peptide linkages. The secondary structure is an α-helix and is held in this relatively unstrained orientation by hydrogen bonding and sometimes by other secondary bonding forces. Some fibrous proteins are spatially arranged in pleated sheets in which the helical configuration is elongated and pleated. Globular proteins attain their final natural spatial arrangement in the tertiary structure, a seemingly disorganized twisting and bunching of the secondary structure. Some very large proteins are made up of more than one peptide fragment, and these segments are organized into a macromolecule in their quaternary structure.

Changes in proteins occur during food preparation in a number of instances. Enzymes may be used to cleave the protein molecules. The pH of a medium may be changed to bring the protein in a food closer to the iso-electric point, thus causing clotting of the protein as occurs in cheese making. Heat and agitation are means used to bring about denaturation of proteins in foods. Denaturation is a physical change; the change accomplished by enzymatic hydrolysis or acid hydrolysis is a chemical change. Proteins and sugars react together in a browning (Maillard) reaction when they are stored together in mixes for long periods of time. The same browning can be seen in sweetened condensed milk that has been stored for an extended length of time or heated for several hours. Metals also may cause discoloration because of interactions with proteins.

BIBLIOGRAPHY

Crick, F. H. C., and J. C. Kendrew. X-ray analysis and protein structure. *Adv. Protein Chem. 12*:133–214. 1957.

Doty, P. Proteins. *Sci. Am. 197*:173–184. 1957.

Edsall, J. T. Structure of proteins. *Nature 170*:53–55. 1952.

Feeney, R. E., and R. M. Hill. Protein chemistry and food research. *Adv. Food Res. 10*:23–33. 1960.

Fox, S. W., and J. F. Foster. *Introduction to Protein Chemistry*. Wiley, New York, N. Y. 1957.

Grass, J. Collagen. *Sci. Am. 204*, 5:121–130. 1961.

Kendrew, J. C. et al. A three-dimensional model of the myoglobin molecule obtained by X-ray analysis. *Nature 181*:662–666. 1958.

Kretschmer, C. B. Infrared spectroscopy and optical rotary dispersion of zein, wheat gluten and gliadin. *J. Phys. Chem. 61*:1627–1631. 1957.

Lehninger, A. L. *Biochemistry*. Worth. New York, N. Y. 1970.

Low, B. The structure and configuration of amino acids, peptides, and proteins. In *The Proteins,* ed. by H. Neurath, and K. Bailey. Academic Press, New York, N. Y. 1953.

Low, B., and J. T. Edsall. Aspects of protein structure. In *Currents in Biochemical Research,* ed. by D. E. Green, Interscience Publishers, Inc., New York, N. Y. 1956.

Meyer, L. H. *Introductory Chemistry,* 2nd ed. Macmillan, New York, N. Y. 1959.

Paul, P. and H. Palmer. *Food Theory and Applications*. Wiley. New York, N. Y. 1972.

Pauling, L., R. B. Corey, and H. R. Branson. The structure of proteins. *Proc. Nat. Acad. Sci. 37*:205–211. 1951.

Pauling, L., R. B. Corey, and R. Haywood. The structure of protein molecules. *Sci. Am. 191*:51–59. 1954.

Pauling, L. The stochastic method and the structure of proteins. *Am. Sci. 43*:285–297. 1955.

Ramachandran, G. N. and V. Sasisekharan. Conformation of polypeptides and proteins. *Adv. Protein Chem. 23*:283. 1968.

Randall, J. T., R. D. B. Fraser, S. Jackson, A. V. W. Martin, and A. C. T. North. Aspects of collagen structure. *Nature 169*:1029–1033. 1952.

Stein, W. H., and S. Moore. The structure of protein. *Sci. Am. 204,* 2:91–95. 1961.

Szent-Gyorgyi, A. G. Role of proline in polypeptide chain configuration. *Science 126*:697–698. 1957.

SUGGESTIONS FOR STUDY

1. Diagram the *(a)* primary, *(b)* secondary, *(c)* tertiary structure of a protein.
2. Explain the change in protein structure caused by beating egg whites with an egg beater.
3. Why does heat cause denaturation of protein?
4. What changes occur in protein as a result of hydrolysis?

APPENDIX A

Nutritive Values
of the Edible
Part of Foods

[1]From *Home and Garden Bulletin No. 72*. U.S.D.A. Washington, D.C. Revised 1971.

MILK, CHEESE, CREAM, IMITATION CREAM; RELATED PRODUCTS

	Food, Approximate Measure, and Weight (in Grams)	Water (%)	Food Energy (kcal)	Protein (g)	Fat (g)	Fatty Acids Saturated (total) (g)	Unsaturated Oleic (g)	Unsaturated Linoleic (g)	Carbohydrate (g)	Calcium (mg)	Iron (mg)	Vitamin A value (I.U.)	Thiamin (mg)	Riboflavin (mg)	Niacin (mg)	Ascorbic acid (mg)
	Milk:															
	Fluid:															
1	Whole, 3.5% fat 1 cup 244	87	160	9	9	5	3	Trace	12	288	0.1	350	0.07	0.41	0.2	2
2	Nonfat (skim) 1 cup 245	90	90	9	Trace	—	—	—	12	296	.1	10	.09	.44	.2	2
3	Partly skimmed, 2% nonfat milk solids added 1 cup 246	87	145	10	5	3	2	Trace	15	352	.1	200	.10	.52	.2	2
	Canned, concentrated, undiluted:															
4	Evaporated, unsweetened 1 cup 252	74	345	18	20	11	7	1	24	635	.3	810	.10	.86	.5	3
5	Condensed, sweetened 1 cup 306	27	980	25	27	15	9	1	166	802	.3	1100	.24	1.16	.6	3
	Dry, nonfat instant:															
6	Low-density (1 1/3 cups needed for reconstitution to 1 qt.) 1 cup 68	4	245	24	Trace	—	—	—	35	879	.4	20[1]	.24	1.21	.6	5
7	High-density (7/8 cup needed for reconstitution to 1 qt.) 1 cup 104	4	375	37	1	—	—	—	54	1345	.6	30[1]	.36	1.85	.9	7
	Buttermilk:															
8	Fluid, cultured, made from skim milk 1 cup 245	90	90	9	Trace	—	—	—	12	296	.1	10	.10	.44	.2	2
9	Dried, packaged 1 cup 120	3	465	41	6	3	2	Trace	60	1498	.7	260	.31	2.06	1.1	—
	Cheese:															
	Natural:															
	Blue or Roquefort type:															
10	Ounce 1 oz. 28	40	105	6	9	5	3	Trace	1	89	.1	350	.01	.17	.3	0
11	Cubic inch 1 cu. in. 17	40	65	4	5	3	2	Trace	Trace	54	.1	210	.01	.11	.2	0
12	Camembert, packaged in 4-oz. pkg. with 3 wedges per pkg. 1 wedge 38	52	115	7	9	5	3	Trace	1	40	.2	380	.02	.29	.3	0

1. Value applies to unfortified product; value for fortified low-density product would be 1500 I.U., and the fortified high-density product would be 2290 I.U.

MILK, CHEESE, CREAM, IMITATION CREAM; RELATED PRODUCTS—Con.

	Food, Approximate Measure, and Weight (in Grams)		Water (%)	Food Energy (kcal)	Protein (g)	Fat (g)	Fatty Acids			Carbohydrate (g)	Calcium (mg)	Iron (mg)	Vitamin A value (I.U.)	Thiamin (mg)	Riboflavin (mg)	Niacin (mg)	Ascorbic acid (mg)
							Saturated (total) (g)	Unsaturated Oleic (g)	Linoleic (g)								
	Cheese—Continued																
	Cheddar:																
13	Ounce	1 oz.	28	37	115	7	9	5	3	Trace	1	213	0.3	370	0.01	0.13	Trace	0
14	Cubic inch	1 cu. in.	17	37	70	4	6	3	2	Trace	Trace	129	.2	230	.01	.08	Trace	0
	Cottage, large or small curd:																
	Creamed:																
15	Package of 12-oz. net wt.	1 pkg.	340	78	360	46	14	8	5	Trace	10	320	1.0	580	.10	.85	0.3	0
16	Cup, curd pressed down.	1 cup	245	78	260	33	10	6	3	Trace	7	230	.7	420	.07	.61	.2	0
	Uncreamed:																
17	Package of 12-oz., net wt.	1 pkg.	340	79	290	58	1	1	Trace	Trace	9	306	1.4	30	.10	.95	.3	0
18	Cup, curd pressed down.	1 cup	200	79	170	34	1	Trace	Trace	Trace	5	180	.8	20	.06	.56	.2	0
	Cream:																
19	Package of 8-oz., net wt.	1 pkg.	227	51	850	18	86	48	28	3	5	141	.5	3500	.05	.54	.2	0
20	Package of 3-oz., net wt.	1 pkg.	85	51	320	7	32	18	11	1	2	53	.2	1310	.02	.20	.1	0
21	Cubic inch	1 cu. in.	16	51	60	1	6	3	2	Trace	Trace	10	Trace	250	Trace	.04	Trace	0
	Parmesan, grated:																
22	Cup, pressed down	1 cup	140	17	655	60	43	24	14	1	5	1893	.7	1760	.03	1.22	.3	0
23	Tablespoon	1 tbsp.	5	17	25	2	2	1	Trace	Trace	Trace	68	Trace	60	Trace	.04	Trace	0
24	Ounce	1 oz.	28	17	130	12	9	5	3	Trace	1	383	.1	360	.01	.25	.1	0
	Swiss:																
25	Ounce	1 oz.	28	39	105	8	8	4	3	Trace	1	262	.3	320	Trace	.11	Trace	0
26	Cubic inch	1 cu. in.	15	39	55	4	4	2	1	Trace	Trace	139	.1	170	Trace	.06	Trace	0
	Pasteurized processed cheese:																
	American:																
27	Ounce	1 oz.	28	40	105	7	9	5	3	Trace	1	198	.3	350	.01	.12	Trace	0
28	Cubic inch	1 cu. in.	18	40	65	4	5	3	2	Trace	Trace	122	.2	210	Trace	.07	Trace	0

	Measure	Weight (g)	Water (%)	Food energy (cal)	Protein (g)	Fat (g)	Saturated (g)	Oleic (g)	Linoleic (g)	Carbohydrate (g)	Calcium (mg)	Iron (mg)	Vitamin A (IU)	Thiamin (mg)	Riboflavin (mg)	Niacin (mg)	Ascorbic acid (mg)
Swiss:																	
29 Ounce	1 oz.	28	40	100	8	8	5	3	Trace	1	251	.3	310	Trace	.11	Trace	0
30 Cubic inch	1 cu. in.	18	40	65	5	5	3	2	Trace	Trace	159	.2	200	Trace	.07	Trace	0
Pasteurized process cheese food, American:																	
31 Tablespoon	1 tbsp.	14	43	45	3	3	1	1	Trace	1	80	.1	140	Trace	.08	Trace	0
32 Cubic inch	1 cu. in.	18	43	60	4	4	2	2	Trace	1	100	.1	170	Trace	.10	Trace	0
33 Pasteurized process cheese spread, American.	1 oz.	28	49	80	6	6	3	2	Trace	2	160	.2	250	Trace	.15	Trace	0
Cream:																	
34 Half-and-half (cream and milk).	1 cup	242	80	325	8	28	15	9	1	11	261	.1	1160	.07	.39	.1	2
35	1 tbsp.	15	80	20	1	2	1	1	Trace	1	16	Trace	70	Trace	.02	Trace	Trace
36 Light, coffee or table	1 cup	240	72	505	7	49	27	16	1	10	245	.1	2020	.07	.36	.1	2
37	1 tbsp.	15	72	30	Trace	3	2	1	Trace	1	15	Trace	130	Trace	.02	Trace	Trace
38 Sour	1 cup	230	72	485	7	47	26	16	1	10	235	.1	1930	.07	.35	.1	2
39	1 tbsp.	12	72	25	Trace	2	1	1	Trace	1	12	Trace	100	Trace	.02	Trace	Trace
40 Whipped topping (pressurized).	1 cup	60	62	155	2	14	8	5	Trace	6	67	—	570	—	.04	—	—
41	1 tbsp.	3	62	10	Trace	1	Trace	Trace	Trace	Trace	3	—	30	—	Trace	—	—
Whipping, unwhipped (volume about double when whipped):																	
42 Light	1 cup	239	62	715	6	75	41	25	2	9	203	.1	3060	.05	.29	.1	2
43	1 tbsp.	15	62	45	Trace	5	3	2	Trace	1	13	Trace	190	Trace	.02	Trace	Trace
44 Heavy	1 cup	238	57	840	5	90	50	30	3	7	179	.1	3670	.05	.26	.1	2
45	1 tbsp.	15	57	55	Trace	6	3	2	Trace	1	11	Trace	230	Trace	.02	Trace	Trace
Imitation cream products (made with vegetable fat):																	
Creamers:																	
46 Powdered	1 cup	94	2	505	4	33	31	1	Trace	52	21	.6	200[2]	—	—	Trace	—
47	1 tsp.	2	2	10	Trace	1	Trace	Trace	0	1	1	Trace	Trace[2]	—	—	—	—
48 Liquid (frozen)	1 cup	245	77	345	3	27	25	1	Trace	25	29	—	100[2]	0	0	—	—
49	1 tbsp.	15	77	20	Trace	2	1	Trace	0	2	2	—	10[2]	0	0	—	—
50 Sour dressing (imitation sour cream) made with nonfat dry milk.	1 cup	235	72	440	8	38	31	2	Trace	17	277	.1	10	.07	.38	.2	1
51	1 tbsp.	12	72	20	Trace	2	Trace	Trace	Trace	1	14	Trace	Trace	Trace	Trace	Trace	Trace

2. Contributed largely from beta-carotene used for coloring.

MILK, CHEESE, CREAM, IMITATION CREAM; RELATED PRODUCTS—Con.

	Food, Approximate Measure, and Weight (in Grams)		Water (%)	Food Energy (kcal)	Protein (g)	Fat (g)	Saturated (total) (g)	Unsaturated Oleic (g)	Unsaturated Linoleic (g)	Carbohydrate (g)	Calcium (mg)	Iron (mg)	Vitamin A value (I.U.)	Thiamin (mg)	Riboflavin (mg)	Niacin (mg)	Ascorbic acid (mg)
	Imitation cream products (made with vegetable fat):—Con.																
	Whipped topping:																
52	Pressurized	1 cup	70	61	190	1	17	15	Trace	0	9	5	—	340²	—	0	—	—
53		1 tbsp.	4	61	10	Trace	1	1	Trace	0	Trace	Trace	—	20²	—	0	—	—
54	Frozen	1 cup	75	52	230	1	20	18	Trace	0	15	5	—	560²	—	0	—	—
55		1 tbsp.	4	52	10	Trace	1	1	Trace	0	1	Trace	—	30²	—	0	—	—
56	Powdered, made with whole milk.	1 cup	75	58	175	3	12	10	Trace	Trace	15	62	Trace	330²	.02	.08	.1	Trace
57		1 tbsp.	4	58	10	Trace	1	1	Trace	Trace	1	3	Trace	20²	Trace	Trace	Trace	Trace
	Milk beverages:																
58	Cocoa, homemade	1 cup	250	79	245	10	12	7	4	Trace	27	295	1.0	400	.10	.45	.5	3
59	Chocolate-flavored drink made with skim milk and 2% added butterfat.	1 cup	250	83	190	8	6	3	2	Trace	27	270	.5	210	.10	.40	.3	3
	Malted milk:																
60	Dry powder, approx. 3 heaping teaspoons per ounce.	1 oz.	28	3	115	4	2	—	—	—	20	82	.6	290	.09	.15	.1	0
61	Beverage	1 cup	235	78	245	11	10	—	—	—	28	317	.7	590	.14	.49	.2	2
	Milk desserts:																
62	Custard, baked	1 cup	265	77	305	14	15	7	5	1	29	297	1.1	930	.11	.50	.3	1
	Ice cream:																
63	Regular (approx. 10% fat).	½ gal.	1064	63	2055	48	113	62	37	3	221	1553	.5	4680	.43	2.23	1.1	11
64		1 cup	133	63	255	6	14	8	5	Trace	28	194	.1	590	.05	.28	.1	1
65		3 fl. oz.	50	63	95	2	5	3	2	Trace	10	73	Trace	220	.02	.11	.1	1
66	Rich (approx. 16% fat).	½ gal.	1188	63	2635	31	191	105	63	6	214	927	.2	7840	.24	1.31	1.2	12
67		1 cup	148	63	330	4	24	13	8	1	27	115	Trace	980	.03	.16	.1	1

No.	Food, approximate measure	Measure	Grams	Water (%)	Food energy (cal)	Protein (g)	Fat (g)	Saturated (g)	Oleic (g)	Linoleic (g)	Carbohydrate (g)	Calcium (mg)	Iron (mg)	Vitamin A (IU)	Thiamin (mg)	Riboflavin (mg)	Niacin (mg)	Ascorbic acid (mg)
	Ice milk:																	
68	Hardened	½ gal	1048	67	1595	50	53	29	17	2	235	1635	1.0	2200[2]	.52	2.31	1.0	10
69		1 cup	131	67	200	6	7	4	2	Trace	29	204	.1	280	.07	.29	.1	1
70	Soft-serve	1 cup	175	67	265	8	9	5	3	Trace	39	273	.2	370	.09	.39	.2	2
	Yoghurt																	
71	Made from partially skimmed milk,	1 cup	245	89	125	8	4	2	1	1	13	294	.1	170	.10	.44	.2	2
72	Made from whole milk	1 cup	245	88	150	7	8	5	3	Trace	12	272	.1	340	.07	.39	.2	2
	EGGS																	
	Eggs, large, 24 ounces per dozen: Raw or cooked in shell or with nothing added:																	
73	Whole, without shell	1 egg	50	74	80	6	6	2	3	Trace	Trace	27	1.1	590	.05	.15	Trace	0
74	White of egg	1 white	33	88	15	4	Trace	—	—	—	Trace	3	Trace	0	Trace	.09	Trace	0
75	Yolk of egg	1 yolk	17	51	60	3	5	2	2	Trace	Trace	24	.9	580	.04	.07	Trace	0
76	Scrambled with milk and fat.	1 egg	64	72	110	7	8	3	3	Trace	1	51	1.1	690	.05	.18	Trace	0
	MEAT, POULTRY, FISH, SHELLFISH: RELATED PRODUCTS																	
77	Bacon, (20 slices per lb. raw), 2 slices broiled or fried, crisp.		15	8	90	5	8	3	4	1	1	2	.5	0	.08	.05	.8	—
	Beef[3] cooked: Cuts braised, simmered, or pot-roasted:																	
78	Lean and fat	3 ounces	85	53	245	23	16	8	7	Trace	0	10	2.9	30	.04	.18	3.5	—
79	Lean only	2.5 ounces	72	62	140	22	5	2	2	Trace	0	10	2.7	10	.04	.16	3.3	—
	Hamburger (ground beef), broiled:																	
80	Lean	3 ounces	85	60	185	23	10	5	4	Trace	0	10	3.0	20	.08	.20	5.1	—
81	Regular	3 ounces	85	54	245	21	17	8	8	Trace	0	9	2.7	30	.07	.18	4.6	—
	Roast, over-cooked, no liquid added: Relatively fat, such as rib:																	
82	Lean and fat	3 ounces	85	40	375	17	34	16	15	1	0	8	2.2	70	.05	.13	3.1	—
83	Lean only	1.8 ounces	51	57	125	14	7	3	3	Trace	0	6	1.8	10	.04	.11	2.6	—
	Relatively lean, such as heel of round:																	
84	Lean and fat	3 ounces	85	62	165	25	7	3	3	Trace	0	11	3.2	10	.06	.19	4.5	—
85	Lean only	2.7 ounces	78	65	125	24	3	1	1	Trace	0	10	3.0	Trace	.06	.18	4.3	—

2. Contributed largely from beta-carotene used for coloring.
3. Outer layer of fat on the cut was removed to within approximately ½-inch of the lean. Deposits of fat within the cut were not removed.

| | Food, Approximate Measure, and Weight (in Grams) | | Water (%) | Food Energy (kcal) | Protein (g) | Fat (g) | Fatty Acids | | | Carbohydrate (g) | Calcium (mg) | Iron (mg) | Vitamin A value (I.U.) | Thiamin (mg) | Riboflavin (mg) | Niacin (mg) | Ascorbic acid (mg) |
| | | | | | | | Saturated (total) (g) | Unsaturated | | | | | | | | | |
								Oleic (g)	Linoleic (g)								
	MEAT, POULTRY, FISH, SHELLFISH; RELATED PRODUCTS—Con.																
	Steak, broiled:																
	Relatively, fat, such as sirloin:																
86	Lean and fat	3 ounces	85	44	330	20	27	13	12	1	0	9	2.5	50	.05	.16	4.0	—
87	Lean only	2.0 ounces	56	59	115	18	4	2	2	Trace	0	7	2.2	10	.05	.14	3.6	—
	Relatively, lean, such as round:																
88	Lean and fat	3 ounces	85	55	220	24	13	6	6	Trace	0	10	3.0	20	.07	.19	4.8	—
89	Lean only	2.4 ounces	68	61	130	21	4	2	2	Trace	0	9	2.5	10	.06	.16	4.1	—
	Beef, canned:																
90	Corned beef	3 ounces	85	59	185	22	10	5	4	Trace	0	17	3.7	20	.01	.20	2.9	—
91	Corned beef hash	3 ounces	85	67	155	7	10	5	4	Trace	9	11	1.7	—	.01	.08	1.8	—
92	Beef, dried or chipped	2 ounces	57	48	115	19	4	2	2	Trace	0	11	2.9	—	.04	.18	2.2	—
93	Beef and vegetable stew	1 cup	235	82	210	15	10	5	4	Trace	15	28	2.8	2310	.13	.17	4.4	15
94	Beef potpie, baked, 4¼-inch diam, weight before baking about 8 ounces.	1 pie	227	55	560	23	33	9	20	2	43	32	4.1	1860	.25	.27	4.5	7
	Chicken, cooked:																
95	Flesh only, broiled	3 ounces	85	71	115	20	3	1	1	1	0	8	1.4	80	.05	.16	7.4	—
	Breast, fried, ½ breast:																
96	With bone	3.3 ounces	94	58	155	25	5	1	2	1	1	9	1.3	70	.04	.17	11.2	—
97	Flesh and skin only	2.7 ounces	76	58	155	25	5	1	2	1	1	9	1.3	70	.04	.17	11.2	—
	Drumstick, fried:																
98	With bone	2.1 ounces	59	55	90	12	4	1	2	1	Trace	6	.9	50	.03	.15	2.7	—
99	Flesh and skin only	1.3 ounces	38	55	90	12	4	1	2	1	Trace	6	.9	50	.03	.15	2.7	—
100	Chicken, canned, boneless	3 ounces	85	65	170	18	10	3	4	2	0	18	1.3	200	.03	.11	3.7	3
101	Chicken potpie, baked 4¼-inch diam., weight before baking about 8 ounces.	1 pie	227	57	535	23	31	10	15	3	42	68	3.0	3020	.25	.26	4.1	5

No.	Food	Measure	Grams															
102	Chili con carne, canned: With beans	1 cup	250	72	335	19	15	7	7	Trace	30	80	4.2	150	.08	.18	3.2	—
103	Without beans	1 cup	255	67	510	26	38	18	17	1	15	97	3.6	380	.05	.31	5.6	—
104	Heart, beef, lean, braised	3 ounces	85	61	160	27	5	—	—	—	1	5	5.0	20	.21	1.04	6.5	1
105	Lamb,[3] cooked: Chop, thick, with bone, 1 chop, broiled	4.8 ounces	137	47	400	25	33	18	12	1	0	10	1.5	—	.14	.25	5.6	—
106	Lean and fat	4.0 ounces	112	47	400	25	33	18	12	1	0	10	1.5	—	.14	.25	5.6	—
107	Lean only	2.6 ounces	74	62	140	21	6	3	2	Trace	0	9	1.5	—	.11	.20	4.5	—
108	Leg roasted: Lean and fat	3 ounces	85	54	235	22	16	9	6	Trace	0	9	1.4	—	.13	.23	4.7	—
109	Lean only	2.5 ounces	71	62	130	20	5	3	2	Trace	0	9	1.4	—	.12	.21	4.4	—
110	Shoulder, roasted: Lean and fat	3 ounces	85	50	285	18	23	13	8	1	0	9	1.0	—	.11	.20	4.0	—
111	Lean only	2.3 ounces	64	61	130	17	6	3	2	Trace	0	8	1.0	—	.10	.18	3.7	—
112	Liver, beef, fried	2 ounces	57	57	130	15	6	—	—	—	3	6	5.0	30,280	.15	2.37	9.4	15
113	Pork, cured, cooked: Ham, light cure, lean and fat, roasted	3 ounces	85	54	245	18	19	7	8	2	0	8	2.2	0	.40	.16	3.1	—
114	Luncheon meat: Boiled ham, sliced	2 ounces	57	59	135	11	10	4	4	1	0	6	1.6	0	.25	.09	1.5	—
115	Canned, spiced or unspiced	2 ounces	57	55	165	8	14	5	6	1	1	5	1.2	0	.18	.12	1.6	—
116	Pork, fresh,[3] cooked: Chop, thick, with bone	3.5 ounces	98	42	260	16	21	8	9	2	0	8	2.2	0	.63	.18	3.8	—
117	1 chop Lean and fat	2.3 ounces	66	42	260	16	21	8	9	2	0	8	2.2	0	.63	.18	3.8	—
118	Lean only	1.7 ounces	48	53	130	15	7	2	3	1	0	7	1.9	0	.54	.16	3.3	—
119	Roast, oven-cooked, no liquid added: Lean and fat	3 ounces	85	46	310	21	24	9	10	2	0	9	2.7	0	.78	.22	4.7	—
120	Lean only	2.4 ounces	68	55	175	20	10	3	4	1	0	9	2.6	0	.73	.21	4.4	—
121	Cuts, simmered: Lean and fat	3 ounces	85	46	320	20	26	9	11	2	0	8	2.5	0	.46	.21	4.1	—
122	Lean only	2.2 ounces	63	60	135	18	6	2	3	1	0	8	2.3	0	.42	.19	3.7	—
123	Sausage: Bologna, slice, 3-in. diam., by 1/8 inch	2 slices	26	56	80	3	7	—	—	—	Trace	2	.5	—	.04	.06	.7	—

3. Outer layer of fat on the cut was removed to within approximately ½-inch of the lean. Deposits of fat within the cut were not removed.

MEAT, POULTRY, FISH, SHELLFISH: RELATED PRODUCTS—Con.

	Food, Approximate Measure, and Weight (in Grams)	Grams	Water (%)	Food Energy (kcal)	Protein (g)	Fat (g)	Fatty Acids Saturated (total) (g)	Fatty Acids Unsaturated Oleic (g)	Fatty Acids Unsaturated Linoleic (g)	Carbohydrate (g)	Calcium (mg)	Iron (mg)	Vitamin A value (I.U.)	Thiamin (mg)	Riboflavin (mg)	Niacin (mg)	Ascorbic acid (mg)
	Sausage:—con,																
124	Braunschweiger, slice 2-in. diam. by ¼ inch. 2 slices	20	53	65	3	5	—	—	—	Trace	2	1.2	1310	.03	.29	1.6	—
125	Deviled ham, canned 1 tbsp.	13	51	45	2	4	2	2	Trace	0	1	.3	—	.02	.01	.2	—
126	Frankfurter, heated (8 per lb. purchased pkg.). 1 frank	56	57	170	7	15	—	—	Trace	1	3	.8	—	.08	.11	1.4	—
127	Pork links, cooked (16 links per lb. raw). 2 links	26	35	125	5	11	4	5	1	Trace	2	.6	0	.21	.09	1.0	—
128	Salami, dry type 1 oz.	28	30	130	7	11	—	—	—	Trace	4	1.0	—	.10	.07	1.5	—
129	Salami, cooked 1 oz.	28	51	90	5	7	—	—	—	Trace	3	.7	—	.07	.07	1.2	—
130	Vienna, canned (7 sausages per 5-oz. can) 1 sausage	16	63	40	2	3	—	—	—	Trace	1	.3	—	.01	.02	.4	—
	Veal, medium fat, cooked, bone removed:																
131	Cutlet 3 oz.	85	60	185	23	9	5	4	Trace	—	9	2.7	—	.06	.21	4.6	—
132	Roast 3 oz.	85	55	230	23	14	7	6	Trace	0	10	2.9	—	.11	.26	6.6	—
	Fish and shellfish:																
133	Bluefish, baked with table fat. 3 oz.	85	68	135	22	4	—	—	—	0	25	.6	40	.09	.08	1.6	—
	Clams:																
134	Raw, meat only 3 oz.	85	82	65	11	1	—	—	—	2	59	5.2	90	.08	.15	1.1	8
135	Canned, solids and liquid. 3 oz.	85	86	45	7	1	—	—	—	2	47	3.5	—	.01	.09	.9	—
136	Crabmeat, canned 3 oz.	85	77	85	15	2	—	—	—	1	38	.7	—	.07	.07	1.6	—
137	Fish sticks, breaded, cooked frozen; stick 3¾ by 1 by ½ inch. 10 sticks or 8 oz. pkg.	227	66	400	38	20	5	4	10	15	25	0.9	—	.09	.16	3.6	—
138	Haddock, breaded, fried 3 oz.	85	66	140	17	5	1	3	Trace	5	34	1.0	—	.03	.06	2.7	—
139	Ocean perch, breaded, fried 3 oz.	85	59	195	16	11	—	—	—	6	28	1.1	—	.08	.09	1.5	—
140	Oysters, raw, meat only (13-19 med. selects). 1 cup	240	85	160	20	4	1	—	—	8	226	13.2	740	.33	.43	6.0	2
141	Salmon, pink, canned 3 oz.	85	71	120	17	5	1	1	Trace	0	167[4]	.7	60	.03	.16	6.8	—
142	Sardines, Atlantic, canned in oil, drained solids. 3 oz.	85	62	175	20	9	—	—	—	0	372	2.5	190	.02	.17	4.6	—

No.	Food	Measure	g	%														
143	Shad, baked with table fat and bacon.	3 oz.	85	64	170	20	10	—	—	—	0	20	.5	20	.11	.22	7.3	—
144	Shrimp, canned, meat.	3 oz.	85	70	100	21	1	—	—	—	1	98	2.6	50	.01	.03	1.5	—
145	Swordfish, broiled with butter or margarine.	3 oz.	85	65	150	24	5	—	—	—	0	23	1.1	1750	.03	.04	9.3	—
146	Tuna, canned in oil, drained solids.	3 oz.	85	61	170	24	7	2	1	1	0	7	1.6	70	.04	.10	10.1	—
	MATURE DRY BEANS AND PEAS, NUTS, PEANUTS; RELATED PRODUCTS																	
147	Almonds, shelled, whole kernels.	1 cup	142	5	850	26	77	6	52	15	28	332	6.7	0	.34	1.31	5.0	Trace
	Beans, dry: Common varieties as Great Northern, navy, and others: Cooked, drained:																	
148	Great Northern	1 cup	180	69	210	14	1	—	—	—	38	90	4.9	0	.25	.13	1.3	0
149	Navy (pea)	1 cup	190	69	225	15	1	—	—	—	40	95	5.1	0	.27	.13	1.3	0
	Canned, solids and liquid: White with —																	
150	Frankfurters (sliced).	1 cup	255	71	365	19	18	—	—	—	32	94	4.8	330	.18	.15	3.3	Trace
151	Pork and tomato sauce.	1 cup	255	71	310	16	7	2	3	1	49	138	4.6	330	.20	.08	1.5	5
152	Pork and sweet sauce.	1 cup	255	66	385	16	12	4	5	1	54	161	5.9	—	.15	.10	1.3	—
153	Red kidney.	1 cup	255	76	230	15	1	—	—	—	42	74	4.6	10	.13	.10	1.5	—
154	Lima, cooked, drained.	1 cup	190	64	260	16	1	—	—	—	49	55	5.9	—	.25	.11	1.3	—
155	Cashew nuts, roasted	1 cup	140	5	785	24	64	11	45	4	41	53	5.3	140	.60	.35	2.5	—
156	Coconut, fresh, meat only: Pieces, approx. 2 by 2 by ½ inch.	1 piece	45	51	155	2	16	14	1	Trace	4	6	.8	0	.02	.01	.2	1
157	Shredded or grated, firmly packed.	1 cup	130	51	450	5	46	39	3	Trace	12	17	2.2	0	.07	.03	.7	4
158	Cowpeas or blackeye peas, dry, cooked.	1 cup	248	80	190	13	1	—	—	—	34	42	3.2	20	.41	.11	1.1	Trace
159	Peanuts, roasted, salted, halves.	1 cup	144	2	840	37	72	16	31	21	27	107	3.0	—	.46	.19	24.7	0

4. If bones are discarded, value will be greatly reduced.

	Food, Approximate Measure, and Weight (in Grams)	Water (%)	Food Energy (kcal)	Pro- tein (g)	Fat (g)	Satu- rated (total) (g)	Oleic (g)	Lin- oleic (g)	Carbo- hy- drate (g)	Cal- cium (mg)	Iron (mg)	Vita- min A value (I.U.)	Thia- min (mg)	Ribo- flavin (mg)	Niacin (mg)	Ascor- bic acid (mg)
	MATURE DRY BEANS AND PEAS, NUTS, PEANUTS; RELATED PRODUCTS—Con.															
160	Peanut butter 1 tbsp. 16	2	95	4	8	2	4	2	3	9	.3	–	.02	.02	2.4	0
161	Peas, split, dry, cooked 1 cup 250	70	290	20	1	–	–	–	52	28	4.2	100	.37	.22	2.2	–
162	Pecans, halves 1 cup 108	3	740	10	77	5	48	15	16	79	2.6	140	.93	.14	1.0	2
163	Walnuts, black or native, chopped. 1 cup 126	3	790	26	75	4	26	36	19	Trace	7.6	380	.28	.14	.9	–
	VEGETABLES AND VEGETABLE PRODUCTS															
	Asparagus, green:															
	Cooked, drained:															
164	Spears, ½-in. diam. at base. 4 spears 60	94	10	1	Trace	–	–	–	2	13	.4	540	.10	.11	.8	16
165	Pieces, 1½ to 2-in. lengths. 1 cup 145	94	30	3	Trace	–	–	–	5	30	.9	1310	.23	.26	2.0	38
166	Canned, solids and liquid. 1 cup 244	94	45	5	1	–	–	–	7	44	4.1	1240	.15	.22	2.0	37
	Beans:															
167	Lima, immature seeds, cooked, drained. 1 cup 170	71	190	13	1	–	–	–	34	80	4.3	480	.31	.17	2.2	29
	Snap:															
	Green:															
168	Cooked, drained 1 cup 125	92	30	2	Trace	–	–	–	7	63	.8	680	.09	.11	.6	15
169	Canned, solids and liquid. 1 cup 239	94	45	2	Trace	–	–	–	10	81	2.9	690	.07	.10	.7	10
	Yellow or wax:															
170	Cooked, drained 1 cup 125	93	30	2	Trace	–	–	–	6	63	.8	290	.09	.11	.6	16
171	Canned, solids and liquid. 1 cup 239	94	45	2	1	–	–	–	10	81	2.9	140	.07	.10	.7	12
172	Sprouted mung beans, cooked, drained. 1 cup 125	91	35	4	Trace	–	–	–	7	21	1.1	30	.11	.13	.9	8

	Beets																
173	Cooked, drained, peeled: Whole beets, 2-in. diam.	2 beets	100	91	30	1	Trace	—	—	—	7	14	.5	20	.03	.04	.3	6
174	Diced or sliced	1 cup	170	91	55	2	Trace	—	—	—	12	24	.9	30	.05	.07	.5	10
175	Canned, solids and liquid.	1 cup	246	90	85	2	Trace	—	—	—	19	34	1.5	20	.02	.05	.2	7
176	Beet greens, leaves and stems, cooked, drained.	1 cup	145	94	25	3	Trace	—	—	—	5	144	2.8	7,400	.10	.22	.4	22
	Blackeye peas. See Cowpeas.																	
	Broccoli, cooked, drained:																	
177	Whole stalks, medium size.	1 stalk	180	91	45	6	1	—	—	—	8	158	1.4	4,500	.16	.36	1.4	162
178	Stalks cut into ½-in. pieces.	1 cup	155	91	40	5	1	—	—	—	7	136	1.2	3,880	.14	.31	1.2	140
179	Chopped, yield from 10-oz. frozen pkg.	1 3/8 cups	250	92	65	7	1	—	—	—	12	135	1.8	6,500	.15	.30	1.3	143
180	Brussels sprouts, 7-8 sprouts (1¼ to 1½ in. diam.) per cup, cooked.	1 cup	155	88	55	7	1	—	—	—	10	50	1.7	810	.12	.22	1.2	135
	Cabbage: Common varieties: Raw:																	
181	Coarsely shredded or sliced.	1 cup	70	92	15	1	Trace	—	—	—	4	34	.3	90	.04	.04	.2	33
182	Finely shredded or chopped.	1 cup	90	92	20	1	Trace	—	—	—	5	44	.4	120	.05	.05	.3	42
183	Cooked	1 cup	145	94	30	2	Trace	—	—	—	6	64	.4	190	.06	.06	.4	48
184	Red, raw, coarsely shredded.	1 cup	70	90	20	1	Trace	—	—	—	5	29	.6	30	.06	.04	.3	43
185	Savoy, raw, coarsely shredded.	1 cup	70	92	15	2	Trace	—	—	—	3	47	.6	140	.04	.06	.2	39
186	Cabbage, celery or Chinese, raw, cut in 1-in. pieces.	1 cup	75	95	10	1	Trace	—	—	—	2	32	.5	110	.03	.03	.5	19
187	Cabbage, spoon (or pakchoy), cooked.	1 cup	170	95	25	2	Trace	—	—	—	4	252	1.0	5,270	.07	.14	1.2	26
	Carrots: Raw:																	
188	Whole, 5½ by 1 inch, (25 thin strips).	1 carrot	50	88	20	1	Trace	—	—	—	5	18	.4	5,500	.03	.03	.3	4
189	Grated	1 cup	110	88	45	1	Trace	—	—	—	11	41	.8	12,100	.06	.06	.7	9

VEGETABLES AND VEGETABLE PRODUCTS—Continued

| | Food, Approximate Measure, and Weight (in Grams) | | Water (%) | Food Energy (kcal) | Protein (g) | Fat (g) | Fatty Acids | | | Carbohydrate (g) | Calcium (mg) | Iron (mg) | Vitamin A value (I.U.) | Thiamin (mg) | Riboflavin (mg) | Niacin (mg) | Ascorbic acid (mg) |
							Saturated (total) (g)	Unsaturated Oleic (g)	Linoleic (g)								
190	Cooked, diced	1 cup 145	91	45	1	Trace	—	—	—	10	48	.9	15,220	.08	.07	.7	9
191	Canned, strained or chopped (baby food).	1 ounce 28	92	10	Trace	Trace	—	—	—	2	7	.1	3,690	.01	.01	.1	1
192	Cauliflower, cooked, flowerbuds.	1 cup 120	93	25	3	Trace	—	—	—	5	25	.8	70	.11	.10	.7	66
	Celery, raw:																
193	Stalk, large outer, 8 by about 1½ inches, at root end.	1 stalk 40	94	5	Trace	Trace	—	—	—	2	16	.1	100	.01	.01	.1	4
194	Pieces, diced	1 cup 100	94	15	1	Trace	—	—	—	4	39	.3	240	.03	.03	.3	9
195	Collards, cooked	1 cup 190	91	55	5	1	—	—	—	9	289	1.1	10,260	.27	.37	2.4	87
	Corn, sweet:																
196	Cooked, ear 5 by 1¾ inches.[5]	1 ear 140	74	70	3	1	—	—	—	16	2	.5	310[6]	.09	.08	1.0	7
197	Canned, solids and liquid.	1 cup 256	81	170	5	2	—	—	—	40	10	1.0	690[6]	.07	.12	2.3	13
198	Cowpeas, cooked, immature seeds.	1 cup 160	72	175	13	1	—	—	—	29	38	3.4	560	.49	.18	2.3	28
	Cucumbers, 10-ounce; 7½ by about 2 inches:																
199	Raw, pared	1 cucumber 207	96	30	1	Trace	—	—	—	7	35	.6	Trace	.07	.09	.4	23
200	Raw, pared, center slice 1/8-inch thick.	6 slices 50	96	5	Trace	Trace	—	—	—	2	8	.2	Trace	.02	.02	.1	6
201	Dandelion greens, cooked	1 cup 180	90	60	4	1	—	—	—	12	252	3.2	21,060	.24	.29	—	32
202	Endive, curly (including escarole).	2 oz. 57	93	10	1	Trace	—	—	—	2	46	1.0	1,870	.04	.08	.3	6
203	Kale, leaves including stems, cooked.	1 cup 110	91	30	4	1	—	—	—	4	147	1.3	8,140	—	—	—	68

Item	Food, approximate measure, and weight	Measure	Grams	Water (%)	Food energy	Protein	Fat	Sat.	Oleic	Linoleic	Carbohydrate	Calcium	Iron	Vitamin A	Thiamin	Riboflavin	Niacin	Ascorbic acid
	Lettuce, raw:																	
204	Butterhead, as Boston types; head, 4-inch diameter.	1 head	220	95	30	3	Trace	—	—	—	6	77	4.4	2,130	.14	.13	.6	18
205	Crisphead, as Iceberg; head, 4¾-inch diameter.	1 head	454	96	60	4	Trace	—	—	—	13	91	2.3	1,500	.29	.27	1.3	29
206	Looseleaf, or bunching varieties, leaves.	2 large	50	94	10	1	Trace	—	—	—	2	34	.7	950	.03	.04	.2	9
207	Mushrooms, canned, solids and liquid.	1 cup	244	93	40	5	Trace	—	—	—	6	15	1.2	Trace	.04	.60	4.8	4
208	Mustard greens, cooked	1 cup	140	93	35	3	1	—	—	—	6	193	2.5	8,120	.11	.19	.9	68
209	Okra, cooked, pod 3 by 5/8 inch.	8 pods	85	91	25	2	Trace	—	—	—	5	78	.4	420	.11	.15	.8	17
	Onions: Mature:																	
210	Raw, onion 2½-inch diameter.	1 onion	110	89	40	2	Trace	—	—	—	10	30	.6	40	.04	.04	.2	11
211	Cooked	1 cup	210	92	60	3	Trace	—	—	—	14	50	.8	80	.06	.06	.4	14
212	Young green, small, without tops.	6 onions	50	88	20	1	Trace	—	—	—	5	20	.3	Trace	.02	.02	.2	12
213	Parsley, raw, chopped	1 tbsp.	4	85	Trace	Trace	Trace	—	—	—	Trace	8	.2	340	Trace	.01	Trace	7
214	Parsnips, cooked	1 cup	155	82	100	2	1	—	—	—	23	70	.9	50	.11	.12	.2	16
	Peas, green:																	
215	Cooked	1 cup	160	82	115	9	1	—	—	—	19	37	2.9	860	.44	.17	3.7	33
216	Canned, solids and liquid.	1 cup	249	83	165	9	1	—	—	—	31	50	4.2	1,120	.23	.13	2.2	22
217	Canned, strained (baby food).	1 oz.	28	86	15	1	Trace	—	—	—	3	3	.4	140	.02	.02	.4	3
218	Peppers, hot, red, without seeds, dried (ground chili powder, added seasonings).	1 tbsp.	15	8	50	2	2	—	—	—	8	40	2.3	9,750	.03	.17	1.3	2
	Peppers, sweet:																	
219	Raw, about 5 per pound: Green pod without stem and seeds.	1 pod	74	93	15	1	Trace	—	—	—	4	7	.5	310	.06	.06	.4	94

5. Measure and weight apply to entire vegetable or fruit including parts not usually eaten.

6. Based on yellow varieties; white varieties contain only a trace of cryptoxanthin and carotenes, the pigments in corn that have biological activity.

#	Food, Approximate Measure, and Weight (in Grams)			Water (%)	Food Energy (kcal)	Protein (g)	Fat (g)	Fatty Acids			Carbohydrate (g)	Calcium (mg)	Iron (mg)	Vitamin A value (I.U.)	Thiamin (mg)	Riboflavin (mg)	Niacin (mg)	Ascorbic acid (mg)
								Saturated (total) (g)	Unsaturated									
									Oleic (g)	Lin-oleic (g)								
	VEGETABLES AND VEGETABLE PRODUCTS—Continued																	
220	Cooked, boiled, drained	1 pod	73	95	15	1	Trace	–	–	–	3	7	.4	310	.05	.05	.4	70
221	Potatoes, medium (about 3 per pound raw): Baked, peeled after baking.	1 potato	99	75	90	3	Trace	–	–	–	21	9	.7	Trace	.10	.04	1.7	20
	Boiled:																	
222	Peeled after boiling	1 potato	136	80	105	3	Trace	–	–	–	23	10	.8	Trace	.13	.05	2.0	22
223	Peeled before boiling	1 potato	122	83	80	2	Trace	–	–	–	18	7	.6	Trace	.11	.04	1.4	20
	French-fried, piece 2 by ½ by ½ inch:																	
224	Cooked in deep fat	10 pieces	57	45	155	2	7	2	2	4	20	9	.7	Trace	.07	.04	1.8	12
225	Frozen, heated	10 pieces	57	53	125	2	5	1	1	2	19	5	1.0	Trace	.08	.01	1.5	12
	Mashed:																	
226	Milk added	1 cup	195	83	125	4	1	–	–	–	25	47	.8	50	.16	.10	2.0	19
227	Milk and butter added.	1 cup	195	80	185	4	8	4	3	Trace	24	47	.8	330	.16	.10	1.9	18
228	Potato chips, medium, 2-inch diameter.	10 chips	20	2	115	1	8	2	2	4	10	8	.4	Trace	.04	.01	1.0	3
229	Pumpkin, canned	1 cup	228	90	75	2	1	–	–	–	18	57	.9	14,590	.07	.12	1.3	12
230	Radishes, raw, small, without tops.	4 radishes	40	94	5	Trace	Trace	–	–	–	1	12	.4	Trace	.01	.01	.1	10
231	Sauerkraut, canned, solids and liquid.	1 cup	235	93	45	2	Trace	–	–	–	9	85	1.2	120	.07	.09	.4	33
	Spinach:																	
232	Cooked	1 cup	180	92	40	5	1	–	–	–	6	167	4.0	14,580	.13	.25	1.0	50
233	Canned, drained solids	1 cup	180	91	45	5	1	–	–	–	6	212	4.7	14,400	.03	.21	.6	24
	Squash: Cooked:																	
234	Summer, diced	1 cup	210	96	30	2	Trace	–	–	–	7	52	.8	820	.10	.16	1.6	21
235	Winter, baked, mashed.	1 cup	205	81	130	4	1	–	–	–	32	57	1.6	8,610	.10	.27	1.4	27

No.	Food	Measure	Grams	Water %	Food energy	Protein (g)	Fat (g)	Fatty acids saturated	Fatty acids oleic	Fatty acids linoleic	Carbo- hydrate (g)	Calcium (mg)	Iron (mg)	Vitamin A (IU)	Thiamine	Riboflavin	Niacin	Ascorbic acid
	Sweetpotatoes:																	
	Cooked, medium, 5 by 2 inches, weight raw about 6 ounces:																	
236	Baked, peeled after baking.	1 sweet- potato.	110	64	155	2	1	—	—	—	36	44	1.0	8,910	.10	.07	.7	24
237	Boiled, peeled after boiling.	1 sweet- potato.	147	71	170	2	1	—	—	—	39	47	1.0	11,610	.13	.09	.9	25
238	Candied, 3½ by 2¼ inches.	1 sweet- potato.	175	60	295	2	6	2	3	1	60	65	1.6	11,030	.10	.08	.8	17
239	Canned, vacuum or solid pack.	1 cup	218	72	235	4	Trace	—	—	—	54	54	1.7	17,000	.10	.10	1.4	30
	Tomatoes:																	
240	Raw, approx. 3-in. diam. 2 1/8 in. high; wt., 7 oz.	1 tomato	200	90	40	2	Trace	—	—	—	9	24	.9	1,640	.11	.07	1.3	42[7]
241	Canned, solids and liquid.	1 cup	241	94	50	2	1	—	—	—	10	14	1.2	2,170	.12	.07	1.7	41
	Tomato catsup:																	
242	Cup	1 cup	273	69	290	6	1	—	—	—	69	60	2.2	3,820	.25	.19	4.4	41
243	Tablespoon	1 tbsp.	15	69	15	Trace	Trace	—	—	—	4	3	.1	210	.01	.01	.2	2
	Tomato juice, canned:																	
244	Cup	1 cup	243	94	45	2	Trace	—	—	—	10	17	2.2	1,940	.12	.07	1.9	39
245	Glass (6 fl. oz.)	1 glass	182	94	35	2	Trace	—	—	—	8	13	1.6	1,460	.09	.05	1.5	29
246	Turnips, cooked, diced	1 cup	155	94	35	1	Trace	—	—	—	8	54	.6	Trace	.06	.08	.5	34
247	Turnip greens, cooked	1 cup	145	94	30	3	Trace	—	—	—	5	252	1.5	8,270	.15	.33	.7	68
	FRUITS AND FRUIT PRODUCTS																	
248	Apples, raw (about 3 per lb.).[5]	1 apple	150	85	70	Trace	Trace	—	—	—	18	8	.4	50	.04	.02	.1	3
249	Apple juice, bottled or canned.	1 cup	248	88	120	Trace	Trace	—	—	—	30	15	1.5	—	.02	.05	.2	2
	Applesauce, canned:																	
250	Sweetened	1 cup	255	76	230	1	Trace	—	—	—	61	10	1.3	100	.05	.03	.1	3[8]
251	Unsweetened or artificially sweetened.	1 cup	244	88	100	1	Trace	—	—	—	26	10	1.2	100	.05	.02	.1	2[8]

5. Measure and weight apply to entire vegetable or fruit including parts not usually eaten.

7. Year-round average. Samples marketed from November through May, average 20 milligrams per 200-gram tomato; from June through October, around 52 milligrams.

8. This is the amount from the fruit. Additional ascorbic acid may be added by the manufacturer. Refer to the label for this information.

FRUITS AND FRUIT PRODUCTS—Con.

	Food, Approximate Measure, and Weight (in Grams)		Water (%)	Food Energy (kcal)	Protein (g)	Fat (g)	Fatty Acids Saturated (total) (g)	Unsaturated Oleic (g)	Unsaturated Linoleic (g)	Carbohydrate (g)	Calcium (mg)	Iron (mg)	Vitamin A value (I.U.)	Thiamin (mg)	Riboflavin (mg)	Niacin (mg)	Ascorbic acid (mg)
	Apricots:																
252	Raw (about 12 per lb.)[5]	3 apricots 114	85	55	1	Trace	—	—	—	14	18	.5	2,890	.03	.04	.7	10
253	Canned in heavy sirup	1 cup 259	77	220	2	Trace	—	—	—	57	28	.8	4,510	.05	.06	.9	10
254	Dried, uncooked (40 halves per cup).	1 cup 150	25	390	8	1	—	—	—	100	100	8.2	16,350	.02	.23	4.9	19
255	Cooked, unsweetened, fruit and liquid.	1 cup 285	76	240	5	1	—	—	—	62	63	5.1	8,550	.01	.13	2.8	8
256	Apricot nectar, canned	1 cup 251	85	140	1	Trace	—	—	—	37	23	.5	2,380	.03	.03	.5	8[8]
	Avocados, whole fruit, raw:[5]																
257	California (mid- and late-winter; diam. 3 1/8 in.).	1 avocado 284	74	370	5	37	7	17	5	13	22	1.3	630	.24	.43	3.5	30
258	Florida (late summer, fall diam. 3 5/8 in.).	1 avocado 454	78	390	4	33	7	15	4	27	30	1.8	880	.33	.61	4.9	43
259	Bananas, raw, medium size.[5]	1 banana 175	76	100	1	Trace	—	—	—	26	10	.8	230	.06	.07	.8	12
260	Banana flakes	1 cup 100	3	340	4	1	—	—	—	89	32	2.8	760	.18	.24	2.8	7
261	Blackberries, raw	1 cup 144	84	85	2	1	—	—	—	19	46	1.3	290	.05	.06	.5	30
262	Blueberries, raw	1 cup 140	83	85	1	1	—	—	—	21	21	1.4	140	.04	.08	.6	20
263	Cantaloups, raw; medium, 5-inch diameter about 1 2/3 pounds.[5]	½ melon 385	91	60	1	Trace	—	—	—	14	27	.8	6,540[9]	.08	.06	1.2	63
264	Cherries, canned, red, sour, pitted, water pack.	1 cup 244	88	105	2	Trace	—	—	—	26	37	.7	1,660	.07	.05	.5	12
265	Cranberry juice cocktail, canned.	1 cup 250	83	165	Trace	Trace	—	—	—	42	13	.8	Trace	.03	.03	.1	40[10]
266	Cranberry sauce, sweetened, canned, strained.	1 cup 277	62	405	Trace	1	—	—	—	104	17	.6	60	.03	.03	.1	6
267	Dates, pitted, cut	1 cup 178	22	490	4	1	—	—	—	130	105	5.3	90	.16	.17	3.9	0
268	Figs, dried, large, 2 by 1 in.	1 fig 21	23	60	1	Trace	—	—	—	15	26	.6	20	.02	.02	.1	0

No.	Food	Measure	Weight (g)	Water (%)	Food energy	Protein	Fat				Carbohydrate	Calcium	Iron	Vit. A	Thiamin	Riboflavin	Niacin	Ascorbic acid
269	Fruit cocktail, canned, in heavy sirup.	1 cup	256	80	195	1	Trace	—	—	—	50	23	1.0	360	.05	.03	1.3	5
270	Grapefruit: Raw, medium, 3¾-in. diam.[5] White	½ grapefruit	241	89	45	1	Trace	—	—	—	12	19	.5	10	.05	.02	.2	44
271	Pink or red	½ grapefruit	241	89	50	1	Trace	—	—	—	13	20	.5	540	.05	.02	.2	44
272	Canned, sirup pack	1 cup	254	81	180	2	Trace	—	—	—	45	33	.8	30	.08	.05	.5	76
273	Grapefruit juice: Fresh	1 cup	246	90	95	1	Trace	—	—	—	23	22	.5	[11]	.09	.04	.4	92
274	Canned, white: Unsweetened	1 cup	247	89	100	1	Trace	—	—	—	24	20	1.0	20	.07	.04	.4	84
275	Sweetened	1 cup	250	86	130	1	Trace	—	—	—	32	20	1.0	20	.07	.04	.4	78
276	Frozen, concentrate, unsweetened: Undiluted, can, 6 fluid ounces.	1 can	207	62	300	4	1	—	—	—	72	70	.8	60	.29	.12	1.4	286
277	Diluted with 3 parts water, by volume.	1 cup	247	89	100	1	Trace	—	—	—	24	25	.2	20	.10	.04	.5	96
278	Dehydrated crystals	4 oz.	113	1	410	6	1	—	—	—	102	100	1.2	80	.40	.20	2.0	396
279	Prepared with water (1 pound yields about 1 gallon).	1 cup	247	90	100	1	Trace	—	—	—	24	22	.2	20	.10	.05	.5	91
280	Grapes, raw:[5] American type (slip skin).	1 cup	153	82	65	1	1	—	—	—	15	15	.4	100	.05	.03	.2	3
281	European type (adherent skin).	1 cup	160	81	95	1	Trace	—	—	—	25	17	.6	140	.07	.04	.4	6
282	Grapejuice: Canned or bottled	1 cup	253	83	165	1	Trace	—	—	—	42	28	.8	—	.10	.05	.5	Trace
283	Frozen concentrate, sweetened: Undiluted, can, 6 fluid ounces.	1 can	216	53	395	1	Trace	—	—	—	100	22	.9	40	.13	.22	1.5	[12]

5. Measure and weight apply to entire vegetable or fruit including parts not usually eaten.

8. This is the amount from the fruit. Additional ascorbic acid may be added by the manufacturer. Refer to the label for this information.

9. Value for varieties with orange-colored flesh; value for varieties with green flesh would be about 540 I.U.

10. Value listed is based on products with label stating 30 milligrams per 6 fl. oz. serving.

11. For white-fleshed varieties value is about 20 I.U. per cup; for red-fleshed varieties, 1,080 I.U. per cup.

12. Present only if added by the manufacturer. Refer to the label for this information.

| | Food, Approximate Measure, and Weight (in Grams) | | Water (%) | Food Energy (kcal) | Protein (g) | Fat (g) | Fatty Acids | | | Carbohydrate (g) | Calcium (mg) | Iron (mg) | Vitamin A value (I.U.) | Thiamin (mg) | Riboflavin (mg) | Niacin (mg) | Ascorbic acid (mg) |
							Saturated (total) (g)	Unsaturated Oleic (g)	Unsaturated Linoleic (g)								
	FRUITS AND FRUIT PRODUCTS—Con.																
	Grapejuice:—Con.																
284	Diluted with 3 parts water, by volume.	1 cup 250	86	135	1	Trace	—	—	—	33	8	.3	10	.05	.08	.5	1²
285	Grapejuice drink, canned	1 cup 250	86	135	Trace	Trace	—	—	—	35	8	.3	—	.03	.03	.3	1²
286	Lemons, raw, 2 1/8-in. diam., size 165.⁵ Used for juice,	1 lemon 110	90	20	1	Trace	—	—	—	6	19	.4	10	.03	.01	.1	39
287	Lemon juice, raw	1 cup 244	91	60	1	Trace	—	—	—	20	17	.5	50	.07	.02	.2	112
	Lemonade concentrate:																
288	Frozen, 6 fl. oz. per can	1 can 219	48	430	Trace	Trace	—	—	—	112	9	.4	40	.04	.07	.7	66
289	Diluted with 4 1/3 parts water, by volume.	1 cup 248	88	110	Trace	Trace	—	—	—	28	2	Trace	Trace	Trace	.02	.2	17
	Lime juice:																
290	Fresh	1 cup 246	90	65	1	Trace	—	—	—	22	22	.5	20	.05	.02	.2	79
291	Canned, unsweetened	1 cup 246	90	65	1	Trace	—	—	—	22	22	.5	20	.05	.02	.2	52
	Limeade concentrate, frozen:																
292	Undiluted, can, 6 fl. oz.	1 can 218	50	410	Trace	Trace	—	—	—	108	11	.2	Trace	.02	.02	.2	26
293	Diluted with 4 1/3 parts water by volume.	1 cup 247	90	100	Trace	Trace	—	—	—	27	2	Trace	Trace	Trace	Trace	Trace	5
294	Oranges, raw 2 5/8-in. diam., all commercial, varieties.⁵	1 orange 180	86	65	1	Trace	—	—	—	16	54	.5	260	.13	.05	.5	66
295	Orange juice, fresh, all varieties.	1 cup 248	88	110	2	1	—	—	—	26	27	.5	500	.22	.07	1.0	124
296	Canned, unsweetened	1 cup 249	87	120	2	Trace	—	—	—	28	25	1.0	500	.17	.05	.7	100
	Frozen concentrate:																
297	Undiluted, can, 6 fl. oz.	1 can 213	55	360	5	Trace	—	—	—	87	75	.9	1620	.68	.11	2.8	360
298	Diluted with 3 parts water by volume.	1 cup 249	87	120	2	Trace	—	—	—	29	25	.2	550	.22	.02	1.0	120
299	Dehydrated crystals	4 oz. 113	1	430	6	2	—	—	—	100	95	1.9	1900	.76	.24	3.3	408
300	Prepared with water (1 pound yields about 1 gallon).	1 cup 248	88	115	2	1	—	—	—	27	25	.5	500	.20	.07	1.0	109

		Measure	Grams	Water (%)	Food energy	Protein	Fat				Carbohydrate	Calcium	Iron	Vit. A	Thiamin	Riboflavin	Niacin	Ascorbic acid
301	Orange-apricot juice drink	1 cup	249	87	125	1	Trace	–	–	–	32	12	.2	1440	.05	.02	.5	40[10]
	Orange and grapefruit juice: Frozen concentrate:																	
302	Undiluted, can, 6 fl. oz.	1 can	210	59	330	4	1	–	–	–	78	61	.8	800	.48	.06	2.3	302
303	Diluted with 3 parts water by volume.	1 cup	248	88	110	1	Trace	–	–	–	26	20	.2	270	.16	.02	.8	102
304	Papayas, raw, ½-inch cubes	1 cup	182	89	70	1	Trace	–	–	–	18	36	.5	3190	.07	.08	.5	102
	Peaches: Raw:																	
305	Whole, medium, 2-inch diameter, about 4 per pound.[5]	1 peach	114	89	35	1	Trace	–	–	–	10	9	.5	1320[13]	.02	.05	1.0	7
306	Sliced	1 cup	168	89	65	1	Trace	–	–	–	16	15	.8	2230[13]	.03	.08	1.6	12
	Canned, yellow-fleshed, solids and liquid: Sirup pack, heavy:																	
307	Halves or slices	1 cup	257	79	200	1	Trace	–	–	–	52	10	.8	1100	.02	.06	1.4	7
308	Water pack	1 cup	245	91	75	1	Trace	–	–	–	20	10	.7	1100	.02	.06	1.4	7
309	Dried, uncooked	1 cup	160	25	420	5	1	–	–	–	109	77	9.6	6240	.02	.31	8.5	28
310	Cooked, unsweetened, 10-12 halves and juice.	1 cup	270	77	220	3	1	–	–	–	58	41	5.1	3290	.01	.15	4.2	6
	Frozen:																	
311	Carton, 12 ounces, not thawed.	1 carton	340	76	300	1	Trace	–	–	–	77	14	1.7	2210	.03	.14	2.4	135[14]
	Pears:																	
312	Raw, 3 by 2½-inch diam.[5]	1 pear	182	83	100	1	1	–	–	–	25	13	.5	30	.04	.07	.2	7
	Canned, solids and liquid: Sirup pack, heavy:																	
313	Halves or slices	1 cup	255	80	195	1	1	–	–	–	50	13	.5	Trace	.03	.05	.3	4
	Pineapple:																	
314	Raw, diced	1 cup	140	85	75	1	Trace	–	–	–	19	24	.7	100	.12	.04	.3	24
	Canned, heavy sirup pack, solids and liquid:																	
315	Crushed	1 cup	260	80	195	1	Trace	–	–	–	50	29	.8	120	.20	.06	.5	17
316	Sliced, slices and juice.	2 small or 1 large	122	80	90	Trace	Trace	–	–	–	24	13	.4	50	.09	.03	.2	8

5. Measure and weight apply to entire vegetable or fruit including parts not usually eaten.
10. Value listed is based on product with label stating 30 milligrams per 6 fl. oz. serving.
12. Present only if added by the manufacturer. Refer to the label for this information.
13. Based on yellow-fleshed varieties; for white-fleshed varieties value is about 50 I.U. per 114-gram peach and 80 I.U. per cup of sliced peaches.
14. This value includes ascorbic acid added by manufacturer.

FRUITS AND FRUIT PRODUCTS—Con.

	Food, Approximate Measure, and Weight (in Grams)		Water (%)	Food Energy (kcal)	Protein (g)	Fat (g)	Fatty Acids			Carbohydrate (g)	Calcium (mg)	Iron (mg)	Vitamin A value (I.U.)	Thiamin (mg)	Riboflavin (mg)	Niacin (mg)	Ascorbic acid (mg)
							Saturated (total) (g)	Unsaturated Oleic (g)	Linoleic (g)								
317	Pineapple juice, canned	1 cup	249	86	135	1	Trace	–	–	–	34	37	.7	120	.12	.04	.5	22[8]
318	Plums, all except prunes: Raw, 2-inch diameter, about 2 ounces.[5]	1 plum	60	87	25	Trace	Trace	–	–	–	7	7	.3	140	.02	.02	.3	3
319	Canned, sirup pack (Italian prunes): Plums (with pits) and juice.[5]	1 cup	256	77	205	1	Trace	–	–	–	53	22	2.2	2970	.05	.05	.9	4
320	Prunes, dried, "softenized", medium: Uncooked[5]	4 prunes	32	28	70	1	Trace	–	–	–	18	14	1.1	440	.02	.04	.4	1
321	Cooked, unsweetened, 17-18 prunes and 1/3 cup liquid.[5]	1 cup	270	66	295	2	1	–	–	–	78	60	4.5	1860	.08	.18	1.7	2
322	Prune juice, canned or bottled.	1 cup	256	80	200	1	Trace	–	–	–	49	36	10.5	–	.03	.03	1.0	5[8]
323	Raisins, seedless: Packaged, ½ oz. or 1½ tbsp. per pkg.	1 pkg.	14	18	40	Trace	Trace	–	–	–	11	9	.5	Trace	.02	.01	.1	Trace
324	Cup, pressed down	1 cup	165	18	480	4	Trace	–	–	–	128	102	5.8	30	.18	.13	.8	2
325	Raspberries, red: Raw	1 cup	123	84	70	1	1	–	–	–	17	27	1.1	160	.04	.11	1.1	31
326	Frozen, 10-ounce carton, not thawed.	1 carton	284	74	275	2	1	–	–	–	70	37	1.7	200	.06	.17	1.7	59
327	Rhubarb, cooked, sugar added.	1 cup	272	63	385	1	Trace	–	–	–	98	212	1.6	220	.06	.15	.7	17
328	Strawberries: Raw, capped	1 cup	149	90	55	1	1	–	–	–	13	31	1.5	90	.04	.10	1.0	88
329	Frozen, 10-ounce carton, not thawed.	1 carton	284	71	310	1	1	–	–	–	79	40	2.0	90	.06	.17	1.5	150
330	Tangerines, raw, medium, 2 3/8-in. diam., size 176.[5]	1 tangerine	116	87	40	1	Trace	–	–	–	10	34	.3	360	.05	.02	.1	27

No.	Food	Measure	Grams	Water (%)	Food energy (cal)	Protein (g)	Fat (g)	Saturated (g)	Oleic (g)	Linoleic (g)	Carbohydrate (g)	Calcium (mg)	Iron (mg)	Vitamin A (IU)	Thiamin (mg)	Riboflavin (mg)	Niacin (mg)	Ascorbic acid (mg)
331	Tangerine juice, canned, sweetened.	1 cup	249	87	125	1	1	—	—	—	30	45	.5	1050	.15	.05	.2	55
332	Watermelon, raw, wedge, 4 by 8 inches (1/16 of 10 by 16-inch melon, about 2 pounds with rind).[5]	1 wedge	925	93	115	2	1	—	—	—	27	30	2.1	2510	.13	.13	.7	30
	GRAIN PRODUCTS																	
	Bagel, 3-in. diam.:																	
333	Egg	1 bagel	55	32	165	6	2	—	—	—	28	9	1.2	30	.14	.10	1.2	0
334	Water	1 bagel	55	29	165	6	2	—	—	—	30	8	1.2	0	.15	.11	1.4	0
335	Barley, pearled, light, uncooked.	1 cup	200	11	700	16	2	Trace	1	1	158	32	4.0	0	.24	.10	6.2	0
336	Biscuits, baking powder from home recipe with enriched flour, 2-in. diam.	1 biscuit	28	27	105	2	5	1	2	1	13	34	.4	Trace	.06	.06	.1	Trace
337	Biscuits, baking powder from mix, 2-in. diam.	1 biscuit	28	28	90	2	3	1	1	1	15	19	.6	Trace	.08	.07	.6	Trace
338	Bran flakes (40% bran), added thiamin and iron.	1 cup	35	3	105	4	1	—	—	—	28	25	12.3	0	.14	.06	2.2	0
339	Bran flakes with raisins, added thiamin and iron.	1 cup	50	7	145	4	1	—	—	—	40	28	13.5	Trace	.16	.07	2.7	0
	Breads:																	
340	Boston brown bread, slice 3 by ¾ in.	1 slice	48	45	100	3	1	—	—	—	22	43	.9	0	.05	.03	.6	0
	Cracked-wheat bread:																	
341	Loaf, 1 lb.	1 loaf	454	35	1190	40	10	2	5	2	236	399	5.0	Trace	.53	.41	5.9	Trace
342	Slice, 18 slices per loaf.	1 slice	25	35	65	2	1	—	—	—	13	22	.3	Trace	.03	.02	.3	Trace
	French or vienna bread:																	
343	Enriched, 1 lb. loaf	1 loaf	454	31	1315	41	14	3	8	2	251	195	10.0	Trace	1.27	1.00	11.3	Trace
344	Unenriched, 1 lb. loaf.	1 loaf	454	31	1315	41	14	3	8	2	251	195	3.2	Trace	.36	.36	3.6	Trace
	Italian bread:																	
345	Enriched, 1 lb. loaf	1 loaf	454	32	1250	41	4	Trace	1	2	256	77	10.0	0	1.32	.91	11.8	0
346	Unenriched, 1 lb. loaf.	1 loaf	454	32	1250	41	4	Trace	1	2	256	77	3.2	0	.41	.27	3.6	0

5. Measure and weight apply to entire vegetable or fruit including parts not usually eaten.

8. This is the amount from the fruit. Additional ascorbic acid may be added by the manufacturer. Refer to the label for this information.

	Food, Approximate Measure, and Weight (in Grams)		Water (%)	Food Energy (kcal)	Protein (g)	Fat (g)	Fatty Acids			Carbohydrate (g)	Calcium (mg)	Iron (mg)	Vitamin A value (I.U.)	Thiamin (mg)	Riboflavin (mg)	Niacin (mg)	Ascorbic acid (mg)
							Saturated (total) (g)	Unsaturated Oleic (g)	Unsaturated Linoleic (g)								
	GRAIN PRODUCTS—Continued																
	Raisin bread:																
347	Loaf, 1 lb.	454	35	1190	30	13	3	8	2	243	322	5.9	Trace	.23	.41	3.2	Trace
348	Slice, 18 slices per loaf.	25	35	65	2	1	—	—	—	13	18	.3	Trace	.01	.02	.2	Trace
	Rye bread:																
	American, light (1/3 rye, 2/3 wheat):																
349	Loaf, 1 lb.	454	36	1100	41	5	—	—	—	236	340	7.3	0	.82	.32	6.4	0
350	Slice, 18 slices per loaf.	25	36	60	2	Trace	—	—	—	13	19	.4	0	.05	.02	.4	0
351	Pumpernickel, loaf, 1 lb.	454	34	1115	41	5	—	—	—	241	381	10.9	0	1.04	.64	5.4	0
	White bread, enriched:[15]																
	Soft-crumb type:																
352	Loaf, 1 lb.	454	36	1225	39	15	3	8	2	229	381	11.3	Trace	1.13	.95	10.9	Trace
353	Slice, 18 slices per loaf.	25	36	70	2	1	—	—	—	13	21	.6	Trace	.06	.05	.6	Trace
354	Slice, toasted	22	25	70	2	1	—	—	—	13	21	.6	Trace	.06	.05	.6	Trace
355	Slice, 22 slices per loaf.	20	36	55	2	1	—	—	—	10	17	.5	Trace	.05	.04	.5	Trace
356	Slice, toasted	17	25	55	2	1	—	—	—	10	17	.5	Trace	.05	.04	.5	Trace
357	Loaf, 1½ lbs.	680	36	1835	59	22	5	12	3	343	571	17.0	Trace	1.70	1.43	16.3	Trace
358	Slice, 24 slices per loaf.	28	36	75	2	1	—	—	—	14	24	.7	Trace	.07	.06	.7	Trace
359	Slice, toasted	24	25	75	2	1	—	—	—	14	24	.7	Trace	.07	.06	.7	Trace
360	Slice, 28 slices per loaf.	24	36	65	2	1	—	—	—	12	20	.6	Trace	.06	.05	.6	Trace
361	Slice, toasted	21	25	65	2	1	—	—	—	12	20	.6	Trace	.06	.05	.6	Trace
	Firm-crumb type:																
362	Loaf, 1 lb.	454	35	1245	41	17	4	10	2	228	435	11.3	Trace	1.22	.91	10.9	Trace
363	Slice, 20 slices per loaf.	23	35	65	2	1	—	—	—	12	22	.6	Trace	.06	.05	.6	Trace
364	Slice, toasted	20	24	65	2	1	—	—	—	12	22	.6	Trace	.06	.05	.6	Trace
365	Loaf, 2 lbs.	907	35	2495	82	34	8	20	4	455	871	22.7	Trace	2.45	1.81	21.8	Trace
366	Slice, 34 slices per loaf.	27	35	75	2	1	—	—	—	14	26	.7	Trace	.07	.05	.6	Trace
367	Slice, toasted	23	35	75	2	1	—	—	—	14	26	.7	Trace	.07	.05	.6	Trace
	Whole-wheat bread, soft-crumb type:																
368	Loaf, 1 lb.	454	36	1095	41	12	2	6	2	224	381	13.6	Trace	1.36	.45	12.7	Trace
369	Slice, 16 slices per loaf.	28	36	65	3	1	—	—	—	14	24	.8	Trace	.09	.03	.8	Trace
370	Slice, toasted	24	24	65	3	1	—	—	—	14	24	.8	Trace	.09	.03	.8	Trace
	Whole-wheat bread, firm-crumb type:																
371	Loaf, 1 lb.	454	36	1100	48	14	3	6	3	216	449	13.6	Trace	1.18	.54	12.7	Trace

No.	Food, approximate measure, and weight (in grams)	Measure	Grams	Water (%)	Food energy (cal)	Protein (g)	Fat (g)	Saturated fatty acids (total) (g)	Unsaturated Oleic (g)	Unsaturated Linoleic (g)	Carbohydrate (g)	Calcium (mg)	Iron (mg)	Vitamin A (IU)	Thiamin (mg)	Riboflavin (mg)	Niacin (mg)	Ascorbic acid (mg)
372	Slice, 18 slices per loaf.	1 slice	25	36	60	2	1	—	—	—	12	12	.8	Trace	.06	.03	.7	Trace
373	Slice, toasted	1 slice	21	24	60	2	1	—	—	—	12	12	.8	Trace	.06	.03	.7	Trace
374	Breadcrumbs, dry, grated	1 cup	100	6	390	13	5	1	2	1	73	122	3.6	Trace	.22	.30	3.5	Trace
375	Buckwheat flour, light, sifted.	1 cup	98	12	340	6	1	—	—	—	78	11	1.0	0	.08	.04	.4	0
376	Bulgur, canned, seasoned	1 cup	135	56	245	8	4	—	—	—	44	27	1.9	0	.08	.05	4.1	0
	Cakes made from cake mixes:																	
	Angelfood:																	
377	Whole cake	1 cake	635	34	1645	36	1	—	—	—	377	603	1.9	0	.03	.70	.6	0
378	Piece, 1/12 of 10-in. diam. cake.	1 piece	53	34	135	3	Trace	—	—	—	32	50	.2	0	Trace	.06	.1	0
	Cupcakes, small, 2½ in. diam.:																	
379	Without icing	1 cupcake	25	26	90	1	3	1	1	1	14	40	.1	40	.01	.03	.1	Trace
380	With chocolate icing	1 cupcake	36	22	130	2	5	2	2	1	21	47	.3	60	.01	.04	.1	Trace
	Devil's food, 2-layer, with chocolate icing:																	
381	Whole cake	1 cake	1107	24	3755	49	136	54	58	16	645	653	8.9	1660	.33	.89	3.3	1
382	Piece, 1/16 of 9-in. diam. cake.	1 piece	69	24	235	3	9	3	4	1	40	41	.6	100	.02	.06	.2	Trace
383	Cupcake, small, 2½ in. d.	1 cupcake	35	24	120	2	4	1	2	Trace	20	21	.3	50	.01	.03	.1	Trace
	Gingerbread:																	
384	Whole cake	1 cake	570	37	1575	18	39	10	19	9	291	513	9.1	Trace	.17	.51	4.6	2
385	Piece, 1/9 of 8-in. square cake.	1 piece	63	37	175	2	4	1	2	1	32	57	1.0	Trace	.02	.06	.5	Trace
	White, 2-layer, with chocolate icing:																	
386	Whole cake	1 cake	1140	21	4000	45	122	45	54	17	716	1129	5.7	680	.23	.91	2.3	2
387	Piece, 1/16 of 9-in. diam. cake.	1 piece	71	21	250	3	8	3	3	1	45	70	.4	40	.01	.06	.1	Trace
	Cakes made from home recipes:[16]																	
388	Boston cream pie; piece 1/12 of 8-in. diam.	1 piece	69	35	210	4	6	2	3	1	34	46	.3	140	.02	.08	.1	Trace
	Fruitcake, dark, made with enriched flour:																	
389	Loaf, 1-lb.	1 loaf	454	18	1720	22	69	15	37	13	271	327	11.8	540	.59	.64	3.6	2
390	Slice, 1/30 of 8-in. loaf.	1 slice	15	18	55	1	2	Trace	1	Trace	9	11	.4	20	.02	.02	.1	Trace

15. Values for iron, thiamin, riboflavin, and niacin per pound of unenriched white bread would be as follows:

	Iron (mg)	Thiamin (mg)	Riboflavin (mg)	Niacin (mg)
Soft crumb	3.2	.31	.39	5.0
Firm crumb	3.2	.32	.59	4.1

16. Unenriched cake flour used unless otherwise specified.

Food, Approximate Measure, and Weight (in Grams)		Water (%)	Food Energy (kcal)	Protein (g)	Fat (g)	Fatty Acids Saturated (total) (g)	Unsaturated Oleic (g)	Linoleic (g)	Carbohydrate (g)	Calcium (mg)	Iron (mg)	Vitamin A value (I.U.)	Thiamin (mg)	Riboflavin (mg)	Niacin (mg)	Ascorbic acid (mg)
GRAIN PRODUCTS—Continued																
Plain sheet cake:																
Without icing:																
391 Whole cake	1 cake 777	25	2830	35	108	30	52	21	434	497	3.1	1320	.16	.70	1.6	2
392 Piece, 1/9 of 9-in. square cake.	1 piece 86	25	315	4	12	3	6	2	48	55	.3	150	.02	.08	.2	Trace
393 With boiled white icing, piece, 1/9 of 9-in. square cake.	1 piece 114	23	400	4	12	3	6	2	71	56	.3	150	.02	.08	.2	Trace
Pound:																
394 Loaf, 8½ by 3½ by 3 in.	1 loaf 514	17	2430	29	152	34	68	17	242	108	4.1	1440	.15	.46	1.0	0
395 Slice, ½-in. thick.	1 slice 30	17	140	2	9	2	4	1	14	6	.2	80	.01	.03	.1	0
Sponge:																
396 Whole cake	1 cake 790	32	2345	60	45	14	20	4	427	237	9.5	3560	.40	1.11	1.6	Trace
397 Piece, 1/12 of 10-in. diam. cake.	1 piece 66	32	195	5	4	1	2	Trace	36	20	.8	300	.03	.09	.1	Trace
Yellow, 2-layer, without icing:																
398 Whole cake	1 cake 870	24	3160	39	111	31	53	22	506	618	3.5	1310	.17	.70	1.7	2
399 Piece, 1/16 of 9-in. diam. cake.	1 piece 54	24	200	2	7	2	3	1	32	39	.2	80	.01	.04	.1	Trace
Yellow, 2-layer, with chocolate icing:																
400 Whole cake	1 cake 1203	21	4390	51	156	55	69	23	727	818	7.2	1920	.24	.96	2.4	Trace
401 Piece, 1/16 of 9-in. diam. cake.	1 piece 75	21	275	3	10	3	4	1	45	51	.5	120	.02	.06	.2	Trace
Cake icings. See Sugars, Sweets.																
Cookies:																
Brownies with nuts:																
402 Made from home recipe with enriched flour.	1 brownie 20	10	95	1	6	1	3	1	10	8	.4	40	.04	.02	.1	Trace
403 Made from mix.	1 brownie 20	11	85	1	4	1	2	1	13	9	.4	20	.03	.02	.1	Trace
Chocolate chip:																
404 Made from home recipe with enriched flour.	1 cookie 10	3	50	1	3	1	1	1	6	4	.2	10	.01	.01	.1	Trace
405 Commercial	1 cookie 10	3	50	1	2	1	1	Trace	7	4	.2	10	Trace	Trace	Trace	Trace

No.	Food, approximate measure	Measure	Grams	Water (%)	Food energy (cal)	Protein (g)	Fat (g)	Saturated (g)	Oleic (g)	Linoleic (g)	Carbohydrate (g)	Calcium (mg)	Iron (mg)	Vitamin A (IU)	Thiamin (mg)	Riboflavin (mg)	Niacin (mg)	Ascorbic acid (mg)
406	Fig bars, commercial	1 cookie	14	14	50	1	1	1	—	—	11	11	.2	20	Trace	.01	.1	Trace
407	Sandwich, chocolate or vanilla, commercial.	1 cookie	10	2	50	1	2	1	Trace	—	7	2	.1	0	Trace	Trace	.1	0
	Corn flakes, added nutrients:																	
408	Plain	1 cup	25	4	100	2	Trace	—	—	—	21	4	.4	0	.11	.02	.5	0
409	Sugar-covered	1 cup	40	2	155	2	Trace	—	—	—	36	5	.4	0	.16	.02	.8	0
	Corn (hominy) grits, degermed, cooked:																	
410	Enriched	1 cup	245	87	125	3	Trace	—	—	—	27	2	.7	150[17]	.10	.07	1.0	0
411	Unenriched	1 cup	245	87	125	3	Trace	—	—	—	27	2	.2	150[17]	.05	.02	.5	0
	Cornmeal:																	
412	Whole-ground, unbolted, dry.	1 cup	122	12	435	11	5	1	2	2	90	24	2.9	620[17]	.46	.13	2.4	0
413	Bolted (nearly whole-grain) dry.	1 cup	122	12	440	11	4	Trace	1	2	91	21	2.2	590[17]	.37	.10	2.3	0
	Degermed, enriched:																	
414	Dry form	1 cup	138	12	550	11	2	—	—	—	108	8	4.0	610[17]	.61	.36	4.8	0
415	Cooked	1 cup	240	88	120	3	1	—	—	—	26	2	1.0	140[17]	.14	.10	1.2	0
	Degermed, unenriched:																	
416	Dry form	1 cup	138	12	500	11	2	—	—	—	108	8	1.5	610[17]	.19	.07	1.4	0
417	Cooked	1 cup	240	88	120	3	1	—	—	—	26	2	.5	140[17]	.05	.02	.2	0
418	Corn muffins, made with enriched degermed cornmeal and enriched flour; muffin 2 3/8-in. diam.	1 muffin	40	33	125	3	4	2	2	Trace	19	42	.7	120[17]	.08	.09	.6	Trace
419	Corn muffins, made with mix, egg, and milk; muffin 2 3/8-in. diam.	1 muffin	40	30	130	3	4	2	2	1	20	96	.6	100	.07	.08	.6	Trace
420	Corn, puffed, presweetened, added nutrients.	1 cup	30	2	115	1	Trace	—	—	—	27	3	.5	0	.13	.05	.6	0
421	Corn, shredded, added nutrients.	1 cup	25	3	100	2	Trace	—	—	—	22	1	.6	0	.11	.05	.5	0
	Crackers:																	
422	Graham, 2½-in. square	4 crackers	28	6	110	2	3	—	—	—	21	11	.4	0	.01	.06	.4	0
423	Saltines	4 crackers	11	4	50	1	1	1	—	1	8	2	.1	0	Trace	Trace	.1	0
424	Danish pastry, plain (without fruit or nuts): Packaged ring, 12 ounces.	1 ring	340	22	1435	25	80	24	37	15	155	170	3.1	1050	.24	.51	2.7	Trace

17. This value is based on product made from yellow varieties of corn; white varieties contain only a trace.

| | Food, Approximate Measure, and Weight (in Grams) | | Water (%) | Food Energy (kcal) | Protein (g) | Fat (g) | Fatty Acids | | | Carbohydrate (g) | Calcium (mg) | Iron (mg) | Vitamin A value (I.U.) | Thiamin (mg) | Riboflavin (mg) | Niacin (mg) | Ascorbic acid (mg) |
							Saturated (total) (g)	Unsaturated Oleic (g)	Linoleic (g)								
	GRAIN PRODUCTS—Continued																
425	Round piece, approx. 4¼-in. diam. by 1 in.	1 pastry	22	275	5	15	5	7	3	30	33	.6	200	.05	.10	.5	Trace
426	Ounce	1 oz.	22	120	2	7	2	3	1	13	14	.3	90	.02	.04	.2	Trace
427	Doughnuts, cake type	1 doughnut 32	24	125	1	6	1	4	Trace	16	13	.4[18]	30	.05[18]	.05[18]	.4[18]	Trace
428	Farina, quick-cooking, enriched, cooked.	1 cup 245	89	105	3	Trace	—	—	—	22	147	.7[19]	0	.12[19]	.07[19]	1.0[19]	0
	Macaroni, cooked: Enriched:																
429	Cooked, firm stage (undergoes additional cooking in a food mixture).	1 cup 130	64	190	6	1	—	—	—	39	14	1.4[19]	0	.23[19]	.14[19]	1.8[19]	0
430	Cooked until tender	1 cup 140	72	155	5	1	—	—	—	32	8	1.3[19]	0	.20[19]	.11[19]	1.5[19]	0
	Unenriched:																
431	Cooked, firm stage (undergoes additional cooking in a food mixture).	1 cup 130	64	190	6	1	—	—	—	39	14	.7	0	.03	.03	.5	0
432	Cooked until tender	1 cup 140	72	155	5	1	—	—	—	32	11	.6	0	.01	.01	.4	0
433	Macaroni (enriched) and cheese, baked.	1 cup 200	58	430	17	22	10	9	2	40	362	1.8	860	.20	.40	1.8	Trace
434	Canned	1 cup 240	80	230	9	10	4	3	1	26	199	1.0	260	.12	.24	1.0	Trace
435	Muffins, with enriched white flour; muffin, 3-in. diam.	1 muffin 40	38	120	3	4	1	2	1	17	42	.6	40	.07	.09	.6	Trace
	Noodles (egg noodles), cooked:																
436	Enriched	1 cup 160	70	200	7	2	1	1	Trace	37	16	1.4[19]	110	.22[19]	.13[19]	1.9[19]	0
437	Unenriched	1 cup 160	70	200	7	2	1	1	Trace	37	16	1.0	110	.05	.03	.6	0
438	Oats (with or without corn) puffed, added nutrients.	1 cup 25	3	100	3	1	—	—	—	19	44	1.2	0	.24	.04	.5	0
439	Oatmeal or rolled oats, cooked.	1 cup 240	87	130	5	2	—	—	1	23	22	1.4	0	.19	.05	.2	0

No.	Food	Measure	g	%	cal	g	g	g	g	g	g	mg	mg	IU	mg	mg	mg	mg
	Pancakes, 4-inch diam.:																	
440	Wheat, enriched flour (home recipe).	1 cake	27	50	60	2	2	Trace	2	1	9	27	.4	30	.05	.06	.4	Trace
441	Buckwheat (made from mix with egg and milk).	1 cake	27	58	55	2	2	1	1	1	6	59	.4	60	.03	.04	.2	Trace
442	Plain or buttermilk (made from mix with egg and milk).	1 cake	27	51	60	2	2	1	1	1	9	58	.3	70	.04	.06	.2	Trace
	Pie (piecrust made with unenriched flour): Sector, 4-in., 1/7 of 9-in. diam. pie:																	
443	Apple (2-crust)	1 sector	135	48	350	3	15	4	7	3	51	11	.4	40	.03	.03	.5	1
444	Butterscotch (1-crust)	1 sector	130	45	350	6	14	5	6	2	50	98	1.2	340	.04	.13	.3	Trace
445	Cherry (2-crust)	1 sector	135	47	350	4	15	4	7	3	52	19	.4	590	.03	.03	.7	Trace
446	Custard (1-crust)	1 sector	130	58	285	8	14	5	6	2	30	125	.8	300	.07	.21	.4	0
447	Lemon meringue (1-crust)	1 sector	120	47	305	4	12	4	6	2	45	17	.6	200	.04	.10	.2	4
448	Mince (2-crust)	1 sector	135	43	365	3	16	4	8	3	56	38	1.4	Trace	.09	.05	.5	1
449	Pecan (1-crust)	1 sector	118	20	490	6	27	4	16	5	60	55	3.3	190	.19	.08	.4	Trace
450	Pineapple chiffon (1-crust)	1 sector	93	41	265	6	11	3	5	2	36	22	.8	320	.04	.08	.4	1
451	Pumpkin (1-crust)	1 sector	130	59	275	5	15	5	6	2	32	66	.7	3210	.04	.13	.7	Trace
	Piecrust, baked shell for pie made with:																	
452	Enriched flour	1 shell	180	15	900	11	60	16	28	12	79	25	3.1	0	.36	.25	3.2	0
453	Unenriched flour	1 shell	180	15	900	11	60	16	28	12	79	25	.9	0	.05	.05	.9	0
	Piecrust mix including stick form:																	
454	Package, 10-oz., for double crust.	1 pkg.	284	9	1480	20	93	23	46	21	141	131	1.4	0	.11	.11	2.0	0
455	Pizza (cheese) 5½-in. sector; 1/8 of 14-in. diam. pie.	1 sector	75	45	185	7	6	2	6	3	27	107	.7	290	.04	.12	.7	4
	Popcorn, popped:																	
456	Plain, large kernel	1 cup	6	4	25	1	Trace	—	1	—	5	1	.2	—	—	.01	.1	0
457	With oil and salt	1 cup	9	3	40	1	2	1	Trace	Trace	5	1	.2	—	—	.01	.2	0
458	Sugar coated	1 cup	35	4	135	2	1	—	1	—	30	2	.5	—	—	.02	.4	0

18. Based on product made with enriched flour. With unenriched flour, approximate values per doughnut are: Iron, 0.2 milligram; thiamin, 0.01 milligram; riboflavin, 0.03 milligram; niacin, 0.2 milligram.

19. Iron, thiamin, riboflavin, and niacin are based on the minimum levels of enrichment specified in standards of identity promulgated under the Federal Food, Drug, and Cosmetic Act.

Food, Approximate Measure, and Weight (in Grams)			Water (%)	Food Energy (kcal)	Protein (g)	Fat (g)	Fatty Acids Saturated (total) (g)	Unsaturated Oleic (g)	Linoleic (g)	Carbohydrate (g)	Calcium (mg)	Iron (mg)	Vitamin A value (I.U.)	Thiamin (mg)	Riboflavin (mg)	Niacin (mg)	Ascorbic acid (mg)
GRAIN PRODUCTS—Continued																	
Pretzels:																	
459	Dutch, twisted	1 pretzel	16	5	60	2	1	—	—	—	12	4	.2	0	Trace	Trace	.1	0
460	Thin, twisted	1 pretzel	6	5	25	1	Trace	—	—	—	5	1	.1	0	Trace	Trace	Trace	0
461	Stick, small, 2¼ inches	10 sticks	3	5	10	Trace	Trace	—	—	—	2	1	Trace	0	Trace	Trace	Trace	0
462	Stick, regular, 3 1/8 inches	5 sticks	3	5	10	Trace	Trace	—	—	—	2	1	Trace	0	Trace	Trace	Trace	0
Rice, white:																	
Enriched:																	
463	Raw	1 cup	185	12	670	12	1	—	—	—	149	44	5.4[20]	0	.81[20]	.06[20]	6.5[20]	0
464	Cooked	1 cup	205	73	225	4	Trace	—	—	—	50	21	1.8[20]	0	.23[20]	.02[20]	2.1[20]	0
465	Instant, ready-to-serve	1 cup	165	73	180	4	Trace	—	—	—	40	5	1.3[20]	0	.21[20]	—[20]	1.7[20]	0
466	Unenriched, cooked	1 cup	205	73	225	4	Trace	—	—	—	50	21	.4	0	.04	.02	.8	0
467	Parboiled, cooked	1 cup	175	73	185	4	Trace	—	—	—	41	33	1.4[20]	0	.19[20]	—[20]	2.1[20]	0
468	Rice, puffed, added nutrients	1 cup	15	4	60	1	Trace	—	—	—	13	3	.3	0	.07	.01	.7	0
Rolls, enriched:																	
Cloverleaf or pan:																	
469	Home recipe	1 roll	35	26	120	3	3	1	1	1	20	16	.7	30	.09	.09	.8	Trace
470	Commercial	1 roll	28	31	85	2	2	Trace	1	Trace	15	21	.5	Trace	.08	.05	.6	Trace
471	Frankfurter or hamburger	1 roll	40	31	120	3	2	1	1	1	21	30	.8	Trace	.11	.07	.9	Trace
472	Hard, round or rectangular	1 roll	50	25	155	5	2	Trace	1	Trace	30	24	1.2	Trace	.13	.12	1.4	Trace
473	Rye wafers, whole-grain, 1 7/8 by 3 1/2 inches.	2 wafers	13	6	45	2	Trace	—	—	—	10	7	.5	0	.04	.03	.2	0
474	Spaghetti, cooked, tender stage, enriched.	1 cup	140	72	155	5	1	—	—	—	32	11	1.3[19]	0	.20[19]	.11[19]	1.5[19]	0
Spaghetti with meat balls, and tomato sauce:																	
475	Home recipe	1 cup	248	70	330	19	12	4	6	1	39	124	3.7	1590	.25	.30	4.0	22
476	Canned	1 cup	250	78	260	12	10	2	3	4	28	53	3.3	1000	.15	.18	2.3	5
Spaghetti in tomato sauce with cheese:																	
477	Home recipe	1 cup	250	77	260	9	9	2	5	1	37	80	2.3	1080	.25	.18	2.3	13
478	Canned	1 cup	250	80	190	6	2	1	1	1	38	40	2.8	930	.35	.28	4.5	10
479	Waffles, with enriched flour, 7-in. diam.	1 waffle	75	41	210	7	7	2	4	Trace	28	85	1.3	250	.13	.19	1.0	Trace

No.	Food	Measure	(g)		(cal)								(mg)	(I.U.)				
480	Waffles, made from mix, enriched, egg and milk added, 7-in. diam.	1 waffle	75	42	205	7	8	3	3	1	27	179	1.0	170	.11	.17	.7	Trace
481	Wheat, puffed, added nutrients.	1 cup	15	3	55	2	Trace	—	—	—	12	4	.6	0	.08	.03	1.2	0
482	Wheat, shredded, plain	1 biscuit	25	7	90	2	1	—	—	—	20	11	.9	0	.06	.03	1.1	0
483	Wheat flakes, added nutrients	1 cup	30	4	105	3	Trace	—	—	—	24	12	1.3	0	.19	.04	1.5	0
484	Wheat flours: Whole-wheat, from hard wheats, stirred.	1 cup	120	12	400	16	2	Trace	1	1	85	49	4.0	0	.66	.14	5.2	0
	All-purpose or family flour, enriched:																	
485	Sifted	1 cup	115	12	420	12	1	—	—	—	88	18	3.3[19]	0	.51[19]	.30[19]	4.0[19]	0
486	Unsifted	1 cup	125	12	455	13	1	—	—	—	95	20	3.6[19]	0	.55[19]	.33[19]	4.4[19]	0
487	Self-rising, enriched	1 cup	125	12	440	12	1	—	—	—	93	331	3.6[19]	0	.55[19]	.33[19]	4.4[19]	0
488	Cake or pastry flour, sifted	1 cup	96	12	350	7	1	—	—	—	76	16	.5	0	.03	.03	.7	0

FATS, OILS

No.	Food	Measure	(g)		(cal)								(mg)	(I.U.)				
	Butter:																	
	Regular, 4 sticks per pound:																	
489	Stick	½ cup	113	16	810	1	92	51	30	3	1	23	0	3750[21]	—	—	—	0
490	Tablespoon (approx. 1/8 stick).	1 tbsp.	14	16	100	Trace	12	6	4	Trace	Trace	3	0	470[21]	—	—	—	0
491	Pat (1-in. sq. 1/3-in. high; 90 per lb.).	1 pat	5	16	35	Trace	4	2	1	Trace	Trace	1	0	170[21]	—	—	—	0
	Whipped, 6 sticks or 2, 8-oz. containers per pound:																	
492	Stick	½ cup	76	16	540	1	61	34	20	2	Trace	15	0	2500[21]	—	—	—	0
493	Tablespoon (approx. 1/8 stick).	1 tbsp.	9	16	65	Trace	8	4	3	Trace	Trace	2	0	310[21]	—	—	—	0
494	Pat (1¼-in. sq. 1/3-in. high; 120 per lb.).	1 pat	4	16	25	Trace	3	2	1	Trace	Trace	1	0	130[21]	—	—	—	0

19. Iron, thiamin, riboflavin, and niacin are based on the minimum levels of enrichment specified in standards of identity promulgated under the Federal Food, Drug, and Cosmetic Act.

20. Iron, thiamin, and niacin are based on the minimum levels of enrichment specified in standards of identity promulgated under the Federal Food, Drug, and Cosmetic Act. Riboflavin is based on unenriched rice. When the minimum level of enrichment for riboflavin specified in the standards of identity becomes effective the value will be 0.12 milligram per cup of parboiled rice and of white rice.

21. Year-round average.

	Food, Approximate Measure, and Weight (in Grams)		Water (%)	Food Energy (kcal)	Protein (g)	Fat (g)	Fatty Acids			Carbohydrate (g)	Calcium (mg)	Iron (mg)	Vitamin A value (I.U.)	Thiamin (mg)	Riboflavin (mg)	Niacin (mg)	Ascorbic acid (mg)
							Saturated (total) (g)	Unsaturated Oleic (g)	Linoleic (g)								
	FATS, OILS—Continued																
	Fats, cooking:																
495	Lard	1 cup 205	0	1850	0	205	78	94	20	0	0	0	0	0	0	0	0
496		1 tbsp. 13	0	115	0	13	5	6	1	0	0	0	0	0	0	0	0
497	Vegetable fats	1 cup 200	0	1770	0	200	50	100	44	0	0	0	0	0	0	0	0
498		1 tbsp. 13	0	110	0	13	3	6	3	0	0	0	0	0	0	0	0
	Margarine:																
	Regular, 4 sticks per pound:																
499	Stick	½ cup 113	16	815	1	92	17	46	25	1	23	0	3750[22]	—	—	—	0
500	Tablespoon (approx. 1/8 stick).	1 tbsp. 14	16	100	Trace	12	2	6	3	Trace	3	0	470[22]	—	—	—	0
501	Pat (1-in. sq. 1/3-in. high; 1 pat 90 per lb.).	5	16	35	Trace	4	1	2	1	Trace	1	0	170[22]	—	—	—	0
	Whipped, 6 sticks per pound:																
502	Stick	½ cup 76	16	545	1	61	11	31	17	Trace	15	0	2500[22]	—	—	—	0
	Soft, 2 8-oz. tubs per pound:																
503	Tub	1 tub 227	16	1635	1	184	34	68	68	1	45	0	7500[22]	—	—	—	0
504	Tablespoon	1 tbsp. 14	16	100	Trace	11	2	4	4	Trace	3	0	470[22]	—	—	—	0
	Oils, salad or cooking:																
505	Corn	1 cup 220	0	1945	0	220	22	62	117	0	0	0	—	0	0	0	0
506		1 tbsp. 14	0	125	0	14	1	4	7	0	0	0	—	0	0	0	0
507	Cottonseed	1 cup 220	0	1945	0	220	55	46	110	0	0	0	—	0	0	0	0
508		1 tbsp. 14	0	125	0	14	4	3	7	0	0	0	—	0	0	0	0
509	Olive	1 cup 220	0	1945	0	220	24	167	15	0	0	0	—	0	0	0	0
510		1 tbsp. 14	0	125	0	14	2	11	1	0	0	0	—	0	0	0	0
511	Peanut	1 cup 220	0	1945	0	220	40	103	64	0	0	0	—	0	0	0	0
512		1 tbsp. 14	0	125	0	14	3	7	4	0	0	0	—	0	0	0	0
513	Safflower	1 cup 220	0	1945	0	220	18	37	165	0	0	0	—	0	0	0	0
514		1 tbsp. 14	0	125	0	14	1	2	10	0	0	0	—	0	0	0	0
515	Soybean	1 cup 220	0	1945	0	220	33	44	114	0	0	0	—	0	0	0	0
516		1 tbsp. 14	0	125	0	14	2	3	7	0	0	0	—	0	0	0	0

No.	Food	Measure	Grams	Water (%)	Food energy (cal.)	Protein (g)	Fat (g)	Saturated (g)	Oleic (g)	Linoleic (g)	Carbohydrate (g)	Calcium (mg)	Iron (mg)	Vitamin A (I.U.)	Thiamin (mg)	Riboflavin (mg)	Niacin (mg)	Ascorbic acid (mg)
	Salad dressings:																	
517	Blue cheese	1 tbsp.	15	32	75	1	8	2	2	4	1	12	Trace	30	Trace	.02	Trace	Trace
	Commercial, mayonnaise type:																	
518	Regular	1 tbsp.	15	41	65	Trace	6	1	1	3	2	2	Trace	30	Trace	Trace	Trace	—
519	Special dietary, low-calorie.	1 tbsp.	16	81	20	Trace	2	Trace	Trace	1	1	3	Trace	40	Trace	Trace	Trace	—
	French:																	
520	Regular	1 tbsp.	16	39	65	Trace	6	1	1	3	3	2	.1	—	—	—	—	—
521	Special dietary, lowfat with artificial sweeteners.	1 tbsp.	15	95	Trace	Trace	Trace	—	—	Trace	Trace	2	.1	—	—	—	—	—
522	Home cooked, boiled	1 tbsp.	16	68	25	1	2	1	1	Trace	2	14	.1	80	.01	.03	Trace	Trace
523	Mayonnaise	1 tbsp.	14	15	100	Trace	11	2	2	6	Trace	3	.1	40	Trace	.01	Trace	—
524	Thousand island	1 tbsp.	16	32	80	Trace	8	1	2	4	3	2	.1	50	Trace	Trace	Trace	Trace
	SUGARS, SWEETS																	
	Cake icings:																	
525	Chocolate made with milk and table fat.	1 cup	275	14	1035	9	38	21	14	1	185	165	3.3	580	.06	.28	.6	1
526	Coconut (with boiled icing).	1 cup	166	15	605	3	13	11	1	Trace	124	10	.8	0	.02	.07	.3	0
527	Creamy fudge from mix with water only.	1 cup	245	15	830	7	16	5	8	3	183	96	2.7	Trace	.05	.20	.7	Trace
528	White, boiled	1 cup	94	18	300	1	0	—	—	—	76	2	Trace	0	Trace	.03	Trace	0
	Candy:																	
529	Caramels, plain or chocolate.	1 oz.	28	8	115	1	3	2	1	Trace	22	42	.4	Trace	.01	.05	.1	Trace
530	Chocolate, milk, plain	1 oz.	28	1	145	2	9	5	3	Trace	16	65	.3	80	.02	.10	.1	Trace
531	Chocolate-coated peanuts.	1 oz.	28	1	160	5	12	3	6	2	11	33	.4	Trace	.10	.05	2.1	Trace
532	Fondant; mints, uncoated; candy corn.	1 oz.	28	8	105	Trace	1	Trace	—	—	25	4	.3	0	Trace	Trace	Trace	0
533	Fudge, plain	1 oz.	28	8	115	1	4	2	1	Trace	21	22	.3	Trace	.01	.03	.1	Trace
534	Gum drops	1 oz.	28	12	100	Trace	Trace	—	—	—	25	2	.1	0	0	Trace	Trace	0
535	Hard	1 oz.	28	1	110	0	Trace	—	—	—	28	6	.5	0	0	0	0	0
536	Marshmallows	1 oz.	28	17	90	1	Trace	—	—	—	23	5	.5	0	0	Trace	Trace	0
	Chocolate-flavored sirup or topping:																	
537	Thin type	1 fl. oz.	38	32	90	1	1	Trace	Trace	Trace	24	6	.6	Trace	.01	.03	.2	0
538	Fudge type	1 fl. oz.	38	25	125	2	5	3	2	Trace	20	48	.5	60	.02	.08	.2	Trace

22. Based on the average vitamin A content of fortified margarine. Federal specifications for fortified margarine require a minimum of 15,000 I.U. of vitamin A per pound.

No.	Food, Approximate Measure, and Weight (in Grams)	Water (%)	Food Energy (kcal)	Protein (g)	Fat (g)	Fatty Acids Saturated (total) (g)	Unsaturated Oleic (g)	Linoleic (g)	Carbohydrate (g)	Calcium (mg)	Iron (mg)	Vitamin A value (I.U.)	Thiamin (mg)	Riboflavin (mg)	Niacin (mg)	Ascorbic acid (mg)
	SUGARS, SWEETS—Continued															
	Chocolate-flavored beverage powder (approx. 4 heaping teaspoons per oz.):															
539	With nonfat dry milk, 1 oz., 28	2	100	5	1	Trace	Trace	Trace	20	167	.5	10	.04	.21	.2	1
540	Without nonfat dry milk, 1 oz., 28	1	100	1	1	Trace	Trace	Trace	25	9	.6	—	.01	.03	.1	0
541	Honey, strained or extracted, 1 tbsp., 21	17	65	Trace	0	—	—	—	17	1	.1	Trace	Trace	.01	.1	Trace
542	Jams and preserves, 1 tbsp., 20	29	55	Trace	Trace	—	—	—	14	4	.2	Trace	Trace	.01	Trace	Trace
543	Jellies, 1 tbsp., 18	29	50	Trace	Trace	—	—	—	13	4	.3	Trace	Trace	.01	Trace	1
	Molasses, cane:															
544	Light (first extraction), 1 tbsp., 20	24	50	—	—	—	—	—	13	33	.9	—	.01	.01	Trace	—
545	Blackstrap (third extraction), 1 tbsp., 20	24	45	—	—	—	—	—	11	137	3.2	—	.02	.04	.4	—
	Sirups:															
546	Sorghum, 1 tbsp., 21	23	55	—	—	—	—	—	14	35	2.6	—	—	.02	Trace	—
547	Table blends, chiefly corn, light and dark, 1 tbsp., 21	24	60	0	0	—	—	—	15	9	.8	0	0	0	0	0
	Sugars:															
548	Brown, firm packed, 1 cup, 220	2	820	0	0	—	—	—	212	187	7.5	0	.02	.07	.4	0
	White:															
549	Granulated, 1 cup, 200	Trace	770	0	0	—	—	—	199	0	.2	0	0	0	0	0
550	Granulated, 1 tbsp., 11	Trace	40	0	0	—	—	—	11	0	Trace	0	0	0	0	0
551	Powdered, stirred before measuring, 1 cup, 120	Trace	460	0	0	—	—	—	119	0	.1	0	0	0	0	0
	MISCELLANEOUS ITEMS															
552	Barbecue sauce, 1 cup, 250	81	230	4	17	2	5	9	20	53	2.0	900	.03	.03	.8	13
	Beverages, alcoholic:															
553	Beer, 12 fl. oz., 360	92	150	1	0	—	—	—	14	18	Trace	—	.01	.11	2.2	—
554	Gin, rum, vodka, whiskey: 80-proof, 1½ fl. oz. jigger, 42	67	100	—	—	—	—	—	Trace	—	—	—	—	—	—	—

No.	Food	Measure	Weight (g)	Water (%)	Food energy (cal)	Protein (g)	Fat (g)	Saturated (g)	Oleic (g)	Linoleic (g)	Carbohydrate (g)	Calcium (mg)	Iron (mg)	Vitamin A (IU)	Thiamin (mg)	Riboflavin (mg)	Niacin (mg)	Ascorbic acid (mg)
555	86-proof	1½ fl. oz. jigger	42	64	105	—	—	—	—	—	Trace	—	—	—	—	—	—	—
556	90-proof	1½ fl. oz. jigger	42	62	110	—	—	—	—	—	Trace	—	—	—	—	—	—	—
557	94-proof	1½ fl. oz. jigger	42	60	115	—	—	—	—	—	Trace	—	—	—	—	—	—	—
558	100-proof	1½ fl. oz. jigger	42	58	125	—	—	—	—	—	Trace	—	—	—	—	—	—	—
	Wines:																	
559	Desert	3½ fl. oz. glass	103	77	140	Trace	0	—	—	—	8	8	—	—	.01	.02	.2	—
560	Table	3½ fl. oz. glass	102	86	85	Trace	0	—	—	—	4	9	.4	—	Trace	.01	.1	—
	Beverages, carbonated, sweetened, nonalcoholic:																	
561	Carbonated water	12 fl. oz.	366	92	115	0	0	—	—	—	29	—	0	0	0	0	0	0
562	Cola type	12 fl. oz.	369	90	145	0	0	—	—	—	37	—	0	0	0	0	0	0
563	Fruit-flavored sodas and Tom Collins mixes.	12 fl. oz.	372	88	170	0	0	—	—	—	45	—	0	0	0	0	0	0
564	Ginger ale	12 fl. oz.	366	92	115	0	0	—	—	—	29	—	0	0	0	0	0	0
565	Root beer	12 fl. oz.	370	90	150	0	0	—	—	—	39	—	0	0	0	0	0	0
566	Bouillon cubes, approx. ½ in.	1 cube	4	4	5	1	Trace	—	—	—	Trace	—	—	—	—	—	—	—
	Chocolate:																	
567	Bitter or baking.	1 oz.	28	2	145	3	15	8	6	Trace	8	22	1.9	20	.01	.07	.4	0
568	Semi-sweet, small pieces.	1 cup	170	1	860	7	61	34	22	1	97	51	4.4	30	.02	.14	.9	0
	Gelatin:																	
569	Plain, dry powder in envelope.	1 envelope	7	13	25	6	Trace	—	—	—	0	—	—	—	—	—	—	—
570	Dessert powder, 3-oz. package.	1 pkg.	85	2	315	8	0	—	—	—	75	—	—	—	—	—	—	—
571	Gelatin dessert, prepared with water.	1 cup	240	84	140	4	0	—	—	—	34	—	—	—	—	—	—	—
	Olives, pickled:																	
572	Green	4 medium or 3 extra large or 2 giant	16	78	15	Trace	2	—	—	—	Trace	8	.2	40	—	—	—	—
573	Ripe: Mission	3 small or 2 large.	10	73	15	Trace	2	—	—	—	Trace	9	.1	10	Trace	Trace	—	—

	Food, Approximate Measure, and Weight (in Grams)		Water (%)	Food Energy (kcal)	Protein (g)	Fat (g)	Fatty Acids Saturated (total) (g)	Unsaturated Oleic (g)	Lir.-oleic (g)	Carbohydrate (g)	Calcium (mg)	Iron (mg)	Vitamin A value (I.U.)	Thiamin (mg)	Riboflavin (mg)	Niacin (mg)	Ascorbic acid (mg)
	MISCELLANEOUS ITEMS—Continued																
	Pickles, cucumber:																
574	Dill, medium, whole, 3¾ in. long, 1¼ in. diam.	1 pickle 65	93	10	1	Trace	—	—	—	1	17	.7	70	Trace	.01	Trace	4
575	Fresh, sliced, 1½ in. diam., ¼ in. thick.	2 slices 15	79	10	Trace	Trace	—	—	—	3	5	.3	20	Trace	Trace	Trace	1
576	Sweet, gherkin, small, whole, approx. 2½ in. long, ¾ in. diam.	1 pickle 15	61	20	Trace	Trace	—	—	—	6	2	.2	10	Trace	Trace	Trace	1
577	Relish, finely chopped, sweet.	1 tbsp. 15	63	20	Trace	Trace	—	—	—	5	3	.1	—	—	—	—	—
	Popcorn. See Grain Products.																
578	Popsicle, 3 fl. oz. size	1 popsicle 95	80	70	0	0	0	0	0	18	0	Trace	0	0	0	0	0
	Pudding, home recipe with starch base:																
579	Chocolate	1 cup 260	66	385	8	12	7	4	Trace	67	250	1.3	390	.05	.36	.3	1
580	Vanilla (blanc mange)	1 cup 255	76	285	9	10	5	3	Trace	41	298	Trace	410	.08	.41	.3	2
581	Pudding mix, dry form, 4-oz. package.	1 pkg. 113	2	410	3	2	1	1	Trace	103	23	1.8	Trace	.02	.08	.5	0
582	Sherbet	1 cup 193	67	260	2	2	—	—	—	59	31	Trace	120	.02	.06	Trace	4
	Soups:																
	Canned, condensed, ready-to-serve:																
	Prepared with an equal volume of milk:																
583	Cream of chicken	1 cup 245	85	180	7	10	3	3	3	15	172	.5	610	.05	.27	.7	2
584	Cream of mushroom	1 cup 245	83	215	7	14	4	4	5	16	191	.5	250	.05	.34	.7	1
585	Tomato	1 cup 250	84	175	7	7	3	2	1	23	168	.8	1200	.10	.25	1.3	15
	Prepared with an equal volume of water:																
586	Bean with pork	1 cup 250	84	170	8	6	1	2	2	22	63	2.3	650	.13	.08	1.0	3
587	Beef broth, bouillon consomme,	1 cup 240	96	30	5	0	—	—	—	3	Trace	.5	Trace	Trace	.02	1.2	—
588	Beef noodle	1 cup 240	93	70	4	3	1	1	1	7	7	1.0	50	.05	.07	1.0	Trace
589	Clam chowder, Manhattan type (with tomatoes, without milk).	1 cup 245	92	80	2	3	—	—	—	12	34	1.0	880	.02	.02	1.0	—

Item	Food, approximate measure		Grams	Water (%)	Food energy (cal.)	Protein (g)	Fat (g)	Saturated	Oleic	Linoleic	Carbo-hydrate (g)	Calcium (mg)	Iron (mg)	Vitamin A (IU)	Thiamin (mg)	Riboflavin (mg)	Niacin (mg)	Ascorbic acid (mg)
590	Cream of chicken	1 cup	240	92	95	3	6	1	2	1	8	24	.5	410	.02	.05	.5	Trace
591	Cream of mushroom	1 cup	240	90	135	2	10	1	3	1	10	41	.5	70	.02	.12	.7	Trace
592	Minestrone	1 cup	245	90	105	5	3	–	–	–	14	37	1.0	2350	.07	.05	1.0	–
593	Split pea	1 cup	245	85	145	9	3	–	2	Trace	21	29	1.5	440	.25	.15	1.5	1
594	Tomato	1 cup	245	90	90	2	3	Trace	1	1	16	15	.7	1000	.05	.05	1.2	12
595	Vegetable beef	1 cup	245	92	80	5	2	–	–	–	10	12	.7	2700	.05	.05	1.0	–
596	Vegetarian	1 cup	245	92	80	2	2	–	–	–	13	20	1.0	2940	.05	.05	1.0	–
	Dehydrated, dry form:																	
597	Chicken noodle (2-oz. package).	1 pkg.	57	6	220	8	6	2	3	1	33	34	1.4	190	.30	.15	2.4	3
598	Onion mix (1½-oz. package).	1 pkg.	43	3	150	6	5	1	2	1	23	42	.6	30	.05	.03	.3	6
599	Tomato vegetable with noodles (2½-oz. pkg.).	1 pkg.	71	4	245	6	6	2	3	1	45	33	1.4	1700	.21	.13	1.8	18
	Frozen, condensed:																	
	Clam chowder, New England type (with milk, without tomatoes):																	
600	Prepared with equal volume of milk.	1 cup	245	83	210	9	12	–	–	–	16	240	1.0	250	.07	.29	.5	Trace
601	Prepared with equal volume of water.	1 cup	240	89	130	4	8	–	–	–	11	91	1.0	50	.05	.10	.5	–
	Cream of potato:																	
602	Prepared with equal volume of milk.	1 cup	245	83	185	8	10	5	3	Trace	18	208	1.0	590	.10	.27	.5	Trace
603	Prepared with equal volume of water.	1 cup	240	90	105	3	5	3	2	Trace	12	58	1.0	410	.05	.05	.5	–
	Cream of shrimp:																	
604	Prepared with equal volume of milk.	1 cup	245	82	245	9	16	–	–	–	15	189	.5	290	.07	.27	.5	Trace
605	Prepared with equal volume of water.	1 cup	240	88	160	5	12	–	–	–	8	38	.5	120	.05	.05	.5	–
	Oyster stew:																	
606	Prepared with equal volume of milk.	1 cup	240	83	200	10	12	–	–	–	14	305	1.4	410	.12	.41	.5	Trace
607	Prepared with equal volume of water.	1 cup	240	90	120	6	8	–	–	–	8	158	1.4	240	.07	.19	.5	–
608	Tapioca, dry quick-cooking	1 cup	152	13	535	1	Trace	–	–	–	131	15	.6	0	0	0	0	0
	Tapioca desserts:																	
609	Apple	1 cup	250	70	295	1	Trace	–	–	–	74	8	.5	30	Trace	Trace	Trace	Trace
610	Cream pudding	1 cup	165	72	220	8	8	4	3	Trace	28	173	.7	480	.07	.30	.2	2

Food, Approximate Measure, and Weight (in Grams)		Water (%)	Food Energy (kcal)	Protein (g)	Fat (g)	Fatty Acids Saturated (total) (g)	Unsaturated Oleic (g)	Unsaturated Linoleic (g)	Carbohydrate (g)	Calcium (mg)	Iron (mg)	Vitamin A value (I.U.)	Thiamin (mg)	Riboflavin (mg)	Niacin (mg)	Ascorbic acid (mg)
MISCELLANEOUS ITEMS—Continued																
611	Tartar sauce 1 tbsp. 14	34	75	Trace	8	1	1	4	1	3	.1	30	Trace	Trace	Trace	Trace
612	Vinegar 1 tbsp. 15	94	Trace	Trace	0	—	—	—	1	1	.1	—	—	—	—	—
613	White sauce, medium 1 cup 250	73	405	10	31	16	10	1	22	288	.5	1150	.10	.43	.5	2
	Yeast:															
614	Baker's, dry, active 1 pkg. 7	5	20	3	Trace	—	—	—	3	3	1.1	Trace	.16	.38	2.6	Trace
615	Brewer's, dry 1 tbsp. 8	5	25	3	Trace	—	—	—	3	17	1.4	Trace	1.25	.34	3.0	Trace
	Yoghurt. See Milk, Cheese, Cream, Imitation Cream.															

APPENDIX B

Consumer Buying Guides

COST OF EGGS PER POUND

The following table shows you how to get the most eggs for your money. To use it, find the current price for a dozen eggs of that size in the "price" column on the left. That column tells you the price per pound for eggs of that size and that price. For example, if large eggs are being sold at the supermarket for $0.52 for a dozen, they cost you $0.80 for a pound. If medium eggs are being sold for $0.45 for a dozen, they cost you $0.59 for a pound. The medium eggs, then, are a better buy per pound of protein food.

Here's a general rule you can remember at the supermarket: if there is less than 7 cents difference between the cost of a dozen eggs of one size and the cost of the next smaller size, you get more protein for your money by buying the larger size. If the difference is more than 7 cents, the smaller size would be the best buy. Remember to compare eggs of the same grade.

COST OF EGGS PER POUND[1]

	Price per Dozen by Size			Price per Pound
X Large	Large	Medium	Small	¢/Lb
32	28	24	21	19
33½	30	26	23	20
36	32	28	24	21
38	34	29½	25½	22½
41	36	32	27	24
42	38	33	28	25
46	40	35	30	27
47	42	37	32	28
49	44	38	33	29
52	46	41	35	31
54	48	42	36	32
56	50	43	37	33
59	52	46	39	35
61	54	47	41	36
62	56	49	42	37
65	58	50½	43½	38½
68	60	53	45	40
69	62	54	46	41
72	64	55½	47½	42½
74	66	58	50	44
76	68	59	51	45
78½	70	61	52½	46½
81	72	63	54	48
83	74	64	56	49
85	76	66	59	50½
88	80	69	60	52
90	82	72	63	53½
93	84	73	64	56

[1]Based on the following weights: extra large eggs, 27 ounces; large eggs, 24 ounces; medium eggs, 21 ounces; small eggs, 18 ounces. (Reprinted courtesy of Poultry and Egg National Board, Chicago, Ill).

COMPARATIVE COSTS OF CHICKEN PARTS

If the Price per Pound of Whole Fryers, Ready to Cook, Is:	Chicken Parts Are an Equally Good Buy if the Price per pound Is:				
	Breast Half	Drumstick and Thigh	Drumstick	Thigh	Wing
(cents)	(cents)	(cents)	(cents)	(cents)	(cents)
27	38	35	33	36	21
29	41	37	36	39	23
31	44	40	38	41	25
33	47	42	41	44	26
35	49	45	43	47	28
37	52	47	46	49	29
39	55	50	48	52	31
41	58	53	50	55	33
43	61	55	53	57	34
45	63	58	55	60	36
47	66	60	58	63	37
49	69	63	60	65	39
51	72	65	63	68	41
53	75	68	65	71	42
55	78	71	68	73	44

Reprinted from: *Family Economics Review.* September 1971. Agricultural Research Service, U. S. Department of Agriculture.

COMPARATIVE COSTS OF TURKEY PARTS

Turkey Parts and Products Are an Equally Good Buy if the Price per Pound Is:

If the Price per Pound of Whole Turkey Ready-to-Cook, Is:	Breast Quarter	Leg Quarter	Breast	Drum-stick	Thigh	Wing	Boned Turkey Roast		Boned Turkey, Canned	Turkey with Gravy, Canned or Frozen	Gravy with Turkey, Canned or Frozen
							Ready-to-Cook	Cooked			
(cents)	(cents)	(cents)	(cents)	(cents)	(cents)	(cents)	(cents)	(cents)	(cents)	(cents)	(cents)
33	37	35	42	34	40	31	58	76	74	29	12
35	39	38	45	36	43	32	61	80	79	31	13
37	42	40	47	38	45	34	65	85	83	32	14
39	44	42	50	40	48	36	68	90	88	34	15
41	46	44	52	42	50	38	72	94	92	36	15
43	48	46	55	44	53	40	75	99	97	38	16
45	51	48	57	46	55	42	79	103	101	39	17
47	53	51	60	48	58	43	82	108	106	41	18
49	55	53	62	50	60	45	86	113	110	43	18
51	57	55	65	52	62	47	89	117	115	45	19
53	60	57	68	54	65	49	93	122	119	46	20
55	62	59	70	56	67	51	96	126	124	48	21
57	64	61	73	58	70	53	100	131	128	50	21
59	66	63	75	60	72	55	103	136	133	52	22
61	69	66	78	63	75	56	107	140	137	53	23
63	71	68	80	65	77	58	110	145	142	55	24
65	73	70	83	67	80	60	114	150	146	57	24
67	75	72	85	69	82	62	117	154	151	59	25
69	78	74	88	71	85	64	121	159	155	60	26
71	80	76	91	73	87	66	124	163	160	62	27
73	82	78	93	75	89	68	128	168	164	64	27

FRUIT AND VEGETABLE AVAILABILITY

This chart shows when common fruits and vegetables are in supply.

Legend:
- (open box) Means supplies are scarce or nonexistent.
- (diagonal hatch) Means supplies are moderate.
- (crosshatch) Means supplies are plentiful.
- (solid black) Means supplies are exceptionally abundant.

Key below: blank = scarce, M = moderate, P = plentiful, A = exceptionally abundant.

COMMODITY	Jan	Feb	Mar	Apr	May	June	July	Aug	Sept	Oct	Nov	Dec
APPLES	P	P	P	P	P	M	M	M	P	P	P	P
APRICOTS					M	A	A	M				
ARTICHOKES	M	M	P	P	P	M	M	M	M	M	M	M
ASPARAGUS		M	A	A	P	M						
AVOCADOS	P	P	P	P	P	P	P	P	P	P	P	P
BANANAS	P	P	P	P	P	P	P	P	P	P	P	P
BEANS, SNAP	M	M	M	M	P	P	M	M	M	M	M	M
BEETS	M	M	M	M	M	P	P	P	M	M	M	M
BERRIES, MISC.*					M	A	A	M				
BLUEBERRIES						P	P	P	M			
BROCCOLI	P	P	P	P	M	M	M	M	P	P	P	P
BRUSSELS SPROUTS	P	M	M	M					P	P	P	P
CABBAGE	P	P	P	P	P	P	P	P	P	P	P	P
CANTALOUPES					M	A	A	A	M			
CARROTS	P	P	P	P	P	P	P	P	P	P	P	P
CAULIFLOWER	M	M	M	M	M	M	M	M	P	P	P	M
CELERY	P	P	P	P	P	P	P	P	P	P	P	P
CHERRIES					M	A	M					
CHINESE CABBAGE	M	M	M	M	M	M	M	M	M	M	M	M
CORN, SWEET				M	M	P	P	P	P	M		
CRANBERRIES	M									P	A	P
CUCUMBERS	P	P	P	P	P	P	P	P	P	P	P	P
EGGPLANT	M	M	M	M	M	M	M	M	M	M	M	M
ESCAROLE-ENDIVE	P	P	P	P	P	P	P	P	P	P	P	P
ENDIVE, BELGIAN	M	M	M	M	M	M	M	M	M	M	M	M
GRAPEFRUIT	P	P	P	P	P	M	M	M	M	P	P	P
GRAPES					M	P	P	A	A	A	M	M

*Mostly blackberries, dewberries, raspberries.

COMMODITY	Jan	Feb	Mar	Apr	May	June	July	Aug	Sept	Oct	Nov	Dec
GREENS												
HONEYDEWS												
LEMONS												
LETTUCE												
LIMES												
MUSHROOMS												
NECTARINES												
OKRA												
ONIONS, DRY												
ONIONS, GREEN												
ORANGES												
PARSLEY & HERBS**												
PARSNIPS												
PEACHES												
PEARS												
PEPPERS, SWEET												
PINEAPPLES												
PLUMS-PRUNES												
POTATOES												
RADISHES												
RHUBARB												
SPINACH												
SQUASH												
STRAWBERRIES												
SWEETPOTATOES												
TANGERINES												
TOMATOES												
TURNIPS-RUTABAGAS												
WATERMELONS												

**Includes also parsley root, anise, basil, chives, dill, horseradish, others.

Information courtesy of United Fresh Fruit and Vegetable Association, Washington, D.C.

APPENDIX C

Suggested Sources of Educational Materials about Food

American Dairy Assoc.: 6300 N. River Rd., Rosemont, Ill. 60018

American Egg Board: 205 Touhy Ave., Park Ridge, Ill. 60068

American Frozen Food Institute: Communications Division, 111 E. Wacker Dr., Suite 600, Chicago, Ill. 60601

American Institute of Baking: Nutrition Education Department, 400 E. Ontario St., Chicago, Ill. 60611

Ball Corp.: Muncie, Indiana 47302

Best Foods: Consumer Services, International Plaza, Englewood Cliffs, N.J. 07632

Blue Goose Growers, Inc.: 332 E. Commonwealth, Fullerton, CA 92632

Borden, Inc.: 50 W. Broad St., Columbus, Ohio 43215

Carnation Company: Carnation Food Services Center, 5045 Wilshire Blvd., Los Angeles, Calif. 90036

Cereal Institute, Inc.: 135 S. LaSalle St., Chicago, Ill. 60603

Del Monte Corp.: 215 Fremont St., P.O. Box 3575, San Francisco, Calif. 94119

Durum Wheat Institute: 14 E. Jackson Blvd., Chicago, Ill. 60604

Evaporated Milk Association: 910 Seventeenth St., N.W. Washington, D.C. 20006

Florida Department of Citrus: Florida Citrus Commission, Lakeland, Florida 33802

Frozen Potato Products Institute: 111 E. Wacker Dr., Chicago, Ill. 60601

General Foods Kitchens: 250 North St., White Plains, N.Y. 10625

General Mills: Betty Crocker Kitchens, P.O. Box 1113, Minneapolis, Minn. 55440

Gerber Products: Professional Communications Dept., 445 State St., Fremont, Mich. 49412

Green Giant Co.: Home Services Dept., 5601 Green Valley Dr., Minneapolis, Minn. 55437

Grocery Manufacturers of America, Inc.: 1425 K St., N.W., Washington, D.C. 20005

H. J. Heinz Co: P.O. Box 57, Pittsburgh, Pa. 15230

International Multifoods Corp.: Consumer Kitchens, Minneapolis, Minn. 55402

Kansas Wheat Commission: 1021 N. Main St., Hutchinson, Kansas 67501

Kellogg Company: Home Economics Services, Battle Creek, Mich. 49016

Kraft Foods: Educational Dept., P.O. Box 6567, Chicago, Ill. 61680

Lawry's Foods, Inc.: Consumer Services, 568 San Fernando Rd., Los Angeles, Calif. 90065

Libby, McNeill & Libby: Mary Hale Martin Dept., 200 S. Michigan Ave., Chicago, Ill. 60604

Thomas J. Lipton, Inc.: 800 Sylvan Ave., Englewood Cliffs, N.J. 07632

National Canners Assoc.: Home Economics—Consumer Services, 1133 20th St., N.W., Washington, D.C. 20036

National Dairy Council: 111 N. Canal St., Chicago, Ill. 60606

National Fisheries Institute: Promotions Division, 111 E. Wacker Dr., Suite 600, Chicago, Ill. 60601

National Live Stock and Meat Board: 36 S. Wabash Ave., Chicago, Ill. 60603

National Macaroni Institute: P.O. Box 336, Palatine, Ill. 60067

National Peanut Council: Communications Division, 111 E. Wacker Dr., Suite 600, Chicago, Ill. 60601

National Turkey Federation: P.O. Box 69, Mount Morris, Ill. 61054

Pet Incorporated: Pet Plaza, 400 S. Fourth St., St. Louis, Mo. 63166

Pillsbury Company: Dept. of Nutrition, 840C Pillsbury Bldg., Minneapolis, Minn. 55402

Quaker Oats Company: Consumer Service Dept., 345 Merchandise Mart, Chicago, Ill. 60654

Rice Council of America: P.O. Box 22802, Houston, Texas 77027

Standards Brands: Educational Service, P.O. Box 2695, Grand Central Station, New York, N.Y. 10017

Sunkist Growers, Inc.: Consumer Services, Box 7888 Valley Annex, Van Nuys, Calif. 91409

Swift and Company: Martha Logan, Home Economist, 1919 Swift Dr., Oak Brook, Ill. 60521

Tuna Research Foundation, Inc.: Study Program, Suite 1100, 551 Fifth Ave., New York, N.Y. 10017

United Fresh Fruit and Vegetable Assoc., 777 14th St., N.W., Washington, D.C. 20005

U.S. Govt. Printing Office: Washington, D.C. 20402

Vitamin Information Bureau, Inc.: 383 Madison Ave., New York, N.Y. 10017

Western Growers Assoc., 1811 Quail, Newport Beach, CA

Wheat Flour Institute: 14 E. Jackson Blvd., Chicago, Ill. 60604

APPENDIX D
Pigment Structures

Appendix D: Pigment Structures

(R = CH₃ for chlorophyll a; CHO for chlorophyll b)

*Pheophytin forms when magnesium (Mg) is replaced by hydrogen (H)

Chlorophyll

β–carotene

*Carbonyl of anthoxanthins is replaced with hydrogen in anthocyamins

Flavonol (an anthoxanthin)

Cyanidin (an anthocyanin)

APPENDIX E

Commonly Used Names for Retail Meat Cuts and Recommended Standardized Names[a]

Presented here are lists of the commonly used names for retail names of beef, pork, lamb and veal cuts used in different sections of the country, together with the new standardized names recommended by the Industry-wide Cooperative Meat Identification Standards Committee.

The commonly used names are alphabetized by species and are followed in each case by the new recommended standard name, in capital letters. In instances where one "old" name is followed by more than one recommended standardized name, the same name has been used to describe different cuts in different parts of the country. Under the new meat identity program being adopted by the meat industry, each cut will have the same name wherever it is sold.

[a]Courtesy of the National Live Stock and Meat Board, 36 S. Wabash Avenue, Chicago, IL 60603

BEEF
List of Commonly Used Beef Retail Names
With Recommended Standardized Names[a]

A

Arm Chuck Roast
BEEF CHUCK ARM POT-ROAST
Arm Chuck Steak
BEEF CHUCK ARM STEAK
Arm Steak, Beef Chuck
BEEF CHUCK ARM STEAK
Arm Swiss Steak
BEEF CHUCK ARM STEAK

B

Ball Tip Roast
BEEF ROUND TIP ROAST, CAP OFF
Ball Tip Steak
BEEF ROUND TIP STEAK, CAP OFF
Barbecue Ribs
BEEF CHUCK FLANKEN STYLE RIB
BEEF CHUCK FLAT RIBS
BEEF CHUCK SHORT RIBS
Beauty Steak
BEEF RIB EYE STEAK
Beef Bones
BEEF SHANK SOUP BONES
Beef Bottom Round Steak
BEEF ROUND BOTTOM ROUND STEAK
Beef Cubed for Stew
BEEF FOR STEW
Beef London Broils
BEEF FLANK STEAK ROLLS
BEEF PLATE SKIRT STEAK ROLLS,
    BONELESS
Blade Chuck Roast
BEEF CHUCK BLADE ROAST
Blade Roast, Bone In
BEEF CHUCK TOP BLADE POT-ROAST
Blade Steak
BEEF CHUCK BLADE STEAK
Blade Steak, Bone In
BEEF CHUCK TOP BLADE STEAK
Boiling Beef
BEEF PLATE RIBS
Bone-In Club Sirloin Steak
BEEF LOIN TOP LOIN STEAK

Boneless Arm Steak
BEEF CHUCK ARM STEAK, BONELESS
Boneless Beef for Stew
BEEF FOR STEW
Boneless Beef Shanks
BEEF SHANK CROSS CUTS, BONELESS
Boneless Boston Cut
BEEF CHUCK CROSS RIB POT-ROAST,
    BONELESS
Boneless Brisket
BEEF BRISKET, WHOLE, BONELESS
Boneless Chuck Fillet
BEEF CHUCK EYE ROAST, BONELESS
Boneless Chuck Fillet Steak
BEEF CHUCK EYE STEAK, BONELESS
Boneless Chuck Pot-Roast
BEEF CHUCK EYE EDGE POT-ROAST
Boneless Chuck Roast
BEEF CHUCK POT-ROAST, BONELESS
Boneless Chuck Roll
BEEF CHUCK EYE ROAST, BONELESS
Boneless Chuck Steak
BEEF CHUCK UNDER BLADE STEAK,
    BONELESS
Boneless Club Sirloin Steak
BEEF LOIN TOP LOIN STEAK,
    BONELESS
Boneless English Cut
BEEF CHUCK CROSS RIB POT-ROAST,
    BONELESS
Boneless English Roast
BEEF CHUCK SHOULDER POT-ROAST,
    BONELESS
Boneless Rib Eye Steak
BEEF RIB EYE STEAK
Boneless Roast, Bottom Chuck
BEEF CHUCK UNDER BLADE
    POT-ROAST, BONELESS
Boneless Round Bone Steak
BEEF CHUCK ARM STEAK, BONELESS
Boneless Steak, Bottom Chuck
BEEF CHUCK EYE STEAK, BONELESS
Boneless Stew Beef
BEEF FOR STEW

[a]Recommended standardized names are in capital letters.

Boneless Swiss Steak
  BEEF CHUCK ARM STEAK, BONELESS
Book Steak
  BEEF CHUCK TOP BLADE STEAK,
    BONELESS
Boston Cut
  BEEF CHUCK CROSS RIB POT-ROAST
Bottom Chuck Ribs
  BEEF CHUCK FLAT RIBS
Bottom Chuck Roast
  BEEF CHUCK UNDER BLADE
    POT-ROAST
Bottom Chuck Roast, Boneless
  BEEF CHUCK UNDER BLADE
  POT-ROAST, BONELESS
Bottom Chuck Steak
  BEEF CHUCK UNDER BLADE STEAK
Bottom Chuck Steak, Boneless
  BEEF CHUCK UNDER BLADE STEAK,
    BONELESS
Bottom Round Oven Roast
  BEEF ROUND BOTTOM ROUND ROAST
Bottom Round Pot-Roast
  BEEF ROUND BOTTOM ROUND ROAST
Bottom Round Steak
  BEEF ROUND BOTTOM ROUND STEAK
Bottom Round Steak Pot-Roast
  BEEF ROUND BOTTOM ROUND ROAST
Braciole Round Steak
  BEEF ROUND TOP ROUND STEAK,
    BUTTERFLY
Braciole Steak
  BEEF ROUND TOP ROUND STEAK,
    BUTTERFLY
Braising Bones
  BEEF CHUCK NECK BONES
Braising Ribs
  BEEF CHUCK FLANKEN STYLE RIB
  BEEF CHUCK SHORT RIBS
Bread and Butter Cut
  BEEF CHUCK CROSS RIB POT-ROAST
Brisket, Boneless
  BEEF BRISKET, WHOLE, BONELESS
Brisket Center Cut
  BEEF BRISKET MIDDLE CUT,
    BONELESS
Brisket Edge Cut
  BEEF BRISKET EDGE CUT, BONELESS
Brisket First Cut
  BEEF BRISKET FLAT HALF, BONELESS
Brisket Flat Cut
  BEEF BRISKET FLAT CUT, BONELESS

BEEF BRISKET FLAT HALF, BONELESS
BEEF BRISKET MIDDLE CUT,
  BONELESS
Brisket Front Cut
  BEEF BRISKET HALF POINT,
    BONELESS
  BEEF BRISKET POINT CUT,
    BONELESS
  BEEF BRISKET POINT HALF,
    BONELESS
Brisket Point Cut
  BEEF BRISKET HALF POINT,
    BONELESS
  BEEF BRISKET POINT CUT,
    BONELESS
  BEEF BRISKET POINT HALF,
    BONELESS
Brisket Side Cut
  BEEF BRISKET EDGE CUT, BONELESS
Brisket Thick Cut
  BEEF BRISKET HALF POINT,
    BONELESS
  BEEF BRISKET POINT CUT,
    BONELESS
  BEEF BRISKET POINT HALF,
    BONELESS
Brisket Thin Cut
  BEEF BRISKET FLAT HALF, BONELESS
Brust Flanken
  BEEF CHUCK FLANKEN STYLE RIB
  BEEF CHUCK SHORT RIBS
Butler Steak
  BEEF CHUCK TOP BLADE STEAK,
    BONELESS

C

California Roast
  BEEF CHUCK UNDER BLADE
    POT-ROAST
California Roast, Boneless
  BEEF CHUCK UNDER BLADE
    POT-ROAST, BONELESS
California Steak
  BEEF CHUCK UNDER BLADE STEAK
Cap Meat, Rolled
  BEEF RIB ROLLED CAP POT-ROAST
Center Beef Shanks
  BEEF SHANK CROSS CUTS
Center Chuck Steak
  BEEF CHUCK 7-BONE STEAK

Center Cut Pot-Roast
BEEF CHUCK 7-BONE POT-ROAST
Center Shank Soup Bone
BEEF SHANK CENTER CUT
Center Shoulder Roast
BEEF CHUCK SHOULDER POT-ROAST,
BONELESS
Char Broil Steak
BEEF CHUCK BLADE STEAK, CAP OFF
Chip Club Steak
BEEF LOIN TOP LOIN STEAK
Chuck Arm Pot-Roast
BEEF CHUCK ARM POT-ROAST,
BONELESS
Chuck Arm Roast
BEEF CHUCK ARM POT-ROAST
Chuck Barbecue Steak
BEEF CHUCK BLADE STEAK, CAP OFF
Chuck Blade Roast
BEEF CHUCK BLADE ROAST
Chuck Blade Steak
BEEF CHUCK BLADE STEAK
Chuck Boneless Roast
BEEF CHUCK EYE EDGE POT-ROAST
Chuck Boneless Slices
BEEF CHUCK EYE STEAK, BONELESS
Chuck Eye
BEEF CHUCK MOCK TENDER
Chuck Eye Roast
BEEF CHUCK EYE ROAST, BONELESS
Chuck Eye Steak
BEEF CHUCK EYE STEAK, BONELESS
Chuck Fillet
BEEF CHUCK MOCK TENDER
Chuck Fillet Steak
BEEF CHUCK EYE STEAK, BONELESS
BEEF CHUCK UNDER BLADE STEAK,
BONELESS
Chuck for Swissing
BEEF CHUCK SHOULDER STEAK,
BONELESS
Chuck Pot-Roast, Boneless
BEEF CHUCK POT-ROAST, BONELESS
Chuck Rib Pot-Roast
BEEF CHUCK EYE EDGE POT-ROAST
Chuck Roast, Blade Cut
BEEF CHUCK BLADE ROAST
Chuck Roast, Boneless
BEEF CHUCK POT-ROAST, BONELESS
BEEF CHUCK SHOULDER POT-ROAST,
BONELESS

Chuck Roast, Center Cut
BEEF CHUCK 7-BONE POT-ROAST
Chuck Roast, 1st Cut
BEEF CHUCK BLADE ROAST
Chuck Round Bone Cut
BEEF CHUCK ARM POT-ROAST
Chuck Shoulder Roast
BEEF CHUCK SHOULDER POT-ROAST,
BONELESS
Chuck Spareribs
BEEF CHUCK FLAT RIBS
Chuck Steak, Blade Cut
BEEF CHUCK BLADE STEAK
Chuck Steak, Center Cut
BEEF CHUCK 7-BONE STEAK
Chuck Steak, 1st Cut
BEEF CHUCK BLADE STEAK
BEEF CHUCK BLADE STEAK, CAP OFF
Chuck Steak for Barbecue
BEEF CHUCK BLADE STEAK, CAP OFF
Chuck Steak for Swissing
BEEF CHUCK ARM STEAK
Chuck Tender
BEEF CHUCK MOCK TENDER
Clear Bones
BEEF MARROW BONES
BEEF SHANK SOUP BONES
Clod Roast
BEEF CHUCK SHOULDER POT-ROAST,
BONELESS
Clod Steak, Boneless
BEEF CHUCK SHOULDER STEAK,
BONELESS
Club Rib Roast
BEEF RIB EXTRA TRIM ROAST,
LARGE END
Club Steak
BEEF LOIN TOP LOIN STEAK
Corned Beef
BEEF BRISKET CORNED, BONELESS
Country Club Steak
BEEF LOIN TOP LOIN STEAK
Crescent Roast
BEEF ROUND TIP ROAST
Cross Cut Shank, Boneless
BEEF SHANK CROSS CUTS, BONELESS
Cross Cut Shanks
BEEF SHANK CROSS CUTS
Cross Rib Roast
BEEF CHUCK CROSS RIB POT-ROAST
Cross Rib Roast, Boneless

BEEF CHUCK CROSS RIB POT-ROAST,
  BONELESS
BEEF CHUCK SHOULDER POT-ROAST,
  BONELESS
Cubed Flank Steak
  BEEF FLANK STEAK ROLLS
Cubed Skirt Steak
  BEEF PLATE SKIRT STEAK, CUBED,
  BONELESS
Cubed Steak
  BEEF CUBED STEAK

D

Delmonico Pot-Roast
  BEEF RIB EYE ROAST
Delmonico Roast
  BEEF RIB EYE ROAST
Delmonico Steak
  BEEF LOIN TOP LOIN STEAK
  BEEF RIB EYE STEAK
Denver Pot-Roast
  BEEF ROUND HEEL OF ROUND
Diamond Roast
  BEEF ROUND HEEL OF ROUND
Diaphram
  BEEF PLATE SKIRT STEAK, BONELESS
  BEEF PLATE SKIRT STEAK, CUBED,
  BONELESS

E

English Cut Roast
  BEEF CHUCK CROSS RIB POT-ROAST
English Roll
  BEEF CHUCK CROSS RIB POT-ROAST,
  BONELESS
English Short Ribs, Extra Lean
  BEEF CHUCK SHORT RIBS
English Steak
  BEEF CHUCK SHOULDER STEAK,
  BONELESS
Eye Round Pot-Roast
  BEEF ROUND EYE ROUND ROAST
Eye Round Roast
  BEEF ROUND EYE ROUND ROAST
Eye Round Steak
  BEEF ROUND EYE ROUND STEAK

F

Face Round Roast
  BEEF ROUND TIP ROAST
Fancy Ribs
  BEEF CHUCK SHORT RIBS
Filet Mignon
  BEEF LOIN TENDERLOIN STEAK
Fillet Steak
  BEEF LOIN TENDERLOIN STEAK
  BEEF RIB EYE STEAK
Finger Ribs
  BEEF RIB BACK RIBS
First Cuts of Top Steak
  BEEF ROUND TOP ROUND STEAK,
  1ST CUT
Fish Muscle
  BEEF CHUCK MOCK TENDER
Flanken Short Ribs
  BEEF CHUCK FLANKEN STYLE RIB
  BEEF CHUCK SHORT RIBS
Flank Steak, Cubed
  BEEF FLANK STEAK, CUBED
Flank Steak, Cubed, Rolled
  BEEF FLANK STEAK, CUBED, ROLLED
Flank Steak Filets
  BEEF FLANK STEAK
  BEEF FLANK STEAK ROLLS
Flank Steak London Broils
  BEEF FLANK STEAK ROLLS
Flat Bone Sirloin Steak
  BEEF LOIN SIRLOIN STEAK,
  FLAT BONE
Flat Iron Roast
  BEEF CHUCK TOP BLADE ROAST,
  BONELESS
Fore Shank for Soup Meat, Bone In
  BEEF SHANK CROSS CUTS
Fore Shank for Soup Meat, Boneless
  BEEF SHANK CROSS CUTS, BONELESS
Fresh Beef Brisket
  BEEF BRISKET, WHOLE, BONELESS
Full Trimmed Tip Roast
  BEEF ROUND TIP ROAST, CAP OFF

H

Honey Cut
  BEEF CHUCK SHOULDER POT-ROAST,
  BONELESS

Horseshoe Roast
BEEF ROUND HEEL OF ROUND

I

Inside Chuck Roast
BEEF CHUCK EYE EDGE POT-ROAST
BEEF CHUCK UNDER BLADE
POT-ROAST, BONELESS
Inside Chuck Roll
BEEF CHUCK EYE ROAST, BONELESS

J

Jiffy Steak
BEEF FLANK STEAK

K

Kansas City Steak
BEEF LOIN TOP LOIN STEAK,
BONELESS
Knuckle Bone
BEEF SOUP BONE
Knuckle Soup Bone
BEEF SOUP BONE
Kosher Ribs
BEEF CHUCK FLANKEN STYLE RIB

L

Lifter Roast
BEEF CHUCK TOP BLADE ROAST,
BONELESS
Lifter Steak
BEEF CHUCK TOP BLADE STEAK,
BONELESS
Loin Ambassador Steak
BEEF LOIN TOP LOIN STEAK,
BONELESS
Loin Strip Steak, Hotel Cut
BEEF LOIN TOP LOIN STEAK,
BONELESS
London Broil
BEEF CHUCK SHOULDER STEAK,
BONELESS
BEEF FLANK STEAK
London Broils
BEEF FLANK STEAK ROLLS
BEEF PLATE SKIRT STEAK ROLLS,
BONELESS

London Grill Steak
BEEF PLATE SKIRT STEAK ROLLS,
BONELESS

M

Marrow Bones
BEEF MARROW BONES
Meaty Neck Bones
BEEF CHUCK NECK BONES
Medallion Pot-Roast
BEEF CHUCK MOCK TENDER

N

Neck Boiling Beef
BEEF CHUCK NECK POT-ROAST
Neck Bone
BEEF CHUCK NECK BONES
Neck, Boneless
BEEF CHUCK NECK POT-ROAST,
BONELESS
Neck Pot-Roast
BEEF CHUCK NECK POT-ROAST
Neck Pot-Roast, Boneless
BEEF CHUCK NECK POT-ROAST,
BONELESS
Neck Soup Bone
BEEF CHUCK NECK BONES
Neck Soup Meat
BEEF CHUCK NECK POT-ROAST
NewPort Roast
BEEF RIB EXTRA TRIM ROAST,
LARGE END
New York Sirloin Steak
BEEF LOIN SHELL SIRLOIN STEAK
New York Steak, Bone-In
BEEF LOIN SHELL SIRLOIN STEAK
New York Strip Steak
BEEF LOIN TOP LOIN STEAK,
BONELESS

P

Petite Steak
BEEF CHUCK TOP BLADE STEAK,
BONELESS
Pike's Peak Roast
BEEF ROUND HEEL OF ROUND
Plank Steak
BEEF FLANK STEAK

Plate Beef
BEEF PLATE RIBS
Plate Boiling Beef
BEEF PLATE RIBS
Plate Roll
BEEF PLATE, ROLLED, BONELESS
Porterhouse Steak
BEEF LOIN PORTERHOUSE STEAK
Puff Roast
BEEF CHUCK TOP BLADE ROAST,
BONELESS

R

Regular Roll Roast
BEEF RIB EYE ROAST
Rib Bones
BEEF RIB BACK RIBS
Riblets
BEEF RIB BACK RIBS
Rib Eye Pot-Roast
BEEF RIB EYE ROAST
Rib Pot-Roast, Short Cut, 6-7
BEEF RIB ROAST, LARGE END
Rib Roast DeLuxe
BEEF RIB EXTRA TRIM ROAST,
LARGE END
Rib Roast, Oven Ready
BEEF RIB ROAST, LARGE END
BEEF RIB ROAST, SMALL END
Rib Roast, Short Cut, 6-7
BEEF RIB ROAST, LARGE END
Rib Steak
BEEF RIB STEAK, LARGE END
BEEF RIB STEAK, SMALL END
Rib Steak, Bone In
BEEF RIB STEAK, LARGE END
BEEF RIB STEAK, SMALL END
Rib Steak, Boneless
BEEF RIB STEAK, SMALL END,
BONELESS
Rolled Plate
BEEF PLATE, ROLLED, BONELESS
Round Back of Rump Roast
BEEF ROUND BOTTOM ROUND RUMP
ROAST
Round Boneless Rump
BEEF ROUND RUMP ROAST,
BONELESS
Round Bone Pot-Roast
BEEF CHUCK ARM POT-ROAST

Round Bone Roast
BEEF CHUCK ARM POT-ROAST
Round Bone Steak
BEEF CHUCK ARM STEAK
Round Bone Swiss Steak
BEEF CHUCK ARM STEAK
Round Eye Pot-Roast
BEEF ROUND EYE ROUND ROAST
Round Eye Roast
BEEF ROUND EYE ROUND ROAST
Round Eye Steak
BEEF ROUND EYE ROUND STEAK
Round, Full Cut, Boneless
BEEF ROUND STEAK, BONELESS
Round Heel Pot-Roast
BEEF ROUND HEEL OF ROUND
Round Rump Roast, Bone In
BEEF ROUND RUMP ROAST
Round Rump Roast, Rolled
BEEF ROUND RUMP ROAST, BONELESS
Round Standing Rump
BEEF ROUND RUMP ROAST
Round Steak
BEEF ROUND STEAK
BEEF ROUND STEAK, BONELESS
Round Steak, Center Cut
BEEF ROUND STEAK
Round Steak, Center Cut, Boneless
BEEF ROUND STEAK, BONELESS
Round Steak, Full Cut
BEEF ROUND STEAK
Round Tip Roast
BEEF ROUND BOTTOM ROUND RUMP
ROAST
BEEF ROUND TIP ROAST
Rump Steak
BEEF LOIN SIRLOIN STEAK, BONELESS

S

Scotch Tender
BEEF CHUCK MOCK TENDER
Semiboneless Chuck Steak
BEEF CHUCK UNDER BLADE STEAK
Semiboneless Roast
BEEF CHUCK UNDER BLADE
POT-ROAST
7-Bone Roast
BEEF CHUCK 7-BONE POT-ROAST
BEEF CHUCK TOP BLADE POT-ROAST

7-Bone Steak
BEEF CHUCK 7-BONE STEAK
Shank Soup Bone
BEEF SHANK CENTER CUT
Shell Steak
BEEF LOIN TOP LOIN STEAK
Short Cuts
BEEF ROUND TOP ROUND STEAK,
1ST CUT
Short Ribs
BEEF CHUCK SHORT RIBS
BEEF PLATE SHORT RIBS
BEEF RIB SHORT RIBS
Shoulder Clod Steak, Boneless
BEEF CHUCK SHOULDER STEAK,
BONELESS
Shoulder Cutlet, Boneless
BEEF CHUCK SHOULDER STEAK,
BONELESS
Shoulder Roast
BEEF CHUCK SHOULDER POT-ROAST,
BONELESS
Shoulder Roast, Boneless
BEEF CHUCK SHOULDER POT-ROAST,
BONELESS
Shoulder Roast, Thin End
BEEF CHUCK TOP BLADE ROAST,
BONELESS
Shoulder Steak
BEEF CHUCK SHOULDER STEAK,
BONELESS
Shoulder Steak, Boneless
BEEF CHUCK SHOULDER STEAK,
BONELESS
Shoulder Steak, Half Cut
BEEF CHUCK SHOULDER STEAK,
BONELESS
Sirloin
BEEF LOIN SHELL SIRLOIN STEAK
Sirloin Steak
BEEF LOIN SIRLOIN STEAK,
FLAT BONE
BEEF LOIN SIRLOIN STEAK,
PIN BONE
BEEF LOIN SIRLOIN STEAK,
ROUND BONE
BEEF LOIN SIRLOIN STEAK,
WEDGE BONE
Sirloin Steak, Boneless
BEEF LOIN SIRLOIN STEAK, BONELESS

Sirloin Steak, Flat Bone
BEEF LOIN SIRLOIN STEAK,
FLAT BONE
Sirloin Steak, Hotel Style
BEEF LOIN TOP LOIN STEAK,
BONELESS
Sirloin Steak, Pin Bone
BEEF LOIN SIRLOIN STEAK, PIN BONE
Sirloin Steak, Short Cut
BEEF LOIN SIRLOIN STEAK,
WEDGE BONE
Sirloin Steak, Wedge Bone
BEEF LOIN SIRLOIN STEAK,
WEDGE BONE
Sirloin Strip Steak, Bone In
BEEF LOIN TOP LOIN STEAK
Sirloin Tip Kabob Cubes
BEEF ROUND CUBES FOR KABOBS
Sirloin Tip Roast
BEEF RIB ROAST, SMALL END
BEEF ROUND TIP ROAST
Sirloin Tip Steak
BEEF ROUND TIP STEAK
Skirt Fillets
BEEF PLATE SKIRT STEAK ROLLS,
BONELESS
Skirt London Broils
BEEF PLATE SKIRT STEAK ROLLS,
BONELESS
Skirt Steak
BEEF PLATE SKIRT STEAK, BONELESS
Skirt Steak, Cubed
BEEF PLATE SKIRT STEAK, CUBED,
BONELESS
Soup Bone
BEEF SOUP BONE
Soup Bones
BEEF MARROW BONES
BEEF SHANK SOUP BONES
Spareribs
BEEF PLATE SPARERIBS
Spencer Steak
BEEF RIB EYE STEAK
Spencer Steak, Boneless
BEEF RIB STEAK, SMALL END,
BONELESS
Standing Rib Roast
BEEF RIB ROAST, SMALL END
Standing Rib Roast, 6-7
BEEF RIB ROAST, LARGE END

Standing Rib Roast, 6-8
  BEEF RIB ROAST, LARGE END
Standing Rib Roast, 8-9
  BEEF RIB ROAST, LARGE END
Stew Beef
  BEEF FOR STEW
Strip Steak
  BEEF LOIN TOP LOIN STEAK
  BEEF LOIN TOP LOIN STEAK,
    BONELESS

T

T-Bone Steak
  BEEF LOIN T-BONE STEAK
Tenderloin, Chauteaubriand
  BEEF LOIN TENDERLOIN ROAST
Tenderloin, Fillet DeBoeuf
  BEEF LOIN TENDERLOIN STEAK
Tenderloin, Fillet Mignon Roast
  BEEF LOIN TENDERLOIN ROAST
Tenderloin Tip Roast
  BEEF LOIN TENDERLOIN ROAST
Tenderloin Tips
  BEEF LOIN TENDERLOIN TIPS
Tender Steak
  BEEF LOIN TENDERLOIN STEAK
Thick Rib Roast
  BEEF CHUCK CROSS RIB POT-ROAST
Tip Sirloin Roast
  BEEF ROUND TIP ROAST
Top Blade Steak
  BEEF CHUCK TOP BLADE STEAK
Top Chuck Roast
  BEEF CHUCK TOP BLADE POT-ROAST
Top Chuck Steak, Bone In
  BEEF CHUCK TOP BLADE STEAK
Top Chuck Steak, Boneless
  BEEF CHUCK TOP BLADE STEAK,
    BONELESS
Top Rib Roll, Boneless
  BEEF RIB ROLLED CAP POT-ROAST
Top Round Braciole Steak
  BEEF ROUND TOP ROUND STEAK,
    BUTTERFLY
Top Round London Broil
  BEEF ROUND TOP ROUND STEAK,
    1ST CUT
Top Round Roast
  BEEF ROUND TOP ROUND ROAST

Top Round Roast, Center
  BEEF ROUND TOP ROUND ROAST
Top Round Steak
  BEEF ROUND TOP ROUND STEAK
Top Round Steak, Center Cut
  BEEF ROUND TOP ROUND STEAK
Top Sirloin Steak
  BEEF LOIN TOP SIRLOIN STEAK,
    BONELESS
  BEEF ROUND TIP STEAK
Triangle Roast
  BEEF CHUCK TOP BLADE ROAST,
    BONELESS
Trimmed Tip Steak
  BEEF ROUND TIP STEAK, CAP OFF

U

Under Cut Roast
  BEEF CHUCK UNDER BLADE
    POT-ROAST
Under Cut Steak
  BEEF CHUCK UNDER BLADE STEAK
Under Cut Steak, Boneless
  BEEF CHUCK UNDER BLADE STEAK,
    BONELESS

W

Whole Brisket
  BEEF BRISKET, WHOLE, BONELESS

Y

Yankee Pot-Roast
  BEEF CHUCK NECK POT-ROAST
  BEEF PLATE, ROLLED, BONELESS
Yankee Pot-Roast, Boneless
  BEEF CHUCK NECK POT-ROAST,
    BONELESS

VEAL

List of Commonly Used Veal Retail Names With Recommended Standardized Names

B

Blade Roast
  VEAL SHOULDER BLADE ROAST
Boneless Sirloin Roast
  VEAL LEG SIRLOIN ROAST, BONELESS
Boneless Veal Chops
  VEAL LOIN TOP LOIN CHOPS
  VEAL RIB CHOPS, BONELESS
Boneless Veal Loin Roast
  VEAL LOIN ROAST, BONELESS
Breast
  VEAL BREAST
Breast-of-Veal
  VEAL BREAST

C

Chops
  VEAL LOIN CHOPS
  VEAL LOIN TOP LOIN CHOPS
  VEAL RIB CHOPS
  VEAL RIB CHOPS, BONELESS
City Chicken
  VEAL CUBES FOR KABOBS
Cross Cut Shank
  VEAL SHANK CROSS CUTS
Crown Rib Roast
  VEAL RIB CROWN ROAST
Crown Roast
  VEAL RIB CROWN ROAST
Cubed Steak
  VEAL CUBED STEAK
Cubed Veal Steak
  VEAL CUBED STEAK
Cutlets
  VEAL CUTLETS

H

Heel Roast
  VEAL LEG HEEL ROAST

K

Kabobs
  VEAL CUBES FOR KABOBS

Kidney Chops
  VEAL LOIN KIDNEY CHOPS
Kidney Veal Chops
  VEAL LOIN KIDNEY CHOPS

L

Leg of Veal
  VEAL LEG ROUND ROAST
Leg Roast
  VEAL LEG ROUND ROAST
Loin Chops
  VEAL LOIN CHOPS
Loin Roast
  VEAL LOIN ROAST
Loin Veal Chops
  VEAL LOIN CHOPS

R

Rib Chops
  VEAL RIB CHOPS
Riblets
  VEAL BREAST RIBLETS
Rib Roast
  VEAL RIB ROAST
Rib Veal Chops
  VEAL RIB CHOPS
Rib Veal Roast
  VEAL RIB ROAST
Roast, Boneless
  VEAL LEG RUMP ROAST, BONELESS
Rolled Double Sirloin Roast
  VEAL LEG SIRLOIN ROAST, BONELESS
Rolled Roast
  VEAL SHOULDER ROAST, BONELESS
Rolled Rump Roast
  VEAL LEG RUMP ROAST, BONELESS
Rolled Veal Loin Roast
  VEAL LOIN ROAST, BONELESS
Rolled Veal Shoulder
  VEAL SHOULDER ROAST, BONELESS
Round Bone Roast
  VEAL SHOULDER ARM ROAST

Round Bone Steak
    VEAL SHOULDER ARM STEAK
Round Bone Veal Chops
    VEAL SHOULDER ARM STEAK
Rump of Veal
    VEAL LEG RUMP ROAST
Rump of Veal, Boneless
    VEAL LEG RUMP ROAST, BONELESS
Rump Roast
    VEAL LEG RUMP ROAST

S

Scallopini
    VEAL LEG ROUND STEAK
Shank
    VEAL SHANK CROSS CUTS
Shoulder, Boneless
    VEAL SHOULDER ROAST, BONELESS
Shoulder Roast
    VEAL SHOULDER ARM ROAST
    VEAL SHOULDER BLADE ROAST
Shoulder Steak
    VEAL SHOULDER ARM STEAK
    VEAL SHOULDER BLADE STEAK
Shoulder Veal Chop, Round Bone
    VEAL SHOULDER ARM STEAK
Shoulder Veal Chops
    VEAL SHOULDER BLADE STEAK
Sirloin Roast
    VEAL LEG SIRLOIN ROAST
Sirloin Steak
    VEAL LEG SIRLOIN STEAK
Sirloin Veal Chop
    VEAL LEG SIRLOIN STEAK
Steak
    VEAL LEG ROUND STEAK
    VEAL LEG SIRLOIN STEAK
Steakettes
    VEAL LEG ROUND STEAK
Stew
    VEAL CUBES FOR KABOBS
Stew (large pieces)
    VEAL FOR STEW
Stew (small pieces)
    VEAL FOR STEW
Stew, Boneless
    VEAL FOR STEW
Stew Veal
    VEAL FOR STEW

PORK

List of Commonly Used Pork Retail Names
With Recommended Standardized Names

A

Arm Roast
PORK SHOULDER ARM ROAST
Arm Steak
PORK SHOULDER ARM STEAK

B

Back Bacon
SMOKED PORK LOIN CANADIAN
STYLE BACON
Backribs
PORK LOIN BACK RIBS
Bacon Square
SMOKED PORK JOWL
Bacon Square Slices
SMOKED PORK JOWL SLICES
Blade End Country Spareribs
PORK LOIN COUNTRY STYLE RIBS
Blade Pork Chops
PORK LOIN BLADE CHOPS
Blade Pork Steak
PORK SHOULDER BLADE STEAK
Boneless Boston Roast
PORK SHOULDER BLADE BOSTON
ROAST, BONELESS
Boneless Butterfly Pork Chops
PORK LOIN BUTTERFLY CHOPS
Boneless Centers
SMOKED HAM CENTER SLICES,
BONELESS
Boneless Cubed Pork
PORK CUBES FOR KABOBS
Boneless Fresh Picnic
PORK SHOULDER ARM PICNIC,
BONELESS
Boneless Pork Butt
PORK SHOULDER BLADE BOSTON
ROAST, BONELESS
Boneless Pork Butt Roast
PORK SHOULDER BLADE BOSTON
ROAST, BONELESS
Boneless Pork Chops
PORK LOIN TOP LOIN CHOPS,
BONELESS

Boneless Porklets
PORK CUBED STEAK
Boneless Pork Loin Roast
PORK LOIN TOP LOIN ROAST,
BONELESS
Boneless Pork Roast
PORK LOIN TOP LOIN ROAST,
BONELESS
Boneless Roast from Pork Loin
PORK LOIN TOP LOIN ROAST,
BONELESS
Boneless Rolled Butt Roast
PORK SHOULDER BLADE BOSTON
ROAST, BONELESS
Boston Butt Roast
PORK SHOULDER BLADE BOSTON
ROAST
Boston Shoulder
PORK SHOULDER BLADE BOSTON
ROAST
Boston Shoulder, Boneless
PORK SHOULDER BLADE BOSTON
ROAST, BONELESS
Boston Style Butt
PORK SHOULDER BLADE BOSTON
ROAST
Butterfly Pork Chops
PORK LOIN BUTTERFLY CHOPS
Butt Half Fresh Ham
PORK LEG [FRESH HAM] RUMP HALF
Butt Half Picnic, Boneless
PORK SHOULDER ARM PICNIC,
BONELESS
Butt Portion Fresh Ham
PORK LEG [FRESH HAM]
RUMP PORTION
Butt Roast
PORK SHOULDER BLADE BOSTON
ROAST

C

Canadian Bacon
SMOKED PORK LOIN CANADIAN
STYLE BACON

Center Cut
PORK LOIN CENTER LOIN ROAST
Center Cut Loin Chops
PORK LOIN TOP LOIN CHOPS
Center Cut Loin Pork Chops
PORK LOIN TOP LOIN CHOPS
Center Cut Loin Roast
PORK LOIN CENTER LOIN ROAST
Center Cut Pork Chops Smoked
SMOKED PORK LOIN CHOPS
SMOKED PORK LOIN RIB CHOPS
Center Cut Pork Loin Roast
PORK LOIN CENTER LOIN ROAST
Center Cut Pork Roast
PORK LOIN CENTER RIB ROAST
Center Cut Roast, Fresh Ham
PORK LEG [FRESH HAM]
CENTER ROAST
Center Fresh Ham Slices
PORK LEG [FRESH HAM]
CENTER SLICE
Center Loin Chops
PORK LOIN CHOPS
Chops
PORK LOIN CHOPS
Chops End Cut
PORK LOIN BLADE CHOPS
PORK LOIN RIB CHOPS
Chops, Stuffed
PORK LOIN RIB CHOPS FOR STUFFING
Chunk Side of Pork
FRESH SIDE PORK
Cooked Ham Butt Half
SMOKED HAM RUMP HALF
Cooked Ham Center Roast
SMOKED HAM CENTER ROAST
Cooked Ham Center Slices
SMOKED HAM CENTER SLICES
Cooked Ham Shank Half
SMOKED HAM SHANK HALF
Cottage Butt
SMOKED PORK SHOULDER ROLL
Country Back Bones
PORK LOIN BACK RIBS
Country Ribs
PORK LOIN COUNTRY STYLE RIBS
Country Style Spareribs
PORK LOIN COUNTRY STYLE RIBS
Cubes
PORK CUBES FOR KABOBS
Cube Steaks
PORK CUBED STEAK

Cutlets
PORK LOIN SIRLOIN CUTLETS

D

Daisy Ham
SMOKED PORK SHOULDER ROLL
Double Pork Loin
PORK LOIN TOP LOIN ROAST,
BONELESS

F

Family Pack
PORK LOIN ASSORTED CHOPS
Fresh Belly
FRESH SIDE PORK
Fresh Ham
PORK LEG [FRESH HAM], WHOLE
Fresh Ham, Boneless
PORK LEG [FRESH HAM] ROAST,
BONELESS
Fresh Ham Butt
PORK LEG [FRESH HAM] RUMP
PORTION
Fresh Ham Butt Half
PORK LEG [FRESH HAM] RUMP HALF
Fresh Ham Center Cut
PORK LEG [FRESH HAM]
CENTER SLICE
Fresh Ham Center Cut Roast
PORK LEG [FRESH HAM]
CENTER ROAST
Fresh Ham Center Slices
PORK LEG [FRESH HAM]
CENTER SLICE
Fresh Ham Cube Steak
PORK CUBED STEAK
Fresh Ham Shank Half
PORK LEG [FRESH HAM] SHANK HALF
Fresh Ham Shank Portion
PORK LEG [FRESH HAM]
SHANK PORTION
Fresh Hock
PORK HOCK
Fresh Picnic
PORK SHOULDER ARM PICNIC
Fresh Picnic, Boneless
PORK SHOULDER ARM PICNIC,
BONELESS
Fresh Picnic Steak
PORK SHOULDER ARM STEAK

Fresh Pork Arm Roast
   PORK SHOULDER ARM ROAST
Fresh Pork Butt
   PORK SHOULDER BLADE BOSTON
      ROAST
Fresh Pork Hock
   PORK HOCK
Fresh Pork Leg Steak
   PORK LEG [FRESH HAM]
      CENTER SLICE
Fresh Pork Picnic Roast
   PORK SHOULDER ARM PICNIC,
      BONELESS
Fresh Pork Shoulder
   PORK SHOULDER, WHOLE
Fresh Pork Shoulder, Boneless
   PORK SHOULDER ROAST, BONELESS
Fresh Shoulder
   PORK SHOULDER, WHOLE
Fresh Shoulder, Boneless
   PORK SHOULDER ROAST, BONELESS
Fresh Side Pork
   FRESH SIDE PORK
Fresh Side Pork, Sliced
   FRESH SIDE PORK, SLICED
Fresh Spareribs
   PORK SPARERIBS

H

Half Ham Shank End
   SMOKED HAM SHANK HALF
Ham Butt End
   SMOKED HAM RUMP PORTION
Ham, Butt Half
   SMOKED HAM RUMP HALF
Ham Butt Portion
   SMOKED HAM RUMP PORTION
Ham Center Roast
   SMOKED HAM CENTER ROAST
Ham, Center Roast
   SMOKED HAM CENTER ROAST
Ham Center Slices
   SMOKED HAM CENTER SLICES
Ham, Center Slices
   SMOKED HAM CENTER SLICES
Ham Hocks, Smoked
   SMOKED PORK HOCK
Ham Kabobs
   SMOKED HAM CUBES FOR KABOBS
Ham Shank End
   SMOKED HAM SHANK PORTION

Ham, Shank Half
   SMOKED HAM SHANK HALF
Ham, Shank Portion
   SMOKED HAM SHANK PORTION
Ham Sirloin End
   SMOKED HAM RUMP PORTION
Ham Slice, Boneless
   SMOKED HAM CENTER SLICES,
      BONELESS
Hipbone Roast
   PORK LOIN SIRLOIN ROAST
Hock
   PORK HOCK

L

Leg Butt Portion
   PORK LEG [FRESH HAM]
      RUMP PORTION
Leg Center Roast
   PORK LEG [FRESH HAM]
      CENTER ROAST
Leg Fresh Ham, Whole
   PORK LEG [FRESH HAM], WHOLE
Leg of Pork Steak
   PORK LEG [FRESH HAM]
      CENTER SLICE
Leg Roast, Boneless
   PORK LEG [FRESH HAM] ROAST,
      BONELESS
Leg Roast Shank Portion
   PORK LEG [FRESH HAM]
      SHANK PORTION
Leg Roast Sirloin Half
   PORK LEG [FRESH HAM] RUMP HALF
   PORK LEG [FRESH HAM] SHANK HALF
Leg Roast Sirloin Portion
   PORK LEG [FRESH HAM]
      RUMP PORTION
Leg Shank Half
   PORK LEG [FRESH HAM] SHANK HALF
Leg Shank Portion
   PORK LEG [FRESH HAM] SHANK
      PORTION
Leg Sirloin Half
   PORK LEG [FRESH HAM] RUMP HALF
Leg, Whole
   PORK LEG [FRESH HAM], WHOLE
Loin Back Ribs
   PORK LOIN BACK RIBS
Loin Blade Steaks
   PORK LOIN BLADE CHOPS

Loin Center Cut
  PORK LOIN CENTER RIB ROAST
Loin Cut Roast
  PORK LOIN SIRLOIN HALF
Loin End Chops
  PORK LOIN CHOPS
Loin End Roast
  PORK LOIN SIRLOIN ROAST
Loin 5-Rib Roast
  PORK LOIN BLADE ROAST
Loin Pork Chops
  PORK LOIN CHOPS
Loin Pork Roast
  PORK LOIN SIRLOIN ROAST
Loin Rib End
  PORK LOIN BLADE ROAST
Loin Rib Half
  PORK LOIN CENTER RIB ROAST
Loin Roast
  PORK LOIN CENTER RIB ROAST
  PORK LOIN SIRLOIN HALF
Loin Roast, Boneless
  PORK LOIN TOP LOIN ROAST,
    BONELESS
Loin Roast Center Cut
  PORK LOIN CENTER LOIN ROAST
  PORK LOIN CENTER RIB ROAST
Loin 7-Rib Cut
  PORK SHOULDER BLADE STEAK
Loin 7-Rib Roast
  PORK LOIN BLADE ROAST

N

Neckbones Overlay
  SMOKED PORK NECKBONES
New York Style Shoulder
  PORK SHOULDER, WHOLE
New York Style Shoulder, Boneless
  PORK SHOULDER ROAST, BONELESS

O

1/4 Pork Loin
  PORK LOIN ASSORTED CHOPS

P

Picnic
  PORK SHOULDER ARM PICNIC
Picnic Shoulder
  PORK SHOULDER ARM PICNIC

SMOKED PORK SHOULDER PICNIC,
  WHOLE
Picnic Steak
  PORK SHOULDER ARM STEAK
Pigs Feet Smoked
  SMOKED PIGS FEET
Pocket Pork Chops
  PORK LOIN RIB CHOPS FOR STUFFING
Porklets
  PORK CUBED STEAK

R

Rib Cut Chops
  PORK LOIN RIB CHOPS
Rib End Roast
  PORK LOIN BLADE ROAST
Rib Pork Chops
  PORK LOIN RIB CHOPS
Rib Pork Loin Roast
  PORK LOIN BLADE HALF
Rib Pork Roast
  PORK LOIN BLADE ROAST
Ribs for Barbecue
  PORK LOIN BACK RIBS
Roast
  PORK LOIN CENTER LOIN ROAST
Roast Blade Half
  PORK LOIN BLADE HALF
Roast Loin Half
  PORK LOIN SIRLOIN HALF
Roast Rib Half
  PORK LOIN BLADE HALF
Roast Sirloin Half
  PORK LOIN SIRLOIN HALF
Rolled Fresh Ham
  PORK LEG [FRESH HAM] ROAST,
    BONELESS

S

Shank
  PORK HOCK
Shank Half Fresh Ham
  PORK LEG [FRESH HAM] SHANK HALF
Shank Half Ham
  SMOKED HAM SHANK HALF
Shank Portion Ham
  SMOKED HAM SHANK PORTION
Shoulder Roll
  SMOKED PORK SHOULDER ROLL

Sirloin Chops
PORK LOIN SIRLOIN CHOPS
Sirloin End Roast
PORK LOIN SIRLOIN ROAST
Sirloin Pork Chops
PORK LOIN SIRLOIN CHOPS
Sirloin Pork Steaks
PORK LOIN SIRLOIN CHOPS
Slab Bacon
SLAB BACON
Sliced Bacon
SLICED BACON
Sliced Side Pork
FRESH SIDE PORK, SLICED
Smoked Callie
SMOKED PORK SHOULDER PICNIC,
WHOLE
Smoked Ham Butt Half
SMOKED HAM RUMP HALF
Smoked Ham Hocks
SMOKED PORK HOCK
Smoked Hock
SMOKED PORK HOCK
Smoked Loin Pork Chops
SMOKED PORK LOIN CHOPS
Smoked Picnic
SMOKED PORK SHOULDER PICNIC,
WHOLE
Smoked Picnic Shoulder
SMOKED PORK SHOULDER PICNIC,
WHOLE
Smoked Pork Back Ribs
SMOKED PORK LOIN BACK RIBS
Smoked Pork Chops
SMOKED PORK LOIN CHOPS
SMOKED PORK LOIN RIB CHOPS
Smoked Pork Jowl
SMOKED PORK JOWL
Smoked Pork Jowl Slices
SMOKED PORK JOWL SLICES
Smoked Pork Neckbones
SMOKED PORK NECKBONES
Smoked Pork Shoulder Butt, Boneless
SMOKED PORK SHOULDER ROLL
Smoked Rib Pork Chops
SMOKED PORK LOIN RIB CHOPS
Smoked Shoulder Butt
SMOKED PORK SHOULDER ROLL
Smoked Slab Bacon
SLAB BACON

Smoked Sliced Bacon
SLICED BACON
Smoked Spareribs
SMOKED PORK SPARERIBS
Spareribs, Fresh
PORK SPARERIBS
Spareribs, Smoked
SMOKED PORK SPARERIBS
Steak
PORK SHOULDER BLADE STEAK
Streak of Lean
FRESH SIDE PORK
Strip Chops
PORK LOIN TOP LOIN CHOPS
Strip Loin Chops, Boneless
PORK LOIN TOP LOIN CHOPS,
BONELESS

T

Tender
PORK LOIN TENDERLOIN, WHOLE
Tenderettes
PORK CUBED STEAK
Tenderloin
PORK LOIN TENDERLOIN, WHOLE
Tipless Tenderloin
PORK LOIN TIPLESS TENDERLOIN

W

Whole Fresh Picnic
PORK SHOULDER ARM PICNIC
Whole Ham, Smoked
SMOKED HAM, WHOLE

LAMB
List of Commonly Used Lamb Retail Names
With Recommended Standardized Names

A

American Leg
    LAMB LEG AMERICAN STYLE ROAST
Arm Cut Chop
    LAMB SHOULDER ARM CHOPS

B

Blade Cut Chop
    LAMB SHOULDER BLADE CHOPS
Boneless Double Loin Chop
    LAMB LOIN DOUBLE CHOPS,
        BONELESS
Boneless Lamb Leg
    LAMB LEG ROAST, BONELESS
Boneless Lamb Shoulder
    LAMB SHOULDER CUSHION ROAST,
        BONELESS
Boneless Lamb Stew
    LAMB FOR STEW
Boneless Rib Lamb Roast
    LAMB RIB ROAST, BONELESS
Boneless Shoulder, Netted
    LAMB SHOULDER ROAST, BONELESS
Breast of Lamb
    LAMB BREAST
Breast Pot-Roast
    LAMB BREAST, ROLLED

C

Center Roast
    LAMB LEG CENTER ROAST
Chops and Stew
    LAMB SHOULDER COMBINATION
Combination
    LAMB SHOULDER COMBINATION
Combination Leg
    LAMB LEG COMBINATION
Crown Roast
    LAMB RIB CROWN ROAST
Cube Lamb Steaks
    LAMB CUBED STEAK
Cube Steaks
    LAMB CUBED STEAK

D

Double Chop
    LAMB LOIN DOUBLE CHOPS
Double Loin Roast, Boneless
    LAMB LOIN DOUBLE ROAST,
        BONELESS

E

English Chop
    LAMB LOIN DOUBLE CHOPS
    LAMB LOIN DOUBLE CHOPS,
        BONELESS

F

Fore Shank
    LAMB SHANK
French Chops
    LAMB RIB FRENCHED CHOPS
Frenched Lamb Leg
    LAMB LEG FRENCHED STYLE ROAST
French Lamb Chops
    LAMB RIB FRENCHED CHOPS
Fresh Lamb Rib Chops
    LAMB RIB CHOPS
Full Trimmed Leg Roast
    LAMB LEG, WHOLE
Full Trimmed Loin Roast
    LAMB LOIN ROAST

H

Hotel Rack
    LAMB RIB ROAST

L

Leg Butt Half
    LAMB LEG SIRLOIN HALF
Leg Chop
    LAMB LEG CENTER SLICE
Leg of Lamb, Boneless
    LAMB LEG ROAST, BONELESS

Leg of Lamb, Boneless, for
Shish-Ka-Bob
    LAMB CUBES FOR KABOBS
Leg of Lamb Butt Half
    LAMB LEG SIRLOIN HALF
Leg of Lamb, Oven Ready
    LAMB LEG, WHOLE
Leg-o-Lamb
    LAMB LEG, WHOLE
Leg-o-Lamb Sirloin Half
    LAMB LEG SIRLOIN HALF
Leg-o-Lamb Shank Half
    LAMB LEG SHANK HALF ROAST
Leg, Sirloin Off
    LAMB LEG SHORT CUT, SIRLOIN OFF
Leg, Sirloin On
    LAMB LEG, WHOLE
Leg Steak
    LAMB LEG CENTER SLICE
Loin Chops
    LAMB LOIN CHOPS
Loin Lamb Chops
    LAMB LOIN CHOPS
Loin Lamb Roast
    LAMB LOIN ROAST
Loin Roast
    LAMB LOIN ROAST

N

Neck for Stew
    LAMB SHOULDER NECK SLICES
Neck of Lamb
    LAMB SHOULDER NECK SLICES
Neck Pieces
    LAMB SHOULDER NECK SLICES

P

Pinwheels
    LAMB BREAST, ROLLED

R

Rack Lamb Chops
    LAMB RIB CHOPS
Rack Roast
    LAMB RIB ROAST
Rib Chops
    LAMB RIB CHOPS
Rib Kabobs
    LAMB RIB FRENCHED CHOPS

Rib Lamb Chops
    LAMB RIB CHOPS
Riblets
    LAMB BREAST RIBLETS
Riblets Breast
    LAMB BREAST RIBLETS
Rib Rack for Roasting
    LAMB RIB ROAST
Rib Roast, Boneless
    LAMB RIB ROAST, BONELESS
Rolled Double Loin Roast
    LAMB LOIN DOUBLE ROAST,
        BONELESS
Rolled Lamb Breast
    LAMB BREAST, ROLLED
Rolled Shoulder Roast
    LAMB SHOULDER ROAST, BONELESS
Round Bone Chops
    LAMB SHOULDER ARM CHOPS
Round Bone Roast
    LAMB SHOULDER ARM ROAST

S

Saddle Roast
    LAMB LOIN ROAST
Shank Half Leg of Lamb
    LAMB LEG SHANK HALF ROAST
Shisk Kabobs
    LAMB CUBES FOR KABOBS
Shoulder Blade Lamb Chops
    LAMB SHOULDER BLADE CHOPS
Shoulder Block
    LAMB SHOULDER SQUARE CUT,
        WHOLE
Shoulder Blocks
    LAMB SHOULDER ARM CHOPS
    LAMB SHOULDER ARM ROAST
    LAMB SHOULDER BLADE CHOPS
    LAMB SHOULDER BLADE ROAST
Shoulder Chops
    LAMB SHOULDER ARM CHOPS
Shoulder Lamb Chops
    LAMB SHOULDER BLADE CHOPS
Shoulder Roast
    LAMB SHOULDER ARM ROAST
    LAMB SHOULDER BLADE ROAST
    LAMB SHOULDER CUSHION ROAST,
        BONELESS
    LAMB SHOULDER SQUARE CUT,
        WHOLE

Sirloin Lamb Chop
 LAMB LEG SIRLOIN CHOPS
Sirloin Steak
 LAMB LEG SIRLOIN CHOPS
Spareribs
 LAMB BREAST SPARERIBS
Square Cut Shoulder
 LAMB SHOULDER SQUARE CUT,
  WHOLE
Steak
 LAMB LEG CENTER SLICE
Steak-Leg
 LAMB LEG CENTER SLICE
Stew, Bone In
 LAMB SHOULDER NECK SLICES
Stewing Lamb
 LAMB FOR STEW
Stew Meat
 LAMB FOR STEW

T

3-in-1 Lamb Leg Combination
 LAMB LEG COMBINATION
Trotter
 LAMB SHANK
2-in-1 Lamb Leg Combination
 LAMB LEG COMBINATION

Glossary

Acrolein — The eye-irritating substance formed when glycerol is broken down by heat.

Amino acid — Organic acid containing an amino ($-NH_2$) group. The basic building block of protein molecules.

Amorphous candy — Candy with a random organization rather than an organized crystalline structure.

Amylopectin — The branched-chain fraction of starch that is relatively insoluble in water.

Amylose — The straight-chain, relatively soluble fraction of starch.

Carbohydrate — Organic compound composed of carbon, hydrogen, and oxygen. This group includes sugars, dextrins, starch, and cellulose.

Cellulose — A polysaccharide that is an important structural material in plants and a source of roughage in animal diets.

Coagulation — The physical change in a protein effected by several means. The most common ways of causing coagulation in protein foods are by the use of heat and mechanical agitation.

Collagen — White connective tissue in meat that is converted to gelatin by the use of moist heat.

Colloid — A material whose particles are between one and 100 millimicrons in size. Gelatin, egg proteins, and pectin are examples of colloids.

Crystalline candy — Candy with an organized crystalline structure that can be observed under a microscope.

Denaturation — The process of changing a protein molecule from its native state to an altered, less soluble state.

Dextrinization — The process of breaking starch molecules to dextrins by the use of dry heat.

Dextrins — Polysaccharides that are somewhat smaller and more soluble than starch.

Disaccharide—Carbohydrate consisting of two monosaccharides joined together with an α-glycosidic linkage. Sucrose, lactose, and maltose are common disaccharides.

Elastin—Yellow connective tissue in meat which is not broken down or softened by ordinary culinary procedures.

Emulsion—The dispersion of one immiscible liquid in another, that is, a dispersion of oil and water into a continuous and a discontinuous phase.

Enzyme—An organic catalyst (proteinaceous) that speeds or retards a reaction.

Ester—The organic compound formed by the reaction of an organic acid and an alcohol. Fats are esters of the alcohol, glycerol.

Fat—Organic compound formed when three fatty acids are combined with glycerol.

Fatty acids—Organic acids (commonly fourteen to twenty carbon atoms in length) that can combine with glycerol to form a fat.

Gel—A colloidal dispersion that does not flow.

Gelatinization—The imbibition of water and the resultant swelling of starch granules when moist heat is applied to starch.

Glycerol—The organic alcohol (three carbons) in fats.

Hydrolysis—A chemical reaction in which a molecule is cleaved and a molecule of water is utilized. Example: $RC\overset{O}{\underset{OR'}{\big\|}} + HOH \rightarrow RC\overset{O}{\underset{OH}{\big\|}} + R'OH.$

Inversion—The breakdown of sucrose into its two component monosaccharides, glucose and fructose.

Monosaccharide—Carbohydrate consisting of a single chain of carbon atoms (commonly five or six) with a hydroxyl group on all carbons except the aldehydic or ketonic carbon. Examples include fructose, glucose, and galactose.

Organic compound—Chemical substances of varying complexity, composed basically of carbon.

Osmosis—The passage of water through a semipermeable membrane from an area of a low concentration of the dispersed phase to a higher concentration of the dispersed phase.

Oxidation—A chemical reaction in which one of the reactants undergoes the addition of oxygen.

Pectic acids—Polysaccharides with little gelling ability that arise from changes in pectin during the maturation of fruits.

Pectin—Polysaccharides composed of galacturonic acid which have gel-forming properties.

Pectinic acid—One of the organic substances known as pectin.

pH—The positive expression of the negative logarithm of the hydrogen-ion concentration. On the scale, which ranges in value from 1 to 14, 1 is the most acidic and 14 is the most alkaline; 7 is neutral.

Polysaccharide — Carbohydrate consisting of more than ten monosaccharide units joined together with the expulsion of a molecule of water (linkage can be α- or β-glycosidic linkage). Dextrins, starch, and cellulose are in this group.

Protein — A nitrogen-containing organic compound composed of many amino acids linked together by a peptide linkage to form large molecules. Examples include casein from milk, albumen from egg white, and zein from corn.

Protopectin — The pectic substance with limited gel-forming ability which is converted to pectin in the maturing fruit.

Saponify — To hydrolyze a fat (or other ester) into its component alcohol and acids.

Saturated solution — A solution containing all the solute the solvent is capable of dissolving at that temperature.

Sol — A colloidal dispersion that flows.

Starch — Polysaccharide composed of hundreds of glucose units linked with 1,4- and 1,6-glycosidic linkages.

Supersaturated solution — A solution in which more solute is dissolved than the solvent could ordinarily dissolve at that temperature. This condition is achieved by heating the solution to an elevated temperature and then very carefully cooling it under controlled conditions.

Surface tension — The tendency of a liquid to expose the least possible surface area, that is, the tendency to assume a spherical shape.

Syneresis — The separation of liquid from a gel.

Vapor pressure — The force a liquid exerts as its molecules attempt to evaporate from the liquid. A liquid that evaporates readily at a low temperature has a high vapor pressure. Heating raises the vapor pressure until the vapor pressure just exceeds the atmospheric pressure and boiling occurs.

Photo Acknowledgments

The photographs in this text appear through the courtesy of the following corporations and individuals.

Fig. 1.1.   Standard Brands
Fig. 1.2   Kellogg Company
Fig. 1.3   Spice Islands Kitchen
Fig. 2.1   Plycon Press
Fig. 2.2   Taylor Instrument Company
Fig. 3.1   National Coffee Association
Fig. 3.2   National Coffee Association
Fig. 3.3   Ferry-Morse Seed Company
Fig. 3.4a, b   Plycon Press
Fig. 3.5a, b   Plycon Press
Fig. 3.6a, b   Plycon Press
Fig. 3.7   Oneida Silversmiths
Fig. 3.8   Thomas J. Lipton, Inc.
Fig. 3.9 a, b, c Thomas J. Lipton, Inc.
Fig. 3.10   Spice Islands Kitchen
Fig. 3.11   Spice Islands Kitchen
Fig. 4.1   Ferry-Morse Seed Company
Fig. 4.2   Western Growers Association
Fig. 4.3   Western Growers Association
Fig. 4.4   H. J. Heinz Company
Fig. 4.5   H. J. Heinz Company
Fig. 4.6   Ferry-Morse Seed Company
Fig. 4.7   Ferry-Morse Seed Company
Fig. 4.8   Western Growers Association

Fig. 4.9	Dr. Andrea MacKey
Fig. 4.10	Food and Drug Administration
Fig. 4.11	Western Growers Association
Fig. 4.12	Western Growers Association
Fig. 5.1	Sunkist Growers
Fig. 5.2	Dole Corporation
Fig. 5.3	Sunkist Growers
Fig. 5.4	Western Growers Association
Fig. 5.5a, b	Sunkist Growers
Fig. 5.6	Spice Islands Kitchen
Fig. 6.1	California Fig Advisory Board
Fig. 6.2	Sunkist Growers
Fig. 6.3	H. J. Heinz Company
Fig. 6.4	Western Growers Association
Fig. 6.5	California Avocado Advisory Board
Fig. 6.6	Wilson and Company, Inc.
Fig. 6.7	Spice Islands Kitchen
Fig. 6.8	Western Iceberg Lettuce, Inc.
Fig. 6.9	Spice Islands Kitchen
Fig. 7.1	Cereal Institute, Inc.
Fig. 7.2	Cereal Institute, Inc.
Fig. 7.3	Kellogg Company
Fig. 7.4	Cereal Institute, Inc.
Fig. 7.5	Rice Council
Fig. 7.6	Northern Regional Research Laboratory, Agricultural Research Service, United States Department of Agriculture
Fig. 7.7	American Dairy Association
Fig. 7.8	American Dairy Association
Fig. 7.9	American Dairy Association
Fig. 7.10	Stauffer Chemical Co.
Fig. 8.1	American Dairy Association
Fig. 8.2	Borden, Incorporated
Fig. 8.3	United States Department of Agriculture
Fig. 8.4	American Dry Milk Institute, Inc.
Fig. 8.5	Borden, Incorporated
Fig. 8.6	American Dairy Association
Fig. 8.7	American Dairy Association
Fig. 8.8	American Dairy Association
Fig. 8.9	Borden, Incorporated
Fig. 9.1	National Live Stock and Meat Board
Fig. 9.2	National Live Stock and Meat Board
Fig. 9.3	United States Department of Agriculture
Fig. 9.4	United States Department of Agriculture
Fig. 9.5	United States Department of Agriculture
Fig. 9.6	United States Department of Agriculture

Fig. 9.7   United States Department of Agriculture
Fig. 9.8   United States Department of Agriculture
Fig. 9.9   United States Department of Agriculture
Fig. 9.10   National Live Stock and Meat Board
Fig. 9.11   National Live Stock and Meat Board
Fig. 9.12   National Live Stock and Meat Board
Fig. 9.13   National Live Stock and Meat Board
Fig. 9.14   Pepperidge Farms, Incorporated
Fig. 9.15   National Live Stock and Meat Board
Fig. 9.16   National Live Stock and Meat Board
Fig. 9.17   Plycon Press
Fig. 9.18   National Live Stock and Meat Board
Fig. 9.19   National Live Stock and Meat Board
Fig. 9.20   National Live Stock and Meat Board
Fig. 9.21   Spice Islands Kitchen
Fig. 9.22   Spice Islands Kitchen
Fig. 9.23*a, b, and c*   Swift and Company
Fig. 9.24   Cereal Institute, Incorporated
Fig. 9.25   Rice Council
Fig. 9.26   California Fig Advisory Council
Fig. 10.1   John Wiley & Sons, Inc.
Fig. 10.2   United States Department of Agriculture
Fig. 10.3   United States Department of Agriculture
Fig. 10.4   United States Department of Agriculture
Fig. 10.5   Western Research Kitchens
Fig. 10.6   Borden, Incorporated
Fig. 10.7   American Dry Milk Institute
Fig. 10.8   Betty Crocker Kitchens
Fig. 10.9   Sunkist Growers
Fig. 10.10 American Dry Milk Institute
Fig. 10.11 American Dairy Association
Fig. 10.12 Western Research Kitchens
Fig. 11.1   Poultry and Egg National Board
Fig. 11.2   Plycon Press
Fig. 11.3   Universal Foods Corporation
Fig. 11.4   Universal Foods Corporation
Fig. 11.5   Universal Foods Corporation
Fig. 11.6   Betty Crocker Kitchens
Fig. 12.1   California Prune Advisory Board
Fig. 12.2   Universal Foods Corporation
Fig. 12.3   Plycon Press
Fig. 12.4   Betty Crocker Kitchens
Fig. 12.5   Plycon Press
Fig. 12.6   Plycon Press
Fig. 12.7   Plycon Press

Fig. 12.8	Plycon Press
Fig. 12.9	Standard Brands
Fig. 12.10	Standard Brands
Fig. 12.11	American Dairy Association
Fig. 12.12	Standard Brands
Fig. 12.13	Standard Brands
Fig. 12.14	Betty Crocker Kitchens
Fig. 12.15	Betty Crocker Kitchens
Fig. 12.16	Betty Crocker Kitchens
Fig. 12.17a, b	Betty Crocker Kitchens
Fig. 12.18	Borden, Incorporated
Fig. 12.19a, b	Betty Crocker Kitchens
Fig. 12.20	Betty Crocker Kitchens
Fig. 12.21	Betty Crocker Kitchens
Fig. 12.22	Betty Crocker Kitchens
Fig. 12.23	Cereal Institute, Incorporated
Fig. 12.24	California Prune Advisory Board
Fig. 13.1	Borden, Incorporated
Fig. 13.2–5	Belle Lowe. Experimental Cookery. John Wiley and Sons, Inc.
Fig. 13.6	Borden, Incorporated
Fig. 14.1	California Raisin Advisory Board
Fig. 14.2	Ball Corporation
Fig. 14.3	Ball Corporation
Fig. 14.4	Ball Corporation
Fig. 14.5	Ball Corporation
Fig. 15.1	Kellogg Company
Fig. 16.1	American Dairy Association
Fig. 16.2	American Dairy Association
Fig. 16.3	American Dairy Association
Fig. 16.4	Western Research Kitchens
Fig. 16.5	Oneida Silversmiths
Fig. 16.6	International Silver Company
Fig. 16.7	Oneida Silversmiths
Fig. 16.8	1847 Rogers Brothers
Fig. 16.9	International Silver Company
Fig. 16.10	Oneida Silversmiths
Fig. 16.11	International Silver Company
Figs. 17.1, 2	John Wiley and Sons, Inc.
Fig. 19.1	J. T. Colburn of Armour and Company and Baker's Digest
Fig. 19.2	J. T. Colburn of Armour and Company and Baker's Digest
Figs. 19.3–6	C. W. Hoerr
Fig. 20.1	John Wiley & Sons, Inc.
Fig. 20.2	John Wiley & Sons, Inc.
Fig. 20.3	Worthington Foods

Index

Acceptance of food, 2
Acid, in gel formation, 453
  in meat cookery, 247-248
  in starch mixtures, 165
Acid group, 491
Acid hydrolysis, 281, 360, 362, 367-368
  of starch, 464
Acidophilus milk, 177
Acorn squash, 62, 88
Acrolein, 246, 484-485
Actin, 205, 208
Active dry yeast, 300-301
Actomyosin, 205, 208
Additives, incidental, 403-404
  intentional, 402-403
Adenosine triphosphate, 208
Agar, 370
Aging of meat, 210-211
Agitation in frozen desserts, 371-373
Air cell, 267
Alanine, 492
Albedo, 103
Albumen, meat, 303
  wheat, 312
Aleurone, 312
All purpose flour, 314-315
Altitude, effect on boiling point, 12
Amino acid, 419, 491
Amino group, 491
Amioca, 467
Amorphous candies, 360-362, 363
Amphoteric, 492
Amylase, 299, 465, 466
Amylopectin, 463-464, 467
Amylose, 157-158, 164, 166, 462-463
  films, 467

Anatto, 197
Anemia, 421
Angel cake, 291, 333-334
Annise, 52
Anthocyanins, 82-84, 103
  formula for, A48
Anthoxanthins, 82-84, 103
  formula for, A48
Antibiotics, 210
Antioxidants, 402, 482, 485, 486-488
  natural, 487
  role of, 486-487
  technology, 487-488
Apple, 100, 103, 105, 108, 112-113, 117-118, 119
  canning, 386
  coddled, 117
  freezing, 393
  sauce, 117
Apricots, 98, 103, 108, 113
Arabinose, 459, 468
Ariboflavinosis, 423
Arm roast, 249
Arrowroot, 159, 464
Artichokes, 52, 54, 69, 70, 86, 88
  Globe, 52, 54, 86
  Jerusalem, 54
Ascorbic acid, 65, 104-105, 116, 424, 487
Asparagus, 54, 55, 62, 63, 67, 69, 70, 77, 86, 87, 88
  canning, 387
  freezing, 391
Atmospheric pressure, 11-12
Avocado, 100, 102, 103, 108, 113, 116

Bacterial poisoning, 404-409

*Bacterium bulgaricus,*178
Baked Alaska, 286
Baked custard, 280-281
Baked eggs, 277-278
Baking powders, 301-306
Baked products, 309-354
  biscuits, 322-324
  cake doughnuts, 327
  cakes, 333-342
  chiffon cake, 333-335
  conventional cake, 335-342
  cookies, 342-343
  ingredients, 310-319
  mixes, 349-351
  muffins, 320-322
  pancakes, 326-327
  pastry, 343-349
  popovers, 324-325
  quick breads, 319-327
  waffles, 326-327
  yeast breads, 327-333
Banana, 100, 103, 108, 113, 116
  cream pie, 282
  squash, 62
Bar cookies, 342-343
Barley, 145, 147, 152
Barrow, 216
Basic Four Food Plan, 425-428
Bass, 259
Batch freezer, 181
Bavarian cream, 458
Beans, 55, 63, 64, 69, 70, 77, 85-87, 88, 129
  canning, 387
  freezing, 391
Beef, aging, 210
  curing, 211
  cuts, 224-225
  dark cutting, 209, 220
  definition, 215-216
  final temperatures, 234-235
  freezing, 212
  grading, 216-220, 221
  hormones, 207-208
  nutritional composition, 206
  ripening, 210
  standardized names, A50-A57
  timetables, 236, 238-242
Beets, 55, 63, 69, 70, 77, 86, 87, 88
  canning, 387
  tops, 57
Belt drying, 272
Benzoyl peroxide, 313

Beriberi, 423
Berries, 96-97, 117, 380
  canning, 386
Beverages, 23-50
BHA, 402, 487-488
BHT, 487-488
Bibb lettuce, 58-59
Bicarbonates, 15
Biscuits, 322-324
Blackberries, 96
  freezing, 393
Blackstrap molasses, 358
Blade pot roast, 248
Blanching, 390-391
Blancmange, 171
Blastoderm, 267
Blending of fat, 482
Bloom, 267
Blueberries, 96-97, 108, 113
Blue cheese, 190, 191, 195
Boars, 216
Boiling meats, 248-249
Boiling temperatures, 11-14
  factors affecting, 12
Boiling water bath, 383-386
Boston lettuce, 58-59
Botulism, 405, 406, 409
Bovine tuberculosis, 184
Boysenberries, 96
Braising, 247-248
Bran, 146-147
Brazilian coffee, 24
Brick cheese, 191
Brie cheese, 191, 193
Brine, 191
Broccoli, 55, 63, 64, 67, 69, 70, 77, 86, 87, 88, 89
  freezing, 391
Broiler, 250
Broiling, 244-245
Bromelin, 134, 207, 490
Brownian movement, 452
Browning reaction, 179, 498
Brown sugar, 358
*Brucella abortus,*184
Brucellosis, 407
Brussels sprouts, 53, 55, 63, 69, 70, 86, 87, 88
Buffalo fish, 259
Buffet service, 439, 446
Bulgur, 154, 158-159
Bull, 216
Burnt sugar, 359

Butter, 180, 187
Buttercup squash, 62
Butter clam, 411
Buttermilk, 177
Butternut squash, 62
Butters, fruit, 394
Butylated hydroxyanisole, 402, 487-488
Butylated hydroxytoluene, 487-488
Butyric acid, 474-475
B vitamins, 423

Cabbage, 55, 62, 69, 70, 84, 85, 86-88
Caesar salad, 132
Caffeine, 27, 31, 43
Caffeol, 27, 31
Cake, angel, 291, 333, 334
  baking, 337-338
  chiffon, 333-335, 337
  comparison of, 333
  conventional, 333-342
  conventional method, 335-336, 338
  conventional sponge method, 336, 338
  doughnuts, 327
  flour, 313-314
  modified conventional method, 336, 338
  muffin method, 337, 338
  single-stage method, 337, 338
  sponge, 282, 290-291, 333-334
Calcium, 64, 105, 421
Calcium carbonate, 267
Calcium lactate, 191
Calcium oxalate, 64
Calcium propionate, 402
Calf, 215
Camembert cheese, 190, 191, 193
Candies, 360-364
  amorphous, 360-362
  commercial, 369-370
  crystalline, 361-363
  temperature, 364
Candling, 270
Canning, 382-390
Cantaloupe, 99, 103, 109, 111, 113
Capon, 250, 257
Caramelization, 359-360
Caramels, 362, 364
Carbohydrate, 62, 420, 459-471
  cellulose, 468
  dextrins, 461-462
  pectic substances, 468-469
  starch, 462-467
  sugars, 459-461

Carbonates, 15
Carbon dioxide, 105
Carotenes, 64, 65, 81-83
  formula for, A48
Carotenoids, 81-83, 107
Carp, 259
Carrageenan, 370
Carrots, 56-57, 63, 69-70, 77, 83, 86, 88
Casaba melon, 99, 100, 109, 111
Casein, 191
Cassava, root, 159
Catechin, 41, 104
Cattle fat, 479
Cauliflower, 57, 63, 69, 70, 77, 86-88
  freezing, 391
Celeriac, 57
Celery, 57, 69, 70, 88
Celery root, 57
Cellulose, 62, 64, 80-81, 105, 155, 468
Celsius scale, 7
  conversion from, 9
  conversion to, 7-9
Celtuce, 57, 58
Centerpieces, 438
Centigrade scale, 7
Cereals, 145-159
  enriched, 149
  fortified, 149
  nutritional contribution, 149-149
  preparation, 154-159
  processing, 149-152
  restored, 149
  storage, 154-155
Chalazae, 267, 279
Cheddar cheese, 191-192, 194
Cheese, 188-202
  cookery, 198-201
  hard, 191-192
  natural, 189-198
  process, 189, 198
  quality, 182-183
  semisoft, 191
  soft, 191
  souffle, 200, 289, 292
  types, 189-198
Cherries, 98, 108, 110-112, 113
  canning, 386
  freezing, 393
Cherry tomato, 62
Chickens, comparative costs, A41
  definitions, 250
  hormones, 208

selection, 253
storage, 254
thawing time, 254
Chicory, 28, 57
Chiffon cakes, 333-335, 337
Chiffon pies, 284, 348-351
China, 442
Chinese cabbage, 55
Chloride, 210, 313
Chlorophyll, 81-83, 103, 107
  formula for, A48
Chocolate, 46-48
  beverage evaluation, 48
  beverage preparation, 47
  cake, 335
  drink, 177
  Dutched, 46-47
  instant, 47
  milk, 177
  natural, 46-47, 289
  processing, 46
  souffle, 289
  substitution for, 47-48
Chymotrypsin, 207
Cis configuration, 473, 477
Citric acid, 397, 487
Citron, 98
Citrus fruit, 96-98, 104, 118-119
Clams, 259, 411
Clostridium botulinum, 382, 405, 409
Clostridium perfringens, 407, 408
Club cheese, 198
Coagulation, 273, 498
  factors influencing, 273-274
Cock, 250
Cocoa, 46-48
  processing, 46
  substitution, 47-48
Coconut, 113
  oil, 181
Cocozelle squash, 62
Cod, 259
Coffee, 23-38
  buying, 29-30
  constituents, 27-29
  espresso, 37-38
  evaluation, 36-37
  freeze-dried, 29
  grinding, 26, 30
  iced, 38
  instant, 29
  preparation, 30-35

production, 23-26
roasting, 26
soluble, 29-30
storage, 30-31
varieties, 26
whiteners, 182
Coldpack cheese, 198
Collagen, 205, 247, 494, 496
Colloids, 451-458
  emulsions, 451, 454-456
  foams, 451, 456-458
  gels, 451, 452-454
  size, 451
  sols, 451, 452
  types of systems, 451
Compressed yeast, 300
Conalbumin, 499
Conching, 47
Confectioner's sugar, 258
Connective tissue, 205, 261
Conserves, 394
Consumer decisions, 3-6
Contact freezing, 212
Continuous freezer, 181
Convection freezing, 212
Convenience foods, 3
Conventional cakes, 333-342
Conventional method, 335-336, 338
Conventional sponge method, 337, 338
Cooked salad dressing, 140-142
Cookies, 342-343
Corn, 53, 57, 63, 67, 69, 70, 77, 85, 86, 88,
  145-147, 152
  canning, 387
  freezing, 391
Corned beef, 211
Cornish hen, 250
Cornmeal, 152
Cornstarch, 159-160, 163, 464
  puddings, 171-172, 280
  waxy, 160
Corn syrup, 357, 359, 369
Cow, 216
Crab, 259
Cranberries, 97, 109, 113, 397
  canning, 386
Cream, 179-180, 185, 371
  coffee, 180
  foams, 187
  half-and-half, 179
  light, 180
  sout, 180

table, 180
  whipped, 180
Cream cheese, 191, 192
Cream of tartar, 304, 369
Cream pie, 280-282
Cream puddings, 280-282
Cream puffs, 292, 326
Cream soups, 169-171
  tomato, 169-170
Crenshaw melon, 99, 100, 109
Crepes, 327
Crown roast, 235
Cryptoxanthin, 82
Crystalline candies, 361-363
  crystal formation, 365-369
  effect of beating, 366
Crystallization, 355-375
  beating, 366-367
  factors in, 365-369
  ice, 370-374
  in chocolate, 47
  in fats, 476-481
  in frozen desserts, 370-374
  inhibitors, 367-368
  sugar, 365-369
  summary, 374-375
Cube sugar, 357
Cucumbers, 69, 70
Cultured buttermilk, 177
Cultured milks, 177-178
Curdling, 169, 186-187, 499
Curing meat, 211
Currants, 115
Custard, 274
  baked, 279-280
  pie, 280, 348-349, 351
  stirred, 278-279
Cyanidin, 104
  formula for, A48
Cystine, 492

Dairy products, 175-187
  in frozen desserts, 371
  nutritional value, 184
  quality, 182-183
  storage, 185
Dandelions, 57
Dark cutting beef, 209, 220
Date, 100-101
Deep-fat frying, 247
Delphinidin, 104
Denaturation, 491, 496-498

DES, 207
Dessert sugar, 285, 357
Dextrinization, 161, 165
Dextrins, 461-462
Dicalcium phosphate, 306
Diethylstilbestrol, 207-208
Diglyceride, 473, 482
Diphtheria, 184
Disaccharides, 360, 460-461
Dishes, 441-442
Disodium phosphate, 152, 155-156, 198
Disulfide bridges, 494, 495
Double boiler, 2-3, 13-14
Dressings, salad, 137-142
Dripolator coffee, 32-34
Drop cookies, 342-343
Drupes, 96, 98-99
Dry heat meat cookery, 233-247
Drying, 381-382
Dry ingredients, measuring,of, 16-17
Dry milks, 179, 185
  foams, 187
Ducks, definitions, 251
  roasting, 257
  storage, 254
Durum wheat, 147, 154

Edam cheese, 190, 194, 197
Educational materials, A45-A46
Eggs, 266-293
  angel cake, 291-292
  baked, 277-278
  in baked products, 316-317
  coagulation, 273-274
  cost per pound, A39-A40
  cream pies, 280-282
  cream puddings, 280-282
  custards, 278-280
  dipping, 271
  drying, 272
  emulsifier, 139, 292
  foams, 282-285
  freezing, 272
  fried, 275-276
  grading, 267-271
  hard cooked, 274
  meringues, 285-286
  nutritive value, 266
  omelets, 276-277, 287-288
  poached, 276
  processing, 272
  products, 274-292

proteins, 273
scrambled, 277
soft cooked, 274
souffles, 288-290
sponge cake, 290-291
storage, 271
structure, 267
weight classes, 270-271
yolk, 139
Eggplant, 57, 69, 70, 88
Egg white foams, formation, 282
stability, 283-284
stages in formation, 284-285
volume, 282-283
Elaidic acid, 475
Elastin, 205, 206
Embryo, 146, 147, 312
Emmantaler cheese, 195, 197
Emulsifiers, 198, 455-456, 482, 484, 490
Emulsions, 137-140, 454-456
broken, 140, 455
in cakes, 335-336
permanent, 139-141
semipermanent, 138-139
temporary, 137-138, 455
types, 454
Endive, 57, 58, 69
curly, 57
French, 57
Endomysium, 204
Endosperm, 146-147, 312
Enrichment of flour, 313
Environmental causes, food poisoning, 411
Enzymes, 134, 207, 465, 486, 490
hydrolysis, 498
Escarole, 57, 58, 69
Espresso, 29, 37-38
Essential amino acids, 419
Ethylene gas, 107
Etiquette, table, 445
Evaporated milk, 178-179, 185, 371
foams, 187, 458
Extruded cereals, 150

Fahrenheit scale, 7
comparison with Celsius, 8
conversion from Celsius, 9
conversion to Celsius, 9
Family flour, 314-315
Fasciculi, 204
Fats and oils, 206, 420, 472-489
acrolein formation, 484-485

antioxidants, 486-488
in baked products, 319
as inhibitors, 368
blending, 482
chemistry of, 472-474
crystals, 476-478
hydrogenation, 481
hydrolysis, 484
measuring of, 17-18
melting point, 474-475
oxidation, 484
physical properties, 474-479
plasticity, 335, 475-476, 483
polymerization, 484
rancidity, 485-486
refining, 481-482
rendering, 480
shortening value, 482-484
smoke point, 485
surface area, 483
technology, 480-482
tempering, 482
variations, 478
winterizing, 482
Feed lots, 266-267
Ferrous sulfide, 274, 499
Fibrous proteins, 494, 496
Ficin, 207
Fig, 100-101
Filled milk, 181
Fischer structure, 460
Fish, 258-262
cookery, 261-262
fat content, 259
freezing, 212
grading, 260
inspection, 260
kinds, 259
pastes, 211
sauces, 211
selection, 260
shellfish, 259
smoked, 211
storage, 210
Flaked cereal, 150
Flatware, 438-441
Flavedo, 102
Flavone, 81
Flavonoid, 81, 82-84, 103
Flavonol, A48
Flounder, 259
Flour, 163, 310-316

grades, 313
millimg, 312-313
types, 313-314
Fluffy omelet, 283, 287-288
Fluoride, 421
Foams, 187, 201, 456-458, 490
  egg, 282-285, 457
  fat, 296
  frozen desserts, 373
  gelatin, 457
  milk, 187, 457
Fondant, 361, 364
Fondue, 199
Food Additive Amendment, 403
Food composition tables, A1-A38
Food poisoning, 404-412
  animal parasites, 407-410
  bacterial, 404-407
  chemicals, 410
  environmental, 411-412
Food preservation, 379-399
  canning, 380, 382-390
  commercial, 380-382
  freeze-drying, 380-381
  freezing, 380
  irradiation, 381
  jams and jellies, 393-397
  purpose, 379
Food safety, 412-414
Food sanitation, 400-416
  additives, 402-404
  human contamination, 400-401
  safety in home, 412-414
Fortified milk, 185
Fortified skim milk, 177
Fraction of cereals, 151
Free fatty acids, 474, 486
Freeze-dried coffee, 29-30
Freeze drying, 213, 380-381
Freezer burn, 212
Freezing, 390-393
  denaturation, 497
Freezing point, 370, 372
  effect of salt, 372
  sugar, 370
French omelet, 276-277
Fresh Fancy Quality eggs, 267-268
  fried eggs, 275-276
Fritters, 121
Frozen desserts, 370-374
  evaluation, 374
  freezing, 371-373

ingredients, 370
  texture of, 373
Frozen salads, 132
Fructose, 360, 459, 461
Fruit, 96-123
  availability, 103, 113, A43-A44
  browning, 117
  canned, 114
  canning, 382-386
  classification, 96-102
  composition, 102
  dried, 115
  freezing, 392
  frozen, 114, 380
  grades, 108, 114
  infrozen desserts, 371
  labeling, 114
  nutritive value, 104-105
  pigments, 102-104
  production, 105-107
  salads, 130-132
  selection, 107-115
  storage, 115-116
Fryer, 250
Frying temperatures, 11
Fudge, 361, 364

Galactose, 459, 461, 468
Galacturonic acid, 468-469
Gallocatechin, 41
Gamma rays, 381
Garlic, 69
Garnishes, 128
Gastroenteritis, 184
Geese, definitions, 251
Gel, 452-454
  aging, 434
  pectin, 395-396
  setting time, 134-135
  starch, 165, 166
  temperature, 134
  tenderness, 133-134
Gelatin, 132-135, 139, 247, 496
  aspics, 132
  flavored, 132-133
  isoelectric point, 134
  preparation, 132-133
  setting time, 134-135
  tenderness, 133-134
  unflavored, 132-133, 166, 205
Gelation, 452
Gelatinization, 155, 161

effect of acid, 465
heating, 162
hot paste, 162-163
swelling, 161-162
viscosity, 163-106
Germ, 146-147, 151-152
Glassware, 442-443
Globular protein, 496
Glucono-delta-lactone, 306
Glucose, 360, 459-461
Gluten, 311, 314-316, 317, 496
Glutenin, 312
Glycerol, 369, 472, 484-485
monopalmitate, 466
monostearate, 466
Goose, definitions, 251
roasting, 257
storage, 254
Gooseberries, 97
Gonyaulax catanella, 411
Gorgonzola cheese, 191, 196
Gouda cheese, 190, 197
Granulated cereal, 150
Granulated sugar, 357
Grapefruit, 97, 103, 109, 113, 119
Grapes, 96, 99, 109, 113
GRAS list, 403
Gravies, 167-168
Grits, 152, 159
Ground coffees, 30
Gums, 369-370
Gum arabic, 139, 370
Gum tragacanth, 139, 370

Haddock, 259
Halibut, 259
Ham, 211, 215, 244
Hard-cooked eggs, 274
Hard meringue, 285-287
Hard wheat, 314-315, 346
Haugh units, 270
Haworth structures, 459
Heat of crystallization, 365
Heat of hydration, 162
Heat of solidification, 10
Heavy metals, 410
Heifer, 216
Helical configuration, 493-494
Heme, 205, 421
Hemichromogen, 211
Hemoglobin, 421
Hen, 250

Herring, 259
Hexoses, 459-460
Histidine, 492
Hominy, 152, 159
Homogenization, 184-185
Homogenized milk, 184-185
Honey, 357, 359
Honey ball melon, 99, 100
Honeydew melon, 99, 100, 109, 113
Hormones, 207-208
Hubbard squash, 62
Huckleberries, 97
Hulling cereals, 151
Hydrogenated fats, 485-486
Hydrogenating, 481-482
Hydrogen bonding, 494, 495
Hydrogen sulfide, 84
Hydrolysis, 498
acid, 165, 360, 367-368
in fats, 484-485
in jelly making, 396
Hydrolytic rancidity, 486
Hydroxyproline, 494

Ice cream, 180-181
Ice milk, 180
Iced coffee, 38
Ices, 372
Imitation foods, 181
Imitation milks, 182
Immersion freezing, 212
Incidental contaminants, 403-404
Inhibiting substances, 367-369
Inner membrane, 267
Insect contamination, 403-404
Inspection, meat, 213-215
Instant cereals, 152
Instant coffee, 29-30
Instant nonfat dry milk, 182-183
Instant puddings, 162
Instantized flour, 315
Insulin, 421
Intentional additives, 402-403
Interfering agents, 367-369, 371
Intermediate fat crystals, 479
Intermediate temperatures, 10-11
International metric system, 18-19
Inversion, 396
Invertase, 102, 360, 369, 490
Invert sugar, 360, 461
Iodine, 421
Iodine number, 474

Iodized salt, 421
Irish moss, 370
Iron, 64, 105, 499
Irradiation, 381
Isoelectric point, 273, 283, 499
  and coagulation, 273
  gelatin, 134
  gels, 453

Jams, 393, 394
Jellies, 393-397
  fruit for, 394
  gelation of, 395
  improving, 397
  pectin for, 394-395
  pH, 395
  preparation, 396-397
  sugar in, 396

Kale, 57
Kelvin scale, 7
Kneading, bixcuits, 323
  candy, 308
  yeast breads, 328
Kohlrabi, 56
Kumquats, 97-98

Labels, 433
Lactalbumin, 183
Lactic acid, 177, 191, 208
  bacteria, 180
Lactobacillus acidophilus, 177
Lactobacillus bulgaricus, 187
Lactoglobulin, 183
Lactomucin, 183
Lactose, 188, 371, 460-461
Lambs, cuts, 230-231
  definition, 216
  final temperatures, 235
  freezing, 212
  grading, 221
  hormones, 208
  standardized names, A65-A67
  timetable, 238-242
Lard, 477
Latebra, 267
Leaf fat, 479
Leavening agents, 295-308, 319
  air, 290, 295-297
  chemical, 301-306
  egg white foams, 282
  steam, 297-298

yeast, 298-301
Lecithin, 455-456, 466
Leeks, 59
Leeuwenhoek, 298
Legumes, 55, 78, 89-90, 129
Lemon meringue pie, 281
Lemons, 97-98, 109, 113
Lettuce, 57-58, 63, 69, 70, 135
  butterhead, 58, 59
  crisphead, 57
  leaf, 57
  romaine, 57
  stem, 57
Leucoanthocyanins, 104
Liederkranz cheese, 190, 191
Lima beans, 63
Limburger cheese, 190, 191, 193
Lime, 15
Limes, 97, 109
Limit dextrinase, 299
Linolenic acid, 375
Lipases, 151, 486
Lipids in flour, 316
Lipovitellin, 273
Lipovitellinin, 273
Liquid nitrogen, 380
Liquids, measuring of, 17
Livetin, 273
Lobster, 259
Loganberries, 96
Lowfat milk, 177
Lukewarm temperatures, 11
Lumps in starch cookery, 165-166
Lutein, 82
Lycopene, 82, 83
Lysine, 312, 492

Macaroni, 154-155
  and cheese, 200
  enrichment, 149
Mackerel, 259
Magnesium, 421
Maillard reaction, 498
Maltose, 460, 461
Mandarin oranges, 87, 112
Mangoes, 113
Maple flavoring, 358
Maple sugar, 358
Maple syrup, 357, 358
Maraschino cherries, 99
Marketing, 431-433
Marmalade, 394

Mayonnaise, 139-140
Meal management, 417-448
 marketing, 431-433
 meal service, 445-447
 menu planning, 428-430
 nutritional aspects, 428-430
 table appointments, 434-445
 time planning, 433-434
Meal service, 445-447
 blue plate, 445
 English, 445
 family, 445
Measuring, 16-18
Meat, 203-263
 aging, 210-211
 cold storage, 209-210
 connective tissue, 205
 curing, 211
 definition, 215-216
 dry heat cookery, 242-247
 fat, 206
 freeze drying, 213
 freezing, 212
 grading, 216-221
 identification, 222-232
 inspection, 213
 moist heat cookery, 247-250
 muscle, 203-205
 nutritional composition, 206
 postmortem changes, 209-210
 production, 206-209
 proteins, 205
 selection, 221-232
 smoking, 211
 standardized names, A49-A67
 storage, 209-213, 232-233
Meat Inspection Act, 213
Melanin, 87
Mellorine, 181
Melting point, 474-475
Melons, 96, 99, 107, 109, 116, 380
Menu planning, 428-430
Meringues, 285-287, 349
 hard, 285-289
 preparation, 233-250
 soft, 285-286, 349
Metals, 104
Methionine, 492
Metmyoglobin, 205
Metric system, 18-19
 equivalents, 19
 prefixes, 18

Microorganisms, in canning, 382
 reproduction of, 11
Microwave cookery, 92
Milk, 175-187, 201
 acidophilus, 177
 certified raw, 175-176
 chocolate, 177
 cultured, 177-178
 diseases in, 184
 dry, 179
 evaporated, 178-179
 flavored, 177
 homogenized, 184-185
 lowfat, 177
 nonfat, 176-177
 nutritional value, 183
 pasteurized, 184
 processing, 184-185
 products, 175-182
 quality, 182-183
 skim, 176-177
 sweetened condensed, 179
 whole, 175-176
Millet, 145
Milling of cereals, 51, 312
Minerals, 421-423
Minute tapioca, 467
Mixes, 291, 337, 349-351, 498
Modified conventional method, 336, 338
Moist heat meat cookery, 233
Molasses, 357-358
Monocalcium phosphate, 304, 305, 314
Monoglyceride, 473, 482, 484, 485
Monosaccharides, 459-460
Monosodium glutamate, 403
Mother liquor, 369
Mozzarella cheese, 190, 193
Mucin, 267
Muenster cheese, 190, 191, 194
Muffin method, 321, 337, 338
Muffins, 321-322
Mullet, 259
Mushrooms, 58, 69, 70, 88
Mussels, 411
Muskmelons, 99, 102, 111
Mutton, 216, 221
Myoglobin, 205, 211, 496
Myosin, 205, 208
Myost cheese, 193

Napkins, 437
Native proteins, 491

Natural cheeses, 189-198
NDGA, 488
Nectarines, 110, 113
Neufchatel cheese, 191, 192
Niacin, 410, 423
Nitrate, 211
Nitrite, 211
Nitrogen, liquid, 380
Nitrogen peroxide, 313
Nitrosyl chloride, 313
Noncrystalline candies, 360-362
Nonfat dry milk solids, 371
Nonfat milk, 176-177
  foams, 187
Nonpolar groups, 483
Noodles, 154-155
Nordihydroguaiaretic acid, 488
Nut bread, 322
Nutrition in meal planning, 418-428
  Basic Four, 425
  carbohydrate, 420
  fat, 420
  minerals, 421
  protein, 419-420
  RDA, 425-427
  vitamins, 423
Nutrition labeling, 75-76

Oats, 145-147
  processing, 149
O-bone roast, 249
Ocean perch, 259
Oils, in baked products, 319
  in salad dressings, 137-138
  rancidity in coffee, 27
  types, 138
  winterized, 139
Okra, 58, 69, 70, 88
  canning, 387
Oleic acid, 183, 473, 475
Olive oil, 137-138
Omelets, fluffy or puffy, 283, 287-288
  French, 276-277
Onion, 52, 58-59, 63, 69, 70, 78, 84-86, 88
Oranges, 97-98, 102-103, 110, 113
  beverages, 114-115
Osmosis, 137
Osmotic pressure, 117-118, 452
Outer membrane, 267
Ovalbumin, 273
Oven frying, 258
Ovomucin, 273

Oxidation of fats, 484
Oxidative rancidity, 486
Oysters, 259, 411

Palmitic acid, 183, 473
Panbroiling, 246
Pancakes, 326-327
Pan frying, 246-247
Pancreatin, 207
Panocha, 362, 364
Pantothenic acid, 424
Papain, 102, 107
Papaya, 101-102, 113
Parevine, 181
Parmesan cheese, 190, 195, 198
Parsnips, 69, 70, 86, 88
Pastas, 154, 159
Pastes, starch, 165-166
Pasteurized milk, 184
Pastry, edgings, 345
  flakiness, 347-348
  flour, 315
  ingredients, 343-344
  preparation, 344-346
  tenderness, 346
Pattypan squash, 62
Peaches, 98, 103, 110, 113
  canning, 386
  freezing, 393
Pear, 100, 103, 110, 113
  canning, 386
Pearl barley, 152
Peas, 53, 60, 63, 64, 67, 69, 70, 77, 86, 88
  canning, 387
  freezing, 391
Pecan pie, 280
Pectic acid, 62, 394, 469
Pectic substances, 62, 468-469
Pectin, 62, 97, 139, 370, 393, 394-395, 469
Pectinates, 469
Pectinic acid, 469
Pelargonidin, 104
Pellagra, 423
Penicillium camemberti, 191
Penicillium roqueforti, 191
Pentoses, 459
Peppers, 59, 69, 70
Pepsin, 297
Perch, 259
Percolator, 32-35
Perfringens poisoning, 408
Pericarp, 312

Perimysium, 204
Peroxide number, 474
Persian melon, 100, 109
Persimmons, 113
pH, 80-81
Phenol oxidase, 164
Phenylalanine, 492
Pheophytin, 81-83
Phosphate baking powders, 301, 304-306
Phosphorus, 421
Pickles, 383-386
Pies, chiffon, 284, 348, 351
   custard, 280, 348-349, 351
   evaluation, 347-349
   preparation, 344-346
Pigments, muscle, 205
   plant, 81-84
Pike, 259
Pineapple, 100, 101, 103, 110, 113, 116
Place mats, 437-438
Place settings, 443-444
Plastic fats, 335, 475-476, 483
Platinum, 442
Pleated sheet, 494
Plocamo-bacterium yoghourti, 178
Plums, 98, 110, 113
   canning, 386
Poached eggs, 275-276
Poaching fish, 262
POEMS, 465
Polar groups, 483
Polishing of cereals, 151
Pollock, 259
Polymerization of fats, 484
Polyoxethylmonostearate, 465-466
Polyphenols, 27-29, 31, 41, 43, 186
Polysaccharides, 461-469
Polyunsaturated fatty acids, 473
Pomegranate, 100, 102, 113
Popcorn, 146
Popovers, 296, 324-325
Pork, aging, 210
   curing, 211
   cuts, 228-229
   final temperatures, 235
   freezing, 212
   grading, 220-221
   hormones, 208
   nutritional composition, 206
   safety, 215
   standardized names, A60-A64
   timetables, 237-242

Port du Salut cheese, 190
Porterhouse steak, 246
Postmortem changes, 208-209
Potassium iodide, 402
Potatoes, 59-60, 62, 63, 69, 70, 72-75, 77-79,
      86-88
   grades, 75
   nonwaxy, 72-74
   precooked, 467
   salads, 129
   specific gravity, 73-74
   starch, 159-161, 163
   varieties, 73
   waxy, 72-74
Pottery, 442
Poultry, 250-258
   consumer notes, 251-253
   kinds, 250-251
   other methods, 257-258
   roasting, 253-257
   storage, 253
Powdered sugar, 358
Precooked starches, 467
Preparation today, 1-6
   factors in, 7-20
   temperatures used, 9-10
Preservation, 379-399
   canning, 382-390
   commercial, 380-382
   conserves, 394
   freeze-drying, 380-381
   freezing, 390-393
   irradiation, 381
   jellies, 393-397
   preserves, 393-394
Preserves, 393-394
Pressure canning, 386-390
Pressure cooker, 12
Pressure saucepan, 12, 80, 93, 430
Primal meat cuts, 223, 232
Primary structure of protein, 493
Primost cheese, 193
Process cheese, 189, 198
Proline, 494, 495
Propionaldehyde, 84
Propionibacterium shermanii, 197
Propyl gallate, 487-488
Protein, 419-420, 490-501
   browning, 498
   composition, 491-492
   cookery, 142
   denaturation, 490, 496-498

hydrolysis, 498
in cereal, 148
in milk, 183
isoelectric point of, 499
muscle, 205
nutritive value, 490
salad, 132
structure, 494-495
types, 496
vegetable, 64
wheat, 311-312
Protopectin, 62, 80, 394, 469
Provolone cheese, 190
Prunes, 98, 113
Pudding, cornstarch, 171-172
Puffed cereal, 150
Puffy omelet, 283, 287-288
Pumpkin pie, 280
Pyranose structure, 460
Pyridoxine, 423

Quaternary structure of protein, 495
Quick breads, 319-327
biscuits, 322-324
comparison, 320
cream puffs, 326
crepes, 327
muffins, 320-322
pancakes, 326-327
popovers, 324-325
waffles, 326-327
Quick-cooking cereals, 152
Quick-freezing, 212
Quince, 100

Rack of lamb, 243
Radish, 52, 69, 70
Raisins, 99, 381
Rancidity, 211
in coffee, 27
in fat, 485-486
hydrolytic, 486
oxidative, 486
Rapidmix method, 329-330
Rarebit, 197, 199
Raspberries, 96-97, 110
freezing, 393
Rearranged lard, 477, 478, 482
Recommended Daily Allowances, 425-427
Red tide, 411
Refining of fats, 481
Refrigerator cookies, 342-343

Reggiano cheese, 195
Rendering of fats, 480
Rennin, 191, 197
R-enzyme, 299, 465
R groups of protein, 492
Retrogradation, 465-466
Reversion, 486
Rhozyme P-11, 492
Rhubarb, 117
freezing, 393
Riboflavin, 183
Rice, 145-147, 153-154
brown, 153
cookery, 157
enriched, 149, 153
long grain, 147, 158
medium grain, 147, 158
parboiled, 153
polished, 153
short grain, 147, 158
starch, 160-161, 163
wild, 153
Rigor, 208-209
Roaster, 250
Roasting, 233, 236-238, 242-244
Rock Cornish hen, 250
Rockfish, 259
Rock salt, 371
Rolled cereal, 150
Romaine, 58
Romano cheese, 195
Roquefort cheese, 191, 196
Roux, 169
Rubrobrassyl chloride, 84
Rumford, Count, 2-3, 34
Rutabagas, 60, 69, 70, 83
Rye, 145, 147, 310

Saccharomyces cerevisiae, 293-299
Safety, 14
Sago, 159
Salads, 124-144
arrangement, 126-127
color, 127
flavor, 127
fruit, 130-132
garnishes, 128
gelatin, 132-135
high protein, 132
preparation, 135-137
role in meal, 125-126
shape, 126-127

texture, 127-128
types, 128-135
vegetable, 128-130
Salad dressings, 137-142
cooked, 140-142
Salmon, 259
Salmonellosis, 406, 408
Salt, effect on boiling point, 12-13
in baked products, 318
Salts, in denaturation, 497
in gel formation, 453
Sanitation, 10-11, 400-416
additives, 402-403
contaminants, 403-404
food poisoning, 404-412
temperatures, 412-414
Saponification number, 474
Sarcolemma, 204
Sardines, 259
Savoy cabbage, 55-56
Saxitoxin, 411
Scalding temperatures, 11
Scallions, 59
Scallops, 259
Scallop squash, 61
Scarlet fever, 184
Scoring, 245
Scrambled eggs, 276
Scum formation, 186
Scurvy, 424
Scutellum, 312
Secondary structure of protein, 493-494
Self-rising flour, 314
Semolina, 154
Septic sore throat, 184
Sharp freezing, 212
Sheep fat, 479
Shellfish poisoning, 411
Sherbets, 180
Shortening value of fats, 482-484
Shredded cereals, 150
Shrimp, 259
Silver, plate, 439-440
sterling, 438-439
Simmering temperatures, 11
Sinigrin, 84
Single-stage method, 337, 338
Skim milk, 176-177, 185
Smelt, 259
Smoke point of fat, 485
Smoking meat, 211
Soda, 303

Sodium acid pyrophosphate, 304-306
Sodium aluminum phosphate, 305-306
Sodium aluminum sulfate baking powder, 301, 304-305
Sodium citrate, 198
Sodium nitrite, 210, 410
Soft-cooked eggs, 274
Soft meringue, 285-286
Soft wheat, 313-314
Sol, 451, 452
gelatin, 134
starch, 166
Sole, 259
Solidification, heat of, 10
Soluble coffees, 29-30
Solutions, saturated, 363-365
supersaturated, 363-365
true, 12, 363
Sorghum, 145
Souffle, 288-290, 292
cheese, 200, 289, 292
chocolate, 289
Sour cream, 180
Sour dough, 332-333
South American coffee, 24
Sow, 216
Soybeans, 497
Spaghetti, 154-155
Specific gravity, 73-74
Spinach, 57, 63, 64, 67, 69, 77, 85-88
canning, 387
freezing, 391
Split peas, 63
Sponge method, 330
Sponge cake, 282, 290-291, 333-334
Spoon bread, 290
Spray drying, 272, 382
Squash, 60-62, 69, 70, 78, 88
Stag, 216, 250
Stainless steel, 440
Staling, 466
Standing rib roast, 204, 218-219
Staphylococcus poisoning, 406, 409
Starch, 62-63, 102, 142, 159-172, 462-467
amylopectin, 463-464
amylose, 462-463
in baking powder, 303
commercial products, 466
cookery, 161-172
dextrinization, 161
effect of acid, 464-465
effect of enzymes, 465

gelatinization of, 161-166
granule, 161-162, 463-464
pastes, 162-166
precooked, 467
puddings, 171-172
retrogradation, 465-466
special starches, 466-467
sponges, 466
sources, 159
Steam, 297-298
Steamer, 89
Stearic acid, 183, 475
Steer, 216
Steeped coffee, 32, 33
Sterling silver, 438-439
Stewing, 248-249
Stewing hen, 250
Stilton cheese, 196
Stir frying, 87, 91
Stirred custard, 278, 279
Straight dough method, 327-329
Strawberries, 97, 103, 105, 110, 113
   freezing, 393
Streptococcal infections, 407
Streptococcus lactis, 191
Streptococcus thermophilus, 178, 197
Subtropical fruits, 96, 100-102
Sucrose, 299, 357, 360, 371, 460-461
Sugar, in baked products, 317-318
   brown, 358
   cookery, 355-370
   dessert, 285, 357
   effect on boiling point, 12-13
   frosting, 357
   in frozen desserts, 370-371
   in gels, 134, 164-165
   granulated, 357
   maple, 358
   in starch pastes, 164-165
   powdered, 358
   production, 356-357
   reactions, 359-360
   types, 360
Sugar beets, 356-357
Sugarcane, 356
Sulfur dioxide, 84, 99, 105, 115
Sulfate-phosphate baking powder, 305
Sulphured molasses, 358
Summer squash, 60-62, 88
Superglycerinated shortenings, 482, 485
Supersaturated solution, 363-365
Surface active agents, 455, 465

Surface area of fats, 483-484
Surface tension, in emulsions, 454-455
   in foams, 456-458
Sweetened condensed milk, 179, 185, 498
Sweetening power, 357, 461
Sweet fennel, 52
Sweet potatoes, 60, 63, 69, 70, 83, 86, 88
Swiss chard, 64
Swiss cheese, 190, 195, 197, 198
Syneresis, 166, 279, 397, 453-454, 466
Synergists, 487
Syrup for canning, 383

Table appointments, 434-445
   centerpieces, 438
   dishes, 441-442
   flatware, 438-441
   glassware, 442-443
   linens, 434-438
   table settings, 443-445
Table cloths, 434-437
Table queen squash, 62
Taffy, 362, 364
Tangerine, 97, 110, 112, 113
Tannins, 27
Tapioca, 159-160, 163, 164
Tartaric acid, 397
Tartrate baking powder, 301, 303-304
Tea, 38-45
   black, 40-42
   classification, 40-42
   culture, 38-39
   evaluation, 43-44
   green, 42
   iced, 44-45
   instant, 45
   oolong, 42
   preparation, 40-42
   processing, 40-42
   production, 39
Teas and coffees, 446-447
Temperature, 7-14
   boiling, 11-14
   freezing, 10
   frying, 14
   intermediate, 10-11
Tempering of fats, 482
Tertiary structure of protein, 495
Testa, 312
Testosterone, 207
Thermometers, types, 13
Thick white sauce, 267

Thyroxine, 421
Timbales, 168
Time planning, 433-434
Tocopherols, 487
Toffee, 362, 364
Tomatoes, 62, 63, 65, 69, 70, 72, 77,
    83, 86, 88
  canning, 383-386
  cream soup, 169-170, 186
Toxins, 404-406, 409
Trans configuration, 473, 477
Trichinella spiralis, 214, 235, 407
Trichinosis, 250, 407, 410
Triglyceride, 473
Trimethylamine, 210
Triolein, 475
Tripalmitin, 475
Tristearin, 475
Tropical fruits, 96, 100-102
Tropomyosin, 205
Trypsin, 207
Tryptophan, 423, 492
Tuberculosis, 184
Tuna, 259
Turkeys, comparative costs, A42
  definitions, 251
  hormones, 208
  roasting, 253-257
  storage, 254
  thawing time, 254
Turnips, 69, 70
Tyndall effect, 452
Typhoid fever, 184, 407
Tyrosine, 87

Ultrasonic waves, 498
Ultraviolet light, 498
Undulant fever, 184
Unsaturated fatty acids, 473
Unsulphured molasses, 358

Vacuum, effect on boiling point, 12
Vacuum coffee, 32
Van der Waal's forces, 494
Vaporization, heat of, 12
Vapor pressure, 11-12, 456
Variety meats, 241-242
Veal, aging, 210
  cuts, 226-227
  definition, 215
  freezing, 212
  grading, 221

preparation, 250
standardized names, A58-A59
Vegetables, 51-95
  availability, 69, A43-A44
  boiling, 89
  canned, 75-79
  classification of, 55-62
  color, 81-84
  composition, 62-63
  cookery, 79-85
  flavor, 84-85
  freezing, 390-392
  frozen, 75-79
  grades, 75
  marketing, 67
  nutritional significance, 63-66, 79-80
  preparation, 85-93
  salads, 128-130
  selection, 67-78
  simmering, 89-90
  steaming, 89
  storage, 78-79
  survey of, 52
  texture, 80-81
Vinegar, 137
Vitamin A, 64, 104, 423
  in fortified skim milk, 177
Vitamin B_{12}, 424
Vitamin D, 64, 423, 424
  in fortified milk, 177, 185
Vitamin E, 423, 424
Vitamin K, 423, 424
Vitamins, 423-425

Waffles, 326-327
Water, in coffee, 31
  in food preparation, 14-15
  permanent hardness, 15-16
  soft water, 15
  temporary hardness, 15
Water-holding capacity, 204, 209, 490
Waterless cookery, 85
Watermelon, 99, 100, 102, 103, 109, 111, 113
Wax, 402
Waxy cornstarch, 160
Waxy rice flour, 393
Waxy starches, 464
Weeping, 166
Wheat, 145-147, 154, 310-316
  flour, 163, 310-316
  irradiation of, 381
  nutrients, 148

processing, 149
proteins, 311-312
starch, 159-161
types, 147
Whey, 183, 191
Whipped butter, 180
Whipped cream, 180, 185, 187, 458
White fish, 259
White sauces, 166-167
Whiting, 259
Whole milks, 175-176
Wholesome Meat Act, 213
Wholesome Poultry Products Act, 213, 252
Winterized oils, 139
Winterizing of oils, 482
Winter squash, 60-62, 78

Xanthophylls, 82, 83

Yams, 60
Yearlings, 216, 221

Yeast, 298-301
Yeast breads, 327-333
fermentation, 330-331
rapidmix method, 329-330
sour dough, 332-333
sponge method, 330
straight dough method, 327-329
Yellow crookneck squash, 60
Yogurt, 178
Yolk, 267, 456
foams, 282
frozen, 272
index, 270
Youngberries, 96

Zein, 496
Z-enzyme, 299, 465
Zinc, 421
Zucchini, 61, 88
Zwitterions, 492
Zymase, 298